MANAGING DIVERSITY

People Skills for a Multicultural Workplace

Fourth Edition

Norma Carr-Ruffino

Pearson
Custom
Publishing

Cover photos courtesy of PhotoDisc, Inc.

Printed in the United States of America

10 9 8 7 6 5 4 3 2 1

Please visit our web site at www.pearsoncustom.com

ISBN 0–536–63769–5

BA 993437

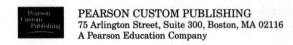
PEARSON CUSTOM PUBLISHING
75 Arlington Street, Suite 300, Boston, MA 02116
A Pearson Education Company

To Fredo, who is always there
To Lorene, who saw good qualities in "different" people
And to Jack, who saw through the eyes of unconditional love

CONTENTS

HOW THIS BOOK CAN CHANGE YOUR LIFE

This book can do more for you than just provide information about changes in the multicultural workplace. It provides tools for you to change your life—if you choose to raise your awareness, change limiting beliefs, and adopt new success strategies. Transformation, or lasting change, can only take place at the level of belief, so this book is designed to help you open up your worldview—and therefore transform it. Such transformation will open up richer relationships with people who hold quite different worldviews.

Is This Book For You?

This book is for you if you see yourself as a workplace leader—now or in the future—whether you take a leadership role as the new member of a work team, the head of an organization, or somewhere in between. This book is for you if you're ready to develop the people power and people skills you need for managing diversity. In this book you'll get the information you need to make informed choices—as well as the processes for broadening your viewpoints and integrating new success skills into your daily interactions.

People Skills You Will Develop

Managing Diversity provides in-depth information, as well as self-awareness activities, for raising your awareness and building your people skills as follows:

- Raising awareness of your own cultural viewpoints and stereotypes
- Recognizing typical values, habit patterns, and concerns of each major cultural group: the dominant U.S. group Euro-Americans, men and women—who are raised in parallel gender cultures, African Americans, Asian Americans, Latino Americans, gay persons, persons with disabilities, older persons, and persons of all sizes and shapes.
- Recognizing each group's burden of myths (that reflect the stereotypes and prejudices of the dominant culture) versus reality, historical background, current demographic profile, and cultural pattern and issues
- Meeting the leadership challenges and opportunities posed by the range of diverse employees in the workplace
- Finding common ground upon which multicultural employees can build productive, trusting relationships
- Developing strategies you can use to overcome barriers and enhance opportunities for members of each group to contribute to team and organizational excellence
- Building productive relationships among team members, coworkers, customers, suppliers, and other business and personal contacts
- Providing a work environment where all types of people can grow and thrive
- Channeling diverse talents, viewpoints, and experiences toward building synergy, enhancing creativity, and developing innovative approaches and products.
- Functioning effectively in multicultural marketplaces—in the U.S. and globally.

What's New in This Edition

Every chapter has been streamlined, reorganized, and/or updated—varying from very little to a great deal.

- Chapter 1 gives updated information on how workplace diversity is evolving, the challenges and advantages of a diverse workplace, and a comprehensive model of the multicultural skill building process. The approaches to dealing with workplace discrimination have been updated and moved to Chapter 5.

- Chapter 2 focuses on cultural differences and similarities, adding new research on cultural differences.
- Chapter 3 brings an understanding of the dominant American culture: Euro-Americans.
- Chapter 4 covers the first two aspects of exclusion: stereotyping and prejudice, how and why everyone within a culture holds similar stereotypes and prejudices. Updates include DNA research and its impact on the myth of race.
- Chapter 5 is new in the sense that it covers the third aspect of exclusion: discrimination. The focus is on discrimination in the workplace, what effects it has, and a range of remedies, including old and new approaches of the melting pot, the legal approach, valuing diversity, and the inclusive multicultural approach (formerly in Chapter 1). New visuals vividly depict the effects of various approaches.
- Chapter 6 on men and women includes new research on male and female management style differences and a new case on Euro-American male issues.
- Chapter 7 on African Americans includes powerful new information on slavery's impact, new demographics, and new online information sources.
- Chapters 8 and 9 on Asian Americans and Latino Americans offer new information about stereotypes versus reality, demographic updates, expanded information on cultural values and issues, and marketplace connection opportunities.
- Chapter 10 on Gay Americans has been dramatically streamlined and updated. It includes new historical and demographic information, a new look at the nature and impact of antigay prejudice, growing up gay, the gay community, the causes of gayness, and gay rights.
- Chapter 11 on Persons with Disabilities has been updated and a new case on wheelchair users has been added.
- Chapter 12 on Older Americans contains new information on mental abilities and retirement demographics.
- Chapter 13 on appearance and Chapter 14 on Managing Diversity are updated.

The People Who Contributed to This Book

I am especially indebted to the following people who gave me feedback and moral support in the long process of developing this book:

- Jane Baack, management professor, San Francisco State University
- Lorraine Dong, Asian studies professor, San Francisco State University
- John Dopp, management professor, San Francisco State University
- Karen Hossfeld, sociology professor, San Francisco State University
- Laurie Pozzi Hull, management consultant, Gig Harbor, WA
- Olive James, library consultant, San Francisco
- Deborah Lowe, marketing professor, San Francisco State University
- Sherron Kenton Bienvenu, communications professor, Emory University, author of Crosstalk
- Anita Silvers, philosophy professor, San Francisco State University
- Barbara Smith, diversity management consultant, San Francisco
- Students in the seminar, Managing Diverse Workers, San Francisco State University, who have given me feedback on these materials over many semesters.
- The staff of Pearson Custom Publishing

Many other friends and family members supported me through their willingness to listen, to comment, and to understand when for days on end I was "committed to the computer" as the project grew and developed. It is truly a privilege to do this work. Just doing it has been a powerful source of personal growth for me. May working through the resulting book be similarly powerful for you, the reader.

Norma Carr-Ruffino, Ph.D.
Department of Management, College of Business
San Francisco State University

CHAPTER 1
Succeeding in a Diverse Workplace

Whatever gets the most attention grows the strongest and lives the longest.
Jach Purcel

American workplace diversity deserves attention. It can be a major source of innovation, global savvy, and profitability—or a source of conflict and chaos. It all depends on us as individuals and together as organizations—on how we respond to workplace changes, and on our ability to build productive relationships with people from many cultures and lifestyles.

Are you paying attention to building your people skills in a diverse workplace and marketplace? Diversity skills are a major factor in that marketable package of skills you need to bring to the workplace. That's because the ability to relate well to all types of people is an essential leadership skill these days—and becoming more important all the time. As a leader in the fast-paced, ever-changing American workplace, what do you need to know about diverse workers? What people skills must you develop?

You've heard that the *way* we work is becoming more technologically based and team oriented, and that global markets affect almost all businesses. You're aware that global markets are changing almost daily, and so are such American market segments as the African American, Asian American, and Latino American markets. These diverse markets and workplaces are increasingly made up of people from various cultures and subcultures.

This diversity creates new challenges for business organizations. The challenges become easier to resolve when you realize that every person in the world belongs to one species—the human species. We are one species and one race, according to the experts. Genetically, we are 99.9 percent alike and therefore deeply connected. Yet each of us is as unique as a snowflake, and we each belong to a particular ethnic group that blends us all together into its own type of cultural "snow." Our individual and cultural differences offer rich opportunities to move into new markets and to boost bottom-line profits. You can learn how to tap into these diversity opportunities.

Think about it. If you were an executive making hiring decisions in this environment, wouldn't you prefer the applicant with diversity people skills? Wouldn't you treasure employees who can form productive relationships with diverse business associates? Wouldn't you want people who can help the company gain and keep its share of these diverse markets?

This increasing diversity you encounter in your workplace will pose some challenges to your ability to do an excellent job, but that diversity can also be the source of amazing career success. You're about to learn the diversity success strategies that make all the difference. But first, start your exploration by answering the questions posed in Self-Awareness Activity 1.1.

Self-Awareness Activity 1.1: What Do You Know About Diversity?

Purpose: To see what you know about the issues covered in this chapter.

Instructions: Determine whether you think the following statements are basically true or false—and think about why. The answers will emerge in this chapter, and the summary at the end of the chapter focuses on these issues.

1. The majority of employees entering the workplace are "white men."
2. Women who work fulltime now make almost as much as their male counterparts.
3. Minorities are fairly well represented at all levels of management these days.
4. To relate well to people from diverse groups, I should first look at how they are different.
5. Few people hold biases and stereotypes about minorities these days.

Back to your career, how is this blossoming diversity affecting workplace relationships? Think of your own relationships. You probably relate best to people you feel comfortable with. And you probably feel most comfortable with people who are most like you. Encountering new and different people can be interesting, stimulating, even exciting. But it can also be stressful, confusing, and frustrating when you don't understand where they're coming from, what they're trying to communicate, and why they do what they do. It can also be uncomfortable when they harbor stereotypes about you—and you harbor stereotypes about them, especially when those stereotypes cause you, or them, to feel and act in prejudiced ways.

Stereotypical thinking, prejudiced feelings, and discriminatory actions are what kept the doors to opportunity closed for so long. Discrimination is a typical outcome of prejudiced thinking, and we all harbor prejudices. It's just the flavor and degree that vary. For we are all products of our culture, and virtually all cultures are ethnocentric, believing "our way is the true way" of viewing reality.

Traditionally business has handled diversity by adopting the "Melting Pot Myth," but people of color and women never "melted in" because they don't look or act like the dominant majority, Euro-American men. In recent decades legal action has opened many doors of opportunity, but it has not necessarily changed the beliefs and attitudes, nor the thoughts and feelings, that led to discrimination in the first place. Savvy leaders in forward-thinking companies value diverse employees for the unique contributions they can make to the company's success. They are crafting a multicultural approach to managing diversity, an approach that welcomes all types of employees—and then appreciates and nurtures them.

What do you need to know? As a leader in a diverse workplace, the most important knowledge you can gain is how to build multicultural skills. What skills do you need? You need those skills that will provide the basis for building productive relationships with all types of people, skills for creating a work environment that provides challenge and support for people from all cultural backgrounds.

HOW THE WORKPLACE IS CHANGING

The workplace is changing in most every way. The kinds of people we see in high powered jobs are more diverse. The way people work together and the tasks they do are changing. And the way business is done throughout the world is changing by the day.

New Faces in New Jobs

People with university degrees and technical expertise come from all types of backgrounds these days. Since the 1960s more and more African Americans, Latino Americans, Asian Americans, and women have been entering college programs and technical areas that were formerly dominated by Euro-American men. As a result, these "minorities" have been moving into managerial, executive, technical, and professional careers formerly closed to them.

The workplace is becoming more diverse in other ways, too. For example, persons with disabilities have been finding ways to use the many abilities they do have and to become productive employees. Many gay persons no longer try to hide their sexual orientation and want to be dealt with as employees who have rights equal to those of straight employees. Older employees now have the right to refuse mandatory retirement and can work as long as they are still productive. Obese persons are beginning to expect and gain some rights to be treated fairly and equally in the workplace. And people are becoming aware of the unfairness of "appearance bias" in general, especially when it's not essentially related to job productivity.

These dramatic changes in the workplace are producing some interesting challenges for everyone, from entry-level employees to top management. All must face the misunderstanding, communication breakdown, conflict, and even failure that can result when people from widely diverse backgrounds must pull together as a team or at least complete some sort of business transaction together. But these changes also offer bountiful opportunities for new levels of growth, innovation, expansion, and productivity. This book is about successfully meeting the challenges and prospering from the opportunities.

More Women and Immigrants

Since the 1960s more and more women work outside the home for most of their adult lives. Some do this because they want careers, even though they may be wives and mothers; some because their family needs their income; and most for both reasons.

More and more ethnic minorities are in the work force because immigration quotas were expanded in the 1960s allowing more Latinos and Asians to become citizens. In 1940 more than 85 percent of people who had come to the United States as immigrants were European, while in 1995, 75 percent were from non-European countries. Most are from Latin American (47 percent) and Asian (22 percent) countries. These immigrants tend to be younger on average and to have more children than the Euro-American population, further expanding their numbers. As of 1999, slightly less than half the California population was Euro-American.

Figure 1.1 shows the ethnic makeup of the population and the work force in 2000, as well as the proportions of Euro-Americans and minorities in the better-paying middle- and top-level management jobs. Although Euro-American women and minorities made up 65 percent of the work force, they held only 30 percent of middle management jobs and 5 percent of top management positions.

Income for these groups reflects the glass ceiling to higher-level jobs still in place in corporate America. Median incomes for full-time workers are shown below (U.S. Census Bureau 1990). The 1999 estimates of the Bureau of Labor Statistics indicated that this pattern of gender and ethnic differences had not changed, as shown in Table 1.1.

TABLE 1.1: Income and Poverty Rates, 1999

	Men	*Women*	*Household*	*Poverty Rates*
All full time workers	$27,300	$15,300	$40,800	12%
Euro-American	30,600	15,900	44,400	8
African American	20,600	14,800	27,900	24
Latino American	18,200	11,300	30,700	23
Asian American	27,700	16,800	51,200	11

FIGURE 1.1: Ethnic and Gender Segments of the Workforce and of Management, 2000

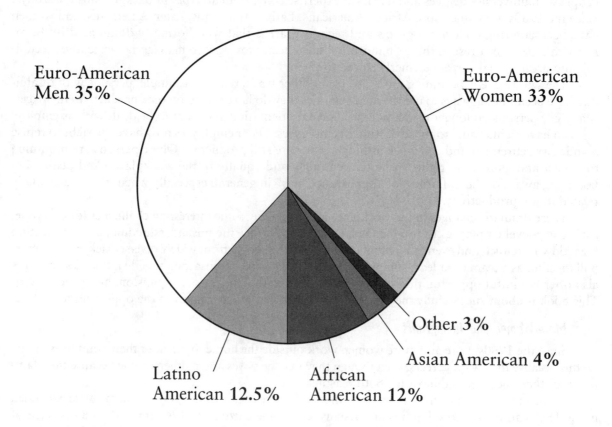

Euro-American Men 35%

Euro-American Women 33%

Other 3%

Asian American 4%

Latino American 12.5%

African American 12%

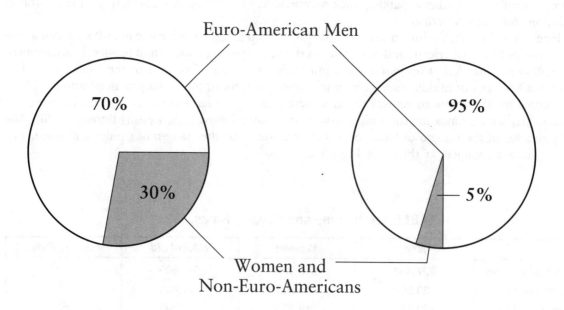

Middle Managers

Top Managers

Euro-American Men

70%

30%

95%

5%

Women and Non-Euro-Americans

Source: *U.S. Census Bureau, 2000; U.S. Dept. of Labor, 2000.*

The trend toward a more diverse population and work force is expected to continue. Of the 26 million new workers coming into the work force between 1990 and 2005, about 85 percent are expected to be women and minorities, according to Labor Department estimates. A handy way to remember the proportions is to think in terms of sixths: Women will account for about four-sixths, minority men more than one-sixth, and Euro-American men one-sixth, as depicted in Figure 1.2.

FIGURE 1.2: New Workers Entering the Workforce, 1990-2005

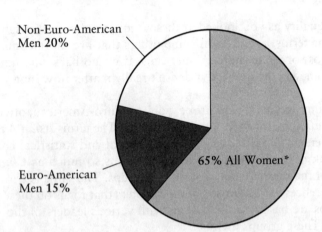

Non-Euro-American Men 20%

Euro-American Men 15%

65% All Women*

*45% Euro-American Women, 20% Non-Euro-American Women
Source: U.S. Bureau of Labor Statistics

Historically, men of European ancestry have run virtually all the major American organizations. They have set the rules of the game in the American culture as well as in corporate cultures. Other types of employees were traditionally kept out of mainstream leadership roles. They worked on the periphery of our organizations as the workers who were told what to do and how to do it, as temporary employees and part-timers. Some were kept out completely—the unemployed and unemployable.

In the past most American businesses functioned primarily within U.S. borders. Now even very small businesses may do much of their business in global markets. Corporate success now depends on building positive, productive relationships with people from many cultures around the planet. Corporate cultures that are open, flexible, appreciative, and savvy about cultural and lifestyle differences have a competitive edge. Having diverse employees at all levels in all functional areas enhances that edge—and is becoming ever more crucial for success and profitability as reliance on global transactions increases.

New Terms that We Use for People

People are very sensitive about the labels others attach to them. Most prefer no labels at all. Yet how do we discuss the issues of cultures and subcultures, of diverse groups in a pluralistic society, of prejudice and discrimination based on group stereotypes? Obviously, verbal communication requires the use of descriptive terms. Such terms tend to change over time in response to social and cultural changes and interactions. African Americans were properly called "Negroes" during the 1800s, politely called "Colored" during the first half of this century, then took the term "Black" for themselves. Women were politely called "ladies" before the women's movement of the 1960s. When group labels are continually used in a limiting, demeaning, scornful, or hostile way, they eventually are resented by the people they refer to. Therefore, if we want to show respect and appreciation for others, we want to use the terms they prefer. This can be difficult since members of a particular group rarely have unanimous opinions about preferred terms.

The terms used in this book are terms adopted by a multicultural task force in a large university that met weekly for many months to work out terminology and basic policy concerning diverse groups. The terms for the largest ethnic groups are listed below and reflect the preferences of activists and leaders from those groups.

- African Americans
- Asian Americans (such as Chinese Americans, Asian Indian Americans)
- Euro-Americans
- Jewish Americans
- Latino Americans (such as Mexican Americans, Puerto Rican Americans)
- American Indians

If you got a sense of equality as you looked at these terms, you're on the right track. The major rationale for these particular terms, rather than some others that are more commonly used, is that we're all Americans, and most of us are native Americans. If we go back far enough, all of us have ancestors who came from somewhere else. And it doesn't really matter how long we or our ancestors have been here.

If your ancestors were immigrants from Europe, you're a Euro-American, often called *white*, and you're a member of the dominant majority in American culture. The terms *Asian American* and *Latino American* are used for convenience in discussing certain cultural and statistical commonalties. Most Asian Americans don't think of themselves as Asian Americans so much as *Chinese Americans* or *Filipino Americans* or one of the many Asian subcultural groups. The same is true for Latino Americans. These subcultural differences are addressed in the chapters that focus on these groups. The terms used for other diverse groups are based on discussions with various leaders of those groups and on a review of current literature. These groups include:

- Persons with Disabilities
- Gay, lesbian and bisexual persons
- Older persons
- Obese persons

When you're relating one-to-one with people from any of these groups, you rarely need to refer to the group or groups they identify with. You're dealing with the individual. However, when you deal with groups or need to discuss groups with an individual, consider beginning with questions about how the person(s) feel about the various names for the groups. Reach some agreement about appropriate labels. Become sensitive to language that some consider racist and sexist, and weed it out of your vocabulary. Every time we use such terms, we reinforce the prejudicial patterns, whether we intend to or not.

Diverse Backgrounds = Diverse Issues

Whether you are an entry-level trainee, a team leader, or a top manager, your success in and enjoyment of your career increasingly depend on how well you understand and relate to a diverse range of people. If you can mentally slip inside their skin for a time and see the world through their eyes, you'll gain great power in understanding their thinking and feeling and the issues most important to them. Here's a brief preview of some of the issues you'll learn about in this book.

Career women often find themselves in catch-22 situations. For example, people expect women to be emotional, indecisive, and vulnerable. But business leaders are expected to be in control of their emotions, decisive, and able to roll with the punches. If women project the typical image, they're not seen as potential leaders. But if they project the "business leader" image, they're often seen as too hard and masculine, even abnormal.

Men are expected to be aggressive, ambitious, and proud. But many corporate cultures are changing in ways that call for leaders who are cooperative and who focus more on challenging and supporting others than on personal achievement. Many men are confused about what companies expect of them, just as they're confused about what the women in their lives expect. The dramatic changes in women's roles have had a major impact on men's lives.

African Americans who have a problem with a "brother or sister" typically take the bull by the horns and confront the issue directly. They go straight to the person, "tell it like it is," and try to work it out immediately. To them this approach is real and honest. But to most other people in a workplace, it may be threatening and may imply anger that might erupt into violence. When Euro-American, Asian American, and Latino American co-workers feel threatened by African Americans' "confrontation, rage, or violence," it's usually because they misinterpret their cultural behavior patterns.

Asian Americans are taught that one of the highest values is to control one's reactions and to become mature enough to put relationships before personal concerns. As a result they may be very indirect about expressing criticism or disagreeing. Often, they don't show or express strong emotion, especially outside the family circle. When Euro-American, Latino American, and African American co-workers conclude that Asian Americans are closed, secretive, inscrutable, and even cold, it's usually because they're unaware of Asian cultural values.

Latino Americans are often stereotyped by Euro-Americans as having a "manana" (literally "tomorrow") attitude. This stereotype implies that they're not ambitious, productive go-getters, as Americans tend to be. Actually, most Latino Americans are hard workers, but they tend to wait for orders from the boss. Their cultural beliefs include greater respect for authority than most Euro-Americans hold—and greater acceptance of themselves as subordinates to a powerful boss. Also, Latinos tend to be more accepting than Euro-Americans of undesirable circumstances, often seeing such situations as God's will. When Euro-Americans judge Latino Americans as lacking initiative, it's usually because they don't understand these aspects of their cultural background.

Gay persons are sometimes avoided by co-workers on the assumption that gays don't have "normal" relationships. Co-workers have made such comments as, "I just don't feel comfortable socializing with Joe (a gay man). Maybe he'll come on to me sexually," or "Maybe he'll get jealous of my friendship with a guy he's attracted to, when to me we're just hanging out." Joe would probably say, "Hey, I'm *me* first and foremost, just a person. My sexual orientation is just one slice of the whole pie that's me. What's more, I'm very sensitive to the discomforts and fears of straight guys." Studies indicate that people in the gay community have a whole range of relationships, as people in any community do, and that overall they're as likely to have "normal relationships" as people from any cultural group.

Persons with disability are thought to be a small minority by most people and are often seen as distinctly "different," even abnormal. Actually, most people have some type of disability, usually fairly minor. Persons classified as "disabled" simply have a disability that affects their ability to perform one or more major life functions, such as walking, reading, or hearing. They're not really "different" from the person who limps around occasionally with back trouble, the person who wears contacts, or the person who doesn't hear too well out of one ear. It's just a matter of degree. Even persons with a severe disability, such as paralysis from the neck down, may learn to live and work independently and often to make significant contributions through their careers.

Obese persons are often as healthy as most adults, depending upon the extent of their obesity and their age. Many cruel myths and stereotypes surround obesity in our culture. The type of discrimination obese employees experience has an element of appearance bias and is related to skin-color discrimination, which is also a form of appearance bias. Obese persons also experience discrimination based on assumptions about what they cannot do, similar to that experienced by persons with disability. Recent court rulings that support the employment rights of obese persons are based on their rights to "reasonable accommodation" under laws that protect the disabled.

Older persons are often assumed to be rigid, dogmatic, and forgetful. Their younger co-workers may avoid them and may wonder why these "old folks" haven't retired or when they're going to retire. Research indicates that aging itself does not cause any significant loss of intelligence, memory, or learning capacity. However, with age one's habits tend to come home to roost. People who abuse or neglect their bodies start paying the price in their later years, while people with good eating and exercise habits tend to remain healthy and vibrant. People who habitually spend much of their time in negative thinking tend to become even more negative with age, while those who work on a positive outlook and self-growth become more delightful to be around.

Other groups that have distinct issues include American Indians, Arab Americans, Jewish Americans, and bi-ethnic persons (those whose parents are from two distinctly different cultural backgrounds). For example, the person whose mother is Euro-American and whose father is African American tends to experience a unique type of cultural conflict while growing up. Because of the limitations of time and space, these other groups are not included in this book, even though they are valuable and important groups.

Every cultural subgroup has its own unique set of values, habits, customs, life circumstances, and issues to resolve. Understanding the key cultural themes and issues of each group can give you great insight and power for building good work relationships and helping other team members do the same.

New Ways of Working Together

In the new technologically oriented companies, employees are more highly skilled and educated than ever. Old hierarchies and authoritarian bosses who dictate orders are fading into the archaic past. More common are:

- self-managing work teams
- leaders who facilitate team meetings and help teams to reach consensus
- consultants and technical experts who function more as professionals than as traditional employees.

Relationships with teammates, customers, and suppliers, and the information that flows among them, are the lifeblood of the organization. Corporations are increasingly built upon trust, collaboration, cooperation, and teamwork. In such organizations, it's more obvious than ever that people are the most valuable resource, that how we work together creates energy and innovation or decay and demoralization, that our interactions spark the knowledge and information that fuel organizational growth and success.

In summary, key trends that point to the need for multicultural leadership skills are:

- A shortage of qualified, educated workers means companies must be more responsive to workers' needs and expectations.

- The U. S. work force is becoming dramatically more diverse at all levels. Workers expect more accommodation to their needs and identities than in the past. Fewer workers are willing to compromise their unique characteristics for the sake of "fitting in" with corporate cultures built exclusively on traditional Euro-American values and norms.

- The global marketplace that now affects most American corporations is intensely competitive, making qualified employees more crucial than ever for providing the quality, innovation, and productivity companies need to compete.

- The growth of these subcultural groups means growth of subcultural market segments. Companies need a work force that "looks like America" to project a multicultural company image, contribute to marketing insights, and relate well to customers from all ethnic and lifestyle groups.

- Success in the global marketplace depends on building profitable relationships with people in all the countries where an organization does business. Diverse people skills are as powerful in the global marketplace as they are in the American workplace. Once you develop such skills, you can easily expand them to include other cultures and environments.

TEN PAYOFFS FOR MANAGING DIVERSITY WELL

You want to be the type of business leader who uses an active, change-oriented multicultural approach. Such leaders are discovering a surprising wealth of payoffs for their organizations. Benefits accrue at all levels: personal, interpersonal, and organizational. They include:

1. attracting and retaining the best available human talent
2. increasing organizational flexibility
3. gaining and keeping greater market share, locally and globally
4. reducing costs
5. improving the quality of management
6. creating and innovating more powerfully
7. solving problems more effectively
8. increasing productivity
9. contributing to social responsibility
10. bottom line: increased profits

We'll explore briefly why and how each of these payoffs is important.

Payoff #1: Attracting and Retaining the Best People

Attracting and retaining the best people as employees requires that organizations meet potential employees' needs, show respect for them as individuals, and use multicultural skills in working with them.

Attracting Qualified People.

As qualified employees become more scarce, employers must become more flexible. They can no longer afford to convey the implicit message, "This is what we offer and how we do things. Fit in or leave." Now they must adapt to potential employees who say, "These are my needs and goals; they must be met if I am to stay."

Retaining High-Potential Employees.

To retain good employees, firms must be truly committed to treating all employees fairly and to valuing diversity. Employers who appear to favor some personal orientations and stifle others risk paying the price of low productivity due to a restricted pool of applicants, employee dissatisfaction, lack of commitment, turnover, and even sabotage. University of Alabama Professor John Sheridan's research indicates that professionals (both strong and weak performers) stay an average of 14 months longer in firms whose main focus is "interpersonal orientation" values than in firms whose focus is "work task" values. Sheridan estimates that the work task-value firms incurred opportunity losses of $6 to $9 million more, over the six-year period studied, than the interpersonal-value firms. Sheridan concludes that it makes more sense to foster an interpersonal orientation culture rather than to try to find individuals who will fit into a work task culture.

Meeting Employee Needs and Expectations.

Nearly five-sixths of new employees will be women and minorities in the coming decade. Most are from a new generation who expect something extra from their careers, namely, meaning and a sense of making a contribution. Most, especially career women, expect to have a personal and family life and are less willing than older generations were to sacrifice all for career success. And most, especially ethnic minorities, are more resistant to fitting into a corporate culture that requires them to squelch important parts of their persona.

These better educated employees want their individual and group needs recognized and met. They want more control over their own destiny, a say in decisions that affect them, and more flexibility in the terms and rewards of employment. They want a fair, open, flexible, responsive, and responsible work environment where they can enjoy the workday as well as be productive. They want to experience the excitement and stimulation of meeting challenging opportunities and problems as well as the security and serenity that come from being appreciated and supported.

Word gets around quickly about how companies treat diverse employees and which companies are the best to work for. People are less likely to stay with employers who don't meet their needs.

Communicating Respect for Others.

One of the basic principles of effective multicultural leadership is to signal respect for the unique characteristics of another's culture. Small gestures can communicate respect, such as greeting persons in their native language, taking time to chat and learn more about a person, and keeping their cultural and personal viewpoints and values in mind as you work together. Doing this effectively requires learning about diverse groups and building skills in relating to group members.

Payoff #2: Increasing Organizational Flexibility

Companies are teaming up, forming alliances to pool their resources and to tighten relationships with suppliers and customers. An alliance may require that two teams or units from two different companies blend together to act as a link between the firms involved. The most frequently cited source of problems with alliances is "different corporate cultures," according to a *Harvard Business Review* survey. Multicultural skills can be applied to working in various corporate cultures as well as working with individuals from various ethnic cultures (Kanter 1991).

Payoff #3: Greater Market Share

Companies that manage diversity effectively are better able to expand their share of markets—locally and globally—and to keep it. For example, the spending power of African Americans, Latino Americans, and Asian Americans is an estimated $650 billion in 2000. In California these three groups make up nearly 50 percent of the population. About half of all business travelers are women. Diverse employees can help to attract and retain these types of customers. Their experiences and perspectives can certainly be valuable in building sales.

Such diversity is the best way to be sure the organization remains flexible enough to capture diverse markets and to provide adequate customer service. Having African American women on the team, for example, may motivate management to respond to growing market niches involving such customers. This happened to Avon in the cosmetics market. Also, customers tend to perceive that someone of their own ethnicity or sex is better able to serve their needs, and this can influence them in choosing one service or product over another. Using diversity to improve marketing skills within ethnically diverse domestic markets can help a company to market more effectively internationally, too. Learning how to be responsive to local markets and to project the right image to them will help the company sharpen its skills for the international marketplace.

Diverse employees can prevent many awkward public relations problems. They can also help in those one-on-one provider-customer interactions that are becoming increasingly common, as companies focus on providing services, information, and custom products to customers. It makes sense for a company to employ a workforce that mirrors its customer base. Having African Americans, Latino Americans, and women on decision-making teams could help prevent these kinds of problems:

- An advertisement for a major telephone company featured a drawing of animals making telephone calls from various continents. A gorilla was making the call from Africa. Many African Americans were incensed.

- General Motors launched a major marketing campaign in Mexico to sell its Chevrolet Nova. In Spanish "no va" means "doesn't go." Almost no one bought.

- A major bank instructed its tellers, all women, to wear straw hats with a band reading "Free and Easy Banking." The word "Banking" was hidden under the turned-up brims. When women realized why customers were snickering, they were upset.

Payoff #4: Reducing Costs

A multicultural approach saves money in the long run and often even in the short run. Diversity efforts reduce the high turnover rate of nontraditional employees and the costs that go with it. The cost of turnover per person has been estimated at $5,000 to $10,000 for an hourly worker and from $75,000 to $200,000 for an executive at the $100,000 salary level. (Auster 1988; Hinrichs 1991; Riskind 1991). When a nontraditional manager is included in a development program or gets a promotion, other non-traditional employees at lower levels notice and feel more hopeful and committed to the company. Such companies are more likely to be sought out by nontraditional recruits, which reduces the costs of recruiting. They also may save money in defending grievances, complaints, and lawsuits regarding discrimination, sexual harassment, and similar problems. In addition to lost time and legal fees for dealing with such problems, other costs are job-related stress, lowered morale, lowered productivity, and resulting absenteeism and turnover.

Payoff #5: Improving the Quality of Management

Knowing they must compete with all comers can encourage the more competent Euro-American men to perform even better, while the less competent ones are screened out. Diversity can prod managers to learn fresh approaches to business problems, to see issues from new perspectives, and to add new contacts to their business networks. Exposure to diverse colleagues can help managers develop breadth and openness. Perhaps this explains why Euro-American men who graduate from universities where African American students comprise 8 to 17 percent of the student body earn roughly 15 percent higher wages than whose who graduate from "lily white" schools (Marshall 1995). Also, much of what an organization learns in trying out a special training program for diversity purposes may later be broadly applied to all employees. For example, we all like to be appreciated for our uniqueness and to be treated with respect.

Payoff #6: Creating and Innovating More Powerfully

Traditional assembly-line industrial organizations required creative thinking from only a few, but post-industrial organizations with their self-managing work teams require it of many. If people from diverse backgrounds are truly respected, supported, and appreciated, they'll be willing to contribute their ideas to group sessions. This in turn gives the group a broader range of diverse ideas to choose from, increases group synergy, and prevents groupthink.

The conclusion that creativity is fostered by diversity is supported by research showing that the tolerance of diversity, defined as judging relatively few behaviors as deviant from norms, is a defining characteristic of innovative organizations (Siegel and Kaemmerer 1978). Diverse teams and organizations typically generate more options, especially more creative options and higher quality ideas—because opposing viewpoints are introduced and resolved. Groupthink is less probable. (Nemeth 1986; Nemeth and Wachtler 1983, Cox, Lobel & McLeod 1991; Wanous & Youtz 1986; Watson, Kumar and Michaelson 1993).

On the other hand, when organizations expect minorities to adapt to a Euro-American corporate culture, they fail to capitalize on the innovative and creative outcomes of a diverse workforce. A multicultural approach, on the other hand, enhances innovative outcomes (Ragins et al 1998).

For best results, relationships among team members must be predominantly positive. However, a certain amount of conflict is natural and inevitable, and if it is managed well, it can be constructive. Excessive group conflict interferes with productivity, closing down communication, wasting energy, and even causing people to leave. But too little conflict may signal complacency, repression, or old approaches to addressing new problems. The challenge is to stir innovation, manage conflict, and prevent breakdown (Jackson 1991).

Payoff #7: Solving Problems More Effectively

Culturally diverse workforces have the potential to solve problems better because of several factors: a greater variety of perspectives brought to bear on the issue, a higher level of critical analysis of alternatives, and a lower probability of groupthink and therefore a higher probability of generating many alternate solutions.

Payoff #8: Increasing Productivity

All the benefits mentioned so far work together to generally increase organizational productivity. Specifically, an effective approach to managing diversity helps diverse teams and individuals to be more productive.

Learning about each employee's unique values, expectations, and goals is essential to effectively working with diverse team members on team projects. It's also essential for leaders in helping others with job objectives, job performance, and career plans. Job performance, dedication, and attendance are boosted when employees perceive they are valued and cared for by their organization. Employees are more productive when they enjoy coming to work, feel happy to be working where they're seen as worthy and competent, and can relax into being themselves. In addition, such employees are more innovative, even without any direct reward or personal recognition. Research indicates that groups that are diverse in terms of ethnicity, age, values, background, and training are more productive and innovative than homogeneous groups (Eisenberger, Fasolo, and Davis-LaMastro 1990).

The Center for Creative Leadership identified twelve companies that showed exceptional leadership in encouraging diversity. All the companies were in the top half of *Fortune* magazine's "most admired" corporations, and 80 percent were in the top 20 percent. Rosabeth Moss Kanter (1983) found that, over a 20-year period, companies with a reputation for progressive human resource practices had more profitability and financial growth than their competitors.

Payoff #9: Contributing to Social Responsibility

The organization can become an agent for change, to make the world a better place. If one organization can thrive by creating an environment where diverse people can work effectively together, this can serve as a model for the entire world. A Los Angeles executive said, "In this area the situation is so desperate and so in need of role models, that if we in corporations can't advance minorities so they can turn around and do what needs to be done in their communities, I don't see any of us surviving. The bigger picture we have to deal with is the minority situation in this country."

Payoff #10: Bottom Line: Increased Profits

Global competition is an established fact of life now. The re-engineering, restructuring, and downsizing of the 1990s reflect the reality that United States business can no longer afford bureaucratic, hierarchical structures with a homogeneous group running the show. We can no longer afford the luxury of paying big salaries to layer upon layer of managers to carry information back forth between workers, managers, and staff experts, information that all can now access through their computers. We're realizing the potential power of setting up informational networks where many workers can instantly interact.

We can no longer afford to pay tiers of high-salaried managers to set goals and make plans for workers and then try to motivate them and keep them productive. We're realizing that work teams and individual workers should be setting their own goals and making their own plans. When they do, they're likely to be self-motivated and work out their own productivity issues.

We can no longer afford to exclude people with the talents and skills we so desperately need for business success. All the benefits they bring to the workplace add up to increased career success and company profits—provided we learn to build productive working relationships with each other.

MEETING NEW CHALLENGES: GLOBAL, NATIONAL, CORPORATE, AND PERSONAL

The problems we're facing in our business organizations reflect problems we're facing at all levels: personal problems, family problems, national problems, and global problems. As we grow in our understanding of diversity in the workplace, of the major roles of beliefs, values, stereotypes, prejudices, relationships, and access to information, we grow in understanding ourselves, our family dynamics, and our national and global priorities. As we gain skill in establishing and nurturing relationships with the whole spectrum of diverse people in the workplace, we gain skill as a national culture in working out the problems now dividing us: violent crime, ethnic conflict, inner-city decay, failing schools. If we learn how to find greater unity and harmony as a nation, we can bring this knowledge to the arena of global culture, where as a community of nations we can apply it in meeting global challenges and creating global harmony and abundance.

Our diversity can be our greatest source of power, and it can also be the source of our disintegration as a culture. In biology we understand the power of a diverse gene pool, but in organizations we are just beginning to learn the power of a diverse pool of ideas, viewpoints, and talents. When we see the growing crime and violence almost everywhere, and the continued divisiveness and prejudice, we begin to understand the price we must pay when we don't find ways to manage our diversity so that we also have unity and harmony. Unity with diversity has always been an ideal in our nation, along with freedom and equality of opportunity. Our challenge in the workplace today is to make these ideals a reality.

No wonder workplace diversity has become a hot topic! Diversity symbolizes the key to our power in meeting challenges and creating the world we want—at every level of existence. Diversity also symbolizes our hopes for the New Millennium, and the changes we need to make in order to meet its challenges and rise to it opportunities.

CAREER SUCCESS: HOW TO BUILD DIVERSE PEOPLE SKILLS

Yes, the work world is a dynamic place, and it's changing more rapidly every day. It's becoming more diverse, more technical, more global, and at the same time more dependent than ever on productive working relationships. As a business leader helping to create an inclusive work environment, your success depends more and more on building your multicultural skills. And that's the purpose of this book, which is based on the model shown in Table 1.1.

TABLE 1.1: Multicultural Skill-Building Model

The Steps	*The Techniques*
1. Become aware of culture's impact	*Self-awareness activities*
2. Learn about own culture's values, ways	*Stereotypes versus reality*
3. Recognize own cultural biases	*Connections to the past*
4. Learn about other cultures' values, ways	*Current profile*
	Cultural worldviews, values, customs, issues
5. Build interaction skills	*Leadership challenges and opportunities*
	Case studies, applying new knowledge at work

Laying the Groundwork

Let's look in more detail at the five-step process for building multicultural skills.

Step 1. *Become aware of culture*—its elements, pervasiveness, and impact, as well as similarities and differences among major cultural groups.

Step 2. *Learn about your own culture*—recognize that the beliefs and customs that you may accept as reality are only one way of viewing the world, the way of your culture.

Step 3. Recognize your own biases, the ways in which you stereotype, assume, judge, and discriminate, so you can own them and move beyond them.

Step 4. Learn about other cultures, the environments of people you encounter in the workplace, so you can recognize when cultural differences may be at the root of problems and so you can appreciate the contributions people from diverse cultures can make to the work situation.

Step 5. Build interaction skills and practice new behaviors through self-awareness activities, skill builder case studies, interviews, and applying your new understandings to actual people situations at work, school, anywhere you encounter diverse groups.

In chapters 2, 3, 4, and 5 you'll work through steps 1, 2, and 3. In chapter 2 you'll start becoming aware of culture's pervasive influence, and learn some key cultural patterns that will help you recognize cultural similarities and differences. In chapter 3 you'll become more aware of key aspects of the dominant Euro-American culture and of typical corporate cultures. In chapters 4 and 5 you'll begin to recognize your own biases and learn about the nature of prejudice. These chapters lay the groundwork for building your skills; they're the necessary background you'll need.

Building the Framework for Seeing through Another's Eyes

In chapters 6 through 14 you'll work through steps 4 and 5. You'll build the multicultural skills framework, a structure for housing your new skills. Here you'll focus on learning about other cultures, building interaction skills, and practicing new skills. The process of learning to see the world through another's eyes is based on asking the right questions, and these chapters are structured to give you some answers.

Key Questions	Chapter Structure
What are the key barriers to career success for this group?	Myths versus reality—that reflect stereotypes, prejudice
How did it get that way?	Connections to the past
What's going on now?	Current profile
What really makes these people tick?	Cultural worldviews, values, customs, issues
How can I build productive relationships with them?	Leadership challenges and opportunities
How can I apply my new knowledge and practice multicultural skills?	Cases, other skill builders

In chapters 6 through 13 you get to learn about the cultures of others, ranging from the parallel cultural worlds of men and women to various African American, Asian American, and Latino American subcultures, to the culture-like lifestyles of gay persons, persons with disabilities, older persons, and obese persons. You'll begin building interaction skills and practicing them. Chapter 14 ties the leadership challenges and opportunities together from an organizational viewpoint. You'll focus on how you can influence the organization toward creating an inclusive corporate culture in which all types of employees can be productive and comfortable.

Making Your Skills Count

But what can one person do? Regardless of youir position, your skills can make a difference. You can take whatever leadership role your situation allows. To begin with, you can notice the contributions of employees from groups that seem to be excluded in some way, and you can talk up their positive qualities. You can tell the stories of those who succeed, helping to make them stars in the company grapevine of myths and legends. You can visibly support them in any way that seems right. You can unfailingly respect their dignity and speak out against disrespect in the form of wisecracks, jokes, putdowns, exclusion, and similar behavior. If you have the power, you can provide information and training for other employees to help them understand and appreciate people from excluded groups.

SUMMARY

The workplace is changing dramatically, with minorities and women moving into all types of positions, including executive, managerial, technical, and professional jobs. In fact, about 85 percent of new employees are now women and minorities. However, 95 percent of top managers in major corporations are Euro-American men, and their income is higher on average. Therefore, equal opportunity and pay have not been achieved yet.

Business relationships are more diverse than ever, and diverse groups have diverse issues that are important to them. Suppliers and customers are ever more international in scope, and they, along with global competition, are changing the way we do business. Self-managing work teams and more highly-educated employees call for leaders and business associates with diverse people skills.

The multicultural approach to managing diversity offers many payoffs for organizations, including attracting and retaining the best available human talent, increasing organizational flexibility, gaining and keeping greater market share, reducing costs, improving the quality of management, creating and innovating more powerfully, solving problems more effectively, increasing productivity, contributing to social responsibility, and boosting the bottom line.

The steps to gaining multicultural skills are to: 1) become aware of culture's impact, 2) learn about your own culture's values and ways, 3) recognize your personal biases toward various types of people, 4) learn about the values and ways of people from other cultures, and 5) build your interaction skills through case studies and on-the-job application of your new knowledge.

REFERENCES

Brislin, Richard and Tomoko Yoshida. *Intercultural Communication Training*. Thousand Oaks CA: Sage, 1994.

Carr-Ruffino, Norma, et al. "Legal Aspects of Women's Advancement" in *Woman Power*. Thousand Oaks, CA: Sage, 1991.

Carr-Ruffino, Norma. *The Promotable Woman*. Franklin Lakes, NJ: Career Press, 1997.

Carr-Ruffino, Norma. "U.S. Women: Breaking Through the Glass Ceiling." *Women in Management Review* 6, no. 5. 1991.

Cox, T.H., S.A. Lobel and P.L. McLeod, "Effects of Ethnic Group, Cultural Differences, Uncooperative and Competitive Behavior on a Group Task," *Academy of Management Journal* 34: 827-847, 1991..

Cox, T. Jr. and C. Smolinski, "Managing Diversity and Glass Ceiling Initiatives as National Economic Imperatives" (Working Paper #9410-01). Ann Arbor, MI: Michigan Business School, 1994.

Eisenberger, R., P. Fasolo, and V. Davis-LaMastro. "Perceived Organizational Support and Employee Diligence, Commitment, and Innovation." *Journal of Applied Psychology* 75, no. 1: 51-59, 1990.

Jackson, S.E. "Team Composition in Organizational Settings" in *Group Process and Productivity*. Thousand Oaks, CA: Sage, 1991.

Kanter, Rosabeth Moss. *The Change Masters*. New York: Simon and Schuster, 1983.

Kanter, Rosabeth Moss. "Transcending Business Boundaries: 12,000 World Managers View Change." *Harvard Business Review*, May/June: 151-164, 1991.

Marshall, Jonathan. "Minority Policy—Gainers, Losers." *San Francisco Chronicle*, July 31, 1995.

Nemeth, C.J. "Differential Contributions of Majority and Minority Influence," *Psychological Review* 93: 23-32, 1985.

Nemeth, C.J. and J. Wachtler, "Creative Problem Solving as a Result of Majority vs. Minority Influence, *European Journal of Social Psychology* 13: 45-55, 1983.

Siegal, S., and W. Kaemmerer. "Measuring the Perceived Support for Innovation in Organizations." *Journal of Applied Psychology* 63, no. 5: 553-562, 1978.

Simons, G.F., C. Vazquez, and P.R. Harris. *Transcultural Leadership*. Houston, TX: Gulf, 1993.

Wanous, J.P. and M.A. Youtz, "Solution Diversity and the Quality of Group Decisions," *Academy of Management Journal* 29: 149-159, 1986.

Watson, W.E., K. Kumar and L.K. Michaelsen, "Cultural Diversity's Impact on Interaction Process and Performance," *Academy of Management Journal* 36: 590-602, 1993.

U.S. Glass Ceiling Commission. *A Report on the Glass Ceiling Initiative*. U.S. Department of Labor, 1991.

U.S. Glass Ceiling Commission. *Good for Business*. U. S. Department of Labor,1995.

CHAPTER 2

Understanding Cultures: Your Own and Others

Individuals, sharing the same belief, form a collective consciousness that can define and shape the world.
Harry Palmer

Culture is the collective programming of individual's minds that determines how a group of individuals perceives reality. In fact, we the people in a culture collectively agree on what reality is. We agree on the beliefs that form the foundation of the culture, on which beliefs are most important, and on what the culture values the most. We agree on the norms, the do's and don'ts, the rules by which people will live and be judged. And these basic agreements differ from culture to culture. Therefore, if you as a leader want to deal effectively with workers who come from various "realities," you must understand their cultures and your own. Cultural understanding gives you some clues about why people from various cultures and subcultures think and act as they do. It will also help you to maintain your balance and poise when culture clash occurs—and help others to maintain theirs.

Culture clash occurs when an employee's sense of rightness is challenged by conflicting beliefs and values held by someone from another culture. The employee may respond with several emotions, such as confusion, frustration, disgust, and anger, which tend to block the resolution of the conflict. Typical outcomes are communication breakdown and poor working relationships. Moreover, if such emotional responses are frequent and intense and are not adequately handled, they can lead to stress and even illness. Being able to recognize cultural patterns and differences can help you handle such cultural conflict, and the accompanying emotions, with greater ease.

You can see that as a leader, you'll do well to move out of your cultural cave, take off your cultural blinders, and enjoy a more universal view of the workplace. That means taking the first step in gaining multicultural skills:

Step 1: Becoming aware of culture and its pervasive influence

In this chapter you'll learn about:

- What we mean by culture and how it affects our lives
- The basic elements of culture
- The ten basic ways that cultures differ:

First, test your current knowledge by completing Self-Awareness Activity 2.1.

Self-Awareness Activity 2.1: What Do You Know about Cultures?

Purpose: To see what you know about the issues covered in this chapter.

Instructions: Determine whether you think the following statements are basically true or false—and think about why. The answers will emerge in this chapter, and the summary at the end of the chapter focuses on these issues.

1. The most important aspects of culture are those that people don't talk about.
2. A myth is a false belief.
3. People from different cultures experience different realities.
4. People in the United States put families and ingroups above individual desires.
5. Most cultures believe in inequality and status differences, seeing this as normal.
6. Most cultures of the world value achievement over interpersonal relationships.

UNDERSTANDING THE BASICS OF CULTURE

The major goal in understanding the basics of culture is to understand that we create it and we learn it and each major cultural group creates it somewhat differently. We'll discuss the key concepts of what culture is; what we mean by the hierarchy of culture, from world culture to corporate culture; and how we learn about our own culture.

What Is Culture?

Culture is like the air we breathe: We take it for granted, rarely think about it, and assume our world viewpoint is merely the human viewpoint. We can work more powerfully with people from other cultures if we understand some key concepts of what culture is all about, how it affects our personal reality, and how we learn the beliefs, values, and rules of our culture. Culture is as pervasive and invisible as the air around us. It's our programmed beliefs, many of them hidden, our mental map, our view of reality.

Culture as Programmed Beliefs

Culture is the collective programming of the mind, the learning process that results in the members of one group of people being different from those of another. Culture is a characteristic, not of individuals, but of people who were conditioned by similar educational and life experiences. A cultural group may refer to a tribe, regional group, minority, majority, or nation. Culture becomes crystallized in the institutions that people build together: family structure, educational structure, religious organizations, associations, forms of government, work organizations, law, literature, settlement patterns, buildings, and even scientific theories. All of these structures reflect common *beliefs* that are rooted in the common culture (Hofstede 1984, 1991).

Culture is learned, but it is far more than mere habits that can be easily changed from the outside, even though it's always changing and evolving naturally from the inside. Different cultures have different ways of organizing life, of thinking, and of conceiving the underlying assumptions about the family, the state, the economic system, and of humanity itself and its role in the universe, as indicated in Table 2.1. Harvard anthropologist E.T. Hall views culture primarily as a form of communication, the link between people and the means they have of interacting with each other (Hall 1981b, 1982, 1989). Many experts say that culture is very closely related to what has been defined as *mind*, and may be synonymous with it.

TABLE 2.1: Content of Culture

> **Consensus reality of a group**
> **How we agree to create our reality**
> **Ways of thinking, feeling, speaking, acting**
> **Obvious aspects and hidden aspects**
> **High priority beliefs = values, the roots or foundation of culture**

Culture as Hidden Programming

Beneath the clearly perceived, highly explicit surface culture, there lies a whole other world, a world of hidden beliefs and motives. When we understand this world, we may radically change our view of human nature. Hall says that culture hides much more than it reveals, and what it hides, it hides most effectively from its own members.

Most people strongly believe that their cultural behavior patterns are "human nature," and resist believing that such behavior is learned and can vary from culture to culture. It's quite common to grow up in a culture while gaining little or no knowledge of the basic laws that make the culture work and that differentiate it from all other cultures. Therefore, most people are unaware of the extent to which culture is a major influence on behavior. We're socialized in our culture without much conscious awareness of being socialized, even programmed. We normally think about our culture only when it comes into conflict with some aspect of another culture (Brislin and Yoshida 1994).

> *The cultural unconscious, those "hidden" cultural systems*
> *that have as yet to be made explicit, probably outnumber the*
> *explicit, conscious systems by a factor of a thousand or more to one.*

Lionel Trilling once likened culture to a prison. When we can define the prison, we can begin to plot our own jailbreak. Culture imprisons us in many unknown ways, but the bars that limit our possibilities are woven of our habits and nothing more—habitual beliefs, attitudes, and ways of thinking and feeling, along with customary actions based on long-forgotten decisions we made (Trilling 1955).

Culture as a Mental Map of Reality

As soon as we're born, our parents begin teaching us about consensus reality, helping us build the mental map we need to function in our particular culture. Anthropologists agree on three characteristics of culture:

- Culture is learned, not innate.
- The various facets of culture are interrelated. If you touch a culture in one place, everything else is affected.
- Culture is shared, and it defines the boundaries of different groups.

There is not one aspect of human life that is not touched and altered by culture. Culture is the medium or context within which humans live (Hall 1981a).

Culture as Personal Reality

How we view reality, and how we create our own reality, is tied to how we are socialized within our culture. Putting together what many anthropologists and psychologists have discovered about reality, one way of picturing its elements is shown in Figure 2.1. The psychological raw materials from which we create reality are aspects of our mind, such as our beliefs, attitudes, thoughts, feelings, decisions, and action choices. The tools for changing our reality are also aspects of our mind, namely our imagination, desires, and expectancy. Through imagination we picture, vision, and dream new, different aspects of reality. Imagination is our tool for creating new ideas and adopting innovative approaches. Our desires fire our motivation and are the basis for our purposes, intentions, and goals. Our expectancy refers to our trust or confidence that we can change aspects of our reality. We use these tools on the content or raw materials of our reality, and the most powerful parts to use them on are the belief part and the action choice part. Beliefs are at the root of every aspect of our reality, so when we change a key belief, we shift our reality. Action choices are also powerful fulcrum points of change because actions tend to get immediate results that we can see and experience, so they may change our reality quickly.

FIGURE 2.1: Elements of Reality: Mental Map

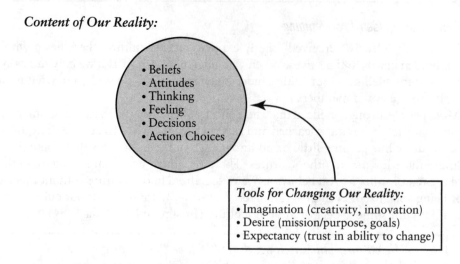

Content of Our Reality:

- Beliefs
- Attitudes
- Thinking
- Feeling
- Decisions
- Action Choices

Tools for Changing Our Reality:
- Imagination (creativity, innovation)
- Desire (mission/purpose, goals)
- Expectancy (trust in ability to change)

Cultural Levels—From World Culture to Corporate Culture

Cultural groups are found at many levels of society:

World culture = humanity; common values and customs found in all cultures

Major culture = a regional or national group that represents a common culture

Subculture = a cultural group within a major culture

Corporate culture = an organization within a major culture

In the past we thought of a culture as a relatively large group of people within a nation or geographic region who spoke the same language and embraced similar beliefs and practices. Now we recognize a diversity and hierarchy of cultures, ranging in size and scope from the whole world to a small corporation. There are about 6 billion people on Earth, living in about 6,000 different cultures, each with its own spoken language. Between 4,000 and 5,000 of those cultures are indigenous tribes, such as the 500 American Indian tribes. They number only about 200 million people, most living as small subcultures within some larger dominant society (World 1993).

Is there really a global culture? Humanity *does* have certain cultural commonalties, so we've always had the potential to become a global culture, but we lacked the necessary frequency and intensity of communication. We are rapidly becoming a global culture in many ways, a trend that's accelerating. Leavitt (1983, 94) states that "a powerful force drives the world toward a converging commonality, and that force is technology." Through advances in communication and transportation, most of us know what's happening in other parts of the world. For example, more than a billion people watch the television news channel, CNN. When the Chinese government clamped down on a student demonstration in Tiananmen Square in 1989, a global audience was watching. People around the world also see the commercials on such stations as MTV and CNN and are more aware than ever of new products becoming available. As a result of such global communication, governments are called upon to be more accountable for their actions. And people in formerly remote, isolated places get in touch with the global marketplace and may want the products and lifestyles it introduces.

Major regions, such as Asia, have many cultural commonalties, a Far East culture, in some ways. Yet within one small nation, Malaysia, there are many subcultures with distinct languages, religious beliefs, customs, and so forth. Likewise, in the United States, although we have a distinct American culture, there are numerous subcultures, such as Vietnamese American.

To complicate matters, we have *corporate* cultures, usually established on the basis of Euro-American male values, norms, and customs, but each having its own flavor and peculiarities. These corporate cultures are changing at an increasingly rapid pace as women and people from various subcultural groups move into positions of power and influence.

Gender as a Cultural Group

Do males essentially live in a different culture from females? Several diversity experts say yes. Evidence indicates that the socialization of people in most societies of the world is greatly influenced by gender, and in each culture the women, as a group, hold a distinctly different worldview from the men (Tannen 1990; Rosener 1990; Cox 1993; Belenky et al, 1986; Fottler and Bain 1980). Here are some specific ways their socialization differs :

- Men and women have different ways of learning and creating knowledge; boys and girls play differently.
- Role modeling behaviors of fathers is different from that of mothers.
- The media portrays men/boys differently from women/girls.

What Makes a Culture? Basic Elements

When you look for culture, what do you look for?
- The values people think are most important
- The heroes and heroines people admire because they personify those values
- The myths and stories about them
- The rituals people engage in every day or on special occasions
- The networks that connect people
- The symbols everyone recognizes as shortcuts for expressing all these other elements.

All these elements of culture underlie how the people in a major culture decide to handle their families, schools, churches, government, housing, business, and science. They're expressed in a culture's art forms, food, dress, play, and every other aspect of life.

A value is an enduring belief that one way of acting or being is preferable to another. A value system is an organization of such beliefs along a continuum of relative importance, a prioritizing of beliefs into a set or cluster. Norms are cultural do's and don'ts about how to act. Some values and their related norms may be talked about but most are just understood.

Heroes, heroines serve as role models. They may also be called champions, stars, or big wheels. They're often seen as fearless leaders or courageous adventurers. They personify the core values and the strength of the organization or group. They become symbolic figures whose deeds are out of the ordinary—but not so far out that people can't identify with them. People like to think, "Maybe I can do that too." Such leaders become great motivators, the people everyone will count on for inspiration when things get tough. They tend to know intuitively how to succeed, to envision the future, to experiment, and to appreciate the value of celebrations and ceremonies.

A myth is a story or saying that usually features a hero or heroine, a story that expresses some value important to the cultural group. It may be a legend that symbolizes a central belief of the culture. It's often more symbolic than factual but may be either. Some myths are based on powerful truths; some on manipulative, hurtful lies; still others on harmless little white lies.

> A *myth* is a story or saying whose function is to bind together
> the thoughts of a group and promote coordinated social action.

Rituals are the "way we do things around here." They include the customary day-to-day actions people take, their expected actions and responses. Core values would have no impact without ritual and ceremony. The unwritten rules of personal communication, the rituals of social interaction, govern relationships between bosses and workers, professionals and support staff, men and women, old and young, insiders and outsiders.

Work rituals spell out standards of acceptable behavior and how such procedures as strategic planning or budgeting or report writing should be carried out. Recognition rituals, such as awards, are more formal. They acknowledge achievements that are valued and signal that the person belongs to the culture. Rituals meet people's need to belong. They help establish and maintain some common values and goals that connect people in the group. A true ritual is always connected to a myth that represents some basic group value. Otherwise it's just a habit that does nothing but give people a false sense of security.

Networks, such as the grapevines, are the primary means of communication within an organization. They tie together all parts of the company without respect to the organization chart. They not only transmit information, they also interpret its significance. In most organizations, only about 10 percent of business takes place in formal meetings and events. The real process of making decisions, gathering support, developing opinions, etc., happens before or after the meeting. Of course, formal networks are important too. They include the formal organization chart, task forces, work teams, professional and trade associations, and similar groupings.

Symbols are shortcuts that remind people of those cultural elements that bind them together. A song, banner, flag, logo, picture, motto, or brand name may bring up corporate values. A nickname or motto may recall a heroine or star. A figure of speech may recall a key myth or ritual. A good symbol can serve to trigger communal thoughts and feelings about a common cause or goal.

How Do We Learn Our Culture?

Cultures have specific ways of teaching values and norms. Primary message systems communicate how the culture views the world and does things. Cultures use such techniques as symbols and *myths* within the message systems, most often communicating through networks of relationships and the grapevine. The methods used to pass on cultural values and norms are education, direction, and role modeling.

The primary message systems that communicate cultural values and norms serve to tell people how to do most everything they do. According to Hall (1982) they are:

- *How we interact with our environment.*
- *How we associate with others,* the way we organize our society and its parts, the role of hierarchy, rank, and status.
- *How we meet our survival needs,* including everything from individual food habits to the economy of a country.
- *How we learn.*
- *How we differentiate male and female behavior.* (Usually when a given behavior pattern becomes associated with one gender, it will be dropped by the other.)
- *How we use space,* our sense of territoriality and personal space.
- *How we use time,* which is tied to life's cycles and rhythms. Whether we focus on a linear, circular, or present-moment approach to time involves how we emphasize the past, present, and future aspects of life.
- *How we play,* relax, enjoy ourselves, and use our leisure time, and what our sense of humor is like.
- *How we defend ourselves* against potentially hostile forces in nature and against destructive forces within ourselves. Defense includes the types of armed forces, law enforcement agencies, religions, and medical practices a culture embraces.

- *How we use things*, including money, transportation, equipment, houses, furniture, clothes, weapons, and all technology.

How we do things communicates to everyone in the culture about our basic beliefs, values, norms, and unspoken rules, as indicated in Table 2.2.

The ways we communicate these basics include symbols, slogans, metaphors, and myths and stories, with heroes and heroines. According to an old Indian saying:

The people must tell their stories and sing their songs or the land (and culture) will die.

The media we most often use are networks and the grapevine, and in recent years written and electronic media. Culture has been handed down for millions of years so the traditional way is by word of mouth.

Three major teaching/learning methods were identified by Hall. Cultures use these methods to convey primary messages and information to succeeding generations: (1) education and training, (2) correction and direction, and (3) role modeling. We educate and train people, beginning in childhood, usually in a very conscious way. We also correct people when they do something the culture considers wrong or improper, and we direct them in the right way to think and act, also primarily in a conscious way. When we serve as role models, it's usually not in order to teach children and others how to think and act; we're just "being ourselves." But toddlers watch their parents, and adults watch their heroes or heroines, to learn from them and to emulate them. Role modeling is probably the most powerful teaching mechanism and we're rarely aware that it's going on.

TABLE 2.2: Essentials of Communicating the Culture

How we do things communicates our:

- beliefs and values
- norms — do's and don'ts
- informal, unspoken rules

The ways we communicate include:

- symbols
- slogans
- metaphors
- myths and stories about heroes/heroines

The media we most often use to communicate are:

- networks of relationships
- the grapevine
- written and electronic means

The teaching/learning methods we use are:

- education and training
- correction and direction
- role modeling

What does this mean for you as a business leader? It means that if you want to create an environment that challenges and supports all types of employees, you must first and foremost be a role model to others. You must hold the beliefs and attitudes that value diversity. Your thinking and feeling, your decisions and day-to-day action choices must reflect your respect for people from all groups. As a leader, it's important to give effective education and training for valuing diversity. It's also important to set up organizational systems that detect and correct discrimination and other diversity problems. But most of all, you must be a role model by "walking your talk."

HOW DO CULTURES DIFFER? TEN MAJOR DIFFERENCES

When we consider all the life forms that we're aware of, it's clear that humans throughout the world are amazingly alike. Yet our differences can make it difficult or impossible to communicate and work together effectively. The purpose of this book is to help you understand where our major differences lie so that you can figure out ways to reconcile and respect differences and to find common ground for working with people from diverse backgrounds. The United States is called the most diverse society in the world. Within our American culture we have many subcultures, each with its own unique set of values and customs. Before exploring some major ways in which cultures differ, do a brief self-analysis about your own cultural orientation by completing Self-Awareness Activity 2.2.

Self-Awareness Activity 2.2: What's Your Cultural Orientation?

Purpose: To determine your personal orientation regarding key cultural factors.
Instructions: For each of the following numbered pairs of statements, circle A or B according to which statement *best* reflects your orientation.

1. A. I create my life by what I do and by what I allow.

    B. I'm just a cog in the wheel of life. Most of what happens to me is outside my control.

2. A. My top priority is to achieve my personal goals.

    B. My top priority is to be a good son/daughter, wife/husband, boss/worker, mother/daughter, that is, to fulfill those roles expected of me.

3. A. I'm happiest when I'm ahead or winning.

    B. I'm happiest when I'm working or playing with friends, family, or coworkers.

4. A. My top priority at work is getting the job done.

    B. My top priority at work is maintaining good relationships with people.

5. A. If a top manager asked me to discuss my ideas, I'd be comfortable.

    B. If a top manager asked me to discuss my ideas, I'd be nervous and uncomfortable.

6. A. People who have talent and work hard can become very successful.

    B. People need the right family background and connections to become very successful.

7. A. My motto is "Nothing risked, nothing gained."

    B. My motto is "Stick with the tried and true."

8. A. I believe that "the exception makes the rule" and rules were made to be broken occasionally.

    B. I believe that we must stick to the rules of the game or we'll have chaos.

Followup: Analyze your responses by reading the answer key at the end of this chapter and the following discussion in this chapter.

Cultural Difference #1: I'm Controlled or I Control?

The most basic beliefs we have are probably about who or what creates our environment and causes the events within that environment. How much is caused by our own attitudes and actions? How much by a Supreme Being? How much is just chance or coincidence? Beliefs about the cause of life events tend to affect every other aspect of culture.

I'm Controlled.

People from I'm-controlled cultures might say, "Things happen to me and I have little control over my life. It depends on my boss, my customer, fate, luck, God's will." Most cultures fall into this camp, including most African, Asian, Arab, and Latino cultures. Women in all cultures are more likely than men to hold this viewpoint. (Tse et al 1988; Delgado 1981; Asante and Asante 1985; Redding 1982; Orpen and Nkohande 1977; Ramirez 1988; Helms and Giorgis 1980; Cote and Tansuhaj 1989).

I Control

People with an internal source of control believe that they determine their own reality, destiny, and life experiences to a great extent, either by what they do or by what they allow to happen, or both. They are therefore relatively autonomous, independent people. People from I-control cultures might say, "What happens to me is up to me. It depends on what I do or don't do. God helps those who help themselves." Most Western cultures, especially Euro-American, and especially men, hold this viewpoint (Rotter 1966; Spector 1982)

Choices for Control?

Euro-Americans, for example, believe that if they can control a situation, they'll have better results. They believe they should have many options, and they want lots of choices in order to feel in control of what happens in their lives. They're more likely to accept theories that blame the victims of poverty or "bad luck." Since we all have a great deal of control over our lives, those who are "disadvantaged" must be making poor choices.

In contrast, Asian Americans and African Americans are likely to believe that in nature some things are random and out of your control. Most Latinos believe that certain things are "God's will" or fate. In these cultures, people say that it's important to recognize the power of random events and have a good attitude about them. You shouldn't blame yourself or others too much. It does no good to blame the reality, because the reality is nature (or God), and nature has its own course. Just because you can make choices does not mean your decisions will pay off.

Asian parents tend to make all the choices for their small children. As a result, Asian children do better on a task if they are told their mothers made preliminary choices for them. In contrast, Euro-Americans mothers allow their very young children to make many choices for themselves. For example, in grocery stores they allow toddlers to choose their own cereal, peanut butter, jelly, and so forth. As a result, Euro-Americans children tend to do better on a task if they make the choices themselves.

Inner Problem or Situational Problem?

Euro-Americans tend to explain a person's behavior in terms of internal disposition, while Asian Americans are more likely to see it as a result of the situation the persons finds himself in. Psychologist Kaiping Peng compared reactions to a tragic situation: A Chinese scholar working temporarily in the United States went on a rampage, murdered several people, and then committed suicide. Euro-Americans and Chinese Americans viewed the event quite differently. Most Euro-Americans agreed that a deep-rooted disturbance in the man's personality must have led him to commit the murders and suicide. He must have had a terrible childhood and suffered abuse. The Chinese woman who had dated him must be glad that she didn't marry him because he was clearly a walking time bomb. He might have murdered her too. This explanation reveals a focus on inner causes, such as mental instability or some "dark" features in the person's nature.

Chinese Americans focused on the murderer's situation as a lonely foreigner with few friends in a strange country, a situation that was very stressful for him. The woman who dated him expressed some regret. She speculated that if she had been there to give him the support he needed, he would never have committed such a horrible deed. This explanation reveals a focus on situational causes.

Most Asians have difficulty understanding the concept of evil. They see everything as being part of a state of flux and change, so they tend to explain behavior in terms of situation and context. As a result, they see the "loser" label that's used by Euro-Americans as very cruel. Also, trying to understand people in terms of their personality traits seems very odd to them. And the concept of an "overachiever" or an "underachiever" is strange. The idea that someone "should be achieving something" is bizarre. How do we know that a person is destined to *be* someone or to make good grades or a lot of money? Because nothing is fixed and everything is in a state of change, your score on an aptitude test is just one index of your abilities on a given day.

Cultural Difference #2: Us–First or Me–First?

This is the most important cultural difference for understanding how people interact with others. Cultures that focus on me-first are called individualist cultures because they believe that each individual must first take responsibility for her or his own life and should have the freedom to succeed or fail. Cultures that focus on us-first are called collectivist cultures because individuals are seen first as members of a family or cohesive group. It's similar to looking at a bouquet. Do you focus first on the whole bouquet with the attitude that one flower alone would be out of context and lost? Or do you focus first on each individual flower and then notice how the group forms a bouquet?

Us–First

"I should first integrate my goals, thoughts, and actions with those of my group. Working within what the group wants and needs, I can try to get what I want and need. People should always stay close to their parents and relatives and never stray far." Hofstede's research indicates that most cultures fall into this camp, including most African, Asian, Arab, and Latino cultures (Hofstede 1980, 1991).

Me–First

"I must first focus on my personal goals. I work toward better things for my family and work team and community, but my personal goals must come first. I'll stay with a group as long as it doesn't block my efforts to meet my own wants and needs. When people grow up, they have to cut the apron strings and make their own way in the world." European cultures fall into this camp, with Euro-Americans being the most individualistic.

Key to People Interactions

Many analysts suggest that the me-first versus us-first aspect of culture is the single most important concept for understanding what goes on when people from different cultures get together. Whether our primary outlook is me-first or us-first greatly influences our goals and priorities. The most important difference between collectivists and individualists is the emphasis they place on the opinions and feelings of group members ("What will they think?)" and the psychological closeness between themselves and others ("How does this affect our relationship?")(Kagitcibasi 1990; Brislin and Yoshida, 1994; Hofstede 1980; Hui 1990; Kim et al 1994).

Collectivist or Individualist?

Individualism and collectivism refer to the degree to which people in a culture believe that a person's beliefs and actions should be independent of the group's thought and action. Us-first collectivists believe that individuals should integrate their thoughts and actions with those of a group; for example, the extended family or the work organization. Me-first individualists are more likely to pursue their own personal goals, while collectivists are more likely to integrate their own goals with those of group members. Certainly, everyone has personal desires and goals they want to pursue and everyone needs to belong to at least one group. The concept revolves around priorities and emphases. What is the relative weight we place on fulfilling the need to belong and the need to do our own thing, especially when these needs conflict?

Euro-Americans, for example, explain human behavior in terms of an individual's experience and disposition, while ignoring the effects of the group situation on behavior. In an experiment Berkeley Professor Kaiping Peng showed people a picture with a single fish that was moving away from a school of fish. He asked people what this fish behavior meant. Most Euro-Americans indicated that the fish was asserting its independence, while most Asian Americans said the fish had been expelled by the school.

Peng showed a picture that included one fish by itself and four fish clustered together. Most Euro-Americans focused their attention on the lone fish, while most Asian Americans focused on the group of fish. Peng asked, "What is the group of fish feeling?" Most Euro-Americans responded by asking, "Which fish?" They found it very difficult to conceive of a group having an emotion. Because they believe that people's feelings should be private and individual, then feelings cannot be expressed by a group.

Happiness?

Euro-Americans tend to feel happy when they're experiencing strong emotions and strong subjective feelings. They're also likely to feel happy when they're experiencing disengaged emotions—feeling different, superior, unique, better, or special. Asian Americans, in contrast, are likely to be happy in relation to their evaluation of social experience. A typical attitude is: "I may feel poorly today and in a bad mood, but my family and society are happy, so I'm happy. If the group around me is happy, my personal mood of the day or hour are not that important." Happiness is likely to involve engaged emotions—getting along with others, feeling connected and bonded and welcomed.

Cut the Apron Strings or Not?

In individualist cultures, members are likely to cut the apron strings when they reach adulthood in a more complete way than do members of collectivist cultures (Hall 1989). For individualists, from birth to death, life is punctuated by separations, many of them painful. Paradoxically, each separation forms a foundation for new stages of integration, identity, and psychic growth. The newborn baby experiences himself and his small universe as one, inseparable. To be truly alive in the Euro-American culture, you must outgrow this state, and the full impact of the process comes when you leave home and establish yourself as an independent person. Conversely, in collectivist cultures, the bonds with the parents, grandparents, and even ancestors are not severed but are maintained and reinforced.

Individual Differences Within a Culture

Remember that some people within an individualist culture may have predominantly us-first collectivist values. Women in all cultures tend to be socialized to be collectivist. People in individualist cultures can also adopt collectivist values from their family, their subculture, their religion, or region. For example, in the United States you may be more collectivist if you live in the South or in a New England village than if you live in New York or Los Angeles (Brislin and Yoshida 1994).

Cultural Difference #3: Tight Ties or Loose Ties?

Cultures vary by how much alike people are, how homogeneous or diverse. This in turn helps determine whether people feel bound together by many ties or only loosely connected with few ties.

Many Ties That Bind = Us–First

"I see people first as part of a particular family or organization or community, and they see me that way. If I fail, the others in my group will 'lose face' and feel shame, so I should try to cover up my failure. If I succeed, the glory goes to my group, not to me." This mindset predominates in Eastern cultures and is held by a majority of the world's people.

"As I grew up, I thought of myself as part of 'we' rather than 'I.' It's important to me to protect my family and close friends and to be loyal to them. I expect them to protect and be loyal to me. Who I am is a member of my family, work group, and community. The ideal way to live is in close relationship with them. I belong to several groups and organizations. I depend on those relationships. We make decisions together, and I believe in those decisions. Who my friends are depends a great deal on the groups I belong to. My status and prestige comes from these relationships. The groups I belong to provide what I need—expertise, order, duty, and security. I'm loyal first to my parents and immediate family, then my relatives, and then the clan or nearby community. Success and satisfaction in life, comes from living up to those loyalties. If I gain material success, I'll share it with my family and close friends."

"When I was a university student, I studied hard to pass exams in order to acquire the status of a degree. Now I seek the satisfaction of a job well recognized. It's very important for me to preserve 'face,' or respect from my family and friends, and to avoid shaming them through my failure. My job life and private life are inseparable. It's okay if my boss inquires about my private life, and I expect the boss to help out with family or personal problems. On the job, relationships are even more important to me than getting tasks done. I must develop a relationship with the people I work with and become adopted into the work group before I can do a good job on my tasks."

In more tightly-woven collectivist societies, individuals are viewed in the context of social relationships, such as the family, the organization, the community. They are less differentiated as a self in contrast with others. "We" is usually more important than "I." An individual's failure causes others to "lose face" and results in shame, so it should be covered up and not seen. This mindset predominates in Eastern cultures, and is held by a majority of the world's people.

Key concepts are protection by the ingroup, loyalty to the ingroup, identity that stems from the group and the social system, membership in groups and organizations as the ideal mode, emotional dependence on organizations, belief in group decisions, friendships predetermined by stable social relationships, and need for prestige within these relationships. The organization or group provides expertise, order, duty, and security. Value standards differ for ingroups and outgroups. People are expected to be loyal first to their parents, relatives, and clan; and life achievement and satisfaction consist of living up to those loyalties.

Individuals perceive themselves as belonging to one or more close ingroups from which they cannot detach themselves. The ingroup may be an extended family, clan, or organization, which protects the interests of its members but in turn expects their permanent loyalty. A high quality of life is defined primarily in family and group terms. Children think of themselves as "we" rather than "I." If you gain success and wealth, you're expected to share it with your ingroup.

When they attend a university, people in a collectivist society are motivated to pass their exams in order to acquire the status of a degree. People seek the satisfaction of a job well recognized. Preserving face, or the respect from one's ingroup, and avoiding shame, are important. Job life and private life are inseparable. The company may intrude in the worker's private life and the worker expects the company to help out with family or personal problems. On the job, relationships take precedence over getting tasks done. An essential precondition for achieving a task is developing a relationship with the other person so he or she can become adopted into the ingroup (Hofstede 1984).

Earthy or Stylized?

Some anthropologists make a further distinction among tightly woven collectivist groups: the "earthy" cultures and the "stylized" cultures. Earthy cultures include American Indian, African, Latino, Pacific Island, and most Arab cultures. Function and style are one, for they value things that are functional and at the same time express beauty or meaning and honor mythology and nature. Stylized cultures include the Chinese, Japanese, Korean, East Indian, and Thai cultures. They feature many close, irreplaceable connections and are highly structured, with strict expectations, roles, and lifestyles. They're based on the most numerous ties of all and on the closest, most binding relationships.

Loose Ties = Me–First.

"I'm unique, one of a kind. Growing up means becoming my own person. If I fail in life, it's strictly my fault, and I would probably feel guilty and want to be by myself till I got over it. What I value most are autonomy, self-reliance, self-identity, emotional independence, and individual initiative."

"When I was a university student, I worked hard in order to master the subject matter for my major. It's important to me to maintain my self-respect and avoid guilt. On the job, I value challenges, individual achievement, and personal ambition. I want the satisfaction of a job well done, especially by my own standards. When I come home, I don't want to think about the job, and when I'm at work, I try to forget home problems. At work, it's all about getting the job done, so I don't have much time for getting to know people or hanging out." These are typical views of people from Western cultures.

The United States is one of the most loosely-knit cultures of modern times. In loosely-knit individualist societies, the individual is highly differentiated from others. Growing up means becoming an individual who is distinctly separate from others. Failure in life is the "sin" of the individual and may lead to guilt and separation. In such a society the collective goals of the family, ingroup, or community are often subordinated to the needs of individuals. This largely Western mindset is held by a minority of the world's people and is most strongly held among Americans. The mindset tends to be stronger in males than in females. Key values are autonomy, self-reliance, self-identity, emotional independence, and individual initiative. Major workplace values are job challenge, achievement, and ambition (Hofstede 1984).

In such *self-interest* cultures, people are loosely integrated (low context). Individuals look primarily after their self-interest and the interests of their immediate family. A high-quality life means individual success, achievement, self-actualization, and self-respect. In the workplace people seek the satisfaction of a job well done, especially by their own standards. When they attend a university, people are primarily motivated by a need to master their subject. Preserving self-respect and avoiding guilt are important. Job life and private life are usually sharply separated. Getting tasks done is more important than spending time on work relationships.

Euro-Americans, for example, tend to see themselves as different from others. Most have a strong belief that they're one of "the chosen" and that positive things will happen to them. A typical attitude is: "I'm not similar to others, but others may sometimes be similar to me." They're likely to say proudly that they're not nonconformists, but they do believe that something unique and different is good. In contrast, Asians tend to think that everyone is more or less alike. A typical attitude is: "Others are just like me and I like that idea."

Researcher Kaiping Peng offered people a free pen for participating in his survey. He showed them five pens, four of which were alike and one different. Euro-Americans overwhelmingly chose the "one-of-a-kind" pen, and Asian Americans chose a pen that was part of the group of four.

Cultural Difference #4: Achievement–First or People–First?

Most cultures place greater value on building and maintaining strong interpersonal relationships than on getting things done. Others value most highly a person's (or group's) achievements. People-first values are found most often in us-first cultures, while achievement-first predominates in me-first cultures. A people-first orientation reflects feminine values, while an achievement orientation reflects masculine values. However, in both types of cultures men dominate the political and workplace arenas, as research indicates that no country or culture is dominated by women in these areas.

People–First = Connecting, Cooperating = Feminine Aspect

"I focus on building and maintaining positive, personal relationships. The type of life I build is more important than the things I accumulate. I value my hunches and intuition. What motivates me is contributing to my family, workplace, and community. I work in order to live rather than live in order to work."

Relationship-oriented cultures focus on building and maintaining positive interpersonal relationships. They also feature gender equality and quality of life other than the material things in life. Intuition is highly valued, service is the chief motivating drive, and working in order to live is more the case than living for one's work.

The Scandinavian cultures are the most people-focused. Roles and viewpoints of men and women are not as separated as in most cultures. Neither men nor women need be to ambitious, competitive, or focused on material success. Men and women may respect whatever is small, weak, and slow. Values within political and work organizations center around interpersonal relationships and concern for the weak.

Research indicates that while Euro-Americans, especially men, tend to be highly competitive in social interaction and in task performance, Latino Americans, African Americans, and Asian Americans favor a more cooperative approach (Cox, Lobel, and McLeod, 1991; Kagan and Madsen 1971; DeVos 1980).

Achievement–First = Focus on Competition, "Things" = Masculine Aspect

"I'm very ambitious, and I believe I'm here to work. Hard work will bring me independence. Men should be assertive, ambitious, and competitive. They should work for material success, and respect whatever is big, strong, and fast. Women should serve and care for the intangible qualities of life, for the children, and for the weak."

Achievement-oriented cultures focus on achievement for men. They define very different social roles for men and women. They tend to be patriarchal, materialistic, performance-oriented, and factual. Independence is the ideal, ambition is the motivation, live-in-order-to-work is the viewpoint, and machismo is valued. Men are expected to be assertive, ambitious, and competitive, to strive for material success, and to respect whatever is big, strong, and fast. Women are expected to serve and care for the intangible qualities of life, for the children, and for the weak. Political and corporate values stress material success and assertiveness.

The most masculine culture by far is Japan's, while the United States culture is considered moderately masculine [Hofstede 1984].

Cultural Difference #5: Equality or Not?

Some cultures, primarily Western ones, are based on the ideal that all persons have equal value and status as human beings. People are therefore entitled to equal opportunity to achieve and advance in the society. Other cultures accept the idea that some people are naturally more powerful, affluent, and privileged than others. They therefore accept the inequality of rank and status in a hierarchical or stratified society. In these cultures people from different levels feel a greater sense of "power distance" than do people who live in more egalitarian cultures.

Inequality = Rank/Status Cultures

"My company's organization chart looks like a pyramid, with a few autocratic leaders at the top and many ordinary workers at the bottom. If my country had an organizational chart, it would look that way too. Our leaders are very strong and powerful. We depend on them to make the right decisions. We expect them to control things. If they asked us what to do, we would assume they were weak and should step down. The leaders we admire are good people, similar to good fathers who take care of things. Of course they live well, with people to take care of menial tasks for them. Such leaders should have the trappings of wealth that go with the territory. I expect my boss to make the decisions, give me clear orders, and to take a personal interest in me and my family. I don't speak up to my boss unless he tells me to. I would never contradict my boss, either at work or elsewhere. My status depends on the status of my boss and my company."

Nearly all so-called under-developed and developing countries have such vertical societies. When people from these cultures move to Western countries to work, they often initially feel lost because their leaders are not so authoritarian and patriarchal. For example, people from Latino and Asian cultures pay more homage to the boss than do people from Western cultures. They may be appalled at the idea of arguing a point with the boss or seeing the boss pitch in to help out in a pinch. They are much less likely to point out potential problems with their manager's decision and may have difficulty speaking up when team decisions need to be made. To them, bosses do the bossing and employees do the work and deviations from that norm imply that one or the other can't do their jobs properly.

In rank/status cultures, power distance is high. Organizations tend to feature hierarchical organizational structures (picture a pyramid), power inequality, autocratic leadership, dependence on leaders, centralized decision making, and the belief that power lies with a few strong leaders. People have strong dependence needs on higher-ups.

While people may aspire to democracy as an impersonal ideal, they expect superiors to behave autocratically and don't expect to be consulted. Ideal superiors are benevolent autocrats or patriarchs, good father types that subordinates can depend on. Superiors are expected to enjoy special privilege and be exempt from certain rules and laws. Status symbols are widely used and contribute to the superiors' authority in the eyes of subordinates. Organizations are identified with one or more powerful individuals. Change comes about by decree from top individuals or by revolution.

Hierarchical cultures are virtually always collectivist cultures. They value deference to authority and sensitivity to status. This is part of going along with the group. Bosses in such cultures may appear arrogant and aloof to individualists, who tend to believe that bosses and employees are basically equal human beings. Such bosses may seem to flaunt the privileges of status, such as fine cars, drivers, and elite dining rooms in contrast to workers who ride the bus and eat from a lunch box (Brislin and Yoshida 1994).

The boss-centered workplace, where the boss calls the shots, is the norm. Workers are not expected to initiate communication with the boss nor to speak up unless called upon to do so. Bosses are respected in and out of the workplace and are not to be publicly contradicted. Employees' status is higher when the status of the boss and the company is higher.

Equality = Democratic Cultures

"My company's organization chart looks sort of like a low box. The organization chart of my daughter's company looks like a web within a circle with the executive team at the center. I believe that my boss has power because he's worked his way up to boss, not because he's better than me. I appreciate it when my boss consults me about decisions that affect me and my job. I like it even more when he lets me or the team make the decisions. I like being independent but I don't mind choosing to be interdependent with my work team."

Equality of power is referred to as small power distance. Key concepts are democratic leadership, independence or interdependence, flat organizational structures, decentralized decision making, and the belief that position power lies in the role, not in the superiority of the person. In general, women are more likely than men to manage in a democratic way (Eagly and Johnson 1990).

In moderately egalitarian cultures—such as in the United States, Japan, and most European countries—consultation is usually appreciated but not necessarily expected. Participative environments are initiated by the participative leader, not by subordinates. Ideal leaders are pragmatically democratic. Moderate status differences and privileges for leaders are acceptable. Rules and laws are expected to apply to superiors and subordinates alike. Change normally starts with the top leaders, but key people throughout the organization must buy into the change if it is to be effective and lasting.

In very egalitarian cultures—such as in the Scandinavian countries, Israel, and Austria—subjecting yourself to the power of others is seen as undesirable. Everyone should have a say in everything that concerns them. Status differences are suspect. Ideal leaders are democratic and loyally carry out the will of their groups. Change comes about through group consensus. Leaders must persuade and influence the group. Former leaders are usually comfortable with accepting new, less powerful roles, for the power differential is in the roles, not the people who fill them.

Cultural Difference #6: Take Risks or Play It Safe?

In cultures that value playing it safe, people like to avoid uncertainty. People are not comfortable with unstructured, unclear, or unpredictable situations, so they adopt strict codes of behavior and a belief in absolute truths in order to avoid such uncertainty.

Play It Safe

"We keep things under control in my culture. We do it by:

- Making sure that everyone knows the rules and not allowing people to break the rules without punishment.
- Making sure that people know what's expected by designating precise relationships, assignments, and schedules.
- Arranging life so that everyone knows what to expect."

"Since change creates many unknowns and uncertainties, we don't like change and try to prevent it by sticking with tradition."

Cultures that value playing it safe are high in "uncertainty avoidance." This term refers to the extent to which people are comfortable with unstructured, unclear, or unpredictable situations, and the extent to which they try to avoid such situations by adopting strict codes of behavior and a belief in absolute truths. Since change creates many unknowns and uncertainties, people in these cultures resist change more than others. They focus on tradition, and therefore the past, and often become quite rigid in these matters.

People in play-it-safe cultures are also generally more active, aggressive, emotional, security-seeking, and intolerant. Greece is the most certainty-oriented culture, followed by Japan. Most European and Latino cultures fall into this pattern [Hofstede 1984].

Take Risks

"'Nothing ventured, nothing gained' is my motto. Rules have their place but there are exceptions to every rule. I like change and new adventure. I like investing in the future and looking forward to possible payoffs. For a business to be successful, people must come up with new ways of doing things, new products and services, and new technology."

Cultures where people are more comfortable with uncertainty tend to be risk-taking cultures. When people don't fear "reasonable" risks, they are more open to change and more forward-looking, anticipating the payoff from their investment in future changes. New ways of doing things, new products and services, and new technology are highly valued.

People in risk-taking cultures also tend to be more contemplative and tolerant, and less aggressive and emotional than those in play-it-safe cultures. The United States has a moderately risk-taking culture, and Singapore is by far the most risk-taking culture studied by Hofstede (1984).

Cultural Difference #7: Time—Dive–Right–In or Step–by–Step?

Some cultures see time as a series of points along a line and people doing one task at a time. Others see time as a circle in which they jump in doing many tasks at one time. The first is a linear, single-task use of time, and the second is a circular, multiple-task use of time.

Dive–Right–In Time

"Time is like a circle, and I use points of time within the circle. Several things may be happening at once in this circle because several people may need my attention at any one time. After all, it's more important to maintain good relationships with others and to complete transactions with others than to do one thing at a time on a preset schedule. Each point in time is sacred but only because I give myself fully to the moment, to the relationships, events, or activities of the moment. An activity simply takes as much time as is needed for its completion, so if the activity is important, the time it takes is irrelevant."

Circular-time cultures include Latino, Middle Eastern, and some Asian and African cultures. In the U. S. workplace, it is likely that many African Americans, Asian Americans, and Latino Americans are circular-time people. While they may necessarily adapt to the Euro-American time orientation when they work in U.S. organizations, they tend to return to their own time orientation for social and family events.

Euro-Americans sometimes feel they don't really have the full attention of a busy circular-time person. They worry that the person may never get around to the most important business at hand. Some feel that nothing seems solid or firm with circular-time people, particularly regarding the future. Often there are changes in the most important plans, right up to the very last minute. In circular-time organizations, systems need a much greater centralization of control because the top person deals continually with many people.

In some cultures, time is determined by repeated cycles of activities, such as the agricultural cycles of planting, cultivating, and harvesting. People in such cultures do not see time as stretching into the future, but focus on the past and present. This orientation is dominant in Cuban, Mexican, and many African tribal cultures.

Step–by–Step Time

"Time is made up of the past, the present, and an infinite future. I pay most attention to the future. Time can be separated into units or steps with fixed beginnings and endings for events. I measure my time and budget it as I schedule appointments, decide on the starting and ending times for events, get to things on time, meet my deadlines, and plan ahead. The best way to use my time is to focus on one thing at a time."

In Western countries, especially the United States, people tend to view time as separable into quantifiable, discrete units or steps with fixed beginnings and endings for events. They place great emphasis on future events and therefore on planning, scheduling, setting target dates, and being prompt. The segmenting of time leads to focusing on one task, appointment, or event at a time (Graham 1981; Cote and Tansuhaj 1989; McGrath and Rotchford 1983).

Step-by-step time is linear, like a ribbon or road of time. It's almost tangible because people talk about manipulating it, scheduling it, using it, and borrowing it. Compartmentalizing time in steps or units allows you to concentrate on one thing at a time, but it also denies you much of the context in which events occur. It permits only a limited number of events within a given period. Thus it can limit your possibilities. Your business life, social life, and even sex life, are apt to be completely time dominated. Linear-time people are less likely to see things in a larger context (Hall 1982).

Cultural Difference #8: Space—Come Close or Back Off?

Cultures differ in how much personal space individuals expect to occupy, how close they stand or sit to one another, and how much physical contact they have. In the workplace this translates into different perceptions about comfortable office sizes and layout and requirements for privacy in work stations (Hall 1982).

Come–Close Space

"I'm from the Middle East. When I talk with business associates and friends, we stand close enough to be able to feel each other's breath on our face and to be able to catch each other's scent. We touch each other a great deal as we interact. My male business associates often embrace instead of shaking hands."

Latino and Middle Eastern cultures tend to be high-contact societies, with more touching permitted and expected than in other cultures. Two men will often embrace instead of shaking hands. People in Latino cultures prefer slightly more distance than those in Middle Eastern cultures, but they like to stand closer and to touch more than do people in Western cultures. Asian cultures like the most space and least public touching of all, according to E.T. Hall.

Back–Off Space

"I'm a Euro-American. When I talk with business associates and social acquaintances, it's usually at arm's length, about two or three feet away. Of course, I'm closer to my lover as well as family members and close friends. I notice that I stand farther away when I want to protect myself or to stay uninvolved. If someone moves too close into my space, I usually feel uncomfortable and back up till I feel comfortable. It really bugs me if a person keeps moving in even after I back off."

Western cultures are basically non-contact societies, according to Hall. In most Western cultures we learn to stand about two or three feet away, an arm's length, when we're at business or social events. Only family members, close friends, and lovers are expected to come closer. We may stand farther away when we feel a desire to remain aloof or protect ourselves. When someone moves into our space, we normally feel uncomfortable and back away till we feel comfortable again.

In most Asian cultures, perhaps because of dense populations, people prefer an even greater distance and less touching with all but family and close friends.

Cultural Difference #9: Communicating—Direct or Indirect?

While there are many variations in communication style, two that stem directly from the key cultural patterns we've discussed are directness and indirectness.

Using Go–Betweens and Implied Messages

"I try to maintain harmony and to get along with people, so I never say things that would offend them. Saying no directly would be offensive, so I try to gently let them know that I'm not terribly enthusiastic about something. To make an initial overture or bring up a sensitive topic, I usually ask someone close to the other person to feel them out first."

People in most cultures use an indirect style of communication, especially in those cultures identified as us-first, people-first, rank/status, and play-it-safe. In us-first cultures with many close ties, many messages can be implied because people have been socialized alike and are on "the same wavelength." And in many cultures, go-betweens are used to broach sensitive topics. In all cultures, women are likely to use an indirect style, such as hinting, implying, keeping quiet in order to keep peace, and mentioning problems or desires to associates of the decision-maker in the hope that they'll "put in a good word."

Going to the Person and Getting to the Point

"I try to build trusting relationships based on honesty and sincerity. It's important to be upfront and genuine in my dealings with people. If I have a problem with a person, or want to make a proposal, I go directly to that person first and try to work it out."

The direct style is typical in Western cultures, especially those that focus on I-control, me-first, achievement-first, equality, and risk taking. Within those cultures men are more likely than women to use a direct communication style.

Cultural Difference #10: How We Make Money = Dependence Level

Whether you—and most of the people in your ingroup—are a farmer, an assembly line worker, or a computer programmer will affect your cultural values and customs. Agriculture is the dominant way of making a living in so-called undeveloped countries, while most developing countries have become industrialized to some extent. The Western nations are predominantly post-industrial. But many countries have large groups that make their living as farmers and other large groups that work in industry (Nirenberg 1993). In many countries there is a peasant-class value system that's quite different from the ruling-class value system, which may have post-industrial values. This economic-structure approach is directly related to the level of dependence that people in a culture tend to feel. In fact, the ten cultural differences tend to fall into three distinct patterns of independence, dependence, and interdependence, as shown in Table 2.3. For further detail on how these factors play out in the workplace, see Table 2.4 at the end of this chapter.

TABLE 2.3: Cultural Differences and Types of Dependence

Dependent Focus	Independent Focus	Interdependent Focus
External source of control: life happens to me **Collectivism:** us-first	**Internal source of control:** I control my life **Individualism:** me-first	**Internal source of control:** I control my life **Combination:** independent persons choose to team up.
Ties: tight, close with ingroup members	**Ties:** loose, few	**Ties:** vary by personal choice
Personal connection first: cooperative, feminine, focus on relationships and intangibles	**Achievement first:** competitive, masculine, focus on material things and tasks	**Combination:** people-first in order to achieve as work teams
Class difference status, rank, defer to authority	**Equality:** democratic, give-and-take authority	**Equality**
Security-seeking: I must avoid uncertainty; leads to being rigid, rules-oriented, w/focus on tradition, the status quo	**Risk-taking:** I can handle uncertainty; leads to openness, flexibility, focus on future change	**Risk-taking**
Time use: circular, multiple-task	**Time use:** linear, single-task	**Time use:** combination linear and circular; flexible
Space use: close for members **Communication:** indirect **Economic system:** agricultural	**Space use:** distant **Communication:** direct **Economic system:** industrial	**Space use:** flexible combination **Communication:** direct **Economic system:** post-industrial

Economic and occupational differences may help explain the cultural complexity we find among people in a supposedly homogeneous nation. Within a nation, region, or culture, various groups may be operating from the ethos that represents their way of making a living, under-girded to some extent by other traditional cultural values. For example, all workers in the United States share in the cultural media—television, film, radio, magazines, and books are readily available to most everyone. Farmers, factory workers, and computer technicians will therefore maintain some common values. But people immigrating from certain Latino, Asian, and African countries may have lacked access to such media and therefore were more segmented and isolated by their economic activities. For example, in China groups in fairly remote areas may be almost entirely involved in agriculture and still adhere to many agriculture-era values. Others, in urban areas, may be focused on manufacturing and therefore on in-dustrial-era values. A few, such as those in Hong Kong, may be focused on post-industrial activities and values.

Agricultural Economy = Dependent Worldview

In many countries that are primarily dependent upon an agricultural economy, the value system of the masses in the peasant class is quite different from that of the elite ruling-class. The masses are quite dependent on the extended family and village groups. They are likely to believe they're con-trolled, put the group first and have many close ties, focus on cooperative relationships, accept status differences, avoid change and risk, view time as circular, like physical closeness, at least with family, and use an indirect communication style. All this adds up to a worldview that's primarily dependent on external forces, the family, and village groups. The dependent pattern was traditionally typical of most women in all cultures and of men and women in Asian, Latino, and African cultures, in fact of most of the world's peoples.

It seems obvious that putting the group first is good for family and group survival, and it can con-trol personal selfishness and greed. A major disadvantage is the lack of personal choice you're allowed in such cultures. For example, in traditional cultures parents and community leaders determined whom you should marry, where you should live, what work you should do, how you should worship. All the major life decisions were made for you. The effect can be to drain away some of your motivation, pas-sion for life, and ability to make your own decisions and take responsibility for their outcomes. Imag-ine the difference between living with a husband or wife you were required to marry versus someone you passionately wanted to marry. Or working in an occupation you were expected to follow versus one you knowingly chose once you were clear about what you really wanted to do in life.

Industrial Economy = Independent Worldview

As a culture moves into a manufacturing-based economy, values shift to a more independent focus that's needed for success in that workplace. People are likely to believe they're in control, put their own goals first, have looser ties with others, focus on competitive achievement, demand equality, take calculated risks to bring needed change, view time as points on a line, keep most people at arm's length, and use a direct communication style. An independent worldview is traditionally typical of men in Western cultures. It allows for greater selfishness and greed, and doesn't do as much to encourage con-cern for others, but it also provides for greater personal power and autonomy. This in turn promotes such skills as taking calculated risks, taking initiative, taking charge, doing independent problem solv-ing and decision making, and taking responsibility for results.

Post-Industrial Economy = Interdependent Worldview

As a culture moves to an information- and service-based economy, it begins to shift to an inter-dependent focus. Some values and customs seem similar to dependence on the surface. But a major dif-ference is that people are aware of their individuality and independence. They have developed the powerful skills typical of people in an independent culture.

People in post-industrial economies are likely to believe they're in control. They may embrace elements of both the me-first and us-first orientations—as autonomous people they choose to put the work team first in order to achieve greater things together. They focus on cooperative relationships in order to achieve greater success. They're also likely to demand equality, take calculated risks, be flexible in how they use time and physical closeness, and use a direct communication style.

Instead of feeling dependent upon a group for survival, people in interdependent cultures have the power and freedom to either work independently or to team up with others. When they choose to team up or form alliances, it's because they believe that choice will allow them to have more fun, or be more successful, or both.

Key differences between dependence and interdependence:

- Group members choose to be part of the group—it's a preference rather than a need—so they bring with them the power of free choice rather than duty or obligation.
- Group members are self-motivated.
- Group members bring the power and skills inherent in an independent lifestyle.

These qualities are especially valuable for the types of work arrangements needed today, such as:

- Self-managing teams
- Entrepreneurial teams
- Project teams
- Business alliances
- Professional networks

Warning: Don't Use Cultural Knowledge to Create New Stereotypes

A little knowledge can be a dangerous thing—or a wonderful thing, if you realize its limitations. Now that you have a little knowledge of cultural differences—and you'll be gaining more detailed knowledge of the largest U.S. subcultures—be sure you use it wisely. When you learn what experts have to say about your own culture, you're sure to think about some aspects, "Oh, no, I don't do that!" Well, that's true for most people. While they live out most of the major beliefs and values of their culture, they'll have their own ideas about some things. There are always some areas where people think independently, or even rebelliously.

Bottom line: Don't use the knowledge you acquire about a culture to create new stereotypes about people from that culture. Focus on each person you meet as an individual, using your knowledge of their cultural background as a sensing device for getting to know the individual, as pictured in Figure 2.2.

Why study cultural differences? Without this knowledge, you'll find that the more diverse your workplace is, the more you get caught in puzzling, conflicting situations without a clue as to how to proceed. You may try to feel your way through the amorphous mass of people's puzzling actions, sometimes engulfed by a swirling ocean of people's mysterious emotions, trying to feel your way through a dense fog of hidden motivations. You feel blocked by the unknowns and can't work your way through to understanding and resolution. Think of your cultural knowledge as threads, lifelines, that you can follow to formulate the

- right questions to ask
- appropriate motivations to explore
- specific feelings to recognize

Used sensitively, cultural information can help you weave together these threads of information to arrive at ways to work with people to resolve problems and conflicts. It can help you figure out how to connect and bond with people and build trusting, productive relationships.

FIGURE 2.2: Focus on the Individual against a Cultural Background

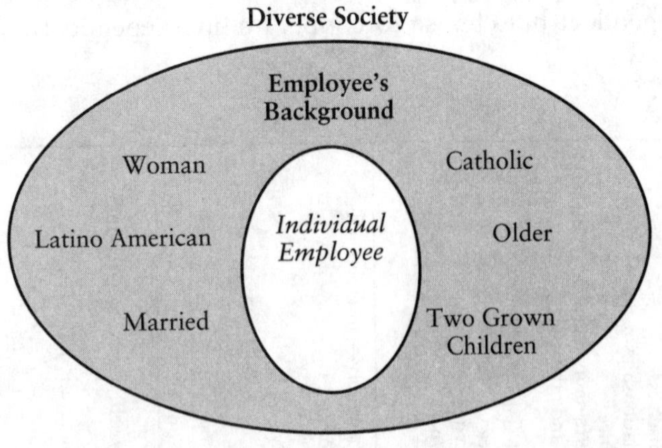

Diverse Society

Employee's
Background

Woman   Catholic

Latino American   *Individual Employee*   Older

Married   Two Grown
                              Children

SUMMARY

The first step in building multicultural skills is becoming aware of culture and its pervasive influence. Culture is programmed beliefs, hidden programming, our mental map, our consensus reality, and our personal reality. Cultures are made up of the key values people believe are important. About 1,000 aspects of culture are hidden within our subconscious minds for every element we're consciously aware of. Heroes and heroines serve as role models that personify certain cultural values and norms. They motivate others to succeed. Rituals and ceremonies indicate to everyone the culture values and the way the people are expected to do things. Networks are the ways people are connected, and grapevines are channels for getting the word around. Cultures use ten primary message systems that communicate values, norms, rituals, and customs from one generation to the next. The message systems are embedded in the ways adults educate youngsters, direct them, and model appropriate behaviors for them.

Numerous commonalties are found across all cultures. Still, cultures can be quite diverse, and going from one to another can be like going into another world. Even within one culture, girls and boys are raised so differently it's as if they're living in parallel worlds—and gender is said to be one of the most basic differences.

Cultural differences can be categorized into ten major areas.

1. I'm-controlled or I-Control reflects beliefs about whether I create my situation or it happens to me.

2. Us-first or me-first refers to a focus on the group or the individual.

3. Tight ties or loose ties looks at how tightly-knit the culture is.

4. Achievement-first or people-first refers to whether the culture values most highly getting things done or nurturing relationships.

5. Equality or inequality refers to the importance placed on rank and status.

6. Taking risks or playing it safe relates to needs for security and clarity.

7. Views of time can range from dive-right-in to step-by-step.

8. How to use personal space may range from come-close to back-off.

9. Communication patterns include directness or indirectness and level of formality.

10. How we make money refers to whether we work in an agricultural, industrial, or post-industrial economy.

The underlying theme that runs through these cultural differences is level of dependence. In cultures with a predominantly agricultural economy, people feel more dependent on each other and nature.

Those in an industrial economy feel more independent, and as the culture moves to a post-industrial economy, as it is in the United States, people become more interdependent. At this level, people are capable of being independent but choose to cooperate interdependently for greater enjoyment or achievement, or both.

TABLE 2.4: The Economic System's Effect on Cultural Values

Values Related to Achievement Vs Relationship:

Agricultural-Era Values— Dependent	Industrial-Era Values— Independent	Post-Industrial-Era Values— Interdependent
Cooperative - win/win	Competitive (win-lose)	Cooperative (win-win)
Worker as member of a family	Worker as automaton	Worker as dynamic colleague
Static role-based relationships (place-bound)	Mechanistic organizations	Organic organizations
Community	Compartmentalization	Integration
Life is a chore/people must earn redemption	Theory X—people are lazy, must be coerced, directed	Theory Y—people can be self-motivated
Survival focus	Profit centered	Value centered
Traditions/ceremonies	Acquiring material goods for family/self	Experiencing events, life
Work relationships—focus on role	Work relationships—focus on secrecy/need to know	Work relationships—focus on openness
People necessary for family survival	People as means to organizational ends	People as ends in themselves
Feelings channeled through ceremonies	Feeling denied/relationships impersonal	Feelings expressed, relationships personal
Right brain emphasis (intuitive, feeling, holistic)	Left brain emphasis (rational, linear, factual)	Intuitive/rational balance
Role modeling (toward an ideal)	Macho modeling (winning)	Androgyny, masculine/feminine balance
Power over nature	Power over others	Empowerment of self and others
Dominance	Manipulation	Collaboration
Personal/community development	Management development	Organization development
People as necessary components	People as expendable resources, liabilities	People as renewable resource/asset
The spiritual aspects of life most highly valued	Material things most highly valued	Ideas most highly valued
Focus on traditions, values, family	Focus on bottom line	Focus on process/goal/person

Values Related to Me-First or Us-First and to I-Control or I'm-Controlled

Agricultural Economy— Dependent	Industrial Economy— Independent	Post-Industrial Economy— Interdependent
Family/community focus	Bureaucracy/hierarchy	Flexible teams/networks
Family/clan centered	Organization centered	Organization as part of society
Family/clan centered	Class centered	Lifestyle centered
Integrated community role	Extrinsic motivation (incentives)	Intrinsic motivation
Social norms—universal	Dependency at work	Autonomy at work
Family/community hold the power	Social norms—universal	Social norms—pluralistic
Work as a function of life	Shareholder/manager hold the power	Stakeholders share the power
Performance judged by elders, neighbors	Work as drudgery	Work as fun
Submersion of self in groups	Performance judged by boss as control factor	Performance judged by self, others, for growth
Product standard—adequacy	Interpersonal game playing	Authenticity
Work—rhythmic	Product standard—planned obsolescence	Product standard—conservation
Diffuse localization of power and activity	Work—routine, often monotonous	Work—creative
Diverse chores	Centralization of power and activity	Decentralization of power and activity
Community oriented	Job specialization	Job enrichment
Risk averse	Isolated, alienated	Committed
Obedience to parent/elder	Risk averse	Entrepreneurial
Workers—role/family centered	Obedience to boss	Respected associate
	Workers—job centered	Workers—profession centered

Values Related to Time and Space Orientations

Agricultural-Era Values— Dependent	Industrial Economy— Independent	Post-Industrial Economy— Interdependent
Viewpoint tied to seasonal/life cycle	Viewpoint short-term, narrow, fragmented	Focus on the long term, the holistic
Permanence—social life static	Permanence—social life slow evolving	Transience—instant intimacy
Provincialism	Provincialism	Cosmopolitanism

Preparation for Skill Builder: What's Your Cultural Identity?

Instructions: Read the information here as preparation for Skill Builder 2.1.

Your cultural identity consists of the groups you identify with and the strength with which you identify with each group. When we take the time to think about it, we can easily name those aspects of our identity that are most important to us. Most people are quite aware of those aspects that make them different from the dominant majority and are considerably less aware of their other facets. For example, Euro-American women tend to focus on being a woman, expatriates focus on nationality, minority men focus on ethnicity, and nonwhite women focus somewhat equally on gender and ethnicity.

Euro-American males are more likely than any other group to focus on individual identification, according to Cox [1993], even when instructed to refer only to group identifications. As Hofstede [1980] showed, individuality is a strong cultural norm for Euro-American men. Also, because they are part of the dominant majority group, Euro-American men face the fewest workplace and socioeconomic barriers, and therefore tend to be less aware of group identities than are members of minority groups. [Alderfer 1982]. The ways in which we differ from one include gender, sexual orientation, physical ability, ethnic heritage, occupational or professional influences, educational and socioeconomic background, and religious, spiritual, or philosophical influences. You have a chance to develop your own cultural profile in Skill Builder 2.1.

The ethnic differences of immigrants tend to recede over time, and each generation born in this country is more Americanized than their parents. However, certain cultural values tend to remain strong. For example, even third-generation Japanese Americans have been found to have relatively high scores on ethnic identification with the Japanese culture, with survey scores virtually unchanged between second- and third-generation respondents. [Matsumoto, Meredith, and Masuda 1970].

Skill Builder 2.1: Your Cultural Profile

Purpose: To identify key aspects of your cultural heritage and identity.

Step 1. If you have not read the preceding section on Preparation for Skill Builder, do so now.

Step 2. Complete the second column of the table below by completing the statements made in the first column.

Step 3. Complete the third column of the table by determining the importance of each specific category for you. [For example, is being a college graduate a major or minor part of your identity?] Place a number, from 1 to 5, beside each category you've listed, according to its importance, using the following guidelines to assign weights:

5 = Major, essential aspect of my identity

4 = Very important aspect of my identity

3 = Fairly important aspect of my identity

2 = Somewhat influential aspect of my identity

1 = Slightly influential aspect of my identity

Step 4. Write a brief paragraph about your cultural profile. Include any thoughts, feelings, surprises, or insights that came to you as you did this Skill Builder.

Aspects of Your Identity

Area of Identity or Influence	Specify Categories	Weight 1 to 5
My **gender** is:		
My **sexual orientation** is (heterosexual, homosexual, bisexual):		
My **ethnic group** is (ancestors' country of origin):		
The **nation** where I was born is:		
The **part of the country** I grew up in is:		
The **occupation** I'm in or want is:		
The **company** I work for is:		
My **religion** or philosophy is:		
My **socioeconomic** class is (middle, lower, upper class):		
My **educational** level is:		
My **parents' educational** level is:		
Other groups or aspects that have influenced my identity are:		

Skill Builder 2.2: Diverse Groups You Need to Learn About

Purpose: To identify those groups of people you need to learn more about, ranging from those you know almost nothing about to those you need no information about.

Step 1. In the first column of the table below are listed types of groups discussed in this book. In the second column, you may want to set up two categories, men and women, and assign them different weights.

Step 2. The third column of the table refers to the degree to which you lack information on each group listed in the first column. Place a number, from 1 to 5, beside each group you've listed, indicating how much you know about this group, using the following guidelines to assign weights:

5 = I know nothing about this group
4 = I know almost nothing about this group
3 = I know very little about this group
2 = I have a fair amount of information and understanding of this group
1 = I have a great deal of information and understanding about this group
and need little or no additional information

Groups I Need to Learn About

Type of Group	More specific identity?	Weight: 1 to 5
Arab Americans		
African American		
American Indian		
Asian American (or subgroup)		
Euro-American		
Latino American (or subgroup)		
Persons with Disabilities		
Gay/Lesbian/Bisexual		
Obese persons		
Older persons		
Persons from other religions		
Persons whose mother and father are from different ethnic groups		
Women's issues		
Men's issues		
Other groups		

Skill Builder 2.3: Identifying Some Perceptions

Purpose: To learn more about your way of thinking.

Step 1. Relax and focus on the words listed below, one at a time. Notice what mental picture, what words, and what feelings you experience when you focus on the words. Jot down the word and note your reactions and associations with it. Do this for all the words.

Stranger, Foreigner, Immigrant, Native, People, Family, Home, Work, Nature

Step 2. Now go back and review your list. For each word, note any judgment, attitude, or belief that came to mind when you first saw the word or that comes to mind now. Do this for all the words.

Step 3. Go back again and review your judgments, attitudes or beliefs. Where do you think each of these originally came from?

Step 4. Write down any thoughts, feelings, and insights that occur to you now that you've completed working with the list of words. What, if anything, did you learn about yourself?

Skill Builder 2.4: Your Sense of Time

Purpose: To increase your awareness about how you and others view and use time.

Instructions: Describe briefly at least one instance when you and someone from a different cultural background experienced conflict, misunderstanding, or problems about time. Use the following list to help you remember your situation:

- Being on time
- Meeting deadlines
- Feeling hurried, rushed
- Using time efficiently
- Using time effectively
- Being "out of sync"
- Feeling impatient over others' slowness
- Focusing on past events, tradition
- Living for the moment, short-range view
- Focusing on the present moment
- Focusing on the future, what might happen
- Focusing on planning, or long-range view
- Other issues about time

Skill Builder 2.5: Your Boundaries

Purpose: To increase your awareness about how you and others view and use personal space.
Instructions: Describe briefly at least one instance when you (or others) experienced conflict, misunderstanding, or problems about personal space, touching, or boundaries. Use the following list to help you remember your situation.

- Invasion of privacy - yours or others
- Discomfort because of lack of privacy
- Invasion of personal body space
- Someone in your face
- Feeling crowded or claustrophobic
- Too much touching
- Invasive touching
- Too much coldness and distance
- Other issues about space, boundaries, or touching

Skill Builder 2.6: Your Values

Purpose: To learn more about yourself and what you want in life.
Instructions: Before you begin, remember that the purpose of this Skill Builder is for you to learn more about you. Don't evaluate, judge, or analyze what comes up; just let what wants to come up do so.
Step 1. Brainstorm. Relax, close your eyes for a few moments and think about these questions:

- What are the aspects of my life that I treasure the most? That I wouldn't want to lose? That I would fight to keep?
- What are those aspects of life that I don't yet have and want most to have? That I would work hard to have?
- What are my values?

Step 2. Write. Don't try to evaluate or analyze the thoughts that occurred to you. Just write them down in whatever sequence you remember them. As more ideas come up, write them down.
Step 3. Categorize. Look over what you've written. Do the items fall into any patterns or categories, such as:

family, friends work, leisure	money, power beauty, truth	intelligence, emotions spirituality

You'll find your own categories, not necessarily these. Work with your list till you see some logical categories; then rewrite your list of values by category.
Step 4. Personalize terms. What would you call the items on your list if you didn't call them values? (desires? goals? beliefs? issues? other?)

Skill Builder 2.7: Cultures You've Known

Purpose: To recognize the hidden aspects of your own and other cultural group.
Instructions: Perhaps reviewing some obvious rites, rituals, heroes, and symbols of the cultures you've belonged to will help you recognize more subtle rites, rituals, etc., in the cultures you encounter. Remember, rites and rituals relate to the need for belonging. A *rite* is any formal practice, custom, or procedure. A *ritual* is any detailed method of procedure that is regularly followed.

Be aware that in every organization, the stronger the rules, rituals, symbols, and heroes, the stronger the effect and influence the organization has on its members' lives.

For each category that is relevant to your own life, such as your nation, school, religious community, family, workplace, identify examples of cultural practices, as exemplified in the National Symbols category below.

Step 1: National Symbols

Rites and Rituals: (What rites and rituals gave you a feeling of national unity—an overall community with common purpose? For example, the national anthem.)

Heroes: (What heroes personified key national values?)

Symbols: (What symbols served to unify, to express values? For example, the flag.)

Values: (What values are expressed by the above?)

Step 2: Pick at least one other area of your life—such as your workplace, school, family, religious community, or social organization—and give examples of important rites, rituals, heroes, symbols, and values.

REFERENCES

Alderfer, C.P. "Problems of Changing White Male's Behavior and Beliefs Concerning Race Relations," in *Change in Organizations*. San Francisco, Jossey-Bass, 1982.

Althen, Gary, *American Ways*. Yarmouth, ME: Intercultural Press, 1988.

Asante, M.K. and K. Asante, eds. *African Culture*. Westport, CT: Greenwood Press, 1985.

Bellah, R.N. et al. *The Good Society*. New York: Knopf, 1991.

Bhawuk, D. and Brislin, R. "The measurement of intercultural sensitivity using the individualism and collectivism concepts." *International Journal of Intercultural Relations*, 16: 413-436, 1992.

Brislin, Richard & Tomoko Yoshida. *Improving Intercultural Interactions*. Newbury Park, CA: Sage, 1994

Cote, J.A. and P.S. Tansuhaj, "Culture Bound Assumptions in Behavior Intention Models," *Advances in Consumer Research*, Vol. 16, 1989, pp. 105-109.

Cox, T.H. and J. Finley-Nickerson, "Models of Acculturation for Intraorganizational Cultural Diversity," *Canadian Journal of Administrative Sciences* 8, 2, 1991, 90-100.

Cox, T.H., S. Lobel and P. McLeod, "Effects of Ethnic Group Cultural Difference on Cooperative Versus Competitive Behavior in a Group Task," *Academy of Management Journal* 34, 1991, 827-847.

Cox, Taylor. *Cultural Diversity in Organizations*. San Francisco: Berrett-Koehler, 1993.

De Anda, D. "Bicultural Socialization," *Social Work*, 29: 101-107, 1984.

Deal, T.E. and A.A. Kennedy. *Corporate Cultures*. Reading MA: Addison-Wesley, 1982.

Delgado, M. "Hispanic Cultural Values: Implications for Groups," *Small Group Behavior*, Vol. 12, No. 1, 1981, pp. 69-80.

DeVos, G.A., "Ethnic Adaptation and Minority Status," *Journal of Cross-Cultural Psychology* 11, 1, 1980, 101-124.

Eagly, A.H. and B.T. Johnson, "Gender and Leadership Style," *Psychological Bulletin* 108, 2, 1990, 233-256.

Feldman, D.D. "The Multiple Socialization of Organization Members," *Academy of Management Review*, 67, 2: 309-318, 1981.

Fottler, M.D. and T. Bain, "Sex Differences in Occupational Aspirations," *Academy of Management Journal* 23, 1980, 144-149.

Goff, J.L. and P.J. Goff. *Organizational Co-Dependence*. Niwot, CO: University Press of Colorado, 1991.

Graham, R. J. "The Role of Perception of Time in Consumer Behavior," Journal of Consumer Research, Vol. 7, 1981, pp. 335-342.

Hall. E.T. *Beyond Culture*. New York: Doubleday, 1981a.

Hall, E.T. *The Dance of Life*. New York: Doubleday, 1983.

Hall, E.T. *The Hidden Dimension*. New York: Doubleday, 1982.

Hall, E.T. *The Silent Language*. New York: Doubleday, 1981b

Hall, E.T. and M.R. Hall. *Understanding Culture Differences*. Yarmouth, ME: Intercultural Press, 1989.

Harris, P.R. and R.T. Moran. *Managing Cultural Differences*. Houston: Gulf, 1991.

Helms, J.E. and T.W. Giorgis, "A Comparison of the Locus of Control and Anxiety Level of African, Black American and White American College Students," *Journal of College Student Personnel* 21, 6, 1980, 503-509.

Hofstede, Geert, "The Cultural Relativity of The Quality of Life Concept," *Academy of Management Review*, 1984, Vol 9, No. 3, 389-398.

Hofstede, Geert, *Culture's Consequences: International Differences in Work-Related Values*. Thousand Oaks, CA: Sage, 1980.

Hofstede, Geert, *Cultures and Organization*. NY: McGraw, 1991

Hofstede, Geert. *Cultures and Organization*. New York: McGraw, 1991.

Hui, C. "Work Attitudes, Leadership Styles, and Managerial Behaviors in Different Cultures" in *Applied Cross-Cultural Psychology*. Thousands Oaks, CA: Sage, 1990.

Kagan, K. and M.D. Madsen, "Cooperation and Competition of Mexican, Mexican American, and Anglo-American Children of Two Ages Under Four Instructional Sets," *Developmental Psychology* 5, 1, 1971, 32-39.

Kagitcibasi, C. "Family and Home-Based Intervention," in *Applied Cross-Cultural Psychology*. Newbury Park, CA: Sage, 1990.

Kanter, R. and B.A. Stein, eds. *Life in Organizations*. New York: Basic Books, 1979.

Kantrow, A.M. *The Constraints of Corporate Tradition*. New York: Harper & Row, 1987.

Kennedy, Carol, "Culture Club: Companies With a Mission to Change," *Director*, December: 40-44, 1989.

Kim, U., H.C. Triandis, C. Kagitcibasi, S. Choi, and G. Yoon (eds.) *Individualism and Collectivism*. Thousand Oaks, CA: Sage, 1994.

Kohls, Robert L. The Values American Live By. San Francisco: LinguaTec, 1988.

McGrath, J.E. and N.L. Rotchford, "Time and Behavior in Organizations," *Research in Organizational Behavior* 5, 1983, 57-101.

Meyerson, D. and D.S. Lewis. "Cultural Tolerance of Ambiguity. Working paper, University of Michigan, Ann Arbor, 1992.

Morgan, Gareth. *Images of Organization*. Thousand Oaks, CA: Sage, 1986.

Morgan, Gareth. *Creative Organization Theory*. Thousand Oaks, CA: Sage, 1989.

Morrison, Terri et al. *Kiss, Bow, or Shake Hands*. Holbrook MA: Bob Adams Inc, 1994.

Nierenberg, John. "Cross-cultural Management Literature May Be Hazardous" *San Francisco State University School of Business Journal* (summer 1993): 47-55.

O'Reilly, C.A., J. Chapman, and D.F. Caldwell. "People and Organization Culture," *Academy of Management Journal*, 34, 3: 487-516, 1991.

Orpen, C. and J. Nkohande, "Self-Esteem: Internal Control and Expectancy Beliefs of White and Black Managers in South Africa," *Journal of Management Studies*, May 1977, 192-199.

Peng, Kaiping, as quoted by Timothy Beneke, "The Culture Club" *Express*, 23, 16: 1-14.

Peters, Tom. *Liberation Management*. New York: Knopf, 1992.

Quinn, R. *Beyond Rational Management*, San Francisco: Jossey-Bass, 1988.

Ramirez, A. "Racism Toward Hispanics" in *Eliminating Racism*, ed. Phyllis A. Katz and Dalmas A. Taylor. New York: Plenum Press, 1988.

Redding, S.G. "Cultural Effects on the Marketing Process in Southeast Asia, *Journal of Market Research Society*, Vol. 24, No. 19, 1982, pp. 98-114.

Rosener, J.B. "Ways Women Lead," *Harvard Business Review*, November-December 1990, pp. 119-125.

Rotter, J.B. "Generalized Expectancies for Internal Versus External Control of Reinforcement," *Psychological Monographs,* No. 80, 1966, pp. 1-28.

Schaef, A.W. and D. Fassel. *The Addictive Organization.* San Francisco: Harper & Row, 1988.

Schein, E.H. "The Individual, the Organization, and the Career," *Journal of Applied Behavioral Science,* 7: 401-426, 1971.

Schein, E.H. *Organizational Culture and Leadership.* San Francisco, Jossey-Bass, 1985.

Siehl, C. and L. Martin. "The Role of Symbolic Management," in J.G. Hunt, D.M. Hosking, C.A. Schriesheim, and R. Stewart (Eds.), *Leaders and Managers.* New York: Pergamon Press, 1984.

Spector, P.E., "Behavior in Organizations as a Function of Employee's Locus of Control," *Psychological Bulletin*, Vol. 91, 1982, pp. 482-497.

Stewart, Edward C. *American Cultural Patterns: A Cross Cultural Perspective.* LaGrange Park, IL: Intercultural Network, Inc., 1992.

Takaki, Ronald. *A Different Mirror: A History of Multicultural America.* Bost: Little, Brown, 1993.

Trilling, Lionel. *The Opposing Self.* New York: The Viking Press, 1995.

Tse, D.K., K. Lee, I. Vertinsky & D.A. Wehrung. "Does Culture Matter?" *Journal of Marketing*, vol. 52, 1988, pp. 81-95.

Wheatley, Margaret J. *Leadership and the New Science*, San Francisco, Berrett-Koehler Publishers, 1992.

Wiebe, Robert H. *Introduction to the Meaning of America.* NY: Oxford University Press, 1975.

Feedback on Self-Awareness Opportunity 2.2: What's Your Cultural Orientation?

1. a. Internal source of control, individualism, independent
   b. External source of control, collectivism, dependent
2. a. Me-first, individualism
   b. Us-first, collectivism
3. a. Achievement first, competitive, individualism
   b. Relationships first, cooperative, collectivism
4. a. Achievements and tasks first, linear time orientation
   b. Relationships first, circular time orientation
5. a. Focus on equality, democratic orientation, direct communication
   b. Focus on class differences: status, rank, deference to authority, indirect communication
6. a. Risk-taking orientation, focus on future change, independence, individualism
   b. Security-seeking orientation, focus on tradition, hierarchy and the status quo, dependence, collectivism
7. a. Equality, risk-taking orientation
   b. Security-seeking, avoid-uncertainty orientation
8. a. Risk-taking, equality
   b. Security-seeking, deference to authority

CHAPTER 3

Understanding the Dominant Culture: Euro-Americans

Many Americans have a great take-charge, can-do attitude,
but it can seem pushy and arrogant in other cultures.
Phillip R. Harris

The American culture was founded by Euro-American men, and their values and customs are still the most dominant. Though it contains many elements of Western culture, meaning European, it has a unique flavor of its own. The pioneering, independent spirit of the founding fathers is an important element, as is the belief in the basic equality of people and their right to be free to pursue the American Dream.

The term "American" as used in this chapter refers to those qualities of the U.S. culture generally agreed upon by such scholars as Gary Althen, R.T. Kohls, P.R. Harris, R.T. Moran, and D.J. Boorstin, who look at American values and customs as compared to those of other national cultures. The cross-cultural research of Geert Hofstede further confirms their work. While American culture is based on the values and customs of the dominant group, Euro-Americans, it also includes some aspects of its subcultures, such as American Indian, African American, Latino American, and Asian American. Although culture changes slowly, the American culture *is* changing to reflect more elements of its subcultures as they become greater in number and larger in size and influence.

Nearly all U.S. corporations and corporate cultures were founded by Euro-American men, and they are still 95 percent of the top managers who run the corporations. Therefore, corporate cultures are also a reflection of Euro-American male values. But corporations are changing because the marketplace is now global and the workplace is culturally diverse. Corporate cultures must become open and flexible enough to profit from that diversity. For example, management researchers such as Taylor Cox and Roosevelt Thomas have discovered that corporate cultures are increasingly moving away from the old attitude: "We're just one big happy family," which usually implies a one-way approach that means, "new employees must adapt to our corporate culture if they want to stay and succeed." They're moving toward a new attitude: "We're learning what it's like to walk in other people's shoes so we can fully appreciate what they need and what they can contribute," which implies a two-way approach that means, "our corporate culture is broad enough and flexible enough to adapt to new employees from a diversity of backgrounds, just as they adapt to us.

An important part of gaining diversity skills is understanding your own cultural programming. Assuming that at least part of your cultural background is Euro-American, you need to address the question, How is being an American different from being some other nationality? The better you understand your own culture, the better you can understand people from other cultures. To function well in a diverse workplace and a global marketplace, you need to attain a worldwide perspective. It's similar to climbing the highest mountain you can find, looking around at other cultures, and then looking at the American culture.

In this chapter you'll complete the second step of the five-step process for becoming a diversity-savvy person:

> ### Step 2. Learning about your own culture

Specifically, you'll learn in this chapter:

- How Euro-Americans view the world and how that differs from other cultures
- What Euro-Americans value the most and how that differs from others
- How Euro-Americans relate to others and how that differs
- How cultural differences affect your company and your job, how corporate acculturation approaches are changing, what works and what does not

First, complete Self-Awareness Activities 3.1 and 3.2.

Self-Awareness Activity 3.1: What Do You Believe about Euro-Americans?

Purpose:

- to get in touch with your beliefs and stereotypes about this group of people
- to experience how judgmental beliefs affect your thinking and feeling processes
- to experience the ways in which your beliefs create your reality regarding other persons, even before you have any interaction with them.

Part I. What Do You Believe about Euro–American Women?

Step 1. Associations

- Relax as deeply as you can: close your eyes and take a few deep breaths.
- Focus on the word "Euro-American (white) woman" and allow a mental picture to come up in your mind's eye. Imagine that you are this woman. Be Euro-American woman.
- Notice your resistances to being this person, and your willingness.
- Notice the words and images that come to mind as you "see" this woman.
- Open your eyes and list 10 to 20 words in the order in which they occur to you.
- Review your list. Mark a plus beside the words that are positive, a minus beside the words that are negative, and a circle beside neutral words.

Step 2. Negative Associations

- Close your eyes and focus again on the image of the woman. Formulate a negative opinion or judgment, perhaps one you typically hold about Euro-American women.
- Notice your *feelings* as you see the person in this negative way. What *thoughts* come up as you focus on the image?
- Write a few sentences about your feelings and thoughts.

Step 3. Positive Associations

- Formulate a positive opinion or judgment, perhaps one you typically hold about Euro-American women.
- Notice your *feelings* as you see the person in this posi__e way. What *thoughts* come up as you focus on the image?
- Write a few sentences about your feelings and thoughts.

Step 4. Insights

- Focus on the differences between your experiences when you hold negative and positive judgments or opinions. What were the differences? What meaning does this have for you, for your beliefs and feelings about people from this group, and about beliefs in general?
- Write your responses in a few sentences; include anything you like about your feelings, thoughts, and insights.

Part II. What Do You Believe about Euro–American Men?

Repeat the phases and steps in part I, this time focusing on the image of a Euro-American man.

Self-Awareness Activity 3.2: What Do You Know about the Euro-American Culture?

Purpose: To see what you know about the issues covered in this chapter.

Instructions: Determine whether you think the following statements are basically true or false—and think about why. The answers will emerge in this chapter, and the summary at the end of the chapter focuses on these issues.

1. A dominant Euro-American value is putting membership in an ingroup ahead of self-interest.
2. Most Euro-Americans tend to see situations in black-or-white terms.
3. Euro-Americans value just "being" even more than doing.
4. The dominant Euro-American view of humans and nature is that we must live in harmony with nature.
5. Euro-Americans in general tend to develop a few deeply committed friendships rather than many friends.
6. Corporate cultures need heroes mainly because people love a good story.
7. Strong corporate cultures are on their way out.

THE EURO-AMERICAN CULTURE: HOW IS IT DIFFERENT?

Euro-American culture differs from other cultures in three basic ways: the way people view the world, the personal values they hold most important, and the way they handle personal relationships. A summary of these values and customs is shown in Table 3.1. Many other cultures hold some, or even all, of these beliefs. What makes each culture unique is the focus and emphasis they place on them and how they express them in their daily lives.

TABLE 3.1: The American Culture

World View	Personal Values	Relationships
Conquering nature	Individualism	Friendliness
Progress	Achievement	Generosity
Change	Self-reliance	Many casual friends
Rationalism	Assertiveness	Arm's-length closeness
Scientific method	Work hard-play hard	Competition
Facts, practicality	Material success	Cooperative achievement
Measuring things	Freedom	Fair play
Quantifying things	Self-improvement	Specialized roles
Either-Or thinking	Keeping busy	Directness
Change Oriented	Staying young	Informality
Future Oriented		

WHAT'S THE TRADITIONAL EURO-AMERICAN WORLDVIEW?

Euro-Americans think of themselves as individuals first, the world as basically inanimate, nature as something to be conquered, material success as the major goal, and "doing" as the preferred state. Most value self-improvement and hard work as the way to ensure a better future for themselves and their families. Euro-Americans believe in scientific and technological "progress," viewing the world in rational, linear, cause-and-effect terms. People from other cultures usually see Americans as pragmatic, factual, and future oriented, with a tendency to view things more in either-or terms than the shades between. The seven aspects of the Euro-American worldview that we'll discuss are:

1. Conquering nature
2. Making progress and welcoming change
3. Using a rational, linear, cause-effect approach
4. Getting the facts and putting them to work
5. Measuring things
6. Thinking in either-or terms
7. Using time to change the future

Worldview #1: Conquering Nature

Making progress often requires conquering nature. Euro-Americans have traditionally gone along with the Western assumption that the external, non-human world is physical, material, like a complex machine with many parts, and therefore does not have a soul or a spirit. Nature, Mother Earth, is not seen as a living entity. Euro-Americans, probably more than any other group, believe the physical environment is there to be used, even exploited, for human purposes, according to P. R. Harris and R.T. Moran (1996). This contrasts with views common in Asia and among American Indians that stress the unity among all forms of life and inanimate objects. They see people as part of nature and the physical world instead of in opposition to them.

Worldview #2: Making Progress and Welcoming Change

Euro-Americans believe in and value progress—scientific and technological developments that improve their material world, according to Gary Althen (1988) and R.L. Kohls (1988). Euro-Americans often use their concept of progress to evaluate themselves and others. This concept is unknown by many in the non-Western world and may be rejected by them. Euro-Americans have traditionally believed that the basic problems of the world are technological and their solution will bring about economic abundance. The final measure of what's good and desirable is how economically feasible or lucrative it is. Progress is usually tied to their struggle to increase their physical comfort, health, material possessions, and standard of living. Also tied to their concept of progress is a feeling of general optimism towards the future, that their efforts can bring about a better future in which there is enough for everyone.

Progress implies change. Euro-Americans have their fair share of resistance to change, yet have pursued institutionalized change to a greater degree than any other society. "New" and "improved" are seen as "better." This acceptance of change shows up in their willingness to relocate. The U. S. is the most mobile society in the world, changing addresses more often than people in any other nation.

Worldview #3: Using a Rational, Linear, Cause–Effect Approach

Euro-Americans believe that everything has a cause-and-effect relationship, as in the operation of a machine. The notion of a natural "happening" has not been familiar or acceptable to most Americans—who see the world as rational in the sense that they believe the events of the world can be explained and the reasons for particular occurrences can be determined. Effective performance in the real world is based on experience and on training and education, which should be practical.

Euro-Americans believe in the scientific method. This means focusing on facts, figures, and techniques as the means to solve problems that represent obstacles to achieving goals. This action orientation leads Americans to look for a simple cause of an event, in order to plug this cause into the problem-solving process and decide on a course of action. Americans like to develop alternative courses of action, anticipate their future effects, compare them, and choose the one that seems best for the purpose at hand. Euro-Americans like action plans that are practical, with results that are visible, measurable, and materialistic. They see action (and the world itself) as a chain of events, a connection of causes and effects projecting into the future. To people from other cultures Americans may seem to sacrifice the end result for the means of getting there, for the scientific method is the only means they trust.

Management scholar Margaret Wheatley (1992) notes that recently some quantum physicists and business leaders have been collaborating to move beyond the traditional scientific method to more holistic approaches to science and management. Based on new discoveries about the interdependence of the web of life, how the mere act of observing a phenomenon can change it, how random events tend to self-organize into coherent patterns, and similar breakthroughs, leaders are focusing more on the importance of intuition, emotional intelligence, human relationships, and similar factors.

Worldview #4: Getting the Facts, Putting Them to Work

Most Euro-Americans don't pay much attention to theories that don't seem to have a practical application. The role of concepts and ideas in American life is to provide direction for purposeful activity. Theories are judged and tested according to their usefulness in daily life. Americans have not followed in the Euro-tradition of evaluating ideas or systems of thought according to the "intellectual consistency" or "aesthetic appeal" that researcher D. J. Boorstin (1960) identified.

Euro-Americans love facts. Their thinking process generally begins with facts and then proceeds to ideas, an inductive process. How good the ideas are depends on how well they work and whether people can bring them into the way they do business. Euro-Americans are somewhat unique in their insistence on practical applications—the continual need to organize their perceptions of the world into a form than enables them to act. They will accept a certain amount of pure science (research for the sake of curiosity), but expect most research to result in technology or products they can use, something that represents "progress." This operational style of thinking leads to an emphasis on consequences and results. "So much for the hypothetical. What's the bottom line?"

Euro-Americans especially resist systems of thought that lose sight of the individual. For example, despite their many programs of governmental responsibility and care for the individual, Americans resist unifying them into a system of ideology, some sort of modified socialism. Instead, they cling to the ideal of individual enterprise.

Worldview #5: Measuring Things

Euro-Americans prefer qualities that can be measured, and they like to see the world in dimensions that can be quantified. Even quality and experience can be at least partially quantified, if only as first or last, least or most. Or we can assign them arbitrary values, such as "a scale of 1 to 7." In business, government, and academia, Euro-Americans tend to use statistics to measure success and failure, amount of work, ability, intelligence, and overall job performance (Althen 1988).

Euro-Americans have managed to create unparalleled economic abundance with the combined focus on externalized achievement and on exploitation and control of the physical environment. Further, they tend to believe in unlimited physical resources, that there's enough to go around for everyone. This expansive view of achievement in a world of economic abundance contrasts sharply with the perception of limited wealth that prevails throughout most of the world. Only recently have large groups of Euro-Americans, such as environmentalist groups, begun to question the sustainability of their abundance worldview. Now, with satellite television carrying pictures of their abundant lifestyle to every corner of the globe, billions of people are beginning to clamor for similar affluence. If the way of life of 250 million Americans is damaging the planet, what will happen if billions choose this way? Will Euro-Americans have to change their beliefs and their ways? (Wheatley 1992)

Worldview #6: Thinking in Either–Or Terms

When you value the scientific method, objectivity versus subjectivity, and measurable outcomes, this allows you to set a numerical cutoff point for whether something is one way or another. This may be one reason Euro-Americans tend to focus on either-or viewpoints rather than many subtle differences. Euro-Americans draw a clear distinction between the subjective or personal and the objective or impersonal.

Euro-Americans often ask such questions as, "Who's your best friend?" or "What's your favorite color?" People outside the culture would generally have difficulty answering such questions because the answer would depend on knowing additional factors, such as the friend you most confide in or the friend you have the most fun with, the color you'd pick for a room or for a suit. Euro-Americans often make judgments or justify actions based solely on personal preference. This tendency is related to the tendency to see the world in terms of either this or that, and it's related to a predisposition to action. Euro-Americans set up unequal dichotomies, with one element valued more than the other; for example, right/wrong, good/evil, work/play, peace/war. These polarities simplify their view of the world, prime them for action, and provide them with their typical method of evaluating by means of comparison.

When it comes to evaluating people, however, Americans allow more shades of gray. Most Euro-Americans are unlikely to give much thought to church views that humans are flawed or evil by nature. They're more likely to see humans as a mixture of good and bad or as creatures of their environment and experience. Most important, Euro-Americans stress the ability to change (Kohls 1988).

Worldview #7: Using Time to Change the Future

Euro-Americans see time as an abstract quality, separate from self. "Time moves fast. It's important to cope with time slipping away. You've got to keep up with the times." Time is something to organize, schedule, use, and save. In business time is money, so being on time and using time efficiently are critical

Euro-Americans are future oriented, believing they can improve on the present and that action and hard work pays off in creating a better future for themselves. They see any unpleasantness in their work, or any stress due to incessant activity, as necessary intermediate steps for change and as progress toward the future. In contrast, Latinos, who have a present orientation, focus more on immediate events. Chinese, who have a past orientation, focus more on traditions (Harris and Moran 1996; Althen 1988).

EURO-AMERICAN VALUES: HOW DO THEY DIFFER?

Becoming an achieving individual is the name of the American game. As the most individualistic culture on the planet, Americans value responsible, autonomous individuals who make their own decisions and go out and achieve in the world. They admire people who work hard, play hard, get rich, and stay young. The six Euro-American values we'll discuss are:

1. Becoming an individual
2. Making their own decisions
3. Valuing achievement
4. Working hard and playing hard
5. Achieving material success
6. Staying young

Value #1: Becoming an Individual

Euro-Americans love their freedom to be autonomous individuals. Closely related are the values of competition and assertion. They admire people who decide what they want and go for it, who are willing to compete and don't easily give up. They generally don't place as much faith in fate or luck as do people in many other cultures. The meaning of their brand of self-reliance is neither translatable nor self-evident in other cultures (Harris and Moral 1996; Hofstede 1984).

Value #2: Making Their Own Decisions

Euro-Americans encourage their children, from the earliest age, to decide for themselves, to make up their own minds. They encourage children to believe that they're the best judge of what they want and what they should do. Therefore, as adults Euro-Americans are likely to view bankers, teachers, counselors, and other experts as people who can give them advice, not as people who should make decisions for them. Euro-Americans expect to choose their own mates, careers, homes, and to some extent, lifestyles. By contrast, in many other cultures, all or part of these decisions are made by parents.

Euro-Americans believe in democratic processes that are fair, give everyone an equal say, and help groups make action decisions. Most believe in majority rule and that people are capable of helping to make good decisions, although many men still accept the chain of command and autocratic decision making in military, government, and business organizations. In contrast, some Asian cultures, such as Japan, reach group decisions by feeling around or groping for a voice, preferably that of the chairman, that will express the group's consensus. In those cultures it's offensive for any one person to urge the group to accept his own opinion about what to do (Kohls 1988).

Euro-Americans believe that personal motivation should come from within. They don't like it when others, such as managers, impose their motives on them, especially when managers issue orders and threats. Euro-Americans value persuasion as the method of coordinating people in organizations. The subtle threat of failure is always in the background, which empowers the manager's persuasive appeals to self-interest and reason. Euro-Americans want to believe that they decide what they must do.

In rank/status cultures, people accept a personal bond between subordinate and superior, which makes the authority figure an acceptable source of motivation. Direct orders, explicit instructions, and demands for personal conformity may be acceptable, and even desirable, in such cultures. In them, the Euro-American preference for persuasion may be seen as weakness on a leader's part, and employee self-determination may be viewed as egotism and a threat to the organization.

Value #3: Valuing Achievement

Euro-Americans like to think they can achieve just about anything, given enough time, money, and technology. Externalized achievement has traditionally been the dominant motivation of Euro-American men, and they use competition as the primary method for driving themselves and others to achieve. Competition is seen by many as the keystone of American culture (Harris and Moran 1996; Althen 1988).

In many non-Western cultures, and traditionally among Euro-American women, affiliation is the primary motivation and way of relating to others. A communal feeling toward each other excludes the incentive to excel over others, either as a member of a group or individually. Euro-American values seem to be evolving, however. For example, many women are learning to accept their need for individual achievement and success. Some men, who formerly felt compelled to be competitive, are becoming more group-oriented and less autonomous in their behavior, as demonstrated in self-managing work teams and other alliances.

Value #4: Working Hard and Playing Hard

Euro-Americans are known to be work oriented and efficient. They act upon persons, things, or situations. Others may see Americans as living at a fast pace, incessantly active. Euro-Americans are likely to fill their waking hours primarily in a *doing* mode, seldom asking if getting all those things done is really worth it. They like the kind of activity that results in accomplishments that are measurable by standards that the culture says are valuable. Euro-Americans believe hard work is rewarded by success, and failure usually means you didn't know how to do it right, you didn't try hard enough, or you're too lazy to care. In contrast, people in some Asian cultures fill their waking hours with a *being* mode. Their focus is on valuing the spontaneous expression of themselves as humans or on developing all aspects of the self toward a higher-level, integrated, whole person.

Euro-Americans are somewhat unique in categorizing activities as either work activities or play activities. Work is pursued for a living. You may not necessarily enjoy it but you must do it and you put it first. In contrast, many non-Westerners rarely allow work to interfere with the amenities of living. For Euro-Americans, play is relief from the drudgery and monotony of work and is enjoyable in its own right. However, Euro-Americans often pursue play with the same seriousness of purpose as they pursue work. They tend to admire the person who "works hard and plays hard" (Stewart 1992).

Euro-Americans currently in their 30s and 40s are more likely to look to both work and play for personal enlightenment and fulfillment, and are now looking for ways to balance their career goals with family and personal priorities. Those in their 20s are the most insistent on balance, being less willing to sacrifice family and personal life for careers or employers. They're most likely to insist that work be fun—and that play be carefree and to make it whatever they want it to be.

Value #5: Achieving Material Success

Euro-Americans consider it almost a right to be materially well-off and physically comfortable. People should have shelter, clothing, warmth, and all the other necessities for material comfort. An important part of the good life is each household unit having its own house, car, and other physical possessions. Euro-Americans spend great time, effort, and money acquiring such comforts. They expect convenient transportation, preferably under their control, a variety of clean and healthful foods, and comfortable homes equipped with many labor-saving devices, certainly including central heat and hot water. They assume that cleanliness is nearly identical with health, if not with "Godliness" (Kohls 1988).

The Euro-American stress on material things is related to the achievement value and to the Euro-belief in private property, one that is highly valued and upheld by an entire legal system. It's difficult for many Euro-Americans to imagine, but some cultures don't even have a concept of private property, and some Asian cultures value a person's "state of grace" much more highly than their material wealth.

However, Euro-Americans under age 40 are more likely than older Euro-Americans to look to other determinants of status, success, and accomplishment; specifically:

- personal satisfaction with their lives
- control of their own lives
- the respect of other people
- a good marriage

Value #6: Staying Young

America is a youth culture. It often seems that everyone wants to look and act about 25. In most cultures, such as Asian and Latino, older persons are nearly always catered to, honored, and even revered. In the United States they're often ignored, even shunned.

Extensive research by the polling firm Yankelovich Partners, Inc. points to possible changes in this value, based on generational differences. They predict a shift toward these beliefs about youth and beauty:

- Age will be beautiful.
- Comfort will be beautiful—people will be less willing to sacrifice comfort to look stylish.
- Beauty will come in many skin tones and ethnicities

Only time will tell how strong these new value trends will become.

THE EURO-AMERICAN WAY OF RELATING: HOW DOES IT DIFFER?

Americans are seen by those in other cultures as friendly and informal, direct and casual, and having have many easy, casual friendships. Their ideal is equality of all people, but in practice they often violate this ideal. Euro-Americans believe in cooperation and fair play, and they tend to fit people into specialized roles. Six specific values involving relationships are:

1. Making many casual friends
2. Preferring arm's-length space
3. Fitting into specialized roles
4. Seeing people as basically equal
5. Cooperating and playing fair
6. Communicating informally and directly

Relationship Value #1: Making Many Casual Friends

Americans are known to be friendly, informal, and generous. They tend to reject the idea of someone being special or privileged merely because of birth. They're more likely to defer to those who have achieved power and affluence through their own merit. The way they dress and greet each other tends to be informal relative to many cultures. Americans are known to be generous, willing to come to the aid of people, and to embrace a good cause.

To Euro-Americans a "friend" may be a passing acquaintance or a lifetime intimate, but they're likely to have many personal relationships that are friendly and informal and to form few deep and lasting friendships (Harris and Moran 1996; Stewart 1992). In contrast, people from many other cultures are slow to form friendships, but once committed, they're friends for life. They will do almost anything for a such a friend, such as loan them money or help them move their household. In these situations Euro-Americans would prefer to hire professional help rather than inconvenience friends (or be inconvenienced, if the situation were reversed). Americans' immediate friendliness, forming of instant friendships, and lack of deep commitment are confusing to people from deep-friendship cultures.

Euro-Americans change friends and membership groups more easily than most. Though they spend a great deal of time in social activities, Euro-Americans generally avoid personal commitments and intense involvement except with one or two "best friends." Their exchange of invitations and gifts is within a loose, informal framework. The quality of their social interactions tends to stress equality, informality, impermanence, and personal detachment. Many Euro-Americans need to express friendship and to be popular in order to feel self-confident. They often judge their personal and social success by popularity, almost literally by the number of people who like them.

Relationship Custom #2: Preferring Arm's–Length Space

Euro-Americans' boundaries are about arm's length. When someone breaks through that boundary, they may feel invaded, and the act often carries sexual or belligerent overtones. The way they use space reflects the desire to have privacy and to maintain some distance in their personal lives. Traditionally, the more space and privacy a person has—both in the workplace and at home—the higher their position probably is. Euro-Americans are more willing than others to sacrifice such benefits as shorter commute time in order to have homes with more floor space and yard space (Stewart 1992; Harris and Moran 1996; Kohls 1988).

Relationship Value #3: Fitting into Specialized Roles

As a primarily industrial economy for the past century, America's workplace roles have been developed and filled with specialists who deal with specific functions and problems. The organizational hierarchy has been like a machine with interchangeable parts; that is, people with specific skills. Until recently, Euro-Americans never thought of an organization as growing out of the unique qualities that people brought to it and their ability to respond to unique opportunities that unfolded in the environment. Instead, they focused on specialized roles in business, the military, and government, particularly where technical skills and complicated equipment are involved. Associates from other cultures often find it difficult to understand the traditional Euro-American insistence on separating planning from implementing. This tendency is changing as America has moved into a post-industrial economy with self-directed teams, which merge these two functions.

Interpersonal relationships have reflected the workplace tendency towards specialization of roles. Euro-American friendships are likely to be based on their role activities, such as work, hobbies, sports, children, charities, games, and political or religious interests. They tend to think of others as co-workers, fellow tennis players, club associates, old school chums, neighborhood friends, PTA parents, etc. This specialization of friends often reflects their reluctance to become deeply involved with more than one or two friends and a wish for privacy. Euro-Americans' separation of occupational and social roles, of work and play, is different from other cultures (Stewart 1992).

Relationship Value #4: Seeing People as Basically Equal

An important theme in Euro-American relationships is equality. Ideally, just the fact of being human gives each person a certain irreducible value, and interpersonal relations are typically horizontal, conducted between presumed equals. However, big business and big government have traditionally been hierarchical and authoritarian, run by able-bodied, straight, Euro-American men, who in practice generally considered themselves the only true equals. When one of them needed to confront another who was a subordinate, he was more likely to establish an atmosphere of equality than are the bosses in rank/status-oriented cultures. However, this value has often not extended to employees who were "too different," such as African Americans or women.

In addition to these contradictions, Euro-Americans have further reservations about total equality: Not everyone is presumed to have equal talent and ability, even though they're entitled to equal rights and obligations. Euro-Americans generally believe, however, that in any group there will be people of ability and leadership potential. They emphasize equality of opportunity more than equality of results or equality of individuals per se. During their history, they've blatantly violated their belief in equality—and they've modified their understanding of it. But the belief remains a pervasive cultural value and the keystone for building an inclusive, profitable workplace (Althen 1988; Harris and Moran 1991; Takaki 1993; Wiebe 1975).

Relationship Value #5: Cooperating and Playing Fair

Although Euro-Americans value competition, they usually compete against a backdrop of cooperation, for competition requires a considerable amount of coordination among individuals and groups. Euro-Americans can do this because they don't commit themselves as wholeheartedly to a group or organization as those from most other cultures. Euro-Americans pursue personal goals while cooperating with others who, likewise, pursue their own. They tend to accept the goals of the group, but if their expectations are unfulfilled, they feel free to leave and join another group. Euro-Americans can adjust their goals to those of other group members for carrying out joint action. This compromise is practical to them, allowing them to achieve a benefit they couldn't attain on their own. Euro-Americans cooperate in order to get things done, but that doesn't imply that they're giving up their personal goals or principles.

Euro-Americans believe you don't have to accept other persons in totality to be able to work well with them. Part of being practical or professional is the ability to work effectively with anyone who can do the job, even if you disapprove of a co-worker's politics, lifestyle, or religious beliefs. It's this trait that allows Euro-Americans to cooperate with a diversity of people in order to achieve specific goals. This is a strength Euro-Americans can build upon to overcome the systemic and subtle discrimination that still exists in the workplace (Harris and Moran 1996; Althen 1988).

Relationship Value #6: Communicating Informally and Directly

The American communication style is known for being informal and direct. Euro-Americans stress a simple vocabulary, a relative disregard for style, and the use of slang to show they (and the other person) are "one of the gang." As a loose-knit, diverse culture, Americans must rely more on the specifics of verbal communication, while tight-knit cultures can rely more on vague, nonverbal signals.

Euro-Americans' informal, direct approach to interacting with others can seem brusque, rude, or confusing to people of other cultures. Compared to others, Americans tend to make fewer discriminations among people—quickly moving to a first-name basis with all and relating with breeziness, humor, and kidding. Their friendly, personal way of treating everyone, even enemies, contributes to a depersonalization.

While Euro-Americans tend to avoid confrontation, once they decide that a situation with another person must be resolved, they're likely to deal directly with the person. This contrasts with the idea of "saving face" and using a go-between or other indirect approaches that are practiced in many other cultures (Harris and Moran 1996; Kohls 1988; Althen 1988).

AMERICAN CORPORATE CULTURES

The evolution from independence to interdependence is reflected in the American business culture generally and in the corporate cultures of leading organizations specifically. *Corporate culture* refers to the values, norms, and principles that underlie an organization's policies and practices. Every organization has its own culture, whether it's a corporation or not, so even if you work in a government agency, a school, or a nonprofit organization, you still work within a "corporate culture," more properly called an organizational culture. A corporate culture is made up of values, symbols, stars and champions, myths and legends, rituals and ceremonies that are often summed up as "what we're all about" and "the way we do things around here" (Deal and Kennedy 1982, 1999). Just as the culture at large ties people together and gives meaning and purpose to their everyday lives, corporate culture is the glue that holds corporations together.

Strong and Weak Cultures

Some corporate cultures are strong, others weak. Even weak cultures influence almost everything in the organization, from who gets promoted to what decisions are made, from how people dress to what they do when they're off.

Weak Cultures

In weak corporate cultures people adhere primarily to their own culture group's viewpoints, norms, and values. People have more freedom to determine how to act. However, the extreme of weak culture is organizational chaos. Some essential values must be shared by members if an organization is to be able to achieve its goals. To survive and thrive over time, organizations need strong cultures. You can identify a weak-culture firm by looking for the following signs:

- No set of beliefs about how to succeed is delineated by the leaders.

- No rank-ordered priority of values is communicated by the leaders.

- No overriding common values are held by the different subcultures in various parts of the company.

- Role models don't serve the culture well. They may be disruptive, even destructive, or don't reinforce key values and beliefs.

- Rituals of everyday work life are disorganized or contradictory. People do their own thing or work at cross-purposes, undermining each other.

Strong Cultures

In strong corporate cultures leaders clearly define and enforce values and norms, giving more direction to how people should act, more reinforcement about what they should do, and perhaps higher penalties for not conforming. The *actions* of management must be consistent with corporate values, because the inconsistencies will be noticed and magnified out of proportion. When messages and actions are consistent, people get the message. Shared values and expectations act as an informal control system that tells people what's expected of them. The result is that people are more likely to view a situation in the same way, to respond similarly, and to expect similar results. They are marching to the same drumbeat, which impacts organizational performance (Peters 1992).

Authoritarian-style strong cultures are those in which management expects people to conform to values and norms that encompass most of their activities. There is a required company way to do almost everything.

Flexible-style strong cultures can be just as strong while still providing for individual work styles. Management clearly showcases a few core values that people must passionately commit to. Around this clear, hard core all else may be fairly fuzzy. People can decide how to achieve job goals as long as methods are aligned with core values. This culture works best with diverse groups because it allows for a greater variety of behaviors.

SHOWCASE
The Body Shop:
Strong Corporate Culture in Action

During the global nineties, successful managers began to see the necessity to focus more and more on managing the corporate culture. They learned to build, enunciate, and promote a strong culture that bonds people together, giving diverse people a core of common beliefs and values, a sense of common purpose. An example of such a strong culture is The Body Shop, a multinational chain of retail stores selling hair and skin preparations. The founder and CEO, Anita Roddick, is the guiding heroine who enunciates the organization's key values. Her constant theme is communication. She focuses on words that are associated with feminine values and concerns: love, family, caring, nurturing, connecting, preserving.

A key value of The Body Shop is to provide quality products at reasonable prices, with honesty and integrity, using natural ingredients, without animal testing. Other key values are respecting the environment, honoring indigenous people through "Community Trade," and giving back to the community in creative, interactive ways. To implement its values, the company has a constantly evolving, but limited, set of humanitarian concerns addressed in a pro-active way. Some examples are (1) helping the Kayapo Indians in the Brazilian rain forest protect their way of life, (2) reducing violence against women, (3) helping the orphans of Romania, (4) supporting AIDS relief organizations, and (5) supporting education in general as well as specific educational projects.

Roddick spends much of her time traveling around the world, visiting employees of the corporate stores and owners of the franchised stores—a total of more than 1,000 stores in more than 40 countries. The force of her personality, her energy, and the goodwill that she projects are strong factors in bonding the far-flung shops together. She continually formulates her beliefs and values into communication themes and common causes that are adopted by people throughout the organization. Franchise owners and key employees are carefully screened, primarily to determine that their beliefs, values, and principles are compatible with those of the organization. Once on board, people are given great freedom in how they carry out the organization's plans. They also have significant input into corporate plans. Their ideas and opinions are sought out and carefully listened to.

Employee training is more aptly described as employee education in The Body Shop. Time devoted to narrow skills training is minimal. Most time is devoted to discussions of broad philosophical concepts and sharing information about important developments in the world at large, as well as within the organization.

Ironically, The Body Shop is often a target of the news media precisely because it stands out as a model of a socially responsible, multicultural organization. A reporter might have much to gain by finding a fatal flaw in its operation. Most of the sniping is ignored, but in 1993 The Body Shop successfully sued a newspaper for false reporting. Also, some individuals respond to glowing reports about The Body Shop's unique culture by searching for negatives, criticizing and picking at its performance, apparently unwilling to believe that the founder could be sincere. As Roddick has said, it's easier to follow the herd than to break out on a new path.

Undermined Cultures of the New Millennium

Greed at the top has undermined the formerly strong corporate cultures of many large corporations (Deal and Kennedy 1999). The culture of any organization is a reflection of the deeply held values and the behaviors of a few people, and in large companies that means the top management team.

In the past, nearly all corporate cultures included an unspoken deal between the company and its employees: "You commit to the company and produce for the company, and the company will commit to you." But in the 1980s and 1990s, corporate top management increasingly made decisions driven by greed and self-interest.

Stock option plans became the main source of executive income. This started out as performance-based compensation that gave an executive a stake in the company. But executives soon realized they could earn really big bucks by making decisions that would cause the stock price to jump the most. Quarterly and annual profit statements directly affect stock prices, so leaders began slashing costs to boost stock prices. Downsizing and outsourcing were key cost-cutting measures that were devastating to the long-term employees whose jobs were axed, downsized, or otherwise jeopardized.

By the late 1990s corporations began focusing on mergers as the solution to every corporate problem, often resulting in mergers of very different, even conflicting, corporate cultures. Such incompatible mergers were nightmares for ordinary employees.

A major result of these developments is that the old patriarchal deal between the corporation and its employees is off. Now there's no deal. Employees must look out for themselves. In large corporations a culture of self-interest at the top and fear at the bottom is common now, which has undermined employee loyalty and trust.

Some Corporate Culture Patterns

Each corporate culture is somewhat unique, depending on the type of business, its context, and its leaders. Deal and Kennedy (1986, 1999) have identified certain patterns, however, that may help you get a handle on learning about a particular company's culture. Table 3.2 presents four typical patterns. Few companies fall completely into one type. In fact, large companies organized functionally will vary in type by department.

TABLE 3.2: Corporate Culture Patterns

Pattern	Characteristics	Examples
High Risk-Fast Lane	• tough • fast-moving • short-term • quick feedback.	Entertainment, professional sports, publishing, venture capital, advertising, construction management consulting, makers of computers, high-fashion clothing, and cosmetics; marketing departments of any firm.
Low Risk-Fast Lane	• high activity • fast-moving • short-term • quick feedback.	All retail stores. Firms that make or sell such products as food, real estate, office equipment, automobiles; sales and production departments.
High Risk-Slow Lane	• big stakes • slow-moving • long-term • slow feedback.	Firms that develop oil, minerals, etc.; insurance funds, biotech, architectural services, computer design, capital equipment; research departments.
Low Risk-Slow Lane	• bureaucratic • process culture • little or no feedback.	Government, utilities, banks, heavily regulated firms such as pharmaceuticals; support staff departments.

High Risk–Fast Lane

This culture is a world where one event or decision can make or break a career, even a company, often overnight. The risk of failure is high, and you know how you did relatively quickly. Examples are shown in Table 3.3. Functional departments within companies that tend toward a high risk-fast lane subculture include marketing, especially advertising.

Timely decisions are crucial, since delaying a decision can mean losing out. The all-or-nothing nature of many decisions encourages values of risk taking and belief in oneself. The majority of these cultures, which focus on speed rather than endurance, attract young employees. High competition, both internally and externally, is the rule. In this world of individualists, the stars are the heroes. Stars are known to be temperamental, and outlaw heroes are common. They may behave outrageously as long as they keep succeeding. Procedures can become temporary havens from the fear of taking risks and making the big mistake that spells disaster. Superstitions abound. Bonding can be exclusive and exclusionary because to change the structure of a group that's been successful might break the magic spell.

The major weakness of this culture stems from the emphasis on quick feedback. The tendency is to put too many resources into short-term projects, neglecting needed long-term investments. The level of competition can also be a weakness if the need for cooperation is overlooked. If superstition gets out of hand, people may start assigning the cause of success or failure to walking under a ladder or carrying a lucky charm and may neglect to rationally analyze what went right or wrong so they can learn from their mistakes. The end result of rewarding people who focus on winning in the short run is that people whose careers might blossom over time can't last. This high turnover makes it difficult to build a strong, cohesive culture.

Low Risk–Fast Lane

These are the cultures that focus on retail markets, either making and selling or just selling. They include virtually all retail stores. Sales and manufacturing departments within organizations that develop this culture. People in these companies take relatively small risks; one sale won't make or break them. They must be active—stay on the move and move fast, and they get quick feedback on whether or not they are succeeding. Sales are good or they're not. The customer bought or she didn't.

The primary values center around customers and their needs, on finding a need and filling it. Competition is fairly high, though not as tough as in a high risk-fast lane culture. The race is to the quick, and people must stay active and take initiative to even stay in the race. The super salespeople are the heroes, and people measure the worth of their activity in volume of sales, not high stakes. People tend to be friendly, fun loving, work-hard/play-hard types. The team is usually more important than the individual star because it takes a team to produce the sales volume the company needs to succeed. Rites and rituals center around contests, meetings, promotions, and conventions, all designed to bolster motivation.

A potential weakness in this culture is focusing too much on quantity volume and neglecting quality. Also, the focus on short-term results often leads to a tendency to focus on short-term goals and solutions. The quick fix is popular. Sales people are not accustomed to digging for the root of the problem when sales are off. They may become disillusioned and switch companies rather than sticking it out until they fix the problem. A strength of this culture is its ability to attract young people looking for a place to prove their stuff. They'll need their stamina in this active culture.

High Risk–Slow Lane

Big stakes, and therefore high risks, are the constant backdrop of this culture, where companies make huge investments hoping for long-term payback. Examples include companies that develop oil and minerals, provide insurance funds, biotech research and products, architectural services, computer design, and capital equipment. It includes most firms that focus on research and development, and the armed services because they spend so much time preparing for wars that may never occur.

Values focus on the future and the importance of investing in it. Because of the high stakes, deliberateness in decision making and action is a key value. The business meeting is the primary ritual. Hierarchy and rank are important.

People who thrive in this culture are as self-directed and as tough as people in the highrisk-fastlane culture, but they have the stamina to endure long-term ambiguity and little feedback on how they're doing. Their moves are measured and deliberate because they need to be sure they're right. Survivors respect authority and technical competence. The heroes tend to be hunker-down heroes, and they are especially important in this culture because they provide psychological support during the rough times that people must ride out. People who will share their hard-won knowledge are valued. Younger employees depend on mentors, who are the foundation of the system. There is great respect for authority that stems from expertise and experience.

Low Risk–Slow Lane

This is a bureaucratic culture. The stakes are low—no one transaction will make or break anyone—and feedback is normally very slow if it ever comes at all. Examples include most of the government, utilities, banks, and other heavily regulated companies such as pharmaceuticals. Functional departments that often have a bureaucratic style include large support staff departments—clerical, office administration, accounting, credit, and similar services. Typically, employees get little or no feedback on how well they're doing until someone blames them for something. This forces them to focus on *how* they do things more than on *what* they do, making it a process culture. Protecting themselves from blame often takes an inordinate amount of their time.

Values center on technical perfection, how you do things, figuring out the risks, and having solutions down pat and the details right. Survivors learn to live in this world where protectiveness and caution are the rule and where doing things (perhaps stupid or irrelevant things) neatly and completely are what's important. They are punctual, orderly, detail oriented, and have good memories. They carry out procedures according to the manual, whether the procedures make sense to them or not. Heroes tend to be hunker-down types who often win out when the political winds shift for the better. For some employees, the job position is the hero rather than the person filling it.

Rituals revolve around work patterns and procedures. Long rambling meetings may be held to talk about the way a decision should be made—the process. Reorganization is one of the most important rituals. Retirement ceremonies for those who hunkered down the longest are important. The tightly structured hierarchies are reminiscent of a class system, and title and formalities are respected. The greatest weaknesses of the bureaucratic culture can be the tangle of red tape and the difficulty employees often have of dealing with the real world of customer needs. They do provide a stability and continuity that help offset the uproar of some of the other cultures.

The Virtual Corporation

The virtual corporation is evolving from the demands of a diverse, post-industrial, technological, global economy. Just as virtual reality is a computerized experience that seems real but takes place in cyberspace, a virtual corporation is "like a real (traditional) corporation." However, much of the work, the meetings, and communication take place on computer screens, fax machines, car phones, voice mail, and video conferences. Work teams may include company specialists, independent contractors, suppliers, customers, and investors. They may be scattered around the globe, change from month to month, and never meet face to face. Or they may be self-managing teams that meet every day. They may work together to develop the plans, set the standards, identify and solve the problems, make the decisions, and provide the products and services. In any case, the degree of success or failure depends heavily on people's relationships with one another.

Of course, this format affects organizational structure. Old rigid bureaucratic hierarchies are melting into fluid, shifting networks of relationships among employees, customers, suppliers, and allied competitors. Table 3.3 shows how manufacturing corporations can fit this model; however, the virtual corporation format is also being adopted by many service organizations. Examples are custom banking, investment services, manufacturers' representatives, wholesale operations, and computer services (Davidow and Malone, 1992).

The virtual corporation is built upon trust, collaboration, cooperation, and teamwork, but it also relies on individual achievement and the ability to be entrepreneurial, and therefore competitive, in outlook. In such organizations, it's more obvious than ever that people are the most valuable resource, that how they work together creates energy and innovation or decay and demoralization, that their interactions spark the knowledge and information that fuel organizational growth and success. And the kinds of people moving into these new jobs are more diverse each year.

TABLE 3.3: Virtual and Traditional Corporation Comparisons—Manufacturing Example

Strategies	
Virtual Corporation	*Traditional Corporation*
Post-Industrial Economic View: Manufacturing base is essential as customers of services and generator of wealth for employees to purchase services.	*Post-Industrial Economic View:* Buy products from other nations where labor is cheaper.
Result: Develop a complex, rich manufacturing and agricultural base, highly automated, few workers.	*Result:* Hollowed-out economy—manufacturing corporations as mere shells for products made in other countries.
Targeted market niches.	Economies of scale.
Engine: Information processing.	Engine: The assembly line.
Lights-out automated factories.	Large factories, many workers.
A few long-term suppliers, many customized models—targeted customers.	Many suppliers, few models of products, many customers.

Products	
Virtual Corporation	*Traditional Corporation*
Virtual products are stored in minds of cooperating teams, in computers, and in flexible product lines.	Products are stored in warehouses and retail stores.
Virtual products are produced instantly and customized to customer demand.	Products supplied weeks or months after orders are placed or plans made—limited, standardized models.

Structure	
Virtual Corporation	*Traditional Corporation*
Fluid, flexible, constantly changing—a web or network of informational relationships.	*Rigid, stable—hierarchical departments filled with job slots, each with a job description and lines of authority.*
Structure meets unique needs of customers.	Structure meets needs of corporation—or a broad average (mass) of customers.
Structure, planning start with customer needs and desires.	Structure, planning start with what corporation wants to do and can do.
Self-managed work teams that may include customers, suppliers, retailers, investors, distributors.	Individual workers, some internal task forces and work teams.
Corporation is a vast network of relationships to carry out ever-changing clusters of common activities.	Corporation is a discrete, separate enterprise.

Human Resources	
Virtual Corporation	*Traditional Corporation*
Most workers (85–90%) in knowledge or service jobs.	Most workers in production jobs.
Change focus to targeted production of customized products and services for "niche" customers.	Retain focus on mass production of standardized products and services for mass consumption.
Most jobs require higher education—broad, general knowledge—multicultural and technological.	Most jobs require secondary education—specialized knowledge.
Requires workers to be informed, responsible, adaptable to change, flexible. Free flow of rich information.	Requires workers to be obedient, fit a job slot, specialized. Managers have access to information they need; pass along minimal information to workers.
Managers as leaders, coaches, facilitators; power lies in people skills.	Managers as directors, motivators, evaluators; power lies in the hierarchy.
Worker freedom, power to control work.	Close supervision of workers.
Built on trust, collaboration, mutual cooperation, teamwork.	Built on protecting self-interest, confrontation between workers and management, adversarial relationships.
Rewards leaders for long-term dedication.	Rewards leaders for short-term manipulation.

How Corporate Cultures Integrate Newcomers

The orientation process informs newcomers about the organization's goals, norms, the way we do things around here. New employees normally must develop specific work skills, learn role behaviors appropriate to their new job, and adjust to the work group's values and norms. Here's where the unspoken, unwritten, and sometimes most important information about getting along should be learned. The values and norms may be more difficult for culturally different members to learn, because minorities are usually not part of the informal social networks of the dominant group. Socialization occurs by such formal methods as training, performance appraisal, and promotion decisions, as well as by such informal methods as rituals, stories, jargon, and role modeling. The purpose of orientation, sometimes called organization socialization, is to align employees with the norms of the organization; it is closely linked to acculturation processes.

Acculturation

Acculturation is a process that occurs when new employees join an organization or when two organizations with different cultures merge. Traditionally, acculturation was accomplished through stories that express key values, and norms—stories about role models, rituals, ceremonies, myths, and symbols. Cox describes four modes of acculturation: assimilation, separation, deculturation, and pluralism (Cox and Finley-Nickelson 1991).

Assimilation. When the organization's culture is the standard of behavior for all persons, assimilation is the mode of acculturation. The goal is to eliminate cultural differences at work. New employees who are culturally different are expected to reject, or at least repress, their conflicting beliefs, values, norms, and practices. It is a one-way adaptation, similar to the melting-pot approach.

Separation. Alienation occurs when new employees are unwilling or unable to adapt to the organization culture. They maintain some separation from it. Cultural exchange is minimal. This is possible where a minority group's members are segregated by job category, and they form their own corporate subculture. To a lesser degree, minority groups from various units may cluster together, voluntarily isolating themselves from the dominant group in order to maintain some cultural autonomy.

Deculturation. A lack of enculturation that occurs when new employees are not significantly affected by either the organization culture or by their cultural group. The corporate culture is weak. New employees' own cultural identity is ill defined, perhaps because they have severed ties with their original socio-cultural group but haven't formed new ties with the dominant culture. Symptoms may be: very little bonding taking place, very weak loyalty and commitment, and high turnover and absenteeism.

Multiculturalism. This is a two-way learning and adaptation process in which both the organization and new employees from various cultures change to some degree to reflect the cultural norms and values of each other. It focuses on mutual appreciation among cultures, the importance of maintaining subcultural identity, and interdependence among the corporate culture and the various subcultures. New employees assimilate a limited number of core behaviors and values, but they also maintain important differences.

Acculturation Factors

How well diverse employees are acculturated depends on many factors, especially the culture's tolerance for ambiguity, the degree to which cultural diversity is valued, the extent of conformity that's required, and how well the employees' cultural backgrounds and the corporate culture fit together.

Tolerance for ambiguity. This refers to the organization's assumptions about whether ambiguities, uncertainties, and paradoxes are "legitimate and normal" (Meyerson and Lewis 1992). Organizations with high tolerance exert less pressure on people to conform to rigid "corporate ways," and they are more tolerant or appreciative of diversity. They are more likely to favor multiculturalism as an acculturation mode. Conflict among different ethnic groups is more likely to viewed as normal and potentially useful as a way to avoid groupthink, rather than as dysfunctional and threatening.

Degree to which cultural diversity is valued. Organizations with a strong "valuing diversity" norm tend to welcome the cultural exchange and interaction that is at the core of the multiculturalism mode of acculturation.

Demand for Conformity. Cultures vary by the extent and degree of conformity they demand of members. Table 3.4 compares some tendencies of typical managers in high conformity cultures with those in low conformity cultures.

TABLE 3.4: Comparison of Management Behaviors: High Conformity and Low Conformity Corporate Cultures

Managers in High Conformity Cultures:	*Managers in Low Conformity Cultures:*
• Have a narrow view of what is O.K. behavior Evaluate, judge, and criticize others	• See many behaviors as O.K. unless they violate a few core values, such as integrity and quality
• Avoid taking risks	• Take calculated risks; encourage others to do so
• Are intolerant of mistakes	• View failure, within limits, as a learning opportunity and part of innovation
• Focus on mistakes	• Pay more attention when people exceed standards than when they don't
• Ignore many positive contributions	• Don't judge ideas until they clearly understand them
• Prescribe the details of how to do things	• React to ideas in ways other than judging them good or bad
• See one right way to do most things	• Encourage people to create new approaches that work

Adapted from Cox, 1993

Cultural fit. This refers to the degree of alignment between two or more cultural patterns, and therefore the degree to which subcultures may comfortably exist within the organization culture. Obviously, fit is best where there is a great deal of cultural overlap between the corporate culture and an employee's root culture, where their beliefs, values, and norms are similar (De Anda 1984). Some authors have identified types of subcultures according to the their degree of fit with a corporate culture (Siehl and Martin 1984). A *reinforcing subculture* is compatible with and strongly reinforces the norms and values of the organization culture. A *refining subculture* shares many of the basic assumptions and values of the organization culture but also holds some that are unique. A *counterculture* embraces basic assumptions and norms that are primarily in conflict with the organization culture and therefore challenges its validity.

When cultural fit is poor, employees must pay the psychological costs of giving up some of their identity and of acting unnaturally. Their choices of how to act become more complex and ambiguous and they tend to experience stress.

Targeted acculturation. Companies can lower turnover rates of diverse employees by targeting acculturation procedures to group and individual needs. Without some special form of orientation, how can women and minorities become properly acculturated? Some companies use formal mentoring programs. Others try to manage job assignments to ensure a progression of sympathetic and supportive superiors. A third strategy is to assign them to a series of problem-solving task forces so they form a series of relationships with their peers that sustain them in their early years with the firm.

How can company leaders influence the culture to accommodate the needs of women and minorities? Some develop explicit guidelines for behavior in situations involving them, and a procedure for making everyone aware of these guidelines. Women and minorities can't become effective members of the culture if they're continually coping with embarrassing situations. Leaders must spell out standards for social behavior in relationships with these new members. They must focus on ritualistic cultural barriers to the acceptance of women and minorities and take specific action to remove these barriers. Leaders must become role models, setting an example of appropriate treatment of minorities and women.

SUMMARY

The Euro-American culture is predominantly a me-first, achievement-first culture that values equality and risk taking. The American way of thinking is predominantly a rational, linear, cause-and-effect approach that relies on measuring things. They believe in getting the facts, preferably measurable ones, and using expertise to conquer nature for a more comfortable, affluent life. Euro-Americans traditionally have thought more in black-or-white terms than in shades of gray. They look toward the future, welcome change and progress, and are beginning to use their individualism in an interdependent way to reach even higher levels of achievement together. Euro-Americans especially value being an individual, making individual decisions, and achieving material success and progress. They therefore believe in keeping busy and in separating work and play. They take a step-by-step, linear view of time and use it by staying busy.

The Euro-American way of relating involves making many casual friends with less intense commitment than in many other cultures. They tend to identify people with specialized roles and to base friendships on specialized activities, such as work, sports, etc. They believe in treating others as equals, cooperating, playing fair, and being direct. In physical terms, their boundary for most colleagues is about arm's length, more distant than Latino and Arab cultures and closer than Asian cultures. Communication tends to be direct and informal.

Corporate cultures contain the same basic elements as larger cultures. They can be strong or weak, depending on the leaders at the top. The type of corporate culture that works best in a multicultural workplace is a strong but flexible culture that insists on conformity to only a few core values but gives a great deal of freedom in how to achieve.

Typical corporate culture patterns depend on whether the company is basically in a high risk or low risk business and whether it must produce results quickly or over time. The virtual corporation is a recent pattern where people often use computers, car phones, faxes, and other electronic equipment in the field, in far-flung small offices, or in home offices, often on a subcontractor, outsourcing, or consulting basis. Therefore the virtual corporation may not look much like a traditional corporation and the culture is accordingly much more flexible and dynamic.

Newcomers into the corporation may be acculturated or assimilated. When they're not, separation or deculturation may occur. Multiculturalism is a two-way adaptation process that values diversity. How new employees are acculturated depends largely on the flexibility and openness of the corporate culture and its leaders' commitment to a multicultural workplace.

Skill Builder 3.1: Interviewing Diverse Employees and Their Managers

Purpose: To gain first-hand knowledge about the challenges and opportunities that a particular group of diverse employees is experiencing in today's workplace—and how managers of those employees view the situation. Determine whether to complete this skill builder on your own, with a partner, or as a team member.

Instructions:

1. **Select a diverse group** that you want to know more about.

2. **Interview diverse employees.** Find and interview at least two employees from this diverse group, asking about their challenges, problems, and "horror stories," as well as the opportunities, achievements, and "success stories" they have experienced.

3. **Interview their managers.** Find and interview at least two managers who have significant experience managing people from the diverse group you're studying. Ask them similar types

of questions to get their viewpoints of the situation. Ask for tips for managing and working effectively with people from this diverse group.

4. **Gather other information.** Find additional information about the diverse group, and tips for working with them, in library literature and on the Internet.

5. **Write a report.** Organize your research into a report.

6. **Write a case study.** If you got interesting information from the problems and "horror stories" part of your interview, write a case study, similar to the cases you find in this text, concluding with case questions. The case should be written so that it could be used as a skill builder for others who are studying this topic. In a separate section, write your own case analysis— what you see as the major problems and what you recommend as solutions.

Idea-Starters for Sample Interview Questions

Here are some questions that could be used for many types of interviews regarding workplace diversity.

Questions about Managing Diversity

1. Have you ever had employees from the (Asian American, Gay, Disabled, etc.) group on your work team? If so, what did you learn about meeting the needs and desires of people from this group? The unique kinds of contributions they can make? How to help them make that contribution? Unique problems? Ways of solving those problems?

2. Does the organization have any policies or strategies for *attracting* and *hiring* diverse employees in general? Specifically, for certain groups?

3. Does the organization have any policies or strategies for *retaining* people from these groups?

4. Does the organization have any policies for promoting people from these groups?

5. Has the organization adopted any specific plans or programs designed to help minorities and/or women to

    • identify their values, priorities, and thus their career goals?

    • identify corporate career paths that fit their career goals

    • gain experience and training needed to be promoted along chosen career paths?

6. Does the organization provide *training opportunities* specially targeted for these groups?

7. Does the organization have some system to *monitor* whether diverse employees have equal or *fair access to training opportunities* at all levels?

8. Has the organization adopted any *plan or strategy to prepare and move* diverse employees *into the highest levels*?

9. Does the organization provide *training programs* specifically designed to help people deal effectively with a culturally diverse work environment?

10. How would you describe the *corporate culture* here? How does it relate to typical values and priorities of key diverse groups?

11. What do you perceive to be the *greatest barriers* to developing and using (within the organization) the *full potential* of members of these groups?

12. What do you think are the *most important problems* that diverse employees face in adapting to the organizational culture here? General problems? Problems specific to each group?

13. Does the organization focus on *work teams*? If so,

    • Are these self-directed teams?

    • Are minorities and women often part of the teams?

- Is creativity and innovation encouraged?
- Do you think people are more productive when they work in teams?
- How successful are the teams in the organization?

14. When these teams are successful, what are the chief factors? In other words, what makes a successful team click?

Questions for Employees from a Specific Diverse Group:

1. Has the fact that you're a member of your particular ethnic (or other) group had any effect on your *work experience* in this company? In other companies you've worked with? What success stories? What horror stories? Particular problems? Unique solutions?

2. Are there any *specific problems* you can describe
   - in getting hired?
   - getting adequate and fair pay?
   - getting adequate training?
   - getting good job assignments, projects, appointments to committees, and other opportunities that would groom you for promotion?
   - getting promoted?
   - in being accepted by coworkers, management, customers, others?

3. What specific *encouragement or help* has the company given you in the above areas?

4. How would you describe the environment here?

5. Would you encourage others from your ethnic (or other) group to go to work for this company? Why or why not?

Skill Builder 3.2: Diversity Audit: Learning More about an Organization's Culture

Purpose: To learn more about a target organization's culture, perhaps the one you work in or one you're thinking about joining, and to place it into a frame of reference for understanding what's going on.

Name of Target Organization: _____

Step 1. Investigate
Visit the organization and observe or ask questions as follows.

1. *Observe the physical setting.*
   - What's your initial impression?
   - What does the physical layout seem to communicate?   handicapped physically disabled
   - Is the image consistent in all divisions? facilities?

2. *Collect and analyze written materials, such as annual reports, newsletters, news releases, manuals.*
   - What does the company say about itself?
   - What type of culture do written materials reflect?
   - Do you see signs of diversity at all levels in the materials?

3. *Observe reception area procedures.*
   - Formal or informal?
   - Relaxed or busy?

- Elegant or plain?
- What is the receptionist doing? How does she or he interact with visitors?
- What procedures or processes are used with visitors?
- Do visitors wait?
- Do you see signs of diversity so far?

4. *Ask employees questions, such as these:*
   - Tell me about the history of the company. (Notice what facts seem accurate, what myths surface.)
   - What has made the company successful? (Look for company values. Do people generally agree on which company values are most important?)
   - What kind of people work here? Who gets ahead? (Look for signs of diverse role models, descriptions of role models; look for clear agreement about how to succeed. Are role models constructive, serve the company well? Do women and minorities often succeed?)
   - What's it like to work here? How do things get done? (Look for important rites, rituals, meetings, or bureaucratic procedures; do all departmental or team subcultures have some unifying values? Do rites, rules, and procedures encompass or respect the diversity found within the organization?)

5. *Observe and ask, how do people (really) spend their time?*

6. *Ask about career paths:*
   - Who gets ahead? What departments were top people once in? What positions did they hold? Do people from diverse groups get ahead?
   - What do people have to do to get promoted?
   - What does the company reward? competence in key skills? performance against objective criteria? seniority? loyalty? good team player? other?

7. *Find out how long people usually stay in jobs.*

   (Short terms usually mean people are motivated to make their mark quickly and to steer clear of longer-term, slower payback activities. They also can mean people from diverse groups became discouraged, felt they couldn't reach their career goals, and left.)

8. *Find out what people are talking about and writing about.*
   - What are memos and reports about — actual content?
   - What are meetings about? What is actually discussed, who talks to whom?

Step 2. Review and Analysis.

Go over the results of your survey to determine how strong or weak, how conformist or flexible, you think the company is. Use it to help identify companies that are in danger of failing. Look for:

1. *Patterns and themes.* Think about patterns that emerged from the stories and anecdotes that people volunteered. What are the key points? Do most stories revolve around customers? political infighting? individual initiative that was rewarded or punished?

2. *Inward focus.* People don't pay much attention to what's going on outside the company with customers, competitors, new trends. They focus on placating the boss, looking good, getting one up on the people around them. They seem to over-emphasize budgets, financial analysis, or sales quotas.

3. *Short-term focus.* If people spend most of their time and energy meeting short-term goals, then sustainable business receives no support and the company is headed for problems.

4. *Declining morale.* Is turnover high or trending upward? Look at the whole company and at subcultures within the company. Look at the track records of employees from diverse groups,

such as minorities. Poor morale often begins with a lackadaisical attitude, moving on to loud complaints, and finally people start leaving.

5. *Weak culture.* When a culture is weak or in trouble, people get frightened and anxious. This fright shows up in emotional outbursts in the workplace, such as condemning company policy at a meeting or getting angry with coworkers or bosses. Did you hear any stories that indicate that stress, anger, or other emotions are building up? If so, did you get any clues about the causes?

6. *Fragmentation or inconsistency.* When a division is unhappy about how headquarters is handling things or tells jokes about what goes on there, it's usually a sign that the parts of the culture are not integrated into a coherent whole. Signs that normal variations in different functions of the firm are becoming a problem:

- Subcultures (within departments, or sometimes within ethnic groups) are becoming ingrown. Regular interaction among subcultures is declining.

- Subcultures are clashing, publicly trying to undermine each other. The healthy tension among two subcultures has become destructive.

- Subcultures are becoming exclusive. One or more subculture is acting like an exclusive club. People are feeling left out and resentful, not pulling together toward company goals.

- Subcultures act as if their values are more important than company values, not giving key overriding company values top priority.

Skill Builder 3.3: Assessing Corporate Culture Fit

Purpose: To raise your awareness about how various corporate cultures fit the needs of diverse employees.

Begin with how a target corporation fits your needs. Select an organization you want to study or to work in. After you have conducted a survey of the corporate culture (Skill Builder 1), complete the following Skill Builder, using this scale.

moderately important=1   very important=2   extremely important=3

Target Org. A or B? 1, 2, or 3?	My Root Culture A or B? 1, 2, or 3?	Values: What's Most Important	
		A Values	**B Values**
		Doing the work Living for the present Being aggressive Promoting myself Competing Being unemotional Individual goals Taking risks Other	Building relationships Working for future rewards Being passive Being modest Cooperating Expressing emotions Team goals Avoiding risks Other

Step 1. Assessing the organization's values. In the Target Organization column, for each value, assign either an A or B, whichever best represents that organization's value, and a number from 1 to 3 that represents moderate to extreme importance placed on that value by the firm. Add any other organization values you think will affect you significantly.

Step 2. Assessing your values. In the My Root Culture column, repeat step 1 for your own values, modifying your root culture's focus, where necessary, to reflect your own values. Add any other workplace values that are important to you.

Step 3. Estimating cultural fit. Compare the target organization's profile of values with your root culture's profile, and write a brief paragraph about what this means in terms of cultural fit between someone from your culture and this organization.

Step 4. Assessing another person's cultural fit. Think of someone from another culture that you know well. Do steps 1-3 substituting that person's profile for your own. In the paragraph write-up in step 3 include comparisons between your own fit and this person's fit and any insights that occur to you regarding cultural fit.

REFERENCES

Althen, Gary. *American Ways*. Yarmouth, ME: Intercultural Press, 1988.

Boorstin, D.J. *Americans and the Image of Europe: Reflections on American Thought*. New York: Meridian Books, 1960.

Cox, Taylor. *Cultural Diversity in Organizations*. San Francisco: Berrett-Koehler, 1993.

Davidow, W.H. and M.S. Malone. *The Virtual Corporation*. New York: HarperCollins Publishers, 1992.

De Anda, D., "Bicultural Socialization," *Social Work* 29, 1984, 101-107.

Deal, T.E. and A.A. Kennedy. Corporate Cultures. Reading, MA: Addison-Wesley, 1982.

Deal, T.E. and A.A. Kennedy. *The New Corporate Cultures: Revitalizing the Workplace after Downsizing, Mergers & Reengineering*. New York: Perseus Books, 1999

Hall, E.T., and M.R. Hall. *Understanding Culture Differences*. Yarmouth, ME: Intercultural Press, 1989.

Harris, Philip R., and Robert T. Moran. *Managing Cultural Differences*, 4th ed. Houston: Gulf Publishing Co., 1996.

Hofstede, Geert. *Cultures and Organization*. New York: McGraw, 1991.

Kohls, Robert L. *The Values Americans Live By*. San Francisco: LinguaTec, 1988.

Meyerson, D. and D.S. Lewis, "Cultural Tolerance of Ambiguity," Working paper, University of Michigan, *Behavior 5*, 1983, 57-101.

Peters, Tom. *Liberation Management*. New York: Knopf, 1992.

Pettigrew, Thomas. A Profile of the Negro American. Princeton, NJ: Van Nostrand, 1964.

Ramirez, A. "Racism Toward Hispanics" in *Eliminating Racism*, ed. Phyllis A. Katz and Dalmas A. Taylor. New York: Plenum Press, 1988.

Siehl, C. and L. Martin, "The Role of Symbolic Management" in *Leaders and Managers*. New York: Pergamon Press, 1984.

Spector, P.E., "Behavior in Organizations as a Function of Employee's Locus of Control," *Psychological Bulletin*, 91, 1982, 482-497.

Stewart, Edward C. *American Cultural Patterns: A Cross Cultural Perspective*. LaGrange Park, IL: Intercultural Network, Inc., 1992.

Takaki, Ronald. *A Different Mirror: A History of Multicultural America*. Boston: Little, Brown and Company, 1993.

Thomas, Roosevelt. *Beyond Race & Gender*. New York: AMACOM, 1991.

Wheatley, Margaret J. *Leadership and the New Science*. San Francisco: Berrett-Koehler Publishing, 1992.

Wiebe, Robert H. *Introduction to the Meaning of America*. New York: Oxford University Press, 1975.

CHAPTER 4

Stereotyping & Prejudice: How and Why They Occur

Build bridges, not walls.
Nicole Schapiro

As Americans, we have inherited a legacy of prejudice, but we've also inherited a legacy of belief in equality, and the mainstream has grown to accept more and more people as basically equal and therefore entitled to equal opportunity in the workplace. "Minorities" as a whole will soon outnumber Euro-Americans in some states. Leading-edge businesses know they need people from all the diverse groups—as customers and as talented employees who work in all corporate functions and levels.

But our legacy means that no one grows up without developing some degree of stereotyping and prejudice. They are woven into the very tapestry of our culture, springing up from the grass roots of family; filtering down from the top levels of government, business, and society; and feeding back on themselves at all levels in between. The first step to breaking out of this web is for each of us to quit denying that we're prejudiced. Then we can start rooting out those pockets of prejudice and the specific stereotypes that created them. We can start getting new, valid information, focusing more on the positive aspects of each group. We can deal with people from each group as unique individuals, going beyond the stereotypes to the specific cultural background that provides deeper understanding.

In this chapter you'll work on the third step in building multicultural skills.

> Step 3: Recognizing your own biases, the ways in which you
> stereotype, assume, judge, and discriminate.

You're probably aware that to be a valuable employee or business associate, you must move beyond the stereotypes and prejudices that exclude whole groups of people. This involves learning how to bridge the divisive walls of prejudice—and showing others the way. Doing so can bring huge rewards—to you in building success skills and profitable workplace relationships and to your company as you work more productively with people from diverse backgrounds. You'll learn why and how we stereotype, prejudge, discriminate against, and exclude people just because they belong to a particular group. You'll learn how moving beyond assumptions and prejudices can boost success for you and your company. Specifically, you'll learn about:

- Why people avoid and exclude others
- Why we stereotype people
- How you can become aware of your own stereotypes and prejudices
- The connection between the authoritarian personality and prejudice
- How and why people become prejudiced
- How people express prejudices
- How prejudice affects people generally and in the workplace
- How people can move beyond stereotyping to valuing people's differences and building relationships that promote profitable collaboration

Before you begin your exploration, complete Self-Awareness Activity 4.1.

Self-Awareness Activity 4.1: What Do You Know about Prejudice?

Purpose: To see what you know about the issues covered in this chapter.
Instructions: Determine whether you think the following statements are basically true or false—and think about why. The answers will emerge in this chapter, and the summary at the end of the chapter focuses on these issues.

1. Anthropologists generally agree that there are three major races: caucasoid, negroid, and mongoloid.
2. Most aspects of our culture teach us to appreciate others and not be prejudiced.
3. People who believe in strict categories of right and wrong are unlikely to be prejudiced.
4. Prejudiced beliefs are frequently hidden, not in awareness.
5. Being prejudiced affects the personality of the holder as well as the receiver of the prejudice.
6. Members of disparaged groups become resentful toward others.
7. Prejudiced beliefs cannot be changed, but discriminatory actions can.

WHY DO WE EXCLUDE WHOLE GROUPS OF PEOPLE?

We may exclude whole groups of people because we've bought into a stereotyped belief that people from that group are inferior in some way. This means that we prejudge such persons before we ever get to know them. If we don't give them a fair chance on the job, or if our organization is set up in a way that automatically ignores certain groups of people, then we are participating in discrimination against them.

Workplace prejudice is alive and well. Surveys indicate that stereotypes are still prevalent and that most of the Euro-Americans who dominate the workplace tend to believe that other ethnic groups are less intelligent, less hard working, less likely to be self-supporting, more violence prone, and less patriotic than they. The Executive Leadership Council's study found prejudice to be the most serious career hurdle for African American executives. The research organization Catalyst found prejudice to be the biggest advancement barrier women face today (Morrison 1992; Smith 1990; Baskerville and Tucker 1991; Catalyst 1990).

Three terms are often used to describe the separate but related elements of exclusion: stereotypes, prejudice, and discrimination.

Stereotypes: A Way of Thinking

You're exposed to millions of bits of data every second of your waking life. You couldn't function unless you filtered out most of this data and categorized the rest of it. Categorizing data into groups, giving the groups of information recognizable labels, and fitting them into your current knowledge base—these are some ways that your mind must function. So stereotyping, in this sense, is normal and essential. Problems occur when we allow these labels to become rigid, exaggerated, irrational beliefs about a particular group of people. Such rigid stereotypes about people usually lead to prejudice.

Prejudice: A Way of Feeling

When you view a group of people who are different as somehow deficient, that means you are pre-judging individuals before getting to know them. Prejudice, therefore, means judging a whole category of people as basically better-than or worse-than others. Because individuals within a group have many similarities but also many differences, pre-judging them is obviously unfair to the individuals. Prejudice is a way of feeling because it arises from some of our deepest fear-based emotions and triggers still other problem emotions.

Some prejudice is a matter of blind conformity to prevailing cultural beliefs and customs. However, in most cases prejudice seems to fulfill a specific irrational function for people, such as making them feel superior to others or using others as scapegoats for the prejudiced persons' own resentment or guilt. Prejudice usually is tied to a person's deepest fears, although the connection is normally subconscious and therefore hidden from awareness, according to Harvard psychologist G.W. Allport in his classic work on prejudice (1954).

Discrimination: A Way of Acting

Now we get down to actual actions or practices that result in members of a less-powerful group being treated differently in ways that disadvantage them. Discrimination usually refers to behavior that is prejudiced, and the acts that have an effect on people who are targets of prejudice.

Most discussions of prejudice and discrimination are based on the following assumptions (Ridley 1989):

- Prejudice is reflected in behavior.
- Prejudiced acts can be performed by nonprejudiced as well as prejudiced people.
- Prejudice is found in every ethnic group.
- The criteria for judging whether or not a behavior is prejudiced lies in the consequences, not the causes, of the behavior. (We can't prove someone is prejudiced, but we can prove that their acts have a discriminatory effect.)
- Power is a force that is absolutely essential to perpetuate discrimination.

All this implies that a power imbalance is a key aspect of discrimination. As we've seen, civil rights measures are based on this premise and represent attempts to break the cycle of centuries of discrimination.

Discrimination has been built into American institutions and systems. No one is completely immune to its impact, although people from historically disadvantaged groups tend to suffer the worst effects. Civil rights laws have reduced its pervasiveness and intensity, and activist groups are working against it. But groups are made up of individuals, and change begins within one person and expands person by person. The role you play is important (Ponteretto 1993; Allport 1954; Cox 1993).

Vignette: How We Stereotype People

Overheard at a restaurant: *Sorry I'm late—had to wait in line over 10 minutes at the post office. Most of the clerks seemed to be on a break. Well, what can you expect? Postal employees!*
Yeah, really. But they don't bother me—as long as they don't go 'postal' when I'm around!
In the office: *I'm not voting for any of them. They're all a bunch of corrupt crooks.*
You're right—and you can't believe any of their promises.

At a party. *Oh, sure, he's good looking and a great dancer, but I probably won't get involved with him. I hear they're all pretty macho when you really get to know them.*
Uh huh, and most of them have some kind of Mafia connection.

If you're like most people, you're improving the quality of your beliefs and attitudes toward people who have traditionally been devalued in our culture—*and* you want to do better at bridging the gaps and connecting in a positive way with people from diverse backgrounds. You want information about how to build rewarding relationships—whether it's with postal employees, politicians, Italian Americans, African Americans, or others you deal with in your day-to-day activities. You want to link, bond, connect, and ally with people in ways that will build strong relationships.

Moving beyond prejudiced thinking offers many rewards. It can make you a more effective team member, help you give better service to all your customers and associates, and in turn boost your company's profits and success. Clearly, the bottom line reward for moving beyond stereotypes to collaborating with people is the boost to your own career success. A very real bonus is the probability that you'll get more enjoyment from working with people and you'll feel better about yourself.

WHY DO WE STEREOTYPE PEOPLE?

The process of stereotyping allows us to manage complex realities by using categories to store new information, to quickly identify things, to handle multisensory experiences, and to make sense of things. We may attach strong emotion to these stereotypes, even when they're false, and we often use stereotypes to justify our dislike of someone.

Rigid, limiting stereotypes create barriers to really getting to know people, but you can break free. The first step is understanding how this process of stereotyping works in your everyday life.

Making Complex Reality Manageable

When we stereotype, we form large classes and clusters for guiding our daily adjustments. We must deal with too much complexity in our environment to be completely open-minded. We don't have time to learn all about every new person or situation we encounter. Of necessity, we associate them with old categories in our mind in order to make some sense of the world.

Short-Cutting with Categories

We tend to place as much as we can into each class and cluster. Our minds tend to categorize events in the *grossest* manner compatible with the need for action. We like to solve problems as easily as possible, so we try to fit them rapidly into a satisfactory category and use this category as a means of prejudging the solution.

Quickly Identifying Things

A stereotype enables us to readily identify a related object. Stereotypes have a close and immediate tie with what we see, how we judge, and what actions we take. In fact, their whole purpose is to help us make responses and adjustments to life in a speedy, smooth, and consistent manner.

Incorporating Multisensory Experiences

For each of our mental categories, we have a thinking and feeling tone or flavor. Everything in that category takes on that flavor. For example, we not only know what the term *Southern belle* means, we also have a feeling tone of favor or disfavor that goes along with that concept. When we meet someone that we decide is a Southern belle, that feeling tone determines whether we like her more or less than we would if we got to know her on her own merits.

Being Rational—Or Not

Stereotypes may be more or less rational. A rational stereotype starts to grow from a kernel of truth and enlarges and solidifies with each new relevant experience. A rational stereotype can give us information that can help us to predict how someone will behave or what might happen in a situation. An irrational stereotype is one we've formed without adequate evidence or because it met an emotional need. We notice behavior that "proves" the stereotype is true, reinforcing it—for example when the Southern belle bats her eyelashes. As for behavior that refutes the stereotype—for example, when she makes an assertive statement—we either don't notice it at all, or we classify it as a rare exception.

Adding the Emotional Whammy

Our minds are able to form irrational stereotypes as easily as rational ones, and to link intense emotions to them. An irrational idea that is engulfed by an overpowering emotion is more likely to conform to the emotion than to objective evidence. Therefore, once we develop an irrational stereotype that we feel strongly about, it's difficult for us to change that stereotype based on facts alone. We must deal with the emotion and its ties to our deepest fears.

Justifying Dislike

Sometimes we form a stereotype linked to an emotion related to fear—such as hostility, suspicion, dislike, disgust—and set up the framework for prejudice toward an entire group of people based on our experience with one or a few. When people become prejudiced toward a group, they need to justify their dislike, and any justification that fits the immediate conversational situation will do. So we grasp any real or imagined behavior that serves to "prove" the stereotype.

In summary, stereotyping is part of the human need to categorize the massive amounts of information we encounter every day. Categorizing and labeling are ways of making sense of the world and managing the stuff we must do. Stereotyping, when used in this *technical* sense, is a rational thing to do. The problems arise when we make our categories too fixed and our labels too permanent—and what most people call *stereotyping* refers to this fixed, permanent aspect. Rigid stereotyping of groups of people often leads to prejudice and discrimination.

Self-Awareness Activity 4.2: Being Tolerated and Being Appreciated

Purpose: To experience the difference between tolerance and appreciation.

Step 1. Being Tolerated

a. Think of a time when you felt tolerated. Write a few words about it.

b. How did it feel to be merely tolerated? Write a few words about your feelings.

c. How did feeling tolerated affect your relationship with the tolerant person(s)?

Step 2. Being Appreciated

a. Think of a time when you felt appreciated. Write a few words about it.

b. How did it feel to be truly appreciated? Did you feel respected? Write a few words about your feelings.

c. How did feeling appreciated affect your relationship with the appreciative person(s)?

Stereotyping, prejudice, and discrimination create gaps between people, as well as major barriers to tapping the full potential of all the members of a diverse work team or any diverse group. They diminish the potential synergy, innovativeness, and success of such groups (Gadamer 1989; Feagin 1978)

HOW CAN WE PINPOINT OUR PREJUDICES?

Virtually everyone harbors some rigid stereotypes and prejudices. Some prejudice is a matter of blind conformity to prevailing cultural beliefs and customs. However, in most cases prejudice seems to fulfill a specific irrational function for people, such as making them feel superior to others or using others as scapegoats for the prejudiced persons' own resentment or guilt. Prejudice usually is tied to a person's deepest fears, although the connection is normally subconscious and therefore hidden from awareness. Researchers such as G. W. Allport, M.H. Ijzendoorn, and Joseph Ponteretto have uncovered some interesting facts about prejudice:

- Prejudice is found in all types of people and in every ethnic group.
- Prejudice occurs in the mind but can be acted out in ways that exclude others.
- Prejudiced acts can be performed by nonprejudiced as well as prejudiced people.
- The best way to decide if an action is prejudiced is how it affects another person. You can't prove someone is prejudiced, but you may prove that their acts exclude and disadvantage another person.

Key Aspects of Discrimination

You can discriminate by merely being part of an organization that itself unintentionally discriminates through its traditional business practices. This is because of the power-privilege imbalance that automatically favors a dominant majority and disfavors minorities—unless actions are taken to offset the imbalance.

Power Imbalance

A power imbalance is a key aspect of discrimination. Power is a force that is absolutely essential to perpetuate discrimination. For example, an African American clerk may dislike a Euro-American executive and never try to get to know him as a person. Her actions are not called "discrimination" because she does not have the power to take actions that exclude him in ways that disadvantage his career. On the other hand, the executive does have the power to discriminate against her, and that type of power differential is not unusual. Euro-American men still hold nearly all the top-level economic and political power in the United States, as mentioned in Chapter 1. They hold 95 percent of the top-level positions in mid- to large-sized businesses and about 80 percent of the seats in Congress, even though they are about 39 percent of the workforce and 35 percent of the population, according to the U.S. Census Bureau and the U. S. Glass Ceiling Commission. Civil rights measures are based on the fact of power imbalance and represent attempts to break the cycle of centuries of discrimination.

Privilege Imbalance

A privilege imbalance goes hand in hand with a power imbalance, meaning there is a powerful group with distinct privileges that other groups don't have. Most Euro-American men and boys are unaware of the hundreds of privileges they enjoy as members of their group, according to research by Peggy McIntosh; for example:

- When they leave their family or local community in the morning and go out into the world, they can choose to ignore ethnicity, skin color, and other people differences. People from other groups never have that luxury if they want to succeed in the corporate workplace.
- When they set their goals and plans for social, professional, or political achievement, they don't ask whether a person from their ethnic group or gender would be accepted in the situation, and what related barriers they must overcome.
- When they take a job, co-workers assume they got the job because they're qualified, not because they're a diverse employee. Company expectations are that they will probably succeed.
- They don't have to struggle to be visible, valuable, and important. Educational materials consistently testify to the *existence* of Euro-American men and their *contributions* to the United States.

- Anywhere they go in the United States they don't worry about being rejected—just because they're Euro-American men—when they try to join a club, rent an apartment, buy a house, or get a loan. Of course, most rejections are evasive and subtle, but for ethnic minorities they are real.

To better understand the connections between privilege, power, and discrimination, complete Self-Awareness Activity 4.3.

Self-Awareness Activity 4.3: How Privileged Are You?

1. What are some privileges that you enjoy in life? List a few.
2. How do the privileges affect your life? Do they affect your personal power? Ability to achieve your goals? Your success?
3. Which of these (or other) privileges are unavailable to some people because of the group they belong to? Beside each unavailable privilege, write the name of the group.
4. What are some privileges that are unavailable to you that people from certain other groups enjoy? List each privilege and beside it, the group(s) that has access to it.
5. How does this lack of privilege affect your life? Your personal power? Your ability to achieve your goals? Your success?

Some Types of Prejudice

We talk about prejudice in terms of workplace prejudice, sexism, racism, ethnic prejudice, and other ism's.

Sexism

Sexism is prejudice based on gender and is said by some to be the root of all prejudice and discrimination. As children we literally begin learning this form of inequality in the cradle. It doesn't involve a majority and minority, since men and women are relatively equal in number. However, women in all countries are a minority in economic and political arenas and have fewer rights and privileges than men.

Racism: Our Most Dangerous Myth

Racism is typically a problem in societies such as the United States, where there is a predominant majority group and one or more large cultural subgroups. People often use the term *racism* in discussions of prejudice, which raises the question, "How do I know when I'm dealing with someone of another race, and how can I be sure what race they represent?" This brings us to the myth of race.

Myth: Everyone belongs to one race or another. If your parents came from two different races, then you are bi-racial. Americans tend to believe in three great races—caucasoid, mongoloid, and negroid—a system developed in Europe and North America in the 1700s.

Those who try to distinguish between race and ethnicity say that racial traits are inborn, inherited, and given by nature, while ethnic traits are learned, cultural, and acquired through nurture.

Reality: Scientists view race as a folk myth. "Race as a meaningful criterion within the biological sciences has long been recognized as a fiction," according to Princeton professor Henry Gates (1992). In 1997 the American Anthropological Association asked the U.S. government to drop the term "race" from its census categories and to use "ethnicity," which reflects culture. Anthropologist Ashley Montagu has discussed the fallacies and dangers inherent in the whole concept of race in the many editions of his classic book, *Man's Most Dangerous Myth* [1997]. Race is a myth, but much of the discrimination in society still takes place in the name of race.

We now know that modern humans arose in Africa less than 200,000 years ago, and the great migrations took place less than 100,000 years ago. So we don't even come close to having enough genetic diversity to allow for races or subspecies. The only pattern that shows up consistently is a geographic one. As scientists survey traditional homelands, people look similar to those from nearby geographic areas and different from those who live far away. The greater the distance, the more differences in appearance.

As humans moved into new climates, environmental pressures such as sun, wind, and hot or cold temperatures produced different physical appearances, including slightly different physiques. But the environment literally works only on the surface, changing skin, hair, and facial features a bit. Rather than race, scientists like to discuss "clinal variations" or physical types that may be found in one general area of the world but that fade fairly evenly into other types as one moves across the globe. Even geographic patterns of some sets of genes do not match other sets within the group, showing clearly that human populations have been merging, migrating and intermarrying from the start.

Anthropological work on race has produced these facts:

- As human beings, we are all one species that has one set of common ancestors, all originally out of Africa.

- Genetically, we are 99.9 percent alike.

- No one belongs to a pure stock, except a very few people found in remote isolated parts of the earth.

- Most of the variable human characteristics ascribed to race are actually due to cultural diversity and should therefore be regarded as ethnic, not racial.

Much of the racism in the United States involves African Americans, viewed as a separate "race." Yet experts estimate that about 75 percent of African Americans are of mixed heritage, usually having some Euro-American ancestors. Since most of the characteristics that vary from culture to culture are learned, and are not "permanently fixed in our genes," they can theoretically be changed (Allport 1954). "Ethnicity" is much more flexible and changeable than "race."

> *What's in a Name?* The terms *race* and *racism* are not biologically
> meaningful for U.S. subcultures, although racial beliefs are still used by some
> persons as the basis for discrimination. More realistic and conciliatory
> terms are *ethnicity* and *ethnic prejudice*.

Ethnic Prejudice

Ethnic discrimination against minority subcultures occurs when "minority" status carries with it the exclusion from full participation in the society and the largest subculture holds an undue share of power, influence, and wealth in society (Ponterotto et al 1993).

Other ism's

Other *ism's* include ageism, classism or class snobbery, and homophobia, or antigay prejudice. Besides ethnic minorities and women, groups that experience discrimination in the workplace include persons with disabilities, gay persons, older employees, and obese persons. To a lesser extent, persons from lower socioeconomic groups may be targets of prejudice, as symbolized by such derogatory terms as *trailer trash* and *poor white trash*. Prejudices know no boundaries, however, and some people believe that all post office employees are deadbeat bureaucrats, all administrators are corrupt political sharks, and on and on.

WHAT IS A PREJUDICE-PRONE PERSONALITY?

While everyone is prejudiced to some extent, the degree of prejudice varies greatly and a large body of psychological investigation explains why. The original work on the authoritarian personality was done in 1950 and was studied by Harvard professor G.W. Allport. Since then more than 1200 well-accepted scientific studies have been conducted on this topic—far more than for any other personality aspect. Many of these studies, such as those by Dutch researcher M.H. Ijzendoorn, indicate that people who score high on an authoritarianism scale also show a consistently high degree of prejudice against all other cultural groups. Now, complete Self-Awareness Activity 4.4.

Self-Awareness Activity 4.4: Twenty Questions About You

Purpose: To learn more about your personal viewpoint.
Instructions: Mark each item true or false.

1. I have little or no difficulty deciding what's right and wh 's wrong.
2. I thrive on variety and change.
3. I often enjoy being with people that some would call strange or weird.
4. I like my routines.
5. I know how I feel about most situations and don't need to keep thinking about them.
6. I need to know exactly where I'm going and when.
7. I often ask myself why I did certain things, or why I think or feel as I do.
8. I hate it when people change our plans.
9. There is only one right way to do most things.
10. Few actions are totally right or wrong; most actions stem from complex situations and have varying effects.
11. I prefer to focus on a few simple things rather than a wide variety.
12. I can feel comfortable with most situations, even if I'm not sure about what's going on.
13. I don't always agree with people from other groups, but I usually understand why they might think and feel as they do.
14. People basically create the life they have and the sooner they take responsibility for it, the better it will be.
15. I think I know my own strengths and shortcomings pretty well.
16. Most actions can be classified as either proper or improper.
17. People have different ideas about what's proper and improper; that's fine with me.
18. I don't start a job until I know exactly how to do it.
19. I'm comfortable "feeling my way" through a task, if necessary.
20. I need to know what's going on and what to expect at all times.

Followup: To interpret your responses, see the answer key at the end of this chapter and review the discussion in this chapter on the authoritarian personality.

The Highly-Prejudiced Personality

People who are rigid and authoritarian in their beliefs have thinking processes and personality traits that are linked to prejudice. They tend to be more prejudiced than people who are open and flexible. As you begin to understand these key personality traits, you can better understand your own tendencies. Don't be dismayed if you find you're much more authoritarian that you'd like. You can change any belief that you decide doesn't serve you—and you can do it in a heartbeat once you are truly motivated. Understanding the authoritarian personality can also help you to see why some people in your organization are more prejudiced than others. You may be able to help them recognize rigid beliefs and imagine more flexible ones—but the choice to change is up to the individual. Just as no one can make you change, you cannot force change on another.

Thinking Processes

The thinking processes of highly prejudiced people are *in general* different from those of less-prejudiced people. Their prejudice is not likely to be merely a specific attitude toward a specific group—though they may rationalize it that way. More likely, it's a reflection of their whole way of thinking about the world they live in. They're likely to indulge in either-or thinking, such as the following.

- Whenever they think of nature, of law, of morals, of men and women, they think in terms of good/bad, right/wrong, black/white, maleness/femaleness, etc. There's little gray in their thinking.
- They tend to be uncomfortable with categories that encompass variety, and are more comfortable if categories are limited to similar things.
- Their habits of thought are rigid, and they don't change their mental set easily, but persist in their "tried-and-true" ways of reasoning.
- They have a real need for things to be definite and don't cope well with uncertainty in their plans.
- They tend to agree with such statements as "there are only two kinds of people" and "there's only one right way to do something."
- They divide the world into proper and improper.
- They need precise, orderly, clear-cut instructions before proceeding with a task.

Typical Traits

Highly-prejudiced people have what's known as an *authoritarian personality*. The personality profile includes these typical traits [Ijzendoorn 1989].

- rigid beliefs
- intolerant of weakness in themselves and others; power orientation
- highly punishing; aggressive
- suspicious, cynical
- extremely respectful of authority; a strong commitment to conform to the prevailing authority structure
- politically conservative

The Authoritarian Link to Prejudice

Almost invariably, when the parents of authoritarian people have been studied, they're also highly prejudiced against other subcultural groups. The rigid authoritarian cluster of beliefs and attitudes goes back to early childhood experiences in families with these typical characteristics:

- Parents administered harsh and threatening discipline.
- Parents used love and its withdrawal as their major control mechanism to make the child do as told.
- The child was very insecure and highly dependent on the parents.
- The child feared the parents and felt unconscious hostility toward them.

The child gets a double whammy: the setup for developing an authoritarian personality and role models who specifically teach prejudice.

This set of characteristics usually produces an adult with a high degree of anger and a habit of repressing the anger because of insecurity and fear of expressing it directly. Anger must go somewhere, and in this instance it takes the form of displaced aggression against powerless groups. Meanwhile the authoritarian person maintains an outward respect for law and order.

This person typically dislikes uncertainty more than others. Rigid persons don't easily deal with situations that are unclear or difficult to interpret. They see uncertain situations as threatening, while others may see them as nonthreatening or even as interesting, intriguing or otherwise desirable. Rigidity is also referred to as intolerance of ambiguity. Cultural differences obviously create uncertainty about human behavior, and the behavior of diverse others is less understandable and predictable to us than the behavior of those we grew up with. People with rigid personalities are especially likely to view interactions with diverse others as threatening and undesirable (Cox 1993).

Of course, there are exceptions to this profile. Some persons from authoritarian homes are able to choose an open, flexible approach to life. Others, through personal growth, change their beliefs and attitudes in order to become more open, flexible, and accepting of diversity. But it's difficult. Prejudice is clearly more than an occasional incident for people with rigid, authoritarian personality traits. It's embedded in every facet of their personalities. If and when such persons change their prejudiced viewpoints, it follows that they must change their whole life pattern.

The Less–Prejudiced Personality

Tolerant people have adopted thinking processes that are relatively open and flexible, as follows.

- They rarely see things in black-or-white terms but see many shades of gray.
- They're usually comfortable differentiating among the variety within a category.
- They can be comfortable with people and situations they're uncertain about.
- They often empathize with those who are different—and are sensitive to their way of seeing and feeling.
- They're self-aware and assess the quality and meaning of their thoughts, feelings, and actions.
- They tend to take responsibility for what happens to them in life and for the life they create.
- They know their own strengths and shortcomings pretty well.
- They've built a great deal of inner security, have handled threats to their self-esteem with inner strength, and can be at ease with all sorts of people.
- They handle moral conflict pretty well, and so can be fairly flexible and tolerant with the ethical mistakes people make.
- They can tolerate ambiguity, paradox, and uncertainty.
- They feel safe in saying "I don't know" and in waiting until time brings the information or evidence they need.
- They can feel their way through a task, if necessary

If you're a fairly tolerant person, you're likely to fit the following profile fairly well. You were probably raised in a home with a relatively permissive atmosphere. You felt welcomed, accepted, and loved in an unconditional way. While you were reprimanded for certain behavior, you weren't rejected as a person because of that behavior. You accepted your parents on the whole but weren't afraid to criticize their behaviors or beliefs at times. You generally didn't fear or dread your parents' superior power. Of course, there are exceptions to this profile. Some persons from authoritarian homes are able to overcome their upbringing, reject their parents' approach, and choose an open, flexible approach to life. Some, through personal growth, change their beliefs and attitudes in order to become more open, flexible, and accepting of diversity.

Investigators have failed to discover important relationships between prejudice and such variables as age, gender, or income. People with more education tend to be less prejudiced, but the connection is fairly minimal. Prejudice is clearly more than an occasional incident for many people; it's embedded in every facet of their personality. If such persons were to change their prejudiced viewpoints, it would follow that they would be changing their whole life pattern.

HOW AND WHY DO WE BECOME PREJUDICED?

How we become prejudiced is closely related to why we become prejudiced. Some typical reasons are:

- the need to feel superior to someone
- fear of competition for jobs from the disparaged group's members

- general frustration because of low status and resulting hostility
- lack of education leading to a simplistic, stereotypic view of the world
- difficulty dealing with new, uncertain situations and people
- the need to be approved and included by people from the ingroup, most of whom are prejudiced themselves
- the tendency to conform to dominant beliefs and attitudes

As we explore how people become prejudiced, details of the reasons why will emerge.

Prejudice in the United States is probably rooted in the ethnocentric philosophy that values mainstream dominant cultural beliefs and attitudes more highly than culturally diverse belief systems. Our history is riddled with many flavors of overt and covert prejudice, ranging from slavery to segregation to ethnic and sexist jokes. Most prejudice today is of the subtle and hidden form. We might view prejudice as both a group disease and an individual disease. People become prejudiced through the following processes and sources:

- being raised in ways that promote such personality traits as rigidity and authoritarianism
- learning from the culture—family, school, church, media, workplace
- stereotyping
- developing an ethnic identity
- forming ingroups
- becoming ethnocentric
- living in a diverse, rapidly changing society

We Learn Prejudice from Our Culture

People learn to be prejudiced first and primarily at home, but regardless of where they first adopt prejudiced beliefs, reinforcement occurs throughout the culture—within the family and in the media, the schools, the churches, the workplace, the government. Prejudice is reinforced when we see the contributions of certain groups being devalued or ignored and when we hear people use negative adjectives and stereotypes for them. It's kept in place when we don't have access to a broad array of factual and suitable information about other groups—and when our contacts with people from other groups are only superficial.

The Society—Attitudes and Actions

"Racial profiling" is a hot topic these days. It usually refers to police officers detaining, harassing, and arresting African Americans and Latino Americans in situations where Euro-Americans are normally left alone. But "racial profiling" occurs throughout society, not just in police departments. It's a form of stereotyping that is acted out in discriminatory ways. Here are some examples of profiling:

- In retail stores, Euro-American who look affluent are eagerly waited on while Asian Americans may be ignored, and African Americans are followed around by store or security personnel to prevent shoplifting.
- In Euro-American neighborhoods, police are apt to detain African Americans just because they seem "out of place," meaning not in their own neighborhoods.
- In airports and at border crossings, Euro-Americans are the least likely to be detained or subjected to baggage or body searches.
- Arab Americans are the group most likely to be detained as possible terrorists.
- Latino American boys are the group most likely to be detained for possible gang activity.

Family Beliefs and Attitudes

Children learn about the world first from their families. Let's take ethnic stereotyping. Family environments that influence children toward stereotyping include these factors:

- Parents avoid discussing ethnic issues because they are too touchy.
- Friends who visit regularly are all of the same ethnic group.
- When people (friends, media persons) make prejudicial remarks, parents do not confront them.
- Children remain in segregated schools and play groups.
- Parents don't bother to point out the strengths and contributions of diverse cultures.

The Media

Rigid stereotypes are reinforced by television and radio programs, newspaper and magazine articles, and books by these practices:

- Showing minority group members in stereotypical roles.
- Failing to show minority group members in visible professional positions, such as news anchor, or in positive, leading roles in books, plays, series, situation comedies, and other programs.
- Allowing imbalanced coverage of minority communities, with more focus on criminal activities and tensions than on positive events and programs. Failing to portray the full range of a community's culture.

Schools

School systems and school cultures reinforce stereotyping, prejudice, and discrimination in these ways:

- Allowing an administration, faculty, or student body that's not as culturally diverse as the community at large.
- Promoting a learning environment that focuses on only one value system, normally middle-class mainstream Euro-American. (For example, promoting competition above cooperation, emphasizing future time emphasis over past or present, emphasizing individual achievement above group or team orientation.)
- Building the curriculum around European history and the dominant Euro-American culture, paying little attention to cultures of other Americans.
- Ignoring the need for education about ethnic and gender prejudice and discrimination.

The Workplace

The workplace and its corporate cultures reinforce stereotyping, prejudice, and discrimination in these ways:

- Allowing or imposing a glass ceiling that blocks nearly all minorities and women from top positions.
- Encouraging and rewarding only a middle-class and upper-class Euro-American-based value system.
- Tolerating subtle or overt discrimination at the workplace.

The Government

Behavior by the American government that reinforces discrimination includes these practices:

- Not passing, or watering down, equal rights legislation that is needed to promote fairness and equality for diverse groups.

- Halting or undermining affirmative action enforcement before such programs have achieved their purposes.
- Ignoring, minimizing, or downplaying harassment charges.

Churches

Research by G.W. Allport and J.M. Ross shows that many people actually equate bigotry with organized religion because religious views have so often been used as the basis for stereotyping and prejudice. Their research also indicates that churchgoers are more likely to be prejudiced.

Of course, not all churchgoers are prejudiced. Churches vary greatly in their beliefs about ethnic groups. Also, bigotry becomes a personal issue when religion becomes the excuse for ingroup superiority and for outgroup denigration. Such bigotry occurs for ego-related reasons.

Allport and Ross were surprised by their research findings, in the 1950s and 1960s, that the greater a Euro-American's commitment to religion, the more prejudiced against African Americans he or she tended to be. Some studies indicated that people with no religious affiliation showed on average less prejudice than did church members. This was puzzling since virtually all denominations are supposedly based upon love of others.

To explore further, Allport [1967] asked, "Why do people go to church in the first place?" His findings revealed two basic motivations: Extrinsically motivated members use their religion, and intrinsically motivated members live their religion.

Extrinsic religious motivation refers to a self-serving, manipulative approach to religion that conforms to social conventions. The primary value is to enjoy social acceptance and belonging. Church provides members with security, comfort, status, or social support and may mean belonging to a powerful, superior ingroup. This orientation is associated with prejudice toward outgroups.

Intrinsic religious motivation refers to valuing religion as a framework that gives meaning to life, a way of understanding all of life, and guidance for day-to-day living. The primary value is to "love thy neighbor," and there's no legitimate place for rejection, contempt, or condescension. The church's basic creed of brotherhood expresses an ideal that these members sincerely believe in. This orientation lends itself to tolerance and acceptance of all groups.

Many church members incorporate elements of both orientations. Some are there primarily for social reasons, but some deeper meaning also motivates them. Others are there for life meaning and guidance but also enjoy the social and supportive aspects. In the 1990s, G.W. Herek's [1994] analyses confirmed that prejudice or tolerance toward African Americans can be predicted with some accuracy by extrinsic or intrinsic religious motivation.

Herek's studies also indicate that, unlike prejudice toward African Americans, Euro-American prejudice toward gay persons can *not* be predicted on the basis of extrinsic or intrinsic orientation. The major predictor of whether a church member will harbor antigay prejudice is whether or not the church has a fundamentalist orientation. A major aspect of fundamentalism is a literal interpretation of the Bible. For example, when discussing beliefs about gay persons, church leaders and members tend to focus on Bible passages that they believe condemn homosexuality.

We Develop an Ethnic Identity

All of us achieve our identity from a period of exploration and experimentation that usually takes place in adolescence and often continues into early adulthood. Working through this exploration, we come to solidify our decisions and commitments regarding our career and occupations, lifestyle, sexual standards, politics, and philosophy of life or religion. We'll review how most Euro-Americans develop their identity as part of the ethnic majority in American culture. We'll also see how a minority person typically develops an ethnic identity. Both are summarized in Table 4.1

TABLE 4.1: Developing an Ethnic Identity

Euro-Americans	Minority Persons
Little or no ethnic awareness	Identify with Euro-Americans
Ethnic conflict about prejudice	Encounter prejudice, search for own identity
Reaction or retreat from conflict	Attach to own culture
Balance identity to include minorities	Integrate, internalize ethnic identity

How Euro-Americans Develop a Majority Identity

Euro-Americans, or any dominant majority persons, normally experience an ethnic identity process that is different from that of the ethnic minority members. Now assume that you are a young Euro-American and mentally move through the stages of developing an ethnic identity.

Step 1. Before exposure and contact with ethnic differences

In the beginning you don't even think of yourself as an ethnic person. You unconsciously identify with being "a white person" in a culture where most minorities have darker skin coloring, and you accept stereotypes about minorities without questioning them.

Step 2. Ethnic conflict

As you mature, you become acquainted with people from other ethnic groups. You may have noticed that many or all of them don't fit the stereotypes you've held about them. Perhaps you've seen them excluded, castigated, and in many ways treated unfairly.

You may experience conflict between wanting to go along with the beliefs and actions of your biased friends and relatives and wanting to treat minorities with respect and fairness, as essentially equal human beings. So you begin to reexamine many of your assumptions and beliefs about Euro-American people, which in turn leads you to challenge your accepted set of beliefs about "being white." You come face to face with minority issues and are challenged to acknowledge the continuing reality of prejudice in American society and your role in perpetuating the status quo. Key emotions that come up during this stage are confusion, guilt, anger, and perhaps even depression, all related to your belief that you have been a part of the prejudiced establishment. Your anger may be directed inward toward yourself as well as outward toward the dominant culture in general.

If you are male, you will deal with being part of a dominant group that discriminates against women as well as ethnic minorities. You'll face contradictions about how your mother, sister, or close friends and other relatives are viewed and treated by men in the culture. If you are female, you'll get in touch with the bifurcated position of being a member of the dominant ethnic group and at the same time a member of the disadvantaged gender group. On one hand, you'll begin to deal with being part of a system where you have the power to exclude others. On the other hand, you'll probably begin to notice commonalties of women's situation with that of other disadvantaged groups.

Step 3. Reaction or retreat

As a member of the dominant majority, you'll probably have one of two reactions to the feelings that came up in step 2.

- **Reaction.** You take a strong stand for minority issues. You begin to fight or resist the prejudice you see around you and to identify with disadvantaged groups. You feel compassion and empathy for them, which somewhat offsets the feelings of confusion and guilt you were experiencing.

- **Retreat.** You avoid situations that cause you to feel confusion and conflict. You back off from any sort of inter-ethnic contact, returning to the comfort, security, and familiarity of your own culture. You decide life is just easier and less complicated that way. You over-identify with "being white" and feel defensive about the dominant culture. You may fear minorities and feel angry about their behavior.

Step 4. Balancing your identity to include minorities

At some point, you may mature into a more balanced and healthy ethnic identity, especially if you chose the reaction route in step 3. You acknowledge that as a member of the dominant culture, you share responsibility for maintaining prejudice. At the same time you identify with the larger holistic American culture and with a nonprejudiced Euro-American viewpoint: Not all of us want to perpetuate the status quo. You can see positive and negative beliefs and actions in your own group, as well as in minority groups. You now turn your energy and attention to equality issues and become committed to fighting all forms of oppression. You feel flexible and open to learning more about all cultures, including your own.

How Minority Persons Develop an Ethnic Identity

Members of ethnic minorities are bicultural, having an American cultural identity and also an ethnic subcultural identity. Therefore, their process is different from that of Euro-Americans. Put yourself in the role of a young minority person and follow the typical identity development process through four stages.

Step 1. Identifying with the Euro-American majority

At some point in your life, usually as a young teenager before you've had a turning-point inter-ethnic encounter, you're almost certain to identify primarily with the Euro-American majority culture. You prefer their ways of thinking and acting; that is, their standards, norms, and values. It may be that you simply view your ethnic identity as unimportant. Perhaps your unexamined preferences and commitments are based on your parents' values.

Step 2. Gaining minority awareness, encountering prejudice, searching for identity

Somewhere along the line, you become painfully aware of your status as a minority in a prejudicial society. This awareness may be raised either by a single dramatic encounter with an oppressive or prejudicial experience, or it may grow out of an accumulation of more subtle experiences. This awareness triggers a period when you question your status and the values of the dominant culture. You also begin a search for your own ethnic identity.

You're likely to feel confused, embarrassed, and angry. You begin to develop positive prejudice toward your own ethnic group and negative prejudice toward the Euro-American majority. (This phase is especially difficult for children whose father is from a different ethnic group than the mother.) Your negative prejudice is just forming, so you probably don't act it out in prejudiced behavior yet. But you do become tired of the Euro-American system and you want to strengthen your bonds with your own ethnic group, to really belong and feel a part of that culture. You may feel some confusion about teaming up with members of other minority groups.

Step 3. Identifying with and attaching to your own culture

If you've come into adulthood within the past thirty years, you're especially likely to have entered a phase where you committed yourself to your own ethnic group and immersed yourself in that culture. In this stage you endorse the beliefs, values, norms, and customs of your own group, while completely rejecting values and norms of the Euro-American establishment.

This stage is the most intensely emotional. You're certain to direct anger and even rage toward the majority. You feel intense loyalty and pride toward your own group, so much so that you tend to idealize and romanticize your group. Now you're more likely to act in a prejudiced way toward Euro-Americans than in any stage. You're likely to have a separatist attitude; you may participate in political action that calls attention to minority issues; and you may even act out your rage in a violent manner.

Step 4. Integrating and internalizing your ethnic identity

At this stage you do a more realistic reassessment and reappraisal of your own minority culture, the dominant Euro-American culture, and your role in the scheme of things. Out of this reappraisal, you develop a more balanced bicultural identity that integrates the best of both cultures (your minority culture and the dominant Euro-American culture). You internalize this bicultural identity, making it a part of your belief system. If your mother and father come from different minority cultures, then you must develop a multicultural identity, integrating both minority cultures with the dominant culture.

You've run through the intense emotion of the previous phase. The major characteristic of this stage is the development of a secure ethnic identity along with an appreciation of other cultures. Now you're likely to direct your commitment toward cooperative alliances with committed people from the mainstream culture, from your own minority group, and from other minority groups in order to change discriminatory policies and practices. You're likely to work within the mainstream culture to bring about peaceful change.

We Form Ingroups

Even before we develop an ethnic identity, we identify with one or more ingroups. Part of the process of developing an ethnic identity is forming ingroups. What we're familiar with tends to become a value. The familiar provides the indispensable basis of our existence. As early as age five, children develop a fierce sense of loyalty to their ingroup. Members of an ingroup all use the term *we* with the same essential significance.

Ingroup memberships are not set in concrete. At times people have reason to claim one category of membership, and at other times a different or slightly larger category, depending on their need to look good or be accepted. No doubt, you've noticed that certain people in your ingroup squabble among themselves all the time. But if one of them is attacked by someone from outside the group, the former squabblers may join together in defending against or attacking the outgroup enemy. Likewise, two groups that formerly fought each other may join together to fight a third group, a common enemy. In this way members may modify their ingroups to fit their needs. When the needs call for hostile action, the purpose of the newly formed ingroup may be action against a hated outgroup.

The term *ingroup* indicates the sheer fact that you're a member of a group, while the term *reference group* indicates whether you cherish that membership or whether you seek to relate yourself with another group. The terms help us to identify two levels of belongingness. A reference group may be either

- an ingroup that you're happy you belong to, or
- another group that you'd like to belong to.

Some people are always comparing themselves with groups which for them are not ingroups. Some minority persons tend to mold their attitudes around those of the dominant majority, which for them may be a reference group. The dominant majority exerts a strong pull on minorities, often forcing them to conform to majority attitudes. This conformity, however, rarely goes so far as a minority rejecting her or his own ingroup. It does explain, however, why women and minorities sometimes echo the opinions of Euro-American men even when such opinions are against the best interests of women and minorities.

Ingroup memberships are vitally important to individual survival. Through memberships we form a web of habits. When we meet outsiders who follow different customs, we tend to unconsciously say, "They break my habits." Habit-breaking is unpleasant because we tend to prefer the familiar. Most of us feel a bit on guard when other people seem to threaten or even question our habits. Attitudes partial to the ingroup, or to the reference group, do not necessarily require that attitudes toward other groups be antagonistic—even though hostility often helps to intensify the ingroup cohesion. Narrow circles can, without conflict, be supplemented by larger circles of loyalty. Allport (1954) noted that this happy condition is not often achieved, but it remains from the psychological point of view a hopeful possibility.

We Become Ethnocentric

Ethnocentrism can lead to prejudice, but does not always do so. While prejudice assumes different groups are inferior, ethnocentrism assumes your own group is superior. It's a part of developing an ethnic identity. While ethnocentric attitudes are widespread in human society and seem to reflect a universal tendency, studies indicate that Euro-American managers are more ethnocentric than their counterparts in Britain, Australia, and mainland Europe (Ijzendoorn 1980).

Ethnocentrism is the belief that your ethnic group is superior to all others.

Ethnocentrism is a form of ingroup/outgroup bias. Two related factors stand out:

- Such bias can be based on nearly any group identity, such as blue eyes or brown eyes, and does not necessarily imply a long history of prejudice.

- It's a milder form of ingroup favoritism than the more extreme forms of hostile bigotry that are usually associated with prejudice and discrimination.

In her landmark experiment with school children, Jane Elliott (1985) was able to create the main dimensions of ethnocentric behavior in a matter of hours on the basis of a group separation that was essentially arbitrary—whether a child had blue eyes or brown eyes.

Research provides evidence that dominant group members tend to believe that when outgroup people succeed, it's because they got help or got lucky, but when ingroup members succeed, it's because they deserved it, earned it, and had the right traits and skills. In other words, Euro-American males tend to think that when their own succeed in the workplace, it's because of internal traits, but when others succeed, it's because of external circumstances.

Ethnocentrism in the workplace has made it difficult for people other than Euro-American males to make it to the top. For example, several studies indicate that the major barrier is the tendency for Euro-American males at the top to be more comfortable with their own kind (Morrison, White, and Van Velsor 1987; Carr-Ruffino1991).

Ethnocentrism is a human tendency that offers several benefits. If you decide to stick with your ingroup:

- You can better predict and understand others' behavior, because they're like you.

- It's easier to figure out why others in the group do what they do.

- It's easier to establish rapport and build a relationship.

- You're more likely to help others, because people are more likely to help others like themselves than to help "strangers."

People who are high in authoritarian and rigid personality traits and low in moral development tend to be more ethnocentric. They tend to be less tolerant toward, and hold less favorable attitudes toward, members of outgroups, especially minority group members (Ijzendoorn 1989; Brewer 1979; Clark 1975; Greenhaus and Parasuraman 1991).

People who are more open and flexible enjoy a different set of advantages. When you're comfortable and open to interacting with people from outgroups:

- You get to expand your experience and knowledge of other people and cultures.

- You make your work more interesting, exciting, and intriguing.

- You increase your ability to relate to many types of people.

- You boost your social and leadership skills.

- You become more cosmopolitan.

We're Part of a Diverse, Rapidly Changing Society

We learn prejudice from our culture, and the United States provides the ideal climate for this, simply because of its current situation. Research shows that the following conditions provide fertile ground for prejudice to develop—and can exacerbate or intensify existing prejudice in a culture (Ponteretto and Pedersen 1993).

- The society is heterogeneous.

- Upward mobility is allowed and valued.

- Social change is occurring rapidly.

- Communication barriers and ignorance between groups are common.

- A minority group is large or increasing.

- An increasing minority represents direct competition and a realistic threat.

- Exploitation of minorities sustains important interests.
- Customs regulating aggression are favorable to bigotry.
- Traditional justifications for ethnocentrism are available.
- Neither assimilation nor cultural pluralism is favored.

This reads like a current description of American society. We're the most heterogeneous society on earth, and a key value is the opportunity for people to move up if they learn the ropes and work hard. Social change, and every other type of change, is occurring rapidly, especially the family changes caused by women pursuing careers. We've been a segmented society and de facto segregation is still common. Barriers to communication result in ignorance about other groups, which make them easy prey to rumor, suspicion, and stereotype. This process is most likely to occur if the group is also regarded as a potential threat because it is growing and its members are competing with the dominant group in the job market. Internal colonialism has sustained privilege for Euro-Americans, bigotry has been a part of U.S. history, and ethnocentrism is still creating barriers in the workplace. Finally, we're in a state of flux and transition regarding assimilation versus cultural pluralism, both in our corporations and in our communities. Immigrants have found themselves criticized both for maintaining their cultural ways and for pressing for assimilation.

In this section, we've addressed the question, How do we become prejudiced? A review of the processes and influences may leave you wondering, How could we not be prejudiced? The legacy of the patriarchal family teaches us about the inequality and stereotyped roles of men and women just by its very existence. From the cradle, this is part of our enculturation. And the organizations we encounter when we leave our homes have virtually all been founded on the basis of inequality and stereotyped roles. Some psychologists note that prejudice and discrimination at the top level of a society, or an organization, set into motion a continuing cycle of prejudice and discrimination throughout every part (Ponteretto and Pedersen 1993). We can see, then, that prejudice is woven into the very tapestry of our culture. The people with the most influence in sustaining or breaking the cycle are parents in the home and leaders in organizations.

HOW DO PEOPLE EXPRESS PREJUDICE?

When someone is prejudiced, how do you know it? People may express prejudice by denying it or rationalizing it, by acting it out in various ways from mild to devastating, by subtly discriminating, or by using outgroup members as scapegoats.

They Deny and Rationalize

Two common ways of handling the inner conflict that arises when people discriminate against others are

- *denial*: repressing the conflict by denying the prejudice
- *rationalization*: offering defenses for the prejudice, justifying it

People often choose denial because if they admit prejudice, they admit to being both irrational and unethical. No one wants their conscience to bother them all the time. So it's not unusual to hear the person we perceive as being quite prejudiced saying, "I'm not prejudiced, but . . . ."

The most obvious way for people to defend prejudiced beliefs is to gather evidence in their favor. People may select only that evidence that supports their stereotypes. When we rationalize, we may:

- See only those traits, actions, and events that confirm a decision we've already made, and we simply fail to notice those that don't.
- Say it must be true because other people think this way too. "Everybody thinks those people are sneaky" (. . . dirty, stupid, rude), claiming truth by consensus.
- Blame the targets or shift the blame back onto our accusers. "It's their own fault they don't get ahead" (. . .that others shun them, etc.) or "They're just as prejudiced as we are."

- Defend our thinking or action by saying it's the exception to our usual pattern. "Some of my best friends are Platians, but . . . ."

They Act Out

We act out our prejudice toward people from an unfavored group with varying degrees of hostile energy. Talking against such people involves relatively little energy, while actively avoiding them takes more. Stepping up the energy level, we may discriminate against them, physically attack them, or in a rare extreme of hostile energy, participate in exterminating them. While some people would never move to a more intense degree of action, for others activity on one level makes it easier to move to a more intense level.

Talking against

People usually talk against those from outgroups when they're with like-minded friends, and occasionally with strangers. People sometimes disparage an outgroup in order to cement their relationship as part of their ingroup. Talking against includes joking or disparaging comments that express a mild animosity. Name-calling expresses a more intense hostility. The more spontaneous and irrelevant the talking against, the stronger the hostility that lies behind it.

Physically attacking

Actual physical attacks on outgroup members, and other acts of violence or semi-violence, occur far less frequently than the milder expressions of prejudice. However, violent incidents are increasing both in the workplace and in the community, especially against women. They usually occur when people become overwrought and overemotional. However, violence may be calculated to create a reign of terror, to teach others to stay in their place, or to otherwise punish or threaten.

An FBI report cited more than 7,600 hate crimes in 1993. Director Louis Freeh said the total falls far short of the full picture because police forces representing 44 percent of the population did not even report hate crimes. Crimes against people accounted for 70 percent of the offenses reported. The most common targets:

African Americans	2,500
Euro-Americans	1,300
Jewish Americans	1,054
Gay persons	777

Offenders were unknown in 42 percent of cases. Of the known offenders, 51 percent were Euro-American and 35 percent African American (Espinosa and Pimentel 1993).

They Subtly Discriminate

It's not attractive to express prejudice in many social circles, and it can be illegal in the workplace. Therefore, most prejudice today is of the covert and subtle form, sometimes classified as the avoidance prejudice of the liberals and the symbolic prejudice of the conservatives. Psychologically, if you hold your prejudiced beliefs out of conscious awareness, you can hold onto your self-concept as a nonprejudiced, egalitarian person. You can swear you're not prejudiced and define prejudice as an intentional, overt act, the old-fashioned type of prejudice (Blanchard and Crosby 1989).

Avoidance Prejudice among Liberals

A subtle form of prejudice among liberals is called "avoidance prejudice" by some researchers. Even though liberals are all for equality and consider themselves unprejudiced, some possess negative feelings and beliefs about minority groups. Because such people hold egalitarian values and see themselves as tolerant, they usually won't discriminate against other ethnic groups in situations where the policies and procedures describing appropriate behavior are clear and unambiguous. To do so would directly threaten their egalitarian self-image. When the rules of the game are weak, ambiguous, or conflicting, or if such persons can justify or rationalize a negative response on the basis of some factor other than ethnicity, many will discriminate, while holding onto their egalitarian self-image. Business leaders can reduce discrimination within the organization, therefore, by developing clear policies and procedures for the treatment of people from diverse groups. At least that portion of discriminatory behavior that is based on avoidance prejudice will be reduced.

Symbolic Prejudice among Conservatives

Subtle prejudice among conservatives is often called "symbolic prejudice." These conservatives believe that discrimination no longer exists. They also believe that minority groups are violating our cherished American values and are still making unwarranted demands for changing the status quo. According to symbolic prejudice theory, many Euro-Americans acquire negative feelings toward other ethnic groups early in life. These feelings persist into adulthood but are expressed indirectly and symbolically.

Modern conservatives tend to express their prejudice in such symbolic ways as opposition to affirmative action or sexual harassment policies, rather than directly or overtly, as in support for segregation. They reject traditional racist beliefs and they displace their prejudicial feelings onto more rationalizable abstract social and political issues, such as "family values" and "school voucher systems." People who practice symbolic prejudice, like those who practice avoidance prejudice, are therefore relatively unaware of their prejudicial feelings.

They Scapegoat

Most societies seem to encourage, officially or unofficially, the open expression of hostility toward certain groups that serve as scapegoats or safety valves for anger and aggression. Scapegoating is a form of group projection that helps groups to remain ethnocentric by projecting members' shortcoming and failures upon outgroups, blaming them for the ingroup's problems. In addition, most nations have numerous chauvinistic devices that breed ethnocentrism. For example, virtually no history book ever teaches that one's country was ever in the wrong. Geography is usually taught with a nationalistic bias, and claims to achievements in science and the arts are often overblown.

SUMMARY

The third step in gaining multicultural skills is recognizing your own biases, the ways in which you stereotype, assume, judge, and discriminate. Stereotyping is prejudging or assuming certain traits and characteristics about people, based on their ethnic group or other category, and rigid stereotypes lead to prejudice. Prejudice is our tendency to view people who are different as being inferior, while ethnocentricity is the tendency to think your own cultural group is superior. When we discriminate, we act out our prejudice in ways that disadvantage people from disparaged groups.

Although most prejudice is called either *racism* or *sexism*, most anthropologists agree that race has little or no meaning as a practical concept. *Ethnic prejudice* is a more appropriate term. On the other hand, sexism is said by some to be the root of all prejudice because it begins in the home.

How do we become prejudiced? Virtually every aspect of our culture teaches us to be prejudiced, from the differential in mother's and father's status and other family beliefs to the media, schools, workplace, government, and religious organizations. As children grow up, they develop an ethnic identity. Euro-American children usually become aware of ethnic differences after some type of ethnic conflict. They may react by defending minorities or by avoiding future contact with them. Minority children usually identify first with the Euro-American majority until they encounter prejudice and begin searching for their own identity. They may develop resentment toward Euro-Americans or become ashamed of being a minority. Most eventually identify with their own cultural subgroup and later integrate aspects of both cultures.

Prejudice and ethnocentrism are related to the human tendency to form ingroups. A reference group is either your ingroup, if you're happy you belong to it, or another group you want to belong to. People who are most ethnocentric and prejudiced tend to also be most rigid and authoritarian.

The authoritarian person believes in strict categories of right and wrong, good and bad, and other black/white opposites. Such people tend to be intolerant of weakness, highly punishing, suspicious, and extremely respectful of authority. People develop either a relatively authoritarian or relatively open, flexible personality in childhood but can choose to change at any age. The United States provides fertile ground for prejudice to grow because it is an increasingly diverse society, still relatively segregated, and in the midst of rapid change.

How do we express prejudice? Most people are unaware of their prejudices, and denying or justifying prejudice is a typical way of handling the inner conflict that prejudice often creates. People may act out their prejudice in varying degrees of hostility, from talking against others or avoiding them to discriminating against them, physically attacking them, or even participating in programs to exterminate them. People who are unaware of their prejudices may express them quite subtly. Liberals tend to use avoidance prejudice and won't discriminate where policies and procedures are clear. Conservatives tend to resort to symbolic prejudice, opposing for example affirmative action but not advocating a return to legal segregation. Disparaged groups are often used as scapegoats so the dominant group can retain its belief in its superiority.

REFERENCES

Allport. G. W. *The Nature of Prejudice*. Boston: Addison-Wesley, 1954.

Allport, G.W., and B.M. Kramer. "Some Roots of Prejudice," *Journal of Psychology* 22: 9-19, 27, 1946.

Allport, G.W., and J.M. Ross. "Personal Religious Orientation and Prejudice." *Journal of Personality and Social Psychology* 5: 432-443, 1967

Baskerville, D.M., and S.H. Tucker. "A Blueprint for Success." *Black Enterprise,* November: 85-92, 1991.

Blanchard, F.A., and F. J. Crosby. *Affirmative Action in Perspective*. New York: Springer-Verlag, 1989.

Brewer, M.B., "Ingroup Bias in the Minimal Intergroup Situation," *Psychological Bulletin* 86: 307-324, 1979.

Clark, C.X. "Race, Life Style, and Rule Flexibility." *Organizational Behavior and Human Performance* 13: 433-443, 1975.

Cox, Taylor. *Cultural Diversity in Organizations*. San Francisco: Berrett-Koehler, 1993.

Espinosa S., and B. Pimentel, "New Fears About Racist Groups," *San Francisco Chronicle*, August 13: A-1, 1993.

Feagin, Joe R., and Clairece Booher Feagin. *Discrimination American Style: Institutional Racism and Sexism*. Englewood Cliffs, NJ: Prentice-Hall, 1978.

Gadamer, Hans-Georg. *Truth and Methods*, rev. ed., New York: Crossroad, 1989.

Greenhaus, J.H., and S. Parasuraman. "Job Performance Attributions and Career Advancement Prospects" in *Organizational Behavior and Human Decision Processes*, Orlando, FL: Academic Press, 1991.

Herek, G.M. "Assessing Heterosexuals' Attitudes" in *Lesbian and Gay Psychology*. Thousand Oaks, CA: Sage, 1994.

Holmes, Robyn. *How Young Children Perceive Race*. Thousand Oaks: Sage, 1995.

Hopson, Darlene and Derek. *Raising the Rainbow Generation*. New York: Simon & Schuster, 1993.

Ijzendoorn, M.H. "Moral Judgement, Authoritarianism, and Ethnocentrism." *Journal of Social Psychology* 129, 1: 37-45, 1989.

McIntosh, Peggy. *White Privilege and Male Privilege*. Working Paper 189. Wellesley, MA: Center for Research on Women, 1988.

Montagu, Ashley. *Man's Most Dangerous Myth*. Walnut Creek CA: AltaMira Press, 1997.

Palmer, Harry. Living Deliberately. Palm Beach, FL: Star's Edge, 1994

Pettigrew, Thomas. *A Profile of the Negro American*. Princeton, NJ: Van Nostrand, 1964.

Ponterotto, Joseph G. and Paul B. Pederson. *Preventing Prejudice*. Thousand Oaks, CA: Sage, 1993.

"Race Is Not a Biological Distinction," *San Francisco Chronicle,* February 23:A-1,4: 1998.

Ridley, C.R. "Racism in Counseling as an Adverse Behavioral Process" in *Counseling Across Cultures*, 3rd ed. Honolulu: University of Hawaii Press, 1989.

Smith, W.T. *Ethnic Images*. National Opinion Research Center, GSS Topical Report No. 19. Chicago: University of Chicago, December, 1990.

Takaki, Ronald. *A Different Mirror: A History of Multicultural America*. Boston: Little, Brown & Co., 1993.

Feedback: Self-Awareness Activity 4.4

R = Rigid, authoritarian personality
O = Open, flexible personality
Instructions:

1. To get your R score, add up all the R questions you answered true and all the O questions you answered false.

2. To get your O score, add up all the O questions you answered true and all the R questions you answered false.

3. Compare your R and O scores to assess your relative levels of openness and rigidity.

1. R   I have little or no difficulty decided what's right and what's wrong.
2. O   I thrive on variety and change.
3. O   I often enjoy being with people that some would call strange or weird.
4. R   I like my routines.
5. R   I know how I feel about most situations and don't need to keep thinking about them.
6. R   I need to know exactly where I'm going and when.
7. O   I often ask myself why I did certain things, or why I think or feel as I do.
8. R   I hate it when people change our plans.
9. R   There is only one right way to do most things.
10. O   Few actions are totally right or wrong; most actions stem from complex situations and have varying effects.
11. R   I prefer to focus on a few simple things rather than a wide variety.
12. O   I can feel comfortable with most situations, even if I'm not sure about what's going on.
13. O   I don't always agree with people from other groups, but I usually understand why they might think and feel as they do.
14. O   People basically create the life they have and the sooner they take responsibility for it, the better it will be.
15. O   I think I know my own strengths and shortcomings pretty well.
16. R   Most actions can be classified as either proper or improper.
17. O   People have different ideas about what's proper and improper; that's fine with me.
18. R   I don't start a job until I know exactly how to do it.
19. O   I'm comfortable "feeling my way" through a task, if necessary.
20. R   I need to know what's going on and what to expect at all times.

CHAPTER 5

Workplace Discrimination: Its Effects and Remedies

Prejudiced persons' thinking patterns tend to block their own happiness and zest for life—holding onto prejudice creates a joy drain.
Researcher M.D. Kite, 1986

You're probably aware that to be a valuable employee or business associate, you must move beyond the stereotypes and prejudices that exclude whole groups of people. This involves learning how to bridge the divisive walls of prejudice—and showing others the way. Doing so can bring huge rewards—to you in building success skills and profitable workplace relationships and to your company as you work more productively with people from diverse backgrounds. In this chapter you'll learn about:

- How prejudice affects people generally and in the workplace
- How discrimination specifically affects employees' chances to be hired and promoted
- How handling workplace discrimination has changed over time
- How people can move beyond prejudice and discrimination to valuing differences and building relationships that promote profitable collaboration

Before you delve further into the complexities of prejudice, complete Self-Awareness Activity 5.1.

Self-Awareness Activity 5.1 What Do You Know About Discrimination?

Purpose: To see what you know about the issues covered in this chapter.
Instructions: Determine whether you think the following statements are basically true or false—and think about why. The answers will emerge in this chapter, and the summary at the end of the chapter focuses on these issues.

1. Being prejudiced affects the personality of the holder as well as the receiver of the prejudice.
2. Members of disparaged groups become resentful toward others.
3. The best way to end discrimination is simply to have contact with people from the disparaged group.
4. The melting-pot theory has been successful for integrating minorities and women into the workplace.
5. Affirmative action programs normally include quotas for hiring minorities.

6. Affirmative action has been much more powerful than equal employment opportunity for reducing discrimination.

HOW DOES PREJUDICE AFFECT PEOPLE?

Prejudice affects the personalities of the persons who hold the prejudice as well as those on the receiving end. You can work more effectively with people who are prejudiced if you understand the ways that prejudiced thinking influences their life views and their day-to-day actions. You can relate more constructively to people from groups that have traditionally been disparaged in the mainstream culture when you understand how their life experiences may be influencing their behavior patterns.

Effects of Rejecting Others

When you stereotype and reject others as not good enough, the immediate payoff is feeling "better-than," but it's a cheap thrill. After all, the more time you spend with stereotyped, prejudiced, and discriminatory thoughts, the more time you spend in a critical, blaming, judging state of mind. It follows that you'll spend less time in an appreciative, enthusiastic, or joyous state of mind.

The more prejudiced you are, the more you view life through a negative lens. The more your thoughts focus on distaste, dislike, resentment, revulsion, anger, and similar feelings, the more likely you are to experience the anxiety and fear of being despised by others, because that way of thinking is prominent in your experience. Your world becomes more hierarchical, with everyone becoming categorized as better or worse, and people always judging and comparing. You have less space in your mind and less time for the beauty, the joy, the love, the wonder of other beings. As prejudice becomes a habit, you may become more and more critical, and therefore you become more and more isolated because there are fewer and fewer people you can enjoy. You block the possibility of knowing a large part of the world's people with their fascinating variety because you choose to judge so many of them as too strange or not good enough.

Effects of Being Rejected

Feeling rejected and inferior is difficult to deal with, even if you're a Euro-American male. It's more difficult if you're a woman because you're told in thousands of subtle or blatant ways throughout your life that you're inferior in most life areas—just because you were born a woman. If you're a minority, you're not only told that you're inferior, you're frequently rejected—just because you were born into an "inferior" subgroup. The message that you're inferior cannot be hammered into your head day after day without doing something to your character. It may cause you to examine who you really are, to accept yourself, and to become a stronger person for it. Or it may cause you to develop defensive coping behaviors. These persecution-produced traits are not all unpleasant. Some people, even when they're in reaction to rejection, are able to overcome the human tendency to lash out against the unfairness of a dominant majority and to choose responses that are constructive and socially agreeable (Ponteretto and Pedersen 1993; Allport 1954).

Just which ego defenses people develop is largely an individual matter, often coming out of choices made at an unconscious level but sometimes decided upon consciously. At one extreme, you'll find minority group members who seem to handle their status easily, with little evidence that their outgroup affiliation is of any concern to them. At the other extreme, you'll find people so rebellious that they have developed many ugly defenses, so that they continually provoke the very snubs they resent. Most people you meet fall somewhere between these extremes, showing some mixture of acceptance and resistance to their status.

Only to a slight extent can we say that certain types of ego defense will be more common in one outgroup than in another. Every form of ego defense may be found among people of every disparaged group. Allport developed the model shown in Figure 5.1, which distinguishes between ego defenses that cause us to strike out at other persons from those that we turn inward to punish ourselves.

FIGURE 5-1: Model of Responses to Discrimination

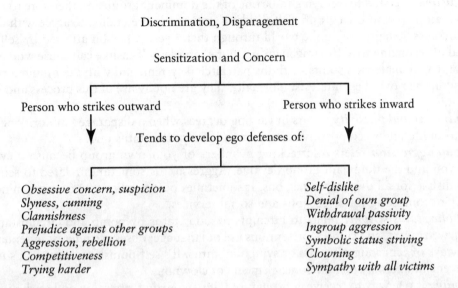

Discrimination, Disparagement

Sensitization and Concern

Person who strikes outward   Person who strikes inward

Tends to develop ego defenses of:

Person who strikes outward	Person who strikes inward
Obsessive concern, suspicion	*Self-dislike*
Slyness, cunning	*Denial of own group*
Clannishness	*Withdrawal passivity*
Prejudice against other groups	*Ingroup aggression*
Aggression, rebellion	*Symbolic status striving*
Competitiveness	*Clowning*
Trying harder	*Sympathy with all victims*

Adapted from Allport, 1954

Ego Defenses That Strike Outward

The basic feeling of members of disparaged groups is one of insecurity, which may lead to being on guard and hypersensitive. Minorities must make many more adjustments to their status than majority members. The latter interact mainly with their own kind and only occasionally with minority group members. The reverse is true for most minorities. In addition, they are more likely to be in a less-powerful position than each of the dominant group members they meet. Preoccupation with the strain of accommodation may become excessive, so that they come to view virtually all members of the dominant group with deep suspicion.

Obsessive concern and suspicion often result in a chip-on-the-shoulder attitude based on the belief, "I've been rejected so often that I've learned to protect myself in advance by not trusting any of you."

Slyness and cunning are responses of some people who are trying to survive or get ahead in a discriminatory environment. In really hostile environments "sneaky" traits may be a passive-aggressive way of gaining petty revenge against more powerful persecutors.

Clannishness, or clustering together with other minority group members, is a natural response to being excluded by the majority group. When people are excluded in work, play, and neighborhood settings, who else can they turn to but their own kind?

Prejudice against other outgroups, especially less-powerful groups, is one way to gain some sense of status and power. When we start with a foundation of inequality, a pecking order naturally develops, with the strong picking on the weaker, and they in turn picking on the still weaker.

Aggression and rebellion occur when people refuse to "take it lying down," and fight back whenever they can. Their frustration breeds aggression. This can be the source of criminal activity and riots. In contrast, some members see the futility of violence and join political or activist organizations that are dedicated to improving the existing situation.

Competing and trying harder are the responses of some minorities. Examples are attending evening classes, studying harder, and working harder than others, trying to make up for an uneven race. Dominant group members may respond with grudging admiration, but they also may accuse the minority of being *too* industrious and clever. Lower-class members of the dominant group may feel envious, resentful, or threatened.

Ego Defenses That Focus Inward

Some minorities turn their feelings and actions inward on themselves or their group. They tend to punish themselves for being inferior or "outcasts."

Self-dislike is related to a craving to be one of the dominant group and therefore to identify more with them than with your own group. Self-dislike is not merely pretending to agree with the dominant group; it involves actually seeing the world through their eyes. A person affected by self-dislike may be ashamed of belonging to a disparaged group. For example, self-dislike can cause women to identify more strongly with male viewpoints, with the patriarchal system, and with their limited roles as being positive and in their own best interests. Normally, they are not aware of this process and would probably deny it.

Withdrawal and passivity occurs in varying degrees when a disparaged minority person decides to retreat from life's more competitive activities and accept the status quo.

Ingroup aggression refers to attacking members of your own group because they possess the traits that you and the dominant group devalue. Aggression is sometimes related to self-dislike that extends to dislike for all disparaged persons. It sometimes occurs when two or more minority groups believe they're competing for scarce jobs and social services.

Symbolic status striving refers to attempts to gain status by pomp and circumstance, a flashy display of jewelry, cars, and clothes; pretentious use of language; obsessive interest in sexual conquests; and other ways of achieving marginal or symbolic status. It's self-punishing because it's not based on solid achievement and may include some elements of clowning.

Clowning is one way to receive good-natured, if patronizing, attention and to show that you are harmless, not threatening. Protective clowning extends into the subgroup itself. For example, some gay persons call themselves and each other *queers*, implying: "If we call ourselves "queer,' it's no longer an epithet that you can use against us." Some African Americans call themselves "niggers," implying: "If we call ourselves 'niggers, we can harden ourselves to the sting of the insult. If we say it often enough, we'll become so hardened we won't ever feel its pain again."

Sympathy with all victims is considered the most positive of these inward-directed ego defenses. People who feel they've been victims of discrimination are usually either very high in prejudice or very low; they're seldom "average." Being a victim disposes you either to develop aggression toward or sympathy with other outgroups. Knowing all too well how it feels to be rejected, many minority persons reach out to other victims and offer support. Examples are Jesse Jackson's Rainbow Coalition and Jewish Americans who joined African Americans to put their lives on the line in the South during the Civil Rights era.

HOW DOES DISCRIMINATION AFFECT EMPLOYEES?

Discrimination against diverse employees not only affects their career progress, it also affects their trust, motivation, and productivity—their relationships with the rest of the workforce. It affects them in every phase and aspect of their work experience. Here are some ways companies exclude diverse employees (Cox 1993).

- recruitment practices
- screening practices
- terms and conditions of employment
- tracking and job segregation
- performance evaluation
- training and development decisions
- promotion practices
- glass ceiling barriers
- diverse standards
- layoff, discharge, and seniority practices
- career alternatives

Recruitment Practices

Word of mouth is still the most common way that people learn about hiring and promotion opportunities. Up to 90 percent of workers find their jobs this way. Studies have concluded that the distribution of white-collar jobs to African Americans depends heavily upon informal networks of information, radiating outward from persons currently employed in upper rank slots. Does word-of-mouth recruiting in your company happen primarily among Euro-American men? What can you do to be sure that minorities and women find out about job opportunities?

Does your company place ads for all types of jobs in minority publications—or just ads for lower-level jobs? When the company makes plans for new facilities, are they ever located at sites that are convenient for minorities? A Civil Rights Commission study of housing (1973) found that "despite a variety of laws against job discrimination, lack of access to housing in close proximity to available jobs is an effective barrier to equal employment."

Screening Practices

Are the diplomas, degrees, and experience that your company requires of applicants really good predictors of whether those people will succeed on the job? If not, and if many minorities or women don't have them, they're discriminatory. Do the aptitude and intelligence tests that your company makes applicants pass really predict job success? The same principle applies here. Because minorities still tend to get an inferior education in the public schools, they're not as likely to do well on screening tests as Euro-Americans. Also, most people who make the tests are Euro-American men from middle-class backgrounds. People from minority subcultures obviously are at a cultural disadvantage in relating to the terminology, examples, cases, and other aspects of such tests. However, they may be quite intelligent, capable of learning how to do the job, and likely to succeed on the job.

Does your company have a strict requirement for applicants to have clean arrest and credit records? Do such screening practices really predict job success or failure? Police department practices often discriminate against minorities, especially African American men and to some extent Latino American men. Such men are more likely to have arrest records even though their behavior may have been as lawful as Euro-American fellow applicants. The same principle applies to credit records. Minorities tend to have lower incomes and to have more difficulty getting credit and maintaining good credit records.

How heavily does your company depend on cumulative employment records in making hiring decisions? Sometimes companies require women and minorities to have experience in areas where they previously have been excluded.

How does your company conduct background investigations of job applicants? If such reports include subjective, vague, and arbitrary assessments from prejudiced persons, they may be unfair to minorities and women.

Terms and Conditions of Employment

Are women and minority men earning approximately the same income as Euro-American men at all levels of the company? On average, they earn about 75 percent, even at the vice-presidential level. Above the "worker" level, they also tend to receive fewer benefits and perquisites.

Tracking and Job Segregation

Does your company still have "women's jobs," "men's jobs," and "minority jobs," even though they're never called that? One example of tracking is the placement of well-educated women in clerical work. Do clerks, secretaries, and administrative assistants have chances to participate in training and development for better-paying jobs? Do they have the chance to get to know people in management? Are they groomed and recruited for higher-level jobs?

To some extent, discrimination in every job phase from recruitment to promotion results in a dual labor market in which women and minorities work disproportionately in occupations and industries with lower prestige, status, and compensation. Within organizations, they typically work in jobs and departments that are less influential and have lower status than those held by Euro-American men. Progress is being made, but we have a long way to go (U.S. Glass Ceiling 1995; Johnson 1987; Buono and Kamm 1983).

Performance Evaluation

Are performance evaluation practices in your company free of bias? Research indicates that successful performance by women on tasks traditionally done by men tends to be attributed to luck, while Euro-American men's performance is more likely to be attributed to their ability. Compared to Euro-American managers, the performance of African American managers is less likely to be attributed to ability and effort and more likely to be attributed to help from others (Deaux and Emswiller 1974; Cash, Gillen, and Burns 1977; Greenhaus and Parasuraman 1994).

Also, evaluations made by Euro-American men are often colored by their stereotyped expectations of the ways women and minorities act. As a result, Euro-American managers often hold women and minorities to tighter standards of behavior than the majority group members. Many women managers say they must "walk a tight rope," feeling their way through the narrow range of acceptable behavior. They see that the men can show more aggressiveness, ambition, competition, and similar traits without being criticized. African American men must show less anger and sexuality to avoid reinforcing stereotypes that cause discomfort. For diverse employees, it amounts to a double standard of acceptable behavior (Baack, Carr-Ruffino, and Pelletier 1993; Morrison, White, and Van Velsor 1987).

Training and Development

Who makes the decisions about which employees will receive various types of training and development opportunities? Are these decisions open and equitable? Or are they colored by stereotypes about which types of persons have the potential and image to be groomed for certain jobs? For example, a study of who gets picked by corporations for midcareer programs at such universities as Harvard, Yale, and Stanford indicated those selected were virtually all Euro-American men. Such practices keep the glass ceiling in place for minorities and women (Carr-Ruffino 1991).

Promotion Practices

How open and equitable are the promotion procedures in your company? In many companies, they're secretive and very difficult for outsiders to understand. Although formal promotion policies and procedures are spelled out in writing by large companies and government agencies, unwritten, informal rules or expectations usually have a much greater impact.

Many studies, past and present, indicate that Euro-American male executives and managers continue to harbor stereotyped views of women and minorities, views that shape the promotion decisions. A woman is disadvantaged if she's married ("We didn't promote her because she has children and her family responsibilities will interfere") and disadvantaged if she's not ("We didn't promote her because she's likely to quit and get married"). Another stereotype is that employees won't accept a woman or minority in a high position. Such subtle discrimination has kept the glass ceiling in place (Carr-Ruffino 1991; Morrison and Van Velsor 1987).

Glass Ceiling Barriers

Several studies, such as those done by two separate U.S. Glass Ceiling Commissions, indicate that the major barrier to promotion up the ladder is the tendency for the men at the top to be more comfortable with their own kind. The reasons for this tendency are:

- They can better predict and understand another's behavior when that other is like them.
- It's easier to figure out why others in the group do what they do.
- It's easier to establish rapport and build a relationship.

- They're more likely to help others in the group, because people are generally more likely to help ingroup members than to help "strangers."

Diverse Standards

Some studies indicate that reasons given for passing over diverse employees are "lack of initiative" or "not aggressive enough," when the real reason involves a misreading of cultural traits. Latino American and Asian American behavior is often interpreted as "too passive" when managers focus on style, not substance. African Americans' style may be seen as "too aggressive." In fact, some studies, such as those by Ann Morrison, have found that different standards of "getting along with others" have been required for African Americans than for others.

Indirect discrimination also occurs when Euro-American male supervisors fail to support and recommend their minority employees for promotion, even though company leaders rely on such subjective evaluations when they make promotion decisions.

Vignette:
"Bid-With" and Unfair Standards

Rich was the first African American compensation manager ever hired by Juno Jeans. Because the compensation manager has access to information on salaries and benefits for every person in the company, top management considers it a very sensitive position calling for someone who is discreet, even secretive. Rich seemed to be a mature man with good judgment and the right kind of experience, so they were willing to give him a try.

Juno employees are given the choice of taking lunch at 12:00 or at 1:00 and many play cards or dominoes after lunch. Most of the clerks and hourly people take their lunch at 12:00, and virtually all the management and professional people take theirs at 1:00. Bridge was the game of choice of the 1 o'clock crowd, while games of the 12 o'clock bunch were as varied as their ethnic backgrounds. The African Americans regularly played Bid-With, a game similar to bridge and generally known only in their community. Rich was a wicked Bid-With player but had never mastered bridge. Because of this he usually joined the 12 o'clock bunch.

The Euro-American executives could not understand why Rich would hobnob with the clerks and maintenance people. To them, it is unwise to become too friendly with people from lower levels, especially when a manager works with sensitive information. It is too easy to relax, forget yourself, and let bits of information slip out. The executives mentioned their concern to Sandra, an African American lawyer in the legal department. She did not agree with their take on the situation. She explained to them that Rich probably just wanted to play Bid-With, and they should not worry about clustering, buddying, blabbing, or similar problems. But the executive's concerns did not go away. Within a few months they found an excuse to terminate Rich.

Sandra discussed the problem with her husband. "It's too bad, but these guys tend to get paranoid any time they see African American employees bonding—or women professionals talking together, for that matter. They'll make joking comments, such as 'Plotting a revolution?' or 'Ganging up on us?' But beneath the humor, I sense they feel threatened by us. Maybe it's a fear of giving up some power and privilege. Poor Rich, his love of Bid-With did him in. And the company lost a really loyal, talented guy, all because top management has these stereotypes about how managers must act."

Layoff, Discharge, and Seniority Practices

What policies and practices does your company follow when they must lay off or fire people? If they use seniority to protect workers who've been there the longest, does this mean that most of those laid off are minorities and women? If not, are older workers the ones who are most likely to lose their jobs? Employees have successfully sued employers for discrimination in both types of situations.

Seniority systems often affect women and minority members more adversely because they typically have less seniority than Euro-American men. The purpose of an organization-wide seniority system is to guarantee that employees with the greatest seniority will receive the greatest protection when cutbacks or layoffs take place. Such guarantees are usually part of a union contract. Yet seniority systems operating today often result in indirect discrimination. Where women and minority persons were barred from certain occupations in the past and therefore have been hired only in recent years, they will be the first to be laid off. This situation is common in organizations with a unionized workforce, such as manufacturing firms and local fire and police departments.

In most other organizations, older workers are more likely to be laid off because they are typically the highest-paid employees. In the process of reengineering, restructuring, and downsizing, companies are often looking for ways to decrease salary expense. Also, when a company computerizes a functional area, the experience and expertise of older workers in that area may become less valuable or even obsolete.

Career Alternatives

Discrimination can even make it more difficult for minorities to choose alternatives to corporate careers when they can't get hired or when they hit the glass ceiling. For example, the Small Business Administration did a study of its loans for 1990 through 1992 and declared that its loan guarantee program had been poorly serving minorities and women. The agency set a goal of at least doubling the number of loans to targeted groups during the coming year (WSJ 1994).

REMEDIES FOR WORKPLACE DISCRIMINATION

Until the 1960s most corporate leaders adhered to the melting-pot approach to deal with workplace diversity. Because this didn't work for women and ethnic minorities, the Civil Rights laws of the 1960s ushered in the legal approach to managing discrimination. Now savvy leaders in forward-thinking companies are going beyond old approaches. Their focus is on valuing diverse employees for the unique contributions they can make to the company's success. They are crafting a multicultural approach to managing diversity—and a corporate culture that welcomes all types of employees to its doors and then appreciates and nurtures them.

Myths vs. Realities

People tend to avoid discussions of workplace discrimination. Many avoid even thinking about it. It should come as no surprise, therefore, that myths about this topic are more prevalent than the realities.

Myth #1: The American workplace is a melting pot. Traditionally business has handled diversity by adopting the Melting Pot myth, but people of color and women never "melted in" because they don't look or act like the dominant majority, Euro-American men.

Myth #2: The equal pay and equal opportunity laws have eliminated workplace inequities. In the 1960s Civil Rights laws began to open many doors of opportunity. However, the laws did not necessarily change the beliefs and attitudes, the thoughts and feelings that led to discrimination in the first place. Many of the people with the authority to make changes have found ways around these laws. And most employees who are discriminated against are unlikely to turn their employer in to a government agency.

Myth #3: If we ever needed Affirmative Action (AA), we no longer need it now. You learned in Chapter 1 that very few women or minorities have made it to the top of middle- to large-sized corporations—even after 30 years of affirmative action programs. On the other hand, large numbers have moved part-way up the ladder, and experts say that affirmative action is the most powerful career boost for them. Until women and minorities are adequately represented at all levels, corporate management still needs the guidance and motivation that affirmative action law provides.

Myth #4: AA imposes hiring and promotion quotas on companies. It's against the law for the federal government to set AA quotas for corporations, and it's against the spirit of the law to hire or promote unqualified people. More details later.

Myth #5: AA is really reverse discrimination. AA opponents often focus on the reverse discrimination myth. They say that because AA requires companies to fulfill quotas, they're forced to hire and promote women and minorities who are often less qualified than the white men who are being discriminated against.

Supporters of AA say it's ludicrous to believe that AA has the long-term general effect of discriminating against the most powerful, dominant group in the workplace. Supporting this conclusion is the fact that Euro-American males run the show in 95 percent of the corporations. Supporters also point out that Euro-American males have always had their own brand of AA—the old school ties, the old boys' network, and other ingroup privileges that few notice.

Myth #6: We can't afford to spend much time or money on diversity initiatives. We must focus on bottom-line profits. Actually, companies that succeed in New Economy markets do it through talented employees. Inclusive, savvy corporate cultures are attracting and retaining the best talent—which translates into greater success and profits.

The Melting–Pot Approach

"But America has always handled its diversity so well," some say. "Why, we're the Great Melting Pot." But the melting pot has been a cruel myth for aspiring career women and for non-European minorities. Who has it worked for? In society in general, it has worked for all immigrants from European countries. In the workplace, it has worked for male immigrants from those countries. European immigrants were expected to learn the American ways so they could be assimilated and absorbed. The goal was to create a seamless American culture and workplace. This worked fairly well for European men because Western cultures have much in common and people from those cultures look much alike. Although the Jewish, Irish, Italian, and Eastern European immigrants experienced some distinct prejudice and discrimination, within a generation or two they blended in.

On the other hand, people of color actually lived in segmented and segregated subcultures and women grew up alongside men in parallel but different worlds. People of color and women simply don't look like Euro-American men, the dominant culture of the workplace, and they were never truly assimilated.

How Do I Recognize the Melting-Pot Myth in a Company?

How can you tell when a company is relying on the melting-pot myth to handle diversity? Look for the following kinds of messages:

- We (Euro-American men) are at the center of the universe here.
- Why should we bother to learn about newcomers? We're busy and we belong here.
- It's the newcomers' job to learn how to succeed here and how to fit in (become like us).
- They have to learn the ropes and speak the language correctly if they want to work here.
- If they learn to do it our way, they won't have any problems.
- Immigrants can be a nuisance to talk to because of their accent and grammar.
- Women's culture is just a subset of whatever ethnic culture they belong to; Euro-American women live in the same cultural world we do.
- The best approach is to ignore cultural differences.
- Our goal is to eliminate cultural differences.
- Managers naturally have an adversarial relationship with workers.
- Managers must do the planning, then control and check on worker performance.

This set of beliefs logically leads to a belief that the person from a different group is wrong or inferior. It causes you to rely on predominant stereotypes of people from other groups, often assuming they're stupid or lazy or stubborn or sneaky. It says to the newcomer, "Get rid of your unprofessional behavior, your odd language, your strange ways."

How Does the Melting-Pot Myth Affect People of Color and Women?

Newcomers in the past have usually bought into the melting-pot belief system, which led them to new beliefs, such as:

- I must become just like the dominant group.
- My native country is inferior; America is better.
- I must fit in, no matter what I have to do.
- I won't teach the children about the old country; let them be Americans.

The immigrants' children picked up on this attitude, and many grew up to be ashamed of their parents' "old country" ways (Simons et al 1993).

When assimilation was either a conscious or unconscious goal in dealing with diversity, the ideal was to ignore differences and treat everyone the same. The biblical Golden Rule was the ideal:

*Do unto others as **you** would have **them** do unto **you**.*

This rule usually works in a homogeneous culture, but in a multicultural workplace life is not so simple, and a more appropriate Golden Rule would be,

*Do unto others as **they** would have **you** do unto **them***

People may prefer to be treated in ways you haven't even thought of—because they may have quite different values and habits than you. You must treat people differently when they are different, if you want to be fair. This is a much more complex and difficult task than treating everyone alike.

What Are the Major Problems with the Melting-Pot Myth?

You can see that the melting-pot ideal has never been ideal for all. Here are some additional problems with this approach:

- Those who don't look the part can't blend in.
- Forcing everyone to take a similar approach leaves untapped potential that could blossom from different approaches.
- In a competitive environment, assimilation is stifling and deadly.
- When diverse newcomers are expected to fit in, they focus on doing the expected or accommodating the norm, on playing it safe, instead of making innovative suggestions.
- Newcomers avoid doing or saying things that might label them as "different."
- The more energy newcomers must expend on adapting, the less they have for developing innovative ideas and personal strengths.
- Talented newcomers tend to go (and grow) where they're appreciated for who they are—to companies with a more supportive multicultural approach.

Obviously, the more diverse the work force becomes, the more important it becomes for organizations to solve the problems presented by the melting-pot approach, to dismantle the traditional barriers to full productivity and contribution, and to develop an approach that's more inclusive.

Vignette: Growing Up Among Many "Pots"

A group of friends who grew up in a North Texas city during the 1940s was reminiscing about their "all-WASP" childhood. Ralph said, "You know, I never knew a Mexican American when I was growing up; never talked to one except for the man who sold tamales from a cart on the street. But I know there had to be a Mexican American community somewhere." Others agreed that this was a com-

*mon experience. Andrea said, "I never had any African American friends either. Of course, that's eas-
ier to understand, with the severe segregation and all. The only African Americans I knew were the
cleaning women who came to our home sometimes."*

The Glue: The American Dream

What about American unity? What glue holds Americans together as a nation? Certainly, two primary values that have pulled immigrants to these shores and kept them here are freedom and opportunity—the freedom to pursue one's own lifestyle and religion and the opportunity to make a decent
living. A whole set of values formed around this American Dream, shaped the society, and is remarkably strong in holding it together. Americans have rallied round a common consumer market and
media. Their political system lets them participate and have influence, and their political-legal system
effectively sets the rules of the making-money game and referees conflicts. Their many interest groups
get to have their say through members' votes and whatever influence they can wield within the system.

The Legal Approach: Equal Opportunity and Affirmative Action

Because the melting pot approach did not provide equal opportunities for people of color and women,
the legal approach was introduced by government in the late 1960s. First came the Civil Rights Act
that established Equal Employment Opportunity (EEO). Later came an executive order establishing Affirmative Action (AA). EEO strengthens the individual employee's *rights* to equal opportunity and better jobs, but the employee must take action to complain about unfairness. AA requires employers to
take action to bring in under-represented groups of people into better jobs. This increases the chances
for a minority employee to *actually get* one of those jobs—without having to file a complaint.

Where people of color and women formerly faced brick walls, doors to opportunity appeared,
so this legal approach has been more effective for their upward mobility than the melting pot approach. Although most business leaders agree that the equal opportunity approach has been generally beneficial, most people don't understand it well. Euro-American men tend to resent it, and many
minorities and women don't know why they need it. How did it all come about and what does it mean?

Equal Employment Opportunity: Good But Not Enough

In 1964 Title VII of the Civil Rights Act established the Equal Employment Opportunity Commission (EEOC) to define and enforce acceptable employment policies and practices, especially as they
affect minorities and women. Businesses with more than 15 employees are subject to this law. EEO was
an important step forward for people of color and women, because people who are discriminated
against can complain to their employers, based on EEOC guidelines. If an employer doesn't satisfy
such a complaint, the employee can go directly to a regional EEOC office and file a complaint there.
If the employee can get other employees to join the complaint, it may become a class action. And if the
EEOC cannot get the employer to resolve the discriminatory issue, the employees may be able to file
a class action lawsuit. The courts then decide on the matter.

The advantage of EEO law is that it gives an employee a direct way to deal with job discrimination. The disadvantage is that it is extremely difficult for an individual to prove discrimination. Those
who go outside the company to complain are usually branded as troublemakers and blackballed
throughout the industry. Although such retaliation is illegal, it is almost impossible to prove when it's
handled by word of mouth and never put in writing. Individuals who pursue this route usually find their
career progress put on hold for years. Often they must change occupations or industries and start over.

In 1991 an amendment to the Civil Rights Act increased the money damages that employees can
receive if they can prove discrimination occurred. Before they could only recover lost back pay with
interest. Now they can receive money for compensatory and punitive damages—if they can prove that
they were subjected to malicious, illegal behavior that resulted in undue stress. Still, the problem is in
the proving.

Affirmative Action: A Major Impact

AA is a legal attempt to open up equal opportunity for three categories of women and minorities:

1. *Students* trying to get into public colleges and universities
2. *Contractors* trying to win bids from government agencies
3. *Employees* trying to get hired and promoted by corporations

Each type of AA has its own complexities. Here is a brief explanation of AA for small business contractors, followed by a more complete explanation of how AA applies to corporate job applicants and employees.

AA for Small Minority Business Contractors

The Small Business Administrations 8a program is a "minority set-aside program" that "sets aside" a certain percentage of federal government contracts to go only to small "disadvantaged" business owners. To qualify, a minority contractor must prove that its business is owned by one or more minority persons and that the owners are also economically and socially disadvantaged. They can retain their special contract status for no longer than nine years.

Minority set-aside programs are also found at state and local levels, and have been bitterly criticized, primarily by Euro-American male business owners. Yet, the main problem with the programs has been that some of the companies that win minority contracts are merely fronts for Euro-American male businesses. The SBA 8a program sets aside only about 3 percent of all federal government contracts for minority bidders—a tiny proportion of the businesses that could qualify. About the same proportion is set aside in the various state and local programs. In the 1990s the Clinton Administration set a goal of giving 5 percent of federal government contracts to small, disadvantaged firms.

AA for Corporate Employees

Because EEO alone does not have a significant impact on the upward mobility of minorities and women, AA was stepped up. AA law is not so obvious as EEO to individual employees. The average employee will never meet with an AA official and never file an "AA complaint." That's because AA works in the background, normally with a human resources administrator, and at times with the top management team, developing an AA program that's approved by an officer from the Labor Department's Office of Federal Contract Compliance Programs (OFCCP). The compliance officer may periodically review the company's progress toward the diversity goals it has set in its AA program, as shown in Figure 5.2. Therefore, individual employees usually don't know that the higher-level job opportunities they found were open to them only because of the company's AA plans and goals.

But what exactly is AA and how does it work? Beginning in 1967 a series of executive orders signed by then-President Johnson empowered AA by:

- requiring AA plans from firms doing business with the federal government
- randomly and periodically monitoring such firms for compliance to plans
- for firms that don't comply, cutting off their federal contracts

Specifically, all federal government contracts include provisions that prohibit employment discrimination because of race, color, religion, national origin, or sex. Any business that enters into federal contracts of more than $50,000 per year must develop an AA plan to hire and promote "under-utilized" minorities, setting goals and time targets, and periodically filing progress reports.

Adequate representation of minorities and women at all job levels usually relates to their proportions in the available workforce. This focus on overall numbers, proportions, and representations takes the pressure off the individual minority person who is not given an opportunity. The individual does not have to prove discrimination. Instead, discriminatory results are implied when, for example, 40 percent of the available work force and of actual employees are women but only 5 percent are managers. The employer would then be expected to set reasonable short- and long-term goals, over a period of several years, to increase the proportion of women in the better-paying managerial, professional, and technical jobs. Figure 5.2 shows how AA works.

FIGURE 5-2: How AA Works

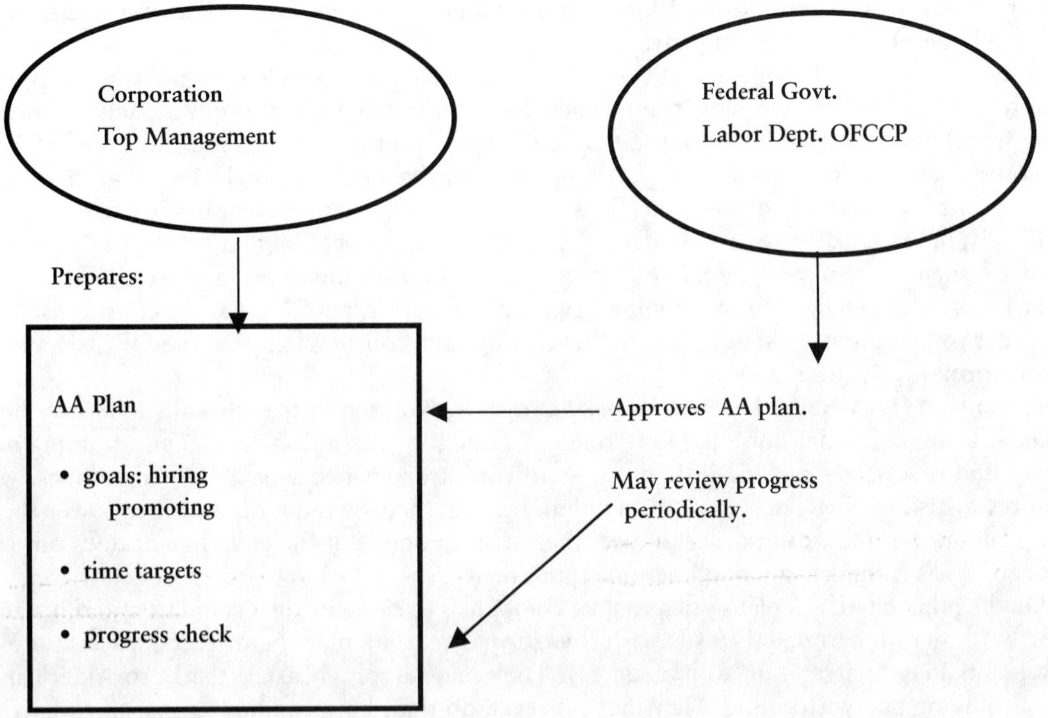

The Rationale for AA

AA provoked immediate controversy and backlash, but it was fairly well established during the 1970s. However, when President Reagan took office in 1981, he signaled a desire to dismantle the system. In response, the bipartisan government body, Commission on Civil Rights, issued the updated statement of principles, "Affirmative Action in the 1980s," which defined six AA principles.

Principle #1: Problem-Remedy Approach. The first AA principle is that discrimination is an entrenched problem that won't be resolved without the AA remedy. It is such a problem that prior to AA few women or persons of color pursued the education and training for higher-level occupations because they could see their investment would not pay off. There would be no jobs open to them, even if they became well qualified.

Principle #2: Color-blind Remedies Don't Work. The second principle is that discrimination is a self-perpetuating process that colorblind laws have not been able to change. Discrimination will never end without AA to break the cycle and to create new, more equitable processes when these factors are present:

- a history of widespread prejudice
- conditions of inequality with Euro-American males
- resulting barriers that have *not* been removed by measures that are color-blind and gender-neutral—that is, by measures that ignore ethnicity and gender.

The main point: Under such conditions as we still have in the United States, remedies for discrimination that insist on *color-blindness* or *gender-neutrality* are not sufficient. The only effective remedy to the problem is a type of AA that responds to discrimination as a self-sustaining process and sets specific hiring and promotion goals for dismantling it. The commission went on to respond to the major criticisms of AA concerning hiring quotas, lower standards, the stigma of AA hiring, and claims of reverse discrimination.

Principle #3: Hiring Quotas Are Illegal. Quotas cannot be imposed on an employer by normal AA law. It is illegal for the government to demand hiring quotas of any private employer. This means that companies set their own numerical goals, which are then approved by a federal contract compliance officer. The goals are not quotas because they are flexible and approximate. If a company doesn't meet its diversity goals, it's not penalized, as long as management can show they're making a good-faith effort to create a diverse workforce. AA programs and goals will end when all groups are reasonably represented at all levels of the company.

Why do most people believe that AA imposes quotas? First, people who politically oppose AA love to refer to quotas because most people consider them unfair. Quotas imply a company must hire anyone from a minority group, even the unqualified—obviously poor practice, and unfair. Second, some companies *do* impose their own quotas because they've neglected their AA program and face a sudden urgency to make up for lost time. This is poor diversity management in the extreme.

Finally, in extremely rare cases of deeply entrenched discrimination that's completely impervious to change—such as the Birmingham Fire Department—minority employees may sue. A judge *may* rule that the nature and extent of the discriminatory problem is so entrenched that the court must set quotas in order to bring about change. This occurs through the court system, not the OFCCP, and is not how the normal AA process works.

Principle #4: AA Never Dictates Lower Standards. Nothing in the law calls for lowering valid standards. Companies that don't use long-range planning for recruiting, hiring, and training minorities may find themselves making little progress toward a diversified workforce. Sometimes, when a federal review is looming, such companies voluntarily set their own quotas and then lower their hiring or promotion standards in order to meet their own quotas. But the government does not require this sort of crisis management, and does not condone it.

On the other hand, AA plans often require companies to examine their standards, and if standards cannot be shown to be related to successful performance, they must be discarded. Certain tests or requirements may be irrelevant to job success. They may simply measure the Euro-American male ways of thinking and performing. They may not even do that, but are simply some sort of screening device with little job relevance.

The use of such invalid tests and standards may deny opportunities to some people for reasons unrelated to merit. In situations where the use of valid standards serves to exclude women and minorities, civil rights law does *not* require the selection of unqualified minorities and women. It does, however, encourage:

- the restructuring of jobs
- the development of new standards that are equally related to successful performance but do not exclude
- the development of training programs that prepare the excluded to meet valid standards.

Within a few years of the passage of the EEOC and AA laws, there was a significant increase in the enrollment of women and persons of color in college, university, and advanced vocational programs that would qualify them for the higher-level jobs that companies were now willing to offer them. Sometimes it took class action suits to get companies to open up their own advanced training programs, but gradually most large companies made some progress.

Principle #5: "AA Stigma" Is Manageable. The Civil Rights Commission addressed the charge that AA further stigmatizes minorities and women when, for example, people adopt the attitude that an African American gained her position because of AA rather than because of merit. Such a woman has difficulty gaining respect and credibility. Often, the problem is actually faulty implementation of AA plans. For example, a woman may be placed as a "token" in a situation where she faces open hostility and/or lack of basic support. When the resulting isolation or failure causes her to quit or be removed, the employer may cite this as the reason for not promoting other women.

Company leaders set the tone by their attitudes toward diverse employees. When they signal respect, trust, and support, others are unlikely to devalue minority capabilities. Even when leadership support is grudging, many minorities and women say that an opportunity with stigma is better than no opportunity at all, which is what they had before AA. To them, throwing out AA means throwing out opportunity. They say that until some proven alternative to AA comes along, the stigmatization argument is invalid.

Principle #6: AA Is Not Reverse Discrimination. The remedial use of goals, timetables, and setting aside a certain percentage of government contracts to go to minorities in order to bring about workplace equity for all ethnic groups has become part of international law. In 1969 the United Nations treaty called *Declaration of All Forms of Racial Discrimination* was passed and became international law. The treaty is clear about measures designed to bring ethnic groups into the mainstream:

> Statement from the 1969 United Nations treaty
> Declaration of All Forms of Racial Discrimination:
> *AA measures shall not be considered discrimination or reverse discrimination.*

The only qualification regarding such measures is that they be removed as soon as they are no longer required. By 1984, 107 nations had ratified it—more than for any other treaty that has emerged from the U.N., but the United States Senate has never seriously debated it nor ratified it.

A similar U.N. treaty calling for the same rights for women was passed in 1979. *The Convention on the Elimination of All Forms of Discrimination Against Women* calls for the same rights for women. It also calls for nations to "embody the principle of equality of men and women in their national constitution or other appropriate legislation." Because Congress also refuses to act on this U.N. treaty, the United States is the only industrialized democracy that has not ratified it (Carter 1995).

In 1999 the United Nations approved a protocol for enforcing the 1979 treaty. Women suffering any form of discrimination that's banned by the 1979 treaty, and who have tried all means of redress in their own countries, may appeal to a U.N. experts' committee. Women's organizations may also appeal on behalf of victimized women. The U.N. committee may launch its own investigation into a member state's conduct if it receives reliable information indicating grave or systematic violations of the rights afforded women. The committee has no power to force a country's government to change. But if the committee finds a complaint justified, it must inform the country and make recommendations for correcting rights abuses.

AA Made a Difference in the 1970s

The track record of AA during the 1970s, when it was enforced with some consistency, indicates that it does open doors for minorities and women without harming business. Figures 5.3 and 5.4 depict the experiences of women and minorities before and after AA. At least four major studies concluded that the law was effective in boosting the careers and economic status of minorities and women. At the same time business suffered no loss in productivity and paid an average of $78 per employee per year for all EEO/AA related activities (Simpson 1984; U.S. Dept. of Labor 1984; Potomac Institute 1984; Leonard 1984a,b, 1985, 1986).

Bette Woody, Wellesley College, concluded that EEO/AA laws played a major role in allowing African American women, who were working predominantly as cleaning women to make a dramatic shift to office positions. Clerical jobs were mostly off-limits for them before AA. In 1960 most worked as cleaning women. By 1980 only 6 percent worked as domestic maids, and 39 percent were in clerical jobs—up from 8.5 percent in 1960. The gap between African American and Euro-American women's earnings narrowed from 80 percent in 1967 to 90 percent in 1985 (Woody 1989).

Did AA lower productivity or raise costs? J. Leonard, U.C. Berkeley (1984a), compared national manufacturing figures for 1966 with those for 1977, when minority males and women had recently moved into jobs formerly held only by Euro-American men. Minority males were roughly 70 percent as productive as Euro-American males but earned only 70 percent the salary, so cost the company no more. Women were 1 percent more productive, but earned only 60 percent the salary, so cost the company 41 percent less on average. Costs overall fell by a fraction of a percent.

In summary, a review of the relative impact that AA, the EEOC, and class action lawsuits had during the 1970s indicates that AA had the greatest impact by far—because of its power to impose penalties that can affect the profits of so many large businesses.

FIGURE 5-3: Before Affirmative Action

Ladder of Opportunity:

High-Level Jobs:
*Euro-American
Males Only*

Dead-End Drudge:

Low-Level Jobs:
*All Others,
Qualified or Unqualified*

With EEO Only (no AA):

- *Employee—discriminated against unfairly*
- *Must handle on own—file company grievance*
- *File a complaint with EEOC*
- *File a lawsuit?*
- *Informal blackballing—7 years in limbo*
- *Start new career in different field*

FIGURE 5-4: After Affirmative Action

Ladder of Opportunity:

*All who are
qualified*

*Those unqualified
for better jobs:*

- *Entry-level jobs*
- *Training to qualify*

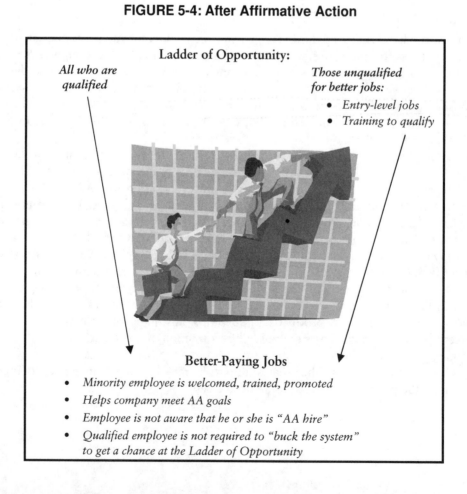

Better-Paying Jobs

- *Minority employee is welcomed, trained, promoted*
- *Helps company meet AA goals*
- *Employee is not aware that he or she is "AA hire"*
- *Qualified employee is not required to "buck the system"
  to get a chance at the Ladder of Opportunity*

AA Was Undermined During the 1980s

From 1980 to 1992 successive Republican administrations chipped away at the foundation of AA from every angle. Several studies indicate that the noticeable, but not spectacular, progress minorities and women had previously experienced became generally stalled during the 1980s (Leonard 1988). In President Bush's administration Secretary of Labor Lynn Martin commissioned a study that found the glass ceiling was much lower than predicted, existing below mid-level positions for most minorities and women, and was generally lower for minorities than for Euro-American women (U.S. Dept. of Labor 1991).

Why Business Retained AA During the 1980s

While most analysts agree that the regulation and enforcement of AA and EEO laws were eroded during the 1980s, they also agree that most employers maintained a high level of interest in them, especially larger corporations that wanted to keep AA plans in place for four reasons:

1. As a practical matter, in corporate political terms, AA plans provide employers with a way to integrate workforces despite internal opposition from some Euro-American males.

2. AA fits with the long-term interests of some corporate human resource planners who want to streamline hiring systems, set and enforce valid standards, apply training requirements, and monitor progress of all workers.

3. Although executives generally resist government regulation, they also understand that government regulatory positions come and go, and that eventually the pendulum would swing back in favor of AA, leaving those employers who had dropped their plans at a disadvantage.

4. Many of the people who moved into positions formerly closed to them because of ethnic or gender discrimination were very productive and effective employees and were generally a bargain in salary terms, because companies still got away with paying them less for basically comparable, or superior, contributions.

Problems with Implementing AA

Problems include poor Human Resource planning by companies and too few penalties for failure to achieve AA goals.

Poor HR Planning. Too many organizations have focused on barely meeting requirements, often flying by the seat of their pants, rather than focusing on valuing diversity and gradually shaping a corporate culture that reflects that value. Many companies have fallen into a frustrating AA cycle that views the workforce as a pipeline and try to fill it with minorities that "fit in," as follows:

- Recognize an AA problem, such as failure to meet targets for hiring or promoting women and minorities, or excessive turnover of these employees, their inadequate upward mobility, or their low morale.

- Respond by recruiting the kinds of minorities who will fit in with the corporate culture, rather than making the corporate culture more flexible and inclusive and establishing practices that meet the needs of these minorities.

After a period of high expectations that the AA problem is being resolved, disappointment sets in when the problem remains or new related problems arise, such as:

- The new recruit doesn't progress as expected.
- Co-workers complain about reverse discrimination or preferential treatment.
- The new recruits sense that others resent them.
- Employees don't give management credit for a good faith effort.

Discouraged, management quits trying and AA efforts are given less attention. After a period, a new human resource crisis appears.

Weak, Infrequent Penalties. Another problem is that few companies are penalized for poor performance in hiring and promoting women and minorities. In fact, since AA began about 30 years ago, the OFCCP has debarred only 41 companies in all types of industries. The agency cannot fine firms unless it finds workers who were denied jobs that they were qualified for. In such cases the workers could get back pay for the period of unemployment. But few workers know of this option and even fewer pursue it.

Bottom Line: AA Is Still Essential

We've mentioned the other major problems of AA, such as the glass ceiling, backlash, and stigma. The bottom line: AA has been the most powerful tool society has ever used to open doors of opportunity where formerly there were brick walls blocking the entry of people of color and women into upwardly mobile career paths. Because of it, the United States has more women managers than any country in the world—and people no longer believe that an African American man or a Latino American woman could not possibly work out as a manager in a Fortune 500 company. Yet in 2000, only four Euro-American women, and no minorities had worked their way up to CEO of such a company. About 95 percent of top managers are still Euro-American men and they're paid 25 percent more than minorities and women at every level, including vice presidents. That means we still need AA. If we as a culture want to complete our path toward equal opportunity for all, we must retain the best of AA and build on it by creating multicultural company climates that are welcoming to minorities and women.

Valuing Diversity Approach

During the 1970s, when companies were opening new doors to diverse persons in order to meet EEO/AA requirements, most of them were still using the melting pot approach, expecting everyone to adapt to their Euro-American male corporate cultures. Minorities and women had difficulty fitting in. Even those who seemed to fit in didn't like the price it exacted, that is, giving up important aspects of their own culture and personality. Company leaders, human resource executives, and corporate consultants looked for ways to encourage productive work relationships and to stem turnover rates of diverse employees. Meeting these needs led to the valuing diversity approach.

Valuing diversity is based on moving beyond tolerance of diverse others to appreciation of what they have to offer. It involves seeing a diverse work force as a treasure trove of valuable opportunities for innovation, networking, marketing savvy, and similar assets. The approach primarily involves a shift in beliefs and attitudes away from "we're all alike (or should be)" to "we're each unique and that's the source of our greatness. The valuing diversity approach focuses primarily on educating people through experiential and informational seminars to make appropriate attitude shifts. It emerged in the 1980s and is still a part of managing diversity.

An Inclusive Multicultural Approach

Beyond the melting pot myth, the legal approach, and even the valuing diversity approach is a more action-oriented approach that we'll call the inclusive multicultural approach. It is based on valuing diversity and goes further to find ways to shift the corporate culture itself, to make it more inclusive and therefore multicultural. The goal is to create a corporate culture that supports and nurtures all types of employees. We'll explore this multicultural approach in detail in Chapter 14. To grasp this evolution of management approaches to diversity, examine Figure 5.5.

FIGURE 5.5: Evolution of Approaches to Workplace Diversity

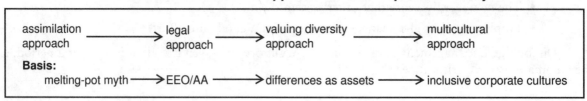

LEADERSHIP CHALLENGE: MOVING BEYOND STEREOTYPING TO PROFITABLE COLLABORATION

You can take a leadership role in helping people in your organization move beyond stereotyping and prejudice by simply being a role model, whether you're the new entry-level employee or the CEO. If you do as Mary Englebreitt suggests and *bloom where you're planted*, you can begin to experience the power of one. It's contagious. And one plus one plus one can soon become a critical mass for change.

You can start by understanding the negative effects of stereotypes on people's performance and the type of contact that tends to heal prejudice. You can then learn powerful action strategies for moving beyond the stereotypes.

Challenge #1: Understand the Effects of Prejudice on Performance

Prejudice and discrimination have a great impact on employee performance. At the deepest level, they undermine employee trust. They also undermine employee motivation and productivity.

Effects on Trust

Prejudice and discrimination sabotage trust. Given our history of intergroup prejudice, trust is more difficult to build across cultural groups than it is within them. "Don't trust Whitey" has long been a motto in many African American families and communities. Minorities tend to feel less free to spontaneously express their opinions and ideas in the workplace. They tend to engage in much more internal prescreening or self-censorship in order to fit into the work group. Euro-American men tend to be unaware that this kind of self-censorship is occurring. Losses to the group generally go unnoticed.

Effects of on Employee Motivation

Minorities generally find it more difficult than Euro-American men do to determine the cause of their events and life experiences, often asking themselves, "Was this event caused by discrimination or by other factors?" This can be a major problem when they attempt to process feedback and to stay motivated: "Is my boss criticizing me because my work is not up to standards or because I'm African American?" Expectancy theory holds that the motivation to perform on a job is a function of three factors:

1. If I put forth enough effort, will it produce the performance level the boss wants?

2. If I achieve the performance level the boss wants, will I get what I want (praise, raise, promotion, etc.)?

3. Is it worth it to me?

Discrimination can interfere with factors 1 and 2. Even if the boss is not influenced by an employee's group identity when he evaluates performance, if the employee believes he is, then that employee's motivational level will almost certainly drop.

Effects on Employee Productivity

We've mentioned Jane Elliott's study of the effects of prejudice on productivity, which is described in the documentary film *A Class Divided*. Elliott separated students into blue-eyed and brown-eyed groups. On the first day, the instructor told the class that the brown-eyed "outgroup" was inferior (they wore collars for clear identification of their status). She reinforced this by various actions, such as giving certain privileges to the "ingroup." On the second day, the roles were reversed. On both days the superior ingroup discriminated against the inferiors, calling them names and ostracizing them in many ways.

The work performance of the so-called inferior group declined significantly after just a few hours of the discriminatory treatment. Test scores of the students went up on the day they were in the advantaged group and down on the day the same students were in the disadvantaged group. The change in behavior of the instructor and fellow students had an immediate impact on the performance of the students. The study highlights, among other things, the effect of leader expectations on performance.

Leader expectations are communicated to employees in several ways:

- The amount of output the leader wants signals expectations (How challenging and desirable are the goals? To what extent does the leader believe the employee can achieve high goals? How supportive is the leader?).

- The overall climate (favorable tone, positive responses, etc.) that leaders set communicates their expectations.

- The amount of input (information relevant to getting the job done) that leaders give employees signals their expectations.

- The amount of feedback (information about how well the employee is doing) that leaders give communicates or implies their expectations.

Leaders have more influence than anyone in the work group in setting an inclusive tone. If we want top performance, there must be no outgroups. Everyone must be a member of the ingroup.

Challenge #2: Understand the Life Experiences of Diverse Employees

If you can meet the leadership challenge of truly understanding what makes women and minority employees tick, you'll then be able to design policies, systems, and practices that are sensitive to their life experiences. You can use approaches that help them overcome such internal barriers as lack of organizational savvy and conflict in balancing career and family demands.

Typical life experiences. These may include:

- a history of oppression
- being excluded from mainstream business (and society, for minorities)
- feelings that differ, in a negative way, from those of Euro-American men
- when moving into new roles, low self-concept, self-esteem, and self-confidence
- being positioned in a one-down status
- being prohibited from, and not encouraged to seek, a better position and status in business, and, perhaps, in society and in life
- being denied equal opportunities

The experience of being in a subordinate position typically leads to certain attitudes and behaviors that become internal barriers to workplace effectiveness. Kanter (1979) concluded from her study of corporations that many of the behaviors attributed to women were actually behaviors typical of powerless employees stuck in dead-end positions. Examples are excessive focus on detail, over-concern with rules and procedures, and excessive interest in gossip about personal lives.

Typical internal barriers. These may include lack of organizational savvy and professional image. Most minorities don't know how to play the game of getting along, such as paying attention to office politics and the agendas of their bosses and peers. They rarely know how to be strategic about their own career development.

They don't assert themselves and their views, so Euro-American men see them as subservient or passive, not willing to take a stand. Women have been reared to support men and seek their approval. Asian Americans and Latino Americans have been raised to respect authority to a greater degree and in a different way than Euro-American men. African Americans are frequently seen as too aggressive, vocal, confrontational, defensive, and pushy by Euro-Americans, though other African Americans wouldn't interpret their behavior that way.

Women who are balancing responsibilities for children with a career can be misunderstood. Leaders need to understand that a slow-down or time-out phase for a woman to have a child doesn't necessarily mean that she's not a candidate for rapid career development later. Companies that are flexible enough to support women in this phase are likely to win their loyalty and commitment.

Challenge #3: Understand the Type of Contact that Heals Prejudice

Segregation of the African American community was for hundreds of years legally enforced in the South and was a way of life in the rest of the country. Informal or de facto segregation was generally the rule for Latino American and Asian American communities until recently. We still have a great deal of de facto segregation in our cities, and even where integration has occurred, it has often been accompanied by misunderstanding, conflict, violence, and crime. Some psychologists have described the peaceful progression of contact between diverse groups as a four-step process (Ponteretto and Pedersen 1993):

1. initial contact, leading to
2. competition, which in turn gives way to
3. accommodation, and finally to
4. collaboration.

Whether or not this peaceful progression occurs depends on the nature of the contact that is established, whether it is casual contact, making acquaintances, simply living or working near each other, or working together to achieve common goals. The types of contact diverse groups typically experience range from conflict and superficial contact to true acquaintance and collaboration.

Type #1: Conflict

Clashes of interests and values do occur between groups, and these conflicts are not in themselves necessarily an expression of prejudice. Also some conflicts grow out of economic competition that is not necessarily rooted in prejudice but, again, tends to aggravate any prejudice that exists.

Type #2: Superficial Contact

This has traditionally been the most common type of contact between ethnic groups. Where segregation is the custom, most contacts are superficial, either because they're very casual or because they're firmly fixed into superior-subordinate relationships. Such contact is more likely to increase prejudice than to decrease it because we tend to selectively notice behavior that will confirm our stereotypes. Therefore, each contact may serve to "prove" that our stereotypes are true. Research indicates that superficial contact often reinforces prejudiced beliefs about the following aspects of outgroup members:

- their physical appearance
- their ability to communicate clearly
- the traits and qualities we assume they have (stereotypes and prejudice)

Reinforces Physical Appearance Stereotypes. Visibility serves as a central symbol of group differences (Allport 1954). The two most visible differences are skin color and sexual characteristics. Such differences can serve as a lightening rod for all kinds of thoughts and feelings about certain ethnic groups or about the other half of the human race. Such a lightning rod enables us to pull together and condense these thoughts and feelings and therefore to think of the outgroup as a cohesive unit. Remember, we tend to toss all we can into a category, for efficiency's sake.

For most of us, our view of others, whether favorable or unfavorable, is influenced by how we perceive their physical attractiveness. We assume that physically attractive people have more social skills, intelligence, and competence, so we're more likely to hire them. Various cultures have somewhat different views of physical attractiveness, which may change with the times, and our preferences reflect those views.

Physical distinctiveness can be a double-edged sword. If being different is viewed positively, it can be an asset that makes one stand out and be remembered. However, being too different or inappropriately different from the majority group will trigger prejudiced responses. For example, the token female sales rep in a male-dominated industry may be more successful because she's "different" and therefore remembered. But if she's "too different," she'll lose customers. Many studies illustrate the importance often placed on physical appearance in the workplace, and the dangers to career success of deviating too far from the majority norm (Cox 1993).

Reinforces Communication Stereotypes. Negative attitudes toward people who are difficult to understand have been linked with discomfort and frustration experienced by the persons who are trying to communicate with them. This applies to people who do not know the dominant language well, people who use "street language," and people with speech disabilities. As a result, others may avoid them or shorten their contact time with them (Cox 1993).

Type #3: True Acquaintance

In contrast, most studies show that true acquaintance lessens prejudice. Specifically, contacts that bring knowledge and acquaintance are likely to engender sounder beliefs concerning minority groups, and, therefore, contribute to the reduction of prejudice. But true acquaintance normally happens only where both parties view each other as basically equal human beings. And conversation must delve deeper into basic values, beliefs, and ways of functioning in the world.

Type #4: Collaboration

Have you ever done teamwork over an extended period with a person(s) from another culture—a team situation where success was important to everyone and all had to cooperate to make it? Didn't you get to know what kind of people those team mates really were? This was contact at the deeper, collaborative level—the type most likely to move beyond stereotyping and prejudice.

Research indicates that Euro-Americans who live side by side with African Americans of the same general economic class in public housing projects are on the whole more friendly, less fearful, and have less-stereotyped views than those who live in segregated arrangements. Merely living together is not the decisive factor. Whether people are jointly active in community enterprises is what counts. The form of the resulting communication is different and makes all the difference in the relationship that develops (Ponterotto and Pedersen 1993).

For example, a public housing project in Los Angeles was converted to private condominiums, which low-income families were able to purchase. Owners established a homeowners association that met regularly for the purpose of making the neighborhood as livable and vital as possible. During the Los Angeles riots of 1992 homeowners took a united stand against any invasion of their neighborhood, and it was spared from vandalism. Residents who were interviewed credited the friendships built by people from various subcultures for the solidarity they displayed during the crisis (*L.A. Times* 1992).

This pattern holds true for contact in the workplace. Only the type of contact that leads people to do things together is likely to result in healing prejudiced beliefs and attitudes. Common goals are all-important. It's the cooperative striving for a goal that engenders solidarity. Participation and common interests are more effective than mere equal-status contact. Self-managing work teams hold tremendous challenge and opportunity to finally break down prejudiced belief systems and establish the unity we so need. But we must meet the challenge of overcoming the barriers to effective collaboration.

> *The key to moving beyond prejudice is working together toward common goals that are highly valued, in situations where people need each other to achieve their goals.*

LEADERSHIP OPPORTUNITY: HOW CAN I PROMOTE COLLABORATION?

If you want to be a leader in your organization, develop the people skills that will enable you to promote collaboration, synergy, and creativity among people. These skills will help you lead people beyond prejudice and discrimination toward profitable ways of working together. Then adopt these seven leadership strategies to accomplish this type of change.

Strategy #1: Promote Tolerance

Work toward openness and acceptance of others, respect their right to have different beliefs and viewpoints, lifestyles and business images, and work styles and job behaviors.

Strategy #2: Be a Role Model of Respect and Appreciation

Be willing to listen to and learn about diverse people and groups, to examine your own ego needs, beliefs, and viewpoints that block your ability to respect and appreciate others, to work collaboratively with others to produce more creative, high-quality results. Be willing to change false beliefs.

Strategy #3: Value Empathy

Be willing to relax into your intuition and listen to its messages as you tune into others, allowing yourself to see things from their viewpoint.

Strategy #4: Promote Trust and Goodwill

Educate yourself and others about the key differences among diverse groups. Value those differences— see them as individual, colorful facets of the kaleidoscope of humanity. Expect everyone to build trust and goodwill in all their interactions—with all team members, business associates, and contacts in other countries.

Strategy #5: Encourage Collaboration

Encourage everyone to work toward common goals for the good of the whole organization, the whole industry, the whole nation, and the world. Value unity, which is not uniformity but individuated integration. See that in unity there can be great diversity. Understand that each part is vital to the integrity of an emerging whole.

Strategy #6: Work Toward Synthesis

Share a vision of people gathering together the separate elements that form the whole project, work team, organization, and industry. See them bringing the whole into active expression. Envision them acting as one to create a new reality—including new projects, processes, products, relationships, and corporate culture. Understand that synthesis is *not* assimilation.

Strategy #7: Create Synergy

Recognize that extra creative spark, that increment of information, knowledge, goodwill, or other benefit that is the by-product of collaboration and synthesis. Use it to carry the team and the organization to new heights of excellence and innovation. Celebrate that added gift, which is more than the sum of what each person brings to the group.

LEADERSHIP OPPORTUNITY: HOW CAN I IMPLEMENT COLLABORATIVE STRATEGIES?

A key diversity skill that you as a leader can bring to the diverse workplace is to recognize your own ethnocentricity, the ways in which you stereotype, judge, and discriminate, and your emotional reactions to conflicting cultural values. Now that you've raised your awareness about the nature of prejudice and ethnocentricity, you're ready to take specific action steps that will move you beyond it. The following are nine action steps that serve to implement the collaborative strategies. Once you, as a leader, work through the action steps yourself, you can serve as a role model and coach for helping others work through them. These action are listed below and then discussed in some detail.

1. Uncover your personal prejudices. Become aware of the ego needs and beliefs that support them and the feelings tied to them.

2. Open your mind. Be willing to listen and seriously consider other viewpoints.

3. Support civil rights measures and inclusive company policies and practices that bring about fairness and equity for disadvantaged groups.

4. Work on your capacity to respect and appreciate diverse people and groups.

5. Explore the ways that respecting diverse people and groups serves your self-interest as well as theirs.

6. Be open to developing your intuition and your capacity for empathy.

7. Learn ways to build trust and make it your top priority.

8. Learn about diverse groups. Pursue multicultural and diversity education.

9. Seek opportunities to collaborate with diverse people and groups and to work toward important common goals.

Action #1: Get in Touch with Prejudiced Beliefs and Feelings

The first step toward becoming more open and accepting of diverse persons is to decide you want to. Then you can begin to notice thoughts that occur when you see certain people, judgmental thoughts that lead to feelings of aversion, dislike, suspicion, and similar feelings that prevent good interaction and block collaborative relationships. Self-awareness activities and skill builders throughout this book are designed to help you in this process. We often hide prejudiced beliefs from ourselves, so uncovering them can be challenging, but it's a challenge worth pursuing.

Action #2: Open Your Mind to Other Viewpoints and Listen

Open-minded persons are relatively rare. They tend to look beyond labels, categories, and sweeping statements. They usually insist on knowing the evidence for broad generalizations before accepting them as true. They are open to new evidence that might lead them to modify a category. Good listeners are just as rare. Most of us take turns talking instead of listening to get another's ideas that we might incorporate into our own. Be willing to listen with an open mind to other viewpoints and to new information that might change your prejudiced beliefs.

Action #3: Support Equal Opportunity Measures

In 1954 Allport stated the belief that legal action can have only an indirect bearing upon reducing personal prejudice. It cannot coerce thoughts or instill personal tolerance. Legal restraints merely say, in effect, "You can have whatever prejudices you like, but you may not act them out to a point where they endanger the lives, livelihood, or peace of mind, of groups of American citizens." Law is intended only to control the outward expression of intolerance. Even so, outward actions have an eventual effect on inner habits of thought and feeling and inclusive actions can result in our opening up our views of limited, stereotyped roles for certain groups. For example, before AA you may have assumed that Latino American women generally didn't have the qualities to be managers. Now you have worked with several of these women who are competent managers, and your earlier stereotyped belief had to shift. Because this process is quite typical, legal action has been one of the major methods of reducing private prejudice as well as public discrimination.

Have you really become informed about the major civil rights laws that affect the workplace and the related policies of companies you've worked for? Or have you settled for basing your opinions on

30-second media sound bites or the glib opinions of co-workers? If you're serious about moving beyond prejudice, you owe it to yourself to become informed about civil rights issues, as well as diversity policies and practices.

Action #4: Express Respect and Appreciation

Once you've opened your mind, the next step is to become comfortable and imaginative in expressing respect and appreciation, primarily through your actions but also through your conversations. Every time you choose to focus on goodwill and trust instead of focusing on fear and mistrust, you automatically move to respecting and appreciating instead of judging and belittling.

Action #5: See Mutual Respect As Mutual Self-Interest

You stand to benefit greatly from moving beyond prejudice, as does your career, your organization, and the planet for that matter. And staying stuck in prejudice, no matter how hidden or subtle, has great costs. You may have learned from bitter failure in a relationship that your stereotypes were in error or that your friends or business associates disapproved of your prejudged categories. You're fortunate if you get such a "change message," for it can help you see clearly that it's in your own interest to change your prejudiced thinking.

Even when you're not confronted by others with your prejudices, and even when you're not consciously aware of them or the effects they have, you probably believe at some level that prejudice conflicts with your deepest beliefs about human value and equality. Most of us, when we catch ourselves in prejudice, don't feel good about it, and if you stop to take a good, hard look at it, you probably don't particularly like yourself when you think and act this way. Except for making you temporarily feel "better than," it's not nearly as satisfying to dislike people and look down on them as it is to appreciate them, collaborate with them, and have fun together. Further, prejudice sets in motion a negative cycle of action and reaction that divides and separates and throws up barriers to building trust. It prevents people from having the productive and harmonious workplace and society that would benefit us all.

Action #6: Open Up to Intuition and Empathy

Clearly, the ability to feel empathy for others can help you to move beyond tolerance to appreciation, and beyond prejudice to collaboration. When you empathize, you intuit how another person sees and feels about a situation; therefore, you're able to experience empathy when you're in touch with your intuitive side. With empathy and intuitiveness, you're better able to understand others and therefore have less need to feel apprehensive and insecure. You tend to gain confidence that you can sidestep unpleasant involvement if the need arises. Accurate perception of how others think and feel gives you the ability to avoid friction and to conduct successful relationships. In contrast, people who cannot empathize are forced to be on guard, to put strangers into categories, and to react to them as a group rather than as individuals. Lacking subtle powers of differentiation, they must resort to stereotyping.

Intuition is never wrong, else it wouldn't be intuition. To come in touch with intuition is similar to listening to your body when it's letting you know it's time to eat, to rest, to exercise. First, give yourself permission to be intuitive. Then, realize that you're most likely to contact your intuition when you're relaxed. So find a time to relax, ask your inner self for intuitive insight, and allow whatever wants to come into your awareness to come in. If you're sincere, answers will come. However, the moment that you set up expectations about *how* the event may occur and *when*, you're immediately limiting your possibilities. So put forth the desire, give yourself permission to ask for it, then be watchful. Intuition is not linear and rational; answers may come in unexpected ways and times. They often come as little flashes or "glimmers" of thought or feeling. Learn to recognize them and to use the power of insight.

Action #7: Build Trust

You build trust by building authentic relationships, in which you respect and appreciate others and show it through words and actions. When you're consistent in your actions and words, keep your commitments, and show respect and appreciation, time after time, then people begin to trust you. Where there is a long legacy of mistrust, it may take years to build trust. It can be destroyed in a moment of betrayal, and the healing process may be difficult or impossible. The best preventive is to consistently choose an attitude of goodwill and trust toward other people.

Action #8: Pursue Multicultural and Diversity Education

Once you begin to understand the typical stereotypes, biases, and barriers that persons from disparaged groups must cope with every day, you can begin to understand more about what their lives are like. Once you become aware of how cultural do's and don'ts affect such persons' self-image, self-esteem, and emotions, you have a better chance of anticipating how your own actions may affect them. The goal of cultural understanding is to be able to walk in another person's shoes for a while, to see the world as that person sees it, and feel what he or she feels. Or to step into a little slice of that person's life and look out at the world from that vantage point.

We've inherited the legacy of prejudice, but we've also inherited the legacy of equality, and we've recently grown to accept more and more people as qualified to be equal. We're approaching the time when Euro-Americans may become a minority in some states, and we face some confusion about our national identity and our future as one people. Euro-Americans, as the dominant majority, can insist on holding onto the past.. That would mean continuing to ignore or discount all American cultures except the Euro-American. For many, it would probably mean hunkering down in separate enclaves.

Alternatively, the American culture can welcome its expansion into a multifaceted culture that acknowledges and values all its ethnic groups. As a nation that has thrived on the concept of expansion, it seems more constructive to expand our notion of cultural literacy to reflect the multicultural heritage of all our people, not just the Euro-American portion. If we take this inclusive approach, there will be no need to hide out in exclusive segregated communities or to cluster into ethnic groups in the workplace.

Action #9: Work with Diverse People Toward Common Goals

You've learned that superficial contact does not help people to overcome stereotypes and prejudices toward a subgroup. What has worked to change prejudiced beliefs and attitudes is working with diverse others on projects that help all participants to achieve common goals. So continually seek opportunities to work together toward common goals—in alliances, teams, partnerships, and other joint efforts.

SUMMARY

What are some effects of prejudice? It causes the prejudiced to live a more limited life than is necessary. In fact, studies indicate they have less zest for life. They block many of the possibilities for exploring diversity in the world, and the sense of curiosity and adventure that goes with it. On the other hand, discrimination causes minorities to distrust the majority because they've felt hurt, betrayed, and rejected time after time. It affects the personality of those who are targets of prejudice in many ways. Some develop ego defenses that strike out at the majority, such as suspicion, slyness, clannishness, aggression, and competitiveness. Others develop ego defenses that are self-punishing, such as self-dislike, attacking or disliking their own group, putting on a superficial show of success, and clowning. And some are motivated to succeed in spite of discriminatory barriers and to sympathize with all victims.

Discrimination affects minorities' career paths at every step, from employment screening and hiring to promotions, layoffs, and discharge. Discrimination in the workplace was ignored in the past. The melting-pot myth has traditionally assumed that all employees would assimilate into a common corporate culture, but people who don't look like the dominant workplace group, Euro-American men, have never "melted in."

To overcome the discrimination and workplace barriers minority employees have experienced, civil rights laws were enacted in the late 1960s. EEO allows employees to directly complain about discrimination, but individuals find this a difficult path that usually entails severe career setbacks. AA works in the background for most employees but has proven much more powerful than EEO in opening career doors. It requires that employers who obtain large federal government contracts to develop and implement AA plans for hiring and promoting minorities. Backlash and resistance to AA have been reflected in claims of reverse discrimination and beliefs that unqualified minorities are hired or promoted into good jobs only to fill "quotas." In reality AA does not condone any of this. The way leaders can prevent these problems is to make a commitment to diversity, to value diversity, and to create inclusive corporate cultures that support employees from all groups.

To move beyond stereotyping, recognize the effects of prejudice on performance, from trust to motivation to productivity. Understand how the life experiences of diverse employees may create certain internal barriers to career success, barriers that can definitely be overcome. Understand the type of person-to-person contact that heals prejudice. Superficial contact with people from disparaged groups may actually reinforce stereotypes and prejudices. The type of contact that reduces prejudice is based on getting to know people in depth and collaborating with them to achieve meaningful goals together. Work teams provide an ideal type of contact for moving beyond prejudice. Adopt and implement collaborative strategies that enable employees to move beyond prejudice to synergy, creativity, and productivity. Take action steps to heal your own prejudice, to become more intuitive and empathic in relationships, and to become a trustworthy ally and role model.

Skill Builder 5.1: Opening Up to New Experiences

Purpose: To help you open up to all types of people. Especially helpful for people who score above average on the authoritarian personality scale.

Barriers	*Motivators*
I don't know what to expect.	It may be fun.
I don't feel comfortable.	It may be interesting.
Maybe they won't like me.	I may learn something.
Maybe I won't like them.	They may like me.
Maybe they won't treat me well.	I may like them.
I may look end up looking foolish.	I may end up feeling better about myself.
I don't know what to say.	I may gain experience, perspective,
I don't know how to act.	understanding, empathy, compassion.
Others:	Others:

The barriers relate to some type of discomfort and ultimately to some type of fear. They cause us to mentally separate ourselves from others, to contract, withdraw. The motivators relate to an outgoing tendency and ultimately to some type of goodwill. They cause us to mentally reach out, to include, and to expand. They often involve curiosity, courage, and sense of adventure.

Step 1. Think of a situation where you did *not* say yes to an opportunity to experience a new situation with people you didn't know well. What were some of the barriers that held you back? Check off the barriers that apply in the list shown here. Add others that you experienced.

Step 2. Think of a situation where you *did* say yes to such an opportunity. What motivated you? Check off the motivators that apply in the list shown here. Add others that you experienced.

Step 3. What happened in the situation you said yes to? Was the experience more positive or negative in your opinion? If more negative, what lessons can you draw from this experience?

Step 4. What might have happened if you had said yes to the situation in step 1? What experiences, opportunities, advantages, lessons might you have missed?

What lessons can you learn from this?

Skill Builder 5.2: Picturing Exclusion and Inclusion in Your Organization

Purpose: To use the power of symbols and pictures to help you better understand your thoughts and feelings about prejudice and exclusion.

Step 1. Draw a picture of prejudice and exclusion in your company. Draw anything you like, but do not use words in the picture. Use colors and symbols to express how people relate to one another, which groups have power, how they use power, and similar aspects.

Step 2. Look at your completed picture and respond to the following:

- What immediate feelings do you experience?
- What thoughts come to mind?
- What does your drawing say about exclusion in the organization?

Step 3. Draw a new picture. Show symbolically how people could relate to each other in ways that express respect, appreciation, and inclusion. Show how personal power, group power, and organizational power might relate, how it might change, how things would look.

Step 4. Look at your completed picture and respond to the following.

- What immediate feelings do you experience?
- What thoughts come to mind?
- What does your drawing say about how inclusion might change the organization?

Skill Builder 5.3: Process for Changing Beliefs

Purpose: For leaders who are ready for advanced personal development work.

Be open to the idea that your hostile feelings, or feelings that separate, might be reflections of your judgments about yourself—that what you dislike in others is what you dislike in yourself. In describing this process, we'll use the term *judgment* to mean categorizing people, things, or situations, as right or wrong, good or bad, blaming or praising others, or making them wrong, bad, or evil on the one hand or right or good on the other. *Discernment* is the term we'll use for making choices.

Step 1: Find the bottom-line belief.

a. Situation

Think of a problem situation involving someone from a "different" group, a situation that you suspect involves prejudice on your part. Describe the situation in a few brief words. Then write in answer to the following questions.

b. Feelings

- How do I feel about the situation?
- How do I feel about the diverse other(s)?
- Why do I feel this way?

For each response, again ask, "Why do I feel this way?" until you sense that you are at the root feeling.

c. Judgments

- How am I judging the person(s)?
- How am I judging the situation?
- How am I making the person(s) wrong or bad?

d. Beliefs

- Why am I making this judgment(s)?
- What belief causes me to make this judgment(s)?

Keep asking "Why? What belief?" until you sense you have found the bottom-line belief underneath the judgment.

Step 2: Take responsibility for the judgmental belief and its results.
Acknowledge that you have created this reality through your beliefs. You have co-created the situation with the other person(s) in that situation. It takes two to create a relationship problem. Allow that idea to permeate your being. Be willing to accept full responsibility for your beliefs and the actions that flowed out from those beliefs.

Step 3: Acknowledge and embrace your judgmental belief.
In your mind, you've been making the person(s) or situation(s) wrong or bad. You've been judging. That's part of being human. To create harmony, you must release your judgment, release the experience of making things good/bad, right/wrong, and move into the experience of accepting what is.

If you want to change what is, you must first acknowledge and accept it. The only way to release judgment is to first recognize and acknowledge that you are judging. If you make yourself wrong for judging, you're still into the experience of judging, only now you're judging yourself. The change process requires you to accept the humanness of your judgment, to embrace it.

Embracing the judgmental belief. By embracing your judgmental belief, you create the freedom to change. Intellectualizing the change process usually will not change a belief, but it is the first step. The change process is to say to yourself, "It's okay to believe this, but now it's time for a change." Then very gently allow the change to occur. Gather the judgmental belief from that judgmental part of yourself into your whole self, your greater self, with love and compassion. A metaphor that is powerful for some people is, "gather it into your light."

Releasing the resistance to painful feelings. A judgmental belief usually fits in with your bottom-line fear, and the belief is often hidden because the fear is hidden, covered with layers of rationalizations, defenses, and other, less-painful fears. When you have great pain, you tend to handle it an extreme way. At one extreme, you express the pain with rage, tears, or anger. At the other extreme, you suppress the pain, ignore it, pretend it's not there until you don't consciously feel it. So you'll normally have a great deal of repressed pain connected to the judgmental belief, and a great deal of resistance to feeling that pain, which for many people wants to be felt in the "pit of the stomach."

Step 4: Feel the feelings.
The process of mentally embracing the judgmental belief with love and compassion lets you relax and let go of the "resistance to feeling pain." Allow yourself to feel any painful emotion that comes up. Don't intellectualize at this point, but move your consciousness out of your head into your stomach area. Go fully into this emotion and then let your consciousness go deeper into other underlying emotions if it wants to.

When you sense these painful emotions have run their course, be willing for your emotional consciousness to move into your heart area. The painful feelings can now give way to feelings of harmony, serenity, peace, and joy. These feelings come up when you truly acknowledge and embrace your judgment and move beyond beliefs that hold your separateness in place. You may experience a sense of oneness. Hang out there for a while so you can fully experience these expansive feelings.

REFERENCES

Allport. G. W. *The Nature of Prejudice.* Boston: Addison-Wesley, 1955.

Allport, G.W. *The Person in Psychology.* Boston: Beacon, 1968.

Allport, G.W., and B.M. Kramer. "Some Roots of Prejudice," *Journal of Psychology* 22. 1946, 9-19, 27.

Allport, G.W., and J.M. Ross. "Personal Religious Orientation and Prejudice." *Journal of Personality and Social Psychology* 5, 1967, 432-443.

Baack, J., N. Carr-Ruffino, and M. Pelletier. "Making It to the Top: Specific Leadership Skills." *Women in Management Review* 8, 2. 1993.

Buono, A.F., and J.B. Kamm. "Marginality and the Organizational Socialization of Female Managers." *Human Relations* 36, 12, 1983, 1125-1140.

Canby, Nicholas. "The Ideology of English Colonization: From Ireland to America." *William and Mary Quarterly*, 3rd series, 30, 4, October 1973.

Carr-Ruffino, Norma. "U.S. Women: Breaking Through the Glass Ceiling." *Women in Management Review* 6, 5, 1991.

Carter, Jimmy. "Keeping Faith with the World's Women." *The Atlanta Constitution* (March 8, 1995) A-11.

Cash, T.F., B. Gillen and D.S. Burns, "Sexism and 'Beautyism' in Personnel Consultant Decision Making." *Journal of Applied Psychology* 62, 1977, 301-310.

Catalyst. *Women in Corporate Management*. New York: Catalyst, 1990.

Deaux, K., and T. Emswiller. "Explanations of Successful Performance in Sex-Linked Tasks." *Journal of Personality and Social Psychology* 29 (1974): 80-85.

Elliott, Jane. *A Class Divided* (documentary videotape). Alexandria, VA: PBS Video.

Erez, Miriam and P.C. Earley. *Culture, Self-Identity, and Work*. New York: Oxford University Press, 1993.

Faludi, Susan. *Backlash*. New York: Doubleday, 1991.

Gates, Henry L., Jr. *Loose Canons*. New York: Oxford University Press, 1992.

Greene, Kathanne. *Affirmative Action and Principles of Justice*. New York: Greenwood, 1989.

Greenhaus, J.H., and S. Parasuraman. "Job Performance Attributions and Career Advancement Prospects" in *Organizational Behavior and Human Decision Processes*, Orlando, FL: Academic Press, 1991.

Grof, Stanislav, and Christina Grof. *The Stormy Search for the Self*. Los Angeles: Jeremy P. Tarcher, 1990.

Gudykunst, W.B. *Bridging Differences: Effective Intergroup Communication*. Thousand Oaks, CA: Sage, 1995.

Johnson, A. "Women Managers: Old Stereotypes Die Hard." *Management Review*, 76, 1987, 31-43

Kanter, Rosabeth Moss. *Men and Women of the Corporation*. New York: Basic Books, 1979.

Leonard, J. "The Impact of Affirmative Action on Employment." Cambridge, MA: National Bureau of Economics Research, reprint no. 535,1984b

Leonard, J. "Affirmative Action as Earnings Redistribution." *Journal of Labor Economics* 3, no. 3 (1985) 363-385.

Leonard, J. *Antidiscrimination or Reverse Discrimination?* Berkeley, CA: Institute of Industrial Relations, Reprint no. 457,1984a.

Leonard, J. "What Was Affirmative Action?" *American Economic Review* (May, 1986): 359-363.

Leonard, J. *Women and Affirmative Action in the 1980's*. Paper presented at the Annual Meeting of the American Economic Association, 1988.

Locke, Don. *Increasing Multicultural Understanding*. Thousand Oaks CA: Sage, 1995.

Los Angeles Times "Neighbors Stick Together," June 2, 1992.

Morrison, Ann, ed. The New Leaders: Guidelines on Leadership Diversity in America. San Francisco: Jossey-Bass, 1992

Morrison, Ann, R.P. White, and E. Van Velsor. Breaking the Glass Ceiling. Reading, MA: Addison-Wesley, 1987.

Potomac Institute. *A Decade of New Opportunity: Affirmative Action in the 1970s*. Washington, DC: Potomac Institute, 1985.

Simpson, Peggy. "Affirmative Action in Action," *Working Woman* (March, 1984): 105.

U.S. Commission on Civil Rights. "Affirmative Action in the 1980s: Dismantling the Process of Discrimination." Clearinghouse Publication 70, 1981.

U.S. Commission on Civil Rights. "Understanding Fair Housing." Washington DC: U.S. GPO, 1973.

U.S. Dept. of Labor, Employment Standards Administration. "Employment of Minorities and Women in Federal Contractor and Noncontractor Establishments, 1975.1980, " unpublished final draft (The Crump Report), 1985.

U.S. Glass Ceiling Commission. *A Report on the Glass Ceiling Initiative*. U. S. Department of Labor, 1991.

U.S. Glass Ceiling Commission. *Good for Business*. U. S. Department of Labor, 1995.

Williams, Robin M, Jr. "Prejudice and Society," in *The American Negro Reference Book*. Englewood Cliffs, NJ: Prentice-Hall, 1966.

Woody, Bette. "Black Women in the New Service Economy," working paper no. 196. Wellesley, MA: Wellesley College Center for Research on Women, 1989.

WSJ. *Wall Street Journal* (June 16, 1994): B1. "SBA Sets New Goals,"

CHAPTER 6

Men and Women: Parallel Cultures

Men and women literally live in parallel, but different, worlds.
Deborah Tannen

Men make up about 55 percent of the U.S. workplace, while women are 45 percent. Researcher Deborah Tannen has spent much of her career exploring how men and women can communicate better with each other. She concluded that men and women communicate differently because they view the world differently—to the extent of actually living in different, parallel worlds. Gender differences are the most basic and pervasive of all differences, a good place to start working on the last two steps for gaining multicultural skills. We'll continue to work on these steps in the remaining chapters.

Step 4. Learning about other cultures you encounter in the workplace, so you can recognize when cultural differences may be at the root of problems and so you can appreciate the contributions people from diverse cultures can make to the work situation.
Step 5. Building interaction skills and practicing new behaviors through self-awareness activities and skill builder case studies.

You're about to deepen your understanding of what it's like to be a woman or man in today's society and workplace and how this experience can affect relationships with the opposite sex in the workplace. You'll learn about the following:

- How stereotypes about men and women compare with reality
- How culture affects male-female traits and status
- How gender roles have evolved and are changing
- How the communication styles of men and women differ
- The resulting differences in worldviews of men and women
- Women's cultural barriers to workplace success
- Men's responses to new roles and expectations
- How men are responding to new expectations in the workplace

- Understanding sexual harassment
- How assertiveness helps to create win-win successes
- Handling the leadership challenges of meeting the needs of women and men
- Rising to the leadership opportunities for building a more gender-balanced workforce and corporate culture

People who have taken the time and effort to learn about our gender differences and similarities say they have boosted their ability to work productively with both men and women. Most of us are not fully aware of our beliefs, attitudes, thoughts, and feelings about these issues. To get in touch with your opinions, beliefs, stereotypes and biases concerning gender and to play with new beliefs, complete Self-Awareness Activities 6.1 and 6.2. Then, to test your current knowledge of gender issues, complete Self-Awareness Activity 6.3. After you've finished this chapter, briefly review these activities to see if any of your responses and insights have changed.

Self-Awareness Activity 6.1: Traits of Men and Women

Purpose: To become aware of your beliefs about gender traits and roles

1. What are the traits or qualities that you like to see in men, traits and actions that you admire or feel comfortable with? List them.

2. What are the traits or qualities that you like to see in women, traits and actions that you admire or feel comfortable with? List them.

Self-Awareness Activity 6.2: What Do You Believe about Women and Men?

Purpose:

- to get in touch with your beliefs and stereotypes about this group of people
- to experience how judgmental beliefs affect your thinking and feeling processes
- to experience the ways in which your beliefs create your reality regarding other persons, even before you have any interaction with them.

Part I. What Do You Believe about Women?

Step 1. Associations

- Relax as deeply as you can: close your eyes and take a few deep breaths.
- Focus on the word "woman" and allow a mental picture to come up in your mind's eye. Imagine that you are this woman. Be woman.
- Notice your resistances to being this person, and your willingness.
- Notice the words and images that come to mind as you "see" this woman.
- Open your eyes and list 10 to 20 words in the order in which they occur to you.
- Review your list. Mark a plus beside the words that are positive, a minus beside the words that are negative, and a circle beside neutral words.

Step 2. Negative Associations

- Close your eyes and focus again on the image of the woman. Formulate a negative opinion or judgment, perhaps one you typically hold about women.
- Notice your *feelings* as you see the person in this negative way. What *thoughts* come up as you focus on the image?
- Write a few sentences about your feelings and thoughts.

Step 3. Positive Associations

- Formulate a positive opinion or judgment, perhaps one you typically hold about women.
- Notice your *feelings* as you see the person in this positive way. What *thoughts* come up as you focus on the image?
- Write a few sentences about your feelings and thoughts.

Step 4. Insights

- Focus on the differences between your experiences when you hold negative and positive judgments or opinions. What were the differences? What meaning does this have for you, for your beliefs and feelings about people from this group, and about beliefs in general?
- Write your responses in a few sentences; include anything you like about your feelings, thoughts, and insights.

Part II. What Do You Believe about Men?

Repeat the phases and steps in part I, this time focusing on the image of a man.

Self-Awareness Activity 6.3: What Do You Know about Gender Issues?

Determine whether you think the following statements are basically true or false—and think about why.

1. The American culture is basically a patriarchal culture.
2. Men focus on reporting information, while women focus on establishing rapport.
3. About 40 percent of top managers are women.
4. Since passage of the Equal Pay Act, there is little difference in the wages of men and women.
5. The men's movement is about restoring the patriarchal system.
6. Balancing masculine and feminine strengths refers to hiring approximately equal proportions of male and female employees.
7. Sexual harassment is rare and refers to bosses giving favors in exchange for a sexual relationship.

Almost from the moment we're born, we begin learning gender stereotypes and myths. Most of us also begin learning about inequality in relationships from the patriarchal system of family, church, and culture. Although the patriarchal system is beginning to change in the United States, boys and girls are still socialized in very different ways. Megatrends that affect all aspects of American society, such as new workplace opportunities for women, are changing our culture. For example, nearly half of all employees are women, and 40 percent of all managers are women. Still, less than 5 percent of top managers are women, and women make an average of 25 percent less than men at all levels. And boys and girls still grow up in two worlds, overlapping but different. These differences cause major misunderstandings at times; for example, when the man focuses on giving and getting information in a conversation while the woman is focusing on giving and getting emotional support. We'll discuss how female activists view these changes; we'll compare this with male activists' views, and we'll look at how gender issues affect both women and men.

What's In a Name? Sex is normally defined as the physical aspects we use to classify organisms according to their reproductive functions, while *gender* originated as a grammatical term referring to a category that includes masculine, feminine, and neuter. For our purposes here, we'll use *gender* to discuss workplace or social issues that stem from the fact that one is a man or a woman, and *sex* to discuss situations that stem more directly from one's sexuality.

STEREOTYPED TRAITS

Self-Awareness Activities 6.1 and 6.2 were designed to give you some insight into your own gender beliefs. Compare them with the typical gender traits and roles that most people expect, whether consciously or not. People expect men and women to express different traits, and the traits they admire in men are often traits they don't admire in women and don't expect women to express.

Male Traits

Typical traits people expect to find in men, according to Gallup Polls (1990) are:

- aggressive
- strong
- proud
- confident
- independent
- courageous
- disorganized
- ambitious

These are also traits traditionally expected of business leaders.

Female Traits

Those traits that people typically expect of women are quite different:

- emotional
- talkative
- sensitive
- affectionate
- manipulative (say men)
- creative (say women)
- moody
- patient
- romantic
- cautious
- thrifty

The traits needed for business success are *not* the traits people expect in women. These stereotypes about traits create barriers for women in the workplace.

STEREOTYPES AND REALITIES

Stereotypes about the roles that men and women should play are as limiting and challenging as the myths about their traits.

Stereotype #1: The typical American family consists of a husband with a career and a wife who stays home and takes care of the two children.

This stereotype reflects traditional male/female roles. The woman belongs at home doing housework and raising children, and the man belongs in the workplace earning a living for the family. This pattern was typical from about 1900 to 1960. Now, only about 15 percent of U.S. families fit that description—and even then only temporarily while the children are very young—making the roles more myth than reality.

Stereotype #2: There are only two types of women: good and bad.

In the past "good women" were placed on a pedestal, called ladies and treated like little madonnas or dolls, while "bad women" were called sluts or whores. There was not much gray area in between. Women who had ever had sex outside of marriage were bad and the others were good. Men, on the other hand, were expected to have sex before marriage, and extramarital sex for them was covertly condoned and even admired. This stereotype tends to define women primarily by their sexual relationship to men. Its vestiges are definitely still in evidence, more in some subcultures and regions than in others.

Stereotype #3: Women's status in society is equal to men's.

The stereotype is that since women got voting rights, equal opportunity, and affirmative action, they've gained equal status. However, we know that less than 5 percent of the top decision makers in business and government are women. And women at all levels average 25 percent less pay than men.

If the media reflects what's going on in society, women are still seen first as sex objects—at least while they're young. Later they're seen as wives and mothers. The media frequently portrays young women as little more than dimwitted bimbos hanging onto a powerful man's arm, or sex objects that help sell cars, liquor, cosmetics, and most anything else. The idea is that buying the product will help a man to attract a young, sexy woman or help a woman to become young-looking and sexy. A 1972 study showed that the role of women in 32 percent of TV commercials was sex object/decoration and in 20 percent it was wife/mother. A 1990 survey of women's opinions of advertising indicates that things haven't changed much (Dominick and Rauch 1972; Crane and De Young 1992). Most say the few ads that feature career women tend to show them as superwomen who do it all, and that advertising generally:

- shows women mainly as sex objects
- does not show women as they really are
- suggests that women don't make important decisions

Stereotype #4: Real men are in control of the situation.

In our patriarchal culture, being in control has had high value. Men have typically been told by men in authority, "You're letting things get out of control," "Control your wife," "You've got to take charge." This myth implies that men are superior. At home they should be master of the house, and in the workplace they should be the managers. More and more American women are expecting to have equal relationships at home and in the workplace. Relationship styles and management styles are changing. The trend is that people are expected to control themselves and to take control of their own lives, then come together as basic equals to collaborate on joint projects. Trying to control others is becoming frustrating and counterproductive for men.

Stereotype #5: Real men don't cry.

People in our culture typically tell little boys that "Big boys don't cry." Neither are they afraid. They are brave and confident. They may get angry and fight back, but they don't whimper or snivel. In hundreds of little ways men get the message that they should not be emotional nor show their feelings. Most boys learn to hide their feelings. By the time they grow up, many have denied their feelings for so long that they're numb to them, out of touch with them.

Once they're men, it's generally all right to show anger in certain situations, such as to get things done or to defend one's honor. And it's acceptable to show some feelings with one's mate in romantic settings. Otherwise, feelings are to be buttoned up, locked in, and kept contained. And that's the major problem with this myth. Unacknowledged and unexpressed feelings don't go away. They build and fester, contributing to stress and its related illnesses.

Stereotype #6: Women are too emotional and soft to be real leaders.

Many stereotypes that are devastating for career women are based on the "too emotional and soft" belief. According to the 1995 Glass Ceiling Commission, these stereotypes are the ones that create the greatest barriers:

- Women are too emotional.
- Women are too passive, too aggressive, not aggressive enough.

- Women aren't tough enough to fill some positions.
- Women can't or won't work long or unusual hours—or relocate.
- Women can't or won't make tough decisions.
- Women can't crunch numbers.
- Women don't want to work.
- Women aren't as committed to careers as men.

These traits are primarily learned traits. They are a matter of style rather than substance.

The impact of this stereotype is still strong. A Gallup Poll done in 2001 indicates that nearly half of Americans would prefer to work for a male boss, while 22 percent would choose a female boss, and 28 percent have no preference. The good news for women is the dramatic change in attitudes since the 1950s, when two-thirds said they preferred a male boss and only 5 percent preferred a woman.

DOES CULTURE DETERMINE MALE-FEMALE TRAITS AND STATUS?

While some traits may have a genetic component, we know that culture plays a large role. In patriarchal cultures, men and women have different status and different roles. Different traits provide a rationale for this and so are emphasized.

Stereotyped Traits

Almost from the moment we're born, we begin learning gender stereotypes and myths. Most of us also begin learning about inequality in relationships from the patriarchal system of family, church, and culture. Although the patriarchal system is beginning to change in the U.S., boys and girls are still socialized in very different ways. And boys and girls still grow up in two worlds, overlapping but different.

People generally expect men and women to express different traits, and the traits they admire in men are often traits they don't admire in women and don't expect women to express. Men's traits—such as aggressive, strong, and independent—are those traditionally expected of business leaders. That's why business women report they must walk a fine line between being considered too feminine and too masculine. The traits they need for business success are *not* the traits people expect or admire in women, as Table 6.1 indicates.

TABLE 6.1: Typical Masculine and Feminine Traits

Feminine Traits	Masculine Traits
emotional	aggressive
talkative	strong
sensitive	proud
affectionate	confident
moody	independent
patient	courageous
romantic	disorganized
cautious	ambitious
thrifty	
(Men also said *manipulative*. Women said *creative*.)	

Adapted from Gallup polls, 1990.

This "traits disadvantage" that business women have dealt with is beginning to recede as companies recognize the increasing importance of some of women's typical traits—such as a focus on personal connections, interpersonal relationships, and nurturing leadership—for managing today's participative workplace, which is increasingly peopled by well-educated employees working in self-managing teams. Men who are very aggressive and ambitious may need to develop more sensitivity and patience. All of us can benefit by becoming more well rounded and balanced, allowing the best of our personalities to emerge from both sides, the feminine and the masculine.

Developing this balance is becoming important for effective modern marriages, too. In the old survival times, men and women needed each other for a balance. Today's power couples, where both partners balance important careers with a fruitful family life, tend to develop themselves as whole persons first, then to form partnerships from preference rather than need.

Traits and Power Differentials

Not only are traits learned, they are affected by the power the culture accords to each group. When we are socialized at home in ways that establish and reinforce a power differential between men and women, male-female interactions in the workplace reflect interactions between the more powerful and the less powerful. For example, why do some women use tears to influence men, while men tend to use logical arguments to influence both men and women? Yes, through socialization, women have been allowed to express emotions and men have not. But also, men usually have more power in male-female relationships and therefore have the upper hand. It may be that women's logic would be ignored and they feel they must resort to tears in order to have effect. Research has led to two major conclusions about gender and power tactics (Peplau, 1991):

Gender affects power tactics. Women are more likely to withdraw or express negative emotions, while men are more likely to use bargaining or reasoning. However, in a partnership between gay men, if one partner perceives himself as less powerful, he is likely to use withdrawal or expressions of negative emotions, and the more powerful partner is likely to use bargaining or reasoning. The same dynamics were found between two women in a lesbian partnership.

Power, not gender, is the issue. Regardless of gender or sexual orientation, people who see themselves as relatively more powerful in a relationship tend to use persuasion and bargaining, while those who feel they are lower in power tend to use withdrawal and emotion.

As Rosabeth Kanter (1979) found in her studies of men and women in organizations, behaviors believed to be typical of women are actually behaviors that are typical of the powerless. Regardless of sexual orientation, a partner with relatively less power tends to use "weak" strategies, such as manipulation and pleading. Those in more powerful positions are more likely to use autocratic and bullying tactics. Signs of conversational dominance, such as interrupting, were linked also to the balance of power. Interruption is not so much a male behavior as a tactic of the powerful. Many studies provide support for the dominance interpretation of sex differences in male-female interaction (Peplau 1991; Howard, Blumstein, and Schwartz 1986; Kollock, Blumstein, and Schwartz 1985).

Gender Differences as a Prototype of Group Differences

All cultures differentiate between male and female behavior, and usually when a given behavior pattern becomes associated with one sex, it will be dropped by the other, according to G.P. Murdock's work. Recently many sociologists and anthropologists have begun to see gender differences primarily as cultural differences and have started applying cross-cultural techniques to solving gender problems. Some researchers, such as Richard Brislin and Tomoko Yoshida, say that gender is not just one of many cultural differences, but the most important cultural difference, the root paradigm of difference, just as the inequality of patriarchy is the paradigm of all inequality among groups.

Instead of seeing women's culture as a subculture within each ethnic culture, they declare that the two most basic cultural groups are women and men. Between these two groups we find the prototypical cultural distinctions, after which all other cultural distinctions are modeled. If organizations can learn to accept and deal with gender differences, all other differences can be handled in due course. On the other hand, a great deal of diversity work remains superficial when gender issues are not first recognized and managed. This is because beliefs about gender influence us in the most fundamental ways about how to be with others and make choices in life.

HOW HAVE GENDER ROLES EVOLVED AND CHANGED?

Women in Western cultures have traditionally been viewed as a wholly different species from men, invariably an inferior species. Those primary and secondary sex differences that exist are greatly exaggerated and are inflated into imaginary distinctions that justify discrimination. In the past most men felt an in-group solidarity with half the humans on earth, other men, and with the other half, an irreconcilable conflict. Lord Chesterfield described the way women were traditionally viewed by men in the eighteenth century (Allport 1954) :

(Women are) *"children grown large, with little reasoning ability. They are to be trifled with, played with, humored, and flattered, as with a sprightly, forward child. Few men ever consult them or trust them with serious matters, though they often make women believe that they do both, which is the source of women's greatest pride. They are mainly concerned with matters of vanity and of love.'*

The Patriarchal System

Patriarchy refers to the rule of a family or tribe by men, and a social system in which descent and succession are traced through the male line. It began by brute force and muscle power. Once established, men's superiority and advantage were institutionalized into every sphere of life. It's being undermined because brain power and relationship power are becoming true power. As men's superiority is undermined, some are resorting to extreme measures to hold onto it, even to physical abuse and rape, according to Robert Bly, Sam Keen, and other men's movement leaders.

Men's movement author Walter Farrell defines a patriarchy as the male areas of dominance, responsibility, and subservience in a culture, reinforced by both genders for the purpose of serving survival needs of both. Patriarchy has given men the authority, privileges, and responsibility that come with being in charge. Women's privileges involved being provided for and protected, if they picked the right man and all went well. Both men and women have been rewarded with "identity" when they followed the rules and punished with invisibility when they failed—or sometimes even death if they rebelled against them. Leaders were picked from the men who best followed the rules (Farrell 1993).

Feminist Movements

Women's groups have arisen from time to time to protest the limitations and unfairness to women and to men that patriarchy imposes. The most recent feminist movement began in the 1960s and has made significantly more progress than any previous movement. Perhaps gender equality is an ideal whose time has come. Feminists come in many political shades and stripes. For our purposes we'll use this simple definition.

> *A feminist is someone who believes in equal rights for women.*

Most feminists believe that the inequality inherent in patriarchy does not serve women's best interests, and that equality in the workplace will lead to equality in the family. They focus on eliminating all discriminatory barriers to women's moving up in the work world as the key to the overall liberation of women. They believe that changes in labor market conditions that women face will force changes in family dynamics. Economic power is a prerequisite to a balance of power in family relationships.

From Patriarchy to Equality

As we've moved from an agricultural economy through an industrial to a post-industrial economy, cultural values have shifted dramatically. The women's movement is a reflection of that basic shift. Marriage relationships are the most influential in a society, because children learn about life and relationships by observing their parents. Leaders of both the men's and women's movements propose that we move beyond patriarchy or matriarchy—beyond hierarchy—to a system that relies on leadership that arises spontaneously from those who are willing and able to lead in particular situations. See Table 6.2.

TABLE 6.2: Traditional and New Male-Female Relationships

	Traditional Marriage Relationships	*New Relationships*
Major goal Relationship focus	Survival Role mates, to create a whole	Fulfillment Soul mates, whole persons, to create synergy
Effect on roles Family obligations	Segregated roles Must have children Woman raises children, man makes money. Woman risks life in childbirth; man risks life in war	Common roles Children are a choice Both raise children and both make money Childbirth relatively risk-free; ideally no more war
Partner choice	Parental influence primary; women try to marry "up"	Parental influence secondary; both marry for love
The contract	Lifetime; no divorce	As long as both parties want to stay together
Status of parties	Neither party can end contract Woman is property of man; man expected to provide and protect Both are subservient to needs of family	Either party can end contract Each equally responsible for self and other Both balance needs of family with needs of self
Emotional expectation	Love emerges from mutual dependence I'll stay no matter what	Love is based on choice I'll stay unless you abuse me or we grow in different directions

Megatrends that Opened Doors

Beginning in the 1960s a series of megatrends combined to accelerate the pace at which women moved into managerial, professional, technical, and leadership roles that had been almost exclusively Euro-American male territory.

Social Change

The 1960s brought major social upheavals. Those that most affected gender issues were greater acceptance of divorce, greater sexual freedom, and greater acceptance of equal opportunity for women and minorities. Such social changes allowed women more freedom of choice. During the 1970s women began moving into many fields of study, preparing for the occupations that were closed to them before AA.

Economic Change

As blue collar jobs moved offshore, growing number of husbands no longer earned an income that would support a family, and their wives went to work. As divorce became more economically feasible for women, an increasing percentage of women became heads of households. For all these reasons, middle-class working mothers, once a sign of liberation, became an economic necessity during the 1980s. As the average worker's take-home pay went down, family income grew an average of less than 1 percent per year, even with many wives working. Buying a home became more expensive and took a larger share of family income, and renters found it more difficult to save up a down payment. An ever-greater proportion of women will continue to enter the workforce and stay there, even when they have small children. This means that working mothers will be the largest potential source of qualified workers for the next decade.

Emphasis on Ethical Values

The excesses of the 1980s—from the spending of a Donald Trump to the grand larceny of Wall Street dealers and savings and loan officers—brought a new respect for ethical principles. Also, biotechnology companies say they are poised to solve many of our health and poverty problems, but people are realizing a corresponding need to define ethical values in order to regulate the industry. Several recent surveys indicate that people believe women can bring special talents to dealing with and cleaning up ethical issues, and that people tend to trust women's ethical standards and level of honesty. This applies to both the business and political worlds. Women represent a "fresh face" without the backroom connections and long years of deal making (Naisbett 1990).

Management Style Change

The underlying theme of all the megatrends is the individual (Naisbett 1982, 1990). While people are working together in more dynamic ways than ever, the trend is for power in work groups to stem from the power of individuals within the groups. Leaders who know how to empower others have an edge. This megatrend makes the natural management style of most women, a plus because:

- Women are usually socialized to win commitment from people rather than to give orders and apply controls.

- Women tend to adapt more naturally to the role of teacher/facilitator/coach than they do to the role of director/overseer.

- Women have historically been trained to focus on helping others achieve success, usually husbands and children.

Impact of Change: Current Socioeconomic Profile

Some of the most dramatic changes in gender dynamics center around new roles for women, higher educational achievement, women as heads of households, and a continuing but slowly shrinking pay gap.

Occupations

Women are 52 percent of the U.S. population and 46 percent of the workforce but only 40 percent of all managers and less than 5 percent of top managers. While most managers, precision production workers, machine operators, and laborers are men, most clerical and service workers are women. Professionals, which include teachers and nurses as well as doctors, lawyers, and accountants are nearly half and half, as are technical and sales workers.

Euro-American men are 35 percent of the population and 39 percent of the workforce; yet they are:

- 92 percent of senior managers in mid- to large-sized corporations (5 percent are women; 3 percent are men of all other ethnic groups)

- 82.5 percent of the Forbes 400 persons worth at least 265 million dollars
- 80 percent of Congress (91% of the Senate, 78% of the House; 12% of Congress consisted of women, 8% percent male "minorities" in 1998)
- 92 percent of state governors
- 70 percent of tenured college faculty
- 90 percent of daily newspaper editors
- 77 percent of TV news directors

According to the 1995 Glass Ceiling Commission, they "dominate just about everything but NOW and the NAACP." It is clear that they hold the most powerful positions in the economic and political arenas.

Nearly 60 percent of wives are in the workforce, raising family income by one-third on average. Women with dependent children are more likely to work than women with adult children. And women are increasingly likely to delay marriage and children in order to finish college and establish themselves in a career.

Education

Although there has traditionally been a male-female education gap, with more men getting degrees, the gap had closed for 1990 graduates, with women slightly outnumbering men. The fields where women graduates increased the most dramatically are business and science, as shown in Table 6.3.

TABLE 6.3: Men and Women—Occupations and Education, 1990

Relative proportions of men and women:	Male	Female
In total population	48%	52%
In the workforce	54	46
Managers	58	42
Professionals	46	54
Technical	46	54
Sales	51	49
Clerical	23	77
Service	37	63
Production, craft (electrician, plumber, etc.)	90	10
Machine operators	60	40
Laborers	80	20
Received bachelor's degrees	47	53
Psychology	29	71
Life sciences	49	51
Business degree	53	47
Social sciences	56	44
Physical sciences	69	31
Engineering	86	14

Source: U.S. Census Bureau; Women's Bureau, Labor Department.

The Pay Gap

In 1998 women's median weekly earnings were 75 percent of men's—for full-time employees. The pay gap was more or less 60 to 65 percent from the 1950s to 1980. The 10 percent improvement since 1980 probably reflects men's lower pay, women's higher educational achievement, their choice of formerly male-dominated fields that pay more, and the tendency to delay having children and to take fewer years off from careers once children arrive. The pay gap is especially tough for single mothers. And more families than ever were headed by single women—28 percent in 1999, compared to

17 percent in 1990 and 11 percent in 1970. Among "minority" households, the proportion of single mothers is even higher: for African Americans the figure is 44 percent and for Latino Americans, 32 percent, versus 12 percent for Asian American and Euro-American households.

On average, these women had to survive on about one-third the median income of married-couple families. Therefore, they were nearly six times as likely to live in poverty. In fact, at all ages, more women than men live in poverty. For example, women over 65 are twice as likely as older men to live in poverty. And they live longer—by about 7 years on average.

MEN AND WOMEN: GROWING UP IN TWO DIFFERENT WORLDS

Women and men are much more alike than not. Most differences are probably more cultural than physical, and individual men and women vary greatly as to their degree of typically masculine or feminine traits. Still, even though girls and boys grow up side by side, they live in two different experiential worlds. Because we as a culture and as individuals treat boys and girls, men and women, so differently, their experiences and worldviews are dramatically different.

Cultural Socialization of Girls and Boys

We raise boys and girls differently in our culture. They play differently as children. They have different values and experiences as teenagers. Since we are a patriarchal culture, boys gain more respect as they grow into men. As girls grow into women, they have more difficulty being perceived as competent leaders.

Some differences in the ways boys and girls are socialized in the American culture are shown in Table 6.4. Read the table from the top down, by column, since the each column represents a socialization process, by gender, not a comparison of types of experiences.

TABLE 6.4: Process of Growing Up, by Gender

Note: read each column separately.

Girls and Women	Boys and Men
Girls experience a less active childhood than boys.	Boys lead a more active childhood, controlling their world with physical actions.
Girls are taught to be reactive more often than proactive.	Boys are taught to be self-sufficient, autonomous, a closed system.
Girls learn to experience lines of power going from women to men; power is gained through men.	Boys learn to ignore their needs to be dependent.
Girls learn to think ahead about how people might respond, to "psych out" situations, to be "schemers."	Eventually, males begin to deny they even have dependency needs.
Girls are encouraged to believe that a man's approval is more valuable than a woman's.	Males lose touch with the feelings that accompany dependency needs, then with other feelings.
Teenage girls begin competing with each other for male attention.	Boys and men become task-oriented, compartmentalized, mechanical, and highly rational.
Girls and women learn they're expected to be selfless helpers, not have needs for great space, territorial or psychological.	As a result men become quite dependent on women as the emotional, nurturant "translators" or bridges between men and family members, men and others.
Women learn to live for and through others, to define themselves in terms of their relationships with others.	

Based on the work of Warren Farrell and Julie Matthaei, 1993.

Teenage Differences

Many of the old stereotypes and socialization patterns are still in place for teenagers of the 1990s. Peggy Orenstein's research (Carroll 1994) indicates that girls routinely report feeling:

- resignation about the greater power that society grants boys
- resignation about society's acceptance of boys' greater assertiveness and power to disrupt
- pressure to emphasize appearance and minimize brains to win favor
- pressure to acquiesce in second-rate status
- fear of failure in science and math

Boys and Men: More Respect

As boys grow into men, their time and activities gain respect and tend to be viewed as important, while girls' time and activities are seen as less important. This tendency is tied to the fact that beginning with the Industrial Revolution, men went off to work they got paid for, while women stayed home and did not get paid. In our society income is seen as an indicator of a person's importance and value. Women are expected to be respectful of men's more important responsibilities. As little boys become adults, they take on the parent role with women, serving as their protectors. Men are thus seen as competent and tend to indulge women. On the other hand, as little girls become women, they retain much of the child role, needing to be protected and indulged, and thus they are seen as less competent than men.

Girls and Women: Lower Status

Many studies, such as those by Alice and Rosalind Loring, have shown that males are considered more competent than females, at least outside the home. In one study (Kohn 1988) people were asked to evaluate an article, some copies with a woman's byline and identical copies with a man's byline. The article with the male byline was rated as better by 98 percent of the evaluators.

In another study of mixed-group conversations, 97 percent of interruptions were made by men. There were fewer interruptions when women were speaking with women or when men were speaking with men. In mixed-group studies of who does most of the talking, men talk from 58 percent to 92 percent of the time. Most women are unaware of this type of domination, perceiving that they did a fair share of the talking in 75 percent of the situations (Eisen 1984).

Men are allowed to take the lead and dominate in many subtle ways, as Deborah Tannen's research confirmed. For example, both men and women tend to regard topics introduced by women as tentative, whereas topics introduced by men are treated as material to be pursued. Men use humor to take the lead. They tend to remember and repeat jokes, using the opportunity to take center stage and gain control. Most women tend to forget jokes, rarely try to repeat them, and serve as supportive audience, laughing at the jokes men tell.

The many ways that males and females have learned to behave differently are summarized in Table 6.5.

TABLE 6.5: Male and Female Tendencies

	Men's Tendencies	**Women's Tendencies**
Relationships	Self-focused	Other-focused
	Focus on individuals	Focus on group
	More impersonal	More personal
	Need more distance	Need more closeness
	Fear engulfment	Fear abandonment
	Over-identify with work	Over-identify with people
	Do what I please	Do what others approve
	More independent	Dependent/interdependent
	Like group activities more	Have more intimate friends
	More aggressive toward others	Trust each other more
	Make war	Make peace
	Define self by job	Define self by relationships
	Seek the spotlight	Prefer the sidelines
	More competitive	More cooperative
	Money a measure of masculinity	Money a tool
	Want respect for achievements	Want to be liked
	Love sports and games more	Love shopping more
Method of Supporting	Challenge others	Agree with others
Method of Disagreeing	Confront others	Comply with others
Thinking and Feeling	More rational	More emotional
	Express feeling less	Express feelings more
	Worry less	Worry more
	Express anger	Repress anger
	Thinking more linear, narrow	Thinking more global
		More cross-brain ability
	Focus more on facts	Focus more on intuition
	Greater visual-spatial ability	Greater verbal ability
	Less depression	Handle stress better
	Like the way they look	More concerned about looks
	Take more risks	Tend to avoid risks
Communication	*Initiate more*	*Listen more*
	Talk about things	Talk about people
	Talk more in public	Talk more in private
	Take words at face value	Search for hidden meaning
	Direct language	Circumspect language
	Interrupt women	Let men interrupt
	Decide now, on their own	Decide after group input
	Gossip about work lives	Gossip about personal lives
	Give advice for problems	Give sympathy for problems
	Make direct put-downs	Make backbiting put-downs
	Tell jokes more	Apologize more
	Figure it out themselves	Seek assistance
	Toot their own horn more	Nag more
	Intimidate more	Avoid confrontation more
	Being right is more important	Being liked is more important
	Comfortable giving orders	Uncomfortable giving orders
	Comfortable with hierarchy	Don't like hierarchy
	Don't talk about ailments	Discuss ailments more

Based on the work of Chris Evatt, Carol Tavris, Alice Eagly, Cynthia Epstein, 1992, 1987

MALE-FEMALE COMMUNICATION STYLES: HOW THEY DIFFER

As a result of their different socialization patterns, men and women interpret and relate to their environments differently. Men tend to take more initiative, which results in their being more self-protective and assertive (Gove 1985). They tend to be more focused, future-oriented, and objective, with a greater urge to master. Other major differences in viewpoint and focus, according to Deborah Tannen's groundbreaking research, are:

Women's Focus	Men's Focus
• Connection	• Status
• Establish rapport	• Report information
• Cooperate	• Compete
• Play down my expertise	• Display my expertise

An awareness of these tendencies can help us to understand why men and women often see things so differently. Awareness also helps us to foresee possible misunderstandings and communication breakdowns and in turn helps us to improve male-female relationships and to communicate more effectively. Let's explore Tannen's findings in more detail.

Connection or Status?

Women live in a world of intimacy and men in a world of status concerns. Women, in their world, focus on connecting with others via networks of supportive friends. Much of their communication is aimed at minimizing differences and building on commonalties and agreements. The ultimate goal is to attain maximum consensus and to function in relationships where people are interdependent. Men certainly have their old boy networks, but their world of status places higher priority on independence, where the purpose of much communication is on giving or taking orders. The ultimate goal is to attain more personal freedom.

Rapport Talk or Report Talk?

Women like "rapport talk" because it establishes or maintains connections with others . The focus is on feelings and includes personal thoughts, reactions to the day's events, and the details of her life. Men prefer "report talk," because it provides factual information that the listener needs to know and what's going on in the world. Women's major aim in listening is to communicate interest and caring; men's major interest is to get information. Women will frequently reveal their weaknesses, especially when the other person is feeling discouraged. The rationale: Sharing such personal information will make the other feel equal, and thus closer. Men nearly always feel that revealing a weakness would just lower their status in the other person's eyes.

Cooperative or Competitive?

Women's words and actions often revolve around giving understanding, while men's are more likely to revolve around giving advice. These tendencies are probably based on the different ways men and women measure power. Women view helping, nurturing, and supporting as measures of their power. The activities they engage in include giving praise, speaking one-on-one, and private conversations. The main arenas for these activities are the telephone, social situations, and the home. Men perceive different measures of their power, such as having information, expertise, and skills. The activities they engage in include giving information, speaking more and longer, and speaking to groups. The main arenas for these activities are the workplace and public places.

In the work arena, women tend to approach decision making in a participative way: "I cannot and should not act alone when it comes to important decisions." Men tend to feel they must act alone and must find their way without help. Women focus on mastering their jobs and increasing their skills, consulting and involving others in the process, and developing positive relationships with their peers. Men tend to focus on competition and power, hierarchy and status. Women may not stand up for their rights because they want to avoid conflict. Men are less likely to be afraid of conflict and more willing to confront issues in order to clear the air. Men are more likely to be intimidating to others, while women are more often perceived as approachable.

Women are more likely to be uncomfortable in taking the initiative. Because women tend to be more accommodating and self-sacrificing, they are also more likely to allow frustration to build. To overcome problems arising from these tendencies, women can develop assertiveness skills and habits. Men need clear facts in the communication process. They experience more difficulty in coping with unclear situations and expressing mixed feelings. To overcome these difficulties, they can get in touch with their emotions and intuitive side.

Expertise: Play It Up or Down?

A major source of power for managers, professionals, and other leaders is their expertise. Women tend to downplay their expertise, act as if they know less than they really do, and operate as one of the group or audience. Men are more apt to display their expertise and act as if they know more about their area than others in the group know. They're more likely to be comfortable taking center stage.

The male expert's main goal is to persuade, and he often firmly states his opinions as facts. In contrast, when female experts speak with males, their approach tends to be assenting, supporting, agreeing, listening, and going along. They want to emphasize similarities between themselves and listeners and to avoid showing off. Their concerns: "Have I been helpful? Do you like me?" The male experts' approach tends to be dominating, talking more, interrupting, and controlling the topic, whether they are speaking with males or females. They want to emphasize their superiority and display their expertise. Their concerns: "Have I won? Do you respect me?"

The typical female response to male experts' communication is to either agree or disagree. On the other hand, male listeners usually don't understand that the female expert's main concern is to not offend, so the males often conclude that she is either indecisive, incompetent, insecure, or all of the above. They respond by offering their own opinions and information and by setting the agenda themselves; that is, they incorrectly perceive a power vacuum and try to take over.

Support by Agreeing or Disagreeing?

Women tend to show support by agreeing with others, while men help out by disagreeing to reveal problems and provide alternatives. Women's feedback style tends to be more positive and plentiful . They keep a running feedback loop going with such responses as "mmmm, uh huh, yes, yeah." They ask questions, take turns, and give and want full attention. They usually agree, and they laugh at humorous comments. They focus on the meta-message even more than the literal message. Men give fewer listener responses. They are more silent and listen less. They are more likely to challenge statements and to focus on the literal message.

Because women listen so attentively, they may think a man's silence implies concentration on their meta-message, when in fact he may not be listening. Later she says, "But I told you all about that yesterday!" Most men challenge any statement they disagree with, so a man tends to interpret a woman's silence as consent or agreement. Later, when her actions are incompatible with her "agreement," he concludes that she is insincere or changeable: "Women!" As we begin to understand the different worlds that men and women live in, we can begin to find ways to bridge such communication gaps.

Communication Style: Tentative or Assertive?

With their focus on rapport, connection, intimacy, and playing down their expertise, women's communication styles tend to be more tentative than men's. Because the business world is accustomed to an assertive male approach to communication, women's credibility   undermined by a tentative, overly polite, uncertain, or indecisive approach. Several studies indicate that women perpetuate the lower-credibility stereotype with the following types of behavior:

- *Women ask more questions,* about three times as many as men on average.

- *Women make more statements in a questioning tone,* with a rising inflection at the end of a statement.

- *Women use more tag questions;* that is, brief questions added at the end of a sentence: "... don't you think?" "... okay?" " ... you know?"

- *Women lead off with a question more frequently.* "You know what?" "Would you believe this?"

- *Women use more qualifiers and intensifiers.* Qualifiers or "hedges" include "kind of, sort of, a little bit, maybe, could be, if." Such qualifiers soften an assertive statement, but also undermine its assertiveness. Intensifiers include *really, very, incredible, fantastic, amazing,* especially when those words are emphasized. The meta-message is: "Because what I say, by itself, is not likely to convince you, I must use double force to make sure you see what I mean."

Researchers Alice H. Eagly and Chris Evatt have noted striking similarities between the conversation of women with men and the conversations of children with adults. They conclude that women tend to express their thoughts more tentatively and work harder to get someone's attention, which may in turn reflect basic power differences.

On the other hand, it's not unusual for men to carry assertiveness too far and to be perceived as overbearing or authoritarian. The most effective conversational approach for leaders is usually one that conveys *both* their sensitivity as well as commitment to their beliefs and statements. Both women and men become more effective when they communicate assertively, expressing their thoughts and feelings clearly but with respect for the thoughts, feelings, and rights of others.

Male–Female Management Styles: How They Differ

Men and women managers are somewhat different in their management skills and in their leadership effectiveness, according to a study of thousands of managers (Kabacoss 1998). First, the skill differences: on overall managerial skills, women rate higher on people-oriented skills, while men rate higher on business-oriented skills.

On leaderships traits and management style, women managers were rated higher on productivity orientation and getting results, while male managers scored higher on organization vision and strategic planning. Ratings were made by bosses, peers, direct reports, and the managers themselves. More details follow.

Strengths of Women Managers

Women were generally rated better than men on overall skills, people skills, and five categories of leadership traits and management style.

Overall Skills

In overall skills, peers and direct reports rated women higher, but no differences were found in ratings by bosses. Here are descriptions of the skills that were assessed:

1. **Effectiveness as leader/manager**—total level of performance against expectations, total impact in role

2. **Future potential**—ability to go beyond present level, probability of being a major resource to the organization
3. **Credibility with management**—inspires confidence, communicates well, delivers on promises, thinks in similar ways as management

People Skills

In people skills, all three observer groups—bosses, peers, and direct reports—rated women managers higher than male managers. The following skills were assessed:

1. **Sensitivity**—perceives other people's feelings, shows concern, has insight, is helpful, avoids hurting people's feelings
2. **Likability**—easy, friendly, quick to smile, good-hearted
3. **Willingness to listen**—understands quickly, acknowledges communication, seeks out others' views
4. **Diversity skills**—works well with people from different backgrounds, cultures, belief systems, or lifestyles
5. **Team player**—willing and able to act as a team player, complements the efforts of others, contributes to team performance
6. **Developing people**—allows room for mistakes, stimulates growth, challenges positively, delegates authority
7. **Getting results through people**—delegates effectively, sets high standards, organizes efforts well
8. **Advocacy for team**—defends team members appropriately, sells their views to management, protects them from arbitrary decisions
9. **Invoking enthusiasm**—gets people involved and committed, is persuasive and inspiring
10. **Credibility with peers and subordinates**—inspires confidence, is trusted and respected, delivers on promises

Leadership Traits and Management Style

Everyone surveyed—peers, bosses, direct-reports, and the women themselves—agreed that women managers rate higher on these traits:

1. **Enthusiasm**—operating with energy, intensity, and emotional expression; keeping others enthusiastic and involved
2. **Communicative**—stating clearly what you want and expect from others, clearly expressing your thoughts and ideas, maintaining a precise, constant flow of information
3. **Feedback**—letting others know directly what you think of them, how well they are performing, and if they are meeting your needs and expectations
4. **Dominance in getting results**—pushing vigorously to achieve results through being forceful, assertive, and competitive.
5. **Production**—valuing achievement, holding high expectations for self and others, pushing self and others to achieve at high levels

Strengths of Male Managers

Male managers were rated higher in the business skills and on six aspects of leadership traits and management style.

Business Skills

In business skills, bosses and peers rated men higher, but their direct reports rated men and women about the same.

1. **Business "smarts"**—instinct for making money, exploiting business opportunities, being wily in business dealings

2. **Financial understanding**—understands and can deal with financial issues such as budgeting, accounting, costs, P&L statements

3. **Perspective**—seeing the big picture and interconnections between one's own goals and company goals, strategic orientation, anticipating problems

4. **Effective thinking**—learning rapidly, dealing well with concepts, getting quickly to the heart of an issue, being acute

5. **Effective decision making**

6. **Resourcefulness**—seeing how to get and use organizational resources, perceiving organizational power and dynamics, networking, building alliances

Leadership Traits and Management Style

Male managers got significantly higher mean scores than women on the following traits:

1. **Conservativism**—studying problems in light of past practices to ensure predictability, reinforcing the status quo, minimizing risk

2. **Innovativeness**—feeling comfortable in fast-changing environments, being willing to take risks and to consider new and untested approaches

3. **Strategic approach**—taking a long-range view, broad approach to problem solving and decision making through objective analysis, thinking ahead, and planning

4. **Restraint**—maintaining a low-key, understated, quiet interpersonal demeanor

5. **Delegating**—enlisting the talents of others to help meet goals by giving them important activities and enough autonomy to use their own judgment

6. **Cooperation**—accommodating the needs and interests of others by being willing to defer performance on your own goals in order assist other team members with theirs

Male–Female Management Similarities

Only two traits showed no gender differences. They are:

1. **consensual**—valuing the ideas and opinions of others, collecting their input as part of your decision-making process

2. **authority**—showing loyalty to the organization, respecting the opinions of people in authority, and using them as resources for information, direction, and decisions

For nine of the traits, assessments of male and female managers were mixed, but showed more similarities than differences:

1. Technical orientation
2. Structured systematic approach
3. Tactical approach
4. Control methods
5. Management focus
6. Empathy
7. Self-contained
8. Persuasive
9. Outgoing

CULTURAL BARRIERS TO WOMEN'S CAREER SUCCESS

Most career women must overcome both internal barriers and external barriers to workplace success that are rooted in the American culture. Internal barriers include self-limiting beliefs about women's abilities and roles. External barriers include the glass ceiling, inflexible work arrangements, and pay disparity.

Self-Limiting Beliefs

Traditions from the past affect today's career woman in two basic ways: (1) how she pictures herself and, therefore, the roles and behaviors she's comfortable with, and (2) what others expect of her—their preconceived notions of her abilities, traits, strengths, and weaknesses and their resulting beliefs about proper roles and behaviors. These traditional beliefs and expectations often lead to problems with self-limiting and conflicting beliefs. Leaders who understand how such beliefs create internal barriers are in a better position to help women overcome them. Self-limiting beliefs many women still hold include:

- I should not be ambitious.
- I should wait to be asked.
- I should never parade my achievements and expertise, nor "toot my own horn."
- Women aren't supposed to be good in math, finance, computer, mechanical, technical, engineering, decision-making, and other male fields.
- I should stay out of office politics.
- I don't need to nose around in the inner workings of the company (the hierarchy, chain of command, sources of power, career paths).
- It's best to just let others have their way rather than cause a scene.
- I need to steer clear of risky ventures.
- Criticism of my work or ideas is a criticism of me.
- All I need to get ahead is to improve myself and work hard.
- If I do good work, my boss will notice and promote me.

Some women have beliefs that cause them to personalize events, criticism, and messages of others, to react emotionally, and to act out such emotions. These are beliefs typical of the powerless, regardless of gender, and usually are picked up from the women in the family and community.

Some women have difficulty understanding how upward mobility works. If they've rarely worked on teams, they may have beliefs about self-development that prevent them from recognizing the necessity of networking and teamwork. They may neglect developing a power base, and they may not see how they can meet personal goals through helping the team achieve organizational goals.

Conflicting Beliefs

Certain conflicting beliefs that can lead to fear of success tend to be unique to women and may include:

- I want a successful career *BUT* Men don't want relationships with strong, achieving career women.
- I want a successful career *BUT* Prince Charming may come along, sweep me off my feet, and carry me away to live happily ever after.
- I want a successful career *BUT* Good wives and mothers stay home and take care of the home and kids.

The beliefs that limit women and cause conflict all stem from cultural beliefs, values, and stereotypes about women. Therefore, even when women move beyond such beliefs, they must daily cope with people who still hold similar beliefs. Building a network of supportive friends and co-workers can help career women retain a sense of balance and self-confidence as they juggle career demands with home demands. An understanding, supportive manager can make all the difference. Sometimes the manager can take the lead in helping a woman employee recognize the beliefs that may be holding her back.

Pay Inequity

Information in the current profile section of this chapter indicates that although the United States leads the world in proportion of women managers, we are not as advanced in providing pay equity. Median income for full-time women workers was only 75 percent of male workers' income in 1998. Some argue that women generally have less training, experience, and job commitment than men, and that this accounts for the pay gap. However the 75 percent figure represents every management level.

> *Women vice-presidents earn only 75 percent of male vice-presidents' income.*

It's highly unlikely that women who have made it to the vice-presidential level have less training, experience, and job commitment than their male peers. In fact, some studies indicate that most women who make it this far must have higher qualifications than their male peers (U.S. Census Bureau 1998; Russell 1991).

Some analysts believe that in general women are less committed to careers than men because women take primary responsibility for raising children, which requires them to interrupt their careers. A Census Bureau study indicates that the earnings were the same for women with no work interruption as those who had at least one work interruption of six months or more since age twenty-one. The Census Bureau concludes that structural factors and discrimination, rather than discontinuous employment, explain the earnings gap. And much of the female "gain" reported in some studies actually reflects declining median male wages during the 1980s. On the other hand, the pay gap for younger women is less than that for older women, and it's less for women in rapidly growing, high-tech industries.

The Glass Ceiling

Fortune magazine's recent survey found only 19 women among 4,012 directors and highest-paid executives, 0.5 percent, not much better than in 1978 (0.16 percent). Although the United States leads the world in percentage of women managers, the 40 percent figure can be very deceptive for the following reasons:

- Most women managers are at the lowest managerial levels—lower paying, entry levels, such as working supervisor and first-line supervisor.
- Only 25% of managers were women in the 200 largest companies
- Only 33% of managers were women in the 38,059 companies reporting to the EEOC in 1992.
- Only 5% of vice presidents are women.
- Only four Fortune 500 companies were headed by women in 2000, up from none a few years earlier. That's less than 1%.
- Only 7.5% of all women employees work as managers, compared to 15% of all male employees.
- Women managers' pay lags behind men's at every level, averaging about 75 percent.
- When women move into an occupation in significant numbers, the occupation goes down in status and pay and men tend to move out of it. Conversely, if an occupation loses status and pay for other reasons, women are more likely to be hired into it.
- Women are likely to hit a glass ceiling to top-level, and even middle-level, positions. Therefore, few women are making it beyond lower-level management, and may have

little hope of doing so in the near future. The women who make up the "five percent of top managers" include women who started their own firms (U.S. Labor Department 1991, 1995).

My survey (Carr-Ruffino 1991) of women managers revealed that 90 percent think the glass ceiling is the most important issue facing women managers. Virtually all who did not head their companies (80 percent) said women were underrepresented at the top in their firms. The major reason given was the reluctance of the men at the top to include women. The following barriers to the top were considered the most important ones to overcome, in the order listed:

- Top management harbors stereotypes about women, especially regarding ability to gain acceptance in a top role, level of career commitment, and decision-making ability.

- Women are often excluded from key informal gatherings where information and opinions are exchanged, deals made, etc.

- Women's contributions and abilities are not taken as seriously as men's.

- Women have more difficulty finding mentors.

- Women don't get equal opportunities to serve on important committees and project teams.

Leaders who want to attract and retain the best-qualified women must eliminate the stereotypes, attitudes, and practices that create a glass ceiling. Even those women who don't aspire to the top prefer to stay in companies that have opened all the doors to qualified women and have helped them move up.

Two recent surveys of male and female managers of large American companies found that although women expressed a much higher probability of leaving their current employer than men, and had higher actual turnover rates, their major reason for leaving was lack of career growth opportunity or dissatisfaction with rates of progress. Effective leaders are sensitive to career women's needs and are open to helping them meet those needs.

Inflexible Working Arrangements

Women become frustrated when the demands of work and demand for blind corporate loyalty conflict with other valuable parts of their lives and prevent their full participation in the organization. Some corporate systems and practices are designed for men whose wives handle most family responsibilities. Some are designed by men who are workaholics and expect others to be. Such expectations are unreasonable for women who can't ignore family responsibilities but are committed career professionals.

Good employees can be retained through the child-bearing years if leaders are flexible, accepting, and supportive of family needs. Asking for flexible alternatives or family benefits should not be the kiss of death to career ambitions, but it is in many companies. For example, women who take maternity leave are 10 times more likely to lose their jobs than employees on other kinds of medical leave. In addition pregnant women are often transferred, demoted, harassed, or fired. On the other hand, many new mothers don't return at the end of their leaves because leaves are unrealistically brief; they need more time with the baby. "Mommy-track" and part-time work are usually the boring, low-level grunt work that blocks chances of gaining the skills required to advance professionally. All these practices and attitudes must change if a firm wants to attract and retain career women who also become mothers.

If women are to have uninterrupted careers, rather than just jobs, they need these kinds of advantages:

- Adequate maternity and family medical leave, usually much more than the three months of unpaid leave required by law

- Help in obtaining affordable, quality child care, such as day-care on the job site

- Flexible job structures and benefits, such as flextime, job sharing, part-time arrangements, contract work, and home offices
- Comparable pay and benefits
- Equal opportunity to advance
- Other work/life measures such as eldercare resource and referral and supportive managers

Working Mother magazine (1999) notes that companies offering such benefits are the best ones for fathers as well as mothers. The magazine has been citing the "Best Companies for Working Mothers" since 1986, beginning with only 30 companies, now 100. Companies are getting it; for example, those with on-site child care numbered 60 in 1999, up from only 4 in 1986. The main reason? They need to attract and retain talented women, as well as fathers who are determined to balance a career with home life.

Rather than lose competent women who go through a phase of needing more time for their small children, some companies are giving them whatever they need to do part or all of their work in a home office—fax machines, computers, car phones. Some women can pack the work into three or four days instead of five. Some need to come into the office once or twice a week for meetings. Some women hire a sitter to help out while they work at home. The major advantages: They're near their children, they can handle crises and illnesses themselves, and they don't spend time and energy commuting every day.

MEN'S RESPONSES TO NEW ROLES AND EXPECTATIONS

Surveys by David Gates and Robert Speer give insight into men's reactions to new gender roles and expectations. About half of Euro-American men think they're losing influence and job advantage, while only a third of other respondents think that.

Losing Power: Personal vs. Collective

Recent surveys indicate that the major dilemma men are wrestling with is the power problem—the profound difference between personal and collective power. Most men do not feel very powerful; they report that they are:

- having a harder time making a living than their fathers did
- dealing with a boss telling them what to do
- trying to figure out how to be what woman want: sensitive as well as strong; soft and cuddly as well as firm and "manly."

As a result, many men feel they've failed in their gender role. Men's movement leaders say the women's movement has triggered changes for men in every life area, and most haven't adjusted to it yet. Men look around them and see that they're in danger because men are 83 percent of the homeless, 90 percent of AIDS deaths, and 94 percent of prison inmates. They're three times as likely as women to be murdered, likely to live seven years less than women, and much more likely to die of alcoholism, heart attack, or suicide (Farrell 1993).

In fact men live in a more violent world than women. The more violent the crime, the more likely the victim is a man. Yet men aren't allowed to see themselves as victims. After all, collectively they hold the power in the United States. And if a man is Euro-American, his complicity in maintaining the patriarchy is even greater, for the simple reason that Euro-American men continue to dominate in business, government, and the professions.

Yet, because so many men feel personally powerless, some are threatened by feminism and resist changes designed to give women more collective power. Men also live with the knowledge that women are afraid of men. Decent, protective men still know that it's men who make it dangerous for women to walk city streets alone at night, men who rape and assault and beat them so that they are forever frightened. These are some of the contradictions that men must live with; there are many others.

Feeling Pressure to Perform and Pressure to Change

When men were asked "What are the biggest pressures on men today?" answers indicated that men are feeling much pressure these days, and it's coming at them from all directions. Traditional pressures remain: to succeed in careers, to provide for families, to be strong and courageous and protective. Men also seem to feel a great deal of pressure from women to change their ways, their very natures, and they don't fully understand what's expected of them. Many don't know how to be sensitive or vulnerable and still be the strong protector, the man in control. Adding to these pressures is their sense that it's becoming harder to make a good living, the planet is being destroyed, and politics is a mess.

When males were asked "Have men been helped or hurt by feminism?" the researchers got emphatic responses from both sides. The majority felt that feminism has generally helped both sexes by allowing us to see beyond traditional roles and stereotypes. About 25 percent were vehemently anti-feminist, blaming the movement for promoting anti-male and anti-family attitudes. Still others held that change is always a double-edged sword, and the full impact of feminism is yet to be felt.

When the researchers asked men, "What are the best and worst things about women?" replies focused on empathy, support, warmth, and nice bodies. But many revealed a deep hurt and resentment for the changing roles women have assumed. And for some, women's emotionalism is a drawback.

Unemployed men commit suicide at twice the rate of employed men. Among women, suicide has no correlation to employment status. Men's self-worth is more tied to their jobs. They often feel humiliated, violated, helpless, angry, and guilty over job loss. At all ages men's higher suicide rates are likely to be tied to lack of emotional support systems. Men often bond by giving each other criticism, women by giving each other support.

Being Groomed for Violence

Men are more likely to be subjected to violence throughout their lives. In fact, they're trained from childhood to endure and aspire to situations that include violence. Men's advocates suggest some ways in which we subject men to violence and reward them for being violent:

- unnecessary circumcision (without anesthesia) of baby boys
- violent sports (for school boys), such as football, hockey, and boxing
- approval by girls and parents when boys excel at violent sports
- government money to schools to support violent sports and military ROTC
- the draft of young men into military service
- entertainment dollars to adult males for violent activities such as rodeos, car racing, football, boxing, ice hockey, and violent films and television programs
- media glorification of men who use guns and easy access to guns in society

Historically, the "killer male" was essential to survival, marriage, and the family. In the future the communicative male will be essential. Men's movement author Walter Farrell says, "For the first time in human history, what it takes to survive as a species is compatible with what it takes to love." Some men's movement leaders say it's time for us to ask, How do we want our future to be and how do we adapt? All of us have the potential for killer-protector and for nurturer-connector. What will encourage males to develop the nurturer-connector within them? A good start is for each of us to notice when men and boys express nurturing-connecting attitudes, to openly appreciate men and boys who act in nurturing-connecting ways, and to reward them appropriately.

Experiencing Barren Father–Son Relationships

More and more men are becoming aware that the way they were raised affects their leadership style and therefore their careers, as well as every other aspect of their lives. For example, some men are beginning to talk about the lack of loving, touching, even liking in their experiences with their fathers.

Some express a very deep sadness and quite a bit of anger that their fathers had never told them that they loved them, were rarely around, and never hugged or kissed them, even when they were little kids. Along with feelings of emptiness and inadequacy because fathers didn't think their sons were "good enough" to justify their love, there was also a loss of role models: "These men just didn't know what men do. Sometimes they learned the most exaggerated male tendencies, such as adopting strict macho behavior. But they certainly didn't learn about father-child tenderness and love," says men's movement leader Bernie Zilbergeld (1993). The upside? These men want to avoid the same mistakes with their sons. They are trying to learn comfortable ways to express love to their own children. And they're becoming more appreciative of women's style of relating to others and its empowering aspects.

Being Denied Emotional Skills

When boy babies are born and for the first few months of life, they are more emotionally expressive than girl babies, according to Harvard Psychiatrist William Pollack (1998). But by the time they're 5 or 6, much of that expressiveness has been lost or repressed.

Male Behavior Models

As a result of cultural norms, boys quickly begin adopting one or more of the four basic male behavior models, according to researchers Deborah Davis and Robert Brannon (Pollack 1998).

1. *Sturdy Oak.* Boys who learn this mode believe they must:

   - be stoic and independent
   - never show weakness
   - don't share pain or grieve openly

As a result they're constantly acting, pretending to be confident even when they feel afraid, sturdy even when they feel shaky, independent even when they're desperate for love, attention, and support.

2. *Give 'Em Hell.* These boys believe they must:

   - be daring
   - show bravado
   - be a macho, high-energy superman
   - be violent in conquering foes

Their heroes are Sylvester Stallone, Jean-Claude Van Damme, Bruce Willis, and similar "action" or "adventure" stars. This mode relies on a false self based on the false belief that real men are biologically wired to act this way.

3. *The Big Wheel.* Boys who adhere to this mode believe they must:

   - achieve status and power
   - wear the mask of coolness
   - act as though all is under control, even if it isn't

As a result, many males push themselves too far in school, sports, or career, often to repress feelings of failure or unhappiness.

4. *No Sissy Stuff.* These boys believe they must:

   - never express feelings or urges that are "feminine"
   - never express dependence, warmth, empathy
   - ridicule and shame boys who do

As a result, these boys can't allow themselves to explore these emotional states and feel forced to shut them out. If they start to break under the strain, they'll probably be greeted with taunts, ridicule, and threats that shame them for not acting like a real man. This is probably the most traumatizing and dangerous model of all. It's a gender straitjacket that blocks males from exploring and expressing normal human feelings, those that are basic to people skills.

The one emotion that boys are allowed to express, even admired for expressing, is anger. This is the one emotion that girls are rejected for expressing. Parents are likely to speak more about sadness with daughters and more about anger with sons, according to the research of Professor Esther Grief of Boston University. As a result, boys feel encouraged to use their rage to express the full range of their emotional experience because they don't feel permission to express the other emotions.

Mother Love Myths

Researchers stress that mother love is essential for developing "real men" who are whole and mentally healthy. There are many myths around mothers doting on their sons.

Myth #1: Mother love makes boys weaker. Reality: It makes them stronger, emotionally and psychologically

Myth #2: Mother love makes boys dependent. Reality: The base of psychological safety it provides gives boys the courage to explore the outside world.

Myth #3: Mother love makes boys act in "girl-like" ways. Reality: It helps them develop their masculinity—the self-esteem and strength of character they need to feel confident in their own masculine selves.

Experts in this field recommend that parents openly express their love and empathy for boy children as well as girls. They can't get too much. Experts stress being there for children, taking time to give them undivided attention and listening fully. Parents could look behind a boy's anger, aggression, and rowdiness to see how he is indirectly asking for help. They can try to read between the lines and create a space where he can talk to them openly. Fathers and older males can create a model of masculinity for boys—a model that's broad and inclusive with a wide range of behaviors and emotional expression. Finally, parents and teachers can value boys as people, not as little men. Expose them to many types of activities and careers that men can choose.

Not Asking for Emotional Support

Father-son arm's-length relationships are just one aspect of the lack of emotional support men typically give and get from one another. Most lack the powerful tool most women use to heal women friends—emotional support for one another. For men, stress often builds, sometimes leading to depression and even suicide.

From adolescence to old age, men are more likely than women to commit suicide. During adolescence, boys' suicide rates go from slightly less than girls' to four times as great. Psychologists speculate that during puberty boys begin to feel intense pressure to perform, pursue, and pay—to be daring and take risks. Boys also sense it isn't acceptable to discuss fears, anxieties, and self-doubt. In 1970 young men aged 25 to 34 committed suicide at twice the rate of young women. In 1990 it was four times the rate. Young men's suicide rate increased 26 percent, while women's decreased 33 percent.

Men older than 65 are 14.5 times more likely to commit suicide directly. They're also more likely to skip needed medication and to get inadequate nutrition and thus die through self-neglect. A husband whose wife dies is about ten times more likely to commit suicide than a wife whose husband dies. Men tend to have fewer intimate friends and family than women, so for men, the loss of love is more devastating.

An Emerging Men's Movement

Many men are confused about what's expected of them now, where the boundary lines are drawn, and how they want to be in this new era. Strong women won't put up with a dominating, dictatorial, or brutal man—but they don't want a weak man either. Men's movement leaders are filling the void with ideas about what men need and with meetings to explore the meaning of being a man today. Most participants are heterosexual, middle-class, midlife Euro-American men (Harding 1992).

Robert Bly, a founder of the men's movement, says the women's movement has been wonderful because it speaks of the pain women feel. Men feel a different kind of pain that the men's movement speaks to. Bly (1992) doesn't want to bring back the patriarchy, but prefers a new society, where male-female status is more equitable rather than the "ruling father, subservient mother" hierarchy.

Long before the industrial revolution, fathers nurtured sons and taught them intimacy and emotional resilience through a community of tribal elders. When men began leaving home every day for the workplace, their sons lost this bonding. The price men have paid for running the country is to "stop feeling, stop talking, and continue swallowing our pain and our hurt and keep dying younger than we need to," according to Bly. He focuses on men's need for a father figure, especially during puberty. He speaks of the importance of male initiation rites, the warrior aspect of the male personality, and the wild man inside. Men must get in touch with their emotions, with how to express caring and nurturing, and with how to ask for it. Some methods of doing that include group processes, retreats, chanting, drumming, body work, and storytelling.

The men's movement is helping some men move into equitable male-female relationships by giving them permission to be vulnerable and intimate. Men who never learned to share their fear are allowed to do so. Talking about feelings is healing, and when the talk is heard compassionately, even more healing takes place. When men have their men's movement weekends to get in touch with the wild man and warrior parts of themselves, they acknowledge the past with its structure, discipline, and ritual that helped men overcome obstacles, protected women, and sustained human survival. The men's movement also helps men move on to the modern age. It encourages men to give themselves permission to ask, "Who do I really want to become? How do I want to get there?" By doing this, they can reach a deeper level of personal power (Keen 1991).

MEN'S RESPONSES TO CHANGES IN THE WORKPLACE

In the past it was extremely unlikely that a man would ever work under a woman manager or be expected to take equal responsibility with his wife for housework or child care—as many do today. On the other hand, men say they were and are expected to do the most dangerous jobs of the society.

Dealing with Women Managers

Recent surveys (*Working Woman*) have asked men what they thought of women managers. Here are some typical comments:

- They obsess on getting one small thing right, and it's blown out of proportion.
- Some are detail-oriented, not conceptual—no sense of corporate mission, the big picture.
- They're too sensitive, take things too personally.
- Some don't get down to business fast enough. First you have to spend time with them on a personal level.
- They're harder on other women. There's more pettiness or jealousy.
- When two women are at each other's throats, it ruins team spirit.
- When women bond together against men, it's demoralizing.
- Unmarried women bosses can make men nervous, especially if their work is their life, and they can work 14-hour days because they have no home life.
- They don't conceal anger or bitterness as well as men.
- We'd rather work for men. Getting a performance review from a woman is like being lectured by mother; it's very castrating.

Studies indicate that men in predominantly male workplaces are more loyal to their companies than men who work with lots of women. It's largely a matter of comfort. Men think they can be themselves around other men, so it's easier to bond. It's also a matter of status because men attach less prestige to professions that attract a large number of women. Men in traditionally male work environments, such as manufacturing plants, are more upset at the prospect of women invading their turf than are men in hospitals, where women have long been a presence (WSJ 1991).

Workplace changes tend to be more traumatic for men than for women because their sense of self-worth is more tied to their work. Changes such as downsizings and layoffs, and the resulting demands to do more work without added pay and the loss of job security add to a sense of powerlessness and betrayal. American men want to feel needed and useful, especially for qualities and abilities that are masculine in nature. They love joint efforts, especially with other men, that result in meaningful productivity. Quiet industry and caretaking are a part of the masculine ethos that baby boomers inherited from their fathers. But the sweeping changes of a global economy run by huge multinational corporations are undermining the sense of mastery, self-confidence, and control that is the other part of the masculine ethos (Faludi 1999).

Meeting Career Demands

A major source of male frustration, and for some resentment and envy, is that they are trapped in the provider role. A married woman with an employed husband has some choice about work—when, whether, and how much to work. If she has children, the family may need or want the money she can earn, but her decision to stay home with the children or to work part-time will normally be admired by friends and neighbors. It will almost never be considered lazy, selfish, or inappropriate. Men say they don't have that luxury.

When men are asked if they would like to take six-month paternity leave to be with their newborn child, nearly 80 percent say yes, if it wouldn't hurt the family economically and if their wife approved (Farrell 1993).

Men are more likely than women workers to agree to relocate to undesirable locations and to work less desirable hours. Full-time working men work 9 hours per week more in the workplace than full-time working women, but the women work about 17 hours per week more in the home. Therefore women typically work 8 hours more per week than men.

Doing the "Worst" Jobs

Of the 25 jobs rated worst in *The American Almanac of Jobs and Salaries* 24 are 95 to 100 percent male-occupied. Ratings are based on a combination of salary, stress, work environment, outlook, security, and physical demands. Worst jobs include truck driver, sheet-metal worker, roofer, boilermaker, lumberjack, carpenter, construction worker, football player, welder, coal miner, and ironworker. Men are expected to brave the hazards and do the dangerous, tough jobs.

- 94 percent of workers who die on the job are men.
- We have one job safety inspector for every 6 fish and game inspectors.
- Every workday hour a U.S. construction worker loses his life.
- Only men are subject to military draft and combat requirements

Holding the "Protector" Jobs

Men protect the innocent and helpless, women and children, and the ability to protect generates respect. But men must cope with the dark side of the world in order to protect, and the price is a loss of innocence.

Men suffer the price of war more than women. The aftermath of war is devastating. After World War I, it was called shell shock; after Vietnam, post-traumatic stress disorder. There's also chemical warfare aftermath, such as Agent Orange and the Gulf War Syndrome. Other results cited by men's movement author Walter Farrell are:

- More Vietnam veterans have committed suicide since the war ended than were killed in the Vietnam War itself.
- About 20 percent of all Vietnam veterans, and 60 percent of combat veterans, were psychiatric casualties.
- In 1978 more than 400,000 Vietnam veterans were either in prison, on parole, on probation, or awaiting trial.
- In 1990 more than 20,000 Vietnam veterans were homeless in Los Angeles alone.

In cultures where men must be protectors, weakness is ridiculed. Young boys search out those with weaknesses, taunting and picking on them. Valuing men as protectors gives us police brutality, the military mentality, and gangs (Farrell 1993).

Men are expected to repress their feelings. The most widely respected cancer research cited by the National Cancer Society finds that cancer is six times more likely to occur among people who repress their feelings than among cigarette smokers (Fischman 1988).

Needing Career–Family Balance

Most men feel a rising pressure to share housework and spend time with their children, since most mothers work outside the home. In 1998 nearly two-thirds of men surveyed said they want the freedom to join women in balancing work-family conflicts during the child-raising years. Men who were surveyed in 1990 reported twice as many work-family conflicts as in 1985. Conflicts include inability to find child care during overtime hours. But few men felt they could be honest with bosses about family demands and often made up excuses such as "other meetings to attend." The message such men want: that they won't be taken off the fast track or considered marginal just because they express work-family concerns and accept family-oriented benefits.

Men need flexibility about relocating, just as women do. The days may be over when companies can insist that moving up the ladder means moving around the country. In 1994 surveyed companies reported that 45 percent of employees turned down requests to relocate, citing family ties or spouse's employment as key reasons, up from 30 percent in 1986. Companies who are retaining good employees are adapting to their needs.

SEXUAL HARASSMENT: UNDERSTAND IT AND PREVENT IT

Before we discuss these aspects of sexual harassment, test your current viewpoint by completing Self-Awareness Activity 6.4.

Self-Awareness Activity 6.4: What Do You Know About Sexual Harassment?

Purpose: To see what you know about sexual harassment.
Instructions: Determine whether you think the following statements are basically true or false—and think about why. Answers are discussed in the following paragraph.

1. Sexual harassment is always about men harassing women.
2. When a manager has an affair with one of his employees, that's sexual harassment.
3. A group of men telling each other sexual jokes is not sexual harassment.
4. If both parties agree to have a sexual relationship, it's not sexual harassment.
5. Sexual harassment is just a misunderstanding about sexual attraction and flattery.

Wherever men and women work, there is a certain amount of sexual interaction on the job. When does it become harassment? When the behavior is unwanted, unsolicited, and nonreciprocal, when it asserts a person's sex role over her or his function as a worker, or when it creates an environment that seems hostile to the employee. Sexual harassment can be about anyone of any gender or sexual orientation harassing an employee. Sexual harassment is about misuse of power, not attraction and flattery.

The Equal Employment Opportunities Commission has identified two types of sexual harassment:

1. *quid prod quo*—"I'll give you job favors for sexual favors" or "I'll take away job favors unless you give me sexual favors."

2. *hostile environment*—sexuality is discussed, displayed, or used in a way that poisons the workplace for you—this can include workplace porn or a boss who has consensual sex with your co-worker, causing an unfair situation for you.

During the1990s, about 75 percent of court cases on sexual harassment were based on the hostile environment form alone, with only about 6 percent based on quid pro quo alone, and 19 percent based on both forms. Examples of sexual harassment from court cases include:

- physical contact such as patting, stroking, hugging, kissing
- comments on a woman's clothing, body, or appearance
- swearing, or "dirty" jokes, pinups, pictures, graffiti, and other visual depictions that are embarrassing or degrading to most women
- indirect harassment caused by being subjected to an environment where sexual harassment occurs even though you are not a target
- favoritism that constitutes a hostile environment; for example, when one employee submits to sexual favors and is rewarded while others who refuse are denied promotions or benefits

Courts have ruled that the standards of a reasonable woman (instead of the traditional "reasonable man") must be used to determine sexually offensive conduct in organizations, when the plaintiff is a woman. The Civil Rights Act of 1991 gives employees the right to jury trials and to limited punitive damages for sexual harassment—in addition to the reinstatement and back pay formerly provided. About 90 percent of sexual harassment complaints are filed by women, and in most cases the male harasser has power over the female harassee.

What Do We Need to Know about Sexual Harassment?

Sexual harassment is pervasive in the workplace. Most surveys indicate that more that half of women employees have experienced it. Sexual harassment is more about power, domination, and hostility than flirting or sexual attraction. A person who is attracted to you in a positive, respectful sense does not harass you.

Men and women view harassment differently. Men have traditionally thought that women who complain of men's sexual advances have somehow asked for it. They have attempted to label such women as a seductress, trouble-maker, bimbo, fantasizer, frustrated wallflower, or voluntary martyr, or nut case. Most women have some sense of the wide disparity between how men and women view sexual harassment and the stereotyped labels that may be pinned on them if they file a complaint. Understandably, most women have refused to file claims, believing that doing so would only make a bad situation worse.

Why Does Sexual Harassment Occur?

The most common causes of sexual harassment stem from people who:

- abuse power in trying to obtain sexual favors
- try to use sex to gain power

- use power to decrease the power of a victim by reference to her or his sexuality and gender identity
- are reacting to a personal crisis
- won't accept that an affair is over
- have a psychological or substance abuse disorder
- are confused about dealing with new gender roles in the workplace

Workplace attractions are certainly not unusual. In fact, a 2001 survey by Vault Inc. indicates that 44 percent of American workers say they've had an office romance and 78 percent think that dating co-workers is fair game. A key word here is "co-worker," meaning not your boss or someone who reports directly to you. That's because having workplace power over someone you are dating inevitably leads to harassment issues. Co-workers will suspect and resent the favoritism, the "reportee" may feel abused when the romance ends, etc.

How Do Men Feel about Sexual Harassment?

Most men feel confusion and concern over sexual harassment. They also object when they think women get away with flirting and men get punished for responding.

Confusion and Concern

Most men are confused about just where the behavioral boundaries are drawn now, and at a deeper level there is an anxiety about changing norms. Some men's movement leaders say the workplace is an easy extension of male adolescence, where boys win attention and other rewards for performing and pursuing. Many are confused by the sudden switch in rules, and some are concerned about the possibility of a woman with some ulterior motive falsely accusing them of sexual harassment.

Many men don't understand how their girlie calendars and pinups in the office constitute harassment. Some assume they merely make women feel inferior by comparison, and that's why they object to them. Women's advocates disagree, saying that pinups signal that sexiness is what counts in the workplace and everywhere else. Such symbols imply that women co-workers are viewed primarily as sex objects rather than fellow human beings and professionals.

The major concern men have is that women can now threaten men with a sexual harassment charge, and they could theoretically victimize men with false accusations of harassment. Companies can certainly set up procedures for investigating and handling sexual harassment complaints that would make it very difficult for men to be victimized and yet provide protection and fairness for women. Conservatives advocate throwing out sexual harassment laws. Liberals say that would be throwing out the baby (women's legitimate problems with men's sexual dominance) with the bath water (women's potential misuse of the laws).

Objections

Men's specific objections to sexual harassment policies include:

- Women still play their old sexual games, without being penalized.
- Women still buy the romance formula of the man pursuing and persisting, the women attracting and resisting, until the man overcomes her resistance.
- Women still send mixed messages, saying "no, no" when they mean "yes, yes" or "maybe."
- Women still dress and behave seductively in the office. Miniskirts, slit skirts, thin blouses, plunging necklines, heavy perfume, and flirting are all provocative. These traditional indirect female initiatives are signals to most men to take direct initiative.
- Sexual harassment laws often create a hostile environment for men, where the females are like children who must be protected by law.

Some men say that if women would communicate honestly and directly, there wouldn't be a problem. One said, "If a woman tells a man directly, with no mixed messages, that she thinks he's sexually harassing her, at least 99 percent of men will stop in that case." Actually, this is difficult for many women because they consider it direct confrontation, which they take great pains to avoid.

Men's advocates say that sexual harassment education needs to focus on the fact that for men to pursue and persist has been functional throughout history. Today, when we are struggling toward equality, it's no longer functional, at least in the workplace. Women need to understand that to attract and resist is natural because it's also been functional throughout history, but it is no longer functional in the workplace.

What Can Men Do to Avoid Problems?

Let's assume men are the ones who worry about being the harasser, although in a small percentage of cases women are the harassers. If you're a man, you can avoid being accused of sexual harassment by using these strategies.

- *Raise your awareness.* Sexual harassment is a rather complex issue, but you can learn enough to stay out of trouble.
- *Respect the word "No."* When you're at work, it's best to forget the old idea that a woman's "no" may not really mean "no" or that it merely makes the conquest more challenging and exciting.
- *Align your attitude.* Are you still harboring the belief that women are inferior? That men should be in control? If so, work on shifting your beliefs to align with current reality.
- *Support clear policies* and training that spell out what harassment is and how the organization will handle it. If you understand sexual harassment, and your company has clear policies about its definition and consequences, you can relax and be yourself (assuming your attitude is in line).
- *Be a role model.* Now that you're savvy about sexual harassment, help other men get it by treating coworkers with respect. For example, refer to women as women, not as "girls," "chicks," "ladies," or similar names. Don't participate in story-telling and jokes that demean women as a group. Let others know you don't want to hear or see women being referred to as sex objects.

What Can Women Do to Avoid Problems?

Women can help ease the situation by becoming aware of men's confusion and complaints and, through a greater awareness, sending clear, straight messages. Some specific recommendations for women are:

- *Avoid the sexual stereotype trap.* Women don't need to automatically and unthinkingly fall into others' expectations about their role. *Sex object* is one of the age-old stereotypes that women can avoid by dressing and acting in a businesslike, professional way. Check flirtatious or femme fatale tendencies at the office door.
- *Avoid sexual liaisons at work.* The objective of the office sex game is to increase the man's status with other men. This is one of the ways a man becomes "one of the boys" who make decisions about promotions and salaries. A woman may therefore increase the status of any man she has sex with and at the same time decrease her own status.
- *Say no tactfully but clearly.* Women can let men know if they don't like being called "honey," "babe," and similar names. Women can send I-messages when they say no to requests for a drink, lunch, dinner, or date: "I like you but I don't go out socially with business friends," "I like you but I never go out with married men," "I value our

relationship but my husband would be hurt if he couldn't share the occasion," "I like you but I'm not comfortable with going beyond a business relationship." The underlying message is you're not interested in sexual involvement and will always say no to such overtures.

What Can Organizations and Leaders Do?

As a leader, you can use your influence to ask that the organization's policies be designed to prevent most sexual harassment and effectively handle cases that do occur. Leaders must be sure that cases are handled professionally, so that everyone's rights are protected. Preventive actions include:

- Management establishes and publicizes a strong policy that specifically describes the kinds of actions that constitute sexual harassment and sets out the consequences for offenders.
- Management suggests that if a manager-subordinate relationship becomes "serious," one party should change jobs, out of fairness to other subordinates.
- Management regularly signals that it is committed to fighting harassment.
- The firm provides training seminars designed to sensitize employees to the issue.
- The firm sets up complaint procedures and mechanisms that encourage private complaints of harassment and that bypass immediate supervisors, who are often the source of the problem.

A 1998 survey of 900 companies indicated that complaints have dropped significantly in companies that take these actions.

What Should a Harassed Employee Do?

Let's pretend the recipient of the harassment is a woman, since that's the typical pattern. A woman in business cannot afford to allow any man to persist in actions that constitute sexual harassment. To do so would signal to other men that such behavior may be condoned and would set a poor example for the entire work team. A woman need not accept such a victim role. Here are some specific steps to take.

Be clear. Say no to overtures, tactfully but clearly. Mean it; give no mixed messages. Object to sexually inappropriate behavior, communication, or symbolism—again tactfully but clearly and directly.

Confront. If objectionable behavior continues, tell your harasser that this behavior must stop immediately. Follow up with a memo documenting what you said and hand it to him in the presence of a witness.

Document. Keep notes of what happened, when, and where. Note who, if anyone, witnessed it. Discuss the incident with any witnesses, to nail it down in their minds. Ask them to make a note about it, with a date.

Confide. If you wish to keep the matter officially confidential while you try to put a stop to the behavior, tell only trusted work associates. Ask them to keep brief notes. These people can later testify on your behalf.

Look for a pattern. Chances are very good that he has harassed other women. Seek out women who have worked with him. Engage in discreet, probing conversations to learn if they have been harassed. If you can establish that he has a pattern of harassment, your case is greatly strengthened.

Report. If the harassment continues, find out who you should report it to, often someone in the human resources department. If you need further emotional support and advice, look for a local women's organization that provides such services.

Consider alternative steps. If you don't like the way your organization handles your complaint, you can carry it further—to the EEOC or to court. Consider consulting an attorney who specializes in such cases. Local women's organizations and bar associations may recommend someone. Some courts have recently allowed class action suits where sexual harassment is common in an organization. Carefully weigh the pros and cons.

Be timely. Determine the statute of limitations for reporting sexual harassment in your state. In most states you must file a claim within six months of the last occurrence.

How Should Complaints Be Resolved?

Guidelines for resolving sexual harassment complaints include:

- Take sexual harassment complaints as seriously as other grievances; investigate them as thoroughly.
- Keep such matters entirely confidential.
- Find out what the complainant wants and try to accommodate her.
- Carefully investigate. Appoint an investigative team: one man, one woman, preferably objective outsiders. Look for documentation, witnesses, confidants, observers.

If the team cannot substantiate that sexual harassment has occurred (she says it did; he says it didn't), tell the complainant why the firm cannot take definitive action and to report any further occurrences or any instances of retaliation. Tell the accused: The organization had a duty to investigate; he is cleared; but if another complaint is filed, it will have more serious implications.

If the team substantiates that sexual harassment has occurred, use disciplinary procedures that are similar to those used in cases of nonperformance of job duties. Normally, the first offense calls for a warning and some sensitivity training. The second offense calls for some form of punishment: no bonus, no promotion, a demotion, docked pay, temporary suspension. The third offense calls for dismissal.

Insure that no one retaliates against the complainant, no matter what the outcome.

ASSERTIVENESS: IMPROVING MALE-FEMALE INTERACTIONS

Women often behave nonassertively and thus are viewed as weak or manipulative. Men often carry assertiveness too far and are seen as overbearing, demanding, or dominating. As a leader in a diverse workplace, you need to understand the basics of assertiveness. Relating to others assertively will improve your own people skills, and you can in turn help others to improve theirs. Women and minorities often need the encouragement to act assertively. Anyone who has been made relatively powerless in society tends to become passive. Making a habit of tactfully asserting yourself is one of the keys to preventing a buildup of frustration, resentment, and stress. It gives you more control over your life and builds self-esteem. Test your assertiveness knowledge by completing Self-Awareness Activity 6.5 now.

Self-Awareness Activity 6.5: What Do You Know about Assertiveness?

Purpose: To see what you know about assertiveness.
Instructions: Determine whether you think the following statements are basically true or false—and think about why. The answers are given in the paragraph that follows.

1. Assertion is getting your way.
2. Nonassertion is being willing to compromise.
3. Aggression is taking the initiative to get things done.
4. I-messages are self-centered messages that often violate others' rights.
5. Not asserting yourself is often desirable because it respects others' feelings.

First, we'll discuss brief definitions of assertion, nonassertion and aggression. Then we'll discuss them in more detail, with some examples.

Assertion is speaking up honestly and directly about what you think, feel, or believe, in ways that respect the rights and feeling of others. It's standing up for your rights, while being considerate of others' rights.

Nonassertion is not speaking up about what you think, feel, or believe, especially when your inaction bothers you when you later reflect upon it. It's allowing others to violate your rights, with no challenge from you. It's letting someone push you around, walk all over you, or not consider your feelings or rights—or to intimidate, demean, or devalue you.

Aggression is carrying assertion too far. It's going after what you want in ways that violate the rights of another— or expressing yourself in ways that intimidate, demean, or degrade another person. It's pushing other people around, using them as a doormat, or not considering their rights or feelings.

As you can see, all the statements made in Self-Awareness Activity 6.5 are essentially false (I-messages are discussed later).

Respecting Your Rights and Others' Rights

The key to assertion is being clear about your rights and then standing up for them. Since people's perceptions of who has what rights in a situation can vary, what happens when rights overlap? The assertive person is willing to listen, discuss the problem, and negotiate a solution that both parties can live with.

Your prime assertive right might be:
You have the right to judge your own behavior, thoughts, and emotions.
You have the right to decide whether and how to express yourself.
You have the responsibility to be totally accountable for the results of these actions.

What are some basic rights that you believe in and that most people in our culture believe in? The Bill of Rights is probably the best expression of our common beliefs about human rights. However, it was basically intended as a list of rights of Euro-American men. Women and minorities have had to fight to be included among the people entitled to these basic rights. What rights do women have that are often violated? Within organizations, managers have certain rights and employees have rights. Think of management and employee rights that you believe in. When you have clear, firm beliefs in the rights of individuals, you have the conviction to assert yourself when your rights are violated. You also have the basis for recognizing and respecting other people's rights.

For example, what do you do when another person tries to break in line in front of you? Do you automatically give way? Do you automatically resist? Or does it depend? Maybe the person previously waited in the line, had to leave for a moment, and just returned. Maybe he or she is in the midst of a minor crisis. Sometimes it's not clear who got there first or why the person is breaking in. Therefore, the two of you have different viewpoints about who is right, and your rights may overlap or be in conflict.

People who tend to be nonassertive rarely see situations as an issue of rights, and they don't know how to stand up for their rights anyway. They may have a compulsive need to "be nice," not cause a "scene," be a martyr, and their actions imply, "my rights, thoughts, or feelings aren't as important as yours." People who tend to be aggressive just want their own way and aren't about to be pushed around. They rarely think in terms of others' rights. Their actions imply, "my thoughts, feelings, and rights are more important than yours."

People who are assertive recognize their own rights and the rights of others and are willing to negotiate, and perhaps compromise, to settle situations where rights conflict or overlap. Such compromises respect the basic integrity of both people, and both get some of their wishes satisfied. This approach helps to avoid the temptation to use assertion to manipulate others in order to get what you want. It often leads to both people getting what they want because people are most likely to become cooperative when they're approached in a respectful way.

Being Assertive

You assert yourself when you stand up for your personal rights and express your thoughts, feelings, and beliefs in direct, honest, and appropriate ways. You do this in ways that don't manipulate, dominate, humiliate, or degrade the other person. Assertion is based on respect for yourself and respect for the other person. You express your preferences and defend your rights in ways that also respect other people's needs and rights. The goal of assertion is to get and give respect, to ask for fairness, and to leave room for compromise when your needs and rights conflict with another person's.

You can assert with empathy to soften the message. "Maybe you have a good reason for wanting to break in, but I was here first." You may need to assert with increasing firmness in those relatively rare cases when people ignore your assertive message. "I mentioned that I was here first. I must insist that you wait your turn." You can use I-messages that express your inner reality without judging, blaming, or interpreting someone else's behavior. Here are some examples of I-messages, in which you take responsibility for your thoughts and feelings. Compare them to the you-messages, which tend to blame and judge the other person.

I-Messages	You-Messages
I have sensitive hearing.	You talk too loudly.
I'm not comfortable talking about sex.	You have a dirty mouth.
I'd like to meet and make plans.	You shouldn't wait till the last minute.
I'd like to go over what we want to get done this week.	You need to manage your time better.
I'd like to prepare for the meeting.	You should send out an agenda.

Your nonverbal messages nearly always convey what you really feel or think. When you're not clear and honest in what you *say*, people receive a mixed message. For example, your voice tone, facial expression, and body language might say, "I'm upset," while your words say, "Oh, it's okay; I don't mind." When you are clear about your rights and say what you really think or feel, using I-messages and other effective assertion techniques, your verbal and nonverbal expressions are in harmony. Your message comes through confidently and congruently. You can be assertive in ways that actually build stronger relationships.

Being Nonassertive

When you don't express your honest feelings, thoughts, and beliefs, or when you express them in such an apologetic, unsure, or self-effacing way that others can easily disregard them, then you're allowing your rights to be violated by your nonassertiveness. By such actions you tell others: *You can take advantage of me. My feelings aren't very important; yours are. My thoughts aren't important; yours are the only ones really worth listening to. I'm nothing; you're superior.*

Nonassertion reflects a lack of respect for your own preferences. In an indirect way it reflects a lack of respect for the other person's ability to take disappointments, to assume some responsibility, or to handle problems. For example, a typical reason people give for not asserting themselves is, "I didn't want to hurt her feelings"—or embarrass him, or upset them. The goal of nonassertion is to please others and to avoid conflict at any cost. When you're being nonassertive, you're often being a victim.

Most experts believe that nonassertion is always accompanied by some degree of resentment that is experienced at some level, whether conscious or not. You resent situations where you don't assume control for your own experience. In other words, you resent your lack of self-control. You store these resentments, small or large, inside yourself. If you don't express them in some way, they build up and you become a pressure cooker of resentful energy. Then an unfortunate person comes along who hands you the final indignity, and you blow up, out of control for all to see. Your explosive reaction is probably as much a surprise to you as it is to others. When you begin to consistently assert yourself, you gain self-control.

Being Passive–Aggressive

Passive-aggressive behavior is a variation of nonassertion. For example, in organizations there are usually some people who smile and agree with the managers, but who undermine them in subtle or sneaky ways. They find ways to quietly sabotage a manager's efforts or projects, usually by not doing their part. They always have a good reason "why not," but meanwhile nothing got done. Passive-aggressive attitudes always result in some type of hostile action.

People who are consistently nonassertive may resort to passive-aggressive behavior because they won't want to face the consequences of speaking up. It may be their way of resisting someone whom they think is trying to dominate them. They may see themselves as the victim of a persecutor. Worst of all, they may secretly stew, fret, boil, or pout—all the while being "nice" and trying to hide their real feelings.

Being Aggressive

Being aggressive is going too far. It's standing up for your personal rights and expressing your thoughts and feelings in ways that belittle the other person or violate his or her rights. Such actions and words are usually inappropriate and often dishonest. Aggressive behavior carries such messages as: *This is what I think; you're stupid for thinking differently. This is what I want; what you want isn't important. Here's what I feel; I haven't considered your feelings.* The goal is getting your way, getting things done, prevailing, winning, or dominating—regardless of the effect on the other person. It's a winner-loser approach. You win by taking needed action without consideration of others, by overpowering, intimidating, belittling, degrading, or humiliating. The result is that other people find it difficult or impossible to express their preferences and defend their rights. You don't really like yourself when you act this way, consciously or not, and others resent it.

Complete Skill Builder 6.4 to test your understanding of assertiveness, nonassertiveness, and aggressiveness.

LEADERSHIP CHALLENGES: BREAKING THROUGH GENDER BARRIERS

Barriers to career success that are often related to gender issues include lack of career planning, pay inequity, glass ceiling issues, lack of proper training, communication blocks, unequal relationships, gender stereotyping, sexual harassment, and career-family conflicts. You can personally help to overcome these barriers by being aware, becoming a role model, and helping co-workers become aware. In the process you and your co-workers will be changing the corporate culture.

Challenge #1: Support Career Planning

Support women and men in developing and implementing their career plans by treating all as valued individuals. Don't assume women are not as career committed as men. Encourage people to answer these questions:

- What do you want from your career?
- What goals do you want to set?
- What contributions do you want to make?
- What events might limit your career efforts in the foreseeable future?
- What sort of work life-personal life balance do you want?
- What can the company do to help?

Career planning may be blocked by self-limiting beliefs. Encourage people, especially women, to overcome self-limiting cultural beliefs. Suggest alternative self-empowering beliefs.

Challenge #2: End Pay Inequity

Pay inequity is endemic in our workforce, a huge problem that no leader could solve alone. However, you can become aware of the ways women have been discriminated against when it comes to pay. You can analyze the compensation packages of all the employees under your influence. And you can use your influence to eliminate inequities and to make sure that women and men receive fair compensation.

Challenge #3: Break the Glass Ceiling

Do your share to end or overcome all the ways—including those many small, hidden, or subtle ways—that the company discriminates against women.

Challenge #4: Give Training

Women need training geared to their particular needs. They may need encouragement to acquire math, computer, technological, and other typically male skills the firm needs. Some women thrive best in all-women classes. Studies indicate that women achieve higher levels of mastery when they take such classes without men around. Women often don't get equal opportunities to attend higher-level management training programs that prepare managers for promotion.

Men need training in people skills and in those aspects of management style that studies indicate need improvement, such as enthusiasm, communication, and feedback.

Challenge #5: Bridge the Communication Gap

Recognize the different ways women and men view the world and communicate about it. Use your knowledge to bridge the gaps. Recognize when a misunderstanding or a miscommunication is rooted in an assertiveness problem. Help to understand and resolve such problems. Relate to others in an assertive manner yourself and teach this approach to others.

Challenge #6: Value Equal Relationships

As a role model and coach you can help men understand the dramatic shifts in male-female relationships at work and at home. Help them to see the advantages of equality in relationships; for example:

- *Shared responsibility,* resulting in less stress for men because they now have help in making the decisions, earning the family income, and other responsibilities that can become burdensome and stressful.

- *More authentic communication* is a natural result of equality in relationships, as Madelyn Burley-Allen's research on assertiveness training indicates.

- *Better relationships with women* can be built as aggressive tactics are replaced with assertive ones, since women are less likely to resort to passive-aggressive responses.

- *More freedom* to develop and express all facets of the self grows from going beyond the limited confines of stereotyped gender traits and roles.

Challenge #7: End Gender Stereotypes

Many men feel a loss of power, are concerned about reverse discrimination, and express difficulties in accepting a woman as their manager. Help men and women drop the old role stereotypes about men's place and women's place. Take the lead in raising awareness of how such stereotypes limit men and unfairly block women. Speak up when you see people acting out the old myths and assumptions about men's and women's traits, their "place," and their limitations.

Challenge #8: Stop Sexual Harassment

Support clear, effective company policies regarding sexual harassment. Make sure that everyone on your team understands the issues and the policies. Be a role model in the way you treat people. If complaints occur, resolve them fairly, and firmly.

Challenge #9: Resolve Conflicts in Career and Family Demands

The core gender issues, both social and professional, can only be addressed when women and men explore and create a partnership where professional and social relationships are managed out of respect for individual talents and needs and aligned with a common vision that includes more than profit making. Such a partnership balances care-taking and bread-winning and views social, emotional, and spiritual needs on a par with economic responsibility. Key areas that we can bring into balance in organizations include:

- men and women having the freedom to strike a balance between work and home
- an ability to move beyond woman as sex object and man as success object
- a balance of men and women taking paternity leaves and maternity leaves without the company stigmatizing them
- organizations that provide more flexible systems and benefits for both men and women, without stigmatizing those who take advantage of them

Most companies must make significant changes to provide the type of flexibility dual career families need. For example, in 1990 only 10 percent of firms with 10 or more employees provided such direct benefits as day care or financial assistance with child care.

LEADERSHIP OPPORTUNITIES: PROMOTING GENDER EQUITY IN THE CORPORATE CULTURE

The differences in worldviews of men and women suggest some possible difficulties for women in most organizations. They are likely to feel pressured to change their work style and leadership style and to experience conflict between leadership and gender roles. If they do become more directive, they are more likely than men to receive negative reactions. Actually, a variety of styles can be effective if the corporate culture values and embraces gender differences.

You can recognize ways in which the corporate culture fails to reflect women's values as well as men's. Help to resolve conflicts and disadvantages this poses for women and to start changing the culture accordingly.

Opportunity #1: Value Gender Differences

For many years women minimized their differences from men and stressed equality, in order to show that they could work as effectively as men and deserve equal treatment and rewards. The men who supported them tried not to notice this most noticeable of differences. Admitting one's differences in the American workplace has traditionally meant accepting inferiority. That's because we tend to jump to the conclusion that differences are either good or bad, rather than a source of interesting possibilities. Those who are different are commonly relegated to the edge of a work group. They may be devalued personally and their contributions ignored.

Opportunity #2: Value Female and Male Traits and Skills

Today's organizations, and those of the future, need a different mix of values, not only because women are present in larger numbers, but because of the ways work itself is changing in the age of the smart machine. Jobs require less muscle and motor skills and more information and people skills. While women continue to acquire many traditional male workplace skills, men must also now master things women have been taught to do well. What these are becomes clearer when we look at organizations run largely by women.

Opportunity #3: Value Female and Male Beliefs and Customs

When women create their own corporate cultures by starting their own companies, researcher J.B. Rosener found that the style that emerges is more democratic and less hierarchical, reflecting these beliefs and customs:

- the basic belief that allowing everyone to contribute and to feel powerful and important is good for employees and the organization
- the tendency to share power and information
- more emphasis on collaborative decision making
- more democratic, participative, consultative management
- more decentralization of decision making and responsibility
- greater concern with process and fairness
- more concern with quality of outcomes, while retaining a pragmatic concern for quantitative outcomes
- less autocratic, domineering, ego-involved management
- less concern with titles and formal authority, more concern with responsibility and responsiveness
- less concern for empire building, power and domination and less consciousness about one's turf

Opportunity #4: Value Female and Male Leadership Styles

Typical male leadership styles have stressed tasks and achievements first. Women's leadership style focuses on people first, tasks second and so is more indirect. Rosener's studies show women leaders achieve higher quality and productivity through these strategies:

- a greater responsiveness and concern for individual feelings, ideas, opinions, ambitions, and on- and off-the-job satisfactions
- skill at enhancing other people's self-worth
- desire to get others excited about their work
- more emphasis on skills as a listener and conversationalist
- high value placed on loyalty, longevity, and interpersonal skills

This represents a balance of masculine and feminine strengths, which would work nicely in today's workplace.

The Bottom Line

Women and men need to work in holistic, balanced organizations that reflect the values and customs of both genders. Such organizations allow and encourage people to develop more of their talents and potentials and to use those talents to achieve personal and team goals.

SUMMARY

Women and men have traditionally been limited by stereotyped roles and traits that culture imposes upon them. In our patriarchal system, babies learn from the cradle that people have unequal power and privilege. However, marriage and family relationships are now moving toward greater equality. The cultural socialization of girls and boys has traditionally been distinctly different, so they grow into men and women who often have difficulty understanding each other's worlds and viewpoints. Research indicates that women tend to be more tentative, relationship oriented, and cooperative, while men tend to be more assertive, factual, competitive, and status oriented. Women managers generally have better people skills, while male managers have better traditional business skills. Women's leadership style is more enthusiastic, communicative and production-oriented, while men's is more conservative, yet innovative and strategic.

Since the 1960s a number of megatrends have resulted in major changes in women's roles. Most women now need to work, and they have greater opportunities in the workplace. Women now hold about 40 percent of management positions but less than 5 percent of top executive posts. Their pay at all levels tends to be about 25 percent less than men's pay. Women's major barriers are the external ones in the workplace, especially stereotyping and lack of support for their family demands. Some of the barriers are internal self-limiting beliefs they learn from the culture.

Many men are having difficulty adjusting to the major changes in virtually every area of their lives, from wives to children to work. Nearly half think they're losing power as a group. Many are no longer sure what "real men" are expected to do, nor what constitutes sexual harassment. Both men and women may experience a buildup of frustration from the pressures, demands, and uncertainties. A positive way to deal with all this is to develop both masculine and feminine strengths in order to become a more balanced person. Another strategy is to learn to interact with each other assertively, without being overly aggressive. Leaders can encourage men and women employees to achieve this balance and to move into an attitude of equality. As this occurs, a new holistic corporate culture can emerge, and in turn a better balanced society. Leaders can also focus on supporting men in adapting to gender changes in the workplace, supporting women in breaking stereotyped molds and achieving career success, and providing both with support to meet emerging family demands.

Skill Builder 6.1: The Case of New Mother Jessica

Jessica is the mother of an 18-month-old child. She is a loan officer with Trust Bank. Jessica had resigned from her previous job because the maternity leave was inadequate for her to make the adjustment to a new baby. When she went to work for Trust Bank, it was with the understanding that it would not be a high-pressure position—no expectation that she would work overtime or make business trips. However, Jessica is beginning to feel pressure to do just that.

Jessica approaches you, her manager, to tell you that she has decided she must resign in order to find a part-time job, about three days a week. She says, "My son needs more of my time and attention just now. I need to work, and I want to work, but I have decided to give his needs top priority for the next year or two."

- As Jessica's manager, what should you do?

Skill Builder 6.2: Alicia Ruiz, Legal Assistant

Alicia Ruiz has been employed at Appleby Associates law firm for nearly a year. She's just been promoted from secretarial assistant to legal research assistant, and she loves her work. She gets along well with the lawyers and other assistants. The only ongoing problem she must cope with is her relationship with *Jake Barnes*, one of the law partners. Lately it's been pretty rough. Jake manages to find more and more opportunities to catch her alone and lean on her—at the water fountain, in the coffee room, and, worst of all, at the elevator in the evening. A couple of times

Jake has really given Alicia a hard time, insisting that she come with him for a drink at the bar around the corner.

As a full partner, Jake is one of the most powerful men in the office, and Alicia doesn't want to turn him against her. Her way of dealing with it lately is to ask her friend *Joe* to wait for her so they can leave together, since they park in the same parking garage. She hopes that if she can avoid Jake for long enough, he'll give up.

Alicia's managing attorney, **Dale Hutchison**, is looking for a file of legal papers and remembers that he gave the file to Alicia. It's urgent that he get some information from the file at once, and Alicia's out of the office. Dale goes to her desk and finds the file on top. He can't avoid seeing a note that Alicia has written on the top sheet of her notepad: *Hi, Could you wait for me again this evening? I'll leave at 5 and just take the work home with me. I don't want "you-know-who" to catch me alone again. Yesterday when I was in the research library, he closed the door and started making disgusting remarks about "heaven between the sheets." Yuk!*

Dale is stunned. Who can Alicia be talking about? And why hasn't she told him she's having a problem with one of the guys? Back in his office, he can't get the incident off his mind. About 30 minutes later he arrives for a previously-scheduled meeting with one of the partners, **Tom Drake**. Since Dale is the first to arrive, he takes the opportunity to discuss the incident with Tom. They both agree that Alicia must file an internal complaint against her harasser.

Later that day, Dale finds time to speak privately with Alicia. "I don't mean to pry, Alicia, but when I was looking for the file on your desk, your note about being harassed was just there. The words just jumped out at me. You know, you don't have to put up with this kind of harassment—and you shouldn't. I'm just so sorry this is happening to you. Tom and I think you should file an internal complaint." Alicia is upset and angry. "Dale, you had no right to discuss this with management, especially without talking to me first. I don't want to bring a complaint. All I would do is make an enemy. It would be his word against mine, and I know who has the power around here!" She stopped, sorry that she had said as much as she had.

"Look, I'll stand behind you. You need to take action to stop this problem."

"I won't have my privacy invaded," said Alicia, "and that's that."

"But the company has to maintain an office that's free of sexual harassment, and as your manager, I'm supposed to report this. It's company policy."

"And I have too much at stake," said Alicia. "I like my job and I want to keep it. Stay out of it, Dale. Let me take care of it."

- What are the major issues here?
- What should Dale do?
- What should Alicia do?

Skill Builder 6.3: Support Networks

Note: Contributed by Scott Stoddard, San Francisco State University

Scott is a manager with Siebert, Inc. He's been with the company for eight years and has been happy with the firm's diversity initiatives, supporting them completely. One of the diversity initiatives is to encourage company support networks for specific diverse groups. So far four successful support networks have emerged: Women's Support Network, African American Support Network, Gay and Lesbian Support Network, and Filipino American Support Network. Siebert Inc. proudly sponsors events that these networks organize, allows members to meet twice a month on company time, and encourages the networks to share their concerns and new ideas with management.

During the past few months several Euro-American male employees have approached Scott asking for permission to start a Euro-American Male Support Network. Membership in this new network would be limited to Euro-American men.

What are the key issues?

If you were Scott, what would you do?

Skill Builder 6.4: Minicases: Is This Sexual Harassment?

Do you think the actions in these four cases constitute sexual harassment? If so, what would you recommend to each party involved?

1. **A male supervisor** occasionally compliments his young assistant with remarks such as "You ought to wear short skirts more often" and "Sit and talk to me a little longer; I'm enjoying the view."

2. **A female doctor** is discharged from a medical residency program. She tries to understand what went wrong. She remembers that she did not react favorably to a supervising professor's invitation to go out for drinks, compliments about her hair and legs, questions about her romantic life. He made comments that seemed to imply that he'd like to help her get through the program, but she sensed that going out with him would be part of the relationship. At first she tried to smile her way through these incidents. Later she gave disapproving looks or turned away. When he kept on, she finally told him one day that she was busy and abruptly walked away.

3. **A male journalist** willingly enters into a love affair with his female supervising editor. She has always rated his work performance as excellent. After a few months he breaks off the affair. At his next performance review, the journalist receives a less-than-satisfactory rating from her.

4. **Rosita, an advertising copy writer,** has been passed over for promotion. A colleague, Hazel, got the job. Rosita is sure Hazel is having an affair with the boss. Several times in the past year, the boss has gone on business trips which called for a copy writer to go along. Each time he took Hazel instead of Rosita, even though in at least one instance Rosita was the one who had done most of the work on the account he was calling on. Rosita has heard talk from other employees. Rumor has it this is not the first affair the boss has had, nor the first time he has promoted a girl friend.

Skill Builder 6.5: Recognizing Assertiveness

Purpose: To apply your knowledge of assertiveness training.
Instructions: Indicate whether you think each response to each of the following situations is assertive, aggressive, or nonassertive.

1. At a meeting, someone interrupts when you're speaking. You say,

    a. Excuse me. I'd like to finish my statement.

    b. Oh, excuse me.

    c. You know, it's rude to interrupt like that.

2. You enjoyed a coworker's presentation. You say,

    a. See you back at the salt mine.

    b. Thanks for your presentation; it gave me a lot of new ideas.

    c. Well, *that's* over!

3. Your women's advocacy group has been trying to get better maternity benefits. A coworker says, " What do you women want anyway?" You answer,

    a. To put chauvinists like you in their place.

    b. I don't get involved in these things.

    c. Fairness and equality.

4. You've been called several times by the same salesperson trying to sell you magazines. This time you say

   a. Would you please not call me again?

   b. You're a disgusting jackass. Why don't you take a flying leap.

   c. This is the third time I've been disturbed, and each time I've told you that I'm not interested. If you call again, you leave me no choice but to report this to the authorities.

5. Asking your boss for a raise, you begin,

   a. Aaah, do you think that you could see your way clear to giving me a raise?

   b. I've been overworked around here for too long, and I'm overdue for a raise.

   c. I'd like to go over this list of extra projects I've completed and work I've reorganized to produce more with less time and money . . . .

REFERENCES

AAUW. *The AAUW Report: How Schools Shortchange Girls*. Washington DC: American Association of University Women, 1992.

Allport, G.W. *The Nature of Prejudice*. Boston: Addison-Wesley, 1954.

Adler, Nancy, and D.N. Izraeli, eds. *Women in Management Worldwide*, Armonk, NY: M.E. Sharpe, Inc, 1988.

Ballentine, Susan and Jessica Inclan. *Diverse Voices of Women*. Mountain View CA: Mayfield, 1995.

Blinder, Martin. *Choosing Lovers*, New York: Avon, 1987.

Bly, Robert. *Iron John: A Book About Men*. New York: Random House, 1992.

Burley-Allen, Madelyn. *Managing Assertively*, 2d ed. New York: John Wiley & Sons, Inc., 1995.

Carr-Ruffino, Norma. *The Promotable Woman*. Franklin Lakes, NJ: Career Press, 1997.

Carr-Ruffino, Norma. "U.S. Women: Breaking Through the Glass Ceiling." *Women in Management Review* 6, 5, 1991.

Carroll, Jerry. "The Secrets of Young Girls." *San Francisco Chronicle*, August 31, 1994, E-1.

Cherry, Robert. *Discrimination: Its Economic Impact on Blacks, Women, and Jews*. Lexington MA: Lexington Books, 1989.

Chin, Steven. "50,000 at Oakland Rally Just for Men," *San Francisco Chronicle*, October 1, 1995.

Crane, F.G. and Susan DeYoung. "Attitudes to Portrayal of Women in Advertising." *International Journal of Advertising*, 1992, 251.

Dominick, Joseph, and Gail Rauch. "The Image of Women in Network TV Commercials." *Journal of Broadcasting*, Summer 1972, 259.

Eagly, Alice H. *Sex Differences in Social Behavior*. Hillsdale, NJ: Lawrence Erlbaum Associates, 1987.

Eisen, Jerry. *Powertalk!* New York: Simon & Schuster, 1984.

Evatt, Chris. *He & She*. Berkeley, CA: Conari Press, 1992.

Faludi, Susan. *Backlash: The Undeclared War Against American Women*, New York: Crown, 1991.

Faludi, Susan. *Stiffed: The Betrayal of the American Man*. New York: Wm. Morrow, 1999.

Farrell, Walter. *The Myth of Male Power*. New York: Simon & Schuster, 1993.

Fausto-Sterling, Anne. *Myths of Gender*. New York: Basic Books, 1985.

Female Executive. Report on sexual harassment survey, 1992.

Ferguson, Andrew. "America's New Man," *The American Spectator*, January, 1992, 26-33.

Fischman, J. "The Character of Controversy," *Psychology Today*, December, 1988.

Gates, David. "White Male Paranoia." *Newsweek*, March 29, 1993, 48-54.

Gove, Walter R. *A Biopsychosocial Perspective*. Vanderbilt University, 1985.

Hamilton, A. and P.A. Veglahn. "Sexual Harassment: The Hostile Work Environment." *Cornell HRA Quarterly*, 33, 1992, 88-92.

Howard, J., P. Blumstein, and Pepper Schwartz. "Sex, Power, and Influence Tactics in Intimate Relationships." *Journal of Personality and Social Psychology*, 51, July, 1986, 102-109.

Jacobs, M.A. "Men's Club." *Wall Street Journal*, June 9, 1994, A-1.

Kabacoss, Robert I., "Gender Differences in Organizational Leadership: A Large Sample Study," American Psychological Association Annual Convention, San Francisco, CA, August 1998.

Kanter, R.M. *Men and Women of the Corporation*. New York: Basic Books, 1979.

Keen, Sam. *Fire in the Belly*. New York: Bantam Books, 1991.

L.A. Times. "Orange Juice War Against Bad Ideas." *Los Angeles Times*, August 14, 1994, M-5.

Lester, Joan S. *The Future of White Men*. Berkeley CA: Conari Press, 1994.

Morrison, Ann, R.P. White, and E. Van Velsor. *Breaking the Glass Ceiling*. Reading, MA: Addison-Wesley, 1987.

Naisbett, John, and P. Aburdene. *Megatrends 2000*. New York: Wm. Morrow, 1990.

Naisbett, John. *Megatrends*. New York: Warner Books, 1982.

Orenstein, Peggy. *Schoolgirls: Young women, self-esteem, and the confidence gap*. New York: Doubleday, 1994.

"Patriarchy: What Is It?" *Men's Council Journal*, special issue, May 1993, 17.

Peplau, L.A. "Lesbian and Gay Relationships" in *Homosexuality: Research Implications for Public Policy*. ed. J. C. Gonsiorek and J. D. Weinrich. Thousand Oaks, CA: Sage, 1991.

Pollack, William. *Real Boys*. New York: Random House Inc. 1998. Wm. Pollack, Ph.D, is Clinical Professor of Psychiatry, Harvard Medical School, clinical psychologist, and co-director of Center for Men, McLean Hospital, Harvard Medical School,

Rosener, J.B., "Ways Women Lead," *Harvard Business Review*, November-December, 1990, 199-225.

Rossman, Marlene L. *The International Businesswoman of the 1990s*. Westport, CT: Greenwood Press, 1990.

Russell, A. M. "Women Vs. Men: Where We Stand Today," *Working Woman*, January, 1991, 66.

Speer, Robert. "What's New with Men?" *Chico News & Review*, April 16, 1993.

Tannen, Deborah. *You Just Don't Understand*. New York: Wm. Morrow, 1990.

Tanner, M. Scot. Expert on Chinese politics in *Business Week*, 1994.

Time. "Indecent Exposure: The Navy Takes a Heavy Rap in the Tailhook Report on Sexual Harassment." *Time*, 141, May 3, 1993, 20-21.

Trost, C., "Firms Heed Women Employees' Needs, *Wall Street Journal*, November 22, 1990, B-1

U.S. Census Bureau. "We the American Women." U.S. Department of Commerce, 1993.

U.S. Census Bureau. " Current Population Reports, Male-Female Differences." Department of Commerce, 1987.

U.S. Census Bureau. "Current Population Reports, Average Earnings of Year-Round Fulltime Workers by Sex and Educational Attainment." Department of Commerce, 1991.

U.S. Women's Bureau, Department of Labor. "Facts on Working Women." 1990, 1992, 1993, 1998.

U.S. Glass Ceiling Commission. *The Glass Ceiling Initiative*. Department of Labor, 1991.

U.S. Glass Ceiling Commission. *Better for Business*, Department of Labor, 1995.

Vanneman, Reeve, and Lynn Weber Cannon. *The American Perception of Class*. Philadelphia: Temple University Press, 1987.

Wilson, William Julius. *The Declining Significance of Race*. Chicago: University of Chicago Press, 1978.

Wilson, William Julius. *The Truly Disadvantaged*. Chicago: University of Chicago Press, 1987.

Working Mother, "100 Best Companies for Working Mothers," October 1999 (see www.workingmother. com)

Working Woman, "How the Men in Your Office Really See You," November 1991,101-103.

WSJ. Report on how men are dealing with women managers, *Wall Street Journal, 1991*.

Zilbergeld, Bernie. Statement by Berkeley psychologist, expert on men's groups, in interview, April 6, 1993.

CHAPTER 7

Working with African Americans

*Negroes not only raised doubts about the white man's value system
but aroused the troubling suspicion that whatever else the true
American is, he is also somehow black.*
Ralph Ellison

About 12 percent of the people in the American workplace are African Americans, which accounts for about one in eight employees. People who have taken the time and effort to learn about the African American community and its values and customs, say they've boosted their ability to work productively with African Americans. Those who belong to the African American culture say studying it has helped them to better understand their own heritage and their strengths.

It's important in today's workplace to develop the level of understanding needed to build good relationships when associates are from another culture whether you are a new entry-level employee or a top executive. A major key is to learn about an associate's culture and get a feel for his or her background. The more skilled you become at interpreting an individual's actions against the backdrop of his or her culture, the greater success both of you can achieve through working together.

The African American community is made up of many elements, and of course no one person expresses all the values and customs discussed here. You may be tempted to use this cultural information to form new rigid categories. To be fair, stay open and flexible as you interact with individual African Americans. Deal with the unique individual, bringing into play your understanding of his or her cultural background.

You're about to get a little taste of what it's like to be an African American in the American society and workplace and how this experience can affect interactions in the workplace. Specifically, you'll learn about these issues:

- How typical stereotypes and myths about African Americans compare with reality
- How the current situation is connected to certain historical events
- Key cultural values and customs that are important to people in this community
- Barriers to career success for African Americans and how to break through these barriers, a leadership challenge

- Assets African Americans may bring to your company and how to use those assets to create win-win successes, a leadership opportunity

First, check your attitudes and knowledge by completing Self-Awareness Activities 7.1 and 7.2.

Self-Awareness Activity 7.1: What Do You Believe about African Americans?

Purpose:

- to get in touch with your beliefs and stereotypes about this group of people
- to experience how judgmental beliefs affect your thinking and feeling processes
- to experience the ways in which your beliefs create your reality regarding other persons, even before you have any interaction with them

Part I. What Do You Believe about African American Women?

Step 1. Associations

- Relax as deeply as you can: close your eyes and take a few deep breaths.
- Focus on the words "African American woman" and allow a mental picture to come up in your mind's eye. Imagine that you are this woman. Be African American woman.
- Notice your resistances to being this person, and your willingness.
- Notice the words and images that come to mind as you "see" this woman.
- Open your eyes and list 10 to 20 words in the order in which they occur to you.
- Review your list. Mark a plus beside the words that are positive, a minus beside the words that are negative, and a circle beside neutral words.

Step 2. Negative Associations

- Close your eyes and focus again on the image of the African American woman. Formulate a negative opinion or judgment, perhaps one you typically hold about African American women.
- Notice your *feelings* as you see the person in this negative way. What *thoughts* come up as you focus on the image?
- Write a few sentences about your feelings and thoughts.

Step 3. Positive Associations

- Formulate a positive opinion or judgment, perhaps one you typically hold about African American women.
- Notice your *feelings* as you see the person in this positive way. What *thoughts* come up as you focus on the image?
- Write a few sentences about your feelings and thoughts.

Step 4. Insights

- Focus on the differences between your experiences when you hold negative and positive judgments or opinions. What were the differences? What meaning does this have for you, for your beliefs and feelings about people from this group, and about beliefs in general?
- Write your responses in a few sentences; include anything you like about your feelings, thoughts, and insights.

Part II. Experimenting with Opinions about African American Men

Repeat the phases and steps in part I, this time focusing on the image of an African American man.

Self-Awareness Activity 7.2: What Do You Know about African Americans?

Purpose: To see what you know about the issues covered in this chapter.

Instructions: Determine whether you think the following statements are basically true or false—and why. The answers will emerge in this chapter, and the summary at the end of the chapter focuses on these issues.

1.   The Civil Rights Act of 1964 was a result of liberal Democrats' demands, led by Kennedy and Johnson.

2.   Since the civil rights measures have been in force, African Americans have dramatically increased their status.

3.   The best predictor of both school grades and SAT scores is ethnicity.

4.   Significant numbers of African American managers and professionals are leaving corporate jobs due to the glass ceiling that prevents their advancement.

5.   African Americans focus primarily on group expression rather than individual expression.

6.   African American communication style tends to be more impersonal and cool than Euro-American style.

7.   Most African Americans need assertiveness training to be most effective in American corporate cultures.

STEREOTYPES AND REALITIES

Most of the stereotypes that African Americans must deal with stem from the legacy of slavery and segregation that is unique to this American subculture. In order to justify slavery, a practice so incompatible with the American ideals of human freedom and equality, some Euro-Americans created degrading stereotypes of Africans. Such beliefs are passed along from generation to generation and die hard.

Although the proportion of Euro-Americans that hold the more extreme stereotypes is continually declining, responses to a recent survey indicate the following beliefs are still prevalent (Thornton and Whitman 1992):

1.   Are Blacks more violent than Whites? Yes, 63 percent

2.   Are they less intelligent? Yes, 53 percent

3.   Are they more likely to prefer to live off welfare? Yes, 78 percent

4.   Do they blame everyone, but themselves for their problems? Yes, 57 percent

5.   Do they tend to be resentful troublemakers? Yes, 51 percent

Bottom line: We have some work to do on changing these beliefs and attitudes.

Stereotypes are rigid, exaggerated, irrational beliefs, each associated with a mental category, such as a particular group of people. Although stereotypes aren't identical to prejudice, rigid stereotypes about people usually lead to prejudice. For example, in the past perhaps a Euro-American observed an abused slave whose rage finally consumed him and who lashed out violently. The Euro-American began saying to others, "African American men are violent." This became a convenient stereotype, a good excuse for keeping African American men under tight rein. Euro-Americans who accepted the violent stereotype didn't notice that most African American men were not violent, even when degraded and abused. But they noted every time one was violent, and each incident confirmed their belief. This is how stereotyping works.

Most Euro-Americans believe that blatant discrimination against African Americans is a thing of the past. But African American leaders consider racial profiling by police a major issue. And within the last few years, many major organizations were found guilty of blatant discrimination, including Texaco, Denny's, American Airlines, Coca Cola, United Parcel Service, Circuit City, Avis, and the U.S. Department of Agriculture.

To get to know what it's like to be an African American, you must understand the stereotypes they deal with every time they leave the family or community circle, or turn on the television, for that matter. To bridge the divisive walls these stereotypes hold in place, you must know what they are, know other realities that balance or refute them, and move beyond myths to a more realistic view of the African American community. The goal here is to appreciate each cultural group's unique value and to strengthen our unity as one culture.

Stereotype #1: African Americans are more violent than others.

A cultural custom that may perpetuate this stereotype is African Americans' preference for using direct confrontation to resolve a conflict. Most Euro-Americans, Asian Americans and Latino Americans prefer more indirect methods. African American behavior is therefore often seen as hostile and militant when it's not. This is reinforced by—and reinforces—the stereotype of African Americans as prone to violence (Foeman and Pressley 1987; Kitano 1976; Hall 1976).

The reality is that certain behavior that is considered assertive and truthful by African Americans is often interpreted by others as anger or rage about to erupt into violence. What feeds this interpretation is:

- cultural differences about how to express concerns and emotions
- the "violent" stereotype itself. We see what we expect to see and ignore actions that don't fit our stereotypes.

While we can prove that African American men have higher criminal arrest and conviction rates, we cannot prove that they are more violent. For one thing, violence is a subjective term. For another many studies indicate that African American men are more likely than others to be arrested and convicted for the same type of activity, according to Marc Mauer's research (1989).

Mauer also concluded that the United States is one of the more violent cultures of the world. More productive that using African Americans as the scapegoats who create violence in society would be addressing violence in the media and society at large.

Stereotype #2: African Americans are less intelligent than others.

In the workplace and elsewhere, Euro-Americans tend to assume that even highly intelligent African Americans are less competent. Some studies indicate that when it comes to Euro-American men helping each other, the other man's *ability* is the determining factor, not the fact that the man is Euro-American. But when it comes to helping African American men, their *ethnicity*, not their ability, is the major determining factor, according to studies by F. A. Blanchard and F. J. Crosby (1989). In a subsequent study using Euro-American women rather than African American men as the partners, researchers found identical patterns.

The reality is that school grades and grades on the SAT exam depend more on socioeconomic status than any other factor, including ethnicity, according to the metastudy done by the American Association of University Women. Children from low-income households, often with no father around, and whose parents have low educational achievement, tend to make lower grades. As socioeconomic status goes up, so do grades—for African Americans, Euro-Americans, boys, girls, and all others.

Learning style is different for many African Americans, according to psychologist James M. Jones. They tend to focus more on rhythms and patterns and recognize patterns better than people from other cultures. They are usually better at oral than written expression, and they tend toward improvisation and creative responses to the world and to the moment. Therefore, they tend to do better on tests where there are clear patterns as well as opportunities for creativity and oral responses.

Many people assume that African Americans value education less than Euro-Americans, since fewer complete high school and college. However, D.G. Solorzano's study indicates that African American high school students, and their parents, have significantly higher aspirations to achieve a college degree than Euro-Americans at the same socioeconomic level. In both groups, the higher the socioeconomic level, the higher the educational aspirations tend to be. Educational progress is improving, according to U.S. Census Bureau figures, but more work must be done in this area.

- 63 percent completed high school in 1990, compared to 51 percent in 1980.
- College enrollment increased 150 percent, from about 4.5 percent to 11 percent, but was only about half the Euro-American rate of 21 percent.
- Educational attainment is about the same for males and females.

Stereotype #3: African Americans are lazy and irresponsible.

As a matter of fact, about the same proportion of African Americans as Euro-Americans hold jobs, but African American men receive only about 70 percent the pay of Euro-American men. African American women receive 62 percent as much. In spite of this wage gap, African Americans are industrious and responsible enough to get and keep jobs in down-sized mean-and-lean corporations that must be globally competitive and productive. Historically, they have done much of the hard labor that helped establish the U.S. economy. This myth goes back to the time when most slaves were treated as subhuman children, denied an education, expected to do exactly as the overseer ordered, and offered little or no reward for working harder and smarter. When some didn't act eager and committed, all were branded lazy and irresponsible.

For well-educated African Americans in corporate America, "lazy" and "incompetent" are two of the most frustrating stereotypes. Many who respond to surveys say they're permitted a much narrower range of behavioral styles to achieve their goals than their Euro-American peers (WSJ 1992). They also become quite frustrated when they perceive they must work twice as hard and must stay in a position longer than necessary—just to prove they're *not* lazy and incompetent and that they *can* handle the next assignment. This stereotype extends to the assumption by Euro-American colleagues that nearly all African Americans are incompetent to handle higher-level responsibilities, as indicated by research studies. Another result: African American professionals are often assumed to be sales clerks, waiters, or other entry-level or menial workers. Social interactions that they enjoy with their colleagues at work may disappear outside the office, where co-workers often literally don't recognize them on the street when they're not in "corporate uniform."

Stereotype #4: They blame everyone else for their problems.

African Americans have been struggling for hundreds of years to rise up from the massive burdens of the past, including 200 years of slavery, and another 100 years of legal segregation that included barriers to well-paying corporate or government jobs. They understand that this history is still affecting their chances to build a successful career and life. While virtually all community leaders focus on self-help programs, most believe the government should help the inner-city underclass to break out of this prison that was not of their own making. This has led to the stereotype of blaming others and expecting "government handouts."

The reality is that African American progress since the civil rights laws of the 1960s has taken two distinct directions: about one-third have made fairly good progress and are part of the hard-working, tax-paying, responsible middle class. These African Americans are not stuck in a victim mentality that blames others for their difficulties. Not all have been so fortunate, however. About one-third are actually worse-off, if anything—mired down in inner-city, underclass poverty and crime—and in dire need of help. The other third are hovering somewhere between underclass and middle class status, most of them struggling to make it on their own. Most community leaders credit the progress that has been made to the people's own bootstrap efforts in combination with civil rights laws and certain successful government programs.

Stereotype #5: Many African Americans are resentful troublemakers.

This stereotype is related to the violent and blaming stereotypes. It's connected to cultural differences in confronting issues and expressing concerns, and to a history of trying to break out of imprisoning discrimination. It's also connected to inner city underclass crime.

The reality is that most people in the African American community believe in speaking up assertively, especially about perceived injustices. Being genuine, expressing the feelings you are feeling, and directly confronting issues are all highly valued and typical patterns in the African American community. During the days of legal and open discrimination and oppression, African Americans did not dare to express these values outside the community. Now that they have more political freedom to do so, younger members are especially likely to feel it's important to be genuine and speak up in such situations. The point is that expressions interpreted as resentful troublemaking by persons outside the community may not be meant that way nor seen that way by African Americans.

To put all this in perspective, these myths are stereotyped beliefs that result in prejudice and discrimination. Euro-Americans and African Americans operate with different definitions of ethnic prejudice. Euro-Americans define it narrowly as "explicit, consciously held beliefs in ethnic superiority." African Americans define it more broadly as a "set of practices and institutions that result in the oppression of a group of people" (Lichtenberg 1992). African Americans say ethnic prejudice is still their principal challenge to moving up in the work world. They say management looks for "safe blacks" to develop and promote and are less willing to take the same risks with African Americans that they take with Euro-American males (Thomas 1991).

CONNECTIONS TO THE PAST

A unique legacy of slavery and legal segregation laid the groundwork for these diehard myths and stereotypes. Of all the U.S. ethnic groups, African Americans have traditionally faced the greatest obstacles, which are built on the foundation of entrenched prejudice and discrimination, usually called racism. The idea that African Americans are of another race is another myth. Business leaders need some background information about the specifics of this form of ethnic prejudice, how it still affects African Americans, and some typical Euro-American rationalizations around it.

> *The Myth of Race.* The "one drop rule" (for one drop of blood) was used well into the 20th century to classify African Americans. But how many African Americans are of pure African stock? In 1930 less than 25 percent of African Americans were of unmixed descent, according to a respected anthropologist (Herskovitz 1930). The Census Bureau has concurred with that estimate. Prior to the 1960s it was illegal for African Americans and Euro-Americans to marry. Yet nearly 75 percent of African Americans had one or more Euro-American ancestors due to sexual unions outside marriage—primarily slave women submitting to sexual demands. Now that intermarriage is legal, it's likely that the percentage of "unmixed" African Americans is much smaller.
>
> What is the actual ancestry of the "average" African American? Studies show it's about 70 percent African, and 25 percent combined Euro-American and American Indian.

The culturally devastating practice of slavery set the stage for the legal segregation in the South and de facto segregation in the North that followed the Civil War. The march toward true equality began the day slavery began, but major breakthroughs came on the heels of an intensified Civil Rights Movement in the 1950s and 1960s.

Slavery

During and just after America's colonial years, about four million Africans were brought over and made slaves. During the first 250 years of our nation, Africans were bought and sold as commodities on a slave market (from about 1615 until Emancipation around 1865). The founding fathers in 1776 designated African Americans as three-fifths human. After the Civil War and Emancipation, during the legal segregation era, they were still seen by many Euro-Americans as subhuman, only a step above the apes but below humans.

The result was a caste system, with African Americans as the "untouchables." The women could wetnurse babies of Euro-American women and prepare the family food, but could not drink from the same public water fountains nor eat at the same establishments. Euro-Americans who protested this treatment of African Americans were branded "nigger lovers" and ostracized or threatened in order to keep them in line.

Slavery had a deep and lasting effect that is clearly present today. Slavery was the culture of the great grandparents of today's African American adults, a culture that affected every aspect of their family life, beliefs about self and the world, hopes and expectations. The culture of slavery also affected everyone else in the United States at the time, and most Euro-American's great-grandparents inevitably handed down the interconnecting beliefs about privilege, inequality, and prejudice—by their attitudes and actions, if not by their verbal teachings. Slavery laid the foundation for the prejudice and discrimination that African Americans must cope with today—and for the resulting social problems many activists are working to overcome.

It began in Virginia, and by the time of the Civil War, 1860, about 92 percent of all African Americans lived in the South, and 95 percent of this group were slaves. In fact, African slaves made up 35 percent of the South's population, while slaveholders were only 5.5 percent of the total. Most slaves provided the essential labor for raising cotton, tobacco, rice, sugar, and hemp. Kept illiterate and ignorant, they were typically told they were incapable of caring for themselves. Most slaveholders liked to picture themselves as kind masters taking care of docile, happy slaves. In reality, many owners were harsh or cruel and most were terrified by the threat of slave rebellion. And many slaves wore masks of docility and deference in order to hide subversive plans (Harding 1980; Takaki 1993).

For African American women, slavery held special horrors. They worked in the fields and factories just as the men did, but many masters viewed them as "breeders" and the only legal source of more slaves after importation of slaves was outlawed in 1808. Their children were not even their own, for the laws allowed masters to separate slave children from their mothers and sell them. And many slave women were used to satisfy the sexual desires of their masters. If these rapes resulted in pregnancy, and the child resembled the master, the woman and her child were likely to be sold. The effect on the adult males in the slave group was to greatly undermine their self-esteem and confidence (Harding 1980; Takaki 1993).

The few slaves who managed to escape headed north toward freedom. But freedom in northern society was only a facade for the reality of caste. African Americans in the North faced segregation, prejudice, discrimination, and violence. They were excluded from the skilled and professional jobs and could find only menial labor. The North was certainly not the promised land of their dreams.

Because virtually every African American is still experiencing the aftermath of the slave experience (Handy 1995), it's important for all of us to understand the impact of being a slave. It included being:

- Uprooted from one's home
- Stripped of one's culture
- Separated from family
- Subjected to deprived and oppressive conditions
- Stripped of voice by enforced silence—required to speak only English, adopt English names, and forgo learning to read and write
- Told to think of self as a slave only
- Blocked from virtually all of life's opportunities
- Brutally punished—in front of other slaves, who had to remain silent—if you resisted

The psychological aftermath and feelings that result from the practice of slavery are far from positive and they tend to separate us. Here are the feelings Kenneth Handy (1995) discovered:

African American	Euro-American
Shame	Guilt
Humiliation	Shame/humiliation
Inferiority	Denial
Anguish	Rationalization
Rage	Anger

We as a culture must discuss and validate this experience before it will be healed. We cannot brush it under the rug, where it will continue to fester. We must go through the joint process of taking responsibility and forgiving before we can move on.

Vignette: A Slave Family's Ordeal

Sarah was a young slave woman who worked in the cotton fields on a plantation in Georgia. She was well aware that her masters and any of his plantation bosses could force her to have sex with them. How could she refuse and still survive? She had somehow escaped this fate until recently when Mr. Jones caught her alone in the barn. Soon after, she realized she was pregnant. Her husband Jake knew something was wrong. When Sarah broke down and told him the story, he felt completely humiliated, so powerless in this situation. Sarah gave birth to a boy, Shane. Everyone noticed what light skin and European-like features he had. Mr. Jones frowned when he heard talk about the baby. The last thing he wanted was his wife noticing a slave child that looked suspiciously like her husband. Soon Sarah and Shane were taken to the slave market to be sold. She was torn apart from her husband, parents, and all the people she knew. She never saw them again.

Self-Awareness Activity 7.3: How Does It Feel to Be Trapped?

Purpose: To find common ground with the people who have the experience of being trapped.

Step 1. The situation. You've read about the experience of African slaves in the United States. They lived constantly with at least two major dilemmas: entrapment and degradation. They were trapped in situations that provided no real personal freedom and almost no alternatives. They were told in many ways that they were inferior. Can you think of a situation in which you felt similarly trapped and/or degraded—physically, emotionally, or psychologically? Write a brief paragraph describing the situation.

Step 2. Thoughts and feelings. Go back to that time and place. Relive the situation. What were some of your thoughts at that time? How did you feel? Write a brief paragraph about your thoughts and feelings.

Step 3. Common ground. Now shift to the situations of African American slaves. Can you imagine what thoughts and feelings you might have had if you were a slave living on a southern plantation around 1800? Can you imagine how all this might affect the way you would raise your children? How even your grandchildren might be affected? Write a brief paragraph about thoughts and feelings that come to mind.

After Slavery: Free but Segregated

Soon after the Civil War, African Americans' life in the South resembled their cousins' life in the North. The major difference was that segregation was de facto in the North and legal in the South. By the 1890s, laws provided for the "Negro's place" in neighborhoods, parks, schools, hotels, hospitals, restaurants, streetcars, theaters, and hospitals. In 1896 the Supreme Court said that such "separate but equal" segregation was constitutional. But African Americans knew that separate was never equal for them. When laws didn't keep African Americans in their "place," vigilantes did. Every year hundreds of African Americans who "stepped out of line" in some way were lynched. In 1909 the NAACP became the first African American organization with the ability to fight for justice in American courts, but its power was very limited.

During World War II there was a mass migration of African Americans from the farms and towns of the South to the cities of the North and West. Even though there was an acute worker shortage, African Americans initially were excluded from skilled jobs in the defense industry. African American labor leaders threatened to march on Washington, and President Roosevelt issued an executive order with the goal of "eliminating racial, ethnic, and religious discrimination in defense industries and in government." By 1945 more than 8 percent of all defense workers were African American. The war resulted in more industrial and occupational diversification for African Americans than had occurred in the 75 preceding years (McWilliams 1964).

Pulled by the employment opportunities in New York, Detroit, Los Angeles, San Francisco, and other urban areas, more than half a million African Americans left the South. At the outset of World War II, 75 percent of them lived in the South, and by 1970 only 50 percent were there. Over 80 percent of the ones who left went to urban areas, mainly to inner cities. This movement triggered violent backlashes, sometimes exploding into ethnic riots. When the war ended, author Maya Angelou wondered, "Can we make it through the peace?" But there would be no turning back to the old ethnic order (Takaki 1993).

The Euro-American Rationalizations

How did Euro-Americans make slavery, segregation, and discrimination compatible with the culture's basic belief that all persons are created equal? The most bigoted Euro-Americans rationalized their ethnic prejudice—and a history of slavery—by denying the humanness of African Americans, viewing them as subhuman and therefore not "persons who are created equal." The less bigoted rationalized prejudice by supporting the "separate but equal" doctrine that provided the basis for segregation through the first half of the twentieth century, ignoring the fact that *separate* for African Americans was far from *equal*. At a more personal, emotional level, many Euro-Americans simply ignored the issue, as if African Americans did not exist (Stewart 1972).

Pettigrew and Martin (1987) determined that more Euro-Americans are against ethnic prejudice than are for it. The problem lies with the great majority who simply go along with the old myths and stereotypes. The specific proportions are:

- 15 percent—extremely prejudiced toward African Americans
- 60 percent—conforming bigots, reflecting the ethnic ideology of the larger society
- 25 percent—against ethnic prejudice in ideology and behavior

Pettigrew and Martin (1987) concluded that persons in the extreme group were motivated largely by authoritarian personality needs. They found that persons in the anti-prejudice category consistently support rights for African Americans. More recent studies also indicate that most Euro-American adults increasingly reject ethnic injustice in principle but remain reluctant to accept and act on measures necessary to eliminate the injustice (Ponterotto and Pedersen 1993). African American leaders often refer to this as the majority's weak will to implement real change.

Robert Terry (1990) points out two current ways that many Euro-Americans rationalize their ethnic prejudice.

- "We're all just people. I'm just a human being first and foremost." The hidden meaning is, "I don't have to take responsibility for what the dominant majority has done and is doing if I ignore my ethnicity and affirm my humanity."
- "I never even notice anyone's color or ethnicity. I believe we should be color-blind. I don't even think of you as Black," implying that if people mention someone's color, they're being racist.

The fact is that Euro-Americans have traditionally been privileged in this culture. And American culture is color conscious. Most people tend to sort others by color, to the advantage of some and detriment of others. African Americans don't have the luxury of ignoring color consciousness. Euro-Americans can choose to ignore what their ingroup has done and how they all continue to benefit from it, but that does nothing toward changing the facts.

When Euro-Americans feel the need to tell African Americans that they don't think about their color, they bring color into the picture. If color isn't important, why comment on it? Let's say Jane Doe makes such a comment to an African American co-worker. If Jane really means, "You're so white in color or in the way you act that I forget about your color," then she's not being color-blind but is absorbing blackness into whiteness. If she means, "I don't discriminate on the basis of color," then she's still not being color-blind but is trying to find a way to express her concern for racial justice.

The bottom line: Valuing diversity means acknowledging and appreciating *all* the differences, including skin color, and moving beyond using physical features as the measure of a person's worth.

The Movement toward True Equality

Actual desegregation did not begin until the African American community began waging an open battle against oppression, now known as the Civil Rights movement. This nonviolent movement led directly to the civil rights laws of the 1960s, and the battle against oppression is still being waged today.

The simple action that ignited and united an entire community, and beyond, occurred in 1955 in Montgomery, Alabama. Rosa Parks boarded a city bus and later refused to give up her seat to a "white man," as city law required and as the bus driver demanded. Such resistance was not new, but the nation's response to it was.

Her arrest led to an explosive protest and boycott of the bus system, led by Martin Luther King, Jr. One year later the court ordered the desegregation of the bus system. African Americans saw that they could transform their situation, and they felt a new sense of confidence.

In 1960 African American students declared a sit-in at a Woolworth's lunch counter, and in 1961 African American and Euro-American "freedom riders" rode together in buses throughout the South to protest segregation. Many were yanked from the buses and brutally beaten by mobs, sometimes before television cameras. In 1963 the conscience of the nation was galvanized by the famous March on Washington. Hundreds of thousands of marchers from all ethnic groups gathered in front of the Lincoln Memorial. As millions watched the event on television, Martin Luther King, Jr., gave his famous "I have a dream" speech.

Vignette

The Legacy of Slavery and Segregation

When we examine the institution of slavery and its power to diminish its victims, we can understand what a powerful impact it had on all Americans. What most people don't realize is the impact that slavery and, later, legal segregation still have on today's culture and workplace. In a 1994 television interview Marie Davis, an officer of the National Association for the Advancement of Colored People (NAACP), said:

There's a perception among white Americans that time has erased slavery's effect. Many people think this was thousands of years ago, but it wasn't really that long ago. My grandfather was born into slavery and freed at the end of the Civil War, when he was still a toddler.

Slavery and the prejudice around it caused most Americans to accept the myth that African Americans are inferior, almost another species. The prejudice that is the legacy of slavery affects virtually all of us today.

Recently my granddaughter came to me, crying because she is black. I never dreamed my granddaughter would be crying like that. Then I cried, too, because I knew what she was going through. I remembered the many times I had cried as a child—cried because I was so hurt.

CURRENT PROFILE

Have African Americans made great progress since the Civil Rights laws of the 1960s were passed? That depends on who you ask and where you look. When asked if real improvement for African Americans was a myth 73% of African Americans agreed, but only 44% of Euro-Americans thought so. When asked if differences in income, job, housing are due to discrimination 75% of African Americans said yes, but only 30% of Euro-Americans agreed (Center 1995).

In fact, there has been a three-pronged progression. Nearly one-third of African Americans have made significant progress and live a middle class life. Nearly one-third have dropped into dire underclass poverty, with the other third somewhere in between. We'll look at African American progress in family income, occupations, business ownership, and education.

Three Tiers: Middle–Class, Under–Class, Struggling Between

Back in the 1960s, President Johnson appointed the Kerner Commission to probe the causes of rioting in the inner cities. The ensuing report said, "Our nation is moving toward two societies, one black, one white—separate and unequal." Thirty years later, a followup report by the Milton Eisenhower Institute (Fletcher 1998) noted that:

- The African American middle class has grown, with many living in the suburbs.
- African American business has expanded.
- The number of African Americans elected to political office has increased.
- But some problems have become more deeply rooted, exemplified by the growing inner-city underclass.

A central feature of African American progress since the 1960s is the simultaneous growth of the middle class and an underclass. Civil rights measures led to distinct improvement and upward mobility for many African Americans. The middle class began growing dramatically. On the other hand, the really poor tended to get poorer. The middle class began moving up and to the suburbs, earning more, sending their children to college, and living better. Meanwhile, the underclass began sinking further into intergenerational poverty, with increasing unemployment rates for young men and a dramatic rise in female-headed families. In 1990:

- 27 percent of African Americans lived in the suburbs
- 57 percent lived in central cities

This is perhaps a fair indication of the proportionate sizes of the middle class and the less affluent. Another indication is the poverty patterns of 1990:

- 27 percent for all African American families
- 11 percent for the married couples
- 45 percent for the female-headed (single mother) families

In 1980 the official poverty rate for all African American families was just under 26 percent, almost the same as in the 1990s, but it was 50 percent for small children, 40 percent for all children and 32 percent for the elderly, a pattern that still continues (U.S. Census).

In 1999 median income patterns reflected the continued poverty of African American women:

- $27,910 for African American households
- $20,600 for African American men
- $14,800 for African American women

Meanwhile the 1999 poverty rate for the African American population was at an all-time low of 24 percent, but still twice as high as the overall U.S. poverty rate of 12 percent.

The Growing Middle Class

Nearly one-third of African Americans are considered middle class. The emergence of a distinct African American middle class was reported in *Time* magazine in 1989. About one-third of all African American households had incomes of $35,000 or more (compared with 70 percent of all Euro-American households) in 1988. African American families living in the suburbs doubled from 13 percent in 1967 to 27 percent in 1990. Some of these people had parents and grandparents who achieved some success as entrepreneurs and professionals serving the African American community. Others somehow broke out of the poverty cycle to go through doors of opportunity opened by civil rights programs.

Closely related to socioeconomic status is home ownership. African American families who get "out of the projects" and foster "pride of ownership" in their children tend to escape the vicious cycle of drugs and crime that plague the ghetto. By 2000, 47 percent of African American families owned their homes, compared with 68 percent of Euro-Americans. The proportion remained fairly stable from 1970 to 1990, when the median value of the African American homes was $50,700, compared with $80,200 for Euro-American homeowners.

Since the 1970s more and more industries have left the cities for the suburbs, and so did more and more Euro-American families, followed by some of the new middle-class African American families. This combination of societal forces has been a major factor in the expansion of the underclass neighborhoods in the central cities. The suburban rings around cities are symbols not only of post-industrialism but also of ethnic and class exclusiveness in a traditionally segmented society. "White flight" refers to the Euro-American tendency to get away from the problems of urban living, including desegregation and other diversity issues, by moving to the exclusive "white" suburbs. Their gradual opening to African American middle-class families is a positive feature, but many of these families report feeling isolated and rejected by their Euro-American neighbors. Many say they feel estranged from the friends and families they left behind in the impoverished inner cities (Billingsley 1992).

These successful middle-class families tend to have a reverence for learning second only to their reverence for the spiritual, according to African American author Andrew Billingsley (1992). They tend to have their origins in the working class, generally in the previous generation. Most are still first-generation middle class. They tend to be more dependent than independent, more employees of others than owners and managers, and have relatively little accumulated wealth. Still, as Billingsley says, the African American middle class is "a major achievement sustained by education, two earners, extended families, religion, and service to others." *New York Times* reporter Isabel Wilkerson (1990) said, "Two main things tend to distinguish black middle-class people from middle-class whites. One is the likelihood that many more of their relatives will come to them for help. The other is that they tend to lack the resources of people who started life in the middle class."

A Growing Underclass

Back in the inner city, at the other end of the scale, are increasing numbers of African Americans who are still trapped in poverty. The followup on the Kerner Commission report revealed the following:

- In assets, the top-ranking 1 percent of Americans have more wealth than the bottom 90 percent put together.
- On an average week in the inner city, most adults do not work.
- About 40 percent of minority children attend an urban school where more than half the students are poor and don't reach minimal academic achievement levels.
- The United States has the largest proportion of prisoners of any nation—1.5 million. About one-third of young African American men are either in prison, on parole, or on probation—far more than are in college, and it costs much more to keep them in prison than in college. Normally the prison experience does *not* lead to improvement.

The major causes of the underclass problem, according to the report, are as follows:

- The1980s politic policies of supply-side, trickle-down economics, which expanded the gap between rich and poor
- Increasing hostility toward affirmative action
- The failure of some social programs, such as enterprise zones and the Job Training Partnership Act

What has worked best, according to the report, are the following initiatives:

- Head Start
- certain after-school programs
- targeted job training
- community-sensitive police strategies

For African American women, the problem of welfare dependency was tied to the increase in single-family mothers and gender inequality in the labor market. Nearly all women were crowded into female-dominated occupations, such as low-wage clerical and sales jobs, making it difficult or impossible for mothers to eke out living expenses *and* child care costs from their meager salaries.

Intensifying the middle-class/underclass disparity, the movement of plants and offices to the suburbs since the 1960s has isolated African American workers from many places of employment. African Americans have also been suffering from the effects of the "de-industrialization of America," with plants relocating to low-wage countries, such as Mexico and Korea.

The loss of blue-collar jobs hit African American men especially hard, because they were concentrated in the smokestack industries, such as automobile, rubber, and steel.

The news media and politicians are doing an impressive job of highlighting the problems of the African American underclass, such as male drug pushers and welfare mothers. The public is quite aware of these issues. However, to focus so heavily on the problems tends to obscure the incredible successes of fully one-third of African Americans who have overcome the most onerous and entrenched barriers in American society to secure a place in the middle class. A focus on the African American strengths behind this major achievement would be productive.

Career Progress

The U.S. Labor Department recently predicted that African Americans will be about 22 percent of new workers entering the workforce in the 1990s and beyond, even though the proportion of Americans who are African American is only 12 percent. From 1900 to 1970 the proportion of African Americans in the population consistently hovered around 10 to 11 percent, so such an increase would be an anomaly. One explanation may be the tendency for children of the expanded middle class to become employed. African Americans are increasingly moving into better-paying occupations, but there is still a significant pay gap, as well as glass ceiling obstacles. The changes in career opportunities and social status have been somewhat different for women than for men.

Employment Rates and Pay Gaps

About the same proportion of the African American and Euro-American populations hold jobs, but African Americans on average make 25 percent less than Euro-American men.

TABLE 7.2: Employment Rates, 1997

	All	*Male*	*Female*
African American	60%	72%	66%
Euro-American	67%	77%	60%

African American men's average income was 80 percent of Euro-American men's, and the women's was only 62 percent (U.S. Women's Bureau 1997). Median family income for African Americans as compared to Euro-Americans rose during the late 1960s and early 1970s, decreased during the 1980s, but is rising again, as shown in Table 7.3.

TABLE 7.3: Median Family Income Ratios, 1960-1997

Median Family Income	1960	1970	1980	1990	1997
Ratio: African American to Euro-American	55%	65%	58%	56%	64%

Source: U.S. Bureau of the Census, 1993, U.S. Bureau of Labor Statistics, 1999.

Movement into Better Paying Occupations

From 1978 to 1990 there was a 52 percent increase in the number of African Americans who held positions as managers, professionals, and government officials. The greatest progress was in government jobs. In 1980, two-thirds of African Americans managerial and professional jobs were working for the federal government. Only 17 percent of managers and professionals as a whole work for the federal government. The proportion of African Americans holding management and professional jobs from 1966 to 1990 is shown in Table 7.4.

TABLE 7.4: Progress in Management and Professional Jobs

African American Employees	1966	1978	1990
% of all managers in firms with 100+ employees	0.9%	3.7%	5.2%
% of all professionals	1.7%	4.0%	5.2%

Source: U.S. Census Bureau, 1993.

Since 1960 an increasing proportion of African Americans have moved into the higher-status, better-paying occupations of manager, professional, technical, sales, and administrative support. Table 7.5 shows the percentage of African Americans in each type of occupation and compares it with the Euro-American distribution. Part of this trend reflects changes in the economy as a whole, away from manufacturing and toward service and information. The decline in proportion of African Americans in service occupations generally reflects a shift out of cleaning and janitorial work into higher-status white-collar and blue-collar jobs. However, as the footnotes to Table 7.6 indicate, African Americans tend to be at the lowest-paid levels of each job category.

TABLE 7.5: Occupations: African American and Euro-American, 1960-1990

Occupation	1960 Af	1960 Euro	1970 Af	1970 Euro	1980 Af	1980 Euro	1990 Af	1990 Euro
Manager, Professional	7.4%	23.8%	14.6%	26.2%	17.9%	28.5%	16.3%	27.2%
Technical, Sales, Administrative Support	8.5	22.7	15.3	24.7	21.3	27.4	28.0	31.3
Service	31.7	9.9	26.0	10.7	23.1	12.1	21.9	12.1
Farming, Forestry	1.0	7.4	3.9	4.0	1.8	2.9	1.6	3.1
Precision production, Craft, Repairs	6.0	13.8	8.2	13.5	9.6	13.3	8.3	12.0
Operators, Fabricators, Laborers	20.4	17.9	23.7	17.0	19.4	13.5	21.5	14.4

Source: U.S. Census Bureau, Statistical Abstract of the United States, 1981, 1991.

Glass Ceiling Obstacles

Progress in corporate America has not kept pace with the government picture, and the glass ceiling has resulted in virtually no African Americans in top positions of top companies. In 1979 the total *number* of African American senior managers in Fortune 1000 companies was three, by 1985 it had increased to four, and in 1990 to five. In 1999 the first African American worked his way up to CEO of a Fortune 1000 company—Lloyd Ward of Maytag. And, high-tech jobs in the New Economy were not readily available to African American, who make up only 3 percent of the technical workforce. Similarly, they account for only 3 to 4 percent of sales reps in the United States.

An African American reaction to the corporate glass ceiling was reported in 1992 (WSJ), when so many managers and professionals were leaving that it signaled a trend. The reasons they give included:

- hitting the Glass Ceiling, lack of opportunity, and upward mobility
- feeling pressured to undermine or drop their African American identity
- having to prove themselves, over and over again, due to being African American
- dealing with the stigma of being an affirmative action hire
- coping with ethnic stereotypes

While learning the language and customs of corporate America may seem like a necessary part of playing the game for Euro-American men and women, for African Americans it can smack of selling out to get ahead. Many report feeling pressured to become "almost white" in order to be accepted, or at best to become "neutral" or to be viewed as an exception to the typical African American type (Bell 1990). They feel the need to change their speech, their dress, their hair in order to fit into the corporate culture. If they go along, they begin to feel some degree of isolation from the African-American community. They don't really belong anywhere and feel "marginal" to all groups (WSJ 1992; Executive Female, 1992).

Men and Women: Differences in Progress and Roles

Comparisons of occupations held by African American men and women are given in Table 7.6. The largest category for women is clerical and for men, laborer. There have been significant differences in the career progress and changing status of men and that of women since the 1960s. While experts tend to agree that both men and women, on average, have improved their socioeconomic status since AA became law, and they have entered many new occupations formerly closed to them, women have made better progress than men. And both men and women have made more progress in government jobs than in corporate jobs.

TABLE 7.6: Occupations of African American Men and Women, 1990

Gender	Managerial Professional	Technical, Sales, Admin Support	Service	Farming Forestry	Precision production, Craft, Repairs	Operators Fabricators Laborers
Men	13.2	18.1	18.1[3]	2.8	14.2	30.5[5]
Women	19.5[1]	37.9[2]	24.9[4]	0.4	2.4	12.4

Source: U.S. Bureau of the Census, 1993.

1. 22% of African American managers/professionals were teachers; most were elementary school teachers.
2. Nearly 30% of African American women employed in technical/ sales/ administrative support jobs were cashiers, secretaries, and typists.
3. 45% of African American men in service jobs were janitors, cleaners, and cooks.

4. Half of African American women in service occupations were nursing aides, orderlies and attendants, cooks, janitors, and cleaners.

5. 30% of laborers were truck drivers, assemblers, stock handlers, and baggers.

Changes in Women's Status

African American women showed a dramatic increase in income, compared to that of Euro-American women, due to occupational shifts. African American women have moved from being primarily agricultural or domestic workers to being office workers. AA opened the doors of America's offices to African American women, and huge numbers of them traded their maid's aprons for pink collars (Carr-Ruffino 1992). However, some researchers say the myth of the double-minority AA advantage is offset by the reality of double discrimination by gender and ethnicity, and sometimes by class. For example, African American women still tend to be:

- placed into training programs for traditionally female occupations
- discouraged from attempting innovative careers
- dependent upon the public sector for employment
- kept out of better private-sector jobs by rigid ethnic barriers

In 1980 more African American than Euro-American married women had outside jobs, they had more children, and they were more likely to be the sole wage earner. In 1990 these trends had not changed. Some researchers have defined a traditional nuclear family as a two-parent family where both parents have married only once and the children were all born after the marriage. In 1990 only 26 percent of African American children lived in such a family, compared to 56 percent of Euro-American children.

Contributing factors are rising divorce rates and decreasing marriage rates. As women's career opportunities have expanded, so have divorce rates. While Euro-American marriage rates have changed very little, rates for African Americans have dramatically dropped. Historically, 90 percent of African American women were married by the age of 44. That rate dropped to 55 percent by 1990. Moreover, the remarriage rate six years after a divorce was only 40 percent for African American women, compared to 60 percent for Euro-American women. African American women are getting married later. For example, the proportion of women in their late twenties who had never married rose from 11 percent in 1970 to 31 percent in 1990.

Changes in Men's Status

Clearly some modest employment gains were made by African American men in the late 1960s and early 1970s. African American men moved out of blue-collar and service jobs, presumably into better paying jobs, by a rate of 12 percent from 1966 to 1973, compared to a rate of 4 percent for Euro-American men (Feagin 1991). But the unemployment rate for young African American men, those from ages 20 to 24 and has remained higher than 20 percent, more than double the rates for comparably aged Euro-American men. And unemployment continues to be a major problem for African American men of all ages. Twice as many African American men are unemployed as Euro-American men; those holding college degrees are three times more likely to be unemployed than Euro-Americans. Unemployment is correlated with a host of underclass problems. For example, African American men are about eight times as likely to be homicide victims as Euro-American men, five times as likely to go to prison, four times as likely to enter a drug abuse treatment center, and nine times as likely to enter a mental institution (Mauer 1989).

Poverty and unemployment seem to be fertile ground for the birth of gangs, drug use, drug dealing, violence, and other crimes. About 25 percent of African American men ages 20 to 25 are in prison or on parole. Ethnic prejudice and discrimination play a part in all this. Studies indicate that African American and Latino American men are more likely to be arrested than Euro-American men, regardless of wrongdoing. By the early 1990s, many articles discussed the fact that young African American males were dying in disproportionate numbers because of high-risk lifestyles, and a number of African American organizations were spurred to action (Billingsley 1992).

Business Ownership

Within the African American community is a large and growing entrepreneurial class. While private business ownership is less well developed in the African American community than in the nation as a whole, it is substantial. And it's built on the strength of achieving, productive African American families. Its promise of future growth is reflected in the dramatic surge of interest among African Americans in attending seminars on how to start and grow a business. Beginning in the 1980s, conferences that normally had focused on upward mobility and promotions for African Americans shifted to seminars on starting a business. Some African American consultants expressed concern about this trend because, "If we are locked out of major corporations, with their enormous influence on the economy and their share of the resources, we're locked out of America" (WSJ 1992).

African American businesses currently tend to be small. The large majority of African Americans can't establish a business of any magnitude because of inadequate assets, net worth, and access to bank loans. The average net worth (assets minus liabilities) of Euro-American families was 10 times that of African Americans in 1990, and less than one-half of one percent of American assets are owned by African Americans. In spite of historical barriers, however, they now own 3 percent of America's businesses.

In 1993 total sales of all African American-owned firms was over $10 billion, although this was only a fraction of one percent of the Fortune 500 revenues of $2.4 trillion. One African American-owned firm was large enough to qualify for the Fortune 500. Beatrice Foods (4,500 workers) with a revenue of $1.7 billion equaled 238th-ranked Pet Foods. The second largest African American-owned firm was Johnson Publishing Company (2,600 workers), publisher of *Ebony* and *Jet* magazines and owner of other businesses, with sales of $294 million. Beatrice was acquired and restructured a few years earlier, while Johnson was started from scratch and grew over the past 40 years (*Black Enterprise*, May 1994).

Supply-side critics point to the lack of external financing available to African American owners. In addition to having fewer assets and thus less collateral to borrow against, most are located in depressed economic areas, where banks don't want to venture. The National Black Chamber of Commerce has cited equitable access to bank loans as a major first step toward business ownership. Demand-side critics say that discrimination limits the ability of African American owned firms to do business with the Euro-American majority, so they're limited to African American customers, who tend to be significantly less affluent than the majority population.

These small African American firms face huge barriers to starting out large enough and to growing large enough. The Internet, on the other hand, offers some lucrative opportunities that don't require huge infusions of capital. A number of African American entrepreneurs are establishing Internet startups, and many are finding success. An added bonus is the anonymity of cyberspace. Customers are only aware of the products and services offered, not the ethnicity of the person offering them.

Education for Careers

Educational progress has been good and is a key to breaking out of the poverty cycle. The proportion of African Americans who have completed high school rose from 51 percent in 1980 to 79 percent in 2000 (compared to 88 percent for Euro-Americans). The high school dropout rate dropped from 16 percent to 14 percent, and college enrollment increased by one and one-half times. Educational attainment is about the same for males and females, but African Americans have a way to go in achieving the same level as Euro-Americans. The proportion who got a university degree in 2000 was 17 percent, compared to 28 percent of Euro-Americans.

After a significant increase in African American college enrollment in the 1980s, the total number began slowly dropping, but enrollment in African American colleges jumped. Although such schools account for only 3 percent of the nation's college enrollment, they were selected by 35 percent of

African American college students in 1990. Students say the main reason is a desire for "the black experience," meaning the self-confidence boost that comes from having African American professors as role models, gaining a sense of African American history, and learning about the contributions African Americans have made to society. Most of the schools are private and expensive. Some students ask, "Why can't we get this in the typical large public university?" (NAEOHE 1990).

Intellectual Achievement Depends on Income

School achievement depends heavily on family economic status, according to a breakthrough study. Table 7.7 shows the correlation between family income and student performance on SAT tests. The authors (AAUW 1992) conclude that

- Socioeconomic status—not ethnicity or gender—is the best predictor of both grades and test scores.

- Public schools must do more to provide educational opportunity for children of low socioeconomic status, who do less well in school regardless of ethnicity or gender.

TABLE 7.7: Family Income Affects School Performance

Average Family Income	Average SAT score
$22,000	750–800
$18,000	550–599
$14,000	350–399
$8,000	200–249

Source: American Association of University Women, 1992 Report.
Selected pairs are used, but missing pairs are consistent with these results.

It would appear that once an African American family is able to break the cycle of poverty and get good jobs, the cycle tends to stay broken for that family. The children do well in school and are therefore likely to get good jobs and earn good incomes when they grow up, which in turn increases the likelihood that their children will do well in school.

Still Segregated

Studies indicate that racially integrated classrooms tend to have positive effects for minorities. Yet in 1990 most African American students were still in classrooms with few, if any, Euro-Americans. And by the late 1990s judges had ended desegregation orders in many school districts. For those who have the advantage of integrated schools, classroom studies of teacher-student relationships have indicated that minority students receive biased treatment. For example, Euro-American teachers tend to give more praise and encouragement to Euro-American students and to accept and acknowledge their contributions to class discussions. Such subtle exclusion can do long-term damage to children's confidence, class performance, and educational aspirations. Although much attention has been paid to problems in the educational system that impacts African Americans, the problems have not yet been solved.

A promising approach might be to study success factors. What if researchers were to focus on African Americans who have broken out of the poverty cycle and find patterns of factors that worked well for them? For example, are there external factors in family, school, or community that affected these members' success patterns? What kinds of internal beliefs and attitudes, thinking and feeling, decisions and choices, are common among the successful? How did successful African Americans use their imagination, desire, and expectations to avoid underclass pitfalls and move up to a better life? If some typical patterns could be found, community leaders use this information to help those who are still stuck. Young people in the underclass could develop similar patterns in their own struggle to break out.

Political Views of African American Status

Why are so many African Americans still caught in underclass poverty? Opinions vary widely about the causes and solutions for this continuing problem.

Conservatives tend to believe that more accurate measures of jobs and income would indicate that the problem isn't very serious. To the extent that problems exist, they reflect the personal inadequacies of African American youths, compounded by the adverse effects of government antipoverty policies, including welfare and minimum wage laws. Any inequity that exists is rooted in African American laziness and disregard for law and order. The conservative prescription is for government to stay out of it because attempts to help amount to handouts, which make the poor dependent on government and are a burden on taxpayers. Poor African Americans who want to will pull themselves up by their bootstraps, and those who don't can suffer the consequences.

Liberals emphasize external causes of the problem, such as declining employment opportunities due to a weakening of economic growth and labor market imbalances. They cite the movement of jobs away from the inner cities to suburbs, Sun Belt states, and low-wage countries. The movement of middle-class African Americans to the suburbs intensifies inner city problems. It reduces the youths' access to role models and to middle-class cultural values. Liberals say that discrimination also continues to be a barrier, and as a result some African Americans naturally become discouraged and demoralized. The problems are too great for African Americans to solve on their own, and it's up to government to help bring an end to inequity.

Black nationalists tend to see the problem as pervasive prejudice. Their concern is for recognition as free human beings. They do not call for integration but rather for true equality that values diversity.

Political differences are said to create difference in perceptions about the status and progress of African Americans (Issues 1999). When asked if they believed job differences, income differences and housing differences between African Americans and Euro-Americans are due to discrimination:

- 70 to 80 percent of African Americans agree
- 30 percent of Euro-Americans agree

When asked is there had been no real improvement in the position of African Americans in the United States:

- 73 percent of African Americans agree
- 44 percent of Euro-Americans agree

About 73 percent of African Americans agreed with the statement, "It makes me mad that affirmative action policies are *needed* in this country because that means that I'm not judged on my merits alone."

What's in a Name? African American

Here are the typical terms for African Americans in historical order:

Negro→ Colored→ AfroAmerican→ Black→ African American.

Negro was used from the time of slavery. *Colored* became the more "polite" term during the first half of the 20th century. *AfroAmerican* was used early in the Civil Rights era, followed by the "Black is Beautiful" era. By the 1990s most African Americans still preferred *Black* (39 percent) or *Black American* (10 percent), but *African American* (34 percent) was growing in favor and is probably predominant today. Those preferring *Black* tend to be the most conservative, those preferring *African American* the most liberal, with those preferring *Black American* somewhere in between (Larkey and Hecht 1991).

THE AFRICAN AMERICAN COMMUNITY: KEY VALUES

Seven typical core values affect how African Americans view themselves, the world, and others, based on work of several African American researchers, including Andrew Billingsley, M.L. Hecht, Thomas Kochman, and J.L. White. Some are rooted in African tribal values. Others are rooted in the need to bond together and to find inner strength and savvy in order to survive the circumstances of slavery and segregation. Here are seven core values typical in most African American communities:

1. *Sharing*, interrelating, interdependence, collectivism
2. *Expressing personal style*, individuality, improvisation, creativity, in a sharing way
3. *Being real and genuine*, tellin' it like it is; learning the truth from direct experience; seeing the good as well as the bad
4. *Being assertive*, speaking up, standing up
5. *Expressing feelings* openly
6. *Bouncing back*, maintaining vitality and resilience, and a positive attitude
7. *Not trusting* the mainstream establishment

Value #1: Sharing and Interrelating

Interconnectedness, interrelatedness, sharing, and interdependence are seen as central and unifying values in the African American community. This is a prominent theme in African American life and language with respect to

- interactive dynamics between speaker and listener
- the power of words to control
- ways of thinking
- timing
- communication skill

Sharing knowledge and endorsing the group are related to collectivism, which means putting family and community relationships above one's own aspirations. It's acted out in the sharing of self and material possessions within the family. It's also expressed in the call-response pattern found in meetings of church members ("Amen! Praise God!") and other groups ("Right on, Brother!") (Halberstadt 1985; Hammer and Gudykunst 1987; Hecht and Ribeau 1984).

Value #2: Expressing Personal Style and Uniqueness

Personal style is important in the way African Americans talk, walk, dress, play, work—in every aspect of life. This uniqueness in personal style and expression celebrates the individual. But the response of family, friends, and community is crucial to the expression. It's meaningless unless done in sync with others. For example, they may develop their own style of dancing, singing, or strutting—basing their style on something the group understands and uses, but adding their own variations. This creative expression of individual style is done amidst others in a sharing way. Jazz improvisation began with this custom. Musicians play a tune together, but one by one the individual musicians take the spotlight and improvise on the theme in their own way.

In contrast, American individualism refers to a more autonomous expression through personal achievement and self-reliance. It might mean that a musician would sit home alone and compose a new piece of music—totally on her own, perhaps later playing it in a performance. It does not rely on sharing the personal expression of individuality with the group in the immediate way that African American "personal style" expression does (Rose 1983; Kochman 1981; Donohue 1985).

Value #3: Being Real and Genuine

At church and at home, African Americans are taught to face up to their circumstances, admit who they really are, and deal with life as it is. Being real and genuine is rooted in a core belief about life: The natural facts, eternal truths, wisdom of the ages, and basic precepts of survival emerge from the experiences of life. Some related common teachings, discussed in L. F. Rose's work, are:

- You can't escape nothing. You got to pay your dues. If you've been through tragedy, it must be you needed it (for personal growth).
- You cannot lie to life.
- You might as well be who you really are, and tell it like it is.
- You learn the truth through direct experience.

Older people, because of their accumulated experiences, are the reservoirs of wisdom. Realness and genuineness are tied to the values of personal style, assertiveness, and open emotional expression. It means African Americans tend to confront problems they care about in a direct, loud, and passionate way. This is respected when it conveys sincerity and conviction (Rose 1983; Kochman 1981).

Value #4: Being Assertive

African Americans value standing up for personal rights and trying to achieve them without harming others. Assertiveness is a key symbol of standing up for yourself in the face of oppression and of taking charge of your own life. Coping with prejudice and discrimination often results in an assertive, determined, confrontational style.

Assertiveness is often expressed in a style that is intense, outspoken, challenging, and forward. It may be done with a loud strong voice, angry verbal arguments, threats, insults, a certain way of dressing, or the use of slang. It can range from calm debates to persuasion to intense expressions of anger.

Actions based on this value often cause misunderstandings outside the community. Others often misinterpret mere assertiveness as a form of violence, blaming, or troublemaking, linking it to those stereotypes. This assertiveness value is related to genuineness and tellin' it like it is, but others may see it as being over-aggressive, coming on too strong, being too argumentative, or stirring up trouble. The most disturbing interpretation is, "Uh-oh, he's about to get violent" (Kochman 1981).

Value #5: Expressing Feelings

African American style is more self-conspicuous, expressive, expansive, colorful, intense, assertive, aggressive, and focused on the individual than the style of most other cultures. Studies indicate that African American use more:

- expressive communications patterns
- direct questions
- public debate and argument
- active nonverbal expression
- emotional intensity
- self-presentations through boasting and bragging

Debates, Arguments, Confrontations

African Americans tend to negotiate more loudly and intensely than others. When African Americans engage in public debate of any kind, their style is often high-key, that is, animated, interpersonal, and confrontational with the effect of expressing and generating emotion. African Americans see their style as natural and sincere expressions of their thoughts and feelings. Since they're accustomed to such expression in their communities, they accept others' passionate style in the spirit in which it's intended: honest engagement, participation, and expression that helps people know each other and ultimately contributes to unity. In general, African American culture allows members much greater freedom to assert and express themselves than do most other cultures (Kochman 1981).

For example the Euro-American culture has standards of quiet "good taste and decorum" as the chief restraining factors—at least in middle-class and upper-class environments. Euro-American style therefore tends to be more low-key; that is, relatively dispassionate, impersonal, non-challenging, and less likely to express or generate as much emotion. Asian Americans are even more averse to open confrontations. Latino Americans are likely to see confrontation as a violation of the need to be "sympatico," which is a style that smooths over differences in order to get along smoothly.

People from these other cultures often interpret African American expressions of anger and their verbal aggressiveness as more threatening and provocative than it's intended. The type of angry verbal disputes, even involving insults and threats, that often occur among African Americans without necessarily leading to violence, would in fact almost always be precursors to violence within the Euro-American, Asian, and Latino cultures.

Boasting and Bragging

Most African Americans distinguish between boasting and bragging. Boasting is typically done with some sense of humor; it's usually exaggerated; and it's not intended to be taken seriously. It's done as a form of play and entertainment used to gain recognition within a group. Bragging is a serious form of self-aggrandizement, and people are expected to back up their claims. Bragging about your ability is okay, but bragging about your possessions or social status is not.

Eye Contact Differences

Have you ever felt that you and an acquaintance were avoiding looking at each other in a conversation? Or staring each other down? Maybe it was unmatched eye contact. When African Americans speak, they tend to look at their partner more than they do while listening, while for Euro-Americans the pattern is reversed.

African American: speak—keep looking, listen—glance away
Euro-American: listen—keep looking, speak—glance away

You can see that when an African American is speaking to a Euro-American, there's too much looking going on. And when the Euro-American is speaking, there's not enough looking going on.

For African Americans, the meaning of this ritual may be: When I speak, I keep close watch to see how you're responding; when I listen, I glance away as I think about what you're saying. For Euro-Americans, the meaning may be: When I speak, I glance away to gather my thoughts; when I listen, I maintain eye contact to show you that I'm really listening.

Of course, when either party has spent a great deal of time with members of the other culture, they've probably learned to adjust their eye contact ritual. Certainly, once you become conscious of the differences, you can learn to adjust.

Value #6: Bouncing Back

Resilience and revitalization are admired and have been a key to survival. Older members are respected because they have

- been through the experiences that can only come with age.
- been "down the line," seen the comings and goings of life.
- survived the cycles of oppression, struggle, survival, backlash, and renewed struggle.
- stood the test of time and adversity, paid their dues, and transcended tragedy
- most, important, learned to "keep on keepin' on."

A lively sense of humor and spiritual beliefs support the bouncing back value.

Value #7: The Dual Culture—Not Trusting the Establishment

The burden of inequality placed upon African Americans is a major contradiction of American ideals. African Americans grow up a part of, yet apart from, American society—in it but not if it, included at some levels and excluded at others. This duality is at the heart of their identity struggle and often generates powerful feelings of frustration, anger, and indignation. It is further complicated by their bicultural value systems, worldviews, and historical legacies. They must try to set up a workable balance between African American and Euro-American values within their lives. Completely denying either one will restrict their life choices. If they focus only on individualism, competition, emotional insulation, power, dominance, and control, they may achieve success but they'll pay a huge price. If they focus only on genuineness, mutual aid, the collective good, and emotional closeness, they'll enjoy inclusion in the African American community but are unlikely to achieve economic success in the workplace. (Baldwin 1992). W.E.B. DuBois (1965, 215) described this dual cultural background as:

. . . this double consciousness, this sense of always looking at one's self through the eyes of others, of measuring one's soul by the tape of a world that looks on in amused contempt and pity. One ever feels his twoness—an American, a Negro; two souls, two thoughts, two unreconciled strivings; two warring ideals in one dark body, whose dogged strength alone keeps it from being torn asunder.

History has taught African Americans to distrust the establishment, to keep their own counsel, and to use caution when communicating outside the community. One result was the use of "code talk" among themselves (White and Parham 1990). For example, "a bad nigger" in African American semantics has traditionally referred to a hero, someone they admire for his or her courage and guts to stand up to "white folks."

Today, the trust gap still shows up in work relationships when African Americans use protective hesitation before they speak up or take action around Euro-Americans. They take time to think about how their words or actions might reinforce negative stereotypes or how they might make themselves vulnerable to betrayal or attack. Where they have a choice, they may avoid working with Euro-Americans. Trust can be built, but it may be a relatively slow and difficult process. One action perceived as betrayal can break the delicate new structure.

Vignette: Seeing Anew Through Informed Eyes

People who have studied the African American culture learn to look for accurate interpretations of behavior. Bill tells about his experience. "I overheard an African American having a telephone conversation the other day. He got so loud and vehement that I became very uncomfortable, even though I wasn't involved. Then I remembered what I had learned about the African American culture. I looked and listened more closely. I saw that he was smiling part of the time and his body was fairly relaxed. Then I shifted my perception, opening up the possibility that he wasn't really angry and about to explode. I began to hear a very different conversation, one in which the guy was just being real and genuine, asserting his thoughts and feelings, and tellin' it like it is."

THE AFRICAN AMERICAN COMMUNITY: TYPICAL CUSTOMS

The core values of the African American community are reflected in typical customs in three major life areas: community life, family life, and personal relationships

Customs in Community Life

The church took on a major role in advocating social change throughout the twentieth century, with ministers becoming leaders in the Civil Rights movement. The church still plays a central role in virtually every aspect of African American life, including major efforts to help the underclass break out of the shackles that keep them in poverty. Most offer an array of self-help programs.

Customs in Family Life

The sharing value is expressed in the practice of seeing relatives and close friends as an extended family, while the distrust factor results in "tough" child-rearing practices.

Extended Families. Among African Americans, the term *parents* often refers to natural parents, grandparents, and others who assume parental roles and responsibilities from time to time. Relationships with key people who are not blood relatives are considered essential to the maintenance of the family. This custom is rooted both in the African American tribal heritage and in the need to withstand the stress spawned by the slavery system and the survival struggles that are still prevalent (Mann 1981).

Child-Rearing Practices. The strict, no-nonsense discipline used by many African American parents, sometimes seen as harsh or rigid to some Euro-Americans, is actually functional and appropriate discipline by caring parents. They see it as preparation for survival in a hostile environment, one that is prejudiced and discriminatory against them (Allen 1981; Willie 1976; Young 1977).

Customs in Personal Relationships

The sharing value means that most African Americans place especially high value on trusting and helping one another. Most have one style for relating to acquaintances and a somewhat different style for relating to friends. And they may appear indifferent or uninvolved in their interactions with persons outside the community (Smith, Willis and Gier 1980; Ickes 1984).

African American Style with Acquaintances

African Americans are guided in their communication with other African American acquaintances, such as co-workers and casual friends, by the following four types of guidelines (Collier 1988).

1. *Follow role prescriptions.* African Americans generally pay more attention to this than Euro-Americans. Still, they place even more emphasis on individual roles that express each person's style than on conventional roles. This reflects their value for expressing personal uniqueness, but within group settings for the purpose of group appreciation.

2. *Be polite.* Politeness is viewed as more an individual than societal trait, and deciding your own rules for politeness is more important to African Americans than it is to other American subcultures.

3. *Watch your words.* African Americans tend to be much more cautious about what they say to people outside the community.

4. *Support "brothers and sisters."* African Americans especially value conversations within the community that are supportive, relevant, and assertive, reflecting the cultural values of sharing and being positive.

African American Style with Friends

African Americans are likely to develop closer, more intimate friendships than do Euro-Americans. They're likely to be more intimate in discussions of school, work, religion, interests, hobbies, and physical condition. On the other hand, Euro-Americans are likely to be more revealing and intimate in discussions of love, dating, sex, and feelings about these issues. African American stress on intimacy may fall into these four types of action (Collier 1992).

1. *Acknowledge the individual.* Allow others to express themselves through assertiveness and individual style and accomplishment. Appreciate their uniqueness and their individual expressions of who they are.

2. *Develop intimacy.* The value of sharing is achieved through talking about family and other personal topics. It includes these kinds of actions:

   - giving and receiving friendly advice, leading to positive feelings
   - taking specific actions to establish trust as the most crucial element of relationships

- expressing sensitivity, support, affirmation, honesty, and brotherhood or sisterhood
- accepting criticisms and requests without compromising the friendship

3. *Be supportive.* Do such things as:
   - offer solutions for a problem or advice on personal issues
   - seek mutual understanding
   - express individuality
   - affirm the other person or the culture
   - establish trust and intimacy

4. *Appreciate the culture.* Focus on the similarities in our beliefs, attitudes, and interests. Express pride in our common roots and the cultural background itself.

Male–Female Relationships

African American culture presumes that all women have a general sexual interest in men and are sexually assertive, so they aren't considered less respectable or more available when they express these traits. African American men are more direct in their expression of sexual interest, and the women aren't insulted by this but generally feel confident about how to reject or accept such overtures. The men are normally not offended by a rejection if it's done in good humor, only by being ignored or rejected in a degrading way.

INTEGRATING AFRICAN VALUES: THE NEW URBAN VILLAGE

A growing movement is afoot in the African American community, a movement that emphasizes African heritage and values and integrates them with American values and the American dream. A comparison of the Eurocentric and Afrocentric views, as developed to community leaders, is shown in Table 7.8 to help explain the idea. Compare the two by entire viewpoint, not belief by belief.

TABLE 7.8: Comparison of Eurocentric and Afrocentric Viewpoints

Eurocentric Viewpoint	*Afrocentric Viewpoint*
Survival of the fittest is central theme. Competition is a major theme in interactions with other humans and nature. Humans devise the battlefields where life is played out. Those who accumulate the most of what costs the most are the winners, the best. War is the ultimate form of competition: Cold War, Star Wars, war on crime, war on drugs Ultimate goal: to be #1, the symbol of achievement and worth.	Humans are one with nature. All entities experience cyclical, periodic, and inevitable changes. In humans these changes are seen as life crises, which are disruptive but can be eased by group rituals of passages from one life phase to the next. The death-rebirth cycle reflects the law of regeneration and applies to all of nature: systems become spent and must be regenerated. When one life phase ends, a new one begins. Rites of passage reflect nature's cycle: separation from the old, transition to the new, and integration of old and new.

Based on the work of George Fraser.

Regarding the Eurocentric ultimate goal, many African Americans say the ultimate illusion of the American Dream is that anyone who is focused, educated, and persistent can fight his or her way to the top and enjoy the distinction of being Number One. If being number one means others are number two, and so forth, then obviously everyone cannot make it.

The urban village concept. This is a recent African American approach. It's grounded in the Afrocentric view but also recognizes that the Eurocentric view sets the rules of the American marketplace. A key principle is of the urban village is:

It takes a village to raise a child.

The keys to success, from this urban village viewpoint, include networking, mentoring, and cooperative economics. The motto is economic empowerment. Virtually every African American church and community organization now operates some sort of economic program, from economic literacy and job training classes to community loan funds. Weekend mentoring programs focus on bringing together urban youth and business persons and other role models.

The urban village concept incorporates Afrocentric rites of passage, especially important for inner city youth, as well as the principles of Kwanzaa.

Kwanzaa. This is a way of life that honors the African heritage for the purpose of encouraging a greater sense of unity, identity, and purpose among African Americans. The seven Kwanzaa principles focus on unity, self-determination, collective work and responsibility, cooperative economics, purpose, creativity, and faith. Many of its symbols and terms come from African tradition, but it's a creation of African Americans that goes back to 1966. Special Kwanzaa celebrations occur from December 26 through January 1.

Kwanzaa and the urban village model are approaches that recognize the realities of African American life in the American society. They are seen by many African Americans as positive, empowering, practical approaches that are grounded in the interdependence and spirituality of an Afrocentric worldview. See www.melanet.com/kwanzaa.

ISSUES IMPORTANT TO THE AFRICAN AMERICAN COMMUNITY

Here is a summary of problems that African Americans ranked most important from a list offered by Princeton Survey Research Associates (Cose 1999).

1. Teenage mothers
2. Lack of jobs that pay a decent wage
3. Decline in moral and religious values
4. Welfare dependency
5. Crime in the neighborhood
6. Racism in society in general
7. Public school education—difficulty getting a good education
8. Social programs—the government should provide more funds for programs with a proven track record, such as Head Start
9. Unmarried parents
10. Racism in the workplace
11. Lack of role models for young people—too few successes in the workplace

LEADERSHIP CHALLENGE: BREAKING THROUGH THE BARRIERS TO SUCCESS

You can play a role in helping African American associates overcome the "less-intelligent" stereotype that leads to lowered expectations for their skill development, promotability, and corporate success. You can also play a role in helping them break through the glass ceiling to better jobs. And, by understanding the typical career phases African Americans experience, you can learn how to support them in overcoming typical personal barriers and corporate-culture barriers at each phase.

Barrier #1: Breaking Out of Lowered Expectations—Success Cycles

A real barrier for many African Americans is the stereotype that they are less intelligent. Many have internalized this belief. All must deal with Euro-Americans in the workplace who hold this stereotype and therefore expect African Americans to be less competent learners and achievers.

You've learned that the higher the socioeconomic status of a family, the higher the grades and SAT scores of their children. Once an African American family is able to break the cycle of poverty and get good jobs, the cycle tends to stay broken for that family. The children do well in school and are therefore likely to get good jobs and earn good incomes when they grow up, which in turn increases the likelihood that *their* children will do well in school. Some predominantly African American schools have identified differences in the failure and success cycles (Howard and Hammond 1988). They've adopted success cycle teaching and learning strategies to help children boost their academic achievement.

Some corporations have adopted these same strategies to help all employees, including African Americans, break out of failure cycles and establish success cycles.

What You Expect Is What You Get

Failure and success cycles are affected by what people expect. Here's what expectancy theory is all about: You, in your manager role, communicate in words and actions your beliefs and expectations about what a worker can achieve. If that worker values your opinion, then your expectations have a powerful impact on that person's skill development and performance. If you believe the co-worker will do well, she's more likely to believe she'll do well, she's more likely to actually do well, and she's more likely to credit her success to her own ability. Belief leads to performance.

If a worker thinks you're an important person, that you have knowledge or you can make a difference, then what you expect can affect the following aspects of her performance:

- how fully she believes she can succeed
- how hard she tries
- how intensely she concentrates
- how willing she is to take reasonable risks, which is a key factor in developing self-confidence and new skills
- how she interprets her success or failure

Failure Cycle

Here's how the failure cycle works: When you believe a worker has inferior abilities and therefore you have lower expectations for him than for others, you set up a failure cycle as follows:

- You assume that he is intellectually inferior, which leads to
- His internalized belief that he is intellectually inferior, which leads to
- Low self-confidence about succeeding at intellectual tasks, which leads to
- Poor performance on intellectual tasks, which leads to
- Avoidance of intellectual tasks

We can therefore conclude that avoidance of intellectual challenge is affected by fears and self-doubt, which are rooted in a history of strong negative stereotypes that Euro-Americans hold about African American's intellectual capabilities.

When a worker expects to fail, or assumes he can't succeed, or believes "I don't have what it takes," here's what's likely to occur:

- He takes a dim view of trying again.
- He loses his motivation and often gives up trying to learn.

- He blames the failure on his own lack of ability (or aptitude and potential) rather than on inadequate or erroneous effort, which is correctable.
- By this process he, in effect, internalizes the low opinion originally held by you (or others).

What makes African Americans unique in this regard is that they are singled out for the stigma of genetic intellectual inferiority. This negative stereotype suggests to African Americans that they should understand any failure in intellectual activity as confirmation of genetic inferiority. No wonder many African Americans shy away from any situation where the rumor of inferiority might be proved true.

FIGURE 7.1: Failure Cycle

Other's assumption that I'm intellectually inferior ⟶
My internalized belief that I'm intellectually inferior ⟶
Low self-confidence regarding intellectual tasks ⟶
Poor performance on intellectual tasks ⟶
Avoidance of such tasks

Success Cycle

African Americans tend to experience greater success when they engage in sports, socializing, and entertaining others because of assumptions and stereotypes that they are "innately" gifted in these areas. Many of them have established success cycles in these areas. But suppose you are an important person in an African American worker's life. Here's how you would set up a success cycle.

- You assume that she can master a job task, which leads to
- her internalized belief that she can master the job task, which leads to
- self-confidence in her ability to master the job task, which leads to
- willingness to put forth effort on the job task, which leads to
- development of job skills

If she has a failure during this process, her self-confidence allows her to see it as merely an error, not a sign of incompetence. Failure is just an opportunity to find out what doesn't work and correct it, a lesson for how to succeed next time.

Your positive beliefs and resulting expectations for her success helps her to build self-confidence. She becomes inspired and willing to put forth the effort necessary to achieve specific job goals, which leads to learning, achievement, and growth in that job area. This achievement becomes the foundation for increased self-confidence in the next cycle, as summarized in Figure 7.2.

FIGURE 7.2: Success Cycle

Assumption by leader that I can master intellectual tasks ⟶
Internalized belief that I can master intellectual tasks ⟶
Self-confidence in my ability to master intellectual tasks ⟶
Willingness to put forth effort on intellectual tasks ⟶
Development of intellectual skills

The success cycle is a process in which success increases self-confidence and effort, leading to even more success, over and over in the upward spiral. It's circular and feeds back on itself, moving upward in a geometrically expanding spiral, as shown in Figure 7.3, Skill Development Cycle.

FIGURE 7.3: Skill Development Cycle

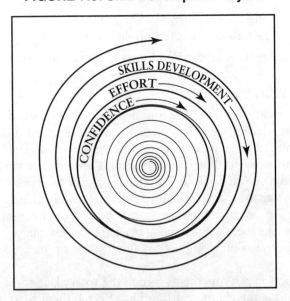

What you can do

Here's how you can encourage a success cycle during the various learning phases:

1. *During the confidence phase.* Begin with your own stereotyped beliefs, assumptions, and expectations. Get them straight. When you're sure you have a "you can" attitude, you'll know your verbal and nonverbal messages are likely to convey positive expectations.

2. *During the effort phase.* Take a positive attitude toward performance evaluation. Encourage African Americans to attribute their successes to ability, boosting their confidence level. Help them to see their failures as either a lack of effort or some correctable error—as a learning tool for creating success the next time around. The key question is, how can I do it differently next time?

3. *During the skill development phase.* Help African American employees to assume responsibility for their own performance and development, and let them know you are there as a resource person. Pay special attention to training and development, bringing in appropriate new opportunities as skills are built. Keep the cycle going.

Barrier #2: Breaking Through the Glass Ceiling

Corporate America cannot yet claim a diverse workplace that looks like America as a whole. African Americans have moved into better-paying occupations but most still hit a glass ceiling at middle management levels or even below, according to government reports.

Barriers to Better Paying Occupations

Looking at the American workforce as a whole, only about 5 percent of *all* managers and professional persons are African American, though they are 12 percent of the population. This includes government jobs, where they have made the greatest progress, so corporate rates are even lower. Still, this is an overall increase of 52 percent since 1978.

The unemployment rate for African American men aged 20 to 24 remained higher than 20 percent well into the 1990s, more than double the rates for Euro-American men. The most common occupation for African American men is laborer and for women, clerical. Since the 1960s women have made better progress than men, most moving from jobs as agricultural or domestic worker to office worker. However, African American women still tend to be:

- placed into training programs for traditionally female occupations
- discouraged from attempting innovative careers
- dependent upon the public sector for employment
- kept out of better private-sector jobs by rigid ethnic barriers

External and Internal Attitudes

In American society traditional prejudice and discrimination toward diverse groups results in a package of feelings and experiences that most members of these groups bring to the workplace. As a leader, you need to be aware of these factors that affect African Americans in a wide range of ways. Some have managed to ignore or rise above most of them. Others may have a problem in one area and none in the others. Knowing what to look for can help you give the right kind of support.

Whether your role is that of manager, team leader, or responsible co-worker, you can identify ways to support African Americans in leaving stereotypes behind and focusing on developing themselves for the next job promotion. The focus may be on increasing their flexibility, networking ability, bottom-line influence, computer literacy, skill in highlighting their own strengths, and other areas relevant to their career plan.

The barriers that most African Americans face in the workplace consist of a mixture of the burdens society has imposed upon them and how that has affected them personally. Most African Americans come to the workplace with some combination of the following factors:

- a history of oppression and exclusion from the mainstream activities of society
- a sense that they're seen as different (in a negative way) from Euro-Americans
- being positioned in a one-down status
- being barred or discouraged from seeking a better position in society—or in life
- lack of equal opportunities
- as a result: lower self-concept, self-esteem, and self-confidence

These problems, and sometimes their solution attempts, have led to other problems, mentioned in surveys of African Americans who have chosen to leave their corporations:

- Hitting the glass ceiling and lack of opportunity and upward mobility
- Feeling pressured to "act white" and to repress their ethnic identity in order to fit in, make others feel comfortable, and succeed
- Feeling misplaced in a corporate culture where work life and social life focus only on Euro-American customs
- Having to prove themselves, over and over again, due to being African American
- Dealing with the assumption, and resulting stigma, that they are an "affirmative action hire"
- Coping with ethnic stereotypes

To succeed in most corporate cultures, African Americans must learn to:

- Pay as much attention to building relationships and monitoring and developing their career strategies as they do to achieving specific job goals
- Market themselves within the company and outside of it
- Network and establish relationships with other people in other divisions
- Tap into the grapevine and keep up with what's going on

Your opportunity as a leader is to encourage and support them in doing all this.

Barrier #3: Breaking Through Blocks at Each Career Phase

You can help African Americans break through career blocks by understanding the career phases typical for African Americans and by giving support at each phase. According to African American managers Jacqueline and Floyd Dickens (1982), African Americans who enter the corporate world typically move through several phases that might be described as:

- *Entry-level* phase—dealing with organizational and personal prejudice
- *Adjustment and frustration* phase—dealing with their own anger and frustration
- *Career development* phase—developing skills in conflict management and management of prejudice
- *Mastery* phase—refining protective hesitation and integrating core skills

Entry-Level and Adjustment Phases

Many African American applicants come to the organization with a positive but naive attitude. They usually encounter personal as well as organizational prejudice and may become angry, hostile, and culturally paranoid. If they decide to stay, they then adjust and plan their growth rather than allow anger and resentment to stifle it. They find ways to recapture their earlier positive attitude, so that negative attitudes cease to be a barrier to learning. Successful African American employees somehow retain a positive attitude even in the midst of prejudiced behaviors.

To succeed in corporate America, managers who are African American, as compared to Euro-American, must pay more attention to building and maintaining relationships. They must put Euro-Americans at ease, for example. Successful African American managers suggest making the first move in building workplace relationships, saying "If you don't reach out, you'll never be a part of important after-hours get-togethers" (Lancaster 1997).

Some Euro-American employees will think African American managers got their job just because they're African American. Nipping this perception in the bud may be best—by bringing it up in a meeting and dealing with the issue of adequate qualifications. About any real problem, it's usually best to speak up, point out the problem, and take issues to higher-level management, if necessary.

African American managers must walk a fine line between accommodating the Euro-American corporate culture and maintaining their identity, expressing it in ways that don't create backlash. African American role models and mentors are a great help, though managers may have to go outside their own company to find one.

- Do you think of African Americans first and foremost as human beings, as individuals, or as African Americans?
- Does your small talk with them cover the whole gamut of topics? Or is it normally confined primarily to African American news items, celebrities, and events?

In the early phases, most African Americans have great difficulty seeing themselves in a leadership position because they've been taught that Euro-American men lead, African Americans follow. They often apologize in various ways for taking leadership or initiative or for being put in even a temporary leadership position. They may have difficulty directing Euro-American males and therefore not be as self-confident as the norm because of discomfort with empowerment. Before they become comfortable with having and using power, their walk may be less assured, their voice tone may lack authority, and their attitude may be more *May I?* than *This is what we can do*. Keep in mind that typically African Americans are required to demonstrate competence at the next level before they are promoted, whereas Euro-American males are typically promoted on the basis of their potential. Ask yourself periodically

- Am I doing my share to see that people are treated equally? That everyone gets a fair chance at plum assignments and promotions?

Even when African Americans achieve the desired results, they typically must devote extra energy to ensure that the results are properly seen by the right people. This is because decision makers often harbor negative stereotypes that prevent them from seeing such achievements.

- Are you open to seeing everyone's achievements and potential?

- Are you helping others to see clearly?

Career Development Phase

Overcoming African American mistrust of the input from Euro-Americans is still an issue for most African American employees, even at the career development stage. They may establish a one-to-one relationship with their manager, but they rarely expand this to a generalized attitude toward all Euro-Americans. During this phase African American employees usually keep their misgivings to themselves, choosing instead to behave in a manner of trust. They need to identify and access one or more mentors.

These employees must develop and use a network of supporters, whether the members are prejudiced or not. A commitment to succeed becomes the prime goal of successful employees. By now they should understand that waiting to be adopted by a Euro-American mentor is risky, so they may need to take the initiative to locate potential people in the organization and find a mentor.

- Are you willing to be a supporter or mentor?

- Are you encouraging others to support African American colleagues?

In this phase, two of the most important job skills to be acquired are *conflict management* and the *management of prejudice*.

If African Americans can't deal with conflict constructively, they're likely to be blamed as a *cause* of any conflict they become embroiled in. African Americans tend as a group to be more open and straightforward in their interactions than do Euro-Americans. They typically want to confront conflict directly and solve the problem quickly. In many organizations however, the norm is conflict avoidance. If so, the African American's style will be seen as inappropriate. African Americans are more likely to confront the other person as soon as they're aware of a conflict situation. If that's inappropriate, they'll do it later in private. Euro-Americans in many corporate cultures will discuss the situation with the other person's boss, and may talk about it with others, before they'll openly confront the person involved in the conflict.

- Are you willing to accept an open, direct style of conflict resolution?

Management of prejudice involves a range of skills most African Americans must develop in order to counteract and neutralize Euro-Americans' demeaning, prejudicial actions. For example, *protective hesitation* is a common African American strategy for dealing with prejudice and the hostile situations it engenders. It's based on the value of distrust of the establishment. The strategy consists of deliberately hesitating before interacting or preparing to interact with Euro-Americans, in order to think about how to protect oneself from possible psychological assault or to avoid reinforcing negative stereotypes about African Americans. Such preventive hesitation involves using caution and preplanning. This behavior has been handed down from parents to children through generations and so comes naturally to many African Americans by the time they're adults. It can be especially helpful at the career development phase when the employee is being assessed for promotion potential.

- Are you willing to understand protective hesitation and to discover the underlying dynamics of prejudice and defense?

The Mastery Phase: Mutual Support

One of the key insights successful African Americans say they used in the mastery phase is that making mistakes or failing is not an option for African American managers. When they fail, they fail for the entire group of African American employees. Most have made protective hesitation a way of life in the corporation. Key to their style is preplanning, careful thought, and caution in relying on

Euro-Americans as resources. Through trial and error, they take their rage and use its energy to help them achieve productive results.

- Are you willing to build trusting relationships by consistently being honest, direct, and supportive?

LEADERSHIP OPPORTUNITIES: BUILDING ON AFRICAN AMERICAN STRENGTHS

As a leader, you need to recognize the strengths that each of your team members brings to the organization and to build on those strengths. African Americans bring many assets to the workplace that can be used in numerous ways. They can contribute to team processes, to the development of networks and business relationships that are especially valuable for the organization, and to connections with the African American marketplace.

Opportunity #1: Planning, Creating, Problem Solving

Work teams must deal with fast-paced change—by recognizing niches, developing profitable products and services, moving in on the right opportunities at the right time, solving problems, and optimizing total quality. The best work teams develop a high level of skill in generating ideas, planning, and problem solving—and they do this through synergy, creativity, and innovation as well as by discipline and application.

You can help team leaders and members recognize the value of African American strengths, such as expressing personal style for the appreciation of the group, being assertive in expressing feelings and ideas, and not giving up. These traits can add to the team's strengths. Some of these traits may seem foreign to those accustomed to typical business traits and approaches.

- You can help your team realize that a different approach can sometimes score winning points, that "differentness" can be an asset.

Opportunity #2: Building Relationships

Relationships are the name of the game in the marketplace. Business is built upon networks of relationships among team members, customers, suppliers, other departments, the community, professional organizations, regulating agencies, and others. African Americans have a special advantage when they apply their tendencies toward: *a people focus, sharing, nonverbal communication skills, and expression of feelings*, as detailed in the earlier values discussion.

For example, in team relationships, African American members can set a tone that could help the team avoid game playing and hidden agendas through focusing on the values of *directness, emotional expressiveness, and sense of justice*. To be most effective, expression of these values may need to be stepped down to an intensity that other team members can accept.

- You can help African Americans members develop appropriate expressions of their strengths.
- You can also provide guidance about expressing the justice and distrust values in ways that avoid the stereotype of the resentful African American or the troublemaker.

Opportunity #3: Connecting with the African American Marketplace

African Americans obviously have an inside edge in understanding other African Americans, the community, and the marketplace. They can contribute great strength to the organization in gaining African American market share. African Americans now represent about $500 billion a year in spending power, and the market is growing. These customers and business persons like to do business with companies that "look like America" and therefore include African Americans. South Africa and other African nations also represent growth market opportunities for many organizations, and African American team members provide an obvious advantage in those markets.

- You can recognize these connections and the related opportunities to use African American employees' understanding of their own cultures and related cultures.

- You can make others aware of these connections and opportunities and use your influence to help African Americans make valuable contributions to the success of your team and your organization.

SUMMARY

The 12 percent of employees who are African American must deal with myths and stereotypes about violence, anger, intelligence, initiative, and style, all part of a heritage of slavery, segregation, and discrimination. African Americans led the Civil Rights movement that opened doors for all disadvantaged groups in the U.S. workplace. As a result, there is a growing affluent African American middle class, about one-third of African Americans, but also a growing underclass of about one-third, with another third struggling in between. African American educational achievement tends to be lower than that of Euro-Americans. Studies indicate that higher socioeconomic status is the best predictor of school grades and SAT scores, so the solution to this problem lies in finding ways to help more African Americans reach middle-class status. Meanwhile, for those who have achieved such status, there's still a glass ceiling to advancement for African Americans in corporate America, and many who hit it are leaving to form their own businesses.

The core values of the African American community are sharing, personal style, being genuine, being assertive, expressing feelings, bouncing back, dealing with a dual culture, and not trusting the establishment. The community is close-knit, and their ways of confronting one another assertively are part of being genuine. This trait is often misunderstood by Euro-Americans as being combative and even a prelude to violence. But it can be a strength, just as vitality and resilience are strengths, that African American employees bring to the workplace and marketplace. These strengths can be especially helpful in team projects and in building networks of relationships.

Leaders can communicate their positive expectations and support for African American employees in order to set up a success cycle. They can help to break the glass ceiling caused by traditional stereotypes, and help African Americans negotiate the typical career phases they experience in mainstream organizations. Leaders must be especially sensitive to the value of distrust of the establishment, and special care must be taken to build trust. Leaders can also help African American employees build on their strengths as they develop other skills and strengths they need to achieve job and career goals.

Skill Builder 7.1: The Case of Jason, African American Manager

Jason has applied for an assistant manager's position at Drysdale Corporation. He's looking for opportunities to learn and grow in his career and wants to leave his current job because such opportunities are lacking. His ultimate career goal is to become CEO of a large corporation. With his degree in business administration and plans to complete an MBA, he thinks he has a chance—if he can find the right firm—even though he's an African American. When Jason is escorted around the Drysdale offices, he sees no African Americans, a few Asian Americans, and one Latino American. Nearly everyone is Euro-American, and they mostly seem too busy to pay much attention to Jason or spend time with him. But Jason really believes in the Drysdale Corporation and decides to accept their job offer.

Soon after he begins work, he notices that ethnic jokes and comments are common at Drysdale. Jason doesn't look like a typical African American because his mother is Euro-American. He speaks up several times, saying he doesn't appreciate jokes and comments that belittle people from any ethnic group. Most of the comments stop, but so does the already-sparse friendliness of Jason's coworkers. While the environment is not particularly warm at Drysdale, Jason still believes he can achieve career success here because he loves the work itself.

Jason knows he's a rapid learner and a responsible person, one who works effectively and efficiently. His performance evaluations during the next year and a half are all excellent and his manager *Ken* seems to be encouraging.

In fact, Jason believes he is one of the most productive workers in the company. He meets his time targets and maintains high work quality. But Jason is getting restless. His work is becoming routine to him and therefore boring. He has asked Ken several times about a promotion and expanded job responsibilities. Ken has been vague, telling Jason to "hang in there and I'll keep an eye out for job opportunities for you." In the meantime, several management positions have opened up at Drysdale and been filled by others.

- What do you think is going on here?
- If you were Jason, what would you do?

Skill Builder 7.2: The Case of Karla, African American Salesperson

Karla is a salesperson at Ellison's Furniture, the only African American on the small sales force of 20 persons. She has been very successful in selling furniture, makes a good salary plus commission, and during the year she has been at Ellison's has made top salesperson of the month three times. Karla enjoys her work but feels isolated from most of her coworkers. Most of them are Euro-American men, and five are Euro-American women. The manager *Daniel* is Euro-American and has been very supportive of Karla's training, development, and sales work. He often praises her work and encourages her to "keep it up."

Rachel is the only salesperson who has seemed willing to spend much time with Karla during coffee breaks or at lunch. While Karla doesn't think of Rachel as a close personal friend, she does view her as more than just a business colleague. She's also a friend.

From time to time Karla has overheard comments of her coworkers about the good times they've had together at various parties and outings that they plan. She can't help thinking about the fact that she is never included. Last week as Karla approached the employees' lounge, she heard someone saying, ". . . at Rachel's party last Saturday . . . ." Karla stopped dead in her tracks. She felt as if someone had punched her in the stomach. What a blow to discover that even her friend, her only "real work friend," had thrown a party and had excluded her.

Daniel has noticed that during the past week Karla has seemed quieter and more withdrawn than usual. He is concerned because he believes that Karla's success as a salesperson is largely due to her outgoing, cheerful personality. When he gets a chance to talk privately with Karla, he says, "Is everything okay, Karla? You've been awfully quiet the past few days."

- If you were Karla, what would you do?
- If you were Daniel, what would you do?

Skill Builder 7.3: The Case of Assistant Manager Doug

Doug is assistant manager of the Nashville branch of Angelo Shipping Company. He's been an employee there for 12 years, since he was 23, and he was promoted to assistant manager a year ago. Last month Doug learned of an upcoming opening in the Atlanta headquarters and applied for it. He believes he has all the necessary qualifications for the position as well as an exemplary performance record. Although there are many African American men working as manual laborers for the company, none are full managers or executives.

John, an executive in the headquarters office, is interviewing applicants for the management position and will make a recommendation to the executive team. Of the four qualified applicants, all but Doug are Euro-American men. John, also a Euro-American, has never worked with an African American manager.

When Doug arrives for his interview with John, he's left waiting in the lobby for an hour. Then a secretary comes in and tells him that John is still interviewing another candidate and will be with him in a while. About 45 minutes later, John appears in the lobby with **Mike** of the Memphis branch. John is talking warmly with Mike, then thanks him and shakes his hand before turning to welcome Doug. They walk to John's office, where John waves toward a chair across from his desk, and Doug seats himself. John and Doug talk for about 10 to 15 minutes, mainly about how Doug feels about his current job and the company. The phone rings. John takes the call, puts his hand over the receiver, and says to Doug, "Thank you for coming in. Could you show yourself out? I must take this call." Doug was shocked, but he found his way out.

A few days later, Doug receives a telephone call from John, who tells him the executive team has selected Mike for the job. He says the executive team felt the position called for someone with Mike's experience. Later, Doug says to his friend Jan, "I know I've been with the company at least as long as Mike, and I've been employee-of-the-month here eight different times. I heard Mike has only won it twice. I don't understand how his experience could be any better than mine. What would make it better?"

- *What is your opinion of John's actions and the executive team's decision?*
- *What do you think Doug should do?*

Skill Builder 7.4: The Case of Sales Rep Evelyn

Evelyn has been one of the outstanding sales representatives for McCord Foods' West Coast region for the past three years. Her immediate supervisor **Rosalie** is in a quandary about what to do. The Houston office needs a sales supervisor with just the kind of experience and qualities that Evelyn has. However, the last time an African American was transferred into a management position at the Houston office, he faced many problems. The major issue was that key customers didn't accept him and he lost a number of accounts. These accounts were with large, traditional food processing and manufacturing firms.

McCord sells spices, flavorings, and other additives to the food industry. The field is very competitive, and accounts are often won and lost on the basis of the personal relationships between sales manager, sales rep, and purchasing agent. The sales manager periodically travels with sales reps to call on major accounts and potential accounts. The sales manager also enters the picture when thorny customer problems arise.

Louis, who is head of the Houston office, was enthusiastic about Evelyn's resume until he heard that she was African American. He called Rosalie and talked over the touchy situation with her. "Maybe it wouldn't be fair to Evelyn to ask her to move all the way down here and then be faced with a no-win situation," he said.

Now Rosalie must make a decision. She knows that two other well-qualified candidates are being recommended for the position, but actually Evelyn is better suited to the job than the others. Shall she recommend Evelyn for the position? Evelyn has a child in the fourth grade, who would have to adapt to a new school and the Houston environment. If it didn't work out, Rosalie would feel responsible.

- *What do you think Rosalie should do?*

REFERENCES

AAUW. *The AAUW Report: How Schools Shortchange Girls*. Washington DC: American Assn. University Women, 1992.

Abrahams, R.D. *Deep Down in the Jungle*. Chicago: Aldine Press, 1963.

Allen, W.R. "Moms, Dads, and Boys," in *Black Men*. Beverly Hills, CA: Sage, 1981.

Baldwin, J.A. "The Role of Black Psychologists in Black Liberation," in *African American Psychology*. Thousand Oaks, CA: Sage, 1992.

Beaty, Paul. *The White Boy Shuffle*. New York: Houghton Mifflin, 1996.

Billingsley, Andrew. *Climbing Jacob's Ladder: The Enduring Legacy of African American Families*. New York: Simon & Schuster, 1992.

Black Enterprise (May 1994).

Blackwell, J.E. *The Black Community: Diversity and Unity*. New York: Harper & Row, 1985.

Blanchard, F.A., and F.J. Crosby. *Affirmative Action in Perspective*. New York: Springer-Verlag, 1989.

Burman, Stephen. *The Black Progress Question*. Thousand Oaks CA: Sage, 1995.

Carr-Ruffino, "Legislative Measures for Women's Advancement" in *Womanpower*. Thousand Oaks, CA: Sage, 1992.

Carr-Ruffino, Norma. U.S. Women: Breaking Through the Glass Ceiling," *Women in Management Review*, 6, 5, 1991.

Collier, M.J. "A Comparison of Intracultural and Intercultural Communication Among Acquaintances," *Communication Quarterly*, 36, 1988, 122-144.

Collier, M.J. "Ethnic Friendships," manuscript submitted for publication, 1992.

Comer, J.P. and A.F. Poussaint. *Raising Black Children*. New York: Penguin, 1992.

Cose, Ellis, "The Good News About Black America," *Newsweek*, June 7, 1999, 29-40.

Cross, Wm. E. Jr. *Shades of Black: Diversity in African American Identity*. Philadelphia: Temple University Press, 1991.

Dickens, Floyd, Jr., and Jacqueline B. Dickens. *The Black Manager: Making It in the Corporate World*. New York: Amacom, 1982.

Donohue, W. A. *The Politics of the American Civil Liberties Union*. New Brunswick: Transaction Books, 1985.

Dovidio, J.F. and S.L. Gaertner, eds. *Prejudice, Discrimination, and Racism*. Orlando, Fla: Academic Press, 1986.

DuBois, W.E.B. *The Souls of Black Folk*, reprinted in *Three Negro Classics*. New York: Avon Books, 1965.

Executive Female. A survey on the glass ceiling, women and African Americans, 1991.

Feagin Joe, "The Continuing Significance of Race: Antiblack Discrimination in Public Places," *American Sociological Review*, 56, February 1991, 101-116.

Fletcher, Michael A. "Kerner follow-up sees wide race gap," *Washington Post*, syndicated in the *San Francisco Examiner*, March 1, 1998, A-6.

Foeman, A.K. and G. Pressley, "Ethnic Culture and Corporate Culture: Using Black Styles in Organizations," *Communications Quarterly*, 35, 1987, 293-307.

Fraser, George. *Success Runs in Our Race*. New York: Wm. Morrow, 1994.

Garner, T.E. "Playing the Dozens," *Quarterly Journal of Speech*, 69, 1983, 47-57.

Glaser, D. "Dynamics of Ethnic Identification," *American Sociological Review*, 23, 1958, 31-40.

Graham, Stedman. *You Can Make It Happen*. New York: Simon & Schuster, 1997.

Graves, Earl G. How to Succeed in Business Without Being White. New York: HarperBusiness, 1997.

Halberstad, A.G. "Race, Socioeconomic Status, and Nonverbal Behavior," in *Multichannel Integrations of Nonverbal Behavior*. Hillsdale, NJ: Lawrence Erlbaum, 1985.

Hall. E.T. *Beyond Culture*. New York: Doubleday, 1976.

Hammer, M.R. and W.B. Gundykunst. "The Influence of Ethnicity and Sex on Social Penetration in Close Friendships" *Journal of Black Studies* 17, 1987, 418-437.

Handy, Kenneth. *The Psychological Residuals of Slavery*, New York: Guilford Press, 1995.

Harding, Vincent. *The Other American Revolution*. Atlanta, GA: Institute of the Black World, 1980.

Hecht, M.L., and S. Ribeau. "Ethnic Communication: A Comparative Analysis of Satisfying Communication," *International Journal of Intercultural Relations* 8, 1984, 135-151.

Hecht, M.L., M.J. Collier, S.A. Ribeau. *African American Communication*, Thousand Oaks, CA: Sage, 1993.

Herskovitz, M.J. *The Myth of the Negro Past*. Boston: Beacon, 1958.

Herskovitz, M.J. *Anthropometry of the American Negro*. NY: Columbia Univ. Press, 1930.

Howard, Jeff, and Ray Hammond. "Rumors of Inferiority: The Hidden Obstacles to Black Success." *The New Republic*, September 9, 1988.

Ickes, W. "Composition in Black and White." *Journal of Personality and Social Psychology* 47, 1984, 1206-1217.

Issues of Public Policy, www.cnbl.org/html/appendices.html, 1999.

Kanter, R.M. *Men and Women of the Corporation*. New York: Basic Books, 1979.

Kenton, S.B. and D. Valentine. *CrossTalk*. Cincinnati, OH: South-Western, 1996.

Kitano, H. *Japanese-Americans*. Englewood Cliffs, NJ: Prentice-Hall, 1976.

Kochman, Thomas. *Black & White Styles in Conflict*. Chicago: The University of Chicago Press, 1981.

Lancaster, Hal, "Black Managers Often Must Emphasize Building Relationships," *Wall Street Journal*, A-1, February 4, 1997.

Larkey, L.K., and M.L. Hecht. "A Comparative Study of African American and Euro-American Ethnic Identity." Paper presented at the International Conference for Language and Social Psychology, Santa Barbara, CA, August 1991.

Lichtenberg, J. "Racism in the Head, Racism in the World." *Report from the Institute for Philosophy and Public Policy* 12, no. 1, 1992, 3-5.

Lynch, F.R. *Invisible Victims: White Males and the Crisis of Affirmative Action*. New York: Praeger, 1989.

Mann, W. "Support Systems of Significant Others in Black Families." in *Black Families*. Thousand Oaks, Ca: Sage, 1981.

Mauer, Marc. Research report on African American problems, 1989.

McWilliams, Carey. *Brothers Under the Skin*. Boston: Little, Brown & Co., 1964.

Myers, Samuel L., ed. *Economic Issues and Black Colleges*. Chicago: Follett Press 1986.

NAEOHE, National Association for Equal Opportunity in Higher Education, 1990.

Pettigrew, Thomas F., and Joanne Martin. "Shaping the Organizational Context for Black American Inclusion." *Journal of Social Issues* 43, 1, 1987, 41-78.

Pinkney, Alphonso. *The Myth of Black Progress*. Cambridge: Cambridge University Press, 1984.

Ponterotto, Joseph G., and Paul B. Pedersen. *Preventing Prejudice*. Thousand Oaks, CA: Sage, 1993.

Rose, L.F. "Theoretical & Methodological Issues in the Study of Black Culture and Personality. *Humboldt Journal of Social Relations* 10, 1982/1983, 320-338.

Smith, D.E., F.N. Willis, and J.A. Gier. "Success and Interpersonal Touch in a Competitive Setting." *Journal of Nonverbal Behavior* 5, 1980, 26-34.

Smitherman, G. *Talkin' and Testifyin': The Language of Black America*. Boston: Houghton Mifflin, 1977.

Solorzano, Daniel G. "Mobility Aspirations Among Racial Minorities, Controlling for SES. *Social Science Review* 75, July 1991, 182-188.

Stanbeck, M., and W.B. Pearce. "Talking to 'the man.'" *Quarterly Journal of Speech* 67, 1981, 21-30.

Stewart, Edward C. *American Cultural Patterns: A Cross Cultural Perspective*. LaGrange Park, IL: Intercultural Network, Inc., 1972.

Stienstra, Tom, A Dramatic Turnaround for State Parks. *San Francisco Examiner*, January 22, 1995, D-12.

Takaki, Ronald. *A Different Mirror: A History of Multicultural America*. Boston: Little, Brown & Co., 1993.

Terry, Robert W. (Detroit Industrial Mission). *For Whites Only*. Grand Rapids, MI: William B. Eerdmans Publishing Company, 1970, 1990.

Thomas, Roosevelt. *Beyond Race & Gender*. New York: AMACOM, 1991.

Thornton, Jeanne, and Davis Whitman, "Whites' Myths about Blacks," *U.S. News & World Report*, November 9, 1992, 41-44.

U.S. BLS, Bureau of Labor Statistics, http://stats.bls.gov, 1999.

U.S. Census Bureau, Current Population Reports. 1991. "Average Earnings of Year-Round Fulltime Workers by Sex and Educational Attainment." February, 1991.

U.S. Census Bureau, Department of Commerce, *We the American Children*, 1993.

U.S. Department of Labor. *A Report on the Glass Ceiling Initiative*, 1991.

U.S. Women's Bureau, Department of Labor, http://www.dol.gov/dol/wb, 1999.

Vas, Kim Marie, Ed., *Black Women in America*. Thousand Oaks CA: Sage, 1995.

West, Cornell. *Keeping Faith*. New York: Routledge, 1993.

West, Cornell. *Race Matters*. Boston: Beacon Press, 1993.

Whitaker, Mark, "White & Black Lies." *Newsweek*, November 15, 1993, 53-63.

White, J L., and T.A. Parham. *The Psychology of Blacks: An African American Perspective*, 2d ed. Englewood Cliffs, NJ: Prentice-Hall, 1990.

Wilkerson, Isabel of the *New York Times* reported in November 1990.

Williams, Gregory H. *Life on the Color Line*: The True Story of a White Boy Who Discovered He Was Black. New York: Penguin Books, 1996.

Williams, Walter. "Career and Opportunities." *Black Enterprise*, February 1992.

Willie, C.V. *A New Look at Black Families*. New Bayside, NY: General Hall, 1976.

Woodson, C.G. *The African Background Outlined*. New York: Negro Universities Press, 1968.

Woody, Bette. "Black Women in the New Service Economy." Working paper no. 196. Wellesley College Center for Research on Women, 1989.

WSJ. "Black Managers Leaving the Fold," *Wall Street Journal*, May 6, 1992, 1A.

Young, V. "Family and Childhood in a Southern Negro Community." American Anthropologist 72, 1977, 269-299.

Online African American Culture

History. Library of Congress research resource including exploration into the African American experience from colonization, slavery and abolition to the explosion of black arts in the 20th century: www.loc.giv/exhibits/african/intro.html

Civil Rights. A national register of historic sites relating to the civil rights movement, including an extensive history of the movement and the people and strategies behind it: www.cr.nps.gov/nr/travel/-civilrights
African American Joint Center for Political and Economic Policy: www.jointcenter.org.

Dates. Part of website Deeper Shade of Black includes a search engine allowing you to investigate dates of interest: www.ai.mit.edu/people/isbell/HFh/black/bhist.html
A timeline beginning in 1527 with events leading up to African colonization and slavery to 1997's Million Women March: www.wanonline.com/blackhistory/1999/tl.html

Culture. A variety of subjects from film and music articles to news and career resources, chats and Web events: www.blackplanet.com

Business. A business-to-business site for minority businesses: www.minority.net
A minority-owned site that helps students prepare for exams: www.cyberstudy101.com

Resources

Major organizations set up to fight the Ku Klux Klan, neo-nazis, and other groups that foster hate crimes:

Southern Poverty Law Center, 400 Washington Ave., Montgomery, AL 36104.

Anti-Defamation League, 823 United Nations Plaza, New York, NY 10017-3560.

CHAPTER 8

Working with Asian Americans

I keep the harmony and pay honor and respect to the manager.
Why didn't he talk to me about the new supervisor job?
Asian American worker

You're likely to have many Asian American colleagues if you live on the East or West Coast or certain urban areas of the country. Only 4 percent of Americans are Asian Americans, but they're clustered in certain cities and regions. People who have taken the time and effort to learn something about Asian Americans, their values and issues, say they've boosted their ability to work productively with these associates.

To help your better understand what it's like to be an Asian American, and therefore to build more empathic relationships, you'll learn in this chapter:

- How typical stereotypes and myths about Asian Americans compare with current reality.
- How the current situation has evolved from past history.
- The major Asian American communities and the key cultural values, customs, and issues that are important to them.
- How you can help Asian American employees overcome barriers to career success.
- How you can help your organization build upon Asian American strengths.

The best use of this information about Asian American cultural patterns is

1. To help you understand how they might view situations or what their actions might mean,
2. To figure out what questions you might ask in getting to know them better
3. To avoid forming rigid ideas and new stereotypes based on this information, and
4. To be open and flexible as you interact with individual Asian Americans.

First, explore your opinions and knowledge of Asian Americans by completing Self-Awareness Activities 8.1 and 8.2.

Self-Awareness Activity 8.1: What Do You Believe about Asian Americans?

Purpose:

- to get in touch with your beliefs and stereotypes about this group of people
- to experience how judgmental beliefs affect your thinking and feeling processes
- to experience the ways in which your beliefs create your reality regarding other persons, even before you have any interaction with them

Part I. What Do You Believe about Asian American women?

Step 1. Associations

- Relax as deeply as you can: close your eyes and take a few deep breaths.
- Focus on the words "Asian American woman" and allow a mental picture to come up in your mind's eye. Imagine that you are this woman. Be Asian American woman.
- Notice your resistances to being this person, and your willingness.
- Notice the words and images that come to mind as you "see" this woman.
- Open your eyes and list 10 to 20 words in the order in which they occur to you.
- Review your list. Mark a plus beside the words that are positive, a minus beside the words that are negative, and a circle beside neutral words.

Step 2. Negative Associations

- Close your eyes and focus again on the image of the Asian American woman. Formulate a negative opinion or judgment, perhaps one you typically hold about Asian American women.
- Notice your *feelings* as you see the person in this negative way. What *thoughts* come up as you focus on the image?
- Write a few sentences about your feelings and thoughts.

Step 3. Positive Associations

- Formulate a positive opinion or judgment, perhaps one you typically hold about Asian American women.
- Notice your *feelings* as you see the person in this positive way. What *thoughts* come up as you focus on the image?
- Write a few sentences about your feelings and thoughts.

Step 4. Insights

- Focus on the differences between your experiences when you hold negative and positive judgments or opinions. What were the differences? What meaning does this have for you, for your beliefs and feelings about people from this group, and about beliefs in general?
- Write your responses in a few sentences; include anything you like about your feelings, thoughts, and insights.

Part II. Experimenting with Opinions about Asian American Men

Repeat the phases and steps in part I, this time focusing on the image of an Asian American man.

Self-Awareness Activity 8.2: What Do You Know about Asian Americans?

Purpose: To see what you know about the issues covered in this chapter.

Instructions: Determine whether you think the following statements are basically true or false—and think about why. The answers will emerge in this chapter, and the summary at the end of the chapter focuses on these issues.

1. Asian Americans are too passive in temperament to be effective business leaders in American corporate cultures.

2. Most Asian Americans in the workplace are more Asian than American.

3. Asian Americans tend to be more unemotional than people from other groups.

4. Early Asian immigrants were considered nonwhite and had to cope with segregation and other forms of discrimination.

5. Most Asian Americans are from China.

6. Traditional Asian Americans expect the manager to be "one of the guys."

7. The "model minority" label reflects the idea that Asian Americans adapt to the American workplace better than African Americans or Latino Americans.

Let's examine some common threads among all Asian American groups. Asian Americans have been in America for over 150 years, before many European immigrant groups. But because they were "different," they were often stereotyped as heathen, exotic, and unassimilable. The Chinese were the first group to arrive in significant numbers, seeking gold, and what happened to them influenced the treatment of the Japanese, Koreans, Filipinos, and Asian Indians, as well as the Southeast Asian refugees who have come since the end of the Vietnam War. Most must cope with similar stereotypes and myths, experience generational differences as new generations become Americanized, hold some common cultural values and behavior patterns, and are affected by some common political issues, including the model minority myth.

STEREOTYPES AND REALITIES

We'll focus on a few of the most common stereotypes that Asian Americans must deal with. These stereotypes reflect some typical Asian stereotypes, and they contribute to the flavor of prejudice and discrimination that Asian Americans face.

Stereotype #1: Asian Americans tend to retain their foreign ways so it's difficult for them to fit in.

Asian Americans have traditionally coped with the exotic, perpetual foreigner stereotype because Euro-Americans have seen them as:

- immigrants who represent a small segment of the American population.
- people of color who bear distinct physical differences.
- people from a culture and lifestyle that is just too different for comfort.
- people who can never be completely absorbed into American society and politics.

Discriminatory laws and practices have reinforced this separateness. In fact, one-fourth to one-half of the members of most Asian American groups were born in this country. Many are even third- or fourth-generation Americans. Further, those bilingual Asian Americans who have recently learned English and still have heavy accents can usually be understood by people who are willing to listen for the rhythm and pattern of their speech. Asian cultures can offer much ancient wisdom to those who are open to different ways of viewing situations. Incorporating different ideas can lead to discovery of new business opportunities and problem solutions.

Stereotype #2: Asian Americans are unemotional and inscrutable.

Euro-Americans often complain that they can't tell what Asian Americans are thinking or feeling, so they're seen as unemotional and inscrutable. This and the "foreign" stereotype are closely related and stem from two sources. The first is the vast differences in English and Asian languages. The other source is the Asian cultural values that call for self-discipline in expressing emotions and for indirectness in communicating. When Asians disagree with you, say no, or convey unwelcome information, they often do it so indirectly and subtly that a Euro-American doesn't know they've done it. Later, if the Asian Americans' actions reflect a lack of agreement, Euro-Americans may conclude that the Asian Americans were evasive, sneaky, dishonest, or even corrupt, when perhaps they were merely being polite.

The reality is that Asian Americans experience the same emotions as other people. The Asian "Face" that Asian Americans present to the Euro-American world is often impassive and hard to read. However this is the Face that American history has taught Asian Americans to present. They have another Face—one that they show to their collective family. This is the Face that is presented most everywhere in their native country. It's more expressive and more understandable.

Stereotype #3: Asian Americans are too passive and polite to be good managers.

This is a career-bashing stereotype with hardly a kernel of truth. One implication is that they're polite and therefore lack the conviction and backbone to stand up to the heat a supervisor must take. Another implication is that they're compliant, therefore passive, which means they don't have the ambition it takes to move up the competitive corporate ladder. The behavior of Asian Americans is often misread by people who don't understand their cultural values and training.

In their own countries, Asians are obviously the business and political leaders. In the United States, Asian American small business owners have established an impressive success record, overcoming great odds. Even women who work on assembly lines can be surprisingly assertive and persistent beneath their "face" of compliance and cooperation, according to recent studies.

Stereotype #4: Asian Americans have learned how to make it in American society by working hard and being thrifty.

Asians are seen as the "good" minority when they're polite, deferent, and technically superior. As the "model minority" they've been more successful than other ethnic groups in penetrating professional ranks. Even though most Asian American professionals have unusually high preparation, they have experienced significant barriers to promotion and upward mobility (Cabezas et al 1989).

The model minority stereotype is true, as far as it goes. On the up side, it makes Asian Americans more acceptable in business and in society in general. But it ignores the complexities and difficulties of their situation, according to Karen Hossfeld's [1994] research. The downside is:

- The "hard worker" image sets up unrealistic expectations that they'll gladly make major sacrifices for their work, work for less than Euro-Americans, work harder, and work longer hours.
- It's easy to assume that such a model minority group has no pressing social or political issues that we must address.
- It causes undue resentment from other minorities.

The reality is that Asian Americans pay a high price for "making it." As a family unit, they work harder and longer for less pay than Euro-Americans and they get less help from society.

Related to the model minority myth is the belief that Asian Americans just want to own their own businesses and acquire real estate—that they don't care about social problems or politics. Results of a recent survey seem to contradict this idea. For example, Asian American responses indicate they attach far more importance to political freedom than to buying a home. They're as happy to work for a U.S. corporation as to be self-employed. And, as we'll see, Asian Americans have viewed the establishment of small family businesses as the only way to survive and get ahead, not necessarily as a choice that's preferable to working for a large corporation. The survey also indicated that Asian Americans *are* concerned about social problems, especially the plight of the homeless (Viviano 1990).

Stereotype #5: Asian Americans can't seem to master English grammar and pronunciation; they have communication problems.

Asian languages are about as different from English as languages can be. Therefore, becoming fluent and proficient is a long, arduous process for Asian American immigrants. Most work diligently and continually to improve their communication skills. In general, they believe in mastering English, and nearly all believe that English should be the only official U.S. language. The reality is that virtually all Asian Americans who here born in the United States are fluent in English and in fact may not be fluent in their ancestral Asian language.

Stereotype #6: Asian Americans are good in technical occupations, but they don't have leadership potential.

This stereotype is a faulty distortion that creates a huge barrier to career mobility. It's related to the idea that Asian Americans are technical coolies, computer nerds, or memorization whizzes, great at crunching numbers but short on people skills and creativity. It stems from the tendency of immigrant students with some language deficiencies to focus on what they *can* do well, which often includes mastering quantitative tasks and usually includes diligently studying, practicing, and memorizing. As a group, Asian Americans do score better than any other group on math tests. But as a matter of fact, Asian American students demonstrate a broad range of aptitudes and talents. Those who were born in the United States do not have the language problem and are likely to gravitate to a wider range of career areas.

Stereotype #7: Asian Americans know about all things Asian.

Some Euro-American business persons tend to look upon the company's "token" Asian Americans as the resident experts on all things Asian American—and Asian, for that matter. This assumes they know everything about the country their parents or grandparents immigrated from, its culture, adaptation of its people to the American culture, and which local restaurants are the best source of its cuisine. For some Asian Americans, this stereotype has become a pet peeve. The reality is that many of them were born in the United States, are more American than Asian, and may be no more of an expert on "things Asian" than the average American.

CONNECTIONS TO THE PAST

Americans have always valued the ideals of equal opportunity and fairness, but reality has not always matched that ideal. From the beginning, Asian immigrants have faced many obstacles to acceptance in America. Recent generations are more Americanized and face fewer barriers to success.

Understanding the Asian American experience requires understanding the processes of their acculturation, how overt and subtle prejudices have constrained their choices, and how each generation has changed the community. Although they become increasingly Americanized and acculturated, Asian Americans have also retained much of their Asian cultural heritage.

Acculturation Processes

Asian immigrants to America have experienced two major processes of acculturation:

- They've had to acquire the values and behavior of Euro-Americans.
- They've had to learn to accept their standing as ethnic minorities.

Many report that they've been seen as people who, because of the skin color and physical appearance, were not allowed to enjoy the rights and privileges given acculturated European immigrants and Euro-American native-born citizens. If they wanted to stay and survive in the United States, they had to learn to "stay in their place" and to act with deference toward those of higher ethnic status; that is, Euro-Americans. Therefore, many of the choices they have made, such as becoming small-business owners or majoring in accounting, have been made within those limits. To fully understand Asian Americans' background as a group, we must be aware of these constraints.

The Chinese: Gold, Railroads, and Exclusion

The first group of Asian Americans were men from China who came during the 1850s California gold rush. Instead of gold, most found work building railroads and doing laundry. There was overt prejudice from the beginning.

Chinese Exclusion Act of 1882. This Act was the first law that prohibited the entry of immigrants on the basis of nationality. The Chinese condemned this restriction as racist and tyrannical. The precedent later provided a basis for the restriction of European immigrant groups such as Italians, Russians, Poles, and Greeks.

Alien Land Acts. The western states, where most Asian Americans lived, passed Alien Land Acts in the early part of this century that barred them from owning land because they were "aliens ineligible to citizenship." Asians were legally classified as "nonwhite" for many purposes, catching them in the segregation net cast around African Americans. Restrictive covenants were written into many deeds making it illegal to sell the property to a "nonwhite."

Miscegenation Laws. State laws prohibited the marriage of people from two different "races," but the main concern was marriage of Euro-Americans to others.

Legal Segregation. School segregation was practiced in districts that had significant numbers of Asians, such as in San Francisco. Asians were usually required to sit in the balcony or on one side of theaters, and some public pools and beaches were off limits to them (Kitano and Daniels 1988).

Racial Profiling. All the discriminatory laws have been repealed, and new laws are in place to prevent discrimination. Still Asian Americans face modern discrimination, such as racial profiling. For example, Wan Ho Lee, a U.S. citizen and Los Alamos scientist who immigrated from Taiwan, was arrested in 2000 for suspicion of espionage. This regarded the leaking of sensitive weapons secrets to China, and the charges were later dropped. Many leaders in the Chinese American community claimed that racial profiling was a major factor, one that Lee's Euro-American colleagues didn't have to face.

The Japanese: Migration, War, and Concentration Camps

The Supreme Court ruled in 1934 that Japanese, Chinese, Filipinos, and Asian Indians were not "white" and therefore did not meet qualifications of the Naturalization Law and so could not become U.S. citizens. At the outbreak of World War II, however, the draft law was amended to allow nonwhites to join. An all-Japanese unit went on to become the most-decorated group in American history.

Meanwhile, their relatives at home were rounded up as "potential spies" and confined in concentration camps. They lost everything except what they carried with them, and of course they could not earn income during the two or three years they were imprisoned. To Japanese Americans, this wartime exile and incarceration was and still is the central event of their history, making it unique among Asian Americans. In 1988 the U.S. government formally apologized to these families and began paying reparations.

Civil Rights Laws of the 1960s

Most of the discriminatory laws were in force until the 1960s. The great changes initiated in the 1960s affected Asian Americans, as they did everyone else. The new Civil Rights laws had a great impact on Asian Americans' options. Higher education opened up to them, and streams of second-generation students poured in, most choosing safe majors in the professions, such as accounting, education, dentistry, or pharmacy. Employment patterns tend to be less discriminatory in professions, where credentials open doors and private practice can be lucrative, especially within one's minority community.

Many occupations previously closed to Asian Americans, such as public school teaching, began to open up, so the phenomenon of second-generation college graduates working at fruit stands began to disappear. College degrees began to mean something and career choices could be planned with some reasonable hope of fulfillment.

Laws forbidding intermarriage were overturned by the Supreme Court in 1967, and "mixed marriages" have become more common. However, most private social clubs were closed to the second-generation, and housing segregation was still a reality until recently.

Generation Gaps

To understand significant differences among the Asian Americans you meet, you must understand the different experiences and attitudes of various generations.

First Generation

Those who immigrated from China or Japan in the early years of this century. They were isolated in their ethnic communities, related exclusively or primarily to other Asian American families, and retained their old cultural ways.

Second Generation

Those born in the 1940s to 1960s are more Americanized but still strongly affected by their Asian cultural heritage. Now mature and aging adults, the second-generation is primarily a low-profile group.

By the end of World War II second-generation Chinese Americans and Japanese Americans finally outnumbered their immigrant parents. Two immigrant groups that were much smaller, Asian Indian Americans and Filipino Americans, often intermarried with other ethnic groups. Their second-generation children, many of bi-ethnic parentage, tried their best to fit into the mainstream.

Young and inexperienced though they were, members of the second generation began to find a voice of their own and to become distinct from their parents' generation. Second-generation members are of course more Americanized but still strongly affected by their Asian cultural heritage.

Third and Fourth Generation

Those born during or after the 1970s are even more Americanized than their parents and grandparents, but they're still distinctly Asian in some ways. Most are definitely more American than Asian. Some are entering occupations once considered closed to Asians, such as advertising, the performing arts, journalism, and broadcasting.

One survey indicates that 47 percent think it's more important to move their family into mainstream American life, while 42 percent think it's more important to maintain traditional Asian ways (Baldassare 1990). Many have never faced the overt discrimination that their parents and grandparents faced. A few have never had close ethnic ties or friendships with other Asian American families. Most go to the university and are eager for good jobs, especially in the professions, such as medicine, engineering, and law.

They're more likely to reflect the influence of their surrounding communities than a strictly ethnic one. Nearly all live in urban areas in the West, especially in California and Hawaii. Although these young people question the lifestyle and certain values of their parents, they're the beneficiaries of the material success of the second generation.

A recent trend is for parents and grandparents to focus on teaching the Chinese culture to the new generation. Wherever you find large Chinese American communities, such as Northern California, you find a growing number of Chinese schools. All teach Chinese language along with such cultural courses as history, abacus, and folk dancing.

Current Immigrants

The contemporary Asian immigration and the refugee influx have been shaped by changes in U.S. immigration laws and by the political, economic, and social agreements made between the countries of origin and the United States since the end of World War II. The United States has favored escapees from communism above all others, such as refugees from Vietnam, Laos, and Cambodia.

Regardless of their reasons for coming, as soon as they arrive, most Asians have quickly made themselves productive. This ability to find niches for themselves is a double-edged sword. Their very success has resurrected some deeply ingrained prejudices and hostility. These contradictions that have characterized Asian American history continue to limit the lives of many Asian Americans today (Takaki 1992).

CURRENT PROFILE: WHO ARE THE ASIAN AMERICANS?

The seven major groups of Asian Americans have many common cultural threads. Many of their values and customs are similar, although each culture also has its unique aspects. Each group came to the United States under somewhat different circumstances and therefore each has faced different situations. Proportion of the U.S. population that is Asian American, and their subgroup proportions, are shown in Figure 8.1.

FIGURE 8.1: Proportions of Asian Americans

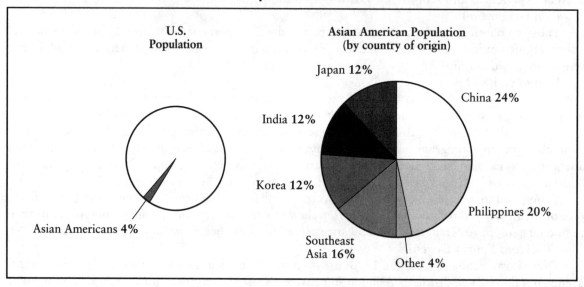

The following facts from the U.S. Census (1994) provide a general demographic picture of Asian Americans.

- *Over half live in the West,* 54 percent, compared to 21 percent of the total population. The U.S. Census Bureau estimates that in 1995 Asian Americans were most populous in the following states:

State	% of State Population
Hawaii	56%
California	13
Washington	6
New York	5
New Jersey	4.5
Illinois	3.2
Texas	2.5

- Most live in a dozen urban areas. The largest Asian American populations in U.S. metropolitan areas, as estimated by the U.S. Census Bureau (1995b) are:

+/- One Million		*+/- 150k to 1/2 Million*		*+/- 100k to 150k*	
Los Angeles	1,340k	Honolulu	526k	Houston	132k
San Francisco	924k	Chicago	256k	Philadelphia	121k
New York	873k	Washington DC	202k	Sacto	114k
		San Diego	198k	Dallas-Ft. Worth	98k
		Seattle	164k		

- *They doubled in number* between 1980 and 1990, due primarily to immigration.

- *Many are foreign born*, 66 percent, with Southeast Asian Americans having the highest percentage and Japanese Americans the lowest.

- *Some are recent immigrants*. Thirty-eight percent entered the United States during the 1980s, mostly refugees. Most live in the West, especially in California.

- *They live longer than Euro-Americans*, whose mean life expectancy is 76, compared to 80 for Japanese Americans and Chinese Americans.

- *They have less crime*. FBI reports indicate that arrest rates of Asian Americans for serious crimes between 1980 and 1985 were well below their proportion in the population. Since the 1930s Asian Americans in California have had lower rates of crime and delinquency than the general population.

- *They're relatively young*. Thirty is the median age, compared with the national median of 33.

- *Most groups have larger families*, on average 3.8 persons, compared to 3.2 for all U.S. families. Five members or more are present in about twice as many (23 percent) of Asian American families as in Euro-American families (13 percent). Hmong families average 6.6 persons, while Filipino, Vietnamese, Cambodian, and Laotian average over 4 persons per family. Japanese had 3.1.

- *Most speak another language*. Sixty-five percent speak another language at home, 56 percent don't speak English well, and 35 percent are linguistically isolated (speak virtually no English). Asian Indian Americans have the lowest proportion speaking another language at home, Hmong the highest.

Education: Higher Achievement than Most

The Asian American devotion to education results in high educational achievement. High school diplomas were held by 85 percent of Asian Americans in 1999, compared to 84 percent of the U.S. population. Averages range from 88 percent for Japanese Americans to 31 percent for Hmong.

Bachelor's degrees were held by 46 percent of the men and 39 percent of the women, compared with 26 percent for all Americans. Asian Indian Americans have the highest rate and Hmong the lowest. Asian Americans do better on quantitative exams than any other group.

Asian Americans Have High Education Levels

They have more high school graduates than average Americans: 85 percent, compared to 81 percent nationally. Averages range from 88 percent for Japanese Americans to 31 percent for Hmong. They also have more college degrees: 41 percent, compared with 22 percent for all Americans (U.S. Census 1995a).

Asian Indian Americans Are the Best Educated

Americans from India, or of Indian ancestry, are the most highly educated group in the United States. Over 65 percent of the men and half the women have degrees, compared to 23 and 18 percent for all Americans. Nearly all speak English, and few have language barriers, which is related to India's history as a British colony. More than 72 percent of them have jobs, compared with 65 percent of all Americans. Nearly half of all foreign-born Asian Indian workers are managers or professionals. This is twice the proportion for all Americans, which is 24 percent. They have the highest per capita income among all Americans, $18,000, after Japanese Americans. Many are part of an Indian "brain drain" that occurred during the 1980s and was caused when India trained more professionals than its businesses could profitably employ.

Fields of Study Vary

Asian American university students enter fields of study similar to the overall population, except there are about twice as many studying physical sciences and engineering, half as many study social science, and only one-third as many study education (National Center for Educational Statistics 1995).

Pay Doesn't Match Educational and Occupational Levels

Although Asian Americans have the highest educational levels, the greatest proportion of family members who work, and the highest concentration in managerial and professional jobs, their income does not reflect these achievements.

Asian Americans Have More Workers. About 67 percent of Asian Americans are employed, compared with 65 percent for all Americans. Groups with an employment rate higher than 70 percent are the Filipino Americans, Asian Indian Americans, and Thai Americans. Twenty percent of Asian American families contain three or more workers, compared with 13 percent nationally.

Self-Employment is High. Over 11 percent of Asian American workers are self-employed, double the rate of other minorities (U.S. Census 1995b).

Asian Americans Hold More High-Status Jobs. About 37 percent of Asian Americans work in managerial and professional specialty occupations, more than the 33 percent of Euro-Americans who hold these types of jobs. Asian Americans are normally distributed across all types of jobs, except in "professional category," where there are twice as many Asian Americans (22.5 percent) as the overall population (11.7 percent). This is due primarily to their higher education levels and the tendency to start their own business or practice.

They work in all major industries, with a normal distribution pattern, except in the "electronic components" industry where there is nearly twice the proportion of Asian Americans (13.5 percent) as the overall population (8.8 percent). Asian Americans make up 2.4 percent of all the employees in the electronics industry.

Asian Americans' Pay is Below Average. Median income per person is $27,700 for men, less than the $30,600 for Euro-American men. For Asian American women it's $16,800, compared $15,900 for Euro-American women. Asian Americans, especially the women, tend to work longer hours than their Euro-American counterparts. Because more of their family members work, the median household income of Asian American families is $51,200, compared to $44,400 for Euro-Americans.

Poverty Rate Is Average. The Asian American poverty rate is 11 percent, compared to 12 percent nationally. Southeast Asian poverty rates range from 35 to 64 percent, with Chinese American and Korean American rates at 14 percent, and rates for Filipino Americans, Japanese Americans, and Asian Indian Americans under 10 percent.

Japanese Americans Are the Most Affluent. By 1990 Japanese Americans were the most successful of any Asian American group by most standards. Their educational attainment ran a close second to the top U.S. achievers, Asian Indian Americans. They had the highest per capita income of any Asian American group, well above the national median. The poverty rate of 7 percent was near the lowest.

A Unique Group: The Hmong

Hmong Hill Tribes from Laos have the greatest challenges. As an aftermath of the Vietnam War, the United States has accepted many war refugees from Vietnam, Cambodia, and Laos. About 60,000 belonged to the Hmong hill tribes of Laos, who lived as semi-nomadic farmers, clearing jungle areas to plant crops. They have a strong family and clan system, and families are traditionally large, so they average 6.6 children, the highest birth rate of any U.S. group. They had no experience with written language until 1960 when missionaries came to Laos, so most speak little or no English and have the lowest educational achievement of any U.S. group. Adapting to a high-tech workplace that's based upon quite sophisticated uses of written information is a major challenge. Only 29 percent of Hmong Americans had jobs in 1990, their average income was $2,600, and most depended on public assistance to survive.

ASIAN AMERICAN CULTURES: COMMON THREADS AND CORE VALUES

There is not one Asian culture. There are at least six or seven major cultures and hundreds of subcultures. The extreme variations in Asian Americans' ways of life make it impossible to identify precise patterns for all. Still, many Asian cultures share a number of characteristics that help describe, but not define, them.

These common threads in the tapestries of Asian societies have been identified by such researchers as Philip Harris, Robert Moran, Ronald Takaki, William Wei, Esther Chow, Loraine Dong, Karen Hossfeld. For example, Asians generally put group concerns above their own desires and put family and group harmony above all else. Asians tend to accept status differences within a social hierarchy, and they revere education for its own sake. They can communicate without being explicit because they live in tight-knit cultures where people are on the same wave length, and they often communicate indirectly in an effort to maintain harmony.

Asian Americans have no common language or religion. Each major Asian ethnic group has its own language and dominant religion, and some groups have several languages and religions. Chinese, Japanese, and Koreans are physically and culturally very similar, stemming from a Confucianist focus on putting family, community, and patriotic duties above personal desires. Beliefs of other major Asian religions, such as Buddhism and Hinduism, tend to foster similar group values. The Vietnamese culture has been strongly influenced by the Chinese culture. India has its own culture, with major influences from the Hindu, Buddhist, and Islamic religions and the former rule of the British. The Philippine culture was influenced by the 300-year rule of Spain with its Catholicism. Even so, both India and the Philippines reflect many common Asian values and cultural patterns.

Individuals are also affected by socioeconomic class and education, by region, by generation, by individual life experiences, and by individual choice. Use the following cultural definitions as valuable background information that can help you formulate the right questions to ask when you're puzzled by the behavior of an Asian American colleague. Resist any temptation to use the information to form rigid stereotypes, and remember to be open and flexible as you interact with individual Asian Americans.

Five key values important in virtually all Asian cultures are:

1. Putting family and ingroup concerns before personal desires
2. Promoting group harmony
3. Accepting the hierarchy and status differences
4. Revering education, thrift, and hard work
5. Communicating vaguely, indirectly, and silently

Value #1: Putting Group Concerns Before Individual Desires

All Asian cultures are collective, depending a great deal upon each other within close-knit families, extended families, and community groups. Members are expected to honor the group by:

- Seeing the group as the most important part of society
- Focusing on a group of people who are working toward a goal as more important than focusing on each one as individuals
- Valuing group recognition and group reward above individual reward
- Emphasizing a sense of belonging to the group and security within the group
- Extending tight, strong family ties to other relatives and close friends
- Placing central emphasis on a strong network of social relationships
- Making public service a moral responsibility
- Viewing personal saving and resource conservation as more important than consumption
- Placing fairness with the group and community above gaining wealth

Expressing Compassion

An important Confucian value involves compassion and benevolence for others, which seems similar to such Protestant values as "love your neighbor as yourself" and "do unto others as you would have them do unto you." However, a key difference is the relationship of the individual to the society as a whole. Euro-Americans believe that individuals should discover what they are good at, set their own standards, and go for it. Asians believe that individuals should use their talents to help the group develop and meet its goals. Success is joining an organization, and being part of a group that becomes successful.

Fitting In

The main point is to fit in with the group. To discourage young ones from going off on their own, parents cite such sayings as, "The nail that sticks up gets hammered down" and "The branch of the hedge that sticks out gets trimmed off."

Walking the Talk

Another difference is that Asians take these values more seriously in their daily lives. They are more constant in consciously reinforcing them throughout life with family altars, rituals, classes, and ceremonies. In Japan, for example, coming of age at 20 is a national holiday with ceremonies that focus on the responsibilities of adulthood.

Value #2: Promoting Group Harmony

Putting the group first naturally leads to the value of putting group harmony first. Customary ways of achieving this goal include the following beliefs and actions.

Disciplined Emotional Expression

Most Asians are taught that harsh words, scolding, temper flares, and similar emotional expressions will cause the other person to lose face and also to lose respect for the speaker. For example, to show your anger is seen as:

- the same as admitting loss of control
- a lapse in training and self-discipline
- a loss of face for you

As a result, in face-to-face relations, Asian Americans tend to maintain the amenities and cordialities, no matter how they are feeling. All this true *unless* things have gone too far—and it's almost impossible for people outside the culture to estimate when things are about to go too far. Only insiders are likely to recognize these subtle signals.

Avoidance of Open Conflict

This includes avoiding personal confrontations, as well as not saying no, not giving others unpleasant messages, or doing this in a very indirect way.

Modesty

Everyone, especially females, is expected to show modesty by:

- Avoiding statements that can be perceived as boasting or self-congratulatory, as in overuse of the words "I," "me," and "mine."
- Being reticent to talk about themselves or their own accomplishments.
- Not drawing attention to themselves.
- Responding to compliments by belittling their abilities.

Self-Effacement

It's often appropriate for persons to act as if they are of lower status in order to show selfless humility and give honor to others. Highly respected people often assume an attitude of self-effacement in social and business contacts. Putting yourself forward is usually viewed as proud arrogance and invites scorn. To make a joke at someone else's expense and to cause embarrassment is highly resented in business. Also, "good" business persons place a higher value on allowing others in the group or community to save face and therefore preserve harmony than on achieving higher sales and profits.

Focusing on Others

The individual is expected to be extremely sensitivity to others' feelings and wishes, giving second place to his or her own feelings and wishes.

Conforming

When persons are flexible, defer to others, or comply with the wishes of others in order to maintain harmony, they show maturity and self-discipline. Asian cultures expect people to conform to the wishes of those of higher status. This maintains harmony even when there is internal conflict between what persons want and what they think they should do. The key thing for you to remember: When an Asian American gives in to another person, it's not necessarily a passive or weak gesture, but is often a sign of tolerance, self-control, flexibility, and maturity.

Giving Back

Mature persons are sensitive to the need to give to others who have given to them, to pay back devotion, generosity, and favors.

Value #3: Accepting Status Differences—The Hierarchy

Protocol, rank, and status are important parts of all Asian cultures, ranging from the extremes of the Hindu caste system to the Confucian system, which states:

- Everyone is expected to honor certain binding obligations to immediate family, relatives, clan, province, and state.
- Society should be structured to minimize deviations from these obligations.
- Women are subordinate to men, sons to fathers, younger brothers to older brothers, wives to husbands, and everyone to the state.
- Elders are especially respected, even revered, pampered, and appeased. Their every wish and desire is catered to whenever possible. Every home, no matter how poor, provides the best room for the honored grandparent.

Across all religions and cultures, the Asian belief in hierarchy includes:

- Valuing a sense of order, propriety, and appropriate behavior between persons of varying status.
- Basing status on occupational position, education, wealth, and family background.

Typical Customs or Behaviors

Typical customs that reflect the status value include:

- When Asians meet someone, they quickly establish whether that person has higher status than they. If so, they show proper deference.
- They address people by their title and first name in all but informal or family situations.
- They respect seniority and the elderly.
- Parents prefer sons to daughters. Daughters go to their husband's family and so lose the value they could bring to their own parents. As children are growing up, parents must protect daughters and can give sons more social freedom.
- Parents must arrange marriages for their children, aiming for partners with as high status as possible.

Respect for the Manager's Status

In the United States, it's appropriate at certain times for managers to roll up their sleeves and work alongside the people to get things done. Pitching in when there's an emergency is a sign you're a good sport, one of the guys. Many Asian Americans, especially the immigrants, would interpret it this way:

- This is an insult to me as a worker.
- You're implying that I can't get the work done the way I should.
- Such work is below your station as a manager.
- I can't have the same respect for you now.
- If you do this again, or do it insensitively, I'll really lose face. I may have to resign.

Value #4: Revering Education, Thrift, and Hard Work

Education is revered in Asian cultures, especially where there's a strong Confucian influence. Being educated is a high moral virtue and is a rigid prerequisite for moving up from lower to higher political and social standing. Scholars are given the greatest respect, have the highest rank, and are often among the most powerful and wealthy in society. Asian Americans therefore:

- value education as a moral virtue
- value position in society and see education as the best way to achieve a good position and some financial security
- consider education an investment in family status

Asian Americans have tended to over-invest in education, given the fact that their income does not reflect as high a rate of return on education as the rate for Euro-Americans. Still, Asian Americans have seen education as one of their few tools for upward mobility in a hostile environment. Also, compared to most Asian countries, education in the United States is an incredible bargain, with tuition-free community colleges and low-tuition state colleges often available. Parents have been willing to make great sacrifices in order to provide a good education for their children.

The Asian attitude toward educational achievement is: Innate ability is not important; hard work is what counts. Beyond education, hard work and persistence in achieving long-term goals throughout life are highly valued. Gaining great wealth is not the goal. Rather, people are expected to fit in with the group and contribute to it by getting the best education and job position that they can, working hard, saving, and investing in order to achieve financial security within the community. This often involves sacrificing short-term pleasures for long-term benefits.

Value #5: Communicating Vaguely, Indirectly, Silently

Asian Americans may sometimes seem vague, indirect, or strangely silent.

Being Vague

In close-knit cultures, such as Japan, where everyone grew up in the same society, people can speak a sort of "shorthand" and be understood. In fact, being direct and making specific references may be seen as insulting. Being vague, indirect, or ambiguous is valued. As a result, people will often leave their sentences unfinished so listeners may mentally form the conclusion for themselves. After all, they know what the speaker is getting at—to "go on and on" might insult the listeners' intelligence. When these tendencies carry over into the U.S. workplace, coworkers can become quite confused.

Being Indirect

You've learned that being indirect is an Asian way of avoiding open conflict and preserving harmony. Pay special attention to situations in which an Asian American associate may need to say no, confront an issue, or deliver some other unpleasant message. Remember that even when that person is trying to be direct in the Asian way, you may still consider it indirect. And their indirect message may be so subtle that you don't get it.

Saying No

To say no is an insult, could damage feelings and disrupt harmony, and is therefore bad manners. Asian Americans may say yes, meaning "I heard you," and then go about doing the opposite with little sense of breaking an agreement. When an Asian American man, for example, disagrees with you, says no, or conveys unwelcome information, he may do it so indirectly and subtly that you won't know it's been done. Later, if his actions reflect a lack of agreement, you may conclude that the he was not only unemotional and inscrutable, but perhaps evasive, sneaky, dishonest, or even corrupt. Probably, he was merely being polite.

- You can help by understanding these vague or indirect communication patterns and asking your Asian American associates to fill in the blanks.

Not Interrupting

If you were listening to a friend and didn't understand something she said, would you wait, expressionless, until she had finished a long explanation, expecting her to take responsibility for your understanding? Probably not. But if all the people you know believe that's the way to listen, then such behavior would be normal. For many Asian Americans, not interrupting is basic courtesy that is essential for conversations to proceed.

- You can help by encouraging Asian American associates to interrupt you in order to ask questions if they don't understand you.

Keeping Longer Silences

When you finish speaking, how do you react when your listener is silent for a minute or more? Most Americans view such long silences as extremely uncomfortable and feel compelled to fill them in with comments or questions. For many Asian Americans, Japanese Americans for example, a few moments of quiet contemplation after listening may be essential, and comments are distracting.

- You can help by becoming comfortable with such silences and refraining from filling such moments with talk.

Other Customs

Other behavioral customs include:

- It's okay to call for someone to come to you by holding out your arm with your palm *down*, using a scratching movement. To turn your palm *up* and use the fingers to motion, which is typical in the United States, is considered rude.

- Meals are often more ritualistic, communal, and time consuming than in the United States. The talk is considered more important than the food.

- Colors and numbers often have different meanings than they have in the United States. For example, white may be used for mourning.

KEY ISSUES IMPORTANT TO ASIAN AMERICANS

Some key issues you should know about because they're important to many Asian Americans include 1) complications of the Model Minority stereotype, 2) changing male-female dynamics and differences, 3) educational concerns.

Issue #1: Model Minority: A Mixed Blessing

In the 1960s, reporters began writing about the high education attainment, high median family income, low crime rates, and absence of juvenile delinquency and mental health problems among Asian Americans. Proponents of this model minority stereotype often ask, "Why can't African Americans succeed like this? (and not bother us)." This stereotype has been a mixed blessing for Asian Americans: it carries with it advantages and disadvantages.

Model Minority Advantages

The main advantages to Asian Americans of the Model Minority stereotype are that it showcases their cultural strengths, especially strengths connected with their success in running small family businesses.

Cultural Strengths

The Model Minority image eventually increased job opportunities for Asian Americans. Business managers say they favor hiring Asian Americans (Hossfeld 1994) because they:

- work hard and are productive
- invest in higher education, even at the cost of financial hardship
- are willing to work unusually long hours
- maintain a frugal lifestyle
- persevere in their goals and their work projects
- identify with the American Dream of hard work leading to a better life.
- save small amounts of money until they can invest in a small business
- use frugal strategies to keep their businesses going

Small Business Ownership

A key aspect of the Model Minority image is Asian Americans' ability to start and hang onto small family businesses. Community credit associations and small family enterprises have traditionally been common in Asian countries. Immigrants who can't find work may use these strategies:

- Join mutual aid associations in the ethnic community, provide needed financing and support, and members agree not to compete. Associations may loan capital, fix business locations and prices, locate employees, and help members in distress.

- Start businesses that are nonthreatening to the Euro-American majority because they're small and they specialize in limited areas.
- Work long hours for a certain minimum income.
- Give jobs first to family, then to extended family, neighborhood, and ethnic group members, in that order.
- Give employees as much job security as possible, with layoffs a last resort.
- Provide job flexibility to free employees to go to school or work at second jobs.
- Make the primary goal a long range one: to sustain the business over the long term.

Factors that limit growth and expansion include:

- Owners' inadequate English skills.
- Dependence on ethnic customers whose per capital wealth is lower.
- Reluctance to go outside the Asian American community to get money that would be needed for business expansion.

Small Business Success

During the 1990s Asian American businesses started up at twice the rate of all U.S. firms. They started with more capital than their Euro-American counterparts, and their owners were better educated, on average. Asian Americans more than doubled their share of contracts awarded under the Small Business Administrations 8a program between 1986 and 1996. One reason is their tendency toward high-tech firms. Although only about 3 percent of federal government contracts are in the SBA 8a program, Asian American firms got 24 percent of them in 1996, compared with 10 percent in 1986. By contrast African American contractors got 37 percent, compared to 50 percent in 1986, and the Latino-American share continued to hover around 30 percent (Sharpe 1997).

How Business Ownership Helped Create a Model Minority

Asian American families who have managed to build and hold onto at least a minimal level of business success have achieved the following advantages:

Protection from discrimination. For most of this century about half the Asian American male population worked for neighborhood small businesses, effectively shielding themselves from the open labor market with its discriminatory practices.

Higher educational attainment. Owners were able to accumulate money to send their children to college. Between 1940 and 1960 there was a dramatic increase in the percentage of Asian Americans who completed high school and went to college.

More opportunities. Small business success and higher educational attainment enhanced Euro-Americans' perception of Asian Americans as productive workers.

Disadvantages: Model Minority Costs

Several disadvantages offset the Asian American success story.

- They get less return on their educational investment than do Euro-Americans. Even though about twice as many have degrees, they average only 70 percent of Euro-American men's income.
- They are disadvantaged in getting the better-paying jobs. The percentage working as service workers, laborers, farm laborers, and private household workers is considerably higher than among Euro-Americans. They are under-represented in the professional ranks and in top management of mid- to large-size corporations.
- Most have a lower living standard than their income implies because 90 percent live in high-cost areas, such as San Francisco and Hawaii.
- More of the family members work than in Euro-American families (3.17 compared to 2.58 in 1997) and they work more hours on average.

- Underemployment is more common. Rather than be unemployed, most will accept low-paying, part-time, or seasonal jobs.
- It overlooks the fact that some recent immigrants, such as Hmong Americans, have major problems.

Political Viewpoints

Why do some scholars and reporters so eagerly focus on Asian American success, while others keep stressing discrimination? The debate is not just over economics but also over political viewpoint.

Those who depict Asian Americans as the model minority tend to be conservatives who believe that American society is indeed an egalitarian one. All people have the opportunity to succeed. Each person must make the necessary effort to achieve material well being. If an individual or group does not make it, it's their own fault.

Liberals, who focus on continued inequality, believe the problem lies primarily within the social, economic, and political system. Before the minority groups have equal opportunity to improve their status, some aspects of the system must change. But systemic change can occur only with a shift in the present balance of power between different groups. Therefore, those who perceive reality in this manner advocate greater political activism.

The answer probably encompasses both viewpoints. We each create our reality in a very important sense. The Asian American woman who has certain attributes and who does the right things, makes the right moves, can indeed overcome all barriers and achieve the success she wants. Connie Chung is one of the few Asian American women to achieve national prominence. But should it have been so much more difficult for her than it is for a Dan Rather? Put another way, why must a Connie Chung be such a "rare bird" in appearance and talent in order to make it, when a Dan Rather can be more "ordinary" and still make it? To what extent can and should we try to level the playing field?

Issue #2: Male–Female Dynamics and Differences

Most Asian cultures are extremely patriarchal and women are significantly more subjugated in these cultures than in the American culture.

Family Culture Clash

Culture clash often affects husband-wife dynamics, especially in families that have immigrated since the 1960s. That's when women's pay and work status began improving and traditional male jobs in manufacturing plants began deteriorating. Problems often arise over these events:

- The wife finds a better-paying job than the husband, upsetting the male status in a hierarchical family structure.
- The wife must learn to be assertive, decisive, and efficient on the job, which conflicts with her role as a shy, patient, and resilient wife and mother.
- Children at school learn they must speak up, express opinions, and ask why in order to succeed, but are expected to keep quiet and do as they're told at home.
- Girls must also speak up at school, but at home they're supposed to be even more reserved and compliant than boys.

Stereotypes of Asian Women Workers

Women who don't have the educational credentials to land better-paying jobs often take manufacturing assembly line jobs. They typically encounter myths, stereotypes, and other barriers to promotion and job satisfaction. For example, research indicates that the formula used by many hiring managers in California's Silicon Valley for entry level manufacturing assembly line operatives can be summarized as "small, foreign, and female" (Zinn and Dill 1994). This means they recruit and hire primarily Asian and Latina immigrant women. Reasons employers give for the hiring policy are based on stereotyped and prejudiced beliefs, especially about Asian American women, as follows:

- Immigrant women are more likely to be content with such jobs. (In fact, most want to advance.)
- They're unqualified for better-paying jobs. (In fact, they're trainable.)
- They have husbands who earn more than they do. (In fact, about 80 percent are the main income earners in their families.)
- Their patience and superior coordination better suits them to assembly line production involving tiny, intricate circuitry.
- Their small size makes it easier for them to sit quietly for long periods, doing small detail work.
- Their strong task orientation, high achievement motivation, and hard work qualify them as reliable production workers.
- They're childlike, obedient, and submissive, good qualities for assembly-line work but not for managerial roles.
- Most U.S. citizens would not be content for long with such boring, low-paying jobs, but Asian American women are.

Reality: Beneath the Passive Surface, Active Achievement

Most Asian American women on assembly lines are actually active, goal-oriented doers, according to several studies. They're disadvantaged in at least three aspects of the social structure, that is, being an ethnic minority, a woman, and within a lower socioeconomic class.

The problems they experience with their supervisors (nearly all Euro-American) stem primarily from the following:

- supervisors' perception of their inabilities
- disrespect for Asian women
- unreasonable work assignments
- unfair performance evaluation
- accusation of job errors
- inappropriate decisions regarding promotion
- intolerance of language accents
- apparent discrimination

How do Asian American women handle the problems resulting from these stereotypes? Here are some facts from Esther Chow's (1994) research:

- About half have no difficulty challenging their supervisor about problems.
- Well over half have difficulty in expressing anger and in demanding their fair share from supervisors.
- Those of higher occupational status have more to lose and more difficulty demanding their fair share.
- Almost all attempt to establish congenial working relationships with people at all levels of the organization.
- Two-thirds have little difficulty in protesting unfair treatment by their Euro-American *co-workers* (as distinguished from their supervisors).
- Most had more difficulty protesting to Euro-American women than to the men, since they tend to consider the women as natural allies and hesitate to break that feeling of camaraderie.
- Only 6 percent said they choose to say nothing to offensive co-workers or to ignore incidents they think are unfair.

A Range of Workplace Styles

Typical styles for dealing with workplace situations are avoidance or indirectness, affiliative, assertive, and confrontational. The style a woman uses depends primarily on how extreme or important the work problem is to her.

Adaptation and Indirectness. Adapting or being indirect seem to fit the passive stereotype. Silence is sometimes a temporary reaction in the process of coping. It may be part of a defensive stand in which they protect themselves from the hurt by pushing their tolerance to the limit. Variations of the approach include avoiding problem situations as much as possible, doing little about them, or hoping a problem will go away. They might write to a supervisor, talk to a supervisor about an offensive co-worker, or make an impersonal telephone call to a co-worker, all in hopes of finding a solution to the problem. Most don't carry this style to the extreme of quitting, which they would see as defeatist. A frequent pattern is to begin by adapting and later to shift to a more active strategy.

Congeniality. Being congenial is a style used sometimes to show willingness to cooperate in solving workplace problems. It involves personal consideration, friendliness, and candidness to achieve some kind of equity with coworkers. Women using this style may emphasize commonalties, such as being women or being Asian Americans, in order to establish rapport, to dispel issues of inequity, and to neutralize feelings of injustice. They are more apt to use this style with Euro-American women than with men.

Assertiveness. Asserting themselves is a direct style for claiming certain work rights and independence. It includes negotiating their time, effort, intellect, commitment, and personal involvement with other workers. About half the women use this style, and they're more likely to do so when they deal with Euro-American male workers than with females. It includes expressing their viewpoints and judgment of a situation, demanding explanations from offensive workers, and focusing their efforts on problem solving. This approach is active, goal-oriented, and a way of taking charge of their own lives. Women using this approach expect to negotiate a solution to a problem. For example, they may want some agreement about work hours that don't interfere with their family obligations.

Confrontation. Confronting the persons involved in the situation is a somewhat aggressive style of fighting prejudice and discrimination at work. The women directly protest against those co-workers they view as insensitive and threatening to their survival. They fight back in the face of apparently overwhelming odds in order to protect their work rights and to show they won't compromise themselves to what they see as others' unreasonable demands. Some even go as far as quitting their job rather than be pushed around, the ultimate form of resistance. They see it as affirming self-respect and human dignity, even above job security.

Issue #3: University Education

Educational issues important to many Asian Americans include getting into top universities and establishing Asian American studies programs.

Getting into Top Universities

Many Asian American high school graduates with straight-As have been unable to get into the nation's top public and private universities. The admission *rate* of Asian American applicants to these universities was lower than that for any other ethnic group during the 1980s. No university has admitted any discriminatory intent, but officials at several have acknowledged that their affirmative action policies and practices may have had an unintentional adverse impact on Asian Americans.

Asian Americans have united to ensure that their educational rights will not be abridged, because access to quality higher education, perhaps more than any other issue, is something they feel very strongly about. Many Asians immigrate to the United States precisely to allow their children to receive such education. Most Filipino Americans, 56 percent, favor affirmative action programs that set quotas for minority admissions to college. Chinese Americans are almost evenly divided on the issue, with 41 percent favoring affirmative action and 43 percent opposing it. Interviews indicated that nearly all Chinese Americans are concerned about discrimination, but many are uncomfortable with using government regulation to alleviate the problem (Baldassare 1990).

Establishing Asian American Studies Programs

Many Asian American university students are asking for a more "relevant" education, meaning a multiethnic curriculum that includes the history of discrimination in the United States and an accurate portrayal of the contributions and struggles of people of color. This interest reflects a new cultural awakening among Asian American students, along with a rising political consciousness. Instead of choosing between their Asian heritage and the American culture, some young Asian Americans are forging a new culture of their own, one that goes beyond a simple blending of East and West. This culture directly reflects the historical experience and current life circumstances of Asians in America. In university courses about Asian Americans, they may get a glimpse of this emerging culture and even be encouraged to help create it.

In the late 1960s and early 1970s Asian American studies courses and programs were established at many West Coast universities. Those at San Francisco State University and at the University of California at Berkeley began as part of the settlement of two long and militant student strikes. What that generation of students, as well as succeeding generations who filled the classes, wanted was a more "relevant" education. By that they meant a curriculum that included the history of prejudice and discrimination in the United States, an accurate portrayal of the contributions and struggles of people of color, and practical training to enable graduates to bring about fundamental social change in their ethnic communities as well as in the society at large. Because of their radical agenda, the programs encountered stiff resistance from curriculum and personnel review committees. A number failed, while others managed to survive but did not grow.

In the late 1980s these programs took a new lease on life when students began demanding a more multiethnic curriculum. Dozens of campuses, including five of the eight University of California campuses, now have some version of an ethnic studies requirement. Students at East Coast and Midwestern universities are also insisting that Asian American studies programs be set up.

Issue #4: Discrimination and Hate Crimes

Some issues that unite Asian Americans across political and ethnic lines include discrimination, the increase in hate crimes, university quotas against Asian Americans, and the maintenance of Asian American studies programs on campuses.

Discrimination

Most Asian Americans say that prejudice and discrimination is *not* a problem in their local area, with 64 percent of Filipino Americans and 51 percent of Chinese Americans saying it's not a problem. However, when asked if qualified members of their ethnic group can rise to the top in local companies, 56 percent of Filipino Americans and 37 percent of Chinese Americans said discrimination was a problem. When asked if the glass ceiling is a problem, about 70 percent of Filipino Americans and 66 percent of Chinese Americans said yes.

While they are not proportionately represented in corporate top management or elected political office, breakthroughs are occurring. For example, in 1996 the first Asian American state governor in U.S. history was elected—Gary Locke, a Chinese American, was elected governor of Washington.

Hate Crimes

Since 1980, increased instances of physical assault, harassment, vandalism, and anti-Asian racial slurs have been reported. The U.S. Civil Rights Commission has stated that "the issue of violence against Asian Americans is national in scope." Three subgroups are especially vulnerable: Southeast Asian Americans, immigrant entrepreneurs (especially Koreans), and various individuals. Many instances of hate crimes against Vietnamese are reported in Texas, California, and Massachusetts. Tensions have built between Korean merchants and residents of mostly African American or Spanish-speaking neighborhoods where many Koreans own stores. They have accused the Koreans of treating them rudely, even roughly. Some have responded with fire bombings and vandalism.

CHINESE AMERICAN WORKERS

About one-fourth of all Asian Americans are Chinese Americans, the largest of the Asian groups. Because of their greater numbers and more extensive history in the United States than other Asian American groups, we'll spend a little more time on this group than the others. We'll review some background information about their immigration experiences, differences among generations, and facts from their current profile.

The First Immigrants: From Gold Mines to Laundries

The Chinese were the first sizable group of Asians to immigrate to America and most settled in the West. Most had been farm peasants in China. However, most who came after the 1940s were more affluent business and professional persons escaping from communism. The earliest immigrants came to California soon after the 1849 Gold Rush to work in the gold mines. Later they were the primary workers who built the railroads and the irrigation canals and levees of the river deltas, laying the groundwork for the agricultural industry.

For many years nearly all the Chinese immigrants were men, who came to earn a nest egg and return to China. But most stayed and since there were so few Chinese women, they formed a bachelor society. The workers were nearly always targets of Euro-American labor resentment, especially during hard times. Ethnic antagonism in the mines, factories, and fields forced thousands of Chinese to set up small stores, restaurants, and service shops, especially laundries, which took little start-up cash. By 1890 the Chinese represented nearly 70 percent of all laundry workers. The "Chinese laundryman" was an American phenomenon. There were no laundries in China. The women there did the laundry, and men in China would have lost social status if they had done it (Ong 1983).

Euro-American workers often referred to the Chinese as "nagurs," and they were often stereotyped as oriental vampires with slanted eyes, a pigtail, dark skin, and thick lips. Like African Americans, they were perceived as heathen, morally inferior, savage, childlike, and lustful. The Chinese were seen as inferior colored people, along with African Americans and American Indians.

In 1880 Congress passed a Chinese Exclusion Act that prohibited further Chinese immigration, even though they represented only 0.002 percent of the total U.S. population. The exclusion act, which was extended indefinitely in 1904, also denied naturalized citizenship to the Chinese already here. Euro-American workers complained about competition from Chinese who would work for less. Many Chinese complained that the "cheap labor" cry was always a falsehood. They said that employers preferred Chinese workers because they were so much more honest, industrious, steady, sober, and painstaking. They said they were persecuted, not for their vices, but for their virtues (Chew 1906).

Subsequent Generations

By the 1920s and 1930s Chinese Americans had become more concerned than ever about their status because they were bringing up an increasing number of American-born children. The dominant Euro-American culture tended to grant more freedom and autonomy to children, as they grew into teenagers and young adults, than the Chinese culture. As in other immigrant families, a generational conflict existed in many Chinese American families over parental authority and the freedom of the American-born children coming of age. Many of them, especially females burdened with stricter limits than males, resented the restrictions on their social lives most of all (Chan 1991).

In the late 1940s to the mid 1960s relatively affluent and well-educated refugees from communism immigrated from China. In the 1990s, most immigrants were either wealthy investors from Hong Kong and Taiwan or poor political refugees from mainland China. Chinese Americans who immigrated as small children generally have no language problem, nor do any of the generations born in the United States. More than half of this group attains at least some college education.

Identity Crisis

Chinese American children reared in America experienced an identity crisis that was intensified by the prejudice that permeated many areas of public life. They were barred from public recreational facilities, such as swimming pools, and forced to sit at the back of movie theaters. Those who participated in athletics usually had to join Chinese teams. One Chinese American gave a typical interview response, "At times I have been called a 'Chink' and I have resented it bitterly and would at times answer back, but recently I have not replied" (Chan 1991, 113). Most troubling, very few second-generation college graduates could find jobs appropriate to their education and training.

Distinct Socioeconomic Classes

By the 1960s Chinese Americans were drifting into two categories. One was educated, relatively affluent, and becoming acculturated to American society. The other was largely uneducated, not affluent, and still retained much of traditional Chinese culture. People in the Chinese American community tended to have either much education or none.

Given the number of well-educated adults, however, the incomes of Chinese Americans were quite low. Although well-trained Chinese Americans could find suitable employment with relative ease, it was still very difficult for them to gain promotion to supervisory and higher administrative positions. Many were clearly overqualified for the jobs they held, and the only conclusion was that employers were reluctant to place Chinese Americans in positions that gave them power over Euro-Americans (Kitano and Daniels 1988).

Since 1960 the most notable developments have been the rapid growth of the Chinese American population, the degree to which it came to be seen as a model minority, and movement to the suburbs. The population increased four fold between 1960 and 1985, due primarily to expanded immigration quotas.

Movement to the Suburbs

A major development since 1980 is the movement of Chinese Americans out of Chinatowns into the suburbs. This move reflects their ongoing acculturation and Americanization. The so-called "miniature Chinatowns" sprouting up in suburban cities are actually small shopping malls, each usually anchored by a large American supermarket. These malls are often financed by Chinese Americans, who may also be some of the shop owners. The homes bought by Chinese Americans who frequent these malls tend to be scattered throughout the neighborhood, a different pattern than the dense homogeneous Chinatown pattern.

Current Profile

Chinese Americans are the largest group of Asian Americans; in fact, until recent decades they were the only large group of Asian Americans. Now they make up 24 percent of Asian Americans, with Filipino Americans running close behind at 22 percent. In 1990 nearly 70 percent of Chinese Americans were foreign born, so most are strongly influenced by Chinese cultural values and practices. Statistical averages of factors that purport to indicate Chinese socioeconomic status can be misleading due to the existence of the two distinct classes discussed earlier. When these two are averaged together, their profile is very similar to that of the average American.

One distinct difference however lies in educational attainment; nearly twice as many Chinese Americans hold bachelor's degrees as the national average, 47 percent of men and 35 percent of women. Such educational attainment is remarkable given the language problems. About 83 percent speak Chinese at home, 60 percent speak English "not very well," and 40 percent are linguistically isolated. Their per capita income does not reflect their higher educational attainment. At $14,900 it's only slightly higher than the $14,100 national median. Their family income is near the national average because more family members work. Nearly 20 percent of families have three or more members in the workforce compared to the national rate of 13 percent.

FILIPINO AMERICAN WORKERS

Filipino culture encompasses a diverse, multi-layered mix of subcultures. Its complex indigenous culture has strong Malay and other Asian influences. This is combined with Spanish and American colonial cultural influences, but since 1950 a clear Filipino cultural identity has been developing.

Current Profile

Most Filipino Americans are hardworking, well educated, and foreign born.

Hardworking. Filipino Americans tend to be very industrious, having the highest percentage of employment (75 percent) of any ethnic group. They also have the highest percentage of families with three or more members working (30 percent), and the lowest rate of poverty (6 percent). Their families average 4 persons, more than the national average of 3.2 (U.S. Census Bureau 1993).

Educated. Filipino Americans are the only Asian American group with more women holding degrees (42 percent) than men (36 percent). This is nearly double the rate of Euro-American men and more than two and one-half times the rate of Euro-American women. In spite of higher education levels, Filipino American per capita income of $13,600 is below the national median of $14,100.

Foreign born. Nearly 65 percent are foreign born, so Filipino values and practices are a strong part of their heritage. Language is not a problem for most. Only 13 percent are linguistically isolated, although 66 percent speak other than English at home. Most Filipino immigrants come from a rural, agricultural environment to urban areas of the United States and must adjust to the differences.

Cultural Values and Practices

Because of the historical Spanish influence, about 85 percent of Filipinos are Roman Catholic, and more than 90 percent have a Christian Malay heritage. The most dominant cultural values are:

- maintaining face or self-esteem
- saving face and avoiding shame
- meeting obligations and reciprocating others' generosity
- cooperating
- respecting authority and elders
- placing the extended family first

Other important cultural values include:

- Personalistic view of the universe and fatalistic view of the future.
- "God will help," a fatalistic reliance on powers beyond self.
- Good luck determines success.
- Sex and marriage are religious concerns; marriages are expected to last.

Let's discuss further the most dominant values.

Maintaining face and avoiding shame. From the Spanish comes a special sense of self-esteem called *amor proprio*, meaning self-love. To maintain self-esteem, some Filipino Americans put great energy into displaying appropriate dress, modesty, and good manners. Shame, called *hiya*, is felt when self-esteem is damaged, and nothing is worse than being shamed. An adult worker may withdraw, becoming less cooperative. If questioned, he or she may feel frustrated and too embarrassed to respond. As a result, Euro-Americans may conclude that they're oversensitive and can't take criticism. Here are some behaviors that may result from *hiya*:

- An employee may not ask questions of a supervisor even if she is not sure what to do
- An employee who is laid off from his job may act violently
- A host may spend more than he can afford for an event
- A student may not disagree in a discussion, even when she feels strongly about the topic

Meeting obligations and reciprocating others' generosity. When a person does something for someone, reciprocal action is usually implicitly expected. When Filipinos don't reciprocate and meet their obligations, they may be shamed. To be called shameless is a serious insult.

Cooperating. Filipinos value cooperation, the ability to get along with people, and are usually very receptive and willing to accept tasks on the job. They may cooperate with the work group at their own expense, and yet be too shy to make friends within the group. They tend to agree with those around them rather than express disagreement, to avoid confrontation, and to be cooperative and compliant. As a result

- Their true feelings may remain hidden from outsiders.
- They may use a go-between to bring up embarrassing or controversial matters.

Respecting authority and elders. Respect for authority and elders and obedience to authority are strong cultural values. They believe older people should be shown respect and allowed to take the lead. They generally seek out elders or other authority figures for approval and protection and for support or advice in making decisions. Filipino American employees, in return for the respect, obedience, and politeness they give the boss, may expect protection and favors, due to the value of reciprocity. Also, they may expect the boss to have an authoritarian management style and may therefore interpret a participative style as evidence of weakness or indecision.

Placing extended family first. Large extended families are common in the Philippines, which has one of the highest birth rates in the world. Family needs and status are placed above individual needs, reflecting the interdependence among family members. Filipinos don't think in terms of accumulating wealth and prestige for themselves, but for their families. Education, which is highly valued, is seen as an investment, primarily to benefit the family.

Communication patterns. Although Tagalog is the major language, most speak English, reflecting the U.S. influence. Filipino Americans follow the pattern found in many Asian cultures of indirectness and the use of a mediator or go-between as a tool of indirectness. To get directly to the point with a supervisor might be seen as disrespectful. They also tend to use flowery language, based on the belief that an impressive command of language is the sign of a cultivated person and enhances one's image, which is similar to the Latino viewpoint.

Use of time. Immigrants from the Philipines often must adjust to punctuality and use of time in the American workplace. In the Philipines, you are considered punctual if you arrive for an appointment within about 15 minutes after the scheduled time. Social events begin an hour or two after the appointed hour. According to Euro-Americans, Filipinos rarely complete things on time despite deadlines. They do get things done in their own time; many Euro-Americans say they do things "almost, but not quite."

On the other hand, most Filipino Americans readily adjust to the punctuality required in the U.S. workplace, as long as expectations are made clear. Their desire to cooperate, respect for authority, and fear of shame impel them to meet the supervisor's expectations regarding punctuality and meeting deadlines.

Expression of feelings. Filipino Americans place great emphasis on feelings or emotions, and generate warmth and friendliness. In this they're more like Latinos than other Asians. Supervisors must be especially careful in giving performance evaluations, critiques, and feedback. It's very difficult for most Filipinos to objectively separate the task at hand, the product, or their performance from themselves as subjective persons. They're likely to interpret a supervisor's objective analysis as a personal attack.

View of nature. Traditional Filipino culture sees humans as part of nature, not dominating it as much as conforming to it and interpreting their experience of nature through religion, family, and other means.

Customs. Some typical Filipino customs include the followings (Andres 1999)

- ***Gifts*** are not opened in front of the giver, which might imply the receiver is materialistic and more concerned with the gift than the act of giving. Also, when multiple gifts are given, comparisons might be made that would embarrass some givers.

- *Home visiting* is often done on a drop-in basis. Guests remove their shoes and are not expected to walk into other rooms without asking for permission.
- *Affection* in public, displayed by couples, is minimal.
- *Handshakes* may be limp, which is socially acceptable.
- *Using the index finger* to beckon people is extremely rude.
- *Lips* may be used to point to things.
- *Nodding upwards* is a common form of greeting.
- *Eyebrows raised* in recognition means "yes."
- *Avoidance of eye contact* implies dishonesty.
- *Smiling,* even for no reason, may be a sign of respect, showing deference and simpatia.

SOUTHEAST ASIAN AMERICAN WORKERS

About one-sixth of the Asian American group emigrated from Southeast Asian countries since the 1960s, most of them escaping the Vietnam War and communism. We'll discuss the unusual conditions of their emigration, their current profile, and the key issue, acculturation.

Background: Refugee Flight

About a million refugees have recently entered the United States from Southeast Asia as a result of the Vietnam War. The war created many political refugees from Vietnam, Cambodia, and Laos. The conditions of emigration may include:

- a recent past marred by years of war, chaos, and political persecution
- panic, fear, crisis, distress
- evacuating under a state of emergency with inadequate time for planning
- problems in transit, perhaps even becoming a "boat person," attacked by pirates and turned away by various governments
- life in temporary centers
- for many, transition from a rural, agricultural society to a modern, industrial or post-industrial society

Because of U.S. involvement in the Vietnam War in the late 1960s and early 1970s, the U.S. withdrawal in 1975, and the subsequent communist takeover of those countries, the United States has taken some responsibility for these political refugees. Immigration legislation in 1975 and 1976 expanded Asian immigrant quotas, and the 1980 Refugee Assistance Act further expanded quotas and provides for federal aid to states during refugees' first few years of residence.

Differences and Similarities among Groups

The first wave of refugees consisted primarily of middle and upper-class South Vietnamese who got out in the 1970s before the U.S. withdrawal, while the second wave contained many more Hmong, Cambodians, and Laotians. People of the first wave are generally more accustomed to western ways, better educated, more affluent, and better equipped to enter the U.S. workforce than those of the second wave. Many among the second wave are having a difficult time.

Vietnamese

Vietnam is largely an agricultural country, but it has more large urban centers than Laos and Cambodia and more people, with a population of 55 million. Over 70 percent of Vietnamese Americans are refugees of the Vietnam War. Many were middle- and upper-class citizens, wealthy or well-connected, and were able to leave South Vietnam before the communist takeover. Most came as family groups, some with large bankrolls and others with only the clothes on their backs. Over half live on the West Coast. San Diego has the largest population and San Francisco the second largest (Vietnamese 2001).

Status in the Vietnamese culture is attained through age and education more than through wealth. The people are oriented more toward intuition than intellect. Here is a brief comparison of Vietnamese and Euro-American worldviews.

Vietnamese Worldview	*Euro-American Worldview*
Humans are basically good but corruptible.	Human nature is evil but perfectible.
Humans should strive for harmony with Nature.	Humans should master Nature.
Past orientation.	Future orientation.
Value attachment to a place, ancestral land.	Value movement, migration, mobility.
Value the process of being or becoming	Value accomplishment, individuality,
Mutual dependence, connectedness.	and self-reliance.

The Hmong Tribes of Laos

Laos is small, mountainous, rural, undeveloped and sparsely populated with only 3 million residents. Most of the refugees are the Hmong, one of the largest hill tribes of northern Laos. They lived apart from mainstream Laotian society, subsisting as semi-nomadic farmers. They're generally described as industrious, independent, and peace-loving people who were swept up in the Vietnamese War because of their strategic location. By 1970 two-thirds of Laos had been bombed, creating more than 600,000 refugees. The fall of Vietnam and the withdrawal of American forces forced about 150,000 Hmong to escape to Thailand, and spend time in refugee camps there, and emigrate to the United States. The influx peaked in 1980. Although most Laotian immigrants are Hmong, others include urban government workers and ex-soldiers.

They have a strong family and clan system, and families are traditionally large. They follow a pattern of male dominance, where the role of the wife is to be devoted to her husband, elders are venerated, and clan and kinship ties are strong. The household, rather than the individual, is the primary unit, and clans serve as mutual aid associations. Most strongly believe in evil spirits, trust their shamans, and distrust modern medicine.

Their supreme commandment is "Hmong have to look after their own." Group solidarity was the cornerstone of Hmong social organization for more than 2,000 years. Living in small tropical mountain villages, most had never seen snow. Yet the U.S. government policy was to disperse them throughout the country, initially in resettlement sites primarily located in flatlands with freezing winters.

It was traditionally taboo to marry within the clan, so dispersal made it very difficult for young people to meet potential marriage partners from other Hmong clans. Many were sent to urban areas where the street violence was abhorrent to them. Their solution was to migrate again, this time on their own. During the early 1980s a third of all the Hmong moved from one city to another. They reunited into clans, formed cohesive communities, founded mutual-assistance organizations, and thoroughly defeated the U.S. government's attempt to scatter them evenly throughout the Melting Pot (Fadiman 1998). The downside: clustering in certain areas strained social services in those locales and created ethnic ghettos.

By 1996 Fresno had 35,000 Hmong, one of the highest concentrations in America. Fresno is the home of agribusiness and not the site of the kinds of small family plots found in the Laotian highlands, where there were no taxes and few bills. In Fresno everything comes due the first of the month. Prejudice against them runs high among the dominant majority as well as among minority groups, triggered by the large number of Hmong, their extremely different ways, and their initial dependence on expensive social services. Hmong are now forbidden to directly resettle in the Fresno area, but about half will probably end up there. On the other hand, many have been moving to North Carolina, where land is cheaper and job opportunities more plentiful.

Perhaps the most unique feature of the Hmong, and the most important for their transition to a U.S. workplace is their traditionally oral form of communication. They had no experience with written language until 1960 when missionaries came to the Laotian highlands. Adapting to a high-tech workplace that's based upon quite sophisticated uses of written information presents a formidable challenge. As an immigrant group with very few tools for adapting to American society, the Hmong have the greatest workplace barriers to overcome. Gaining facility with the English language is the most crucial goal, of course. Although nearly 90 percent were on welfare in the 1980s, they have rapidly learned how to survive on their own.

Cambodians

Cambodia is a small, primarily agricultural country, with a population of about 7 million. In 1979 Vietnamese communists invaded Cambodia, creating more than 3 million refugees. Cambodians who fled to the United States are mainly farmers, although some are skilled trade persons and a few are educated young people.

Current Profile of Southeast Asian Americans

Before 1970 there were about 20,000 Vietnamese in the United States and the number of other Southeast Asians was too small to count. In 1990 more than one million Southeast Asian Americans made up about 16 percent of the Asian American population. Although the U.S. government attempted to scatter them throughout the country, many migrated to the West, especially California.

Large families. They have the highest birth rates of any U.S. group; Hmong American families average 6.6 persons, while Filipino Americans, Vietnamese Americans, Cambodian Americans, and Laotian Americans average more than 4 persons per family, compared to the U.S. average of 3.2.

Less education. The Southeast Asian Americans have the lowest educational level of any U.S. cultural group. Causes probably include the chaos and disruption of years of war in the area they emigrated from, the rural agricultural background of many, language barriers, and their relatively destitute status as political refugees. The differences between educational level of men and women is significant, as indicated in Table 8.1.

TABLE 8.1: Educational Achievement of Southeast Asian Americans by Gender, 1990

Group	% holding a high school diploma or higher		% holding a bachelor's degree or higher	
	Male	Female	Male	Female
Hmong	44	19	7	3
Cambodian	46	25	9	3
Laotian	49	30	7	3
Vietnamese	69	53	22	12
U.S. total	76	75	23	18

Language Barriers. More than 90 percent speak their native language at home. More than 70 percent of Hmong, Cambodians, and Laotians don't speak English very well, and more than half of them are linguistically isolated. About 65 percent of Vietnamese don't speak English very well and 44 percent are linguistically isolated.

Low Incomes. Fewer refugees have jobs than the national average of 65 percent. Only 29 percent of Hmong have jobs, 58 percent of Laotians, 46 percent of Laotians, and 65 percent of Vietnamese. They have dramatically lower per capita incomes than the national average of $14,000. The Hmong average only $2,700; Cambodians, $5,000; Laotians $5,600; and Vietnamese $9,000. It follows that a greater percentage live in poverty: 64 percent of the Hmong, 43 percent of Cambodians, 35 percent of Laotians, and 26 percent of Vietnamese. Surveys of Vietnamese indicate that 92 percent of families with two or more workers are above the poverty line. As recently arrived groups acquire job skills, become employed, and have two or more workers in a family, they too should move out of the poverty category.

Cultural Patterns and Issues

Many Southeast Asian American values and practices are found in other Asian cultures. The primary religion is Buddhism, which is expressed more as a traditional philosophy of values and social relations than attendance at services or professions of belief. The following are general beliefs and behaviors that are especially emphasized by some Southeast Asian Americans, representing tendencies rather than rules:

- Having large, close-knit families, sometimes three generations in one house; it's very common for an extended refugee family to work together and pool resources to attain goals.
- Avoiding public displays of affection between men and women, especially between unmarried couples. Holding hands or touching among women and among men is a sign of close friendship. Greeting by hugging and kissing is not done. Sexual topics are not openly discussed, especially in mixed company.
- In Vietnam, people are introduced by their last name followed by their first name. A married woman retains her own last name, but is often called by her title and husband's last name.
- Being quiet around outsiders. Most Southeast Asian Americans are quite talkative, especially among themselves. The fact that they usually are perceived by Euro-Americans as unusually reserved probably reflects their unfamiliarity with the American culture and their natural reticence as "newcomers."
- Shaking hands upon meeting—for men, not women.
- Viewing a perceived unfairness or betrayal of trust as difficult to forgive or forget.
- Respecting teachers highly, even above parents. They are always referred to and addressed as teacher, never as he, she, or you.

Key Issue: Acculturation

Surveys taken a year after the first wave of refugees entered the United States indicate that major problems in adapting to the American culture were:

- breakup of the family and extended family units
- limits placed on the number of people who can live in one home
- lack of respect by Americans toward the elderly
- absence of friendly American people
- hectic pace in the American workplace
- dependence in America on the automobile and public transportation (difficult to walk or ride bikes from place to place)
- high value Americans place on work and achievement over interpersonal relationships

Factors that affect the acculturation of Southeast Asian refugees include the coercive aspects of their emigration, their need for a cohesive community, culture clashes that affect family cohesion, compatibility with American culture, reactions of other Americans, and occupational and educational fit.

Plans to Return or Stay

Because they were pushed out of their homes, many refugees hope to go back when conditions change. Those who plan to return have a strong incentive to retain their old cultural ways and less incentive to adopt American ways. Younger refugees are acculturating more rapidly than the older ones. Many want to become American citizens and are more hopeful about their future in the United States.

Need for a Cohesive Ethnic Community

U.S. policy was to scatter refugees to avoid backlash from American workers who compete for jobs. Another goal was to settle the refugees as quickly as possible so they could adapt and become self-sufficient. The scattering policy generally didn't work, and most moved to the warm climates they're accustomed to and to urban areas where they could network with other Asian groups. Since 1975 more than 500 mutual assistance associations have been created within refugee communities. They provide support, education, language development, job training, and cultural orientation. Some provide economic assistance in the form of business opportunities and jobs (Baldassare 1990).

Refugees who arrived in family units had the advantages of emotional support and multiple incomes. However, Vietnamese couples have experienced culture clashes that typically occur in families that recently immigrated from Asian cultures. Working wives' new status and children's Americanization can cause problems, reflected in the rapid rise in the divorce rate among Vietnamese couples in America.

Compatibility with the American Culture

The Vietnamese culture encourages responsibility, discipline, and hard work. Vietnamese value facing adversity with courage and stoicism, and they place a high value on education. Like other Asian cultures, they fit into a dominant society through conformity and avoiding confrontation and conflict. Most want a better life for their children and have a high degree of achievement motivation. The Hmong are most unlike Westerners and adaptation for them has been more difficult.

Reception by Other Americans

Some researchers have identified two groups that often feel threatened by new immigrants:

1. Downwardly mobile workers, those who once had more than they now have.
2. Disadvantaged people, the unemployed or underemployed who have always lived on the fringes of society.

In this era of civil rights and valuing diversity, overt prejudice against Asians is relatively rare. However, in an era of de-industrialization and restructuring, job competition can be fierce. American fishermen have clashed with incoming Vietnamese fishermen, some minority farm workers and assembly line workers resent the competition for jobs, and some underclass minorities have complained about the special aid given to refugees. Some middle-class workers seem worried about further erosion of their take-home pay, saying refugees "must be getting a government handout," and therefore they, the taxpayers, must be supporting them.

Asian immigrants cannot merge into the dominant culture as easily as European immigrants. Because they're easily identifiable by their looks as Asians, they don't have the luxury of choosing whether or not to partake of the advantages and disadvantages of being of a distinct ethnic minority.

Refugees have many specific needs that are different from the typical immigrant's needs. However, the things they generally need from the dominant culture are similar to the needs of all minorities:

- sensitivity to their culture and life experiences
- recognition of both the similarities and differences among groups
- understanding that their communication patterns and feelings may not be expressed in the American way, so assumptions may be misleading
- the use of culturally relevant frames of reference for understanding each other
- competent people to process their papers and help them meet governmental requirements

Occupations and Education

The language barrier is the most immediate problem for the refugees, who need to gain the education and skills necessary for job success. Lack of child care has also been cited as a major problem. Because these cultures value hard work and education, most authorities think they will eventually overcome the barriers and become self-supporting citizens.

The most obvious goals for any migrating group are to find good jobs and get a good education for their children. Vietnamese have had the most success in finding jobs because of their urban background. Many are working as assembly line workers, technicians, machine operators, and office workers. Underemployment has been a real problem, as has a lack of Vietnamese in supervisory positions. When previously low-status employees in the home country are given higher job positions than former high-ranking army officers, or when women are in higher positions than men, conflicts occur, especially when directions and orders are given directly.

JAPANESE AMERICAN WORKERS

The Japanese were the second group of Asians to arrive in the United States in significant numbers. Their experiences have both similarities and differences to the Chinese experience.

Myths and Facts

Japanese Americans must cope with the myths and stereotypes that all Asian Americans face, which were discussed earlier, but they face at least two other myths that are specifically held about Japanese Americans.

Myth #1: Japanese Americans are greedy and acquisitive.

This is a variation on the myth that Asian Americans only care about starting their own businesses and buying real estate. The Japanese twist for this myth may reflect the fact that Japanese Americans are the most financially successful of Asian American groups. As mentioned earlier, results of a recent survey refute this myth. Japan today is extremely competitive with the United States in several key industries, and the greedy, acquisitive stereotype is often applied to Japanese business persons. It may be projected onto Japanese Americans, most of whom have virtually no ties with Japanese business.

Myth #2: Japanese Americans are prejudiced toward African Americans.

This myth apparently is based on reports that African Americans who go to Japan to do business report difficulties in dealing with Japanese discrimination. Japan is a very homogeneous society, and few persons of African heritage live there or do business there. Unfamiliarity seems to be part of the problem. More important, most Japanese Americans were born in the United States and do not necessarily have the same viewpoint toward African Americans that Japanese in Japan have.

Background: The Japanese American Experience

The first large group of Japanese that arrived in the United States first migrated to Hawaii as laborers in the late 1800s, later moving on to the U.S. West Coast. In 1900 about 25,000 Japanese lived on the West Coast, mostly men who came to get ahead and planned to return to Japan. By 1920 there more than 100,000, about two-thirds of them in California. Like the Chinese immigrants, most were men working at physically strenuous, low-status, low-paying jobs, mainly in farming and building railroads.

Unlike the Chinese, the Japanese came from scattered rural areas all over Japan and Okinawa. As a group they were somewhat better educated and skilled than the Chinese immigrants. Some were quite skilled in intensive farming, such as truck gardening. Unlike China, Japan had begun the transition toward a modern industrial era. Although the Chinese presence in agriculture diminished after the 1880s, the Japanese became more heavily entrenched as farm owners and tenant farmers.

Community Growth

Due to pressure and negotiations of the Japanese government, immigrants' families were allowed to join them during the period from 1900 to 1924. This balanced the gender ratio and led to the establishment of families. By 1940 the nearly 80,000 second-generation Japanese Americans outnumbered the 47,000 immigrant parents. By 1940 Los Angeles had the largest Japanese American settlement, numbering 37,000, but San Francisco with only 5,000 was the headquarters for the major organizations of each generation.

War and Concentration Camps

The major issue for pre-1940 Japanese Americans was prejudice. Euro-Americans simply did not accept Asian Americans as equals. At the beginning of World War II President Roosevelt signed an executive order to classify Japanese Americans as "enemy aliens" and to intern those on the West Coast in detention camps. The apparent rationale was to protect the United States from Japanese spy and saboteur activity and a feared attack on the West Coast by Japanese submarines. At the same time he urged the men to volunteer in the all-Japanese American combat unit, which went on to become the most decorated U.S. military unit in history (Takaki 2000).

All persons of Japanese ethnicity living on the West Coast, were arrested, regardless of citizenship, age, or sex. They were forced to abandon all their possessions and assets, and allowed to take only what they could carry. In Northern California the first stop was a San Bruno racetrack-stable area called Tanforan, renamed Tanforan Assembly Center. (After the war it became Tanforan shopping mall.)

From there they were sent to one of 10 isolated camps: Gila River, Jerome, or Poston in Arizona; Tule Lake or Manzanar in southeast California; Heart Mountain in Wyoming; Topaz in Utah; Granada in Colorado; Minidoka in Idaho; and Rohwer in Arkansas. The camps were surrounded by barbed wire and were patrolled by armed soldiers, who shot and killed several of the Japanese they were guarding. While they were not death camps, they were concentration camps by most commonly accepted definitions.

Japanese Americans are the only group of U.S. residents ever to be deprived of their constitutional rights without a trial. Yet no individual Japanese American was ever found guilty of espionage nor were any so charged. Italian Americans and German Americans were not confined, even though their homelands were also our war enemies. More than 150,000 Japanese Americans living in Hawaii were left alone, as were the 10,000 who lived east of the Mississippi. Those who were sent to the camps lost virtually all their assets except those they could take with them. Their greatest economic loss was the income they weren't allowed to earn during their internment.

This wartime exile and incarceration was and still is the central event of Japanese American history, making their history unique among Asian Americans. The violation of Japanese American trust, and the extreme level of distrust expressed by the government of their homeland, the United States, was traumatic for those who lived through it. Every year the Japanese American community observes a Day of Remembrance with solemn ceremonies. In 1988 the U.S. government formally apologized to these families and set up a process for reparations.

Current Profile

Japanese emigration peaked around 1910, and by 1970 Japanese Americans were the largest Asian American group in the country. Thirty years later, in 2000, they were the fifth largest group, after those from China, the Philippines, India, Vietnam, and Korea. By then, few were first-generation immigrants. Originally they were heavily clustered in California but now are scattered rather widely.

By most measures of success, Japanese Americans are the most successful of any Asian American group. They have the fewest foreign born (32 percent) of any Asian American group, and the oldest average age, 36 compared to 30 for Asian Americans in general, and 33 for the total U.S. population.

Intermarriage with other ethnic groups, especially with Euro-Americans, has grown rapidly. In fact, 38 percent of the men and 52 percent of the women have married outside their group. The men are most likely to marry women from other Asian groups, while the women are likely to marry Euro-Americans. Since 1980 the number of babies born to a Japanese American and Euro-American parent actually exceeds the number born to two Japanese American parents.

Most speak English at home (57 percent) with only Asian Indian Americans at 85 percent having a greater percentage speaking English at home. However, 33 percent are still considered linguistically isolated.

Japanese American educational attainment is high. Nearly twice the percentage of men hold degrees as the average U.S. male, 43 percent compared to 23 percent. Only Asian Indian American men have a significantly higher educational level. A significantly greater proportion of Japanese women hold degrees than the average U.S. woman, 28 percent compared to 18 percent.

They have the highest per capita income of any Asian American group, at $19,400, well above the national median of $14,100. The poverty rate of 7 percent is just a step above the lowest for all Asian American groups, with the Filipino Americans at 6.4 percent. They have the smallest families, 3.1 compared to the Asian American average of 3.8 and the U.S. average of 3.2. And a relatively small percentage (15 percent) have three or more family members working, compared to the Asian American average of 20 percent and the U.S. average of 13 percent.

Cultural Values

Surveys indicate most Japanese American young people still believe in traditional Japanese cultural values, most of which are typical Asian cultural values. The following values seem to be especially meaningful in the Japanese American culture:

- self-confidence
- sympathy and compassion for others
- fun-loving approach
- craftsmanship, pride in work

KOREAN AMERICAN WORKERS

The Korean American population has increased significantly since 1965. During the Korean War in the early 1950s, millions of peasant refugees fled from their farms to South Korean cities. Many of their children who got professional degrees found inadequate opportunities in their developing economy. When U.S. immigration law was liberalized for professionals in 1965, they flocked to the United States to escape political instability and high unemployment in Korea. They were one of the few immigrant groups in American history that was predominantly urban, educated, and from one generation. Most were Christian, a result of missionary efforts. Most also had some personal savings, military training, and a willingness to work hard.

Current Profile

Nearly 800,000 Korean Americans comprised about 12 percent of the Asian American population in 1990. About 73 percent were foreign born and the average age is 29. More than twice as many Korean American men have degrees as the total population, 47 percent compared to 23 percent. Among women, 26 percent have degrees compared to 18 percent of the total population. About 63 percent hold jobs, compared to 65 percent of all Americans. They have the highest percentage of all Asian Americans in technical, sales, and administrative support jobs. Per capita income is $11,000, somewhat under the $14,000 national median. Poverty rates and families with more than three workers are about the same as the national average.

Cultural Values and Practices

The major religion is Buddhism and there is a strong underlying ethic of Confucianism and Shamanism. Confucianism has especially affected cultural values and practices, and most of these are discussed under Asian American cultural patterns (Harris and Moran 1996).

Inner Feelings, Mood

A concept that is important to understanding Korean Americans is that of *kibun*, literally "inner feelings," with the closest English translation probably being "mood." When the kibun is good, the person functions smoothly and easily and feels great. If the kibun is upset or bad, transactions may come to an abrupt stop, and the person feels depressed, awful. Part of the intention of business people is to enhance the kibun of all parties. To damage the kibun could end the relationship and even create enemies. Class or status is intimately involved in the nurturing of kibun.

Nonpersons

Koreans who fail to follow the basic rules of social interaction are considered by other Koreans to not even be a person—to be a nonperson. Foreigners in a certain sense and to a certain extent are considered by Koreans as nonpersons. Koreans show very little concern for nonpersons' feelings, their comfort, or whether they live or die. Nonpersons are simply not worthy of much consideration. Korean Americans obviously must modify this attitude in order to function effectively in a diverse society; however, some variation of it probably survives and affects relationships.

Use of Names

Newly arrived Korean Americans must adapt to the American use of first names in business situations. To the Confucian, a name is something to be honored and respected, not to be used casually. Therefore, to call someone directly by her or his name is an insult in most social circumstances. A Korean is addressed by her or his title, position, trade, profession, or some other honorary title.

Flattery and Patience

Flattery is a key aspect of doing business among Korean Americans. An important or delicate business matter is always approached gradually. To begin discussing it directly and immediately is considered mere stupidity and will almost always result in failure. A highly skilled business person moves with "deliberation, dignity, and studied motions, and senses the impressions and nuances" that others are signaling (Harris and Moran 1996).

ASIAN INDIAN AMERICANS

About one-eighth of Asian Americans are of Asian Indian heritage. They are the most highly educated U.S. group and nearly all speak English. We'll discuss the two waves of immigrants that came from India, their current profile, and some cultural values and practices.

Background: Sikhs and Professionals

Asian Indians came to the United States in two waves, the first around the turn of the twentieth century and the second after 1965. The first wave were Sikhs from rural areas, and the second wave were educated professionals from urban areas.

The First Wave

About 10,000 Asian Indians emigrated to the United States around 1900. Most were from one region of Punjab, a fertile, prosperous region in North India. Nearly all were Sikhs, a religion that combines aspects of the Hindu and Muslim religions. Highly visible religious customs for males include wearing a long turban, a dagger, and an iron bracelet, and never cutting their hair. About half the immigrants settled in eastern and midwestern cities, especially New York, and worked as merchants and middle-class professionals.

The other half settled in the fertile valleys of California. Following a typically Asian pattern, most were married men who left their wives in India, planning to make money to send back home to buy land. A few of the men took wives after arriving, mostly women from Mexican American farm worker families. Because of cultural differences, these marriages tended to be conflict ridden, and at least

20 percent ended in divorce. They generally experienced the same kind of discrimination as other Asians. For example, the alien land laws made it impossible to own farmland.

From 1914 to 1946 few Asian Indians entered the United States, due to tight immigration laws, and the Asian Indian population in California declined from a high of more than 5,000 to about 1,500. About 7,000 immigrants arrived between 1948 and 1965, mostly close relatives of American citizens. They did not establish new ethnic communities but rejuvenated those in existence.

The Second Wave

Since 1965 a much larger wave has established new communities with few connections with the old ones. Most are not Sikhs, are not farmers, and do not live in the Far West. The 1980 population of nearly 400,000 doubled by 1990 to more than 800,000. Asian American Indians are not dispersed around the country. About a third live in the Northeast, a fourth in the South, a fourth in the Midwest, and a fifth in the West.

Current Profile

In 1990 about 840,000 Asian Indians comprised about 12 percent of all Asian Americans. About 75 percent were foreign born, and the average age was 30. They are the most highly educated U.S. ethnic group, with over 65 percent of the men and 49 percent of the women holding bachelor's degrees or higher, compared to the total population figures of 23 and 18 percent respectively.

Because of India's history as a British colony prior to 1950, most immigrants from India speak English. It's the major linking language in a nation of many languages and dialects. They have the least language difficulties of any Asian American group.

Asian Indian Americans are industrious and are heavily represented in high-status occupations. More than 72 percent of them have jobs, compared with 65 percent of all Americans, and 18 percent have three or more family members working, compared with 13 percent nationally. Nearly half of all foreign-born Asian Indian workers are managers and professionals. This is twice the proportion for all Americans, which is 24 percent, and significantly higher than any other Asian American group.

It follows that Asian Indian Americans have relatively high incomes and few live in poverty. Per capita income was nearly $18,000, compared to about $14,000 for all Americans. Among Asian American groups, only Japanese Americans earned more. Asian Indian Americans had one of the lowest poverty rates, 10 percent compared with 14 percent nationally.

To summarize Asian Indian Americans tend to be:

* strongly committed to maintaining family connections
* highly educated
* concentrated in the professions
* well paid
* trained in India, many part of a "brain drain" during the 1980s, caused by India's training more professionals than its businesses could profitably employ

Cultural Values and Practices

The predominant religion in India is Hinduism. All of these strongly influence the values and practices of the people. In Hindu marriages, the woman is expected to show absolute dedication, submission, and obedience to her husband. Her traditional status in the household is low until she produces a male child. Other traits include:

* Family and friends are much more important than in the West.
* Extended family living is highly valued.
* Friends sense each other's needs and do something about them.

- Speaking your mind to a friend is a sign of friendship.
- Most believe that there are no accidents, that all things are interrelated in a cosmic order.
- Indian women do not expect to be spoken to by men who are strangers; nor is it appropriate for such men to help women out of a car, up steps, etc.
- Women who dare to dance do so only with their husbands.
- People don't address others outside the extended family by first name. The equivalent of *Mr. Bill* or *Miss Linda* is appropriate, as are such titles as *Teacher* and *Doctor*.
- People are expected to be on time.
- Public displays of affection are considered inappropriate.

While Asian Indian Americans have much in common with other Asian Americans, their culture is probably the most distinct because of the influence of Hinduism. There are also many Buddhists, as well as members of other religious groups. There is a strong Muslim influence, especially in Pakistan and Bangladesh, which affects the values and practices of immigrants from those countries.

PACIFIC ISLANDERS

Pacific Islanders who live in the U.S. mainland are a relatively small ethnic group, but still more than 1 percent of the U.S. population. Business people in the West are most likely to encounter Pacific Islanders, since most of them live there, especially in Hawaii and California. We'll review their current profile and some common issues. Then we'll explore the background of the largest population within this group, the Hawaiians.

Current Profile

In the 1990 census, for the first time Pacific Islanders were identified as a distinct group of about 365,000 people living in the U.S. mainland. Their islands of origin are as follows:

Hawaii	58 percent
Samoa	17 percent
Guam	14 percent
Other	11 percent

Most live in the West and a few (13 percent) are foreign born. The median age is 25. Many came to the United States to pursue an education, and 76 percent are high school graduates, while only 11 percent are college graduates.

Most speak English, but 33 percent don't speak it very well, and 11 percent are linguistically isolated. The average family size is four. Most have jobs, but their income is significantly less than the national average and their poverty rate is significantly higher. More than 70 percent have jobs, with 18 percent holding managerial or professional jobs. Their per capita income averages $10,342 and their poverty rate is 17 percent.

Issues Common to Pacific Islanders

Some issues shared by many Pacific Islanders include:

- Education and skills gaps representing the major differences in surviving in their island culture and the high-tech U.S. culture
- Loss of status, rank, and prestige of people who were leaders in the islands
- Low wages and high expenses
- Role and identity problems—hierarchical roles of males are threatened, and identity closely tied to the family is weakened

- Stereotyped as islanders, who are exotic, romantic, heavy-drinking revelers
- Stereotyped as Asians, whose patterns are decidedly different in many ways

What is functional in a small island economy may not be helpful in an urban, technological society. Pacific Islanders' numbers are too small and their resources too slim to develop a separate community and that could develop opportunities for its members. Strong family ties and the belief in helping one another have been an asset for the immigrants.

The Hawaiians: A Multicultural Group

Two hundred years ago Hawaii was the home of a rich, distinct culture, but today it is more multicultural than Hawaiian.

From Distinct Culture to Multiculture

When Captain James Cook, the English explorer, came upon the Hawaiian islands in 1778, he found a thriving, highly stratified culture of more than 300,000 Hawaiians ruled by a class of chieftains. Other Europeans soon followed, including Christian missionaries from New England. By 1890 the great "white man's diseases" had decimated the population, leaving only about 35,000 Hawaiians.

The event that most dramatically changed the Hawaiian social system was the 1848 pact that permitted private persons to buy the land. Much of the land, formerly under the king and chiefs, ended up in the hands of a few Euro-American plantation owners who wanted to grow sugar, pineapple, and similar crops. The sugar and pineapple industries grew rapidly, and the demand for cheap labor changed forever the cultural mix of people on the islands. Most of the Hawaiians were dead, and those who were left generally did not make good laborers. The plantation owners brought in Chinese, Japanese, Korean, and Filipino laborers, many of whom stayed, creating a multicultural population. Today there are almost no "pure" Hawaiians left.

In 1898 the United States annexed Hawaii as a territorial possession. By that time Euro-Americans owned most of the land, were in control of the economy, and ran the political system. The cultural aspects of plantation life were primarily Asian: The languages, games, worship, and attitudes toward family, property, and authority reflected Asian cultural themes. Although Asians were the majority of the population, they were divided by ethnicity and were economically dependent on the plantation owners. What little remained of the native Hawaiian culture was found in the more remote villages.

Twentieth–Century Hawaii

Of all the groups found in twentieth-century Hawaii, the native Hawaiians had the most difficulty in adjusting to the competitive Euro-American culture, and a retreat to the past left them further behind. They began blaming the Asians for their plight and helped the Euro-Americans write land laws discriminating against the Chinese and Japanese, which of course further entrenched Euro-American dominance.

In 1959 Hawaii became a state. The actual numbers of immigrants since then has been difficult to assess. Most who come to the mainland are of mixed ancestry, and their experiences are as diverse as the cultural diversity that they represent. Because of this background, Hawaii is the most multicultural of all the states, and the culture has both Euro-American and Asian American themes.

LEADERSHIP CHALLENGES: OVERCOMING BARRIERS TO CAREER SUCCESS

As a leader you have many opportunities and challenges in working effectively with Asian Americans, in supporting their ability to contribute to work teams, and in building mutual respect and trust. You can help by providing support in overcoming barriers, avoiding typical assumptions and stereotypes, determining the generational status and citizenship status of each Asian American associate, constantly questioning your other assumptions about them, and helping people get to know these valuable co-workers.

Challenge #1: Provide Support in Overcoming Barriers

Some typical barriers to job success faced by Asian Americans include:

- Being typecast as technologists (technical coolies) and therefore not being considered for higher level positions.
- Being discriminated against because Euro-Americans are uncomfortable with their cultural style, which is considered too "foreign and strange."
- Communicating and verbalizing, problems especially crucial with first-generation immigrants.
- Being misunderstood because of their values and behaviors, such as humbleness and passiveness. Such behavior is not necessarily an indicator that they are not qualified for leadership roles.

Challenge #2: Avoid Typical Assumptions and Stereotypes

You've learned about the most typical myths, stereotypes, and assumptions that can hamper good working relationships. Here are a few reminders.

Remember, They're Americans, Not Foreigners

Non-Asian Americans have a tendency to look upon Asian Americans as foreigners because of their Asian appearance. Most Asian-appearing workers you'll encounter will be Asian Americans. They're Americanized in varying degrees and possess varying language skill levels. Keep in mind that they aren't foreigners.

Avoid Assumptions about Language Ability

Some leaders assume Asian Americans are fluent in an Asian language and have problems with English. When Euro-Americans make such comments as "You speak very good English" or "Where did you learn to speak English so well?" Asian Americans who were born and raised in the United States may be understandably taken aback. It's one more reminder that even though they consider themselves as American as anyone, others tend to see them as foreigners.

Asian Americans are often embarrassed or frustrated when others expect them to be bilingual. For example, a worker who is third-generation Chinese may speak little or no Chinese. Let multiple language skills emerge and be used as an asset after you establish the facts.

Most important, when discussing an Asian American employees' skills, qualifications, and career goals, you can help to identify any communication skills or problems that he or she has and try to get remedial training.

Don't Assume They're Cultural Ambassadors

Don't try to make an Asian American worker your token Asian expert. Asian Americans appreciate people who don't assume they're experts in their ancestors' culture, just as they appreciate those who don't assume they're bilingual. For example, Japanese Americans who were born and raised in the United States are not necessarily experts in Japanese cuisine, culture, or politics. They do not necessarily agree with economic or political developments in Japan. Again, it's better to ask about special bicultural expertise than to make assumptions.

Avoid Such Labels as "Oriental"

For many Asian Americans the term Oriental, meaning Easterner, conjures up old Hollywood stereotypes (such as Charlie Chan and Tokyo Rose) depicting mysterious, unknowable, exotic Asians.

It brings up unpleasant memories for many. Also, some consider it Eurocentric, since it describes Asia as east of Europe. A case could be made that it's west of the Americas, and that the Americas are the East to Asians.

Remember, People with Spanish Surnames May Be Filipinos

Many types of people may have Spanish-sounding names. For example, many Filipinos took Spanish surnames during the era of Spanish colonialism. They are not Latinos, although their values and practices probably reflect a Spanish influence.

Challenge #3: Determine Generational Status

There tend to be significant differences between first-generation immigrants and second-, third-, and fourth-generation Americans. By open, direct, but tactful conversations, you can share information about your background and learn about each associate's background. Be sure that your tone or manner is not in any way condescending or patronizing. Getting information can help you to understand the associates' values, viewpoints, and actions. Keep in mind that information you've absorbed about such groups as third-generation Japanese Americans or recently arrived Hmong Americans can only provide general guidelines. Keep an open mind, get to know each individual, and avoid the tendency to use such information to form rigid stereotypes about these people.

Challenge #4: Ascertain Citizenship Status

For workers who are not American citizens or permanent residents, find out about their status, which can help you better understand their background. For example, some initially come as foreign students, then get work visas. Their values and actions therefore tend to stem from Asian values and practices, and they are less Americanized. Companies must sign papers for Asians to keep their work visas, which frequently makes such workers feel dependent on the company. Such workers may be more submissive, obedient, and compliant, a situation some companies prefer and capitalize upon. Take the lead in respecting such workers.

Challenge #4: Question Your Assumptions about Behaviors

Periodically review the cultural values and customs discussed here. Do further research on your own. Question your knee-jerk reactions and assumptions about why an Asian American acts a certain way. For example, in the American business culture "silence is consent," and if someone doesn't speak up about a decision being made during a meeting, we assume he or she has no objections. But in Asian cultures "silence is golden," and "maintaining harmony is virtuous."

Check your assumptions, and then ask some tactful questions to learn what's really going on. Above all, you can look beyond surface behaviors and get to know Asian American team members personally in order to help them develop their talents and make appropriate career plans.

Challenge #5: Help People Get to Know Asian American Co-workers

You can take a leadership role and influence others in the workplace by providing information about Asian American myths and realities, their cultural patterns and strengths, and guidelines for building productive relationships with them. Occasionally review the Asian American values and practices you have just learned. Do further research on your own.

You can help others get to know Asian American associates by including them on team projects. This can provide for in-depth contact with other employees and increased comfort levels.

LEADERSHIP OPPORTUNITIES: BUILDING UPON ASIAN AMERICAN STRENGTHS

You can learn to recognize Asian Americans' potential contributions and respond by building on typical Asian American traits, recognizing Asian American values as strengths, applying some leadership strategies, and helping Asian Americans make marketplace connections.

Opportunity #1: Build on Typical Asian American Characteristics

Some Asian American characteristics that are especially important in business are that they generally

1. have an interest in long-range benefits.
2. are steadfast, once they decide upon who and what is the best choice.
3. stick to their word.
4. are punctual.

What can you do to build on these characteristics?

- You can identify situations in which these traits are an especially good fit.
- You can point out the good fit to Asian American associates and to others.
- You can help them verbalize to team members the value of developing these practices.

Opportunity #2: Recognize Asian American Values as Strengths

Nearly all values and behavior patterns represent a two-sided coin in the workplace. One side is the advantages these can bring to the career achievement and organizational contribution of the employee. The other side is the barriers they could erect. You can learn to recognize the cultural and individual values and behaviors of team members. You can figure out ways to enhance them and bring them into the work situation in constructive ways. Here are some ideas.

Obligation to Family

Work with the value of strong obligation to family. In most American corporate cultures, workaholics are rewarded and people who do not consistently put the company first are viewed as lacking commitment. While most Asian Americans place high value on hard work and perseverance, when family members need them, family obligations must come first.

- You can understand and respect Asian American priorities regarding family and work. By doing so, you're likely to win the respect and loyalty of these employees.

Hard Work and Cooperation

Respect their values regarding hard work and cooperation. Some managers take advantage of the Asian American tendency to value hard work and cooperation by piling on the work. Asian Americans are patient, but not stupid. Eventually such exploitation will backfire.

Most Asian Americans emphasize trust and mutual connections, a major aspect of building cooperative business relationships.

- You can help them put their value for trust and mutual connections to good use for the team, the organization, and for their own careers.

Modesty and Humility

Understand their values of modesty and humility. By American corporate culture standards, many Asian Americans may appear to be too passive and too lacking in self-confidence and ambition to be given tough assignments that call for traditional leadership skills. In Asia such qualities are seen as positive, and the American standards are likely to be seen as egocentric and arrogant, as pushing or imposing oneself on others. First- and second-generation Asian Americans tend to value modesty and humility more highly than later generations.

In Asian countries the typical American can-do attitude may be viewed as too bold or individualistic. People from Asian cultures are more likely to explain optimism in low-key ways. They may say, "This is a very difficult challenge, and I'm trying, even though I may not be able to do it." Euro-American managers who are sensitive to such differences will not jump to the conclusion that Asian American employees lack self-confidence and motivation simply because they don't project the can-do attitude that's typical of Euro-Americans, men especially.

Properly used, such values as modesty and humility can be quite appropriate for facilitative team leaders. Further, such values do not mean that the worker lacks self-confidence, ambition, or assertiveness, qualities that vary among Asian Americans, just as they do among Euro-Americans. Asian Americans merely tend to express them in a more low-key, indirect manner. Similarly, Euro-American managers usually reward employees who tactfully question the status quo, speak up, take initiative, or find a better way of doing things. Asian Americans do not necessarily behave in this manner.

- You can help find ways to reward and motivate Asian American employees who are not as verbal or assertive as Euro-American.
- You can help show them when and how to be assertive.

Indirectness and Respect

Understand the values of indirectness and respect. Instead of assuming that that they are devious, uncommunicative, or dishonest, get to know them as individuals so you can reach a deeper understanding of the values of indirectness and respect in their communication patterns. Another aspect of respect involves the use of space and touching. Asian cultures like more space between persons when communicating and less touching than is typical in the United States.

- Upon meeting, a slight bow or brief handshake is appropriate.
- Follow their lead about how far apart to stand or sit from each other.

Emotional Expression

Understand how they express emotions. You have learned that Asian Americans are less likely to express emotions than are people from other cultures. To maintain harmony they avoid openly expressing such emotions as anger, resentment, and jealousy. In addition, they may hide their emotions when they sense they're in a "hostile foreign environment" that causes them to feel vulnerable, intimidated, or threatened. People from all cultures are likely to show less emotion, as a protective device, when they feel like a foreigner or minority. You can help by:

- seeing them first as Americans and as a part of the group you're working with.
- helping them to explore and express feelings that need to come out and be dealt with in order to build honest, trusting, work relationships.

Opportunity #3: Apply Leadership Strategies

Here are some strategies that may be especially appropriate for Asian American workers.

Enhance Boss–Worker Relations

Explain deviations from traditional boss-worker practices. Asian cultures tend to be more hierarchical and status-oriented than current American corporate cultures. Most corporations have moved beyond the old authoritarian boss-obedient employee model that still fits the pattern of many Asian cultures.

If you're a supervisor, have a conversation with Asian American employees in which you share your ideas of the leader-worker relationship. Once you understand their expectations, you can help them to understand your own deviations from that expectation. For example:

- If they expect the boss to make all decisions, you can explain why workers in this company participate in decision making.
- If they would be personally humiliated if you pitched in to help complete a task, you can explain how this is viewed in the corporate culture and what it means.

Use a Team Approach

Good teamwork integrates cultural differences. One way to bridge the gap between Euro-American emphasis on individual initiative and Asian American emphasis on obedience to authority is to structure tasks so they can be performed by teams. Gradually introduce independent decision making by doing it as a group. Working in teams can also help Asian Americans and co-workers get to know each other at deeper levels, which breaks down walls of prejudice. It can also take advantage of Asian Americans' group-oriented values and skills.

- You can suggest opportunities for working together in teams.
- You can encourage Asian Americans to contribute their group-oriented values and traits to help the team become more close-knit and productive.

Uncover Relationship Problems

Help bring problems to the surface. Harmony and compliance are two Asian American values that have upsides and downsides. A downside can be an unwillingness to confront relationship problems. Most Asian Americans are taught that in troublesome situations, they should act as though nothing has happened. If they acknowledge a relationship problem, then they must take action, and action may be extremely serious. As a result, they tend to be long-suffering and patient, but resentment may build. In team situations it's usually important to bring problems and troublesome feelings to the surface and to deal with them—if they're important enough to an individual to eventually create communication and relationship barriers.

- You can work with Asian Americans in developing such team-related skills.

Provide Assertiveness Training

You have learned that even minimally educated Asian American women can be assertive on the job when they believe it's necessary or desirable. But because Asian cultures focus on humbleness and subordinating personal desires for group interests, Asian American employees often need some training about the role of assertiveness in the American workplace. For more than 20 years, Euro-American women have benefited from such training. Asian American employees also respond well to assertiveness training and can reap similar benefits.

- Help provide assertiveness training by your own examples and explanations.
- Encourage your organization to provide formal training sessions.
- Encourage Asian American associates to attend such training. If the situation is touchy, you may want to go yourself and ask them to come with you.

Build Trust

Our history of prejudice and discrimination may have created some trust barriers in inter-cultural relationships. When Asian Americans perceive that a Euro-American is trying to "buddy up" to them, they may respond internally with some distrust and suspicion. If you're a Euro-American, you must find ways to overcome this barrier.

- Begin by raising your awareness of the ways in which messages can be misunderstood or misinterpreted, and give special attention to clear communication.

- Then be very consistent in your messages and positions, and always follow through on agreements. Trust is built through the experience of another person as honest, fair, consistent, and reliable. Letting someone down, even once, can shatter newly-built trust.

Show Concern

Express sincere personal concern. Cooperative relationships are normally personal ones. Get to know Asian American workers as people in order to understand their goals and needs, which are usually tied to family status and needs. In this way you show that you understand the value of cooperation and want to establish a cooperative relationship.

- Establish personal relationships with Asian American associates.
- Find out what's most important to them and make their priorities a major part of your discussions and of the relationship.

Communicate Clearly

Cultural differences often cause misperceptions and misunderstandings. Therefore, you must find ways to send clear, unmixed messages that involve requests, assignments, expectations, or explanations. Then you must check for understanding in ways that uncover misperceptions.

- If in doubt, be very specific and factual in making requests and giving instructions. Don't say, "You might want to think about doing xyz." Ask, "Can you do xyz before you leave today? How does that fit your schedule?"
- Check for understanding. Don't ask questions that can be answered yes or no; for example, "Is that clear?" Ask questions that clearly establish whether the person understands, such as "How do you plan to go about doing that?"

Select Motivators and Rewards

Consider each employee's values when you choose the motivators and rewards you use. Rewards such as individual recognition may not be as effective for motivating Asian American employees as they are with Euro-Americans. The same is true for perks and benefits.

- You can talk with Asian Americans about their values, goals, and expectations.
- Together you can develop rewards that they value and that serve as effective motivators for them.

Opportunity #4: Make Marketplace Connections

Many companies are realizing the potential of the growing Asian American market, and nearly all U.S. companies are doing more and more business with Asian countries in the global marketplace. This increased trade has created interest in Chinese language courses, which are growing faster than for any foreign language. Chinese now ranks fifth in popularity, after French, Spanish, German, and Japanese.

Asian American employees tend to have a special touch with Asian clients due to cultural similarities. They are also an invaluable resource in developing strategies and action plans for doing business in such markets. Most Asian Americans welcome such opportunities to improve their job prospects.

Help Them Connect with the Asian American Marketplace

Asian Americans have greater buying power than their share of the total population. Companies such as Coca-Cola and AT&T have established Asian American marketing departments and have tried to reach Asian American communities with donations and advertisements. Companies are targeting the rapidly increasing Asian American clientele. They are putting more Asian American models in their television commercials and advertisements. Some are looking to Asian American culture—art, music, dance, clothing designs, movies, and food—for inspiration and to make connections with the Asian American markets (Min 1995).

- You may be able to help your organization to recognize and use Asian American employees as a valuable resource and connection in such efforts.

Help Them Connect with Asian Countries

Virtually all economists expect Asian countries to play a more important role as American economic partners in the twenty-first century. Some locations that are emerging as economic tigers are Singapore, Taiwan, Hong Kong, and South Korea. New trade relations with China are opening up a market of over a billion people (Min 1995).

- You may be able to help your organization see that Asian Americans employees can provide insights into these global markets and can serve as valuable links.

SUMMARY

Asian Americans must deal with many stereotypes and myths, such as they're too passive to be good American leaders, they're unemotional and inscrutable, they're "foreign," good at math, and "technical coolies." Much of this is a matter of style rather than substance. Actually Asian Americans are assertive when it's important and acceptable to be assertive, and they respond well to assertiveness training. Asian Americans have the same emotions as other people, but their values and training determine how they express themselves. Consideration for others' feelings and concern for harmony cause them to limit their emotional expression. Many have focused on technical skills until they could overcome language difficulties, but third- and fourth-generation Asian Americans tend to have good language skills.

Asian Americans have dealt with overt prejudice since Chinese immigrants first came to the United States about 150 years ago. The segregation and discrimination imposed reinforced their tendency to retain tight-knit families and communities. They've therefore retained many of their cultural values and patterns. Still, third- and fourth-generation Asian Americans tend to be quite Americanized. As a group, they have higher educational achievement than average. Although they hold higher-status jobs than average, they make less than Euro-Americans in comparable jobs, which reflects some workplace barriers that still remain.

Common cultural themes of all Asian cultures are putting group concerns before individual desires, promoting group harmony, accepting the hierarchy and status differences, revering education as a moral virtue, and communicating vaguely, indirectly, and silently.

The model minority stereotype has been a double-edged sword for Asian Americans, creating a belief that they are productive workers but leading to unfair expectations that they'll work harder for less than other employees. The myth has been used to blame African Americans and Latino Americans for their lower socioeconomic achievement. The model minority image is misleading and complex. On average Asian Americans do have higher educational and income levels than other groups. However, more of their family members must work to achieve these levels, and their education does not given them payback in income at the same rate as Euro-Americans. Asian Americans' success in small business has helped them to achieve higher education and some financial security in spite of discrimination. Women are expected to be especially modest and compliant, but most are strong and will be assertive and even confrontational when necessary.

Chinese Americans are the largest of the Asian American groups and have been here the longest. In fact they were the only Asian American group of any size for 100 years. They established Chinatowns in several cities, with their own small businesses and mutual aid associations. Filipino Americans are almost as large though they came later. They retain many Asian cultural patterns, as well as patterns similar to Latino Americans because of several hundred years of Spanish rule. Most Southeast Asian Americans arrived since the 1960s as refugees of the Vietnam War. Their backgrounds range from urban professionals to Hmong hill people. Japanese Americans began arriving just after the Chinese and are considered the most successful of the Asian American groups by most measures. Korean Americans are from a predominantly Confucian culture but most are Christians. Most have come since 1965. Asian Indian Americans are mainly urban professionals. They have the highest educational achievements of any U.S. group and most hold degrees. Pacific Islanders are a relatively small group that live primarily on the West Coast.

Leadership challenges include helping Asian American employees overcome the traditional workplace barriers, especially the myths and stereotypes. Opportunities include recognizing their values as strengths, explaining corporate cultures that may be confusing to them, and helping them to bring their issues out in the open to discuss. Their understanding of Asian cultures can be invaluable in doing business in Asian marketplaces.

Skill Builder 8.1: The Case of Doug Fong, Asian American Manager

Doug Fong is a restaurant manager for Jollytime Corporation. Jollytime consists of a chain of over 250 fast food restaurants throughout the United States Its corporate mission is to provide quality fast food at competitive prices and quality service. One of its strategies for quality control is to send "mystery shoppers" to every restaurant at least twice a month. These employees check on quality of food, cleanliness of restaurant, and quickness of service. Two managers operate each restaurant, a day manager and a night manager. Restaurants are categorized as low-level, medium-level, or high-level based on the following criteria: gross sales, annual profit, percentage of increase in sales and in annual profit, and scores assigned by mystery shoppers.

Doug Fong is a first-generation Asian American who lives in the San Francisco area. He's been with Jollytime for ten years and is respected by the other managers. Seven years ago he was promoted to manager of a low-level restaurant in the East Bay suburb of Concord, whose residents are primarily Euro-American but are also somewhat multicultural.

After two years he was transferred to a medium-level restaurant in the Hunters Point area of San Francisco, an area dominated by African Americans. Restaurant profits increased 13 percent the first year and 15 percent the second year. The top executive team was impressed with Doug's ability to handle the challenging Hunter's Point location, and at the end of two years transferred him to a "less hectic" restaurant in the Sunset district, where he has been working for three years. Doug told a colleague, "I was sad to leave the Hunter's Point location because I had built a trusting relationship with my employees and my customers. There were a few trouble makers around, but I really didn't have any problems."

Residents in the Sunset are primarily Euro-American but also multicultural with a significant Asian American population. During the following three years under Doug's leadership, the Sunset district restaurant is ranked third, then sixth, and then second on the top 50 list of all Jollytime restaurants. Profits increased in each of these three years, and mystery shopper ratings have been outstanding. Doug has done well in managing a diverse group of employees. They speak well of him. For example, Kevin, a Euro-American food server, says, "Doug is a great manager; he treats everyone fairly." And Ruben, a Latino American cook says, "I've worked with Doug for nearly three years and he knows how to motivate people."

Doug's career goals include moving up to district manager and then to division manager. He's become more and more devoted to his job, often working 12-hour days. This is rather ambitious given the fact that Doug's educational background includes only a high school diploma. However, he's a rapid and avid learner. For example, he does all the accounting for his restaurant, and the auditors have always approved his work and even praised it.

A district manager oversees 10 to 12 restaurants. In an average day, the district manager may go over current operations and improvement plans with several restaurant managers. The job requires good interpersonal communication skills and knowledge of accounting principles, including budgeting.

Doug has never asked for a promotion. He has operated on the belief that his hard work and excellence speak for themselves and that he'll be offered a promotion when the time is right. In the past two years, two district manager positions opened up, and the outgoing managers picked their successors. All the district managers that Doug has met are Euro-American men with college degrees.

Jim Davis was one of the outgoing district managers. His job had been to oversee restaurants in Oakland, which is predominantly African American. Doug decided to overcome his reticence and speak to Jim about the possibility of taking his place. Jim told Doug, "You're an extremely well-qualified manager—no doubt about that. But maybe the Oakland area is not the best place for you." Jim obviously doubted that Doug was assertive enough to handle the employees there. He said, "Let's wait for an opening in an area that's predominantly Asian American or Euro-American. That would be a better fit." A few weeks later *Jordan Jones*, a Euro-American, was named new district manager for the Oakland area.

Now, a year later, the buzz is that Jones has failed miserably in overseeing the Oakland restaurant managers and he'll be replaced soon. *Jack Barnes*, the division manager will name the replacement.

- What are the key issues in this case?
- If you were Doug Fong, what would you do?
- If you were Jack Barnes, what would you do?

Skill Builder 8.2: The Case of Linda Vuong, Asian American Cashier

Linda Vuong has been working for two years as cashier for Computer City, one of a chain of retail electronics stores. It is located in a neighborhood populated primarily by Chinese Americans. In fact, all of the 20 employees, including its managers, are Chinese American, except Linda, who is Vietnamese American. Most of the employees are in their early twenties, attend college, and help support their families. Linda is majoring in business administration and hopes the company will soon promote her to assistant manager. She takes her job seriously, is very customer oriented, and cooperates well with co-workers.

Wallace is one of the store's three assistant managers and is Linda's immediate supervisor. One of the assistant managers is leaving next month, and Wallace is recommending Linda for the job. In his written evaluation that he submits to *Guy*, the manager and co-owner of the franchised store, Wallace includes the following:

- Linda has continuously demonstrated quickness and efficiency in performing job tasks, which include taking customer orders promptly, packaging smaller items properly, and maintaining a clean work environment
- Linda has good customer skills
- Customers praise her performance
- Linda is a team player, helping her co-workers and offering advice on how to improve communications with difficult customers

Guy seldom interacts with Linda and in fact spends minimal time communicating with employees except to exchange greetings. The exception is that he loves to gossip about the local Chinese American community with a few "insider" employees who speak Cantonese. He rarely speaks English to people in the company except to those at an equal or higher level than he. Guy is a concerned employer, paying attention to salaries, work loads, work schedules, and career opportunities within the company, especially for those employees he feels closest to. However, Linda has never had a chance to discuss her career ambitions with Guy.

Linda has not received a pay increase in 16 months. Guy recently instructed Wallace to delegate more work duties to Linda in order to relieve some of the other employees from job tasks. Not only is Linda expected to do more work without an increase in hours worked, her schedule is often changed to accommodate the requests of other employees who want to attend to personal matters. Linda is hoping all these problems will be solved if she can just get an assistant manager position. This promotion would also allow her to expand her skills and abilities.

Max, one of Linda's co-workers, also wants the assistant manager job. He's definitely in the running even though Wallace has rarely given him high performance ratings. Wallace has had to talk with Max several times about excessive tardiness. However, Max gets along well with Guy, often chatting and gossiping with him in Cantonese about mutual friends and acquaintances.

Today, Guy calls Wallace to his office and says, "I know you've recommended Linda for the assistant manager position, but I don't think she's quite ready for it. You know, Max has great communication skills, and I think he's better equipped to supervise our employees. Max reads people well, he knows how to get close to people, and that's what we need."

- What are the key issues in this case?
- If you were Guy, what would you do?
- If you were Linda, what would you do?

Skill Builder 8.3: The Case of Office Whiz Connie

Connie has been working for six years for Crystal Fizz, a manufacturer of drink mixes. She is one of six employees in the plant office, the youngest at age 27 and the only Asian American. Connie has learned how to do most all the major functions in the office and likes her job. However, she's become disillusioned with the work environment. If it weren't for the good pay and benefits, she'd be gone. In fact, she's thinking about looking for a job elsewhere.

Bob, the owner and manager, a year ago hired *Jim*, who performs duties similar to the ones Connie does. Soon Jim was making comments that disturbed Connie, such as "I can't understand what you're saying half the time," and "Why don't you do things the American way—whatever the American way is?" Connie's response has been to ignore and avoid Jim as much as possible. However, Jim was soon being consulted by Bob about various company decisions. Bob sometimes takes Jim with him to important business meetings. Connie is never included in this way, and she recently discovered that Jim makes about 10 percent more than she.

Company employees get four weeks of vacation. Before Jim came, Connie never took all four weeks at one time because of office demands. It was typical for her to come into the office even when she could have taken some time off, simply because there was much important work to be done. Now she finds she doesn't care about that any more. She came back from a four-week vacation last month, and she plans to take all the time off she has coming to her. She feels that she is being treated unfairly and has no real chance of advancement.

- What do you think are the major problems here?
- What should Connie do?
- What should Bob do?

REFERENCES

Andres, Tomas D. *Understanding Filipino Values: A Management Approach.* Franklin, MI: Cellar Book Shop, 1985. www.cellarbook.com

Baldassare, Mark. "Ethnic Groups Slow to Assimilate." *San Francisco Chronicle*, March 27, 1990, A-1.

Baldwin, Beth C. *Patterns of Adjustment.* Orange, CA: Immigrant and Refugee Planning Center, 1984.

Blinder, David, and Catherine Lew. "Asian Americans: Exit Poll." *San Francisco Chronicle*, November 6, 1992, A-1.

Brannen, Christalyn and Tracey Wilen. Doing Business with Japanese Men. Berkeley CA: Stone Bridge Press, 1993.

Brislin, Richard W., and Tomoko Yoshida, eds. *Improving Intercultural Interactions.* Thousand Oaks, Ca: Sage, 1994.

Cabezas, A., T.M. Tam, B.M. Lowe, A.S. Wong, and K. Turner, "Empirical Study of Barriers to Upward Mobility for Asian Americans in the San Francisco Bay Area," in G.M. Nomura et al (Eds.), *Frontiers of Asian American Studies*: 85-97. Pullman, WA: Washington State University Press, 1989.

Chan, Sucheng. *Asian Americans: An Interpretive History*. Boston: Twayne Publishers, 1991.

Chew, Lee (interview), "Life Story of a Chinaman," in *The Life Stories of Undistinguished Americans as Told by Themselves*. New York, 1906.

Chow, Esther Ngan-Ling. "Asian American Women at Work." in *Women of Color in U.S. Society*. Philadelphia: Temple University Press, 1994.

Corporate 1000: A Directory of Who Runs the Top 1,000 U.S. Corporations. Washington, D.C.: The Washington D.C. Monitor, Inc., 1985.

Dong, Lorraine. Professor of Asian American Studies, San Francisco State University, interview, 1992.

Fadiman, Anne, "Hmong Odyssey," *Via*: 70-74, March/April, 1998.

Gudykunst, W.B. *Bridging Japanese/North American Differences*. Thousand Oaks CA: Sage, 1994.

Gungwu, Wang. *The Chineseness of China*. New York: Oxford University Press, 1991.

Harris, Philip R., and Robert T. Moran. *Managing Cultural Differences*, 4th ed. Houston: Gulf Publishing Co., 1996.

Hossfeld, Karen, "Hiring Immigrant Women: Silicon Valley's 'Simple Formula.'" in *Women of Color in U.S. Society*. Philadelphia: Temple University Press, 1994.

Hurh, Won Moo, and Kwang Chung Kim. *Korean Immigrants in America*. Cranbury, NJ: Fairleigh Dickinson University Press, 1984.

Kitano, Harry H.L. and Roger Daniels. *Asian Americans: Emerging Minorities*. Englewood Cliffs, NJ: Prentice Hall, 1988.

Kumagai, regarding emotional expression, 1981.

Kristoff, N.D. and Sheryl Wudunn. *China Wakes*. New York: Random House, 1994.

Markus & Kitayama. Comments on emotional expression and values, 1991.

Min, Pyong Gap, ed. *Asian Americans: Contemporary Trends and Issues*. Thousand Oaks, CA: Sage, 1995.

Morrison, Ann. *The New Leaders*. San Francisco: Jossey-Bass, 1992.

National Center for Educational Statistics, 1995, www.ed.gov/nces

Nguyen, Liem T., and Alan B. Henkin. "Refugees from Vietnam." *Journal of Ethnic Studies,* 9, no. 4 (1982): 101-16.

Ong, Paul. "Chinese Laundries as an Urban Occupation in Nineteenth Century California." in *The Annals of the Chinese Historical Society of the Pacific Northwest*. Seattle: 1983.

Reid, T.R. *Confucius Lives Next Door*. Vintage, 2000.

Russell, John. "Narratives of Denial: Racial Chauvinism and the Black Other in Japan." *Japan Quarterly*: 416-28, Oct.-Dec. 1991.

Sharpe, Rochelle, "Asian Americans Gain Sharply in Big Program of Affirmative Action," *Wall Street Journal*: A-1, September 9, 1997.

Stuart C. Miller. *The Unwelcome Immigrant: The American Image of the Chinese, 1752-1882*. Berkeley, CA: 1969.

Takaki, Ronald. *A Different Mirror: A History of Multicultural America*. Boston: Little, Brown Co., 1993.

Takaki, Ronald. *Double Victory: A Multicultural History of American World War II*. New York: Little, Brown, 2000.

Tannen, Deborah. *You Just Don't Understand*. New York: Wm. Morrow, 1990.

Tyson, James and Ann. Chinese Awakenings. San Francisco: Westview Press, 1995.

U.S. Census Bureau, Department of Commerce. *We the American . . . Asians*, and *We the American . . . Pacific Islanders*, 1993.

U.S. Census Bureau, Department of Commerce. www.census.gov, 1995a

U.S. Census Bureau, Department of Commerce. *Current Population Reports*: 60-80, 1995b.

Vietnamese 2001: www.ins.usdoj.gov/graphics/publicaffairs/newsrels/

Viviano, Frank. "Poll Contradicts Stereotypes." *San Francisco Chronicle* (March 27, 1990): A1.

Wang, Gungwu. *The Chineseness of China*. Oxford, New York: Oxford University Press, 1991.

Wei, William. *The Asian American Movement*. Philadelphia: Temple University Press, 1993.

Young, Jared. *Discrimination, Income, Human Capital Investment, and Asian-Americans*. San Francisco, CA: R & E Research Associates, Inc., 1978.

Zinn, M.B., and B.T. Dill. *Women of Color in U.S. Society*. Philadelphia: Temple University Press, 1994.

CHAPTER 9

Working with Latino Americans

Latino Americans love their Spanish language and value the warmth and romance of their culture, even as they aspire to the American dream.

Jack Forbes

About 12.5 percent of the employees in the workplace in 2000 were Latino Americans—about one in every eight people you'll meet. Latino American communities include people from many countries. While most of their values and customs are woven from common Latino threads, each country also has its own unique design. For example, you'll find distinct cultural differences among Latino Americans from Mexico as compared to those from Puerto Rico or Cuba or other origins. And of course no one person expresses all the values and customs discussed here. This information can give you a deeper, broader understanding of Latino Americans you may meet. However, you already know the necessity of dealing with each person as a unique individual from a particular cultural background.

As you explore the topics of this course, try to begin seeing the world as a Latino American might see it—according to information gleaned here from scholars of that community. Specifically you'll learn:

- How typical stereotypes and myths about Latino Americans compare with reality.
- How the current situation is connected to certain historical events
- Major Latino American communities, such as Mexican American and Puerto Rican American, their differences and similarities
- Worldview beliefs, values, and customs that are important to people in these communities
- Values and customs for conducting personal relationship
- Some key issues that are important to many Latino Americans
- Barriers to career success for Latino Americans and how to overcome them by meeting cultural needs
- How to use Latino American strengths as opportunities to create win-win successes

First, get in touch with your beliefs and knowledge about Latino Americans by completing Self-Awareness Activities 9.1 and 9.2.

Self-Awareness Activity 9.1: What Do You Believe about Latino Americans?

Purpose:

- to get in touch with your beliefs and stereotypes about this group of people
- to experience how judgmental beliefs affect your thinking and feeling processes
- to experience the ways in which your beliefs create your reality regarding other persons, even before you have any interaction with them

Part I. What Do You Believe about Latino American Women

- Relax as deeply as you can: close your eyes and take a few deep breaths.
- Focus on the word "Latino American woman" and allow a mental picture to come up in your mind's eye. Imagine that you are this woman. Be Latino American woman.
- Notice your resistances to being this person, and your willingness.
- Notice the words and images that come to mind as you "see" this woman.
- Open your eyes and list 10 to 20 words in the order in which they occur to you.
- Review your list. Mark a plus beside the words that are positive, a minus beside the words that are negative, and a circle beside neutral words.

Step 2. Negative Associations

- Close your eyes and focus again on the image of the Latino American woman. Formulate a negative opinion or judgment, perhaps one you typically hold about Latino American women.
- Notice your *feelings* as you see the person in this negative way. What *thoughts* come up as you focus on the image?
- Write a few sentences about your feelings and thoughts.

Step 3. Positive Associations

- Formulate a positive opinion or judgment, perhaps one you typically hold about Latino American women.
- Notice your *feelings* as you see the person in this positive way. What *thoughts* come up as you focus on the image?
- Write a few sentences about your feelings and thoughts.

Step 4. Insights

- Focus on the differences between your experiences when you hold negative and positive judgments or opinions. What were the differences? What meaning does this have for you, for your beliefs and feelings about people from this group, and about beliefs in general?
- Write your responses in a few sentences; include anything you like about your feelings, thoughts, and insights.

Part II. Experimenting with Opinions about Latino American Men

Repeat the phases and steps in part I, this time focusing on the image of an Latino American man.

Self-Awareness Activity 9.2: What Do You Know about Latino Americans?

Purpose: To see what you know about the issues covered in this chapter.
Instructions: Determine whether you think the following statements are basically true or false—and think about why. The answers will emerge in this chapter, and the summary at the end of the chapter focuses on these issues.

1. Most Latino Americans are too emotional and excitable to be leaders in American corporations.
2. Most Latino Americans are originally from Mexico.
3. The largest Latino American population is found in New Mexico.
4. The value that's most important to Mexican Americans is achievement.
5. *Machismo* refers to being the boss.
6. *Simpatico* refers to giving sympathy to poor persons.
7. When communicating, Latino Americans tend to speak indirectly.
8. Latino American workers tend to buddy up to the boss.

STEREOTYPES AND REALITIES

Some typical stereotypes about Latino Americans are:

- They're too passive, polite, and lacking in conviction to be good leaders
- They're too emotional and excitable to fill leadership positions
- The men are macho and the women easily intimidated
- They're qualified only for menial jobs

Most of these stereotypes are either false or they're distorted, partial truths. They often stem from misunderstandings about the ways certain cultural values and customs affect Latino Americans' attitudes and actions. Cultural style, such as passive politeness, is often misinterpreted as leadership inadequacy, such as inability to take initiative and be firm.

Although stereotypes aren't identical to prejudice, rigid stereotypes about people usually lead to prejudice. Latino Americans must deal with these stereotypes and stereotypes every time they leave the family or community circle. Understanding this aspect of their life can help you move beyond stereotypes to bridge the divisive walls they hold in place. The ultimate goal is to appreciate Latino Americans' unique value to the workplace and to strengthen workplace unity.

Stereotype #1: Latino Americans are too passive, polite, and lacking in conviction to be good leaders in the workplace.

Reality #1: This stereotype focuses on style, not substance.
Reality #2: The dozens of Latino nations throughout the world function quite effectively with Latino leaders
Reality #3: Euro-Americans and others can learn what these behaviors really mean and how they can enhance team relationships and other workplace situations. For example, the values of harmony and positive interpersonal relationships that are so important to Latinos have always been important in the workplace and are increasingly crucial to business success.
Reality #4: Latino Americans do learn to adapt to American corporate cultures and to be appropriately assertive in that arena. Euro-American and other leaders can help them adapt.

Stereotype #2: Latino Americans are too emotional and excitable to be leaders.

Latino Americans generally hold views about expressing emotions that are different from Euro-Americans' views. More on this later. The resulting behavior is a difference in style, not substance, and the same realities apply here as in the passive/polite stereotype.

Stereotype #3: Latino American men are macho and the women easily intimidated.

Although Latinos generally are viewed as passive and polite, the men are often stereotyped as being macho with their women—and with each other in bars and similar settings. They're said to have a quick smile and quick knife and love to fight. The machismo stereotype is that the male is strong, in control, and provides for his family, while the woman is submissive and lacking in power and influence.

Reality #1: This stereotype has not been fully researched, and some studies indicate that male dominance in marital decision making is not the rule among Latino American couples. Also, machismo style is changing along with changing economic realities and new job opportunities for Latino American women.

Reality #2: Latino cultures have their own brand of patriarchy, as do all the world's cultures. The "quick knife" stereotype is mainly a phenomenon of youth gangs, found in every culture. They're a small minority of the population and rarely affect co-worker relationships.

Reality #3: Latino Americans, especially the largest group, Mexican Americans, tend to be one of the most cooperative, accepting groups in the United States, and getting along is one of their highest values. This is true for both the men and the women.

Stereotype #4: Latino American workers are qualified only for menial jobs.

Related stereotypes are, *They can't speak English well, They have only the most menial-level skills, They're not productive, They have a "manana" attitude.*

Reality #1: Latino Americans are a diverse group. Many of them have been in the United States for generations and are highly educated. Some groups, such as Cuban Americans, have business qualifications comparable to Euro-Americans. Recent immigrants frequently have language, education, and skill barriers to qualifying for better jobs. But companies operating in urban areas with large Latino immigrant populations have found that providing remedial education and job training results in a pool of skilled, loyal workers.

Reality #2: When Latino Americans feel they are part of an ingroup, they tend to be extremely loyal. Studies indicate that most identify with the American dream of getting ahead, which means they're willing to learn the skills and approaches it takes—including how to be productive and meet time requirements.

What's in a Name?

The government now recognizes **Hispanics** as a distinct ethnic group for civil rights purposes. The difficulty with this term is its root word *Spain*, which for Latino activists brings up painful memories of colonial conquest and domination. Most prefer the term **Latino**.

Until 1970, government census records counted Latino Americans as "white," and so demographic information about them was virtually nonexistent. Leaders of the Chicano (Mexican American) movement won the separate designation battle in 1970 but lost the terminology battle and had to settle for *Hispanic*. However, by 2003 the Census Bureau must switch over to the term *Latino* and in 2000 was using the multiple designation Spanish/Hispanic/Latino. The change to *Latino* still fails to distinguish *Latino Americans* from the other Latinos of the world.

CURRENT PROFILE:
WHO ARE THE LATINO AMERICANS?

The Latino American population consists of three large groups—Mexican American, Puerto Rican American, and Cuban American—as well as smaller groups from many countries. Generally, it is relatively young, fast-growing, and concentrated in a few states, mostly in cities. Educational levels and language ability vary by group. Most have lower than average income, higher poverty rates, and face job discrimination, according to U. S. Census Bureau reports.

A Diverse Population of Many Subgroups

You already know that about 12.5 percent of all Americans are Latino Americans. However, they are most likely to think of themselves as Mexican American or some other name that indicates their country of origin. Major Latino American groups by relative size are displayed in Figure 9.1. The "other" category includes about 100,000 descendants of Spanish settlers. Many of them have ancestors who lived in the West before it became part of the U.S. Their profile is different because they were never immigrants to the U.S.

FIGURE 9.1: Proportions of Latino Americans, 2000

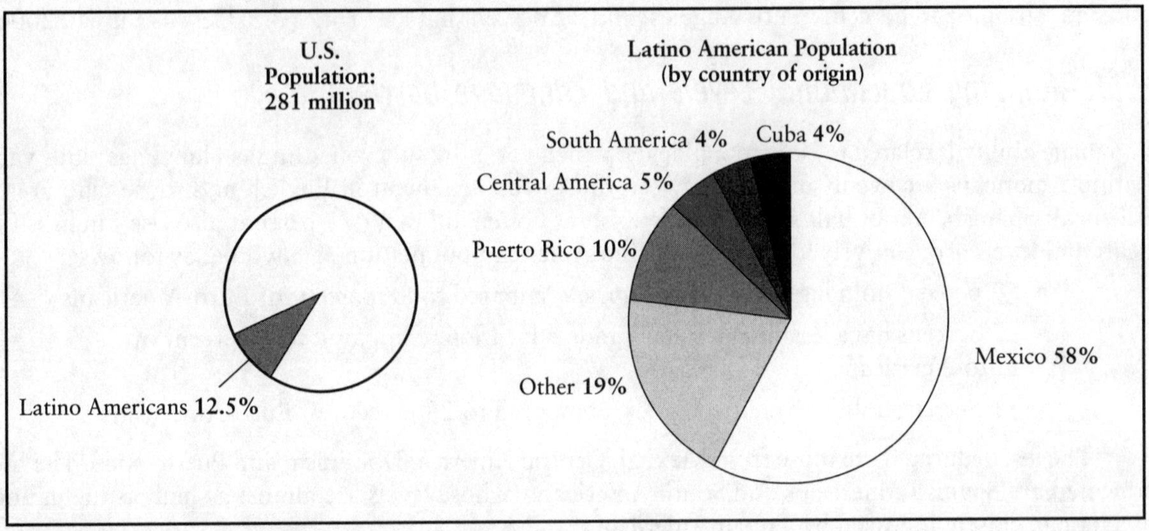

Source: "The Hispanic Population in the United States," U.S. Census Bureau, March 2001.

Fast-Growing and Young: Babies and Immigration

Around 1900 there were less than 250,000 Latino Americans in the United States, fewer than the number of Swiss immigrants. By 2000, there were more than 35.3 million or 12.5 percent of the U.S. population, more than the entire U.S. population of 1850, which was about 22 million.

The Latino American population grew by 57 percent between 1970 and 1990, and again by 58 percent from 1990 to 2000—when the U.S. population total increased by only 13 percent. This rapid growth is expected to continue because of the Latino American group's relative youth and higher birth rate. Here are some facts from Census 2000:

- 35 percent were under age 18, compared to 26 percent of the U.S. population
- Their median age was 26, compared to 35 for the entire U.S. population.
- They produce nearly twice as many children as Euro-Americans, 3.3 compared to 1.9.

Concentrated in a Few Areas

How likely you are to work with a Latino American depends on where you live. Table 9.1 shows the regions where Latino Americans are most likely to live and the proportion of the total population in each of those regions.

Region	Proportion of Latino American Population That Lives Here	Proportion of Total Population That Is Latino Americans
West	43%	25%
South	33%	12%
Midwest	9%	11%
Northeast	15%	2%

Most Mexican Americans (55 percent) live in the West, especially in California and Texas, but nearly a third (32 percent) live in the South. Most Puerto Rican Americans (61 percent) live in New York, and most Cuban Americans (74 percent) live in the South, especially in Florida.

The tradition of most Latino immigrants has been that of rural peasant, mostly from Mexico. But by 1980, because of their migration to work in U.S. cities, most became urban dwellers. In America's 10 largest cities, an average of one in every four people is of Latino origin: about 60 percent in Miami and San Antonio, 46 percent in Los Angeles, and 27 percent in New York (U.S. Census Bureau 2000).

Wide-Ranging Educational Levels and Language Barriers

Language ability is related to educational level, which varies by subgroup. English language skills vary. Latino Americans are evenly divided between those who are fluent in English and those who aren't. All speak Spanish. About half still speak Spanish at home, although 75 percent also use English. Educational levels are relatively low for the Latino American population as a whole, as follows:

- 57 percent hold high school diplomas, compared to 88 percent of Euro-Americans
- 27 percent have less than a ninth-grade education, compared to 4 percent of Euro-Americans
- 11 percent hold university degrees, compared to 28 percent of Euro-Americans

The least educated are those from Mexico, Central America, Dominica, and Puerto Rico. The best educated are Spanish Americans and South Americans, whose levels are almost as high as the national average, closely followed by Cuban Americans.

Education is highly valued by all Latino American groups, even though they have the lowest educational level of any U.S. group. Studies indicate that more Latino American high school students want a college degree than do Euro-American students at the same socioeconomic level. And Latino American parents' aspirations for their children's education is just as high as Euro-American parents'.

Job Discrimination, Lower Income, and Relative Poverty

Latino Americans are twice as likely as Euro-Americans to work as minimally skilled or skilled laborers. Conversely, Euro-Americans are twice as likely to hold managerial or professional positions. Here are some facts from the Census Bureau about Latino American workers:

- 20 percent work in service occupations, compared to 12 percent of Euro-Americans.
- 22 percent work as laborers and operators, compared to 12 percent of Euro-Americans.
- 14 percent work in managerial or professional occupations, compared to 33 percent of Euro-Americans

- Management jobs in U.S. companies of more than 100 employees: Latino Americans hold less than one percent, though they are 12.5 percent of the U.S. workforce.

Only about half as many Latino Americans as Euro-Americans earn more than $35,000, and nearly three times as many live below the poverty line.

- 23 percent earn $35,000 or more, compared with 50 percent of Euro-Americans.
- 23 percent live in poverty, compared with 8 percent of Euro-Americans.

Causes of poverty include fewer job opportunities for the less skilled and educated—and lower wages for those who do have jobs. Single mothers have high poverty rates, and 30 percent of Latino American families are headed by single mothers, compared to 20 percent of Euro-American families. The earnings ratio of Latino Americans to Euro-Americans has been in a decline for several years, with the pay gap increasing by one-half percent per year. Median family income in 1999 was $30,735, much lower than the Euro-American $44,366. Still, about 75 percent of Latino American families fall in the middle to upper income category.

LATINO CULTURES: COMMON WORLDVIEW VALUES

The most important values to most Latino Americans are the focus on family, ingroup loyalty, and getting along with family and ingroup persons. They love their culture, their language, and their tradition, so most have strong feelings about holding onto their ethnic heritage. In a 1980s survey, most Latino Americans expressed a deep desire to pass on to their children their cultural and religious traditions, especially the Spanish language and respect for elders. Passing on the tradition of commitment to the family ranked high, but not as high as passing on the language.

You'll better understand Latino personal values if you first understand their basic worldview—how they see reality. Basic to what Latino countries have in common is the influence of Spanish culture, which includes an aristocratic hierarchy based on a powerful patron who protects his subjects. They in turn serve him and owe him their loyalty. Therefore, the societies that developed in the Latino countries normally consisted of a small, privileged group of the served and a mass of underprivileged servers (Gann and Duignan 1986). Some common themes we'll explore are:

- *Worldview*: maintaining the status quo of the powerful and powerless and patriarchy, with a focus on the present moment, the future's up to God's will.
- *Relationships*: the highest values are family, ingroup loyalty, and getting along.
- *Spiritual life*: fatalism, destiny; a thin veil between physical world and spirit world.

Worldview Value #1: Closeness to the Spirit World

Latino spiritual beliefs are closely tied to the Catholic church, a belief in fate, and a unique attitude toward the relationship between life and death (Harris and Moran 1991; Gann and Duignan 1986).

The spirit world lives alongside Latino Americans, particularly Mexican Americans, in their everyday lives. They perceive less distinction between the living and the dead than do most Euro-Americans. They believe the dead are just beyond the veil of physical reality and there's nothing to fear from these spirits of relatives and friends.

They celebrate afterlife and death symbols—such as ghosts, skeletons, and skulls—in their holidays. They wear the symbols as costumes, similar to some of our Halloween costumes, and use them as themes in toys, confections, songs, and dances. Latino Americans tend to think of death as "passing on" and treat it as an old friend or special person. They frequently joke about death and include the theme in their play. This theme is related to their fatalistic sense of life and death, and draws on some aspects of a worldview that originated in their ancient Indian past.

The Mexican American relationship with death and the dead may be better understood by studying how they observe the Day of the Dead in early November as part of a three-day celebration. First, they observe Halloween, along with other Americans. The next day is known as All Saints Day, and they observe religious rites. The following day is the Day of the Dead, the most important of the three days. Rituals may include altars set up in churches, homes, and shop windows, an all-day picnic in the cemetery, a candlelit procession in costume, and an all-night vigil in the cemetery. Many Latino Americans believe that the spirits of family and friends who have passed on are present at these events and that their spirits in fact move in and out of the physical world all the time.

The Roman Catholic Church remains one of Latin America's major cultural institutions and has played a large role in shaping the various cultures of all Latin nations. Priests tend to be more involved in the family lives of Catholic churchgoers than are church leaders in other denominations. Most professing Christians in Latin America are Catholics, as are about 80 percent of Latino Americans. Their religious commitment varies widely, from indifferent to highly committed. Most are nonpracticing.

Erosion of beliefs and practices increases with the second-generation Latino Americans. In recent years an increasing number are joining Protestant churches, primarily those of an evangelical, fundamentalist nature (Gann and Duignan 1986).

Worldview Value #2: A Sense of Destiny or Fatalism

Latinos are less likely than Euro-Americans to believe they're in control of their own destiny. This dependence on fate or destiny stems from ancient American Indian mysticism combined with a Latino interpretation of Roman Catholic church teachings.

Many believe that outside forces govern their lives, for life follows a preordained course and human action is determined by the will of God. Those who hold this belief are therefore willing to resign themselves to the "inevitable," bow to fate, and take what comes. This is in direct contrast to the typically Euro-American belief that "God helps those who help themselves," or that people create their own reality to a great extent.

Fatalism can result in an attitude that Americans often interpret as passivity, procrastination, or laziness and that they attribute to a *mañana* tendency (tomorrow's good enough for me). After all, if it's God's will, if it's written in the stars, why fight it? This belief is tied to the acceptance of unequal status we'll discuss next.

Worldview Value #3: Hierarchy and Status

A sense of hierarchy and status is a strong element in virtually all Latino countries. (Harris and Moran 1991; Hofstede 1980). People are born into an upper or lower class, and the middle class in most countries is small but growing. Traditionally the masses live in destitute poverty and the elite live with great wealth. The upper classes are more formal and elaborate than in the United States The work you do is directly related to your social class; therefore, to do manual labor, such as helping out as a house guest or pitching in to help an office worker would be undignified and inappropriate.

In recent years nearly all of the political unrest, upheaval and terrorism in Latino countries has centered around attempts to break down the hierarchy. Opposing groups try to break the hold of the rich aristocracy and multinational corporations on the wealth of the land.

Accepting one's place

Latino Americans tend to accept their social status, even when it's extremely inferior to that of the ruling class. They tend to value the stability that comes with everyone knowing their place and staying in it, living up to societal expectations. Social climbing is frowned upon, and people who are seen as "trying to get ahead" are not admired. Such attempts, if successful, are seen as disturbing and disruptive, threatening the relative social position of many people. Climbing also appears as crass materialism and greed to many, and it shows disdain for sensitive human relationships.

Showing respect or respeto

People show respect for someone of superior status by their voice tone and manner. The traditional belief is that the reason people are poor or rich, have power or don't, is because of God's will.

A patron is a man of power or wealth who receives loyalty from people of lesser status. He may be the boss, a politician, a landowner, or a businessman. The patron makes the decisions, and others don't question him. Where Americans attempt to minimize differences between persons due to status, age, sex, etc., Latino Americans tend to stress them.

Accepting the powerful superior

Those in positions of authority maintain their leadership by their ability to dole out resources to their followers and to help and protect them when they need it. The relationship is reminiscent of a parent-child relationship. The authority figures tend to set clear standards and boundaries for compliance with their policies and rules.

Patriarchal values may explain why Latino Americans tend to express less tolerance for gays and lesbians than do Euro-Americans in recent surveys. On the other hand, Latino Americans tend to be more tolerant regarding skin color. Social class is not tied to skin color in Latin American countries as it has been historically in the United States.

Power distance

Where Euro-Americans attempt to minimize differences between persons due to status, age, or gender (sometimes called "power distance"), Latino Americans tend to stress these differences. Latino Americans tend to show greater deference and respect toward certain respected or powerful groups of people, such as the rich, the educated, the older, and toward certain professions, such as doctors, priests, teachers. They place a higher value on conformity and obedience, and they support autocratic and authoritarian attitudes from those in charge of organizations or institutions. People generally fear disagreeing with those in power. The less powerful try to meet all the expectations of the powerful.

Trusting the government

The acceptance of social status, so traditional in Mexico and most other Latino cultures, is reflected in most Latino Americans' view of government's role. In a recent survey most Latino Americans agreed with most Euro-Americans that individuals are responsible for providing for their own needs. However, nearly twice as many Latino Americans as Euro-Americans felt the government should provide jobs, and significantly fewer Latino Americans expressed distrust of government.

Worldview Value #4: Expressing Emotions or the Passion Factor

Latino Americans highly value their emotions. The culture encourages them to fully experience their feelings and places fewer restrictions than Euro-American culture on expressing feelings—especially the ones that reflect caring and passion for life.

Several studies seem to confirm that this passionate tendency still exists in Latino Americans. For example, studies indicate that Latino Americans who respond to surveys are more likely to choose the extreme response categories (strongly agree, strongly disagree) than the middle categories, to a greater extent than Euro-Americans. Overall, the less time Latino Americans have spent in the United States, the more they prefer to make extreme choices. They see the use of the middle categories (somewhat agree) as a way of hiding a person's real feelings by presenting them in moderated terms. This indicates that Latino persons value their feelings, are encouraged to fully experience them, and have fewer restrictions about expressing them—especially the ones that reflect caring and passion for life—than Euro-Americans. The research results also imply that that the longer Latino Americans live in the United States, the more they tend to modify the way they express emotion.

Worldview Value #5: Space—Up Close and Personal

In general Latino Americans like to be physically closer to others than do Euro-Americans, and so they stand closer together when they converse. This preference is related to their close, mutually dependent relationships, and their frequent expression of warm feelings. They are a contact culture that feels comfortable when physically close to others. Therefore, when they brush close to another, moving into what Americans would consider personal body space, there would be no reason to say, "excuse me," as most Americans would. Latino Americans are also more likely to touch each other during a conversation.

Differences in personal space affect the emotional reactions of people in interactions. Latino Americans may seem too pushy as they close in on Euro-Americans, who in turn may seem cold and distant as they back away.

Worldview Value #6: Time—Who Knows What the Future Holds?

Mañana (literally, "tomorrow") doesn't refer to procrastination or laziness, but to the concept that the future is indefinite. In Latin countries it's not unusual for a business person to promise to give you a product or service by the deadline date you want even though they're unlikely to be able to meet the deadline. The main reason for agreeing is to make you happy in the moment. The backup reasoning is that the future is very uncertain, and some miracle may occur that will enable them to meet the deadline. Therefore, they know they can make you happy now, and they might be able to make you happy then.

Latino Americans typically focus more on the present moment than do Euro-Americans. Latino Americans spend less time thinking about the future and planning for it, partly because they see the future as too uncertain to do much planning. This view is related to their sense of fate. The typical Euro-American approach is to start with now and project thoughts into the future. The past is past; it doesn't need to get in the way. Latino-Americans are more concerned with tradition and more willing to continue with things as they have traditionally been. An example is the willingness of the poor masses in Latin American countries to accept their lot in life, although this view has been changing somewhat in recent years.

Meeting time deadlines and being on time for work and business appointments is generally the same for Latino Americans as for Euro-Americans. The main difference in attitudes toward promptness is in social situations, where it is typically less important for Latino Americans. The focus there is on relating to people in the moment, so the passage of time is not in immediate awareness.

The bottom line: Euro-Americans are considered to be generally future oriented because they stress planning for the future, being able to delay gratification, being on time, and making efficient use of time. Present-oriented Latino Americans put less emphasis on these traits and tend to have a more flexible attitude toward time. They feel they are on time even if they arrive 15 or 20 minutes after the appointed time. They place greater value on the quality of interpersonal relationships than on the length of time in which they take place. Highly efficient or time conscious people may be perceived as impolite or insulting. (Marin et al. 1991).

Worldview Value #7: Adopting the American Dream

Most Latino Americans buy into many aspects of the American Dream. They also express a deep desire to pass on to their children their cultural and religious traditions, especially the Spanish language and commitment to the family. First-generation Latino Americans are naturally less Americanized or acculturated than those of the second- and third-generation, for obvious reasons, but certain aspects of the Latino culture tend to be important across generations. This leads to a merging of the Latino and American cultures.

The Acculturation Process

Immigrants go through a stage of crisis or conflict due to culture shock, followed by finding a way to adapt to American culture, such as:

- *assimilating* completely the American culture
- *integrating* the American and Latino cultures
- *rejecting* American cultural patterns

The ability to speak English has become a reliable shorthand measure for evaluating how successfully a Latino American has acculturated, such as:

- *assimilating* English, speaking it almost exclusively
- *integrating* the old and the new by becoming bilingual
- *rejecting* the new, continuing to speak Spanish almost exclusively

The higher the education level, the more successful the acculturation tends to be. Acculturation is important because it affects Latino Americans' mental health status, levels of social support, political and social attitudes, crime rate, and workplace skills. Integration generally works better than assimilation or rejection.

Integration: A Blend of Values

While Latino alienation, anger, and rage exist, most Latino Americans identify themselves with the United States. Only about a third of them identify themselves as Mexicans, Cubans, or Latinos first and Americans second. Most see their heritage as more Euro-than Indian, just as Euro-Americans do. This raises the question: Are most Latinos predominantly Spanish, Indian, or a unique blend? Anthropologists seem to agree that approximately 95 percent are at least part Indian, but the Spanish cultural influence is strong. The cultural mixture of Indian and Euro-elements that occurred in Latin American countries has further blended with the Euro-American in the United States to produce a value system within Latino American communities that is itself a blend.

The American Dream

Despite the prejudice and discrimination that have resulted in segregation and lower socioeconomic status than the mainstream, most Latino Americans believe they're better off in the United States than they would be in their country of origin. On the whole they tend to be law-abiding citizens. They love their Latino heritage but identify primarily with Euro-Americans and value the American Dream. Most parents work hard to send their children to school. They want them to learn a profession and become solid citizens.

LATINO AMERICAN WAYS: PERSONAL RELATIONSHIPS

Latino Americans place the highest priority on relationships, family, getting along, relating in a personal way, and protecting their honor, while machismo is still a factor in male-female relationships and among male peers. Communication patterns are often indirect and always sensitive to others' feelings.

Relationship Value #1—Familismo

The Latino culture is collective, so relationships are the most important value, and family obligations rate higher than individual aspirations. Family and group closeness is their most important priority. Family comes first, and extended family next. There's a much stronger sense of mutual dependence and undying loyalty than among most Euro-Americans, including greater respect for older members. And extended families are more common. (Triandis 1984a; Triandis et al 1982; Cohen 1979; Grebler et al 1970; Mannino and Shore, 1976; Valle and Martinez 1980).

Familismo includes three types of value orientations: (1) feeling obligated to provide material and emotional support to extended family members, (2) relying on relatives for help and support, and (3) constantly checking with relatives about the way they see various behaviors and attitudes and being influenced by their perceptions and feelings.

Family First

The family is the center of personal existence, more so than for most U.S. families. Latino Americans' identities are closely tied to that of their family and its members. The tight bonds of love and loyalty may exclude outsiders to a greater degree. The family may include many more members than most Euro-American families: Grandparents and great-grandparents stay close and aunts, uncles, and cousins may be almost as close; even some close friends may be included. Family business is considered private, and to discuss it with outsiders would be a betrayal. Families are inward-focused and members rely on these relationships for their emotional security. Within the family, members tend to be quite open, honest, and communicative. Parents exercise strong authority.

Mutual Dependence

Latino Americans typically have high levels of mutual personal dependence that includes these factors:

- relying on relatives for help and support
- feeling obligated to provide material and emotional support to relatives
- being highly sensitive to family relationships
- constantly checking with relatives about the way they see various behaviors and attitudes
- being influenced by relatives' perceptions and feelings
- feeling what family members feel—mutual empathy
- conforming to relatives' beliefs and wishes
- sacrificing for the welfare of the family or ingroup members
- trusting the members of the ingroup
- expecting that members will ask each other for assistance and that they'll give it when asked

This value helps to protect each person against physical and emotional stress by providing natural support systems. As a result, Latino Americans place highest value on building interpersonal relationships in ingroups that are nurturing, loving, intimate, and respectful. While Euro-Americans value such relationships, they also value more confrontational and segmented relationships as an aid to independent growth (Hofstede 1980; Marin and Marin 1991).

Undying Loyalty

Latino Americans have incredibly strong ties and loyalties to family and friends. If an employee is asked to transfer to another location, many people in an extended family may be involved in the decision. If an employee loses his job or is transferred, the whole family may quit. If one is mistreated on the job, fellow employees who are also relatives will react as if they were personally being mistreated. As a result, disputes can have a more complex quality than Euro-Americans are accustomed to. The net effect may be for Latino Americans to hold back their true thoughts and feelings until they can stand it no longer. Then they may strike out in ways they later regret. Therefore, they may go to great lengths to avoid disputes or use a third party to intercede or to mediate a dispute.

Relationship Value #2—Simpatico: Getting Along

Getting along with others is extremely important to Latino Americans. They tend to acquiesce to the wishes of others and to agree with them in order to maintain *simpatico*, a Latin form of harmonious relationship. Most try to do what's expected by the culture and to be courteous. A potential problem for people from other cultures is figuring out what Latino Americans are *really* thinking and feeling before resentment builds to the breaking point and the relationship is severed.

Acquiescence

Getting along with the wishes of others, regardless of your own opinions and feelings, is important. It may include providing the answer you think another person wants to hear, whether you think it's factual or not. This is a rather extreme type of response frequently used by Latino Americans, especially by less-educated immigrants, men and women alike. They're more likely to acquiesce than the better educated, more acculturated ones (Landsberger and Saavedra 1967).

The willingness to conform to others' expectations is highly valued in Latino cultures, but so is the willingness to rebel at those rare times when too much has been too much for too long. Latino Americans conform because they want to please and support important others and because they want others to think well of them and accept them. In a high context culture a frequent concern is, "What will they say?"

Simpatico

The Latino cultural value of simpatico encourages acquiescence that promotes smooth, pleasant social relations. Simpatico persons are:

- polite and respectful
- don't express criticism, confrontation, or assertiveness
- show a certain level of conformity and empathy for the feelings of other people
- try to behave with dignity and respect toward others
- value working toward harmony in interpersonal relations

Latino Americans therefore are more likely to give socially desirable responses, avoid face-to-face confrontations at all costs, and view assertiveness quite differently than Euro-Americans do. Small talk before and after discussing business is extremely important for building empathetic relationships.

Latino Americans tend to report that they carry out socially desirable actions and avoid reporting less desirable attitudes and behaviors. They tend to provide the "correct" answer as they perceive it, independent of their actual experiences. Mexicans residing in Mexico are more likely to express socially desirable responses than are Mexican Americans. Also more likely to acquiesce are those in lower socioeconomic levels, indicating that acculturation may modify this tendency (Ross and Mirowsky 1984; Triandis et al. 1984b).

Courtesy

Latino Americans place great importance upon courtesy and therefore offer more profuse thanks, praise, and apologies than Euro-Americans are accustomed to. Elaborate courtesies are common and constant among the upper and middle classes. Lower class people may reserve such treatment for special occasions and for "superiors" and strangers.

Relationship Value #3—Personalismo: Relating in a Personal Way

To relate well to people from a Latino culture usually means relating everything to them on a personal level. Instead of talking in generalities, you would talk in terms of

- how situations relate to them personally
- their families
- their town
- most of all, their personal pride

Especially for the male, the more the communication is personalized, the more successful it's likely to be. In fact, Latino Americans usually trust only those with whom they have a personal relationship, for only those persons can appreciate their soul. You may have to establish a personal relationship with any Latino American you want to do business with.

When doing business in Latino countries, Euro-Americans find they must spend more time building rapport than usual before they can move to discussing the business at hand. This tendency has some carryover, of course, to Latino Americans who immigrated to the United States. Latino Americans tend to avoid at all costs having face-to-face confrontations or unpleasantness with business associates, co-workers, or friends. (Cox 1993; Zurcher et al. 1965).

Relationship Value #4—Reluctance to Self-Disclose

The value of *personalismo* does not mean that Latino Americans will say what they're really thinking and feeling to people outside their ingroup. The value of *simpatico* and power distance means they're less likely than Euro-Americans to self-disclose. When people reveal personal information, they become vulnerable to how the listener will use that information, and their *amor proprio*, or personal honor, could be damaged. Males are even less likely to self-disclose than females, especially with someone they're likely to interact with in the future, or in culturally unfamiliar situations. When Latino American males do self-disclose, it's usually with Latino American females, who pose the least threat of responding with scorn, rejection, or other blows to self-respect (LeVine and Franco 1981; Franco et al. 1984; Constantino et al. 1988).

Relationship Value #5—Machismo and Gender Roles

Most agree that gender roles are more strictly defined in Latin cultures than in the United States. Men's higher status is more noticeable, they're more dominant, they're allowed more sexual freedom, and there are greater differences in men's and women's socially acceptable activities, attributes, roles, and occupations. The degree and importance of these values varies from one Latino culture to another.

Machismo

The machismo pattern of behavior represents male power and an attitude toward the world, especially toward women. While Latino men generally have a poetic, romantic side, the machismo aspect is aggressive and sometimes insensitive. This image consists of virility, courage, competitiveness, a readiness to fight, and a determination to conquer. Men are expected to be assertive, to be leaders, to be in control, and to earn the respect of other men by their masculinity. Machismo is basically about men impressing each other. In business this means that a man should be forceful, confident, unafraid, and take the lead among groups consisting of women and men of lower status.

The *machismo* stereotype is that the male is strong, in control, and provides for his family, while the woman is submissive and lacking in power and influence. In Latino countries, both boys and girls are socialized to admire this image, and Latino husbands virtually always "wear the pants" in interactions with the outside world. It follows that men are less likely to participate in household and child care responsibilities than in Euro-American households. However, if the wife is a strong Latino woman, she may actually control the home, children, and husband. And Latino American women tend to be stronger than their counterparts in Latino countries.

The dark, extreme side of *machismo* involves wife-beating, excessive gambling, fighting, heavy drinking, a tendency to have children with other women, and male-male sex. Some sociologists think the underlying roots of machismo lie in male-male relationships: how men "traffic in honor and how men negotiate status with one another, how men hammer out the measurements of their standing as a man" (Lancaster 1993). Tannen's work regarding the male focus on status seems to support this idea.

Domestic Abuse

A 1995 study concluded that domestic violence occurs in at least 30 percent of Mexican families as well as Mexican American immigrant families (WSJ 1998). In most Mexican states, domestic violence is not grounds for divorce, and there is no legal way for a wife to gain protection from an abusive husband. The divorce rate in Mexico is one-tenth the U.S. rate, and among recent Mexican immigrants the rate is scarcely higher than in Mexico. A strong Latino belief is that even physical and mental abuse should be borne in order to keep the family together. Family and friends reinforce pressure from the culture for the wife to stay in an abusive marriage. Many parents say, "Don't divorce. We would be ashamed to have you in this family if you did." Mexican women say that husbands are forever, no matter how badly behaved. Many mothers tell their daughters, "Your husband is your cross to bear for the rest of your life."

Male–Male Sex

Most boys in Latin America, by the time they come of age, are veterans of recreational sex, seeking ever-new thrills, according to recent research (Paternostro 1999). To some of these men, having sex with many women is somewhat better than monogamy. But the utmost expression of manhood is having sex with a man. In the eyes of a Latino macho man—anti-gay as he traditionally is—having sex with a man does not make him gay or bisexual. So long as he is the penetrating party, rather than the penetrated party, it marks him out as a sort of super-heterosexual. Few stop this practice after marriage. As a result, monogamous women in Latin America are at higher risk of contracting HIV (from their husbands) than female prostitutes. Housewives make up 80 percent of female patients in at least one Colombian AIDS clinic. The Hispanic AIDS Forum in New York distinguishes, in its list of risk groups, between "homosexual men" and "MSMs"—men who have sex with men but consider themselves straight.

Women's Lot

Women are restricted by traditional views about their sexuality, assertiveness, and work roles. "Madonna or whore, no in-between, that's how we're seen," say liberated Latino women. The Madonna, or good woman, marries as a virgin and martyrs herself to her family. She accepts men as the dominant ones and experiences her lot as saintly suffering. Women are therefore expected to be reserved and modest with men outside the family. Assertive women are generally disliked.

Latino Americans are more likely than Euro-Americans to believe that mothers should not have outside jobs. In an extensive survey of Latino Americans, a little more than half said they didn't think married women with children should have the opportunity to pursue their own careers, even if they were able to look after their home and family while doing so. On the other hand, women who do work nearly always have a greater say in family decisions than those who don't. In Mexico and some other Latin American countries, a major shift seems to have begun in the late 1990s, a movement toward greater acceptance of women as administrators, managers, and business owners. This movement is reminiscent of women's progress in the United States in the 1970s.

Relationship Value #6—Communication Patterns

Latino Americans often speak indirectly out of concern for others' feelings and consideration for others' sensitivity to criticism. They may use speech to impress, follow some unique nonverbal patterns, and have clear expectations about how to say hello and good-bye.

Speaking Indirectly. Latino Americans are frequently indirect in their communication with strangers and outsiders. It may appear evasive, but it's intended to be courteous. It may be difficult to determine exactly what they are thinking and feeling. They may use a go-between in order to communicate unpleasant messages or to make requests.

High Concern for Feelings. Latino Americans may tell you what you want to hear, regardless of the "truth," out of great concern for your feelings. This reflects their belief that their own opinion doesn't matter as much as respecting your feelings and giving you the response you'd like to have. This conflicts with the American value of "telling it like it is."

High Sensitivity to Criticism. How Latino Americans take criticism is closely tied to the relative status of the people involved. Usually if criticism comes from a higher-status person, it's accepted sheepishly; if it comes from an equal it may be treated with humor; and if it comes from a lower-status person, it may not be tolerated since this would signal weakness and invite more criticism and even derision.

Saying Hello and Good-bye. If several people are in a group when you arrive, you're expected to go around and greet everyone, shaking hands, or if you know them well enough, embracing them. The "Hi, everyone" greeting would be considered rude. Likewise, upon leaving, you're expected to say good-bye to each person individually.

LATINO AMERICAN ISSUES

Many issues are important to Latino Americans, but four issues that will help you better understand your co-workers are: 1) how to overcome segregation and discrimination, 2) how to improve their knowledge and skills, 3) how to improve their workplace status, and 4) how to overcome recent immigration backlash. The causes of these socioeconomic disparities are related to their younger average age, inadequate schooling, larger families, the large percentage of immigrants, and the related language barrier. Although Latino American citizens have made impressive progress since the 1950s in educational attainment and occupational mobility, many Mexican Americans remain at a persistent, substantial disadvantage. These issues are discussed in books by such researchers as Clete Daniel, Gregory De Freitas, and Carey McWilliams and in U.S. Government reports.

Issue #1. Overcoming Segregation and Discrimination

The long history of discrimination against Latino Americans, together with the antagonism toward Latino cultures, especially the Mexican and Puerto Rican cultures, expressed by many Euro-Americans, has served to heighten their alienation from the dominant culture. While this discrimination has never been as formally overt as that against African Americans and American Indians, informal discrimination has yielded similar results. Three separate government studies conducted in 1942 found that Latino Americans were probably the most ignored and destitute U.S. group—economically, intellectually and socially.

Occupational Segregation

The huge differences in wage levels and worker expectations between the United States and most Latino countries, especially neighboring Mexico, has always motivated workers to migrate to the United States. Discrimination against Mexican Americans has never been as formally overt as that against African Americans and American Indians. Informal discrimination, however, has often yielded very similar results.

The typical practice in the Southwest has been for an employer to hire Mexican Americans by the group—as work gangs, crews, or families—doing those menial jobs which are heavily manual, dirty, seasonal, and dead-end (McWilliams 1975). Where unions existed, they usually excluded them or established work rules that barred them from opportunities to compete with Euro-Americans. The better paying craft unions, in particular, were closed to Mexican American workers. These patterns became self-reinforcing over time. Because Mexican Americans were hired in large numbers for the worst jobs, they became stereotyped as being only good for those types of jobs.

During World War II, President Roosevelt's executive order regarding fair employment practices was mainly in response to African American demands. However, Clete Daniel (1991) says that Latino Americans were actually facing the greatest potential for mistreatment on each of the four bases proscribed by the executive order—religion, color, national origin, and race. The three million Mexican Americans living in the United States during the 1940s were virtually all Catholics, with Indian/Spanish skin coloring, and a Mexican national origin that had been disparaged by Euro-Americans for many years. To confuse the issue, the government couldn't decide whether Latino Americans were fellow "whites" or a race apart. Three separate government studies conducted in 1942 found that Mexican Americans were probably the "most submerged and destitute group in the United States—economically, intellectually and socially" (U.S. Government 1942).

Today Mexican Americans and Puerto Rican Americans remain disproportionately concentrated in blue-collar occupations and in such industries as manufacturing, mining, and agriculture, where employment opportunities are declining. Overt discrimination has decreased, but traditional business practices often result in discrimination that blocks upward mobility.

Residential Segregation

Occupational patterns determine residential patterns. For example, prior to 1950 most jobs available to Mexican Americans were in isolated rural areas of the Southwest. Latino Americans who resided in urban areas could only afford to live in camps or the worst parts of town. Occupational barriers meant they could hardly hope to ever afford much better. As a practical reality, therefore, most were segregated in barrios and barrio schools, just as African Americans were segregated in ghettos and ghetto schools. Since 1950 the Latino American population has rapidly urbanized, but segregation is still common.

The Unnoticed Minority

In 1940 about 90 percent of Mexican Americans lived in five Southwestern states, one of the most intense concentrations of any American subgroup—a pattern that continues in modified form to this day. People in the other forty-three states rarely encountered Mexican Americans and were hardly aware of their existence. Even in the Southwest, they were isolated from the mainstream of American life (Daniel 1991).

Difficulty in gaining access to adequate labor market statistics has been another barrier for Chicano advocates trying to get national attention and political action. To document the degree and nature of discrimination, they must be able to adequately assess both the present patterns and the trends over time. To make such assessments, they must have reliable statistics. Only since 1950 have relatively reliable census statistics been available for Latino Americans. Not until 1970 did the U.S. Department of Labor begin publishing statistics on its manpower programs with a Hispanic category.

Welfare benefits are rarely available to needy Mexican Americans because most of those who need it are either illegal immigrants or noncitizens (Aponte 1991). Recent immigrants tend to earn the lowest incomes and have the most barriers to upward mobility. Most are either speak virtually no English or don't speak it fluently. They tend to be from rural areas and have difficulty adapting to urban life. They rarely have the job skills needed to gain stable employment and make adequate wages. And many lack a high school diploma. Because of male underemployment and unemployment, an increasing percentage of immigrant mothers now work (Santiago and Wilder 1991).

Lack of Political Clout

Latino Americans have traditionally been wary of the U.S. government and have stayed quiet or underground, without political voice. Only 7 percent of registered Latino Americans voted in the 1996 general election (Paulette 2000).

Inadequate education is a hurdle to exercising power in the American political system, the main arena for bringing about needed change. Despite their solidarity and pride of heritage, full participation is impossible as long as many of them lack adequate education, English literacy, citizenship papers, or clear legal status.

On the other hand, Latino Americans are now the largest ethnic group in Los Angeles, 45 percent. Relatively few were in the habit of voting when an anti-immigrant California proposition was passed. Such political passivity is changing, and voter turnout in 1998 was 52 percent for California Latino Americans, compared to 27 percent for Texas Latino Americans (Chronicle 1999). The community began speaking of electing a Latino American as mayor of Los Angeles.

After the 1998 elections, Latino Americans numbered 22 in the U.S. House of Representatives, about 5 percent, and none in the Senate. The unnoticed minority is gaining some visibility and political power.

Issue #2. Improving Knowledge and Skills

The language barrier and lower educational achievement of some Latino American workers accounts for a larger share of their earnings differential than is true for other groups. Continuing high dropout rates and low college enrollments indicate that Latino Americans will be the group most damaged by the shift to a better educated, highly skilled workforce (DeFreitas 1991). Key barriers are:

- recent immigration
- language barriers and difficulties
- poverty-level family incomes

- higher unemployment in the family
- early marriage and early pregnancy
- immigrants' deficient educational preparation in home country
- poor achievement levels in U.S. segregated schools
- biased treatment in integrated U.S. schools

Latino Americans place a high value on education, even though they have the lowest educational level of any U.S. group. Studies indicate that Latino American high school students report significantly higher aspirations to get a college degree than Euro-American students whose families are at the same socioeconomic level. In both groups, the higher the socioeconomic level, the higher the educational aspirations tend to be. About the same percentage of Latino American and Euro-American parents want their children to attend college, again controlling for socioeconomic status (Solorzano 1991).

Issue #3. Improving Workplace Status

When we compare the workplace issues of Latino Americans to those of Euro-Americans, several major factors stand out: higher unemployment, lower economic status, problems of new immigrants, educational discrimination, the need for job skills, and employment discrimination.

Employment Barriers: Mexican Americans

Mexican Americans have made impressive progress since the 1950s in educational attainment and occupational mobility. However, many remain at a persistent, substantial disadvantage. Recent immigrants tend to earn the lowest incomes and have the most barriers to upward mobility. Most either don't speak English well or speak almost no English. They tend to be from rural areas and have difficulty adapting to urban life. They rarely have the job skills needed to gain stable employment and make adequate wages. And many lack a high school diploma. Welfare benefits are rarely available to needy Mexican Americans because most of those who need it are either illegal immigrants or noncitizens. Due to male underemployment and unemployment, an increasing percentage of mothers now work.

Employees have been fired for speaking Spanish in an "English-Only" workplace. The "English-Only Movement" is part of a backlash to increased immigration, as well as to the numbers of Latino Americans who do not speak English. Case law based on "The Spun Steak Case" established that under federal law, employers may demand that their employees speak only English, but this policy must be necessary for conducting business. This case also established that the EEOC rules assert that employers may not prohibit employees from speaking their native language in informal situations (Duncan 2000).

Employment Discrimination

Workplace discrimination persists because, even if employers do not themselves hold discriminatory attitudes, the practice of using stereotyped beliefs that minorities have lower-than-average productivity will result in employers ranking individual minority group members lower than other job applicants. Inside the company, employer discrimination usually involves the confinement of minorities to less skilled, more unstable job titles and slower promotional tracks, rather than differential treatment of minorities and Euro-Americans in the same jobs.

Mexican Labor in United States and in Maquiladores

Today a sizable portion of the labor supply in the Southwest is Mexican American. In some areas, such as south Texas and southern California, Mexican Americans are a rapidly growing proportion of the labor force, and in some areas they are the largest segment. The huge disparities in wage levels and worker expectations between the United States and Mexico motivate Mexican workers to migrate to the United States

Such disparities also motivate U.S. manufacturers to build plants called *maquiladores* in special industrial zones in northern Mexico near the U.S. border. In return, U.S. firms agree to not compete with Mexican manufacturers by not selling these products in Mexico. The U.S. government cooperated initially by reducing tariffs on these products when they were brought into the United States. Now, through NAFTA (North America Fair Trade Agreement), it has eliminated import duties.

Issue #4. Overcoming Immigration Backlash

Nearly a third of Latino Americans are first-generation immigrants with limited English proficiency that significantly hinders their socioeconomic progress. Controversy rages over the cost to taxpayers of providing social services to these immigrants. People also worry about overpopulation straining the country's resources and *illegal* immigrants, who use many social services but don't pay into the income tax and property tax accounts that fund such services. On the other hand, studies indicate that the long-run economic benefits these immigrants generate for the average U.S. taxpayer outweigh any short-run costs. "Immigration backlash" eases whenever the economy improves, but it remains a sensitive issue for many Latino Americans.

MEXICAN AMERICANS

Mexican Americans are the largest of the Latino American groups, 58 percent, or nearly 21 million people. They are the largest minority group in the Southwest, where their influence on culture and society is quite visible. Today most Mexican Americans have immigrant roots; they or their parents or grandparents came from Mexico to *El Norte* in search of a better life. Los Angeles has more people of Mexican origin than any city in the world except Mexico City and Guadalajara (Chronicle 1999). Statistics used in the following discussion of Mexican Americans and other Latino Americans are based upon U.S. Census publications.

Background

After the Mexican-American War in the 1840s, the border between the two countries was moved, and many residents of northern Mexico were suddenly told they were living in the Southwest United States, foreigners in their own land. They were caught in the path of the "manifest destiny" to expand U.S. territory to the Pacific Ocean. During the first decade of this century, many Mexican farmers lost their land, leading to a civil war in Mexico that devastated the economy and triggered a migration of peasants to the United States. The Mexican population grew from about 175,000 to more than a million between 1900 and 1930. These immigrants were generally segregated and exploited as cheap labor by the Euro-Americans. During the Great Depression, Mexicans became the target of deportation programs designed to rid the country of illegal aliens. The purpose was to reduce the labor pool and preserve the few remaining jobs for legal citizens.

Current Profile

Mexican Americans are the fastest growing segment of the population, increasing by 147 percent between 1970 and 1990, compared with a 114 percent growth for all Latino Americans and 16 percent for non-Latinos. They increased by 53 percent from 1990 to 2000, about the same as other Latino American groups.

They have the lowest educational level: Only 44 percent hold high school diplomas and 6 percent hold degrees. About 25 percent of Mexican Americans and Puerto Rican Americans live below the poverty line, significantly more than other Latino American groups.

Compared to other Latino American groups, they have the largest proportion of native-born citizens (67 percent) except for the Spaniards (83 percent). About 7 percent are foreign born who became citizens, and 26 percent are foreign-born residents who are not citizens. About half speak English fluently. The longer they or their families have lived in the United States, the more acculturated they are, and the more likely they are to speak English fluently.

Cultural Themes and Issues

Mexican Americans have a strong cultural heritage. It's extremely important to them. They love their Spanish language and value the warmth and romance typical of their culture. But is it predominantly Spanish, Indian, or a unique blend? Anthropologists estimate that about 75 percent of Mexicans are meztizos, meaning of mixed European and Native American descent. They have perhaps the strongest sense of national identity of all Latinos, although they occupy various levels of prosperity and social standing. The small percentage of citizens of purely European ancestry—about 10 percent of the population—are often referred to as the Thousand Families. They have always controlled the country's political power and economic wealth, just as the Spanish did 300 years ago. Here are estimates of the proportion of the three major ethnic groups in Mexico:

Meztizos (mixed European and American Indian)	75%
European ancestry	10%
American Indian ancestry	15%

Mexican Americans have nourished and sustained Mexican cultural characteristics to a greater extent than other ethnic group, keeping alive their language, identity, and values. This stems partially from the fact that the Southwest was the home of some before it was part of the United States. Another factor is the common border, over a thousand miles long, with continual flows of people back and forth. The most noticeable ethnic feature of Mexican Americans is the pervasive retention of the Spanish language.

Key Value Themes

One study found that the cultural values of Mexican Americans have been strongly influenced by a folk or rural culture in which organized and continuous striving for future monetary gains plays little part (Bullock 1971). This folk pattern of living, especially among the poor, promotes a mixture of individualism and family unity that leaves little room for an interest in the broader community. The welfare of the family is a key focus, along with the duty of older children to help support the family, even if it means dropping out of school. Mexican Americans generally focus less on involvement in the schools and other societal institutions than do Euro-Americans. Class has been a binding influence for the masses: "We're all the same—poor."

Mexican Americans' cultural values and patterns are virtually the same as the Latino American values discussed earlier. Special importance may be given the following values (Ramirez 1972).

- *Relationships* between individuals are more important than competitive, materialistic, or achievement goals. Latino Americans in the Southwest have a high context, highly involved culture, where people constantly monitor members' emotional states.

- *Family* ties are especially strong.

- *Machismo* and a patriarchal family and social structure are strong but they're changing along with changing economic demands and women's new job roles.

- *Ethnic loyalty*, a sense of solidarity and pride in their unique heritage, is strong.

Changing Male–Female Dynamics

Male dominance of the family traditionally emphasized physical occupations as opposed to intellectual endeavors. Women were discouraged from competing in male-dominated occupations. However, beginning in the 1970s some women began organizing and supporting one another in breaking out of some of these traditional limitations. And wives are often able to find jobs more readily than the men, sometimes at higher pay. By the end of the 1990s, these efforts were paying off in the upward mobility of women in the business world.

Religion

Religion in Mexico is a unique blend of Catholicism and ancient beliefs handed down by the Mayans and Aztecs. God is deeply personal, caring for each person through specific saints. Home altars are decorated with *santitos*, images of saints dear to the family. Mexican Catholics believe that the Virgin Mary, Virgen de Guadalupe, has a particular concern for Mexicans and protects them.

Valuing the American Dream

Mexican Americans as a group tend to be law-abiding citizens who love their Latino heritage but identify primarily with Euro-Americans and value the American Dream. Despite the prejudice and discrimination that have resulted in segregation and lower socioeconomic status than the mainstream, most believe they're better off in the United States than they would be in Mexico.

The Chicano Movement

In the 1960s and 1970s Chicano activists confronted discrimination and its effects. The movement sparked a new interest in the Latino American culture, but it did not succeed in its original objective of converting the Mexican American masses. The early Chicano intellectuals had underestimated their own people's belief in the American system, identification with Euro-American values, and their conservatism. The average Latino American voter simply did not view U.S. society as one of the most repressive, intolerant, and prejudiced in the world.

Nor did most Mexican Americans identify themselves with the American Indian, and they had never done so in the past. The cultural mixture of Indian and European elements that occurred in Mexico also blended with the Euro-American in the United States to produce a value system within the Mexican American community that is itself a blend. The rejection of Euro-American values by the Chicanos, therefore, is seen by some Mexican Americans as a rejection of one element of their own culture (Gann and Duignan 1986).

Above all, Chicano activists didn't seem to understand the strength of the social conservatism that inspires the mass of ordinary people in the barrios. Most parents who work hard to send their children to college have no desire to see them become rebels. They want them to learn a profession and become solid citizens. In fact, just after the height of the movement, a 1983 *Los Angeles Times* poll showed that only a small percentage of Mexican Americans choose to identify themselves as Chicanos. While Latino alienation, anger, and rage exist, overall the Mexican Americans identify themselves with the United States. Only about a third of them identify themselves as Mexicans or Latinos first and Americans second. The poll showed that only about half of California Latino Americans were even aware of the movement, about the same rate of awareness as other citizens.

PUERTO RICAN AMERICANS

Puerto Rican Americans are now the second largest Spanish-speaking community in the United States. They number nearly 3.4 million and constitute 10 percent of the Latino Americans on the U.S. mainland.

Past Connections

Puerto Rico was a Spanish colony for 400 years, and shortly after 1900 became an American affiliate, its citizens American citizens. The island is shifting from an agricultural to an industrial economy. Spanish is still by far the strongest cultural influence, which has only slightly waned during this century. The island culture is a microcosm of Latin America, a culture in transition. Therefore, many Puerto Ricans "swing between extremes of apathy and frantic activity, hide hostility and frustration, and lean on fantasy" (Harris and Moran 1991, 86).

The migrations to the mainland began in the 1930s, most immigrants coming from the poverty level. They're primarily Catholic, from low-skill rural backgrounds, and many are dark skinned. On the island, about 20 percent of Puerto Ricans are considered African American and 16 percent "mixed blood." Those who emigrate to the United States tend to have better educational and employment credentials than the average African American on the island, but most experience downward mobility after they arrive in the United States.

In earlier decades nearly all Puerto Ricans landed in New York and stayed there. In 1950 about 80 percent lived in New York, but they've become more dispersed in the past two or three decades. In 1970 about 65 percent lived in New York and in 1980 only 50 percent. The others live primarily in New Jersey, California, Florida, and Illinois. When they moved out of New York, most moved up, both socially and economically.

Current Profile

Still, the majority of Puerto Rican adults in the mainland United States are first-generation immigrants who face considerable prejudice and discrimination. In 2000 there were over 2 million Latino Americans living in New York City, and 37 percent of these were Puerto Rican Americans.

The Puerto Rican American population has grown much faster than the non-Latino population but much slower than either the Mexican American or the total Latino American populations. The growth rates for all groups slowed after 1990.

	Population Growth	
	1970–1990	1990–2000
Puerto Rican American	76%	25%
Non-Latino population	16%	13%
Mexican American	147%	53%
Total Latino American	114%	58%

Education and Income

Educational attainment was significantly above the Latino American average, with 64 percent holding diplomas and 10 percent holding degrees. After the Spaniard group, they have the largest proportion of members who speak English well (60 percent).

About 30 percent of Puerto Rican Americans earn more than $35,000, compared with 50 percent of Euro-Americans, and 20 percent of Mexican Americans. Yet they have the largest number of people, 26 percent, living in poverty, a few more than the Mexican American group (24 percent). The reason is likely linked to the 1990 census finding that Puerto Rican Americans had the smallest number of members living in family households (56 percent) with 37 percent living in female-headed households. And Puerto Rican women had the lowest median income of any Latino American group

Relatively high unemployment among Puerto Rican men is also a factor in the poverty picture. Puerto Rican workers' concentration in declining manufacturing industries in the Northeast seems has been a factor. (De Frietas 1991).

Issue #1: Prejudice and Discrimination

On the surface, it appears that Puerto Rican immigrants would have an easier adjustment than the Europeans who immigrated to New York earlier. Puerto Ricans are U.S. citizens. They don't experience the traumatic shock of being illegal, like many Mexicans, or being "screened" at Ellis Island, as were Europeans in the past. (After screening, families were sometimes split up and the sick or "unsuitable" sent back home.)

Puerto Ricans seemed well adapted to fit into America's multicultural society because the Puerto Rican community contains persons of every possible color and complexion: people of European appearance, people with light-brown skin, and people with dark or black skin. The Puerto Rican upper and middle classes are generally more light skinned than the rest but by no means universally so. Most of the poverty-stricken people in the mountain towns are of European descent. There are no iron-bound distinctions, as is typically true in the United States. Intermarriage is common, class counts for more than color, and there is less concern over skin color than in the English-speaking world.

Once Puerto Rican immigrants arrive in the United States, all that changes. Discrimination based on skin color has encouraged dark-skinned Puerto Ricans to place special emphasis on their Spanish linguistic legacy in order to differentiate themselves from African Americans. There has often been rivalry between the two groups for jobs, between opposing neighborhood gangs, and between welfare recipients. They've had to cope with a cold climate dramatically different from their island warmth, and with a cold people, in contrast to the interpersonal warmth so common in their Latin culture. A common complaint is, "The weather is very cold here, just like the people."

Many Puerto Ricans, therefore, have great difficulty adjusting to New York, even when they're healthy and able to work. They often feel unwelcome and more discriminated against than Cubans and Mexicans. In New York City more than a million Puerto Ricans live in some of the city's most undesirable conditions. They are widely stereotyped as muggers and troublemakers and suffer from ethnic discrimination, especially those with darker skin tones.

Issue #2: Breaking Out of Poverty and Gaining Skills

Puerto Ricans often lack fluency in English, transferable skills, and formal education. Unskilled Puerto Ricans tend to benefit economically by leaving the island and settling in New York. But upwardly mobile Puerto Ricans often do better by returning home and many do after a while.

By 1960 half the Puerto Ricans families in New York were receiving welfare, and one-fourth of their children received some form of welfare assistance. Most didn't want to go on welfare when they arrived on the mainland. They have always preferred to work, and they place high value on dignity, independence, and self-respect.

By 1970, whatever the stereotype, the bulk of Puerto Ricans in America did not belong to the underclass, and they neither shunned work nor broke the law. High fertility rates were concentrated among those who didn't finish high school. While the Puerto Rican Americans were one of the youngest and more poorly educated groups, they earned comparable incomes when compared with people of the same age and education. Those who did move up did it through education. Many second-generation Puerto Ricans went to college, then into various professions or public service. Many attained distinction in sports, entertainment, business, and academia. The proportion of semiskilled and unskilled workers declined significantly between 1950 and 1970, and the percentage in skilled and white collar occupations went up.

Beginning in the early 1980s, more and more professional people began to settle on the mainland. For example, more than half the engineering graduates on the island took jobs in the United States in 1983. As a result, the popular stereotype of the unskilled or semiskilled Puerto Rican immigrant has less and less relevance to the facts.

CUBAN AMERICANS

Cuban Americans are the smallest, 4 percent, of the three major Latino American groups. They are also the best educated and most affluent. Most Cubans in the United States arrived since 1960, when there were only about 30,000 here. Now there are one and a quarter million.

Current Profile

Cuban Americans over age 25 are the Latino American group most likely to have at least a high school diploma, 73 percent as compared to 57 percent for the total Latino Americans. Still, 88 percent of all Euro-Americans over 25 have graduated high school. It follows that among Latino Americans, they have the most members working in managerial and professional occupations. Cuban Americans have the higher proportion (36 percent) earning over $35,000, as compared with 23 percent of all Latino Americans and 49 percent of Euro-Americans. They are generally an older group with smaller family households, and more likely to live in the suburbs than the inner city.

Most were born in Cuba and more than half of those have become citizens. Nearly half the Cuban-born members entered the United States during the 1960s to escape communism, and nearly all the others have entered since 1970. Most settled in the Miami area. Many also moved to the eastern states, especially to western New York, Jersey City, Newark, and Bridgeport, and to a lesser extent to Los Angeles and Chicago.

Soon after Fidel Castro came to power in Cuba in 1959, people of the middle and upper classes began leaving. In fact, more than a million left, about 10 percent of Cuba's population. The overwhelming majority came to the United States

The early emigrants in the 1960s were from varied backgrounds but many were business or professional persons, and entrepreneurs. Those who left were far more likely to be relatively well-educated urban professionals than was the average island resident. They averaged three more years of schooling than Mexicans immigrating at the same time. About 11 percent were professionals or business owners, compared to 1 percent of Mexicans. Meanwhile 12 percent of Mexicans were farm workers compared to 2 percent of Cubans. There were many skilled blue-collar workers from both countries.

The first wave was soon joined by disillusioned members of the revolutionary regime as Castro became more aligned with the USSR. By the end of the 1970s there was a substantial Cuban American community, numbering more than legal immigrants from the whole of Latin America. Immigrants during the 1970s were primarily from the working class, including many skilled workers. Most had to settle for lesser jobs during their first two years. The Cuban American population swelled from about 30,000 in 1959 to about 600,000 by 1980 to 1,070,400 by 1990, and 1,242,000 by 2000. (U.S. Census Bureau).

Where Cuban Americans have created their own communities and established a middle-class or upper-class lifestyle, they've experienced little discrimination. However, Black Cuban Americans apparently believe that racial oppression in the United States is more severe than in communist Cuba. In the 1950s about 72 percent of Cuba's population consisted of people of European heritage. In the U.S. Census of 1970, almost 95 percent of Cuban Americans in the United States were of European heritage.

Cuban Success Story: Revitalizing Miami

Most Cuban Americans live in urban areas, and their capital is Miami, often called "Little Havana." By 1980 almost 60 percent of Miami's population was of Latin American origin. On average, Cuban Americans living outside Miami have a better formal education and higher income than those in Miami. But far from placing a burden on the city, the immigrants transformed its economy.

Before 1959 Miami depended mainly on tourism and money spent by retired persons who moved to Florida from the Northeast. The Cuban Americans used their enterprise and skills to turn Miami into the "new capital city of Latin America." Increasing numbers of Latin American tourists fill the city's hotels. Latin American businessmen are investing huge sums in real estate, about $1 billion a year by 1980. Miami became "the banking center" for investors from Central and South America. More than 100 multinationals doing business with Latin America have established headquarters in Miami. By 1982 international commerce was generating more than $4 billion a year in state incomes and had created 170,000 jobs.

By 1980 nearly half the Cubans in Miami worked for Cuban-owned firms and 21 percent were self-employed. Their wages were somewhat higher than those who worked in non-Cuban firms.

Cuban Professionals

In Miami and elsewhere educated Cuban Americans lost no time in moving up to the status they had enjoyed in their native land. By 1978, about 30 percent of Cubans worked in middle-class occupations as professionals, administrators, managers, and proprietors, as compared to 20 percent in 1970.

Cuban Americans are making an important contribution to American cultural life as artists, university professors, journalists, and other professionals. But they haven't tried to build a new Cuban

American culture, comparable to Mexican American culture. Most consider themselves exiles who will return to their homeland after its liberation but are grateful for their freedom and prosperity in the United States. The mass emigration of these intellectuals became a cultural disaster for Cuba. Most of them are not right-wing conservatives but people of every shade of opinion, including many who had originally supported Castro. Most regard socialism as morally superior to capitalism, at least in the abstract, and continue to regard the United States as a bastion of reaction.

OTHER LATINO AMERICANS

The 10 million other Latino Americans include those from South America, Central America, and the Dominican Republic. During the 1970s and 1980s, more than 1.2 million people emigrated from Central and South America and the Spanish-speaking Caribbean Islands, swelling their U.S. numbers to 2.2 million. That group now numbers about 3.9 million (U.S. Census Bureau).

Central Americans

About 5 percent of all Latino Americans, 1.7 million people, are originally from Central America. Most, 39 percent, are from El Salvador, 22 percent from Guatemala, and 13 percent from Honduras. These are among the smallest and poorest countries in Latin America. Most Central American immigrants are young men, married but traveling without their families, planning to work and save for a couple of years before returning. Most take minimum-wage blue-collar jobs, but these earnings are four times what they could earn at home. Nearly 90 percent work in crews composed of legal and illegal Latino aliens. Most say they intend to return again to work in an American city (Gann and Duignan 1986).

South Americans

More than 1.4 million immigrants from South America live in the United States, comprising 4 percent of all Latino Americans here. Colombians are by far the largest group of South Americans in the United States, comprising about a third, or nearly 470,000 people. Those arriving in the United States appear to be heavily urban, with educational and occupational levels well above the Colombian average. Significant numbers of people have also emigrated from Ecuador, Peru, Argentina, and Chile.

Dominican Americans

Over three-quarters of a million people (765,000) in the United States are from the Dominican Republic. Only 15 minutes by air from Puerto Rico, Dominicans have a close relationship with their Puerto Rican neighbors. Over half the current population of Dominican Americans entered during the 1980s due to political unrest on the island. Many were unskilled workers from rural areas, and they replaced the Puerto Ricans as the most disadvantaged group of Latino Americans. The elimination of many low-wage, manual U.S. manufacturing jobs created severe employment problems for these immigrants.

LEADERSHIP CHALLENGES: MEETING CULTURAL NEEDS OF LATINO AMERICANS

Latino American barriers include trying to meet both job and family obligations, a communication style that may conflict with goal achievement and providing accurate information, unwillingness to confront conflict, and promotion anxiety.

Need #1. Meeting Family Obligations

Work is important to most Latino Americans. They want the American Dream. But family comes first. Therefore, when it comes to the following kinds of issues, the Latino American is more likely than the Euro-American worker to put family concerns first, which affects:

- job relocation that requires the family to move
- overtime work that conflicts with family obligations
- the need to be absent in order to deal with family problems, illnesses, or emergencies

Co-workers and managers must put this in perspective in order to understand the true dynamics of the situation.

Latino American workers will generally consult with the family when deciding to take a job, to seek or accept advancement, and whether to leave a job. For you to understand and work with Latino American employees, you must know about and understand their family concerns that impact work decisions and performance.

In Latino cultures people are hired and promoted based primarily on family and personal ties. Latino American employees may expect the company to give their relatives and close friends preferential treatment. Managers may need to explain differences in company policy and in U.S. corporate cultures.

Need #2. Communicating Organizational Needs for Goal Achievement and Accurate Information

Latino cultures tend to value accurate data less highly than the American business culture. Most Latino business persons see nothing unusual or harmful in withholding information in order to gain or maintain power. While goals are important, the process of achieving the goals and the symbolic messages implied by various aspects of the process may be more important. In contrast, the success of U.S. corporations often hinges on effective and efficient goal achievement, doing what works, getting accurate data and passing it on to those who need it to do the best job. These values are so pivotal that Latino American employees may benefit from special training sessions on these topics.

Need #3. Seeing that Their Style Is Not Their Substance

Latino Americans can seem overly passive to some Euro-Americans because of the contrast in relationship styles. For example, when you combine the value of simpatico with that of power distance—the sense of status difference between supervisor and employee—you'll often find Latino Americans not speaking up in the same way her Euro-American peer does. Unless he's quite Americanized, a Latino American won't say anything that would imply criticism or contradiction of his supervisor—even if he knows the boss has probably made an uninformed and unwise decision. His supervisor might be tempted to label him as too passive for promotion, or even worse, too incompetent.

What this supervisor can do is communicate to the employee about such cultural differences and smooth the way to assertive contributions. Latino Americans have a deep understanding of family relationships. The supervisor, therefore, might compare the supervisor-employee relationship with the ways that brothers or cousins or sisters relate within the family—an equal relationship with one taking the lead.

Need #4. Turning Conflict Avoidance into Resolution with Sensitivity

The Latino value of simpatico compels most Latino Americans to avoid interpersonal conflict on the job. They try to emphasize positive behaviors in agreeable situations and de-emphasize negative behaviors in conflictive circumstances. This affects methods of conflict resolution and needs to be addressed in work team situations. Latino American employees need to understand why conflict is being addressed openly instead of ignored. They need to be reassured about the organization's need for openness, the expectation of openness, and why it is valued. Also, the team needs to respect Latino American members' sensitivities and find ways of resolving conflict that all can accept comfortably. Latino American workers may lead others in finding ways to combine openness with sensitivity and compassion.

Need #5. Dealing Constructively with Promotion Anxiety

Career development has some unique aspects for Latino American employees. For one thing, the employees, especially the men, may see more risk than Euro-Americans in applying for a promotion. If they don't get it, they not only experience a loss but their self-respect will suffer. Also, they may believe they'll be seen as competitive and too ambitious by their peers. Latino Americans tend to view competition as disruptive, leading to imbalance and disharmony. To overcome such barriers, leaders can begin working on career development with employees from the beginning. At periodic one-on-one meetings, career goals and ways of meeting them can be discussed. In this way, each step of development and advancement comes about naturally and the threats are diluted.

LEADERSHIP OPPORTUNITIES: BUILDING ON LATINO AMERICAN STRENGTHS

You can help Latino Americans use their love of group affiliation to enhance work teams and bring in their sense of honor, good name, and idealism to achieve at higher levels, You can relate to them in ways that show respect for Latino American values and issues, and you can help them make connections with Latino and Latino American marketplaces.

Opportunity #1. Enhance Work Team Relationships

Bring into play Latino Americans' cultural values of group loyalty, *personalismo*, and *simpatico*.

Highlight the Group Value.

The tradition of small group loyalty among Latino Americans offers a valuable opportunity for leaders to promote group values.

- Latino Americans place a very high value on belonging to a group and on cooperation and harmony within the group. Once they feel they are an accepted part of a work team, they are very comfortable functioning in this structure.
- For best results, Latino Americans need to feel personally close to the people in the group; otherwise, their first loyalty will lie elsewhere.
- Once they're committed to the team, motivational appeals and rewards geared to the team and the employee's contributions to the team can be the most powerful.
- Latino Americans tend to feel extreme loyalty to their ingroups. On the other hand, they may have difficulty adapting to an impersonal culture and to large groups in which personal recognition rarely occurs.

Remember, Latino Americans tend to give higher importance to relationships than to tasks. Keep the points in mind:

- Ask yourself, on a regular basis, How you can make the relationship value an asset?
- Ask, How can I create opportunities for them to work on tasks with others or to share projects?
- When delegating, coaching, and giving feedback, speak to them in terms of relationships where possible.

Promote Assertive Expression

Latino Americans' reluctance to self-disclose can pose a problem for optimal team functioning. Use *personalismo* to overcome it. Members often must know what's going on inside each others' heads in order to solve problems and keep operations flowing smoothly. When the corporate culture respects and values Latino Americans, their culture, history, and beliefs, then they are more likely to reveal their thinking and feeling to other team members.

Encourage Decision Making

In Latino cultures those in authority make the decisions, and subordinates don't pass judgment on leaders' ideas or question their decisions, as this would imply a lack of confidence in their judgment. Sometimes U.S. managers think they've communicated to Latino American workers that they can make certain decisions, only to find that the decisions are simply not made. In your manager role, you may need to appeal to Latino Americans' wish to be *simpatico*. You can explain in detail the decision-making process. You can reassure Latino American employees about when they can make certain decisions, when the team expects them to participate in making decisions, and when you expect their input, feedback, or questioning of ideas and decisions.

Opportunity #2. Appeal to Honor, Good Name, and Idealism

Co-workers and managers who offer feedback, evaluation, comments, or criticisms of Latino Americans' work would do well to understand and remember the importance of personal dignity, honor, and good name. If this is violated, the employee may feel compelled to leave. It may be futile to try to separate the person from the work or the end result. Latino Americans are likely to take criticism personally no matter how objective you try to be. Therefore, try these tips:

- Make the feedback personal but supportive and offered with great understanding and empathy
- Always give such feedback in private.
- Always offer it in a supportive, warm, concerned way.
- Always treat them as adults.

The idealist aspect of Latino culture can be an advantage when it motivates Latino American employees to support the organizational vision and mission, and to achieve the goals and standards set by the group or the company. Their idealism can inspire and energize other employees.

Opportunity #3. Show Respect for their Values and Issues

Values around hierarchy and status, personalismo and simpatico, are important in work relationships. Also, women managers need to understand effective ways of interacting with Latino American men.

The Manager and Respeto–Status

Respect for status and authority runs deep in Latin cultures, but respect for the person, regardless of position, runs even deeper. Latino American employees generally expect that the boss will be demanding. They often expect the boss to tell them what to do and to exercise fairly close direction until it's done. On the other hand, they can be led to use their own initiative if the leader makes it clear what types of initiative are expected and that this does not conflict with the leader's authority. The combination of challenge and support can help them to be productive and feel comfortable on the job. Such an approach is likely to establish an effective working relationship and engage the Latino American's sense of strong loyalty.

Relationships with Personalismo

When a manager is generally warm, friendly, and encouraging with a Latino American employee, that deeper personal respect tends to develop. Otherwise, such employees may assume the manager is displeased with them. On the flip side, when the manager allows the employee to express his or her personality and share personal concerns, a greater rapport develops.

Since almost all relationships are more personalized in Latin America than in the United States, Euro-American leaders may have difficulty understanding the implications of simpatico. In American business cultures, people tend to value the separation of business matters from personal relationships and concerns. However, it's quite possible to balance the Latino Americans' need for their leaders to show personal understanding and warmth and the Euro-American leaders' need for some professional distance. The reverse is also true. Euro-American employees can understand that the Latino American manager's concern for their personal and family matters is not intended as a prying or controlling ploy. It's the leader's way of showing proper concern for each person.

Relationships and Simpatico

A certain charm is seen as crucial for dealing effectively with others and such *simpatico* is a quality that increases one's status. In fact, it's the surest form of acceptance in Latino culture. On the other hand, rudeness or insensitivity in a leader is shocking to Latino Americans. To them courtesy is synonymous with education, and they would wonder how such a rude person could ever be given a responsible position. Latino Americans greatly admire leaders who can get the job done while exercising smooth social skills that boost the employees' self-esteem and honor.

The Woman Manager of Latino American Men

While machismo is often a misunderstood stereotype and is changing, it is still a factor to consider. Latino American men may have more difficulty than Euro-American men in dealing with a female manager. They are likely to react negatively to being corrected or criticized, especially where other men can hear, since this would be seen as a major attack on their honor. The more assertively the woman comes on, the more difficult it is for the employee. Therefore, women managers need to be especially sensitive to these feelings and to search for positive, tactful ways to achieve their purposes.

Occasionally a Latino American employee will make sexual overtures. It's important for the manager to keep in mind the implications of the Latino good woman-bad woman concept. She can nip such advances in the bud with clear I-messages, such as "I never get romantic with another employee; it wouldn't be fair to the others." She can continue to be warm and friendly, making sure she is also businesslike and professional, sending the clear nonverbal message, "I like you and respect you and I will not have a romantic or sexual relationship with you."

Opportunity #4. Help Make Connections to Latino Marketplaces

With about 75 percent of Latino American families in the middle- to upper-income brackets, Latino American spending power in 1998 was between $350 and $400 billion and growing. The U.S. media has responded dramatically to this market. New Spanish-speaking television and radio stations are popping up, especially throughout the Southwest. Many established magazine publishers—such as *Newsweek*, *People*, *Cosmopolitan*, and *Popular Mechanics*—have launched Spanish versions. And the National Association of Hispanic Publishers estimated there were over 1,000 Latino American newspapers in 1997.

The U.S. Latino American market is huge. Even greater are the markets in all the other Latino countries. NAFTA and other trade agreements are opening up greater-than-ever trade opportunities with those nations. Latino Americans obviously understand Latino cultures better than anyone, and they're more likely than others to have key connections in Latino communities. They can be of invaluable help in dealing with those markets, customers, suppliers, and other associates. Corporate representatives who can speak the language and know the customs offer the company a valuable competitive edge.

SUMMARY

About one in eight Americans is a Latino American. This is the fastest growing minority group because of immigration and fertility rates. Myths and stereotypes center around traditional roles as menial workers, emotional temperaments, and the tendency to be perceived as passive or docile. The large majority are Mexican Americans who live primarily in the Southwest, followed by Puerto Rican Americans in the New York area, and Cuban Americans in Florida. New immigrants usually have a language barrier, are young, and often have low educational achievement.

Latino American worldview values center around a closeness to the spirit world and a sense of destiny or fatalism. Only God knows, and death hovers around the other side of a thin veil, as do the spirits of those who have passed on. The Latino American worldview is built upon acceptance of a social hierarchy consisting of a few privileged elite and a mass of relatively powerless workers. Respect for superiors and a sense of distance between the elite and the masses is common. Emotions are honored and expressed, and the passion factor is important. The use of space is up close and personal in warm relationships with family, extended family, and business associates. Beliefs about time include the belief that the present moment is to be appreciated because the future is indefinite and unknown. Most Latino Americans immigrated because of their belief in the American Dream and are eager to integrate into the American culture while still honoring and preserving their core values and their love of the Spanish language.

Relationship values are the most important values for Latino Americans. Life centers around the family, including extended family, mutual dependence and undying loyalty are expected. *Simpatico* refers to getting along. Being agreeable, acquiescing to the wishes of others, especially those more powerful, and being courteous are all extremely important to promoting smooth social relations. Everything is translated into personal terms and personal relationships. In more formal relationships, Latino Americans tend to be reserved. Therefore, the idea that they're too emotional to hold leadership roles is mistaken. Machismo refers to male domination in male-female relationships, and the need for males to have a "manly" status with other men. This is changing along with changing work roles for men and women. In communicating, Latino Americans tend to speak indirectly, have a high concern for feelings, are highly sensitive to direct criticism, and make sure to acknowledge everyone when saying their hello's and goodbye's.

Current issues center around overcoming a tradition of segregation and discrimination—in workplaces, schools, and housing. Improving their educational opportunities and upgrading their knowledge and skill levels are crucial to achieving other goals. Improving their workplace status and overcoming employment discrimination is a critical issue. A recent issue is overcoming immigration backlash.

Mexican Americans are by far the largest Latino American group. Especially important to them are relationships, family ties, machismo, and ethnic loyalty. The Chicano movement brought attention to Mexican American issues, but most identify more with the American Dream than with the movement.

Puerto Rican Americans are the second largest Latino American group. Their growth rate slowed during the 1990s but still exceeds the total U.S. population. Educational attainment was significantly above the total Latino American figure, but poverty rates were the highest. Poverty is connected with the fact that one-third of Puerto Rican Americans live in female-headed households.

Cuban Americans, the third largest Latino American group, are a unique success story because many were business owners and professionals who immigrated to Florida to escape Fidel Castro's communist regime. They revitalized Miami with their skills and Latin American business contacts.

A major leadership challenge is meeting the cultural needs of Latino Americans, helping them to overcome workplace barriers to success. Needs include meeting family obligations, understanding the importance of sharing information and achieving job and company goals, learning how to turn conflict avoidance into conflict resolution, and learning how to deal with promotion anxiety.

Leadership opportunities include helping Latino Americans enhance work team relationships by building on their strengths of group loyalty, *personalismo* and *simpatico*. It includes helping them to express themselves assertively and to participate in group decision-making. Another opportunity is appealing to the honor, good name, and idealism of Latino Americans. Also important is showing respect for their values and issues. A major opportunity is encouraging Latino American employees to use their cultural knowledge and contacts to help the company capture new and expanding Latino markets—both in the United States and in Latino counties.

Skill Builder 9.1: The Case of New Manager Luis

Luis has been manager of the claims department for three months. He's on his way to the office of his immediate supervisor, *Gale*, for their monthly planning and evaluation session. Walking down the hall, his mind is filled with events of the past few months and what he wants to discuss with Gale.

When Luis applied for the management job, he had five years' experience with National Life Insurance. He had taken the screening exam for the new position and did well on both the written and oral portions. One of Luis' co-workers, *Richard*, also took the test and told Luis that he had done great on it.

Richard had come to National about a year before Luis and had trained Luis in some claims department procedures. Luis learned quickly and they soon had a friendly rivalry going. When their boss Gale was recruited from outside the company, Richard told Luis he heard it was because of pressure to place more women in higher positions. He said the company had recently gone through a government review of its affirmative action program and was found lacking. Richard said, "They brought Gale in mainly because she's a woman." Luis agreed with Richard at the time because he didn't really know the story and he didn't want to argue about it.

Four months ago, Richard told Luis that he really expected to get the claims department manager's job because he had such a good track record with the company and he also had more seniority than the other seven candidates. When Luis got the job, he became Richard's immediate supervisor. Luis felt uncomfortable giving Richard direction. He knew Richard was probably at least as well qualified as he to be boss. He worried about it quite a bit the first month. But he told himself that he must be the most qualified for the job; otherwise, he wouldn't have been selected.

During the second month, Luis noticed that Richard and several other employees seemed reluctant to follow his instructions. Luis attempted to meet them halfway by asking why they weren't doing certain things as he had directed, what they felt should be done, etc. Sometimes it seemed as if these few employees didn't take him seriously. He could see that efficiency and productivity were beginning to be affected by their resistance and balkiness. Time and time again Luis told himself that it would take time for his former co-workers to get used to him as their manager and for him to become adjusted to his new role and responsibilities.

Then just last week, Luis overheard a conversation in the lounge. Richard was talking with a co-worker and didn't realize Luis was in the next room:

I don't know about this affirmative action. Why would anyone want to use the past as a reason why they haven't gotten ahead educationally or economically? I think it's time we all stood up for ourselves and accomplish or fail on our own merit, instead of some people falling back on excuses. Why should we American males be discriminated against just because of past history? If people want everyone to be treated equally, then they can't be given an extra advantage at the same time. I know my test scores were higher than some of these people who are being promoted, but they get promoted anyway—just so some job-climbing administrator can brag about his political correctness and make his track record look good. Worst of all, it just amazes me that Luis actually thinks he deserved that promotion.

Luis was stunned at the time. He started thinking about the number of Latino Americans in company management. He could think of only one. Maybe Richard was right. Maybe he really wasn't qualified enough to handle the new job.

- What do you think are the major problems in this situation?
- If you were Luis, what would you do?
- If you were Gale, what would you do?

Skill Builder 9.2: The Case of Evelyn Sanchez, Supervisor

Evelyn Sanchez is a Customer Services Supervisor for Buckman's, a large mail order house. Her duties include making sure that work is distributed and completed under strict deadlines, approving certain transactions, and reviewing employee's work. She is required to set quarterly goals for herself and to train employees to cross-sell to customers in ways that meet their needs.

Evelyn's team includes ten employees of diverse backgrounds, including African American, Euro-American, Latino American, and Asian American. Most of the employees are bilingual. *Rosita*, a Latina American, is hired as a new member of Evelyn's team. One day when Evelyn stops by to check on how Rosita is doing, they lapse into speaking their native Spanish. *Ophelia*, an African American team member, is working nearby. She feels uncomfortable because she doesn't know what the two were saying. It's no big thing, and she tries to forget her discomfort. However, Evelyn comes by almost every day and has a brief conversation in Spanish with Rosita. Finally, Ophelia mentions her discomfort to Evelyn. She says, "I feel really left out when you two speak on and on in Spanish—and it keeps happening. I wish we could all speak the same language around here."

Evelyn replies, "Lighten up, Ophelia, we're not talking about you nor are we sharing secrets. We're just chatting, and it's good for our heart and soul to be able to converse in our beautiful *Castellano* now and then."

Ophelia becomes more disturbed each day as Evelyn and Rosita have their little Spanish conversations. She decides to complain to *Gene*, the general manager.

- What are the key issues here?
- If you were Gene, what would you do?

Skill Builder 9.3: The Case of Gino George, Sales Rep

Gino George, is a sales rep for Delcor, a telecommunications company. Five years ago he completed a degree in business administration and went to work in the finance department of Delcor as a junior accountant. He was the only Latino American in his department, and he got along well with his co-workers. He earned good performance reviews and merit increases and two years ago applied for and got the sales rep job.

Gino likes being a sales rep. He especially likes getting a commission on every sale he makes. Because he's a good salesperson, his salary is significantly higher than it was as an accountant. Gino is proud of the fact that he can help his Euro-American co-workers when they must deal with Spanish-speaking clients. In fact, Spanish-speaking clients have learned to ask for Gino, making him a valuable asset to Delcor.

On the other hand, being the only Latino American makes Gino feel somewhat isolated. For example, co-workers frequently "forget" to inform him of meetings or to invite him to group events. Few of them talk with him about anything outside of business matters.

Recently Gino was going over some files in the office. A couple of sales reps entered the adjacent cubicle and Gino overheard their conversation. Jeff said, "I heard that Dave's raising our sales quotas for the spring quarter. Business is always slow in the spring. How are we going to sell more than last year? If we don't meet that quota, we won't get our bonus." Ralph replied, "I think it's Gino's fault. He just gives Dave ideas. If he weren't such an eager beaver, Dave wouldn't start thinking that the rest of us should do better." "Yeah," said Jeff, "Any ideas on how we can send Gino back to the accounting department? Let him count beans!"

Gino is very upset by the news that his co-workers view his achievements so negatively. He hates being viewed as a trouble maker and difficult person. He decides to pull back on his sales efforts and to be satisfied with barely meeting his quotas.

Today Dave receives the news that he's being promoted and that he should recommend a replacement to take over his job. As Dave goes through the performance evaluations of all his team members, he narrows the choice down to Gino or Jeff.

Jeff has a high school diploma, experience as a salesperson with one other company, and has been with Delcor for three years as a sales rep. He gets along well with co-workers and is well accepted as "one of the gang."

Gino is better qualified, with his bachelors degree that includes technical expertise in the telecommunications field. He has been building a better track record as a sales rep than Jeff has, but the co-workers don't seem to be as receptive to him as they are to Jeff.

Dave calls Gino and Jeff into his office. He tells them that they're both in the running for the job and sets up times to interview each of them separately. Gino is concerned. He really wants the promotion, but he's worried about being accepted in the managerial role. On the other hand, if Jeff gets the job, he'll probably offer Gino little or no support and encouragement. He'll probably make it tough for Gino.

- What are the key issues in this situation?
- If you were Gino, what would you do?
- If you were Dave, what would you do?

REFERENCES

Aponte, Robert. "Urban Hispanic Poverty: Disaggregations and Explanations." *Social Problems* 38, November 1991, 516-529.

Bullock, Paul. "Employment Problems of the Mexican-American," in *Mexican Americans in the United States*. 1971.

Chronicle, San Francisco, "California Century" series, August 31, 1999, A-1.

Cohen, R. *Culture, Disease and Stress Among Latino Immigrants*. Washington, DC: Smithsonian Institution, 1979.

Condon, J. *Good Neighbors: Communicating with the Mexicans*. Yarmouth, ME: Intercultural Press, 1985.

Cox, Taylor. *Cultural Diversity in Organizations*. San Francisco: Berrett-Koehler, 1993.

Daniel, Clete. *Chicano Workers and the Politics of Fairness: The FEPC in the Southwest, 1941-1945*. Austin, TX: University of Texas Press, 1991.

De Freitas, Gregory. *Inequality at Work: Hispanics in the U.S. Labor Force*. NY: Oxford University Press, 1991.

Duncan, Mary Cheatham, "Hispanics and the American Workplace," www.unc.edu/courses/hnrs030/duncan.html, 2000

Forbes, Jack D. *The Chicano Worker*. Austin: University of Texas Press, 1977.

Gann, L.J., and Peter J. Duignan. *The Hispanics in the United States: A History*. Boulder, CO: Westview Press, 1986.

Grebler, L., et al. *The Mexican American People*. New York: Free Press, 1970.

Harris, Philip R., and Robert T. Moran. *Managing Cultural Differences*, 3d ed., and *Instructor's Guide*. Houston: Gulf, 1996.

Hero, Rodney. *Latinos and the U.S. Political System*. Philadelphia: Temple University Press, 1992.

Hofstede, Geert. *Culture's Consequences: International Differences in Work-Related Values*. Thousand Oaks, CA: Sage, 1980.

Lancaster, Roger N. *Life is Hard*. Berkeley, CA: University of California Press, 1993.

Landsberger, H.A., and A. Saavedra, "Response Set in Developing Countries," *Public Opinion Quarterly* 31, 1967, 214-229.

LeVine, E., and J.N. Franco, "A Reassessment of Self-Disclosure Patterns Among Anglo Americans and Hispanics," *Journal of Counseling Psychology* 28 (1981) 522-524.

Mannino, F.V., and M.F. Shore, "Perceptions of Social Support by Spanish-Speaking Youth with Implications for Program Development." *Journal of School Health*. 46, 1976, 471-474.

Marin, G., et al. "The Role of Acculturation on the Attitudes, Norms, and Expectancies of Hispanic Smokers." *Journal of Cross-Cultural Psychology*, 20, 1989, 399-415.

Marin, Gerardo, and Barbara VanOss Marin. *Research with Hispanic Populations*. Newbury Park, CA: Sage 1991.

McWilliams, Carey. *North from Mexico*. 1975.

Morales, Rebecca, and Frank Bonilla. *Latinos in a Changing U.S. Economy*. Thousand Oaks, CA: Sage, 1993.

Morrison, Ann. *The New Leaders*. San Francisco: Jossey-Bass, 1992.

Padilla, A.M. "The Role of Cultural Awareness and Ethnic Loyalty in Acculturation," in *Acculturation*. Boulder, CO: Westview, 1980.

Padilla, A.M., Ed. *Hispanic Psychology*. Thousand Oaks, CA: Sage, 1995.

Paternostro, Sylvana. *Land of God and Man: Confronting Our Sexual Culture*. New York: Dutton, 1999.

Paulette, Thomas. "In the Land of Bratwurst, a New Hispanic Boom," *Wall Street Journal*: A-1, March 15, 2000.

Polls: Latino National Political Survey, 1993; *Wall Street Journal-NBC*, 1993.

Ramirez, Henry M. "America's Spanish Speaking: A Profile." *Manpower*, September 1972, 33.

Ross, C.E., and J. Mirowsky. "Socially-Desirable Response and Acquiescence in a Cross-Cultural Survey of Mental Health." *Journal of Health and Social Behavior* 25, 1984, 189-197.

Santiago, Anne M., and Margaret G. Wilder, "Residential Segregation and Links to Minority Poverty: The Case of Latinos in the U.S." *Social Problems* 38 ,November 1991, 492-515.

Shorris, Earl. *Latinos*. New York: W.W. Norton Co., 1992.

Solorzano, Daniel G. "Mobility Aspirations Among Racial Minorities, Controlling for SES." *Social Science Review* 75 (July 1991): 182-189.

Triandis, H.C. "Role Perceptions of Hispanic Young Adults" *Journal of Cross-Cultural Psychology* 15 (1984a): 297-320.

Triandis, H.C., et al. "Simpatia as a Cultural Script of Hispanics." *Journal of Personality and Social Psychology* 47 (1984b): 1363-1375.

Triandis, H.C., et al. *Dimensions of Familism Among Hispanic and Mainstream Navy Recruits*. Chicago: University of Illinois, 1982.

U.S. Bureau of Labor Statistics, http://stats.bls.gov, 1999.

U.S. Census, Department of Commerce. *We the Hispanics* and *We the American Children*, 1993.

U.S. Census, Department of Commerce. *The Hispanic Population in the U.S.*, 2000.

U.S. Department of Education. *The Condition of Education*. Washington, DC: GPO, 1989.

U.S. Government reports: (1) David J. Saposs, "Report on Rapid Survey of Resident Latin American Problems and Recommended Program," Office of the Coordinator of Inter-American Affairs," in Reel 28, HQ Files, FEPC Records, April 3, 1942, 1. (2) "Spanish-Americans in the Southwest and the War Effort," in Reel 48, HQ Files, FEPC Records, June 1, 1941, 1. (3) "Report on the Spanish-Speaking Peoples in the Southwest," in Reel 70, HQ Files, FEPC Records, Field Survey March 14 to April 7, 1942, 13.

Valle, R., and C. Martinez, "Natural Networks Among Mexicano Elderly in the U.S." in *Chicano Aging and Mental Health*. Washington, DC: GPO, 1980.

Viviano, Frank. "Poll Contradicts Stereotypes." *San Francisco Chronicle* (March 27, 1990): A-1.

Weber, David (ed.). *Foreigners in Their Native Land: Historical Roots of the Mexican Americans*. Albuquerque, NM: 1973.

WSJ. Vargas, Alexia, "Split Decision," *Wall Street Journal*, November 19. 1999. A-1.

Zurcher, A.L., et al. "Value Orientation, Role Conflict, and Alienation from Work." *American Sociological Review* 30, 1965, 539-549.

Resources

Council of La Raza, a civil rights organization.

Hispanic Center for Corporate Response, Washington D.C.

StarMedia.com, a Web site serving Latinos worldwide.

CHAPTER 10

Working with Gay Persons

Gayness is not the illness; judgment is the illness.
Scott Stewart

Gay men, lesbians, and bisexuals, referred to collectively as gay persons, are often called the invisible minority because they don't *look* different from others in their ethnic group. About one in every 50 persons you work with is a gay person—2 percent, or 5 million Americans, according to the best estimates of researcher R. T. Michael and associates. However, if you work in a major metropolitan area, as many as one in every 10 to 20 persons you meet may be gay.

To become comfortable with gay associates, and in turn to build good working relationships with them, you need get a feel for their lifestyle, community values, and background. The more skilled you become at interpreting co-workers' actions against the backdrop of their lifestyle experiences, the greater your chances of working well together. The goal of this chapter is to help you understand what it's like to grow up gay and to be a gay person in today's workplace—according to scholars from that community. Keep an open mind and try to begin seeing situations as a gay person might view them. Specifically, you'll learn:

- How typical stereotypes about gay persons compare with reality
- How these myths have come about and how they impact people
- What it's like to grow up gay
- Key aspects of the gay community
- Recent findings about why some people are gay
- How people manage a gay identity in the workplace
- Legal rights gay persons do and do not have
- Barriers to career success for gay persons and how to break through those barriers
- Assets gay persons may bring to your organization and how to use those assets to create win-win successes

First, test your opinions and knowledge by completing Self-Awareness Activities 10.1 and 10.2.

Self-Awareness Activity 10.1: What Do You Believe about Gay Persons?

Purpose:

- to get in touch with your beliefs and stereotypes about this group of people
- to experience how judgmental beliefs affect your thinking and feeling processes
- to experience the ways in which your beliefs create your reality regarding other persons, even before you have any interaction with them

Part I. What Do You Believe about Lesbian Women?

Step 1. Associations

- Relax as deeply as you can: close your eyes and take a few deep breaths.
- Focus on the word "lesbian" and allow a mental picture to come up in your mind's eye. Imagine that you are this woman. Be lesbian woman.
- Notice your resistances to being this person, and your willingness.
- Notice the words and images that come to mind as you "see" this woman.
- Open your eyes and list 10 to 20 words in the order in which they occur to you.
- Review your list. Mark a plus beside the words that are positive, a minus beside the words that are negative, and a circle beside neutral words.

Step 2. Negative Associations

- Close your eyes and focus again on the image of the lesbian woman. Formulate a negative opinion or judgment, perhaps one you typically hold about lesbians.
- Notice your *feelings* as you see the person in this negative way. What *thoughts* come up as you focus on the image?
- Write a few sentences about your feelings and thoughts.

Step 3. Positive Associations

- Formulate a positive opinion or judgment, perhaps one you typically hold about lesbians.
- Notice your *feelings* as you see the person in this positive way. What *thoughts* come up as you focus on the image?
- Write a few sentences about your feelings and thoughts.

Step 4. Insights

- Focus on the differences between your experiences when you hold negative and positive judgments or opinions. What were the differences? What meaning does this have for you, for your beliefs and feelings about people from this group, and about beliefs in general?
- Write your responses in a few sentences; include anything you like about your feelings, thoughts, and insights.

Part II. Experimenting with Opinions about Gay Men

Repeat the phases and steps in part I, this time focusing on the image of a gay man.

Self-Awareness Activity 10.2: What Do You Know about Gay Persons?

Purpose: To see what you know about the issues covered in this chapter.

Instructions: Determine whether you think the following statements are basically true or false—and think about why. The answers will emerge in this chapter, and the summary at the end of the chapter focuses on these issues.

1. You can always tell gays by the way they act, dress, and talk.
2. Gay persons tend to influence young people to becoming gay.
3. The American Psychological Association takes the position that gays are mentally disturbed and need therapy.
4. With the proper therapy and motivation, gays can become heterosexual.
5. Boys raised by domineering mothers and weak or absent fathers usually become gay.
6. If a person has one or two sexual experiences with someone of the same sex, he or she is gay.
7. Most researchers conclude that gay persons are born with a gay orientation.
8. Gay persons are protected from workplace discrimination throughout the United States.

STEREOTYPES AND REALITIES

Gays must deal with some of the most vicious and degrading stereotypes and myths, and they probably suffer from more distorted or invalid stereotypes than any group. The effects are devastating, and antigay prejudice ranges from trivial snubs to violence. While most Americans still do not approve of a gay sexual orientation, they are against discrimination and for equal treatment in the workplace.

Many of the stereotypes reflect beliefs about outgroups in general, usually portraying outgroup members as both threatening and inferior to members of the dominant ingroup. Adam (1978) and others found that gays, African Americans, and Jews all are perceived as animalistic, hypersexual, over-visible, heretical, conspiratorial, and inclined to physical and mental disease.

Stereotype #1: Gays cluster in certain occupations.

Many people believe that gay men flock to the occupations of hair stylist, designer, dancer, and similar creative, "feminine" jobs. In fact, the gay men who happen to choose such occupations are more likely to come out for the simple reason that gays are more accepted in those jobs. Meanwhile, people are unaware of the gay men in the more masculine occupations because most stay in the closet in order to survive. Evidence suggests that gays and lesbians do not cluster in a few occupations but are found in a wide range of different occupations as diverse as the general population. A survey of 4,000 gay persons found more gay men and women in science and engineering than in social services; 40 percent more in finance and insurance than in entertainment and arts, 10 times (1,000%) more in computers than in fashion [Fortune 1992]. The true part of this myth is that some gay employees feel forced to cluster in certain jobs or departments because they feel safe there and unsafe in other, perhaps more appropriate, areas (McNaught 1993).

Stereotype #2: People who associate with gays are probably gay themselves.

This belief is sometimes called "courtesy stigma" or stigma by association. When heterosexuals associate with gays, only to be suspected of being gay themselves, they may respond with anger or they may back off. Courtesy stigma, therefore, can create barriers to gays' establishing the support networks and mentor relationships they need for career success. It can block competent researchers from addressing gay issues because of the tendency of the general public to assume that heterosexuals would not be interested in these topics. Closet gays' reaction to courtesy stigma is frequently fear of disclosure and thus avoidance of association with other gays.

Stereotype #3: Gays in sensitive or high-level jobs are a security risk.

This stereotype is downright vicious in its impact. No evidence has appeared to support the belief that gay persons represent an increased security risk. But the myth persists in this form: Gay employees try to keep their homosexuality a secret; therefore, they are easy blackmail targets for con artists and spies, which in turn makes them a security risk, so they shouldn't be hired or promoted into sensitive or high-level jobs. Author G. Herek reasons that if this were true, the fair solution would be to remove the stigma from homosexuality and protect them from discrimination, not to use the "potential blackmail target" rationale for inflicting further discrimination (Herek 1993). In 1995 President Clinton signed an executive order barring the use of this criterion for personnel decisions involving placement of federal employees.

Stereotype #4: Gay persons don't have normal, lasting relationships.

This stereotype depicts gay persons as people drift from one sexual liaison to another, ending up alone when they're old. Studies indicate that most gay persons very much want to have enduring, close relationships and many do. Between 40 and 60 percent of gay men are currently involved in a steady relationship, and between 45 and 80 percent of gay women are so involved. In fact 75 percent of gay women are so involved according to most studies. The few studies that have included older gay persons have found that relationships lasting 20 years or more are not uncommon.

Research also indicates there are no significant differences between heterosexual and gay persons on any of the measures of relationship satisfaction. Further, when couples were asked the best things and worst things about their relationships, researchers found no significant differences in the responses of gay and heterosexual couples, all of whom reported a similar range of joys and problems. The point is not that all gay couples are happy and problem-free but that they are not any more prone to relationship dissatisfactions and difficulties than are heterosexual couples.

Another aspect of this myth is that gay persons don't have normal relationships with friends and therefore don't have strong support networks. While they do experience psychological stress from social rejection and stigma, most have made significant progress in overcoming these obstacles and creating rich, satisfying social networks. Overall levels of support received by gay men and women were similar to and slightly higher than those reported for heterosexual men and women (Peplau 1991).

Stereotype #5: Gay men act feminine and lesbians act masculine.

Most heterosexuals believe that gay persons possess the characteristics of their opposite sex. They also believe the reverse side of the coin, that men who act feminine are likely to be gay and women who act masculine are likely to be lesbian. In fact, gayness itself does not establish the types of sexual roles and behavior people will adopt. The expression of sexuality is diverse and functions along a continuum, rather than in an either/or manner. To refute the myth we can recall how the late film star Rock Hudson shocked the world when he came out, especially the women fans who idolized him as the essence of masculine attractiveness.

A conflicting stereotype is that gay partners take on clear husband and wife roles, which seems unlikely if both gay male partners act feminine, and likewise if both lesbian partners act masculine. In fact, masculine-feminine roles have sometimes been important in the past, but in recent years gender-linked roles have sharply declined. In fact, most gay couples today actively reject traditional husband-wife or masculine-feminine roles as a model for enduring relationships. Most are in dual-earner relationships, with neither member the exclusive breadwinner and each having some economic independence. Any specialization of activities is based on individual skills or interests rather than sex-role stereotyping. While many partners report that there is some sense of a masculine-feminine or husband-wife fit, it's subtle. The most common relationship pattern is the friendship model that emphasizes companionship, sharing, and equality.

Stereotype #6: Gay sex is immoral and gay persons are promiscuous.

This is a religious or philosophical belief and therefore cannot be rationally proved or disproved. Constitutional rights concerning the separation of church and state provide some protection in the legal system and in the workplace against discrimination based on such personal beliefs.

A percentage of the population engages in promiscuous sex, at least during a certain phase of their life, regardless of sexual orientation. The sexual behavior of gay persons who are in the closet, especially married persons, usually stems from their fear of discovery and the resulting need for secrecy and anonymity.

Related to the belief that gay sex is immoral is the belief that AIDS is God's punishment for gay persons. In fact, anyone can contract AIDS; it just happened to gain a foothold in the gay community first. Ignorance about the disease has led to the myth that people who come into contact with gay persons are exposing themselves to AIDS. However, AIDS can only be contracted through sexual intercourse or through the bloodstream. Therefore, casual contact in the workplace is not a threat.

Stereotype #7: Gay persons are a bad influence on children.

The extreme form of this belief is that gay persons are sexual perverts and therefore tend to be child molesters. Scientific studies have repeatedly disproven this stereotype. Each year a few straight and gay persons are convicted of child molestation, and sexual orientation is not a factor.

One aspect of this myth is the idea that gay men are looking for very young men and boys as partners. Research indicates that a majority of gay men aged 18 to 24 prefer a male partner who is older, a majority of those aged 25 to 34 prefer a same-age person, and of those older than 35 about half prefer a younger partner. It was found that the degree of emphasis on youthful partners varied with the social setting and reflected the diversity of the gay community. It also probably reflects the tendency of older men in the larger American culture to prefer younger partners (Harry and DeVall 1992).

Another fear is that gay persons will influence children and youth to become gay. This false fear is the basis for trying to bar gay persons from becoming teachers, counselors, and youth group leaders—and to deny gay parents their child custody rights. Since the preponderance of evidence suggests that sexual orientation is fixed by biology early in life, this myth has no basis in fact nor experience. No evidence exists that a gay teacher or parent could convert a child, even if he or she tried.

Related to the "bad influence" myth is the belief that gay persons shouldn't be allowed to raise children. Until recently courts routinely denied parental rights to gay persons. Some judges have based their decisions on the rationale that such children would be teased and stigmatized by other children and adults. Chief Justice Burger once said that the Constitution "cannot control such prejudices but neither can it tolerate them. Private biases may be outside the reach of the law, but the law cannot, directly or indirectly, give them effect" (Palmore 1985 p. 62).

Related myths about lesbians as parents include:

- They don't care for children in maternal ways
- They hate men and deny their children access to positive male role models
- Their lesbianism is a sort of illness that makes them unfit to be parents

New ideas about family life have opened up the idea of gay persons having an active family life that includes children. Research on gay parents clearly indicates that their lives are remarkably like those of heterosexual parents. Far more similarities than differences are found. Studies indicate that lesbian mothers do not differ significantly from heterosexual mothers in maternal attitude, self-concept as parents, attitude toward marital and maternal interests, current lifestyles, and child rearing practices. Lesbian mothers are more likely than heterosexual mothers to be child-centered (as compared to adult centered or task centered). There is no evidence that a lesbian mother is more likely to negatively influence her child's development, nor that the child is more likely to become gay.

What's in a Name? The American Psychological Association's (APA) Committee on Lesbian and Gay Concerns in 1991 adopted the following guidelines for terminology recommended to psychologists:

- *gay male* and *lesbian* rather than *homosexual*
- *gay persons* when referring to lesbians and gay men as a group
- *antigay prejudice* instead of *homophobia*.
- *bisexual* when referring to persons attracted to both same-sex and opposite-sex partners

The term *homophobia* is still used by many persons when referring to prejudice and discrimination against gay persons. Homophobia originally meant an irrational fear of same-sex eroticism, an appropriate use of the term. But in the 1970s it came to mean a fear or dread of gay persons, a prejudice against gay persons, or a general intolerance and disapproval of gay persons. The term *phobia* is not descriptive of such emotions.

PAST CONNECTIONS

During the past 50 years beliefs about gay persons have rapidly evolved from "They're mentally ill sexual deviants whose lifestyle is depraved and illegal" to "They have a right to express their sexual orientation and most are solid citizens." Antigay prejudice is more common among certain segments of the population than others, and it negatively impacts both the holders and receivers of the prejudice.

Milestones in History

Here are some key events in gay history.

- 1952 American Psychological Association (APA) classifies gayness as a mental illness rather than a choice to be "sexually perverted" and "depraved."
- 1969 Stonewall riots and first Gay Power meeting, New York.
- 1970 Gay pride parade in New York attracts 10,000 gay persons.
- 1973 APA announces that homosexuality is no longer considered a mental illness.
- 1990 APA states that gay persons cannot change their sexual orientation. They can choose to suppress it but pay a high price emotionally and psychologically. That choice is virtually always based on self-hate internalized from the culture.
- 1982 Gay Games are founded.
- 1992 President Clinton issues an executive order ending "gay security risk" as a rationale for personnel decisions and proposes removing the military's ban on gay persons.
- 1997 Ellen DeGeneres comes out.

Stonewall: A Turning Point

Stonewall refers to four days of gay riots that occurred in New York in response to a routine police raid on a Greenwich Village gay bar called Stonewall Inn. Since then, Stonewall has become the symbol of gay resistance to oppression and gay empowerment around the world. To gay persons, it marks the birth of the modern gay political movement, "that moment in time when gays and lesbians recognized all at once their mistreatment and their solidarity," in Martin Duberman's words.

From Extremism to Reformism

Within months after Stonewall, a liberation movement emerged. Gay persons formed the Gay Activists Alliance, the Gay Liberation Front, and the Gay Academic Union—and other organizations sprang up later. Liberationists were political extremists who wanted to radically change American culture by changing or eliminating common concepts of gender and sexual orientation. They viewed "coming out of the closet," in which their sexual orientation had been hidden from public view, as an intermediate step in a process of releasing the ambisexual potential in everyone. They said that antigay prejudice is just heterosexuals' rejection of their own latent homosexuality or homosexual desires. Liberationists declared that for heterosexuals to move beyond such prejudice, they needed to confront their own sexuality. In summary, liberationists said to heterosexuals, All persons can go either way, gay or straight, and your rejection and fear of gayness are rooted in your denial that this is true for you. As a matter of fact, scientific research results since the 1970s have not supported the viewpoint that everyone is potentially bisexual.

Most gay persons came to see the liberationists as enraged persons lashing out at all straights, overreacting to the pain and rejection they had experienced as gay persons. Most gay persons were more attuned to the reformist movement. Reformists adopted a strategy of minority group politics that envisions gay persons as members of a subculture with its own needs, goals, and interests that deserve to be recognized and met within the larger culture. A major goal is protection from employment discrimination. Reformists view heterosexuals' antigay prejudice as a rejection of members of an outgroup, similar to ethnic prejudice. Change involves challenging heterosexuals' misconceptions about gay persons and prejudice toward them.

Cultural Breakthroughs

Gays have historically been rejected in all types of male competitive sports. The Gay Games was founded in 1982 in San Francisco as a gay alternative to the Olympics and has been held every four years since. By 1998, when the games were held in Amsterdam, over 15,000 competitors performed before 200,000 visitors (Associated Press 1998).

In 1997 Ellen DeGeneres, the girl-next-door comedian, came out as a lesbian and launched a sitcom television show in which she played the openly lesbian lead role. Gay rights groups hailed it as a turning point in American pop culture.

CURRENT PROFILE

In the past almost no one would admit to being gay, for obvious reasons, so accurate demographic information was impossible to gather. We know more now about how many gays there are and what their lives are like.

The 2 Percent Estimate

The Kinsey studies of sexuality in the 1950s indicated that gays were perhaps 10 percent of the population, but these statistics are now questioned. A recent extensive and well-respected survey indicates that:

- 2.8 percent of men are gay
- 1.5 percent of women are gay
- 2.15 percent of all persons are gay

This proportion of gay persons holds true for all ethnic groups, economic categories, social classes, age groups, and other demographic categories.

Higher Educational Levels and Jobs

By the 1990s research by Beverly Green and G.M. Herek indicated that as a group, out-of-the-closet gays are highly educated and function effectively in responsible, well-paid occupations. They achieve significantly higher educational levels than the population at large. About 60 percent hold college degrees, compared with about 20 percent of the total population. Significantly more of them hold well-paying professional jobs and jobs that require creativity and innovation.

Lower Pay for Comparable Work

Researcher Dr. Lee Badgett reported on a nation-wide poll found that gay men's wages were 27% lower than wages received by straight men of the same race and region who had comparable educational attainment and job positions. Badgett explored the pervasive notion that gay persons form an economic elite. After examining data from seven different surveys, she finds that none support this stereotype.

THE NATURE AND IMPACT OF ANTIGAY PREJUDICE

Antigay prejudice is the key barrier to gay persons being accepted in society. It affects every aspect of their lives. To understand antigay prejudice, you need to know why people prejudge gay persons, which people are likely to be most prejudiced, and the effects it has—on those who prejudge as well as on gay persons.

Why Are People Prejudiced?

Reasons for prejudice against gay persons include:

- I believe in traditional gender and sex roles and feel threatened by gay couples.
- A man should act like a real man, and a woman should act like a real woman.
- I feel uncomfortable with gay persons. I'm not sure what to say or how to act.
- Maybe they'll come on to me.
- Maybe they'll be jealous if I'm friends with a same-sex person they're attracted to.
- Maybe I'll get AIDS by being around them.
- I have to show disapproval of gays so people will know for sure I'm not one.
- Lesbians believe women don't need men. That really bothers me.

Who Is Likely to Be Prejudiced?

People with antigay attitudes are more likely than others to have the following characteristics:

- male, older, less well educated
- reside in rural areas, the Midwest, or the South
- don't personally know a gay person
- describe themselves as high in assertiveness and low in "feminine" traits
- members of a conservative religious denomination
- strongly religious

G. M. Herek's research indicates that the major predictor of whether a church member will harbor antigay prejudice is whether or not the church has a fundamentalist orientation. A major aspect of fundamentalism is a literal interpretation of the Bible. For example, when discussing beliefs about gay persons, church leaders and members tend to focus on Bible passages that they believe condemn homosexuality. Critics argue that such interpretations ignore other core Biblical values, such as *"judge not that you be not judged," " love your neighbor as you love yourself,"* and *"do unto others as you would have them do unto you."* Others charge that Biblical interpretations vary widely, passages can be taken out of context, and almost anything can be proved by quoting the Bible.

What Does Antigay Prejudice Do to People?

The picture of prejudice is not pretty. When gay persons are excluded, ridiculed, or assaulted due to antigay prejudice, the impact on their lives can range from the mild to the devastating, from difficulty adapting to the workplace culture to deep psychological damage. The people who hold onto antigay prejudice are affected too. They typically experience more guilt, discomfort, and a draining away of joy than do less prejudiced people, according to research by M.D. Kite and K. Deaux. And they can cause conflict and discomfort for straight coworkers who view gayness as normal in a certain segment of the population.

> *Prejudiced person's thinking patterns tend to block their own happiness and zest for life—holding onto prejudice creates a joy drain.*

Is Antigay Prejudice Decreasing?

National opinion surveys suggest that people's attitudes toward civil rights for gay persons are often independent of moral judgments about homosexuality. Even though the gay lifestyle is unacceptable to 53 percent of Americans, according to a 1992 Gallup poll, Herek (1991) reported that most agree that gay persons should have equal employment opportunities and free speech rights. Other research indicates that about half the people would be uncomfortable working with gay persons and from 35 to 45 percent would be comfortable (Roper 1987; *Los Angeles Times* 1985).

One research study that tested people for level of prejudice and tolerance indicated that both tolerant and intolerant persons are usually willing to *meet* a gay person, though the intolerant ones were uncomfortable working with gay persons. About half the gay persons in a 1989 poll said they have experienced some form of discrimination because they're gay. But 85 percent of straight people don't even know that in 40 states it's currently legal to fire a gay person based solely on sexual orientation (Greenburg 1996). Table 10.1 indicates how people's attitudes toward certain gay rights, including employment rights, are becoming more accepting.

TABLE 10.1: Increasing Public Acceptance of Gay Rights

	1977	*1985*	*1989*	*1998–9*
For equal rights for gay persons	56%	59%	71%	83%
Against equal rights for gays	33%	28%	18%	20%
For guaranteed equal treatment under the law in jobs and housing	60%	66%		75%
Against guaranteed equal treatment under the law in jobs and housing	28%	22%		
For hiring gays as elementary teachers	27%		42%	61%
For allowing gays in the clergy	36%		44%	
For allowing gays in the military	51%		60%	70%
For allowing gays as doctors	44%		56%	75%

Source: Herek 1991; Cahill 2000.

WHAT'S IT LIKE TO GROW UP GAY?

Growing up gay usually involves a process of gradually becoming aware of gayness. In virtually all phases, gay persons must deal with the damage to self-esteem caused by rejection and prejudice.

Living through the Phases of Gay Awareness

Virtually all gay persons go through four distinct phases of dealing with their sexual orientation.

Stage #1—Denying

In the past most gay persons denied their gayness because of its devastating consequences. This involves blocking the recognition of same-sex feelings in a variety of ways. Some maintain these defensive strategies indefinitely and hold back their same-sex feelings, consuming huge amounts of psychological energy in the process. Those in denial usually marry and have children, making a valiant effort to fit into a straight world.

Stage #2—Recognizing

Most openly gay persons say they first became aware of same-gender attraction before adolescence. In fact, nearly half of gay men say they were sexually attracted to males before they learned there were such sexual relations in the adult world. Gay adolescents who overcome denial will begin, by stages, to gradually tolerate the fact that they're having significant same-sex feelings.

Stage #3—Experimenting

Next comes a phase of experimenting with same-sex feelings and activities. Some gay persons increasingly feel that same-sex feelings are normal for them. Obviously, parents and society don't socialize children to be gay, and gay youngsters are not prepared to deal with antigay prejudice and the wounding of self-esteem.

Stage #4—Accepting and Coming Out

The coming out process represents a shift in the person's core sexual identity and may trigger intense emotional distress. Denial of same-sex feelings may recur from time to time, but as they begin to accept their same-sex feelings, they develop a sense of identity as gay persons. Ideally, this gay identity is successfully integrated and accepted as a positive aspect of who they are. Those who are able to accept their sexual orientation and "come out," usually join gay support networks and have access to healing acceptance within the gay community. Studies indicate that gay persons who are more open about their sexual orientation have higher levels of self-esteem and psychological well-being.

Dealing with Antigay Bias

A study of 4,159 high school students found that students who identified themselves as gay, lesbian, or bisexual are:

- More than four times as likely to have been threatened with a weapon at school.
- Nearly five times more likely to have been absent from school because of safety concerns.
- Three times more likely to have attempted suicide in the past year.
- Twice as likely to engage in risky behavior—such as having unsafe sex or using drugs before age 13. About 50 percent of gay students said they had engaged in more than five forms of risky behavior, compared to less than 25 percent of straight students.

The study was commissioned in 1998 by the National Centers for Disease Control and Prevention.
Gay rights organizations have been facing the issue of how to protect gay youth whose schoolmates attack them verbally or physically. Legal ground is being carved out to help gay students, using

constitutional claims to equal protection as well as Title IX of the Civil Rights Act, which is the main law against sex discrimination and sexual harassment. Parents of abused gay youths are beginning to file lawsuits, and school districts that have not made a good faith effort to stem the problem are being held liable. Two states, Massachusetts and California, have passed specific laws to protect such students from harassment.

Dealing with the Damage to Self-Esteem

Most gay persons are socialized in a middle-class environment, yet the adoption of middle-class values traps them in antigay prejudice. Becoming aware of their gayness inevitably means their self-esteem is wounded. All around them, gay teenagers see their straight friends' sexuality being anticipated, embraced, and cultivated, while their own sexuality is not. Dating, becoming engaged, marrying, and having children hold joyous implications for others, but not for them. The result of this devaluation and neglect is often a sense of loss: loss of self-esteem, loss of initiative, and loss of the belief that they're entitled to a full life.

When gay persons use the closet as a long-term survival tool, they lose the spontaneity we all need for authenticity in relationships. The constant pressure to conceal parts of the self and the constant dread of being found out creates stress. Coming out is a great relief for gay persons, but the downside is facing direct antigay prejudice. This can lead to lower self-esteem, self-rejection, and new types of stressors. The major way most gay persons handle this is by joining the gay community and building support networks.

WHAT'S THE GAY COMMUNITY ALL ABOUT?

Gay persons who come out of the closet tend to migrate to gay communities in major metropolitan areas. Gay persons within this community have as wide a variety of lifestyles as the rest of the population. They have close friends in support networks that loosely form a gay community, as well as straight friends and associates outside the community. Singles may frequent a gay bar scene, while couples tend to focus on their relationships and sometimes on parenting roles.

The Gay Community

The gay community consists of many distinctive groups. Friendship binds the members of each group together in strong, ongoing relationships. Couple relationships may be stable and long-lasting. Noncouple members may be linked within the group and between groups by tenuous but repeated sexual contacts or by supportive friendships. As a result of these bonds and their relatively small numbers, gay persons within a city tend to know of each other. They have a number of common interests, values, and customs. Such communities have links to each other across the country and even internationally.

Most openly gay persons function in two cultures—the larger culture and the gay community—and may be considered bicultural. Most spend at least half their leisure time with other gay persons. A common pattern is to have two sets of friends, one straight and the other gay. Ethnic minorities who are gay have even more complexities to deal with.

Support Networks

Forming community with other gay persons is an important part of self-acceptance. For gay persons, it relieves their sense of being uniquely different and allows them to jointly form a set of beliefs about sexuality that counter the negative beliefs of the dominant culture. The main function of a gay community or group is psychological, to provide a social environment of acceptance and support, which gay persons cannot find elsewhere.

Gay Couples

A steady couples relationship is claimed by about half of gay men and three-fourths of lesbians, and many establish lifelong partnerships as they mature. Within the gay community, couple relationships are given a status similar to that of marriage. The two partners are sexually available to each other on a continuing basis, expect that the relationship will be relatively long-lasting, and present themselves as a social couple. Being out of the closet makes this possible. In fact, the gay promiscuity stereotype stems from the fact that being in the closet means one must indulge in secret sex whenever the opportunity presents itself.

Gay Parents

Many gay persons have married in hopes of overcoming or curing their gayness and having a "normal" life with children. Why would gay married persons later accept their gayness and come out of the closet? The most common reason is falling in love with a same-sex person. Once this happens, the married gay person tends to move from a covert, highly compartmentalized lifestyle, with all the surface appearances of suburban married life, toward an openly gay life. Divorce is a part of this movement, but most retain a commitment to their children and responsibility for them to the extent that the courts will allow.

In some states gay persons may adopt children. Regardless of how they become parents, almost all gay parents report that their children are straight and are typical for kids of their age and gender. Most have positive relationships with their children, try harder to create a stable home life and are more egalitarian, but otherwise are basically the same as straight parents, according to studies by T.S. Weisner, J.E. Wilson-Mitchell, and others.

Community Issues

Five issues that are especially important to the gay community:

1. How people think of gayness: are you born with it or do you choose it?
2. How to counter the myths and stereotypes that result in anti-gay prejudice
3. How to gain equal rights in the legal system—workplace rights, military rights, partnership rights, and parenting rights.
4. How to become accepted in the workplace, to come out of the closet
5. How to manage a gay identity in the workplace, once out of the closet

ARE PEOPLE BORN GAY OR STRAIGHT?

Whether people are born gay or choose a gay lifestyle is perhaps the most crucial issue in the gay community's political struggle for equal legal rights. The major groups that are attempting to block gay political efforts use the rationale that homosexuality is learned and chosen. That belief supports their religious belief that homosexuality is a perversion and a sin against God and family values. They say gay persons therefore need counseling to help them become heterosexual or to abstain from sex altogether. The gay community vigorously refutes this viewpoint and sees it as their major barrier to achieving equal rights.

Recent scientific findings indicate that genes and hormonal events prior to birth are instrumental in establishing sexual orientation, though people can and do choose to experiment. You can better understand sexual orientation by seeing it as one of the layers of human sexuality, by seeing each sexual quality in terms of a continuum rather than in either-or terms. This will help you assess the arguments offered by nature theorists, who believe that genes and hormones are the primary determiners of sexual orientation, and compare them with arguments of nurture theorists, who believe people learn to be gay and/or choose that orientation.

Sexual Factors: How Deep and to What Degree?

Sexuality is most realistically viewed as having five layers of depth, the deeper layers being more innate, an unchanging part of us, and the superficial layers being potentially changeable, as shown in Figure

10.1. All sexual factors can also be expressed in relative degrees of intensity, from slightly-to-very male or female, slightly-to-very gay or straight, etc. (Seligman 1994; Gonsiorek and Weinrich 1991; Gonsiorek and Rudolph 1991; Haldeman 1991).

FIGURE 10.1: Layers of Depth in Sexuality

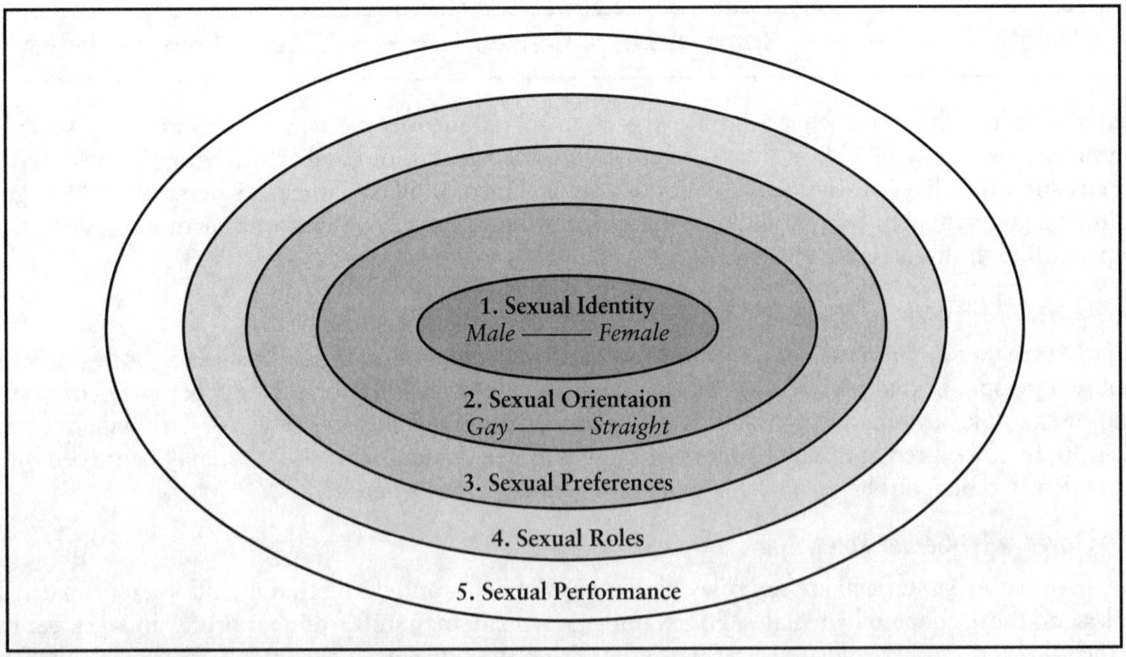

1. Sexual Identity
Male ——— Female

2. Sexual Orientaion
Gay ——— Straight

3. Sexual Preferences

4. Sexual Roles

5. Sexual Performance

Based on the work of J.C. Gonsiorek and J.R. Rudolph, 1991.

Layer #1—Sexual Identity: Male to Female

The deepest, core layer refers to whether we identify ourselves as male, female, or transsexual. Scientists describe the miniscule proportion of persons who are transsexual as men or women who are physically indistinguishable from average men or women but who believe they're trapped in the body of the wrong sex. Some of them choose to have sex-change operations and do in fact change their sexual identity from male to female or vice versa. On the other hand, for nearly all persons, sexual identity, being male or female, is the least changeable aspect of their sexuality.

All our forms and questionnaires offer only two gender choices: male or female. But we all know some people who seem extremely masculine or feminine and others who seem much less so. On the sexual identity continuum, people who are extremely masculine or feminine would fall at either end, with many people in between and transsexuals at the center, as shown in Figure 10.2. Being male or female, then, is not simply an either-or situation.

FIGURE 10.2: Continuum of Sexual Identity

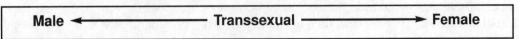

Male ◄——————— Transsexual ———————► Female

Layer #2—Sexual Orientation: Gay to Straight

Wrapped around the core sexual identity layer is sexual orientation, meaning who turns us on—men, women, or both. A very small proportion are described as bisexual. Some bisexuals may be attracted to both men and women; others to either a man or a woman at any one time frame of their life.

We say a person is either gay or straight. But some people are more confirmed in their gayness than others. The Institute for Sex Research devised a seven-point scale to represent the *continuum of homosexuality*, with 0 indicating exclusive heterosexuality, 4 or 5 predominant homosexuality, and 6 or 7 exclusive homosexuality. On the sexual orientation continuum, the large majority of the population is at the straight end. At the gay end are 2.15 percent who are exclusively gay. In between are bisexuals and people who have had some gay experiences. For example, nearly one-third of all men, and about 10 percent of all women, report they have had overt same-sex experiences, most during their adolescent years.

FIGURE 10.3: Continuum of Sexual Orientation

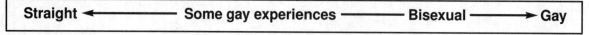

Sexual orientation is somewhat more flexible than sexual identity. Some straights are "less straight" than others and may be able to "choose" a gay orientation, although nearly all gay persons say that in retrospect they have always been gay and it's not a choice. Similarly, some gay persons are "less gay" than others and switch to a straight sexual orientation after they've had one or more gay relationships, although this is relatively rare.

Layer #3—Sexual Preferences: What Turns a Person On

Moving away from the core, we find the particular types of scenes, fantasies, or body parts that arouse a person. Sexual preferences can and do change more readily than the deeper layers of sexuality. For example, a woman, when she's 20, may be turned on sexually by men with dark hair, but when she's 30, men with red hair may be more attractive to her. A man, when he's 20, may be turned on by dependent women, but he may prefer more independent types when he's 30.

Layer #4—Sexual Roles

Even more superficial are sex roles, those ways of being and doing that are adopted primarily by males and those adopted by females. For example, a woman may shift from her professional career role to the wife and mother role as she returns home from the office each evening. A man may shift from football coach to family cook when he returns home.

Layer #5—Sexual Performance

At the most superficial layer we find the different ways that people behave when the time seems right for making love. Both men and women may choose from many behaviors that they think will make love-making more exciting or satisfying or comforting, for example. People can and do vary these behaviors regularly—from the way they flirt to the way they help their partner reach fulfillment.

The Causes of Sexual Orientation: Genes and Hormones

Back to the major issue, now, of whether some people are born gay or choose to be gay. To begin with, how can we explain the fact that gays are found in every society even though no known society socializes children into a homosexual role? None has ever set up gay role models. For example, American parents, after years of teaching their little boys about male sex-ways and their little girls about female sex-ways, have traditionally been shocked and disappointed upon learning their child is gay.

If persons are not socialized into the role of homosexual, it doesn't seem likely that they *choose* their sexual orientation. If this is true, then persons who are predominantly gay can no more *will* themselves to become straight than straight persons can will themselves to become gay.

The idea that gayness is fixed before birth and is biologically based is the prominent belief among scholars today. Some research indicates a genetic basis for homosexuality. Other research points toward hormonal influences before birth.

Genes

Scientists have detected a "gay gene," as reported by Dean Hamer of the National Cancer Institute. They do not claim that it is solely responsible for gayness, nor that any gene can dominate any behavior trait. They are saying that genes influence behavior through indirect and complex paths that require inputs from the physical body, the environment, and the culture.

Gayness in Identical Twins and Siblings

Studies of the sexual orientation of identical twins point to a genetic basis for gayness, according to J.M. Bailey. Since identical twins occur when the mother's egg divides after conception, these twins begin life with identical genetic material. If gayness occurred only because of one or more "gay genes," then theoretically every identical twin who is gay would have a gay sibling. Actually, about half of those who are gay have a twin who is also gay. This indicates that gayness is not entirely genetic. On the other hand, if genes played no part, we would expect that only 2 percent of gay twins would have a gay sibling because that's the incidence of gay persons in the general population. The fact that about 50 percent of gay identical twins have a gay sibling makes a strong case for the important role that genes must play in determining sexual orientation.

Hormones

Hormones secreted in the mother's womb during pregnancy affect the hormone balance of the child and whether that child will eventually be sexually attracted to opposite-sex or same-sex persons, according to researcher Martin Seligman.

Other Clues

Scientists looking for physical clues to sexual orientation have examined everything from finger length to left-handedness to inner ear structure. Berkeley psychologist S. Marc Breedlove has concluded that differences in finger lengths are correlated to a prenatal basis for sexual orientation. Lesbians on average have a more masculine finger length pattern than straight women, reports Breedlove, indicating that they were exposed to more fetal androgen. Dr. Ray Blanchard of Toronto found a tendency toward left-handedness in gay subjects. Some scientists have found differences in the inner ears of lesbian and straight women.

Bottom Line: Human sexuality is complex, and scientists don't know yet how all the factors interact to produce a person's sexual orientation.

The Nature–Nurture Controversy

In 1998 President Clinton issued an executive order forbidding discrimination against gay persons in the federal workforce. Republican members of Congress began an immediate campaign to pass legislation that would undermine this order.

Full page ads began running in newspapers throughout the country. They were sponsored by a dozen or so church and family organizations and quoted Republican Senate majority leader Trent Lott's statement that homosexuality is a sin. The ads urged gay persons to change their sexual orientation (Paid Ad 1998). The Ex-Gay Movement was born.

A *Newsweek* poll (Leland 1998) reveals that most people view gayness as much more flexible than do gay persons themselves, as shown in Table 10.1.

TABLE 10.1: Contrast in Gay-Straight Beliefs about Nature-Nurture

Agreed with the statement:	Overall Population	Gay Respondents
Homosexuality is something people are born with, not the result of upbringing or environmental influences.	33%	75%
Gay men and lesbians can change their sexual orientation through therapy, willpower, or religious conviction	45%	11%

Dr. Robert Spitzer, a Columbia University psychiatrist, conducted a telephone survey of 200 gay persons who claimed to have achieved a change to heterosexual attraction that had lasted at least five years. Asked why they wanted to change their sexual orientation, the large majority, 80 percent, cited both religious conflict and lack of emotional satisfaction from the gay lifestyle. Also about two-thirds of the men and one-third of the women wanted to get or stay married. Their main indication of success in the changeover was a lower frequency of looking at same-sex persons with desire. Still, nearly a third of the men said this still occurs at least a few times a month. About 66 percent of the men and 44 percent of the women said they had "good heterosexual functioning" in the past year (Spitzer 2001). Critics countered that these statistics do not reflect a change in sexual orientation: changing one's behavior because of social pressure does not equal permanent change.

MANAGING A GAY IDENTITY IN THE WORKPLACE

A central career focus for gay persons is managing their sexual identity. Gays who are in the closet must deal with the stress of "living a lie," while gays who come out must deal with people's reactions, according to author R. Rich and others.

Gays in the Closet

Most gays stay in the closet. About 76 percent of gay men and 81 percent of lesbians who participated in a study said that they conceal their sexuality at work (Senate 1994). For those who haven't come out, vigilance is constant. They must devote great energy to pretending they have a lifestyle they don't or avoiding the lifestyle issue altogether. The fear of disclosure is ever present, resulting in anxiety and stress.

Counterfeiting a Straight Identity

How do gay persons manage to stay in the closet without raising suspicion? Many create fictitious spouses or opposite-sex lovers. Some complain about their status as a confirmed single, as someone unlucky in love, as a man with an old war wound, or as a woman with an inconsolable broken heart from an early tragic love affair.

Many corporate cultures make being straight and "coupled" a prerequisite for acceptance and involvement. Invitations to business-related events include mates or dates. If gays accept these invitations, they must make up an excuse for not having a mate, or they must bring an opposite-sex mate to keep up the pretense. If they shun such events to avoid the discomfort, important career opportunities can be lost.

Gay pretenders often complain that their social lives don't reflect their inner reality. Not surprisingly, they feel they're treated as if they are "someone else."

They pay the price of enormous wasted energy from the effort needed to keep up the pose and the anxiety over possible discovery. They also must cope with the ethical problems implicit in living a lie. Perhaps most crucial, they must deal with the feelings of isolation and detachment that result from not being "who you really are."

Dodging the Issue

Gay persons who evade the issue of gayness tend to avoid all discussions of sexuality and to insist that others respect their privacy. They withhold the sexual information that people usually exchange in conversations, information about wives and husbands, girlfriends and boyfriends. They try not to answer such personal questions without people *realizing* they're not answering. Strategies include changing the subject and asking the questioner a question, perhaps softening their evasions with humor.

They have no way of knowing what conclusions others have made about avoidance of personal talk. They wonder, but never know, if others think they are gay. They may have no work-related social contact at all, leaving them feeling alone and separate. Most eventually bump into a glass ceiling imposed by their social isolation. They just don't quite "fit in" with upper management.

Gays Who Come Out

Gays generally carefully calculate the risk before they come out at work. According to such authors as J.D. Woods and J.H. Lucas, when gay persons first come out, they experience great relief but must immediately deal with antigay prejudice. They do find strategies for coping, and virtually all say that coming out is worth it.

Calculating the Risk

Coming out is anxiety filled and liberating at the same time. Gay persons say that when their sexual orientation is disclosed (whether by choice or because someone guessed it or told others), their first response is apprehension and anxiety about their job and the workplace. They don't believe being gay affects their work performance but that prejudice against them does. Most believe their career progression will be slowed or blocked. In fact, about one in three gay persons who have come out say they have experienced some form of job discrimination.

As the awareness and coming-out process unfolds, gay persons' natural tendency is to want to end the deception. They calculate the probable effects of coming out on their job security. Those who are most likely to come out have one or more of the following factors that provide some security. They:

- are self-employed
- have professional credentials
- work directly with customers, so their dependence is dispersed across many persons outside the company.
- hold jobs that have concrete measures of success
- have unique, irreplaceable skills that are needed by the company or within the industry

Facing the Reactions

The most immediate reactions gay persons face when they come out can include

- becoming the target of verbal abuse and nonverbal hostility
- increased stress levels stemming from harassment
- a backlash of negative attitudes
- being fired or demoted
- being heaped with effusive sympathy and support

Professionals may find their effectiveness compromised and their authority undercut. Teachers often feel that they must always be on guard. For example, they may think twice before giving a student a hug and saying "Great job," because it could be misinterpreted.

Over 40 percent of gay persons who have come out report anti-gay discrimination from co-workers (Peeples 1985)

In the long run, they must still spend much energy managing their gay identity, and most of them must also deal with being a token gay in a straight work group. The most important strategy gays adopt is to build a support network, although being gay makes this more of a challenge. Strategies for managing the fact that they're admittedly gay include minimizing their gayness, making it seem "normal" to straights, and offering it as an asset to the firm.

Minimizing Gayness

Some minimize the visibility of their sexuality with the goal of lessening their vulnerability. They fear that if they become too visible, or if gay persons in the organization appear too numerous, they will trigger hostility. They say there's a big difference for most straight persons in knowing about a gay person's sexuality and actually engaging in conversations on the subject, seeing them with a gay partner, and especially seeing them touching, dancing, or embracing. Most straight persons feel safer when gays limit discussions of their gayness to veiled comments and insinuations.

Normalizing Gayness

Gayness is the natural sexual orientation of more than 2 percent of the population, but most straight persons don't think of it as normal. Therefore, many gay persons use a strategy of subtly influencing others to see gayness as normal. They talk about their relationships and lifestyle in terms that highlight similarities to straight life, speaking of family, romance, civil rights. They speak of many of the same concerns as co-workers, such as making house payments, dealing with "in-laws," or finding a date. Their purpose is to transform the unusual into the commonplace and acceptable and to give co-workers a framework for thinking about gay lifestyles. In doing this, they get away from the focus on their "different" sexual orientation so that others may see the similarities between gay and straight relationships and relate to them as people first. Just like straight persons, gays know that beneath their sexual self is a core self that is more essential and encompassing, a more complete and complex self. They have the strong belief: "Whether I'm gay or not, I'm still *me*."

Making Gayness an Asset

A few gay persons are able to showcase their gayness as an advantage to the company. For example, they may highlight their multi-faceted connections with the gay community and marketplace and with talented gay professionals who might be recruited as employees, consultants, or suppliers.

Heaving a Sigh of Relief

Despite the hassles of discrimination virtually all gay males who have come out say they don't regret the decision. The most important result is an overwhelming sense of relief at being finally open, followed by reduced stress, enhanced self-image, and feelings of freedom. Gay persons who come out experience less anxiety and depression, have more positive self-concepts, and feel better able to fully experience their emotions and interests (Schmitt and Kurdek 1987; McDonald et al 1973).

WHAT LEGAL RIGHTS DO GAY PERSONS HAVE?

Worldwide, there are at least eight nations that have national civil rights laws to protect all gay employees from workplace discrimination: Denmark, France, Israel, New Zealand, Norway, South Africa, Sweden, and Netherlands. In the United States gay persons are not included in federal Civil Rights laws that protect other groups from discrimination in employment, housing, parental matters, military service, and other areas.

Only a few states have laws that specifically protect gay persons from discrimination, and only three states provide for gay employees' partners to have access to the same benefits (such as health plans) that married partners enjoy. In most states they must face formidable barriers to parental rights. Many states retain old laws that make gay sex a crime, even though most Americans believe that both gay and straight persons have a fundamental right of privacy for adult, consensual sex.

Struggling for Equal Employment Rights

The most crucial issue that affects gay persons' daily lives, is employment discrimination. The employment-at-will doctrine holds that employer and employee enter an agreement as legal equals because the employee can quit "at will" and the employer can fire "at will." In most states it remains a serious obstacle to worker protection from arbitrary and "at whim" personnel decisions. Table 10.2 gives a summary of current protections.

Federal Protection

In the past decade or so, Democratic lawmakers and Presidents have favored protection for gay persons, while Republicans have fought against it. Here are some highlights:

- Congress has repeatedly refused to include sexual orientation in the anti-discrimination legislation of the Civil Rights Act.

- In 1998 President Clinton signed an executive order banning discrimination against gay persons solely on the basis of sexual orientation. Upon taking office in 1993, he signed orders banning hiring barriers based on the old "security risk" stereotype, as well as a ban against discrimination in the military.

- Clinton also proposed the Employment Non-Discrimination Act (ENDA), which extends the civil rights protections given other groups to gay persons and which must be passed by Congress before becoming law. The proposed law does not include the military, religious institutions, or small businesses with fewer than 15 employees. Still, Congress had not passed ENDA as of 2001. Though presented every year since 1994, it still had not passed when Congress adjourned in 2001.

State and Local Protection

In 40 states it is legal for a private employer to fire a worker for being gay, and there is no recourse in the courts. Only in 10 states is it specifically illegal: California, Connecticut, Hawaii, Massachusetts, Minnesota, New Hampshire, New Jersey, Rhode Island, Vermont, and Wisconsin—plus the District of Columbia. In addition, about 50 cities and counties protect gay persons working in all types of organizations (NGLTF 2000).

State government workers are protected in 19 states (including the 10 just listed). The additional nine states are Colorado, Illinois, Louisiana, Maryland, New Mexico, New York, Ohio, Pennsylvania, and Washington. In addition, about 30 cities and counties have such protection.

TABLE 10.2: Employment Discrimination Rights for Gay Persons, 2000

Type of Protection	Protection
Federal protection in all organizations	No
Federal protection for federal government workers	Yes
State protection in all organizations	10 states + D.C.
State protection for state government workers only	9 states
Cities and counties with laws to protect in all organizations	50
City or county protection for local government workers only	30

Source: National Gay & Lesbian Task Force, www.ngltf.org, May 2001.

Pursuing Family Rights

Gay activists are fighting for basic equal rights for gay couples. They point out:

- Gay partners cannot file joint income tax returns

- Gay employees usually cannot include their partners in their health plans.

- When gay persons become seriously ill or die, their partners can't legitimately take time off to attend to the illness or funeral.

- When gays are hospitalized, their partners may be barred from their bedside by hospital staff because they're "not a family member."

- They are often denied custody, or even visitation rights, of their own children and are not allowed to adopt children in most states.

Domestic Partner Laws

Domestic partner benefits have recently been established for government employees in three states: California, Delaware, and Vermont. The number of employers with domestic partner benefits increased to 3,557 in 2000, 25 percent more than in 1999, when there were 2,856 (Human Rights Campaign 2000).

Marriage Laws

One step beyond domestic partner rights is legal marriage rights. At least four nations legalized same-sex marriages during the 1990s: Denmark, Norway, Sweden, and Netherlands. The Danish parliament, as pioneers, took the stand that you cannot make anyone homosexual who is not homosexual and that gay marriage is not a threat to the community. In 2000 Vermont legalized same-sex marriages, the only state to do so, though Hawaii had come close. Vermont businesses experienced an immediate boost in tourist dollars because 80 percent of the licenses went to thousands of out-of-state gay couples. In backlash, by 2001 more than 30 states had passed "defense-of-marriage" laws specifying that same-sex unions sanctioned elsewhere are null and void within the state.

Fighting Backlash

Alliances between certain religious groups and Republican politicians form the major backlash movement. They are fighting on a range of legal fronts, from antigay discrimination laws, to gays in the military, to domestic partner and marriage laws.

These activists claim that laws making it illegal to discriminate against gay persons actually require religious employers to violate their personal moral standards. These employers would not hire or promote gay persons on moral grounds, but nondiscrimination laws would require them to do so on legal grounds. On this basis, antigay political groups have sprung up with the purpose of blocking laws that establish civil rights for gay persons (G. Herek 1991; W. Paul 1982).

For example, antigay groups persuaded Colorado voters to pass a controversial measure in 1992. It prohibited local governments from passing laws to protect gay employees from discrimination. This was a huge blow to the gay community because at least eight other states prepared similar initiatives. In response, gay rights activists got a court injunction against the law, and in 1994 the Colorado Supreme Court invalidated it. The Court said the measure singled out a class of people for denial of basic rights and thereby violated the equal protection clause of the Constitution. This marked the first time a state supreme court had validated gay rights—and the U.S. Supreme Court later upheld the ruling.

In 1995 the Republican Party published a platform that media analysts labeled "aggressively anti-gay" (Tuller 1996). The 2000 platform retained anti-gay language opposing civil rights protections based on sexual orientation and gay marriage. It also declared that "homosexuality is incompatible with military service" (Dunham 2000).

To further their resistance to the Gay Rights Movement, some Republican politicians and religious groups joined forces to showcase the old idea that homosexuality is a sin and a perversion. They preach that people can choose to be gay or not, and they put great energy into urging gay persons to convert and join the Ex-Gay Movement.

Resisting Private Sex as a Crime

In 2000, same-gender sexual conduct—private, adult, and consensual—was still a crime in 24 states, in many instances a felony punishable by up to 20 years in prison. The right of states to enforce such laws was upheld by the U.S. Supreme Court in 1986. The gay community was stunned when the Court upheld Georgia's right to criminalize private gay sex by consenting adults. The Court relied on Judeo-Christian history and literature and characterized gay persons as a threat to the American family and not a legitimate alternative to traditional patriarchal family life. This in spite of the fact that opinion polls since the 1980s showed that most Americans believed that both gay and nongay persons have a fundamental right of privacy for adult, consensual sex.

Speaking Out in the University

A tradition of academic freedom in public universities has provided gay students with more protection when they're on campus than most any other place. Gay persons on university campuses have a right to meet, create formal student groups, advocate gay rights, and socialize together. Federal and state courts have ruled that these are constitutionally protected free speech and free association rights. Courts have also required state universities and colleges to provide equal space and equal funding to gay student groups, as they do to other types of legitimate student groups. At least 100 universities have policies forbidding discrimination based on sexual orientation, and at least 46 schools have programs in gay and lesbian studies, according to the National Gay and Lesbian Task Force.

LEADERSHIP CHALLENGE: OVERCOMING SPECIFIC WORKPLACE BARRIERS

Your gay associates face many barriers in the workplace, most stemming from cultural myths and stereotypes. These barriers use up energy, drain productivity, and block profitable collaboration, so it is important for you to do your part in removing them.

Barrier #1: Prejudice and Discrimination That Drain Corporate Assets

Most gay persons remain in the closet at work. In fact 81 percent of lesbians and 76 percent of gay men fear they would be the victims of job discrimination if they came out at work. About one in three gay persons who have come out say they have experienced some form of job discrimination.

Talent Drain

Gay persons look for workplaces where it's safe to be themselves. They may move toward a "gay ghetto" within the company where they can socialize with others who are on the edges rather than in the mainstream. Eventually most look to other companies that meet their needs and offer opportunities for growth. Gay employees are especially likely to leave companies that:

- condone antigay prejudice, yet require extensive business-related socializing
- have vaguely defined managerial roles but stress social skills that assume everyone is straight

Many gay employees leave such limiting corporate cultures to expand their careers in:

- smaller companies
- gay-run businesses
- their own business
- corporate cultures that treat gays fairly

This represents an important talent drain.

Energy Drain

Antigay prejudice creates an expensive diversion of human resources. Gay persons must learn to suppress ideas and actions that might invite suspicion, to monitor the way they dress and every word they say. Managing their identity at work consumes enormous amounts of energy, time, and personal resources. In prejudiced corporate cultures, closet gays must disguise their lifestyles or avoid the issue of sexuality altogether. Open gays must deal with various types of prejudice and discrimination. All must cope with high levels of stress that could be eliminated by a supportive work environment. The drain on energy and thus productivity is clear.

Productivity Drain

Prejudice also poisons work relationships and fosters misunderstanding. In its presence many gay employees feel forced to either deceive, disengage, or resign, taking with them whatever investment the company has made in their development. For straight persons, prejudice sets up limited behavioral boxes that may seem comfortable and safe but that stifle ways of thinking and behaving that might fall outside the boundaries. What a waste! The bottom-line result of antigay prejudice is to create walls of silence and mistrust, which in turn lowers productivity.

- Antigay prejudice stems primarily from lack of information about gay persons and the gay community. Everyone needs access to training that provides this information. You can help encourage your associates to pursue such training.

Barrier #2: Blocks to Spontaneity—Seeing Gays as Abnormal

Gay persons need to be seen as persons who are just as normal as straight persons. Sexuality is only one dimension of human beings. Although it is certainly a major dimension, time spent in actual sexual activity is very small in the whole scheme of things. Gay persons are as highly individualistic as the population at large, with the same variety of interests, abilities, and traits.

Gay persons' sexual orientation, by itself, is disruptive only when others despise them for it. When gayness is feared and despised, everyone may become fearful about actions which might be viewed as symptoms of gayness. For example, when any type of same-sex affection and closeness may be viewed with suspicion, spontaneous collaboration among employees is inhibited. This is especially true for men, where standards of "manliness" compel them to remain relatively distant, competitive, and independent. Where men's tendencies to express their feelings or to nurture others might be devalued, men tend to suppress them. Masculinity can become a burden when men perceive they must constantly take charge of situations, speak their minds, and view compromise and accommodation as signs of weakness.

- The solution is simple but not always easy to implement: *Accept gayness as a normal expression of human sexuality for some people.* When gay persons are as valued as anyone else, people don't need to worry about appearing gay.

Barrier #3: The Sexual Double Standard

The Myth: The workplace is essentially asexual.
The Reality: Dating, engagements, weddings, mates, spouses, marriages, and children are discussed everywhere in the workplace, always from the straight person's viewpoint.

The Myth of the Asexual Workplace

Most people believe that ideally sex or sexual orientation should have nothing to do with the workplace, yet the symbols of straight sexuality are everywhere. In fact, personal and professional roles are not at all separate in most corporate cultures. The interactions there are colored by sexual possibilities, expectations, and constraints. Sexuality is often on display, explicitly or implicitly, in dress and image, jokes and gossip, looks and winks, fantasies and affairs. Sexuality is there in the range of persuasive behaviors we call flirtation or seduction and those coercive behaviors we call sexual harassment.

Actual sexual contact at work is rare. Yet we humans *are* sexual creatures, even though we're much more than that, and our interactions are always colored by sexual possibilities. We can't help but bring our sexuality to work. It often underlies such intangible assets as rapport, familiarity, charisma, and "chemistry." When we channel it constructively, it can be the source of intense feelings of personal commitment and loyalty to the work team.

The Sexual Double Standard

The myth of asexual workplace leads to a hidden double standard for expressing sexuality: it's generally okay for straight persons and not okay for gay persons. For example, it's okay for straight persons to discuss their sexual partners, such as husbands, wives, and lovers, and the children produced from such unions, but it is not acceptable for gay persons to do so. This is based on the belief that being straight is normal and desirable, but being gay is not.

Questions about marital status are a matter of course in professional circles, part of getting acquainted. When a man speaks of his wife at work, others interpret this as a statement about his social role as husband, not about his sexual performance as a straight man. People typically inquire about how he met his wife, how long they've been married, and similar facts. His sexual relationship is so socially acceptable, it's treated as asexual. When a gay man speaks of his male partner, the focus tends to be on "unnatural sex."

This double standard compels gay persons to remain silent while others talk about family life. Gay persons must mask and repress their sexuality while others do not. For example, many gay persons won't entertain co-workers at home because it's too risky, especially if they haven't come out. Some say, "I'd love to invite people from work to my home, but I can't because I don't know that their reaction to my partner would be."

One reason gay persons like working in San Francisco or New York is the tendency for people who live there to mind their own business. They simply view what others do outside of work as those persons' private business, which they may choose to discuss or not. Many gay persons say they love the indifference. It's so much better than judgment or pity. Because of their early experiences with censure and worse, their sexuality is always an issue with them, a perpetual threat in the straight world, something to be constantly monitored there.

Any kind of double standard is perceived as unfair by those it discriminates against. Gay employees, to feel as valued and accepted as others, must feel free to discuss their personal lives in the ways that other employees do. Everyone in the company needs information about the sexual double standard and how it affects gay employees.

- You can help set the tone by accepting gay associates' lifestyles. Your attitude will come through and will allow the gay person to feel at ease in discussing personal-life events as you and other co-workers do.

- When referring to employees' couple relationships in general, consider using the term "partner," which is inclusive, instead of "husband" or "wife."

Barrier #4: Walls of Silence That Deaden Creativity

Discomfort and avoidance of gay issues are typical in many corporate cultures. One danger is that people will get in the habit of not talking in order to avoid sensitive, sexual topics. This spills over to not talking about business topics. Such walls of silence tend to deaden relationships, and they deaden the synergy and creativity that can spring forth from lively interactions. They expand the productivity drain.

Like all forms of prejudice, antigay prejudice creates barriers between different groups of people, ensuring that they will have a distorted, insufficient understanding of one another's needs and talents. The bottom line result is an atmosphere of mistrust. Prejudice denies gay persons and co-workers the kind of trust and rapport that would enable them to discuss problems frankly. The result is a "spillover of silence."

- You can help to cure the prejudice and discrimination that builds these walls by being willing to openly discuss gay issues, by communicating regularly with gay associates, and by focusing on building rapport and trust.

Barrier #5: Treating Gay Persons as Tokens

Over half the gay persons in a recent survey said that a major reason they came out was their desire to educate others about gay lifestyles. Others refuse to come out precisely because they don't want to do "all that explaining." Some who come out find that being a symbol or token of the entire gay community means they can't quite be themselves after all, even though they're "out." They sense that co-workers are probing, testing their attitudes about gayness in general. Some token gays feel they're being dissected and examined, and that they're "on," performing, instead of just being themselves.

Token gays are likely to become lightning rods, targets for co-workers' attitudes toward the entire category of gay persons. Their mere presence may raise related issues beyond their immediate work performance. Whether gay persons are in the closet or out, fear of discrimination, together with impaired self-esteem, can motivate them to work harder and be better. Some suffer from double or triple stigma, such as also being a woman and an African American, and work even harder to compensate. But the pressure takes its toll, and burnout can be a result.

- You can help set a tone of acceptance. Treat gay persons as individuals whose achievements and failures reflect the person, not the gay community. Help educate others about the unfairness of viewing people as tokens.

Barrier #6: Hostile Corporate Cultures and Gay Ghettos

When gay persons perceive the corporate culture to be hostile, they may seek refuge in a safe job or position. They may find a protected niche in a large organization, stay out of the spotlight that goes along with high-visibility assignments, broad decision-making responsibilities, and major promotions. They may gravitate to departments that have a reputation for tolerance or in which other gay persons are clustered, sometimes called gay ghettos.

In ghetto-type jobs, the required skills are likely to be hands-on type with clear job duties, and performance can be measured more objectively in terms of sales figures or concrete tasks completed. Therefore, these jobs are safer, more secure and can provide a haven of tolerance in a larger, more biased organization. But comfortable niches nearly always have glass ceilings and walls all around them, in this case "lavender glass."

- You can help to eliminate gay ghettos by encouraging a corporate culture that values and welcomes gay persons—and people from all types of groups.

Barrier #7: The Lavender Glass Ceiling

The "lavender" glass ceiling is what gay persons say blocks them when they reach a certain level of responsibility, so they never go higher. As managers and professionals move toward the top, reputation is everything. Careers are ruined by the perception that people are not "playing on the team" (are gay). Many say that the executives above them feel uncomfortable with bringing gay persons into the inner fold. Some executives rationalize that clients or employees won't accept a gay person at a high level, that relationships are more sensitive at that level, and that the company image might suffer.

Leading-edge companies don't fire people for being gay, but most gay persons are sure that gayness creates a lavender ceiling. And, knowing your job is safe is not the same as having a "warm, fuzzy environment" where people accept you as you are and therefore give you an equal chance.

LEADERSHIP OPPORTUNITIES: BUILDING ON GAY PERSONS' STRENGTHS

As a leader, you need to recognize the strengths that each of your team members brings to the organization and to build on those strengths. Gay persons bring many assets to the workplace that can be used in numerous ways. They can contribute to creative team projects, to the development of networks and business relationships that are especially valuable for the organization, and to connections with the gay community and marketplace.

Opportunity #1: Follow the Lead of Savvy Organizations

Do you want to help your organization stem the talent drain? You can provide company leaders with examples of how other leading-edge companies are attracting and keeping talented gay employees.

Microsoft

"When we lose a viable employee, we've probably lost upward of two million dollars," said Microsoft's diversity director. The world's largest computer software company set a goal in 1990 of making sure that gay professionals have everything they need to stay productive, and their diversity program is an integral part of that strategy.

Lotus

In the early 1990s Lotus recognized that many gay employees have the same deeply-committed relationships that married employees have. The company allows gay employees to include their partners in their health plans and similar benefits. It was the first major publicly-held U.S. company to do so. Since then a number of large companies have made similar changes in their policies.

Levi Strauss

In the early 1990s Levi Strauss became the largest employer to recognize gay partners for purposes of employee benefits, such as health care and life insurance. A gay employees' association was formed with company encouragement. Each year the members hold a Gay Pride Celebration at the San Francisco headquarters facility, which top management attends.

Such leading companies as Apple Computer, AT&T, Digital, DuPont, Hewlett Packard, Oracle, and Xerox—as well as smaller firms—now have gay employee organizations and nondiscrimination policies. These high-tech companies are painfully aware that their most talented employees can easily switch jobs and go to competitors that provide a more tolerant social atmosphere and better benefits. Competition is the newest reason for companies to offer domestic partner benefits. Top managers also know the high cost of replacing highly trained engineers and other technical workers. Companies that fall behind can expect a talent drain.

Opportunity #2: Recognize That Gay Persons Have High-Value Skills

As a practical matter, nearly all companies must have business reasons for focusing attention on a problem and for spending time or money on solving it. Companies are most likely to combat prejudice when they have economic incentives for doing so.

Gay persons are over-represented in the pool of highly educated, well-qualified employees, possibly representing 5 to 10 percent of such workers, according to Robert T. Michael's survey. This is precisely the type of worker that's getting harder and harder to find and keep. Companies need a reputation for diversity in order to be able to hire and keep high-potential gay employees. So long as prejudice, and double standards block their career paths, the collective creativity, knowledge, and energy of millions will be lost to companies.

Gay employees have much to offer in business situations where a knowledge of the gay community is needed. They are likely to have an inside track on how to market products to gay customers, how to provide services to them, the implications of AIDS, and other business issues that involve gay persons. In addition, they can energize work teams. Most have experiences and insights that don't come with conventional lives—a cutting-edge sensibility, freedom from marital responsibilities, and a sensitivity and compassion for members of outgroups.

Opportunity #3: Help Gay Employees Build a Corporate Support Network

Gay persons can have the same problems in building support networks as other minorities. People are most comfortable with others like themselves. Therefore, it may be difficult for gay persons to make key connections and to find mentors. This may be especially true in non-accepting corporate cultures because other gay employees tend to hide out in order to avoid backlash, and other employees tend to avoid guilt by association. However, in flexible corporate cultures that encourage minority employee groups, gay employee associations tend to spring up. Such groups are providing many of the same benefits provided by support networks within the gay community at large, as well as specific workplace benefits.

Opportunity #4: Encourage Company Benefits for Gay Employees' Partners

To the gay or lesbian who is in a loving, long-term relationship, working for a company that provides benefits to state-recognized spouses but not to same-sex partners creates an atmosphere that devalues their couple relationship. Also, corporate antidiscrimination policies regarding gay and lesbian employees would almost certainly have a positive psychological impact on them. The change would probably trigger some negative backlash among certain straight employees in the short term. Top management support for an accepting, nonprejudiced environment, however, can produce positive results for all employees in the long run. Clearly, an accepting environment is likely to result in higher productivity for gay workers.

Opportunity #5: Promote Education about Gay Issues

Most employees base their opinion of gay persons on common stereotypes and myths. Leaders can provide educational seminars for all employees to inform them of the facts and to initiate discussions of concerns and of new attitudes. A frequent concern is AIDS anxiety, a key fear many people have regarding gay persons. The antidote is facts and figures. For example, AIDS is no longer a predominantly gay disease; it infects all segments of the population. It's not normally contagious and is spread only through very specific types of activities, almost none of which normally occur in the workplace. Savvy companies are building AIDS awareness into company policy, providing informative training sessions for all employees, and giving them written materials that explain the issue.

Opportunity #6: Help Create a Savvy Corporate Culture

A corporate culture is based on some basic beliefs and values of its founders and leaders that are accepted generally by most employees. These values are expressed in everyday rituals of communication and interaction, the stories that are passed around about the "big wheels," and the people who are allowed into the grapevines and inner circles. Values are also expressed in corporate policies and procedures and the ways they are carried out.

One example of changing the corporate culture is to change the belief that gayness is abnormal to the belief that it is normal for some persons. As a result, you and others in the company value gay employees as normal, contributing associates. In turn, you accept their family and community activities as normal and become comfortable with discussing them in the same ways you talk with others about their lives

Gay persons most need to work in a corporate culture that accepts them as valuable persons, one that values nonjudgmental caring of one human being for another. They need to feel as welcome and included as straight persons feel.

Assess the Culture

All organizations benefit by looking squarely at the basic assumptions and beliefs that underlie their goals, values, and boundaries and questioning their fairness. You can use your influence to encourage such questioning and the adoption of needed changes in the corporate culture.

- You can encourage your associates to analyze the corporate culture to see how it encourages or allows antigay prejudice. You can jointly identify barriers gay persons encounter and ways to remove the barriers. You can find ways to make the culture safe for gay persons, and to open up new opportunities for profitable collaboration.

Heal Antigay Prejudice

Gay advocates say the workplace issue should not be one of denying sexual orientation but rather respecting all persons' rights to privacy and to a harassment-free environment. You can help your organization face the gay workplace rights issue. If your organization needs to move beyond antigay prejudice, you can help by encouraging specific company actions designed to reduce prejudice and eliminate discrimination.

- You can serve as a role model, setting the example of being as fair as possible in all your dealing with gay persons.
- If you're a supervisor, you can make personnel decisions based on individuals' work performance and potential, not sexual orientation, and encourage others to follow your example.
- Encourage company leaders to establish clear policies that ban antigay discrimination and specific procedures for implementing such policies.

Make It Safe for Gay Applicants

Gay persons need to "come out" at the time of hiring in order to be most productive within an organization. If they feel they must come in as closet gay persons, they may gain respect and credibility as straight persons in the organization, based on their skills, creativity, and competence. This credibility may be decimated if they later come out because co-workers may think they've been deceived all along and trust is shattered. The leading-edge companies that are attracting talented gay applicants have a reputation for accepting gay employees as normal, valuable contributors. They have created corporate cultures that reflect this belief.

- You can encourage your associates to adopt this belief, which in turn will impact the corporate culture.

SUMMARY

Gay persons must cope with many stereotypes and myths, such as gay men act feminine and lesbian women act masculine. Gays don't cluster only in certain occupations, though they naturally gravitate to companies, businesses, and jobs where they feel most accepted. Gay persons tend to be better educated and hold higher-level types of jobs, though they actually earn less, on average, than their straight counterparts. People who associate with gay persons are no more likely to be gay themselves than those who don't associate with gays.

Gay persons have a wide range of relationships, including long-term, committed ones, and ones in which gay couples raise children. Research indicates that children raised by gay parents have no major problems and are not more likely than other children to become gay adults. Gays are not more likely than heterosexuals to molest children.

The people most likely to harbor antigay prejudice are older, less well-educated men who are strongly involved with fundamentalist religious groups. Antigay prejudice has many negative effects on gay persons and on the persons who hold the prejudice, but there is increasing acceptance of gay persons in the workplace. In the 1950s gayness was considered a mental illness that might be caused by domineering mothers and weak or absent fathers. But in 1972 the American Psychological Association took the position that gays are not mentally disturbed nor in need of therapy to change their sexual orientation.

Growing up gay is a confusing, painful process for most gay persons, and cultural prejudice creates self-esteem problems for them. Most initially deny the fact that they're sexually attracted to same-sex persons. However, those who come out are able to identify with the gay community, which is a healing and empowering process. The gay community is as diverse as the heterosexual community.

The core gay issue in American culture is, Why are some people gay? First, we must look at the layers of sexuality and the continuum aspect of each layer. Rather than being either male or female, there are degrees of maleness or femaleness. Instead of gay or straight, there are degrees of gayness, as well as degrees of every other sexual layer.

Then we can examine the Nature versus Nurture theories. People in the Nurture camp think that people become gay primarily because of their environment, experiences, and role choices. Most conservative religious leaders adhere to the Nurture theory, which they say upholds their belief that the Bible condemns homosexuality. This means that it's a condition that can and should be prevented or cured.

Nature theory advocates think gay persons are probably born gay, even though they may not realize this until adolescence. Their gayness may be due to hormone conditions in the womb, being endowed with a "gay gene" at conception, other unknown factors, and probably some combination of these elements. Most researchers tend toward the Nature theory, which, if correct, means that it's perfectly normal and natural for about 2 percent of the population to be gay—some more exclusively gay than others.

The struggle for acceptance in the workplace is a major issue. Gay workers must deal with prejudice and discrimination in every career aspect. They must cope with the sexual double standard that allows straight workers to discuss wives, children, and family events, while gay workers' personal lives are "off limits." This, combined with the "couples expectation," is especially difficult when advancement depends partly on social skills. Managing their gay identity is an ongoing issue for gay workers, whether they're in the closet or out. Pretending they're heterosexual or dodging the issue brings on the problems of "living a lie." Those who've come out often use such coping strategies as building a support network, minimizing their gayness, making it seem as normal as possible, and making their gay connections and insights a marketing asset to the company.

Struggling to gain equal rights is also an important issue. In 2000 there was federal protection for federal government employees, but still no protection for corporate employees under the Civil Rights laws. Ten states prohibited discrimination in both private and government jobs, and another nine states provided protection for state government employees only. Sexual conduct between same-sex persons was a crime in 24 states, gay partners could not legally marry except in Vermont, and in most areas they had few or no family or parental rights.

Skill Builder 10.1: The Case of Gay Rumors

You are a supervisor in the computer section of a large bank. One of your best computer technicians, *Diane*, has worked there for three years. She has been an excellent worker up to now. Lately, however, her productivity has fallen off and she has called in sick several times. The other day you noticed a cartoon about lesbians stuck on the wall near Diane's desk. You've also overheard some gossip in the restroom implying that Diane might be a lesbian.

- What actions, if any, should you take?
- Outline at least two scenarios and the follow-up actions you would take in each instance.

Skill Builder 10.2: The Case of Clients' Comfort Zone

Carmen studies the file folder on her desk. As head of the Western Regional office of the Hartford Company, a lending and investment firm, she must decide how to handle a touchy situation. She's thinking about *Jayson*, one of her most productive employees. Jayson has been in the special customer department for two years, dealing with customers who have a net worth of $200,000 to $1 million. He has done an excellent job of handling these customers' needs to invest their available cash and to get loans for business or home-buying purposes.

Don, in the custom portfolio department, is being promoted and transferred, and Carmen has been considering who should take his position. Don deals only with customers who have a net worth of over $1 million. This is a different group, mostly older and more conservative than the customers Jayson has been working with. The only problem Carmen worries about is the fact that Jayson is a gay man. Carmen knows that at least one or two of Don's customers have made antigay comments. She's concerned not only with the possibility of losing some customers, she wonders if it's fair to Jayson to throw him into such a sensitive situation.

- If you were Carmen, what would you do?
- If you were Jayson, how would you view this situation?

Skill Builder 10.3: The Case of Frank, a Gay Assistant

Frank is hired in February as an administrative assistant at Graphics Express, a Palo Alto, California, software firm. He considers it an excellent opportunity because the company has made a commitment to provide him with career development opportunities and to give him the backup resources he needs to carry out his projects. The resources include clerical help. Frank and his supervisor **Bradley** hit it off well, and Frank looks forward to a successful, rewarding career at Graphics Express.

Frank makes no secret of the fact that he's a gay man—because he prefers to start off on an honest basis with his co-workers. Soon after he comes to work, however, one of his co-workers, **Jennifer**, begins making derogatory comments about gays to him. Frank tries to ignore these put-downs, but Jennifer escalates them to direct insults about Frank's sexual orientation. The comments upset Frank. He discusses them with his partner, saying "It hurts to be treated this way in this day and age. I thought that in this city and this company I would be left alone." Frank and his partner agree that the best response is to continue ignoring Jennifer's negative comments and to focus on doing a good job.

The situation takes a turn for the worse, however, when **Katie**, who works closely with Jennifer, brings some disturbing news to Frank. Katie says that Jennifer frequently complains about Frank to others when she's in the employee dining room-lounge. Katie says, "Frank, I hate to be the one to tell you, but I think you should know. Jennifer's saying you're unfit to represent the company to customers because you're gay. She says you tarnish the company and all of us with your perverse lifestyle."

This time Frank decides he must take action. It's one thing to put up with remarks directed solely at himself, but mudslinging in the presence of all his co-workers is more than he can take. He schedules a meeting with **Jeff**, the human resources director, and informs him of the situation. Jeff promises to look into it. This meeting takes place in early May.

In late May, Frank's supervisor Bradley is promoted. Frank shares Bradley's elation over the promotion, but when he hears who will take Bradley's place, his heart sinks. His nemesis Jennifer will be his new supervisor. Frank decides to try to make the best of it, to ignore Jennifer's hostility, and to do the best job possible.

By the end of June, Frank can see that his goals are becoming more and more difficult to achieve. Jennifer is giving Frank more and more assignments, often menial and tedious ones, and makes it clear that Frank is expected to complete them by deadline without receiving additional clerical help or overtime. The final straw comes when Jennifer tells Frank he can no longer depend on the help of Deborah, the clerk who has worked most closely with him in the past.

This occurs in late July, and Frank immediately goes to Jeff, the human resources director. Frank brings Jeff up to date on the situation, saying: "Jeff, you said you'd look into this problem of Jennifer's hostility toward me. It was difficult enough when she was merely slandering me. Now she's in a position of direct power over me, and she's setting up impossible performance standards for me. The situation has become so stressful that I have great difficulty sleeping, and I've been putting in such long, hard, tension-filled days that I'm beginning to feel drained all the time.

What can you do to relieve this situation?" Jeff promises to investigate the situation but makes no further commitment.

Now, in August, Frank is trying to decide his next move. He feels exhausted, he's had a respiratory infection for six weeks, and his doctor tells him he must get more rest.

- What are the key issues in this situation?
- If you were Frank, what would you do?
- If you were Jeff, what would you do?

Skill Builder 10.4: The Case of Edna, Lesbian Employee

Edna has been working for Whizware, a Silicon Valley software company, for two years. She is 26 years old and for a long time refused to believe that she was a gay person. She married her high school sweetheart but the marriage ended in divorce after a year or so. Now Edna is living with her lesbian partner *Janice*. The relationship is good, and Edna finally feels comfortable about her sexuality. However, she has not told anyone about her sexual orientation except a few close lesbian friends.

Whizware has many liberal policies, including flextime, three-week vacations, and a relaxed dress code. Most of the employees are under age 40. Recently the company encouraged a gay support group to form. Edna was astonished that out of about 350 employees, 52 attended the first meeting. While this turn of events is heartening to Edna, the response of many co-workers is not. Most of what she hears is pretty nasty and hateful, with few accepting or supportive comments.

Having a divorced status has helped Edna to pass for a heterosexual. She says, "I don't deliberately lie, but when my colleagues talk about child care and how hard it is to find reliable help, I can safely murmur something about being glad I didn't have children when I was married. But at the same time I can be sympathetic to their problems, which of course I am."

The longer Edna is employed by Whizware, the more difficult it is for her to maintain her counterfeit identity. The workers tend to know a great deal about each other's lives outside the office. Edna knows, however, that most people are more interested in talking about themselves than hearing about other's lives, so she staves off friendly curiosity by showing more interest of the details of their lives than she actually feels. She says, "Most of my co-workers respect my privacy and assume I'm mourning my failed marriage."

Edna periodically travels to Vancouver and Dallas as part of her job of training clients in the use of Whizware products. Occasionally a colleague or executive will travel with her. Recently *David Southam*, Vice President, accompanied her to Vancouver. As Edna says, "He had a little too much to drink and definitely became too friendly. I had a tough time convincing him that 'no' means 'no.'"

Edna has never heard any office gossip about Southam being a womanizer, but she's concerned that he may seek revenge for her rejection of his overtures. If he does, and if her lesbian relationship with Janice becomes known to him, she would be especially vulnerable. Southam made several antigay remarks while under the influence and clearly was against the gay support program recently instituted at Whizware. After thoroughly bashing the program, he said, "*#* faggots, who needs 'em?" He also made several nasty cracks about *Jane Goodman*, one of the founders of the gay support program. Edna is terrified of the prospect of being regarded in the same devastating way by Southam. On the other hand, when Southam is sober and on the job in Silicon Valley, he's well respected. However, Edna wants to avoid traveling with him in the future.

Edna's partner Janice suggests that Edna could file a sexual harassment complaint against Southam, which could solve any future travel problems. This prospect horrifies Edna, who says, "I'm just gonna try to get out of traveling with him." She knows this might not be possible because one of Whizware's best clients is located in Dallas. The strategy for keeping this client satisfied depends on Edna's technical knowledge combined with Southam's customer relations skills.

- What are the key issues in this situation?
- If you were Edna, what would you do?

REFERENCES

Achilles, Nancy. "The Development of the Homosexual Bar as an Institution." in *Sociology of Homosexuality*. New York: Garland, 1992.

Adam, B.D. *The Survival of Domination: Inferiorization and Everyday Life*. New York: Elsevier, 1978.

American Psychological Association. Minutes of the Council of Representatives. *American Psychologist* 30, 1975, 633.

Associated Press, "Gay Games in Full Swing," *San Francisco Chronicle*: A-2, August 2, 1998.

Badgett, Lee. *Industrial and Labor Relations Review*, July, 1995.

Badgett, M.V. Lee. *Income Inflation: The Myth of Affluence Among Gay, Lesbian, and Bisexual Americans*. National Gay & Lesbian Task Force <www.ngltf.org>, 1998.

Bailey, J. Michael. Northwestern University, see Archives of General Psychiatry, March, 1993.

Cahill, Sean. *What's At Stake for the Gay, Lesbian, Bisexual, and Transgender Community in the 2000 Presidential Elections*. <www.ngltf.org> 2000

Deaux, K., and L.L. Lewis. "Structure of Gender Stereotypes: Interrelationships Among Components and Gender Label." *Journal of Personality and Social Psychology* 46, 1984, 991-1004.

Duberman, Martin. *Stonewall*. New York: Dutton, 1993.

Dunham, K.J. and R.E. Silverman, "Private Campaigner," *Wall Street Journal*, August 6, 000.

Fortune, "Chicago Research Firm Surveys Gays," December 16, 1992, 45.

Firskopp, Annette and Sharon Silverstein. *Straight Jobs, Gay Lives*. New York: Simon & Schuster, 1996.

Gebhard, Paul H. "Incidence of Overt Homosexuality in the United States and Western Europe." in *Sociology of Homosexuality*. New York: Garland, 1992.

Gonsiorek, J.C. and J. D. Weinrich, eds. *Homosexuality: Research Implications for Public Policy*. Thousand Oaks, CA: Sage, 1991.

Gonsiorek, J.C., and J.R. Rudolph. "Homosexual Identity: Coming Out and Other Developmental Events," in *Homosexuality: Research Implications for Public Policy*, Thousand Oaks, CA: Sage, 1991.

Green, Beverly, and G. M. Herek, eds. *Lesbian and Gay Psychology*. Thousand Oaks, CA: Sage, 1994.

Green, R. "The Immutability of (homo)Sexual Orientation: Behavioral Science Implications for a Constitutional (legal) Analysis," *Journal of Psychiatry & Law* 16, 1988, 537-568.

Greenburg Research poll conducted for the Human Rights Campaign, November 1996.

Gross, Larry, and S.K Aurand. *Discrimination and Violence Against Lesbian Women and Gay Men in Philadelphia and The Commonwealth of Pennsylvania*. Philadelphia: Philadelphia Lesbian and Gay Task Force, 1992.

Haldeman, D. "Sexual Orientation Conversion Therapy for Gay Men and Lesbians: A Scientific Examination" in J. Gonsiorek and J. Weinrich (eds.), *Homosexuality: Research Implications for Public Policy*, Thousand Oaks, CA: Sage, 1991.

Hall, M. "The Lesbian Corporate Experience." *Journal of Homosexuality* 12, 1989, 59-75.

Hamer, Dean, and P. Copeland. *The Science of Desire: The Search for the Gay Gene and the Biology of Behavior*. New York: Simon & Schuster, 1994.

Harry, Joseph, and Robert Lovely. "Gay Marriages and Communities of Sexual Orientation" in *Sociology of Homosexuality*. New York: Garland, 1992.

Harry, Joseph, and William DeVall. "Age and Sexual Culture Among Homosexually Oriented Males." in *Sociology of Homosexuality*. New York: Garland, 1992.

Herek, G. "Sexual Orientation and Military Service." *American Psychologist* 48, 1993, 538-5410.

Herek, G. "Stigma, Prejudice, and Violence Against Lesbians and Gay Men" in *Homosexuality Research Implications for Public Policy*. Thousand Oaks, CA: Sage, 1991.

Hetherington, C. E., Hillerbrand and B.D. Etringer. "Career Counseling with Gay Men," *Journal of Counseling and Development* 67, 1989, 452-454.

Kite, M.D. "Age, Gender, and Employment," Paper presented at the meeting of the American Psychological Association, Boston, 1990.

Kite, M.D., and K. Deaux. "Attitudes Toward Homosexuality." *Basic and Applied Social Psychology* 7, 1986, 137-162.

Leland, John and Mark Miller, "Convert?" *Newsweek*: 47-49, August 17, 1998.

Loznoff, Maurice, and W.A. Westley. "The Homosexual Community" *in Sociology of Homosexuality*. New York: Garland, 1992.

Marcus, Eric. *Is It a Choice?* New York: HarperCollins, 1993.

McDonald A.P., Jr., J. Huggins, S. Young, and R.A. Swanson. "Attitudes Toward Homosexuality." *Journal of Consulting and Clinical Psychology* 40, 1973, 161.

McDonald, G.J. "Individual Differences in the Coming Out Process for Gay Men." *Journal of Homosexuality* 3, 1982, 47-60.

McNaught, B. *Gay Issues in the Workplace*. New York: St. Martin's Press, 1993.

McWhirter, D.P., and A.M. Mattison. *The Male Couple: How Relationships Develop*. Englewood Cliffs, NJ: Prentice-Hall, 1984.

Michael, Robert T., J.H. Gagnon, E.O. Laumann, and G. Kolata. *Sex in America: A Definitive Survey*. New York: Little, Brown & Co., 1995.

National Gay & Lesbian Task Force, www.aalu.org/issues/gay/gaylaws.html,1999.

NGLTF: National Gay & Lesbian Task Force, www.ngltf.org, 2000

Paid Ad (see as an example), *San Francisco Examiner*: A-22, August 15, 1998.

Palmore, 466 U.S. at 433. For an application of Palmore in a lesbian mother case, see S.N.E. v. R.L.B. 699 P.2d 875 (Alaska, 1985).

Paul, W. "Minority Status for Gay People: Majority Reactions and Social Context," in *Homosexuality: Social, Psychological, and Biological Issues*. Thousand Oaks, CA: Sage, 1982.

Peeples, A Survey of Perceptions of Civil Opportunity Among Gays & Lesbians in Richmond Virginia (Research Task Force & the Commission on Human Relations, City of Richmond, 1985), as cited in *Comstock*, p. 53.

Peplau, L.A., and S.D. Cochran. "A Relational Perspective on Homosexuality" in *Homosexuality/Heterosexuality: Concepts of Sexual Orientation*. New York: Oxford University Press, 1990.

Peplau, Letitia Anne. "Lesbian and Gay Relationships" in *Homosexuality: Research Implications for Public Policy*, Thousand Oaks, CA: Sage, 1991.

Rich, R. "Compulsory Heterosexuality and Lesbian Existence." *Signs* 5, 1990, 631-660.

Scandura, T.A. "Mentorship and Career Mobility." *Journal of Organizational Behavior* 13, 1992, 169-174.

Schmitt, Patrick J., and L.A. Kurdek. "Personality Correlates of Positive Identity and Relationship Involvement in Gay Men." *Journal of Homosexuality* 13, 4, 1987.

Seligman, Martin. *What You Can Change and What You Can't*. New York: Knopf, 1994.

Senate ENDA hearing, 103rd Congress, Anthony Carnevale cited a 1992 study conducted in Philadelphia, 1994.

Signorile, Michelangelo. *Queer in America*. New York: Doubleday, 1993.

Silverstein, C. "Psychological and Medical Treatments of Homosexuality" in *Homosexuality: Research Implications for Public Policy*, Thousand Oaks, CA: Sage, 1991.

Spitzer, Robert. Study of ex-gay persons, announced at the annual meeting of the American Psychiatric Association, May 9, 2001.

Tuller, David, "New Wave of Outings in Politics," *San Francisco Chronicle*: A-1, October 26, 1996.

Weisner, T.S., and J.E. Wilson-Mitchell. "Nonconventional Family Lifestyles and Sextyping in Six Year Olds." *Child Development* 61, 1990, 1915-1933.

Woods, J.D., and J.H. Lucas. *The Corporate Closet*. New York: The Free Press, 1993.

Yankelovich Partners. Income survey, 1994.

Resources

Advocate, The, a national magazine.

Human Rights Campaign, a gay rights group

GLAAD, Gay & Lesbian Alliance Against Defamation

National Gay & Lesbian Task Force www.ngltf.org

CHAPTER 11

Working with Persons with Disabilities

*Persons with disabilities are in a different situation, not necessarily a less
fortunate one—in the deeper, eternal sense.*
Carolyn Vash

About one in every 16 persons you're likely to encounter in the workplace is a person with a disability. In 1997 about 51.6 million Americans had disabilities that fall under the Americans with Disabilities Act (ADA) definition: "a physical or mental impairment that substantially limits one or more of the major life activities." About 26 million are considered severely disabled. One-third of all persons with disabilities, about 16 million, were employed in the workplace in 1992. (U.S. Census)

Strictly speaking, everyone has some type of impairment, perhaps a missing toe or finger, mild nearsightedness, or difficulty learning advanced mathematics. The people classified as disabled are impaired in a major life function. For some, the difference this makes in their lives is relatively minor; for others, such as quadriplegics, it's enormous.

A major key to building profitable relationships is to learn about an associate's community and get a feel for his or her background. The more skilled you become at interpreting an individual's actions against the backdrop of his or her background, the greater success both of you can achieve through working together. Keep in mind that there are many types of disability and each person deals with their disability in a somewhat unique manner. Avoid the temptation to use this lifestyle information to form new rigid categories.

As you explore the follow topics, designed to help you understand what it's like to be a person with a disability, try to begin seeing situations as you think a person with a disability would view them. Specifically, you learn:

- How typical stereotypes about persons with disabilities compare with reality
- Major reasons why people devalue and exclude persons with disabilities
- How the current situation is connected to certain historical events
- What it is like to be a person with a disability
- Key facts about the Independent Living Movement
- What you should know about the Americans with Disabilities Act (ADA)

- Barriers to career success for persons with disability and how to break through these barriers
- Assets that persons with disability bring to your company and how to use those assets to create win-win successes

To raise your awareness about how you perceive persons with disability, and to determine what you already know about them, complete Self-Awareness Activities 11.1 and 11.2.

Self-Awareness Activity 11.1: What Do You Believe about Persons with Disabilities?

Purpose:

- to get in touch with your beliefs and stereotypes about this group of people
- to experience how judgmental beliefs affect your thinking and feeling processes
- to experience the ways in which your beliefs create your reality regarding other persons, even before you have any interaction with them

Part I. What Do You Believe about Women with Disabilities?

Step 1. Associations

- Relax as deeply as you can: close your eyes and take a few deep breaths.
- Focus on the word "disabled woman" and allow a mental picture to come up in your mind's eye. Imagine that you are this woman. Be woman with disability.
- Notice your resistances to being this person, and your willingness.
- Notice the words and images that come to mind as you "see" this woman.
- Open your eyes and list 10 to 20 words in the order in which they occur to you.
- Review your list. Mark a plus beside the words that are positive, a minus beside the words that are negative, and a circle beside neutral words.

Step 2. Negative Associations

- Close your eyes and focus again on the image of the woman with a disability. Formulate a negative opinion or judgment, perhaps one you typically hold about such women.
- Notice your *feelings* as you see the person in this negative way. What *thoughts* come up as you focus on the image?
- Write a few sentences about your feelings and thoughts.

Step 3. Positive Associations

- Formulate a positive opinion or judgment, perhaps one you typically hold about women with disabilities.
- Notice your *feelings* as you see the person in this positive way. What *thoughts* come up as you focus on the image?
- Write a few sentences about your feelings and thoughts.

Step 4. Insights

- Focus on the differences between your experiences when you hold negative and positive judgments or opinions. What were the differences? What meaning does this have for you, for your beliefs and feelings about people from this group, and about beliefs in general?

- Write your responses in a few sentences; include anything you like about your feelings, thoughts, and insights.

Part II. Experimenting with Opinions about Men with Disabilities

Repeat the phases and steps in part I, this time focusing on the image of a man with a disability.

Self-Awareness Activity 11.2: What Do You Know about Persons with Disabilities?

Purpose: To see what you know about the issues covered in this chapter.
Instructions: Determine whether you think the following statements are basically true or false—and think about why. The answers will emerge in this chapter, and the summary at the end of the chapter focuses on these issues.

1. The definition of a person with a disability is "anyone with a physical impairment that limits the range of tasks he or she can accomplish."
2. Employees with disabilities tend to have better records of punctuality, attendance, and turnover, but they're somewhat less productive than other employees.
3. Society has always attempted to rehabilitate and integrate persons with disabilities.
4. The large majority of persons with disabilities, even those with severe disabilities, can become independent and productive.
5. Only about 30 percent of persons with disabilities are currently employed.
6. The federal Americans with Disabilities Act requires employers to make special accommodation for the disabled, which is proving very costly for employers.
7. Job applicants with disabilities must provide a medical history to potential employers.
8. If you see that a person with a disability needs help, give it at once.

STEREOTYPES AND REALITIES

Persons with disability say the limitations of their disability are not nearly as devastating as the stereotypes, devaluation, and exclusion they experience from the people they encounter.

Stereotype #1: Persons with severe disabilities are childlike, dependent, and in need of charity or pity.

In fact, many persons with severe disabilities have a great deal to contribute and are able to work and to manage their own lives through the Independent Living Movement, which you'll learn about later.

A related myth is that a disability is a constantly frustrating tragedy. In fact, many persons with disabilities say that a disability need only be an inconvenience *if* it is dealt with as an inconvenience. Developing intelligent accommodations is one way to accomplish this. Although severe disabilities pose huge challenges, even they can be viewed primarily as a challenge to be overcome rather than a hopeless tragedy. For example, world-renowned physicist Stephen Hawking has stated that his disabling condition left him with not much to do but use his mind creatively and productively. Carolyn Vash, who has an impairment, suggests that we view her as being in a *different* situation, not necessarily a *less-fortunate* one—in the deeper, eternal sense.

Stereotype #2: Persons with disabilities are unable to lead normal lives.

Most persons with disabilities can live relatively normal lives and want to do so. Most are impaired in only one functional area. They tend to compensate for their impairment in numerous ways. They're able to do most things as well as anyone and usually can do some things better. Many people with disabilities view their limitations as a fact of life but go to work and participate as actively in society as they can. Persons with disabilities are increasingly better educated, with 75 percent completing high school in 1994, compared with 60 percent in 1986 (*Business Week* 1994).

Stereotype #3: Persons with disabilities can only do menial or entry-level jobs, and most don't want to work.

In fact, persons with disabilities are successfully employed at almost all levels in nearly every field. More than 90 percent of net new job openings in the 1990s are in information-intensive and service occupations, and at least 90 percent of persons with disabilities are capable of filling such jobs.

Most want to work, regardless of the extent of their impairment, and see work as a major route to self-fulfillment. They want to find work that draws on their skills and talents and helps them live a more abundant life. Dissatisfaction with life is reported by four times as many adults classified as having disabilities as other adults. This dissatisfaction is related to their desire to work and to live a normal life. About 80 percent of adults with disabilities who do not work say they would rather have a job.

Stereotype #4: Employees with disabilities create safety risks, increase costs, and are less flexible and productive than other workers.

In fact, a review of 90 hands-on studies reveals that compared to other employees, persons with disabilities (Cox,1993; Green and Johnson 1987):

- have better safety records
- do not normally cause increased health care costs
- have equal or better turnover and absentee rates
- have equal or better job assignment flexibility
- are productive; more than 90 percent of 1,451 workers at DuPont rated as average or above average on overall job performance
- have better average attendance records than those of nondisabled employees

Stereotype #5: Employees with disabilities are more difficult to work with.

Two large surveys of managers and co-workers of persons with disabilities indicate the following (Harris 1986, 1987):

- Eighty percent of managers say they are no more difficult to supervise than others.
- Fifty percent of managers rate the following quantities as *better than* those of other workers: willingness to work hard, reliability, punctuality, and attendance.
- Eighty percent of co-workers say they are just as productive as others.

WHAT'S IN A NAME?

Labels can hurt, especially when their effect is to isolate people from the rest of society. The terms we use to refer to persons with disabilities can be loaded with unintended meanings. Most activists prefer terms that are descriptive rather than euphemistic, emotionally neutral rather than charged, and words that don't elicit negative stereotypes (Longmore 1985a).

Preferred Terms	Terms to Avoid
• Persons with Disabilities	• Differently Abled
• The Disabled (as a protected class)	• Physically Challenged
• Sight Impaired, Blind	• Handicapped
• Mobility Impaired	• Crippled, Lame, Gimpy
• Hearing Impaired, Deaf	• Deaf and Dumb
• Emotionally Impaired	• Insane, Crazy
• Neurologically Impaired	• Moron
• Mentally Impaired	• Retard

The term *persons with disabilities* is preferred when referring to the group as a whole because it focuses on them as persons first, rather than on their disability. The use of the term *the disabled* is acceptable when referring to them as a protected class. Such terms as *differently abled* and *physically challenged* are not descriptive and attempt to avoid the issue. They're politically correct in the worst sense. *Handicapped* was considered acceptable for a time, but the word stems from the phrase *cap in hand* and carries a connotation of begging. Now most persons with disabilities avoid it. Such terms as *hearing impaired* or *sight impaired* are specific and descriptive. They're often more accurate than deaf or blind because they refer to those with varying degrees of impairment, as well as those with total loss of an ability. The worst terms carry emotionally devastating stereotypes and tend to focus on the negative: deaf and dumb, crippled, limp, lame, gimpy.

WHY ARE PERSONS WITH DISABILITIES EXCLUDED?

People tend to shun, be prejudiced against, or devalue people who are different. This is especially true when the persons are different because they have less of something than most people have. But people who have more than most others may also be devalued. People who are exceptionally rich, brilliant, beautiful, or even kind are suspected and punished by some people. Most every culture seems to display this tendency.

Most devaluation refers to regarding someone as inferior, a lesser being, not very capable, not very useful, possibly burdensome, not beautiful, and generally one down. Devaluation follows close behind outright oppression when it comes to psychologically damaging consequences. It is the most common and devastating attitude facing persons with disabilities. They consistently experience devaluation in the eyes of others, and therefore in their own eyes unless they can protect themselves from self-deprecation—whether their disability is physical, sensory, or mental in nature.

The form and degree of devaluation is heavily influenced by the surrounding culture. Devaluation can be blatant or subtle. The Nazis blatantly killed disabled people. Most societies are so subtle that their devaluative practices have gone unrecognized as such for many years until the new breed of activists began to call attention to them. The prevailing philosophical or religious beliefs of the culture have a distinct effect on how people view persons with disabilities (Vash 1981). In both the East and the West, for example, it has been common to segregate the disabled into their own schools and workplaces.

Western Viewpoint

Most Western religions and philosophies hold that we each have only one life to live. Therefore, being disabled has other implications, from "It's just God's will and we can't know why" to "It's God's punishment for something the victim did or something the victim's parents did" to "It's a tragedy because we're here to enjoy life."

Western cultures, such as the dominant culture of the United States, place a high value on standard modes of reasoning, a cultural model of physical beauty, and the physical, material world. Such values tend to create barriers to good relationships and to communicating with persons with certain impairments (Vash 1981; Althen 1988).

Many people in our culture view people as a personality inside a body. When one or both of those has been damaged "permanently," not much is left. Societies and individuals who are more spiritually oriented understand that the spirit is not damaged just because the body or personality is damaged.

Materialistic people are especially likely to believe that persons with disabilities continually mourn their misfortune, perhaps as long as they live. This is simply not the case for most persons with disabilities. Therefore, the implied belief that persons with disabilities are sad victims of terrible life circumstances erects a communication barrier between the believer and those persons.

Eastern Viewpoint

Some Eastern philosophies and religions include the idea of reincarnation into multiple lives. Many believe that before coming into a new lifetime, at a spiritual level we choose our parents, our body, and our total life situation. We do this in order to learn certain lessons and have certain experiences that deepen our awareness and understanding and promote our spiritual growth. Disability thus becomes a growth experience. This is not to say that all Asians view disability in this manner. It is to say that some persons with disabilities have found this viewpoint to be more constructive and empowering than the Western view.

When persons without disabilities believe they're more fortunate than persons with disabilities, they tend to feel pity, which implies superiority. People with this viewpoint may feel threatened when a co-worker with disabilities excels, or they may assume that the co-worker was excused from meeting the usual standards. On the other hand, some people view persons with disabilities as merely being in a *different* physical situation, not necessarily a less fortunate one—in the deeper, eternal sense. Such viewpoints allow us to relate to persons with disabilities as peers, colleagues, and equals.

Media Influences

In the past, films and television programs often presented persons with disabilities as villains, criminals, monsters, and tragic figures. All these stereotypes express the idea that disability involves the loss of an essential part of the person's humanity. The figures were often portrayed as almost subhuman. Think of Captain Hook, the hunchback of Notre Dame, mentally impaired Lennie in *Of Mice and Men*. Here disability implied the loss of moral self-control, often through bitterness and isolation that results from the fear and bigotry of others.

During the 1970s and 1980s we saw in increase in programs where persons with disabilities chose suicide as an escape from their "living death," or "vegetable existence," even though they retained many life functions. In many films disability implied total physical dependency and separation from the community, and the victims were unable to adjust to their disability. Death was presented as the only logical and humane solution to a horrible situation. Other dramas focused on bitter, self-pitying victims whose families eventually got tough in order to help the person with disability adjust and cope. The focus was usually on victims who worked courageously and achieved remarkable feats.

Both types of stories featured overcoming adversity, based on the concept of disability as primarily a problem that requires the person with the disability to accept the situation and find the emotional resources to cope and overcome. Social stigma and devaluation were not the issue and society was let off the hook.

A few recent productions have directly dealt with the issue of prejudice. Others have presented persons with disabilities as normal persons who happen to have some functional impairment. Deaf and paraplegic persons have been portrayed as attractive and sexual, entering relationships out of the strength of their own identities. Certain activist groups are trying to influence media decision makers to focus on these more realistic aspects of disability.

Fear of Becoming Disabled

People don't like to think about losing control of their destiny or that the hand of fate could strike them as well as the person with a disability who they see before them. This fear can lead to extreme discomfort and distress upon even seeing persons with disabilities, much less spending time with them. What people fear, they tend to shun and stigmatize. Fear can also lead to blaming the disabled for their predicament. Some people find comfort in believing that persons with disabilities must have brought it on themselves through sin, carelessness, or self-sabotage. In turn, they can tell themselves that they would never bring such a disaster upon themselves, and this makes them feel more in control and safer.

Unfamiliarity and Discomfort with Persons with Disabilities

When people have had little or no experience with persons with a certain type of disability, the unfamiliarity can be disconcerting. People are frequently confused and uncertain about how to act and what to do. Some avoid making eye contact with such persons because they got punished for "staring" when they were children. How many mothers have grabbed their child's arm and snapped, "Don't stare! It's rude." How many have said, "Shhh! Don't ask!" when their naturally curious child blurted out questions and concerns upon seeing a person with a disability? Parents' comments are well meaning, but they teach their children to ignore anyone with a disability.

Unfamiliarity can cause people to focus on the equipment surrounding some people—braces, crutches, wheelchair—and keep them from really seeing and tuning into the person. It can cause people to look at an interpreter, leaving out the hearing-impaired person, instead of viewing the translator as a mechanism for communication and focusing on the person they're communicating with. In all these cases, the person with the disability gets little or no eye contact and becomes something of a nonperson.

To help you imagine what it's like to have a disability, complete Self-Awareness Activity 11.3.

Self-Awareness Activity 11.3: What If You Became Impaired?

Purpose: To increase your awareness of the experiences of persons with disabilities.

Step 1. Various Activities. List some barriers you would face in a typical day if you lost your ability to walk, your vision, or your hearing. Consider how you would manage the activities shown in the column to the left if you had each of the impairments shown on the right. What barriers would you have to overcome in each case?

	Mobility Impaired	Visually Impaired	Hearing Impaired
• getting up in the morning, getting ready			
• getting to work or school			
• doing your work, communicating, etc.			
• having lunch			
• using the restroom			
• other activities? (list)			

Step 2. Getting Dressed. Put on a tight blindfold, or close your eyes and don't peek. Go through the motions of getting dressed. What problems do you experience? Which are the most difficult? *Step 3. Sight and Sound.* While watching a television drama, try the following experiments.

- Wear a blindfold for 5 or 10 minutes.
- Mute the sound for 5 or 10 minutes.

What are the key differences between no-sight and no-sound? What insights does this experience suggest to you about visual and hearing impairments?

EVOLUTION: FROM VICTIM TO ACTIVIST

Cultural attitudes and policies toward persons with disabilities have changed dramatically in this century (Longmore 1987). Persons with disabilities say that the most serious barriers to living reasonable lives and doing their work are not necessarily their own physical or psychological disabilities. The worst barriers are external: other people's stereotypes and attitudes and the buildings, vehicles, walks, steps, and restrooms they must negotiate. Some highlights of historical change include:

Before 1850	Traditional moral attitude: take care of the disabled.
1850s	Provide special schools for the trainable.
1880s	Institutionalize the disabled in large centers.
1880s–1920s	Involuntary confinement and sterilization.
1930s	Rehabilitation for some. Sight-impaired advocates fight for participation in society.
	F.D. Roosevelt, who uses a wheelchair, is elected U.S. president.
1940s	World War II opens doors to disabled workers because of manpower shortages; March of Dimes, Cerebral Palsy associations are formed.
1950s	Focus on rehabilitating and adapting to the environment.
1960s	Disabled-rights advocates organize to change their environment; Urban Mass Transportation Act, Architectural Barriers Act encourage access.
1970s	Federal law requires access and accommodation from some employers and organizations; some states pass similar laws; Independent Living approved by Congress and some states.
1980s	Independent Living Movement; Air Carriers Access Act.
1990s	Federal ADA requires access and accommodation from most employers and in nearly all public buildings.

From Institutionalizing to Rehabilitating

The traditional moral attitude toward adults with disabilities was to take responsibility for their care. Social reform efforts of the 1850s sought to establish special schools for those children with disabilities who were considered trainable. In the 1880s there was a move to switch from small centers to large, more economical institutions that could accommodate more people, with the attitude that defective persons should be removed from the mainstream of society. Subsequent legislative drives from 1880 to 1925 focused on enforcing involuntary confinement and sterilization to prevent "defective" persons from having children.

Rehabilitating

The Rehabilitation Act of 1918 focused on World Ward I veterans with disabilities. Proponents of vocational rehabilitation assumed that people with disabilities could overcome them and become wage earners if given training. The major goal was to prepare people to work so they could pay back the government's investment; it did not seek to offer generalized assistance.

Rehabilitation became a part of the solution for persons with some types of disabilities, but after rehabilitation, they were given only the most menial jobs. During World War II, because of the extreme manpower shortage, workers with disabilities filled a variety of jobs. Studies indicated they incurred less absenteeism and tardiness than other workers and that their productivity was good. After the war, these work reports "got lost" and it was back to the old "moral" attitudes.

From Accepting Disability to Adapting

By the late 1950s it became unfashionable to talk about *accepting* disability. *Adapting* to or *coping with* became the preferred terminology. This thinking led in part to the disabled-advocates revolution. Some saw that counseling would not solve the problem if, in the end, people with disabilities still could not get from one point to another because there wasn't an accessible bus service or they couldn't get up the stairs. The world was not a very reasonable place to live for the disabled, so advocates began to shift the emphasis from modifying the disabled to modifying the world around them.

Adapting While Changing the Environment

"Persons with disabilities" became a movement in the 1960s. They also became a minority group with culture-like features, such as dominant values, cultural themes, and key issues. Emerging from their former victim roles, disability activists brought about important legislative changes. Looking to the future, their goal is to remove as many of the barriers to a normal life as they can.

Transformation: From Victims to an Activist Minority

A new day dawned for persons with disabilities in the late 1960s, as it did for many groups. Many of them began viewing themselves as part of a minority group that must manage its own brand of stereotypes and discrimination from others, develop and affirm its own values and issues, and take charge of its own destiny (Longmore 1985a, 1985b, 1987). Once the disabled started talking to each other, most of them concluded that:

- Other people with disabilities are valuable and worthwhile.
- They themselves weren't the only exceptions to those negative stereotypes that they had previously accepted.
- All persons with disabilities have valuable experience and information to share.
- In unity there is strength.

They began to fight in the civil rights mode of other minorities, to formulate their rights, and to demand protection for those rights. They campaigned for and won new laws during the 1970s. A 1973 federal law addressed the issue of making some public places accessible to persons with disabilities and eliminating discrimination, but it applied only to organizations receiving federal funds. It did not include most stores, restaurants, and theaters, nor did it include private corporations, except those involved in federal contracts. Soon after the 1973 law was passed, several states passed similar laws. California's law, considered an outstanding model, deals mainly with providing physical and program access to the disabled. School administrators began installing ramps and elevators instead of counseling people with disabilities to stop wanting to attend classes held upstairs. Managers began to remove discriminatory hiring practices instead of advising applicants with disabilities to start liking the few jobs they would be allowed to do.

Breakthrough: The Americans with Disabilities Act

The Americans with Disabilities Act (ADA), which was passed in 1990 and became fully effective in 1994, expanded accessibility to jobs and activities in virtually every major arena. It's an amendment to the Civil Rights Act, not a part of affirmative action law that stems from executive orders. It's therefore enforced by the EEOC. Complaints not resolved through the EEOC may be resolved in the courts through EEOC lawsuits.

Future Aspirations: To Bring Down Barriers

Now activists are clear that if the disability cannot be changed, then it must be accepted, as must any other reality, pleasant or unpleasant, if the person is to survive and grow. What they don't accept is the unnecessary handicapping imposed upon people with disabilities by a poorly designed or unaccommodating world or by their own failures to accept what is and go on from there. Nor do they want to be dependent from cradle to grave because this can severely limit their growth and contributions. Activists have made significant progress toward reducing all types of barriers to a quality existence: barriers that existed in the legal, welfare, and educational systems, barriers created by modes of architecture, transportation, employment, housing, shopping, and recreation. Most important, activists initiated the Independent Living Movement (ILM), which we'll discuss later. The United States is the most highly individualistic of nations, so independence has the highest value here, and the ADA and the ILM reflect that.

WHO ARE THE DISABLED? CURRENT PROFILE

Virtually everyone has been or will be disabled at some point in their lives, as mentioned earlier. Virtually all persons with disability want to live as normal a life as possible. Most want to work, regardless of the extent of their impairment. When they do hold jobs, they tend to be productive and to have better-than-average attendance and turnover records (Myths & Facts 1992).

The Legal Definition

To be protected under the ADA, persons must fit one or more of these descriptions:

- They have a physical or mental impairment that substantially limits one or more of the major life activities, such as seeing, hearing, speaking, learning, walking, dressing, or feeding oneself.
- They have a record of such an impairment.
- They are regarded as having such an impairment.

The ADA definition is broad and includes such chronic conditions as diabetes, heart disease, HIV, AIDS, past (but not present) drug addiction and alcoholism, and mental and emotional illnesses. It's directed mainly to those who are hearing-impaired, sight impaired and mobility impaired, which is about 1 percent of working-age adults (Minton 1994). However, the ADA is intended to protect anyone who encounters discrimination in the workplace because of a physical or mental disability, if that person could in fact do the job with some sort of reasonable accommodation. It could potentially cover 25 percent of all workers

We may get some sense of the types of disabilities people experience at various ages by examining information regarding people who receive disability payments. Business leaders need to be aware that persons with disabilities who have been working all or much of their adult lives are not eligible for disability payments unless their disability becomes significantly worse. Managers should not assume that if they lay off persons with disabilities, they'll be able to collect disability payments.

The great majority of persons receiving disability payments suffer from four broad health conditions—mental disorders, heart disease, musculoskeletal disease (primarily arthritis), and cancer—as shown in Table 11.1. The ADA is expected to benefit older workers the most, since that group has the highest percentage of persons with disabilities. About 22 percent of people 55 to 64 years old receive disability payments, compared to 6 percent of people 25 to 34 years old.

TABLE 11.1: Breakdown of Reasons People Receive Disability Payments

	All	*Younger* *<50*	*Older* *50–64*
Mental disorders	28%	40%	17%
Heart disease	18	7	25
Arthritic disease	19	12	23
Cancer	3	3	4
All other	32	38	31

Source: Mitchell, 1993.

The Mental Treatment Gap

Mental disorders are the most neglected of the major disabilities. Nearly two-thirds of all people with diagnosable mental disorders do not seek treatment, according to a report issued by the U.S. surgeon general, Dr. David Satcher (Pear 1999). His study found a huge gap between the need for mental health services and their availability, A major theme of the report is that mental health must be part of mainstream health care, not an afterthought.

Mental disorders were defined as health conditions marked by alterations in thinking, mood, or behavior that cause distress or impair a person's ability to function. They include attention deficit disorder, hyperactivity disorder, phobias, depression, and Alzheimer's disease.

Mental disorders are not character flaws but are legitimate illnesses that respond to specific treatments. They appear in all types of families, of all social classes, and all backgrounds. The "cruel and unfair stigma attached to mental illness" is "inexcusably outmoded and must no longer be tolerated," according to the report. Pear suggested that a major factor for such stigma is the fear that people with mental disability will become violent. Yet there is "very little risk of violence or harm to a stranger from casual contact with an individual who has a mental disorder," according to the report.

WHAT'S IT LIKE TO BE A PERSON WITH A DISABILITY?

You've learned that 51.6 million Americans with disabilities that fall under the ADA definition, about 26 million of whom are severely disabled (U.S. Census 1992). About 16 million persons with disabilities were employed. This means that two-thirds of adults with disabilities are not working, which is the highest unemployment rate of any minority. About 80 percent of those who aren't working say they would rather have a job. Dissatisfaction with life is reported by four times as many adults classified as having disabilities as other adults (WSJ 1994).

Being a person with a disability is like being any other person, only with an impairment that prevents you from performing one or more major functions. For all severely disabled persons, it's having normal reactions to abnormal situations. Otherwise, your experience as a person with disability depends on the following types of factors:

- *Type of disability*: severity, stability
- *Inner resources*: temperament, self-image, self-esteem, gender, education, skills, creativity
- *Environment*: family support, access to a community of persons with disabilities, cultural attitudes, available technology, government funding

Facing Abnormal Situations

Human beings are more alike than different, regardless of variations in their physical bodies, sensory capacities, or intellectual abilities. Some abnormal situations are biological, such as having multiple sclerosis, which involves progressive nerve deterioration. Some are environmental, such as inaccessible entrances. Other abnormal situations are social, such as having a salesperson ask your companion, not you, what size you wear.

Not being able to get a job is an economic example. Some abnormal situations are obvious, such as a restroom door you can't get through. Others are subtle, such as people using or not using the word cripple when you're around. Some may be pleasant, such as being allowed to board the airplane first. Others are unpleasant, such as not being allowed to board at all. Persons with disabilities are continually perceiving and experiencing things that the majority of people around them cannot validate. Unless they are in regular contact with people who are similarly disabled, their sense of isolation and the lack of consensus for their ideas and feelings are added to the list of abnormal situations.

Type of Disability

The type of disability refers to the time and type of the onset of the illness or accident, which abilities are impaired and which are not, the severity and duration of the affliction, and the way society views it (Vash 1980).

Time and Type of Onset

Some persons are born with disabilities. They grow gradually to recognize that they are different from most other people in negatively evaluated ways. Others become disabled after a short or long lifetime of being "normal." The disability may occur in a catastrophic moment or over a period of illness.

To some, having been born disabled seems somehow less respectable than acquiring a disability later on. Such persons are more likely to be subjected to isolation, unusual child-rearing practices (such as overprotection or rejection), and separation from the mainstream in family life, play, and education.

Many become disabled after a close brush with death, which often has a powerful influence on their life. Some feel guilty for having survived to be a burden. Others feel an intensified faith and sense of purpose.

Functions Impaired

The extent to which the disability interferes with physical attractiveness is a key determiner of the disability experience. Sensitivity to its lack or loss can exceed the pain felt about the functional disability.

The functions impaired directly affect other experiences the person has. For example, deaf people describe the loneliness of being "left out" even when physically present in a group. Blind persons may speak of their terror of pitfalls they can't see, and wheelchair users of curbs they can't get up or down.

Severity, Duration, and Status

There is not a direct, consistent relationship between severity of disability and the intensity of reaction to it or quality of adjustment to it. One person can assimilate total paralysis with fair equanimity, while another is devastated by the loss of a finger. Varying degrees of severity do create different kinds of situations for people to respond to, somewhat independently of personal dynamics.

Some people are temporarily disabled, others are permanently disabled, and some fall into a gray area where some day their impairment may be reparable. For those people, the most depressing influence is often the not knowing. One spoke of living a "provisional existence of unknown limit," saying, "I was convinced that I would eventually walk, but the uncertainty of how long it would take was a most depressing factor."

Persons who are disabled perceive a status hierarchy of disabilities, with polio and spinal-cord injury at the top and mental retardation and cerebral palsy at the bottom. When a disability causes you to walk and talk like a drunk, you get a lot of rejection.

Inner Resources

To learn how inner resources affect the disability experience, we might ask such questions as:

- What kinds of temperaments do persons with disabilities have?
- What is the spiritual or philosophical base in their lives?
- What personality traits do they have that will influence the type and intensity of their reactions to being disabled?

The inner resources of persons with disabilities dramatically affect how they experience their disability. They include ability to adapt to the disability, self-confidence built in early childhood, personal interests and values, ability to express emotions, gender, and other personal variables.

Ability to Adapt

How well a person is able to adapt to the loss of abilities and to enjoy the abilities that remain is an important inner resource. Whether key activities can be continued obviously plays a big role in what inner resources can be tapped. What alternate activities are available is also an important factor. Inner strengths that help people to adapt may include high energy level, strong career motivations, life history of emotional stability, many artistic talents, social poise, and leadership ability or potential.

Psychological Support

Inner resources and emotional stability are established early in life. Those who are disabled as children need more psychological support than most children. When they are taught to believe that they're "as good as anyone else and can do anything they want to do," they gain self-confidence to disregard the taunting of other children. The early years of confidence help them combat the doubts and rejections they experience later on.

The hit movie *Forrest Gump* was an exposition of this idea. Forrest was mentally impaired, but his mother made sure that he joined mainstream society. She repeatedly told him that he was not inferior. One of the many mottoes she taught him was, "Stupid is as stupid does." She taught Forrest to do good deeds because actions speak louder than words and to value the goodness of his inner self.

Interests, Values, and Goals

People tend to adjust more easily if they have a wide range of interests, such as physical interests, intellectual pursuits, vigorous activity, rigorous creativity, passive pastimes, and active involvements. For one thing, they're more likely to find some things they can still do that interest them. People who sustain spinal-cord injuries through adventurous, potentially dangerous activities are apt to be most intolerant of a physically inactive life. People from cultures that highly value physical or sexual prowess are more devastated by this disability than those whose traditions stress scholarly or other sedentary pursuits.

Ability to Express Emotions

What emotions do persons with disabilities tend to feel? Disability has the power to elicit the full range of human emotions, from fear, anger, and sorrow to relief and even joy. Chronic depression is the worst. Periodic fear, embarrassment, or righteous indignation are improvements over that.

Almost all persons with disabilities experience anxiety about survival as well as episodes of rage. Some rage against themselves, their own incompetence to do what others take for granted. They may rage against the universe for being unjust. Some turn their rage against other people for not helping or for helping inappropriately. Some of today's disabled peopled have been called an "angry generation," expecting change to come faster than it ever does and seething inside when it doesn't. Some say that even justified anger isn't good for them over the long term, but they feel they need its impetus to sustain their demands for change.

The ways of expressing and acting out emotions are unlimited. The specific trigger to feelings varies from one person to another. Because disability normally brings strong emotions, being able to express them is important for mental and physical health.

Being Male or Female

Being male or female does not imply better or worse reactions, only different ones. It's more acceptable for women to be helpless in our culture because of the greater social acceptance of a passive, dependent lifestyle for women than for men. Women also tend to have the advantage of being more in touch with their feelings and expressing them more freely. However, women's advantage is virtually destroyed by the far greater demand placed on women to be physically perfect specimens, beautiful in face and figure. By definition, women with physically disabilities cannot hope to meet this social ideal.

Other Personality Variables

Such variables as flexibility, adaptability, maturity, and their opposites influence reaction to change generally, and this includes the changes imposed by disability. Personality variables will affect what meaning persons with disabilities give to the fact that they're disabled. The person who views disability as a punishment from God for past sins will feel differently about it than the person who views it as a test or an opportunity for spiritual development.

Reactions that people with disabilities have to their disability continue as long as the persons and the disability do. There is not some point in time when the person has "adjusted." Reactions simply change with each step in the learning process.

The Environment

At the most primitive level of existence, the ability to get around to find food and shelter is the basic requirement for independent survival. In civilization we must also be able to communicate with other people who are essential for our survival. We're dependent on our immediate environment as well as the greater cultural environment. Persons with disabilities are especially dependent on adequate funds, programs, laws, and technological developments to provide what their impairments prevent them from providing for themselves.

The Financial Environment

The financial assets of persons with disabilities make a crucial difference in the type of experience they have. Money can solve many disability problems. With enough money, persons with disabilities can buy all the equipment and gadgets available to help them do what they need to do. And they can pay other persons to do what's left. A major problem with disability is that it's often difficult to make money. A person's welfare and experiences are therefore greatly influenced by the family's social standing and power base in the community, parental acceptance of the person's disability, and their willingness and ability to offer practical and moral support.

The Disability Community

The larger community of persons with disabilities has been emerging as a subcultural group since the 1960s. It began with the activism of people such as Ed Roberts and Paul Longmore. It expanded with the Independent Living Movement. In every major metropolitan area, persons with a specific type of disability can probably find a small community of persons with a similar disability. Such communities can provide invaluable information, support, and inspiration.

The Culture

We've discussed the importance of cultural beliefs and attitudes toward the disabled. Predominant beliefs and attitudes are the direct cause of psychological and physical barriers on the one hand and their removal on the other.

The Physical Environment—Accessibility

The main issue for mobility-impaired people is accessibility, and safety is the main issue for the visually impaired. Inaccessibility has implications for survival. For example, if wheelchair users cannot get into a building, they can't get a job there. If they can't get over the curbs, up the stairs, or into the restrooms, they literally cannot function even though they have many other abilities. The most typical ways people with disabilities cope with problems of inaccessible or unsafe facilities are by:

- minimizing their own disabilities by developing every possible adaptive skill
- keeping up the good fight to get remaining environmental barriers removed

Some wheelchair users are interested in the development of wheelchairs that climb steps. Most prefer to see ramps and elevators wherever steps are used. What do wheelchair users do if they're working in an upper floor of a skyscraper and fire breaks out, rendering all the elevators unusable? Some feasible plans do exist, but they're rare. When deaf passengers take an unknown bus route, how can they know when they reached their street destination? These are the crucial emergencies and everyday problems that disabled-rights advocates are trying to resolve.

Community and Regional Influences

The size and location of the community where the person lives are important. A small town may offer a quality of human support that is lost in the big city, but it may also lack the equipment and services that persons with disabilities need. Also important are the extent to which the community has been willing and able to eliminate mobility barriers, to mainstream children with disabilities into the public schools, and similar actions.

Other factors that affect the quality of life include the services that local voluntary organizations make available, television and telephone services available for the hearing impaired, the type of transportation that's available, and whether activist organizations are around. The climate and typical building styles also can have a significant impact on how persons with disabilities fare.

The Bureaucracies

The various bureaucracies that persons with disabilities must deal with may include live-in institutions and social service agencies.

Institutions. Living in an institution has a profound impact on the disabled person's experience. Few, if any institutions, are ideal. By their very nature they tend to restrict residents' freedom and violate their privacy. Few people go there by choice. Giving up one's autonomy, even for a time, can have long-lasting, negative effects. In an institution, the staff tends to make most of the crucial decisions about the patients' lives. Those patients who are most willing to cooperate with the staff, therefore, may eventually be the least prepared to resume effective, assertive autonomy when they return to the outside world. Those who have been in institutions say it's the attendants who make the most difference in their quality of life while there (Vash 1980).

Social service agencies. The disabled must often interact with agencies that provide vitally important services. These interactions can be supportive, but they can also be stressful. According to disabled advocate Carolyn Vash, when dealing with agencies "in order to receive the benefits they need, disabled people must tell all, hand over the reins, and oftentimes swallow much, possibly for a very long time" (Vash 1980, 36).

Technological Support

How well the culture is able to provide the latest in technological tools, aids, therapies, cures, and other responses to the cause and aftermath of the disability makes a great difference in resolving functional problems. The U.S. culture provides a great deal of independence and convenience through motorized wheelchairs, powered lifts, electronic magnifiers, talking calculators, portable teletypewriters, computers, and similar aids.

Recent technological breakthroughs. Motorized wheelchairs have opened up dramatic new opportunities for the mobility impaired. For the sight impaired, Braille, audiotape, specialized computers, and other electronic or optical devices have greatly reduced the need for personal services, such as readers. Hearing-impaired persons' communication problems are yielding more slowly to technological intervention than those of the blind. They continue to need interpreters to convey information that's presented orally. Signing is a tiring activity and is ideally done by one person for not more than an hour at a time. What's needed is a portable device that will decode speech and turn it into a visual readout. There is still much televised information with no closed captioning for the hearing impaired.

Public transportation is making strides in assisting users with both short-distance and long-distance travel. The kneeling bus, which lowers a wheelchair-sized platform to curb level, has opened up many opportunities. Many housing functions are becoming computerized. In education, computers provide self-paced learning and easy access to libraries of information. Computers have also made employment more feasible, including home-based employment. Flexible work schedules, job sharing, and other programs to accommodate parents and older workers can also accommodate persons with disabilities.

Future technological probabilities. Technology holds enormous potential for easing and enriching the lives of persons with disabilities. For devices and equipment to be affordable under current business methods, they must be standardized, mass produced, and mass marketed. Individual needs often require unique technological solutions, and devices developed on a problem/solution basis cannot be standardized. Therefore, it's nearly impossible to mass produce and mass market such devices. However, under new business methods using computer-assisted design and manufacturing, customizing, or creating variations on a theme, is becoming economically feasible. New strategies to meet global competition by customizing can also be applied to the equipment or medical-device needs of persons with disabilities.

Technology will affect all aspects of a disabled person's life, such as education, health care, transportation, housing, occupations, and recreation. Some specific trends include:

- increased diversity among people, resulting from more individualized education and media
- easier access to all kinds of information
- decreased routine labor and physical labor
- less reliance on mass production of products and more access to custom-made products
- better communication devices, including computers with multimedia (screen, keyboard, and voice) input and output, resulting in a reduced need for physical transportation
- fewer large organizations and buildings and more use of the home as a place to learn and to work

Each of these trends will influence the future of persons with disabilities and their ability to live productive, independent lives.

WHAT'S THE INDEPENDENT LIVING MOVEMENT?

Throughout most of our history, people who were so severely disabled as to need an attendant had only two options:

- to be cared for by family or friends
- to live in a maintenance-care institution

The alternative of being provided with funds to live as an independent adult did not yet exist. By 1980 independent living was becoming the standard as a result of laws that recognized the human and monetary needs of the disabled.

Disability activists are owning their problem, saying they would rather take care of it themselves, and are demanding their rights. They have made their needs known to government entities at all levels. Their thesis is that people with disabilities, as the ones who share the needs, are uniquely qualified to plan ways of meeting those needs. They want to predominate in the advisory boards of professionally run agencies. They want to take over the key jobs of providing services to the disabled. The new type of service organization consists of independent living programs operated by and for the disabled (Crew and Zola 1983).

Showcase

Ed Roberts' Success Story

In 1962, when Ed Roberts, paralyzed from the neck down, applied for help from the California Department of Rehabilitation, they said no. The counselors argued that it was "infeasible" to think that Ed would ever be able to work. But Ed was persistent; he was accustomed to fighting such battles. At age 14 he had polio and heard the doctor tell his mother, "It would be better if Ed died because he's going to be a vegetable." Right then Ed decided that if he was going to be a vegetable, he'd be an artichoke: prickly on the outside, with a tender heart. His motto was "I'm paralyzed from the neck down, not from the neck up." He used his tough mind and soft heart to fight for disabled persons' rights and to change forever their place in society.

Ed had to persuade his high school principal at Burlingame High to give him his diploma even though he had not completed required classes in physical education and driver's education. He won that battle, and in 1962 he won the battle to get into the University of California at Berkeley, one of the top-ranking U.S. universities. On Ed's first day he was lifted out of his wheelchair and carried up the steps to Room 201 of Cal Hall. A local newspaper headline read, "Helpless Cripple Attends UC Classes."

Later, he organized a group of mobility-impaired students who called themselves the Rolling Quads. They in turn started the Physically Disabled Students' program at UC Berkeley, with the main goal of solving all problems that created barriers to academic achievement. They provided such services as finding attendants, accessible apartments, and 24-hour emergency wheelchair repair service. A broken wheelchair could mean weeks of missed class sessions.

When Ed graduated from UC Berkeley in 1972 he and fellow students founded the Center for Independent Living. It became the model for similar centers across the nation. Ed also founded the Independent Living Movement. In 1975, he became the head of the California Department of Rehabilitation, the very same state agency that had at first opposed helping him go to school. He held that position for seven years, until 1982.

In 1984 Ed Roberts was awarded a MacArthur Foundation "genius" award of $225,000, which he used to establish the World Institute on Disability, an influential policy and research center based in Oakland, California. When he died at age 56 in 1995, colleagues called him "the Gandhi of the disability rights movement."

Self–Determination as Keystone

The independent living program is a community-based program with significant consumer involvement that provides services that persons with severe disabilities need in order to increase their self-determination and to minimize their dependence on others.

Persons with disabilities are now running many of the programs that offer a wide range of services never before offered to persons with all types of impairments. Some disability advocates, for example, help others find their way through bureaucratic red tape and regulatory obstacles. Others help severely disabled clients locate, select, and supervise personal attendants. Housing counselors help the disabled locate appropriate, accessible places to live. Transportation counselors, interpreter services, support groups, and peer counseling services are other types of programs that are found in some cities.

Other services include readers, advocacy or political action, financial counseling, training in independent living skills, equipment maintenance and repair, social or recreational opportunities, and information about other necessary services and products. The services are designed to serve the needs of persons in a particular community so that they need not move to a regional, state, or national facility. There are residential programs and transitional programs, as well as independent living centers. Persons with disabilities do most of the directing and managing and much of the staffing.

Independent Living Arrangements

The independent living setup can be as large and formal as an apartment complex of several hundred accessible, fully equipped units that offer extensive personal services and are planned along with adjacent accessible shopping and employment facilities. It can be as modest and informal as one person with a disability living in an ordinary apartment and having an agreement with a neighbor to provide needed morning and evening attendant care. Many in the disabled community believe that the full range of possibilities should be made available to allow for individual choice.

Individual choice is the keystone of independence. The independent living concept specifically includes the provision of needed assistance from other people that, when given, allows even very severely disabled people to live free from the control or determination of others. The goal is for persons with disabilities to take charge of their own lives and to allow them to contribute to an improved destiny for all people with disabilities.

Training for Assertive Communication

Assertiveness training offered by community organizations is becoming common for persons with disabilities. They are learning to speak up for their rights rather than leave the job to professional rehabilitators and other concerned advocates who are not themselves disabled. For example, they learn as patients how to interview physicians who say little or say it in technical jargon. They learn to get necessary information upon which to base their own decisions. They learn as students how to get helpful cooperation from teachers when they are physically unable to fulfill course requirements in the usual ways. As citizens, they learn to get the help that they're entitled to from agencies, without triggering resistance from agency workers. Persons with disabilities often rely on funds and services from public agencies, and failure to get what they need can mean poverty or institutionalization.

Training to Supervise Personal Service Employees

Supervisory training is essential for tactfully and assertively dealing with personal service employees, and community service organizations often provide this training. Many persons with disabilities must hire and supervise attendants, readers, drivers, or interpreters. Abuses are reported regularly, such as mistreatment, unreliability, exploitation, quitting without notice, and subtle cruelties of withholding help. This occurs when disabled employers don't know how to screen out poor risks during the hiring process or how to create a rewarding job for those they do hire. They must make the job intrinsically rewarding because the public funds provided often don't constitute a living wage. To survive, psychologically as well as physically, people using personal service providers must develop skill in their selection and supervision.

Education for Career Success

During the past few decades, public education for young people with disabilities has progressed from no education at all, to special education in segregated classrooms, to a concerted effort to integrate students with disabilities into mainstream schools. Major problems resulting from segregating disabled students from the mainstream include:

- Employers cannot imagine that job applicants with disabilities could function in their work settings because they never saw them functioning in school.
- Employees have trouble relating to co-workers with disabilities because they had no opportunities for contact from their earliest years.
- Students with disabilities do not get an equal education.
- Orientation toward college preparation is usually virtually absent.

The ILM recognizes that persons with disabilities must have access to optimal educational experiences in order to become self-sufficient.

Integration into Work and Community Life

The goal of the inner and outer struggles of the disabled is to break out of poverty and restrictive environments that offer nothing to do and no one to do it with. The goal is to stay out of institutions and back bedrooms and break into the mainstream of everything—school, work, politics, and love affairs. The ultimate goal is to live a more or less normal life in a fairly normal community. Integration into the workforce can be managed in a variety of ways, often in a gradual, step-by-step manner. An emerging trend is for employers to participate in this process by giving on-the-job training to the disabled. These trends are discussed in the last part of this chapter. A related goal is to change society's image of persons with disabilities—from that of pathetic victims to a more positive image of "people like you and me, who happen to have a disability." As such, they're entitled to basic human rights. The disabled have the right to participate, to give and receive, and to take risks like anyone else. The ADA, which we'll discuss next, is based on this belief.

To raise your awareness of how you react to wheelchair users and how you relate to them, complete Self-Awareness Activity 11.4.

Self-Awareness Activity 11.4: Relating to Wheelchair Users

Purpose: To raise your awareness of your reactions and attitudes toward persons who use wheelchairs.

Instructions: Have paper and pen handy. Follow the directions for each step and jot down brief answers to the questions.

Step 1. Person in a Wheelchair

a. Relax by closing your eyes and breathing deeply. Think of a person in a wheelchair and focus on this mental image. Notice the thoughts and feelings that come up.

b. Open your eyes and write a few brief sentences about the thoughts and feelings that came up, as well as your answer to this question:

- *What did you see first when you pictured a wheelchair user: A wheelchair? A person within a wheelchair? Or a person?*

Step 2. Person in a Lounge Chair

Repeat Step 1, but this time think of a person sitting in a lounge chair. When you write about your thoughts and feelings, answer this question:

- *What did you see first when you pictured a lounge chair user: A lounge chair? A persons within a lounge chair? Or a person?*

Step 3. Person in a Wheelchair and Person in a Lounge Chair

Repeat step 1, but this time think first of a person in a wheelchair and then think of the same person in a lounge chair. Shift the mental image back and forth several times. When you write about your thoughts and feelings, answer this question:

- *How did shifting the mental image affect your thoughts and feelings about the person? How did it affect the way you position the person within you own mind and therefore how you're likely to relate to such a person?*

THE ADA—WHAT YOU NEED TO KNOW

The 1990 federal Americans with Disability Act (ADA) applies to virtually all government and private business operations. Its main provisions are set out in five sections or titles, as shown in Table 11.2.

TABLE 11.2: The Americans with Disabilities Act

Section	Purpose
Title I. Employment	Prohibits employment discrimination.
Title II. State and Local Governments	Requires accessibility and prohibits employment discrimination, similar to the 1973 law.
Title III. Public Accommodations	Requires accessibility to restaurants, theaters, stores, etc.
Title IV. Telecommunications	Requires accommodations, such as telephone relays for the deaf.
Title V: Miscellaneous	Catchall section with a variety of technical provisions.

The ADA definition of disability is broad and subject to interpretation by the courts. It is directed mainly to those who are hearing impaired, sight impaired and mobility impaired, all of whom comprise about 1 percent of working-age adults. However, it can include people with such chronic conditions as diabetes, heart disease, HIV, AIDS, past (but not present) drug addiction and alcoholism, and mental and emotional illnesses. It could potentially cover 25 percent of all workers.

Most large corporations have set up ADA task forces to ensure that all the provisions are met. Some smaller business owners have formed regional groups by type of business, such as restaurant, clothing store, or grocery store owner associations. Such associations plan their response to the ADA with the help of professionals, such as consultants and attorneys, and take the large-corporation viewpoint in handling the changes. For example, some send newsletters to employees to inform them of the provisions of the act, proper etiquette in dealing with persons with disabilities, hiring techniques, what the business is doing to adhere to the act, and other helpful information.

Keystone: Equal Opportunity and Reasonable Accommodation

The major stated goal of the ADA is for organizations to manage their affairs in a manner that includes all groups of applicants and workers with disabilities, where reasonable accommodation can make inclusion possible. The major factor that determines if an accommodation is reasonable is whether it imposes an undue hardship on the employer. Another ADA goal is to increase the employment rate of persons with disabilities in order to reduce the cost of government subsidies to them and to enable them to enjoy a more productive, satisfying lifestyle. The major provisions of the ADA are:

1. to require employers to clearly state bona fide job requirements
2. to provide equal opportunities for qualified persons with disabilities who can meet the job requirements
3. to provide reasonable accommodations that will allow otherwise qualified persons with disabilities to do the job, as long as such accommodations don't cause undue hardship for the employer

Clearly Stating Job Requirements

Job descriptions are a key factor in preventing unnecessary discrimination against the disabled. Essential job functions must be clearly spelled out. If physical ability is essential, the exact activities must be specified; for example, "lift a 5-pound packet 5 to 10 times a day." Requirements that are not truly necessary to do the job must be eliminated.

Providing Equal Opportunity

The ADA states that a job candidate may not be discriminated against on the basis of disability, history of disability, or perception of disability. In the past, most employers would not consider hiring candidates who have been in mental institutions, who have a history of epileptic seizures, who have attended classes or schools for the mentally retarded, or have similar indications of disability. The tendency was to see only the potential problems and ignore the positive contributions such persons can make.

The ADA bars discrimination in all aspects of employment, including hiring, compensation, training, and promotion. Employers also must give disabled employees equal access to employee benefits, including medical insurance. The law also protects family members from discrimination, such as an employer's assumption that caring for a disabled relative will be a job distraction.

Providing Reasonable Accommodation

Title I of the ADA focuses on "reasonable accommodation" by employers for disabled workers, where such reasonable accommodation will allow them to do the work. All employees must be given reasonable accommodation, whether they're new employees, have been with the company for some time, or become impaired after being hired.

Reasonable accommodation can occur during the recruiting and hiring phase and includes accommodation in job descriptions, medical tests, employment tests, job interviews, and all other pre-employment activities.

Human resource professionals must determine ways to make testing and interviewing procedures realistic and fair for all persons. Persons with disabilities who are fully competent to meet the demands of a job may have difficulties in completing the normal job-screening process successfully. Be sure that testing procedures actually measure those performance capabilities that are required by the target job and that tests are required for bona fide job requirements only.

Medical Screening

Companies cannot perform medical screening prior to hiring a person. That means they cannot require applicants to provide a medical history, nor can they require them to pass any short of medical test. After hiring, medical screening and other types of screening are permitted only if all workers are included. Those who are thought to be disabled cannot be singled out.

Employment Tests

Reasonable accommodation must be provided for persons with disabilities. For example, reasonable accommodation for visually impaired persons might include reading the test to them or providing the test in large print or Braille. Tests must truly measure whether or not candidates have the ability or potential to be successful on the job.

Job Interviews

Interviewing procedures must protect persons with disabilities from discrimination. For example, interviewers cannot legally ask job applicants about such matters as physical or mental impairments, medical history, drinking habits, or phobias. What if an applicant voluntarily discloses a disability? The interviewer is not legally allowed to follow up with questions about the disability. It is *not* all right to ask directly about a disability, but it *is* all right to ask persons with disabilities whether they can and would do a particular type of work or job and how they would manage the job. There is a fine line between legal and illegal questions here, for *the interviewer cannot ask what kind of accommodation the applicant might need to perform the job until a conditional job offer is made.* After this point, applicants can be asked to demonstrate or describe how they would do the job. If applicants indicate the need for an accommodation, the employer must either provide reasonable accommodation for the demonstration or allow the applicants to merely describe how they would perform this function.

On-the-Job Accommodations

The key questions for employers are:

- What are the one or two things I must do as an employer in order to give this person an opportunity to succeed?
- How can I level the playing field for this person?

Reasonable accommodation for some jobs, especially professional or technical positions, might be as easy as providing an amplified telephone receiver or larger computer screen. It is frequently an action as simple as providing flexible scheduling for work arrival and departure. It might include providing an interpreter for a hearing-impaired worker to attend a training session or reassigning job functions so that a wheelchair user handles telephone calls while another employee stores and retrieves folders in file cabinets.

Protection from Undue Hardship

The ADA states that employers are not required to make accommodations that would cause them undue hardship. This exemption applies when the measures necessary to allow a disabled person to do a job are unduly expensive or interfere with a business necessity. The major test is how the accommodation would affect the entire budget of the organization. Most cases of undue hardship occur in small businesses. Some don't have the profit margin, cash flow, or capital cushion to take such measures as remodeling a building or providing readers or interpreters. What constitutes undue hardship is decided on a case-by-case basis, since the range of disabilities and types of jobs are so vast that no set of legal formulas could begin to cover them. Some guidelines may eventually be worked out through precedents set in court cases.

The Cost: Mostly None or Small

Most accommodations cost nothing at all, and the great majority are easily made by even the smallest businesses. Often it's as simple as allowing more flexible times to arrive and depart from work or rearranging a work area. Studies of costs, reported by Joseph Shapiro, indicate the following:

- Fifty-one percent of all accommodations cost nothing.
- For the other 49 percent, the average cost of an accommodation was $300.
- Less than 1 percent of accommodations cost $5,000 or more.

Many companies are discovering that just by being flexible and opening up their attitudes toward persons with disabilities, they gain workers who are highly committed, productive, and loyal.

Protection for the Few or for All?

Over 90 percent of plaintiffs who filed cases under the ADA during the 1990s lost, according to an American Bar Association study of 1,200 such lawsuits. Most involved the core issue the ADA was passed to address: people with medical conditions seeking some accommodation from an employer in order to continue working.

By the end of 1999 the U.S. Supreme Court had ruled on three of the five such cases on its docket. The verdict? If you have a disability that can be corrected by medicine or devices such as eyeglasses, you're not "disabled" within the meaning of the law, and you can't use the ADA.

One problem is court definitions of disability. According to Fordham University law professor Matther Diller (1999), many judges are not viewing the ADA as the civil rights law that Congress mandated, but as another piece of benefits legislation to which only a few are entitled—those who fall under some court definition of "disabled." Here are some examples of this interpretation problem:

- A law professor with a paralyzed left hand, arm and leg as the result of a stroke wasn't "disabled," since he continued to work: he wasn't entitled to use the ADA.
- A woman with breast cancer was not "disabled," said the court, since she managed to continue working. Thus she had no right to a "reasonable accommodation."
- An employee with AIDS wasn't allowed to bring an ADA lawsuit challenging his dismissal because he'd gotten Social Security disability benefits: that was tantamount to saying he "couldn't work," said the court. Thus he had no right to file an employment

lawsuit. (Yet he and other plaintiffs are simply struggling to do exactly what in other contexts society demands that people do: look for a job, rather than sit at home collecting benefits.)

- A plaintiff with a spastic colon aggravated by multiple sclerosis wasn't entitled to an accommodation that would permit her to arrive at her clerical job 20 minutes late. The court said her condition did not qualify as a "disability."

There are hundreds of other similar cases. Courts have decided that people with cancer, multiple sclerosis, strokes, hemophilia, carpal tunnel syndrome, brain damage, and back and arm injuries aren't really "disabled." In making such decisions, they're falling prey to the stereotype that "being disabled means you can't work." This definition is a legacy of benefits laws and not at all the concept under civil rights law, which protects everyone.

"The courts have seized upon the definition of disability as a way to stop cases and, in effect, shield an employer's conduct from scrutiny," says Diller. Making people prove they're disabled in order to get the benefit of the law—that's making it into a benefits law, not a civil rights law, says Professor Robert Burgdorf, Jr. (1999), who helped draft the ADA. What makes anyone eligible for protection under the ADA is the same thing that makes any of us eligible for protection under the laws against racial or age discrimination: We're eligible to use the law once we run into discrimination. Granted, the ADA was passed primarily to help people disabled in one or more major life function, just as the Civil Rights laws were passed primarily to help the plight of African Americans, but in all such cases these laws are meant to protect anyone who encounters the type of discrimination a particular law addresses.

What the ADA calls for—re-tooling work so that the "essential functions of the job" are defined and that people are allowed to use a range of strategies and technologies to carry out those functions—is such a far-reaching, egalitarian idea that we aren't ready, it seems, to grasp its full implication: that the ADA is really the most egalitarian of laws. It's aimed at creating an accessible society for all of us. Many courts have not really accepted the premises of the ADA.

LEADERSHIP CHALLENGES: OVERCOMING BARRIERS TO CAREER SUCCESS

Persons with disabilities report that major barriers to their career success include making co-workers comfortable with their disability, finding adequate transportation to and from work, getting the technological support they need, and getting on-the-job training as well as the ongoing training and development that builds the skills they need.

Barrier #1: Making Co-workers Comfortable

The sensitivity and socializing issues are related to corporate culture and to level of employee awareness. Companies that have taken a leadership role in disability issues are providing training sessions for all employees in order to raise their awareness and provide skills for working effectively with this group. Influencing corporate culture change can open up many opportunities to utilize the talents of persons with disabilities—as well as other groups that are disadvantaged in the workplace.

Barrier #2: Finding Adequate Transportation

Transportation barriers are probably the simplest to overcome. Major cities now must modify their public transportation systems to provide lifts and ramps for persons with mobility impairments. Also, managers can work with these employees to solve transportation problems.

Barrier #3: Getting Technological Support

You know that technology can substitute for sensory and motor capacities, which opens up occupational options previously considered unavailable to those with certain disabilities. They are therefore able to engage in higher-level and more demanding kinds of work. With computer modems, fax machines, and similar technology, many computer-based types of work can be done at home, which eliminates the transportation barrier.

Barrier #4: Getting On-the-Job Training

Taking a broad view of how to integrate persons with disabilities in the mainstream workplace, leaders have identified five levels on an ascending scale of increasing integration:

1. Home-based or homebound employment, which is being upgraded with the advent of computer and telecommunications technology

2. Sheltered workshops that hire predominantly workers with disabilities

3. Semi-integrated units in mainstream industry that offer some disability-related accommodations and some shelter

4. Fully integrated employment in mainstream industry with some disability-related accommodation

5. Competitive employment with no disability-related accommodation

Sheltered workshops and semi-integrated work units can be provided by companies that need committed workers. The growing trend in such work preparation programs is to use mainstream industry as the setting for work training, evaluation, and adjustment, instead of using rehabilitation facilities. The trainees get acclimated to actual business situations, and employers and employees get to know the trainees through the relatively nonthreatening training process. Actual job performance sampling is also the best predictor of job success and the best way to identify problem areas and needs for further training.

These types of programs are used by the *crews* programs (Community Rehabilitative Employment Work Sites) This type of training program provides a gradual shift from rehabilitation training to on-the-job training to regular employment. About 70 percent of trainees in *crews* programs have mental disabilities, such as learning problems or retardation. They work in groups at workshops located in centers for persons with mental impairments. They are trained and supervised by trainers familiar with the skills needed by particular industries, such as assembling and packaging skills. Once trainees become productive, they are paid by the center to perform work for affiliated private businesses, who in turn pay the center.

Barrier #5: Getting Ongoing Training and Development

Some studies, such as those by S. Stace, indicate that most organizations are less likely to provide training and development opportunities to employees with disabilities than to other employees. This reinforces a tendency for persons with disabilities to define their viable career options rather narrowly. Leaders can encourage broader definitions of career goals, help persons with disabilities to develop career plans, and provide appropriate training and development opportunities. Reasonable accommodation in the training function can pay off handsomely.

LEADERSHIP OPPORTUNITIES: BUILDING ON THE STRENGTHS OF PERSONS WITH DISABILITIES

It makes good business sense to accommodate persons with disabilities, for they usually make excellent employees who enrich the company talent pool. Highly qualified persons with disabilities are most likely to apply to companies that have corporate environments that are friendly to them. They're most likely to be productive in such companies and to stay with them. Corporate cultures are likely to change when leaders recognize the many benefits that employees with disabilities bring to the organization, from skills and commitment, to connection with a multi-billion-dollar marketplace.

A step in changing the culture is for employees to attend training sessions that provide information about persons with disabilities. Such training should set the stage for adopting positive attitudes toward persons with disabilities and using positive language when referring to them. You and your company can follow the lead of successful companies in changing the culture and help persons with disabilities to make marketplace connections.

Strategy #1: Provide Diversity Training for All Employees

Employee training should include exploring the beliefs, myths, and stereotypes that lead to devaluation of the disabled; giving accurate information about current facts, trends, issues, and profiles; and developing approaches that help co-workers appreciate all persons with disabilities and work effectively with them. Training should include positive attitudes and language as well as specific information on how to relate to and assist people with various specific disabilities.

As co-workers become better able to see beyond a person's abilities or disabilities and to form relationships with the "normal" core person within, the quality of work life is further enhanced. Training should include some guidelines for personal interactions with the disabled. For example, helpers should not rush in and take over when they think a person with disability needs help, such as finding the way or getting through a door. They should ask whether and what type of help is needed. The FAQs at the end of this chapter gives some suggestions for assisting persons with various types of impairment.

Strategy #2: Adopt Positive Attitudes Toward Employees with Disabilities

The following are some constructive attitudes that business leaders can adopt for working with the disabled, attitudes that leaders can encourage among all employees.

Realize that people with disabilities are not all alike.

They have some common experiences and they are also highly diverse. On the one hand, many ask to be considered in the same vein as an ethnic minority. Most belong, in varying degrees, to a disabled community, with distinct cultural values, vocabulary, in-jokes, mutual support, and common issues. On the other hand, they ask that we also think in terms of diversity, for their disabilities and abilities range widely. Each person has his or her individual strengths, weaknesses, and peculiarities.

Focus on what people can do.

The traditional tendency is to focus on the impairment. Cooperate with these employees in taking a can-do attitude. Focus also on what people, disabled and non-disabled, can do together. See persons with disabilities as basically normal people who happen to have lost some function. Recognize that this does not define their character. They are people first, and their disability is only something they must cope with; it's not who they are.

Move through fear of disablement.

Be aware of the fear of many people, perhaps your own unconscious fear, of being around persons with disabilities. Others typically do not want to be reminded, "There but for the grace of God go I. This could happen to me." Almost everyone has fear around the issues of body image and brain power.

Accept persons with disabilities as normal persons.

Don't think of them as sick, as patients, as victims, or as abnormal. Remember that we all have some disability; it's just a matter of degree. Most persons with disabilities can marry, have sex, have children, and live many aspects of a "normal" life. The key is that they must work in order to have a full life. Their resources must be used in order for them to gain the sense of purpose, meaning, and achievement that all people want in life.

Explore possibilities for persons with mental retardation.

Even the mentally retarded can usually do some sort of meaningful work. Some are classified as "high functioning mentally retarded" or "high functioning Down's syndrome."

Never treat persons with disabilities as if they're childlike or childish.

Some persons with disabilities, especially the mentally impaired, may appear childlike to some people because of certain mannerisms that go along with their impairment. Respect for them as adults is essential. So are realistic assessments of their capabilities and the tailoring of assignments, expectations, and guidance to fit their level of ability.

Focus on the benefits.

Research reported by Taylor Cox indicates that employees with disabilities tend to be:

- very enthusiastic—because they're happy to have real employment
- eager to succeed—they're adaptable and cooperative
- absent and tardy less
- a terrific resource—one that has been wasted in the past

This adds up to highly committed, loyal employees.

Strategy #3: Use Positive Language

Certain language habits tend to focus on a person's disabilities rather than to focus on the person and to support stereotypes. Avoid such phrases as "John is a diabetic," and use instead "John has diabetes." When you say that someone *is* an alcoholic, arthritic, drug addict, or mental retardate, the implication is that he or she is nothing more than that. More realistic language is "Sue has a drinking problem" or "Jan has a learning impairment." Prefer the active to the passive, such as "person who uses a wheelchair" instead of "person confined to a wheelchair." Say "He is a wheelchair user" instead of "He is wheelchair bound."

Use tact in dealing with disabilities. In some cases, persons with disabilities do not want to deal with their disability. They don't want to talk about it or be reminded of it. This presents the greatest challenge for the manager. You can imply and communicate a complete acceptance of the disability, a willingness to work with it and to accommodate—without forcing the employee into unwanted discussions.

Strategy #4: Follow the Lead of Successful Companies

Hewlett Packard is on the top ten list of corporations that actively recruit from a pool of disabled workers. Their leaders say that the "HP Way" is to treat persons with disabilities with dignity and respect. It was among the first large corporations to set policies for a disability-sensitive workplace. This includes holding seminars to inform all employees about various types of disabilities, developing a mentorship program, and supporting an employee network for employees with disabilities. You can encourage people in your company to take similar actions.

Strategy #5: Make Marketplace Connections

Many companies overlook the U.S. disability market of nearly 52 million people, not to mention a global market estimated at 850 million people. Your company may find that employees with disabilities are a valuable resource for understanding this market arena. They can help the company create communication bridges for marketing to persons with disabilities. In 2001, disabled Americans' spending power was more than $1 trillion. Yet many companies have made no efforts to target this huge market. Those who do are likely to find some profitable niches.

Companies that design products and services for disability markets often find an even larger general market for the same or similar products and services. This principle is sometimes called universal design. Designs that work for persons with disabilities are also frequently more workable for the rest of the population. Examples include big-buttons telephones, voice-recognition and voice-output computers, safer bathtubs, easier-to-open boxes, and easy-to-grip tools. Special service designs can also apply to larger markets. For example, personal services targeted at disability markets, such as grocery shopping and home meal delivery, can also fill a need for working mothers and others.

Among the models featured in ads of leading companies are people who obviously have some disability. Studies indicate that 52 percent of households pay more attention to advertising messages featuring people with disabilities (Atlanta 1998). Nordstrom's uses disabled models in its catalogs. A Benetton ad campaign featured students from Institut St. Valantin, a school for the disabled in the Bavarian Alps. Allied Domecq in Europe hired a blind man for its campaign for Sauza tequila. General Motors, AT&T, IBM, Sears, and Kmart are also using models with disabilities. Meanwhile, some retail stores are catering to shoppers in wheelchairs by lowering the height of their counters.

All of this signals a real turning point in public attitudes. Gone are the days when people with disabilities were kept from public view, hidden away in institutions and private homes. In the past 25 years, that has changed in many parts of the world, as new laws and organizations work to help those with disabilities be welcomed into the mainstream for the many contributions they can make.

SUMMARY

Persons with disabilities are those who have a physical or mental impairment that substantially limits one or more of the major life activities, or a record of such impairment, or are regarded as having such an impairment. They're generally stereotyped as childlike, dependent, and in need of pity and not leading normal lives. At work they're often stereotyped as being capable of only menial jobs, a source of greater safety risks, costs, and other difficulties. The realities are that most want to work and to lead lives that are as normal as possible. Their abilities and motivations to work are as wide-ranging as that of the general public with the exception of their having an impairment in one or more activities. Managers and co-workers report that they are just as productive and cooperative as other workers, and they tend to have better records of punctuality, attendance, and turnover. Before the 1930s most persons with disabilities were confined to institutions. Disability activists have brought about a realization that when certain accommodations are made, most persons with disabilities can become relatively independent and productive.

At least 52 million Americans fall under the ADA definition, and about one-third of these are employed. Leaders and coworkers need to understand what it's like to be a person with disabilities, to become aware that they are normal persons except for a specific impairment. They want to be viewed as a person, not as "a disabled." The ILM was founded to help persons with disabilities take charge of their own lives, to form their own subculture, and to remove barriers to living and working on their own. New technology, especially computer-based technology, is helping more and more persons with even severe disabilities to achieve these goals.

The ADA is intended to end discrimination against persons because of their disabilities when reasonable accommodation will allow them to function effectively on the job. The law protects employers from undue hardship in providing such accommodation. Most accommodations cost nothing and those that do cost an average of $300. During the job recruitment phase, companies can no longer do medical screening or require medical histories. After hiring, workers with disabilities cannot be singled out for medical tests and screening. Reasonable accommodation must be made for applicants taking employment tests, and such screening tests must truly predict the likelihood of job success.

The major challenge for leaders is finding ways to help employees with disabilities to eliminate and overcome barriers to their productivity and effectiveness. This includes training to help co-workers feel knowledgeable and comfortable, helping persons with disabilities find adequate transportation, and providing the technological support and on-the-job training they need. The major opportunity leaders have is building upon the strengths of persons with disabilities. This includes providing adequate diversity training for all employees, adopting positive attitudes and language, adopting successful policies and practices, and helping persons with disabilities make marketplace connections. The main thing to remember when you want to personally assist a person with disability is to first ask what kind of help they would like.

Skill Builder 11.1: The Case of Severely Disabled Judy

Judy was paralyzed from the neck down. She must have help getting out of bed, getting dressed, and getting into a motorized wheelchair. Judy says that she still has the greatest ability of all: her mind, which is as sound as ever. She says if she can find a way to attend the university, she will get a degree in public administration and she wants to have a career in that field. She has come to you, a vocational counselor at the state Department of Rehabilitation as the first step in getting the funding she needs from the state in order to pursue this educational and career goal. Your responsibilities are:

- *Regarding education:* to predict the possibility and probability that an applicant will actually complete the educational program he or she enters.
- *Regarding occupation:* to predict the possibility and probability that an applicant will actually get and retain a job in the proposed field.
- *Regarding funds:* to allocate scarce state funds for rehabilitation in a manner that produces the best results for persons with disabilities and for society.

Considering Judy's situation and your responsibilities,

- What will your decision be?
- What will you say to Judy?

Skill Builder 11.2: The Case of Paul, Who Becomes Disabled

Paul works for the San Francisco AIDS Foundation as a developmental system associate. He's been there for nearly three years and his work has become an asset to the foundation. He is solely responsible for overseeing the data base system, which he helped create. His responsibilities include tracking donations and generating the foundation's budget reports and income statements. Paul's performance evaluations have always been excellent.

A little over a year ago Paul was diagnosed with Aggressive Liver Disease. This disease eventually results in liver failure. Paul is waiting for a liver transplant and hopes a donor will make one available within the next three to five years. Last year Paul took a four-month medical leave of absence to get his disease under control. Since his return, he has managed to keep his performance up to par, even though he must miss work for his doctor's appointment each week. The main physical problems that Paul is currently experiencing are fatigue and the nausea caused by the drugs he must take.

Paul knows he cannot continue working forty-hour weeks, and the commute to and from work is an energy drain he'd like to avoid. Paul starts thinking that he could do most of his work at home. He would need a computer, modem, and dedicated telephone line. He researches this idea and determines that this would require an initial investment of $2,500 plus about $20 per month in telephone charges. Paul is thinking about asking for a meeting with his manager *Claudia* and requesting that the foundation provide him with the equipment for a home office. As far as he knows, no other employee has ever asked to do most of their work from a home office. However, Paul is concerned that if he doesn't make better use of his failing energy, he'll be required to go on disability leave until his liver transplant comes through.

- What are the key issues here?
- If you were Paul, what would you do?
- If you were Claudia, what would you do?

Skill Builder 11.3: The Case of Visually Impaired Manager Jill

Jill Dovetsky is the Human Resource Manager of Spirit Clothing Co. She has been visually impaired since a very young age and in fact is almost totally blind. In spite of this, Jill earned a degree in business administration and worked her way up to Human Resource Manager within five years of joining Spirit.

Jill has had a positive influence on the company's policies toward persons with disabilities, and Spirit's workforce includes one of the highest proportions of employees with disabilities in the industry. Last month, on November 15, the Accounting Department Manager announced his retirement plans. Jill has met with the Spirit executive team and determined that they want a manager who will bring in "new blood," someone fairly young with recent university training but also a good track record in the field. They want someone with new ideas, new energy, and hopefully someone who will stay with the company for many years.

Jill has interviewed many applicants for this job and is leaning toward *Amy* as the probable best fit. She's now in the process of interviewing three finalists for the position and would like to make the selection before the Christmas holidays. She schedules a 5:30 p.m. meeting with Amy. The interview goes well. Amy seems to have most of the right answers to Jill's questions and responds satisfactorily to the few concerns that Jill has about Amy's qualifications.

They've been chatting for well over an hour when *Rick*, Jill's assistant knocks on the door and enters the room. Rick says, "Hey, why are you two sitting here in the dark?" As Rick turns on the lights, Amy lets out a sigh of relief, and it seems to Jill that a heavy weight is lifted from Amy's shoulders. Jill responds, "Well, you know me, Rick, lights or not, it's all the same to me. Amy, I must apologize for forgetting the time of day. But surely you know it's okay to remind me?" Amy seems quite flustered and stammers, "Oh, that's okay, it's . . . it doesn't matter."

Later, when Jill discusses the incident with Rick, he said, "Amy seemed very nervous and uncomfortable when I came in. I saw a definite sense of relief when I turned on the lights." Jill said, "Mmmm, too bad. We have several persons with disabilities in the Accounting Department—and in fact many throughout the company. The person we hire for this management job must know how to deal with disability situations and issues."

- What are the key issues in this case?
- If you were Amy, what would you have done?
- If you were Jill, what would you do now?

Skill Builder 11.4 Alisa at Touch-Up

Touch-Up Inc. has just opened a new branch and is looking for a Human Resources Director. One of the requirements for the new position is the ability to work from 50 to 70 hours per week and to maintain a heavy workload at times.

Alisa has applied for the position because it would advance her career. She is a 31-year-old Euro-American woman who uses a wheelchair because of paralysis in her lower legs. She joined Touch-Up two years ago as a personnel assistant in the Human Resources Department. She has received several promotions for excellent job performance and has maintained a heavy workload.

Joe also applied for the position. He has been with the company for a year as a sales person and in this position has put in very long work hours. He worked in the human resources department of Actel Company a few years ago.

Ted, the CEO, interviewed both Alisa and Joe. Alisa noticed that Ted seemed uncomfortable during the interview, which was much briefer than she had expected. Ted really didn't give her an opportunity to discuss why she thinks she is an ideal person for the new position.

A few days later, Ted announced that Joe would fill the new position.

- What are the key issues here?

- If you were Ted, would you have done anything differently?

- If you were Alisa, would you have done anything differently? What would you do now?

BONUS: FREQUENTLY ASKED QUESTIONS (FAQS) ABOUT PERSONS WITH DISABILITIES

FAQs about persons with disabilities reflect the need to understand specifics of working effectively with such persons, according to disability advocates Chalda Maloff and Susan Macduff. Here you'll find answers to FAQs about persons with 1) mobility impairments, 2) visual impairments, 3) hearing or speaking impairments.

FAQs About Persons with Mobility Impairments

Q: How do I offer help to a person with disability? Or should I?

- Offer help; it's never the wrong thing to do. It can always be declined if not wanted, but always ask *first* if the person wants you to help and take *no* for an answer.

- If help is wanted, ask specifically what you can do and how to do it, or suggest something and get agreement.

- If you assist another helper, remember the person with the disability is in charge.

- Handle the helping situation as unobtrusively as possible; avoid a "circus."

Q: How do I help persons using wheelchairs, crutches, etc.?

- Never grab their appliances except in cases of obvious immediate physical danger.

- After helping, stay a moment and make sure matters are in hand before leaving. Let the person know you are leaving.

Q: Should I open doors for persons with mobility impairments?

- Everyone can use help with doors at times.

- Hold the door itself, rather than their arm or wheelchair—until the person is completely inside.

Q: How can I be considerate of people who use wheelchairs?

- Avoid blocking aisles and other spaces that a wheelchair user needs to access—don't block with them briefcases, wastebaskets, etc.; push chairs under tables or desks; be aware.

- When having a conversation with a wheelchair user, try to seat yourself in front of the person, so you can talk eye to eye. If you must stand, step back so the person isn't required to look up to you.

- Reaching elevator buttons may be impossible for a wheelchair user; offer to help.
- Users of non-motorized wheelchairs may need help getting up inclines or around barriers, but never begin pushing a wheelchair without asking permission.
- Never release the chair without warning, so the wheelchair user is always in control.
- Be sure you know exactly where the person wants to go.
- Begin pushing a wheelchair cautiously if you are not familiar with it. Go slowly at first; wheelchairs can gain surprising momentum.
- Note the size and protrusions of the chair, such as protruding foot plates. Pay attention to the terrain, such as step-downs, and watch where you're going.
- When entering a crosswalk in a street, remember the wheelchair user's feet may be further out than you think and may be dangerously close to passing traffic.
- Going up steps, lean the chair back to raise the front wheels and push the chair up frontwards.
- Going down steps, ask if the person prefers going down frontwards or backwards. Either way, raise the front wheels and keep them up until the entire chair is down the step. The occupant should always be tilted toward the back against the backrest instead of toward the front where there is no support.

Q: How do I show consideration for persons who walk with difficulty?

- When approaching steps, walk alongside them and offer your arm, which they can grasp, giving them control and support. Grabbing their arm can upset their balance.
- If more help is needed, put your arm around their waist.
- Any time a person falls, ask how you can assist, or offer your arm for the fallen person to take if he or she needs it. Don't grab the person.

Q: What should I consider when I'm planning activities that require mobility-impaired persons to go to unfamiliar places?

- Mobility-impaired persons need to know in advance whether they will encounter a difficult barrier—such as inadequate parking places, ramps, and restrooms.
- Find out what kinds of parking arrangements they need.
- Wheelchair users need access to restrooms with hallways and doors wide enough for the chair, enough space inside the stall, and perhaps a handbar by the commode.
- Never insist on simply carrying a disabled person over, around, and through obstacles. They may find it demeaning, unpleasant, or even scary—and it could be dangerous for both of you. All of us prefer to be independent and self-possessed.
- When in doubt, ask the disabled person for some tips on places that are accessible and comfortable.

FAQs about Persons with Visual Impairments

Q: What should I consider when giving directions to visually impaired co-workers?

- The single most useful thing you may be able to do is to furnish relevant information about the immediate surroundings. Often just a few words will do.
- Furnish simple information without hesitation, anytime it seems appropriate.
- When giving directions, be sure you really know where the target location is.
- Find out what types of directions are most helpful; this will depend on what the person can see or not see. Use numbers, where possible. Ask yourself, How many blocks

down the street? How many doors down the hall?

- Give directions that are as specific as possible. Describe turns or curves as *left, right, clockwise,* etc. Terms such as *north* or *south* will probably be irrelevant.
- Describe anything out of the ordinary along the way, such as possible safety hazards.
- Tell persons with some vision about large, noticeable landmarks.
- Be as complete as necessary without overloading the person with information.
- If you think the place is simply too hard to find, offer to take them there.

Q: What should I do when I'm walking with a visually impaired person?

- City streets pose one of the biggest hazards for visually impaired persons. Offer your arm, but do not clutch the person's arm. Be sure you understand which street the person wants to cross.
- Don't leave the person until she or he is safely up the opposite curb.
- If the person does not take your arm, walk closely enough for her or him to reach over and touch you. Avoid getting separated in crowds.
- If the person takes your arm, walk slightly ahead to guide the way and proceed normally. Never push the person ahead of you.
- Avoid sudden turns or jerky movements.
- Tell the person when it's time to step up, step down, or step around some obstacle.
- Watch for overhead obstacles, especially with a taller companion.
- When approaching steps, elevators, or other possible barriers, pause and briefly describe what's ahead.

Q: What should I know about helping persons who use canes?

- If a person touches your foot with a cane, step aside and let her or him pass.
- Don't touch a cane without permission.
- When walking with a person who uses a cane, offer your arm.

Q: What should I know about helping person with guide dogs?

- Guide dogs and service dogs are used by a minority of visually impaired persons to help them get around and by mobility impaired persons to perform certain tasks.
- A guide dog is on duty any time it's wearing a harness.
- Take care to do nothing that will interfere with the dog's performance. Have faith in the dog and do not interfere unless there is a genuine emergency.
- Don't disrupt the routine and training by touching, feeding, petting, playing with, speaking to, or commanding the dog unless you're encouraged to do so.
- If you have a dog, keep it away from the guide dog.
- When walking with someone who is using a dog, offer your arm.

Q: What should I consider when I'm communicating with visually impaired persons?

- Be aware that they rely on sound and touch to know what's going on.
- When you first meet a visually impaired person, feel free to shake hands. You might say, "May I shake your hand?" to cue them that you're extending your hand.
- When you meet the person thereafter, identify yourself, and any others you are with.
- When you would normally hand a business associate a business card, brochure, or other written material, give the visually impaired person the option to accept. You might offer to stay a moment and help interpret the material.
- When you enter the presence of visually impaired persons, speak to them and let them

know you're there. Otherwise they may be unduly jolted when they hear you make some noise. Also, let them know when you're leaving.

- When leaving in a public place, say how long you'll be gone. Consider whether you need to offer to guide the person to a place where he or she can wait comfortably.
- When visually impaired persons hear your voice, they may be unsure whether you are talking to them or to someone else. They may remain silent rather than respond to comments they think might be meant for someone else.
- Address them by name when you're in a group or in public. If you don't know their name, stand directly in front of them and begin speaking. You may also gently touch their arm or repeat yourself to be sure they understand.
- Don't yell.
- Offer to describe visual sights.
- Speak up tactfully when some aspect of their grooming seems unpremeditated.

Q: When making plans that include visually impaired persons, what should I keep in mind?

- If you're planning to meet outside the office, the key issue is likely to be transportation. Give some advance notice so they can arrange for a ride.
- If you're not sure whether a visually impaired person would be able to attend an event, ask. Invite them and allow them to make the decision; then respect their wishes.
- At restaurants, remember to offer help in reading the menu and calling the server.

FAQs about Persons with Hearing or Speaking Impairments

Q: What do I need to know generally about working with persons with hearing or speaking impairments?

- Most people with speaking impairments have normal hearing, and many hearing-impaired persons have excellent speech skills, particularly those whose hearing impairment is not of long standing or is not severe.
- When you initiate a direct conversation with communication-impaired persons, begin by asking, orally or in writing, how best to communicate.
- When introducing communication-impaired persons to others, make every effort to introduce only one or two persons at a time. Try to find a quiet spot and pronounce names slowly and distinctly.
- If you're asked to make a telephone call for a communication-impaired person, get the key information first, perhaps asking the person write it.
- Before you hang up, check to be sure the message is complete, and after you hang up, give a complete report.

Q: What do I need to remember about lip-reading?

- When talking to persons who use lip-reading, position yourself about three or four feet directly in front of them with adequate light on your face so they can see your lips.
- Face them squarely without looking down or turning your head.
- Keep your hands away from your mouth and avoid eating, smoking, or chewing gum.
- Be aware that lip-reading is tiring, so avoid long monologues. Use a give-and-take format. Take a break during longer conversations.

Q: What do I need to remember about communicating nonverbally?

- Your eyes are especially expressive, so remove dark glasses, hats, etc. Maintain a natural and relaxed manner without straining to exaggerate.
- If nonverbal communication is inadequate, find other methods.
- When both speaking and using gestures, be sure the gestures correlate with the speech. Random motions throw the listener off balance, trying to sift them from the real clues.

Q: How about writing out messages?

- Writing out messages is slow but is sometimes used. Be creative when you communicate in writing. Often a simple diagram, picture, or map is most effective.
- Watch the person's face as he or she reads your message, just as you would do if you were speaking, so you can gauge the understanding and reaction.
- When persons begin writing to you, don't talk or otherwise distract them until they finish. Allow them to finish writing before you try to read the message, and read the entire message before you begin to answer.
- In a group, offer to read the person's written message aloud to others.

Q: How should I communicate when a professional interpreter is used?

- Professional interpreters who use sign language may be used by people with severe impairments. When you speak through an interpreter, your key goal should be to respect the dignity and autonomy of the impaired person who is the "listener." The interpreter is merely a device in this situation, a tool.
- Face the hearing-impaired person and speak as though no interpreter were present.
- Direct all your comments to the listener, the person with whom you have business, saying, for example, "Your project is being reviewed." The interpreter will relay these exact words to the person.
- Never direct comments intended for the listener to the interpreter, saying "His project is being reviewed." This has the effect of excluding the listener, implying that he is a helpless bystander.
- Remember to look at the listener, not the translator, and to speak to her or him in direct address, using *you*, not *he* or *she*.
- Avoid engaging an interpreter in side conversations that exclude the other person.
- Remember that with any translation process is difficult. Choose simple, specific words to be as clear and direct as possible, avoiding slang.

Q: How about communicating by telephone?

- A telecommunication device for the deaf (TDD) is used by many people with speaking or hearing impairments for communicating by telephone. If you don't have a TDD, you can still communicate through the device by going through a voice exchange system, available in most cities.
- Regular telephone communication with a hearing-impaired person is often possible without translator equipment, if the person has enough hearing ability.
- Organize your message ahead of time so you can convey it in a concise, direct manner.
- Try to quiet the noise at your end.
- Talk directly into the receiver clearly and firmly. Speak moderately slowly and pause at the end of a sentence.
- Be prepared to spell, rephrase, or use more creative ways to get your message across.
- If you have trouble hearing or understanding, ask for clarification as soon as you start getting lost.
- Keep the conversation short unless you are encouraged to extend it.

Q: *How do I plan and conduct meetings that include communication-impaired persons?*

- Select a room with good acoustics and a minimum of extraneous noise.
- Check ahead of time to determine what devices, such as interpreters, are needed.
- Offer the people with impairments preferential seating, where they will have a good view of speakers. Ask what they prefer.
- Ask speakers to stay in one spot rather than pacing the floor, for lip-readers.
- Pay special attention to the use of visual aids, handouts, charts, illustrations, and other communication aids.
- Write down new words or terms as you introduce them; it is almost impossible to lip read an unknown word.
- Write down important facts.
- Repeat all comments or questions from other people in the room before you respond to them.
- If you sit next to a hearing-impaired person in a meeting, be as quiet as possible. If you must communicate with the person during the meeting, write a brief note.
- Allow the hearing-impaired person to observe any notes you're taking.
- Afterwards, offer to answer questions.
- Make occasional eye contact with speaking-impaired persons, to see if they have anything to contribute to the discussion.
- If they can't speak up quickly, you can create a break in the conversation and encourage them to participate.
- If you sit next to a speaking-impaired person, offer to ask questions for her or him during the meeting.

Q: *How do I work effectively with persons with hearing impairments?*

- The first step is getting their attention without startling them. Stand in front of them and say their name loudly, but don't shout. If you don't know their name, stand directly in front of them and begin speaking. You may also gently touch their arm or repeat yourself to be sure they understand..
- If they don't respond, tap them lightly on the arm or shoulder. If you're not in touching range, wave your hand and try to make visual contact. You may also get attention by knocking on the desk or rapping on a nearby wall, as many are sensitive to such vibrations. Flipping the light switch will get the attention of everyone in the room, so use this method with greater selectivity.
- Effort and concentration are needed by hearing impaired persons in order to understand the speech of others. Conversing at length while walking down a hall or street may be exhausting or impossible.
- You may be able to help as an interpreter when a hearing-impaired person is trying to understand someone with a foreign accent or a child with a high-pitched voice.
- Giving needed information is one of the most helpful things you can do—especially about any sound that may spell danger, such as honking horns, sirens, and alarms—but also information that comes over public address systems, radio, and other sources where lip reading is impossible.

REFERENCES

Althen, Gary. *American Ways*. Yarmouth, ME: Intercultural Press, 1988.

Atlanta Paralympic Organizing Committee, as reported in "New Opportunities for Disabled People," *The Futurist*: 7, Dec 1998.

Berkeley, CA, City of. Survey of ADA costs, 1992.

Brown, S.E. "Creating a Disability Mythology," *International Journal of Rehabilitation Research*, 15: 227-233, 1992.

Bureau of National Affairs, Inc. "The Americans with Disabilities Act: A Practical and Legal Guide to Impact, Enforcement, and Compliance," Washington, DC, 1990.

Burgdorf, Robert L. "The ADA is a Civil Rights Law," *Electric Edge* magazine, www.ragged-edge-mag.com/extra/edgextraburgdorf.htm, September 1999.

Business Week, May 30, 1994: pp. 63-93. "The New Competitive Advantage."

Business Week, April 12, 1993, "Business Has to Find a New Meaning for 'Fairness.'"

Cox, Taylor, Jr. *Cultural Diversity in Organizations*. San Francisco: Berrett- Koehler Publishers, 1993.

Crew, Nancy M., and Irving Kenneth Zola. *Independent Living for Physically Disabled People*. San Francisco: Jossey-Bass, Inc., 1983.

Diller, Matthew, "Judges don't understand the ADA," *Electric Edge magazine*, www.ragged-edge-mag.com/extra/edgextradiller.htm, September 1999.

Green and Johnson 1987

Hahn, Harlan. "The Politics of Physical Differences," *Journal of Social Issues* 44, 1:39-47 1988.

Hahn, Harlan. "Toward a Politics of Disability." *Social Science Journal* 22:87-105, 1985

Harris Poll, 1986, 1987.

Hopkins, Kevin, and Susan Nestleroth, supplement in *Business Week*: p. 24, October 28, 1991.

Longmore, P.K. "A Note on Language and the Social Identity of Disabled People," *American Behavioral Scientist* 28, 3: 419-423, January/February 1985a.

Longmore, P.K. "Screening Stereotypes: Images of Disabled People." *Social Policy:* pp. 32-37, Summer 1985b.

Longmore, P.K. "Uncovering the Hidden History of People with Disabilities," *Reviews in American History*, pp. 355-364, September 1987.

Maloff, Chalda, and Susan Macduff. *Business and Social Etiquette With Disabled People*. Springfield, IL: Charles C. Thomas Publisher, 1988.

McDonough, Hugh H. "Hiring People with Disabilities." *Supervisory Management:* pp. 11-12, February 1992.

McGovern, John. "Justice Department Publishes Final Rules on the ADA," *P&R:* 12-73, November 1991.

McKee, Bradford. "Achieving Access for the Disabled." *Nation's Business:* pp. 31-34, June 1991.

Minton, Eric. "Implementing a Can-Do Attitude." *Hemisphere:* p. 31, July 1994.

"Myths & Facts: About People Who Have Disabilities." Chicago: National Easter Seal Society, 1992.

Mitchell, Olivia S., ed. *As the Workforce Ages*. Ithaca, New York: ILR Press, 1993.

Pear, Robert, *New York Times*, as reported in *San Francisco Chronicle*: A-1, December 13, 1999.

Potter, Edward E. *A Compliance Guide to the Americans with Disabilities Act*. Washington, DC: Employment Policy Foundation, 1991.

Ragged Edge, The: The Disability Experience from the Pages of the First Fifteen Years of the Disability Rag. ed. Barrett Shaw. .

Shapiro, Joseph. "The New Civil Rights." *Modern Maturity:* pp. 28-35, November-December 1994.

Shapiro, Joseph. *No Pity: People with Disabilities Forging a New Civil Rights Movement*. New York: Times Books, 1993.

Stace, S. "Vocational Rehabilitation for Women with Disabilities." *International Labour Review* 126, 3: 301-316, 1987.

Vash, Carolyn. "Sheltered Industrial Employment" in *Annual Review of Rehabilitation*. New York: Springer, 1980.

Vash, Carolyn. *The Psychology of Disability*. NY: Springer Publishing Co., 1981.

Vash, Carolyn L. *Personality and Adversity*. New York: Springer Publishing Co., 1994.

WSJ. "Labor Letter" in *Wall Street Journal*: p. A-1, June 7, 1994.

Resources

Computer Learning Center, Cerebral Palsy Center, 4500 Lincoln Avenue, Oakland, CA 94602, www.slip.net/~cpcoak, Email: cpcoak@slip.net

Disability History Website. www.disabilityhistory.org. Created by Patricia Chadwick and Stephen Dias of Oakland, CA.

Disability Rag & ReSource. *Ragged Edge* magazine, *Electric Edge*, online version, www.ragged-edge-mag.com

Read Me a Book Website. www.readmeabook.com created by Dick Stein.

Stepping Stones. Growth Center, 1720 Adeline St., Oakland, Ca 94607. (Mission: bringing persons with developmental disability into the mainstream of society).

We magazine. 372 Central Park West, Suite 6B, New York, NY 10025, www.wemagazine.com, e-mail editors@wemagazine.com. A monthly magazine that focuses on issues of persons with disability.

World Institute on Disability, 510 16th Street, Suite 100, Oakland, California 94612, phone (510) 763-4100.

CHAPTER 12

Working with Older Persons

*What if we began to value older persons as fountains of wisdom, support, and vitality . . .
and to expect that they would continue to grow, develop, and
unfold as they did earlier in life?*

Betty Friedan

Older Americans are the fastest-growing population group. Nearly half of all Americans are older than 40 and so are protected by age discrimination laws. Nearly one-third are older than 50, and baby boomers, as they turn 50, are dramatically increasing the size of this group. Now that it's illegal to force persons to retire, and medical breakthroughs help people stay vital at every age, more people are working into their 70s and 80s. All this means that more and more of your co-workers are likely to be persons older than 50.

Older workers who keep their skills and knowledge up to date are likely to have higher incomes than younger workers. But those who don't are more likely to lose their jobs. If they do, they then face more intense problems than their younger counterparts with unemployment, underemployment, and lowered wages. Those who keep their jobs may face age discrimination, management resistance to investing in training for older workers, and a resulting lack of new job skills. They must cope with the generation gap that can occur as new generations of younger workers enter the workforce. Older workers must also deal with retirement expectations—their own, their organization's, and the culture's—and decisions around retiring, not retiring, partially retiring, or starting a new career.

People who have taken the time and effort to learn some facts about older persons say they have boosted their ability to work productively with such persons. Supervisors say such information helps them understand how to help older employees to keep learning, stay motivated, and continue contributing to the organization. Co-workers, teams, and organizations gain a leading edge when they learn how to utilize the wealth of experience, knowledge, and talent that many older employees bring to the workplace.

In this chapter you'll explore what it's like to be an older person in the American workplace. You'll also learn about basic generational differences so that regardless of your age, you can bridge generation gaps. Remember, the more open you are to putting yourself in the place of others and seeing things the way they might see them, the better your ability to feel comfortable with people of all ages and to build productive work relationships. Specifically, you'll learn:

- How typical myths and stereotypes about older persons compare with reality
- How the current situation is connected to certain historical events

- Generation gaps and how to bridge them
- How ageism in the workplace affects older persons and organizations
- What you should know about the Age Discrimination Employment Act
- How skills obsolescence affects older employees employment and wages
- When and why people retire and the need for more options
- How to build on the strengths that older employees bring to the organization

Before we explore these fascinating aspects of working with people from other generations, complete Self-Awareness Activities 12.1 and 12.2.

Self-Awareness Activity 12.1: What Do You Believe about Older Persons?

Purpose:

- to get in touch with your beliefs and stereotypes about this group of people
- to experience how judgmental beliefs affect your thinking and feeling processes
- to experience the ways in which your beliefs create your reality regarding other persons, even before you have any interaction with them

Part I. What Do You Believe about Older Women?

Step 1. Associations

- Relax as deeply as you can: close your eyes and take a few deep breaths.
- Focus on the word "older woman" and allow a mental picture to come up in your mind's eye. Imagine that you are this woman. Be older woman.
- Notice your resistances to being this person, and your willingness.
- Notice the words and images that come to mind as you "see" this woman.
- Open your eyes and list 10 to 20 words in the order in which they occur to you.
- Review your list. Mark a plus beside the words that are positive, a minus beside the words that are negative, and a circle beside neutral words.

Step 2. Negative Associations

- Close your eyes and focus again on the image of the older woman. Formulate a negative opinion or judgment, perhaps one you typically hold about such women.
- Notice your *feelings* as you see the person in this negative way. What *thoughts* come up as you focus on the image?
- Write a few sentences about your feelings and thoughts.

Step 3. Positive Associations

- Formulate a positive opinion or judgment, perhaps one you typically hold about older women.
- Notice your *feelings* as you see the person in this positive way. What *thoughts* come up as you focus on the image?
- Write a few sentences about your feelings and thoughts.

Step 4. Insights

- Focus on the differences between your experiences when you hold negative and positive judgments or opinions. What were the differences? What meaning does this have for you, for your beliefs and feelings about people from this group, and about beliefs in general?

- Write your responses in a few sentences; include anything you like about your feelings, thoughts, and insights.

Part II. What Do You Believe about Older Men?

Repeat the steps in part I, this time focusing on the image of an older man.

Self-Awareness Activity 12.2: What Do You Know about Older Persons?

Purpose: To see what you know about the issues covered in this chapter.
Instructions: Determine whether you think the following statements are basically true or false—and think about why. The answers will emerge in this chapter, and the summary at the end of the chapter focuses on these issues.

1. Older workers are no more forgetful than younger ones.
2. Older workers have more difficulty adapting to change.
3. Older workers are prone to frequent absences because of age-related conditions and illnesses.
4. Older workers have fewer work accidents than younger workers.
5. Extensive training for older workers doesn't pay off because they don't learn as well and they'll retire soon anyway.
6. Older workers have more job security and higher pay than younger ones.
7. Workers who retire before age 65 tend to live longer than those who don't.

STEREOTYPED MYTHS AND REALITIES

Betty Friedan (1993) and Steven Sandell have surveyed a number of interesting studies of age discrimination. They found that most of the myths and stereotypes about older persons are either false or distorted, partial truths. In fact, most stem from the high value the American culture places on youth and appearance and the tendency to avoid facing one's own aging and eventual death.

Remember, although stereotypes aren't identical to prejudice, rigid stereotypes about people usually lead to prejudice. For example, you've heard that people lose their mental abilities after a certain age. When older co-worker Joe forgets an appointment, you think "Uh-oh, Joe's losing it." But when younger worker Janet forgets an appointment, you think "We all forget sometimes. She must be really busy." Each time a "Joe" forgets, your belief is reinforced, and soon you develop a rigid belief that all older persons lose their mental abilities and become forgetful. The ultimate goal in becoming aware of myths and stereotypes is to refute those that are false or rigid and to move beyond them to appreciating each generation's unique value and contribution to the workplace.

Myth #1: People quit learning when they get old.

One of the most untrue and degrading myths is "You can't teach an old dog new tricks," closely related to the myth that "Anyone over 35 is a technological dinosaur." It's common and career-devastating for management to ignore training for older workers—and for older workers to believe training won't pay off for them. In fact, while the most rapid rate of learning occurs at very young ages, the capacity to learn remains high throughout life. They're not only trainable and retrainable, but also a unique resource.

Intellectual performance

Intellectual performance remains robust throughout life for healthy people. From age 30 onward there is a slight mental slowdown in reaction time, but older workers compensate by increasing their speed on certain complex repetitive tasks. Other functions, such as vocabulary choice, get better with age, and the brain continues to develop throughout adult life. Some brain cells die each year, but connecting branches between them—pathways for the nerve impulses that create thought, feeling, and memory—keep sprouting and spreading, more than compensating for the loss of cells.

Forgetting names and poor concentration are not connected with normal aging. They're often connected with new priorities, more years of information, more names to sort through, and heavy work loads. Actually, 92 percent of persons older than 65 show no significant mental deterioration. Only about 8 percent have such symptoms as partial memory loss and slowing reaction time.

Research uncovered by author Betty Friedan indicates that age actually brings some positive changes in certain mental abilities. The type of intelligence that involves experience, meaning, knowledge, professional expertise, and wisdom continues to increase even though speed in completing IQ tests may decline. Older workers bring a lifetime of experience to the learning situation. That's why they tend to be better at problem solving, to draw on more information for decision making, and to be good mediators.

Further, people do *not* deteriorate in either basic mental competence or intelligence, even in their eighties, *if* they remain healthy and continue to be physically and mentally active and stimulated. For example, through mental activity, people can continue to develop vital new brain connections until the end of life and even reverse deterioration. Yet the false stereotypes of older persons may keep them from seeking or getting continuing education and the right kind of health care.

Avoiding Alzheimer's and the Nun Study

Among people over age 65, only 10 percent have Alzheimer's, but the incidence rises to about half of those over age 85. A breakthrough long-term study of nearly 700 retired nuns is being conducted by researcher David Snowden (Lemonick 2001). He has linked the essays they wrote as young women entering the order to their emotional and intellectual capabilities and tendencies, which are in turn linked to the likelihood that they will develop Alzheimer's and similar brain disorders. Here are some preliminary suggestions about how to prevent the onset of these disorders:

1. **Thinking.** Encourage rich density and complexity of ideas—to stimulate and exercise the brain's connections. Engage in an active intellectual life, if possible beginning with a college education, that values creative thinking.

2. **Feeling.** Learn how to think and act in ways that trigger positive emotions, spending more and more time in ever more expansive emotional states such as joy and peace.

3. **Acting.** Engage in active mental work and play. Choose interesting and challenging work that you like (better yet, that you love); hobbies that are engaging, absorbing, and fun such as crossword puzzles, card games, mind games; challenging craft and building projects.

4. **Learning.** Continually learn new information and skills, such as new languages, vocations, hobbies, avocations, teaching, tutoring

5. **Relating.** Keep developing close relationships with family and friends and maintain close contact.

6. **Protecting Head.** Avoid head trauma by using helmets, seatbelts, airbags, etc.

7. **Preventing.** Check your family history for signs and Alzheimer's to determine if you must take more preventive measures than usual.

Myth #2: Older workers are more rigid and dogmatic.

Evidence indicates that dogmatic behavior is unrelated to age. What is related to age is a tendency to become more caring, accepting, and mellow. This means that older persons tend to handle crises better than younger workers and to see the humor in life's slings and arrows.

Nurturing, Accepting

People are more likely to mentor others and become more accepting of life as they age. Carol Ryff's studies indicate that men and women tend to change their behavior during middle age to focus more on mentoring younger persons, showing more concern for guiding the next generation and feeling more of a sense of responsibility to younger persons. Beyond middle age, people tend to become more accepting of life, to adapt to the triumphs and disappointments of being human, and to view past events as inevitable, appropriate, and meaningful (Ryff 1985). While basic character traits tend to be stable, people's experiences and personal development become more varied with age.

Appreciative of Respect

An implication of the rigid myth is that older workers resent being told what to do by younger managers. In fact, no one really likes being told what to do, and younger workers are more apt to respond negatively. Older workers do appreciate receiving some respect for their years of experience. When managers get them on their side, they're less likely than younger workers to be vying for the manager's position, to quit, or to be disloyal. Their accumulated wisdom can be very helpful to managers and co-workers.

Creative

Also implied in the rigid myth is that older workers are not very creative. In fact, creativity and intellectual activity is still vital in persons older than 100, according to a Social Security Administration survey of such people. When creativity is encouraged and rewarded, and when the environment is structured to enhance it, older workers bring a greater richness of ideas, stemming from their abundance of life experience (Friedan 1993).

Myth #3: Older workers are less productive, just coasting to retirement.

In 1998 over 100 leading image consultants were sent pictures of gray-haired men—along with pictures of the same men with darker hair. Their reaction? While they assumed that 49% of the dark-haired men would be "very capable," they gave only 27% of gray-haired men that rating. Scripps Howard News Service (1998) reported that researchers expected gray-haired women to fare even worse, due to gender bias.

Gray-haired persons, and those who otherwise look older, are seen as less capable and less productive than they were when they were younger, but research refutes this myth. There is no significant performance decline that's caused by aging in the case of engineers, scientists, blue-collar workers, clerical workers, and production workers. And several studies suggest that older paraprofessionals and clerical workers outperform younger workers.

U.S. Department of Labor studies reveal that age has little effect on manual-labor workers through age 50, and declines in productivity after age 50 never exceed 10 percent, on average. A study of 1,700 managers working in diverse organizations showed that when managerial performance is measured in terms of such bottom-line indicators as return on total capital, growth of stockholders' equity, earnings per share, and sales growth, no significant differences in performance could be related to the age of managers.

A similar myth is that older employees are less energetic and enthusiastic. For some older persons, but not all, some age-related decline may occur in speed and accuracy of movement, perception, hearing, vision, and certain types of problem-solving skills. However, researchers have concluded that these declines would affect performance in only a few jobs requiring extremely high levels of sensory or cognitive skills. Workers older than 60 are functionally able to excel in nearly all occupations, drawing on years of experience and good judgment. Overwhelming scientific evidence, reported in *Retirement Living* indicates that older workers:

- enjoy higher morale
- have a greater sense of organization commitment
- are more involved in their jobs
- rate work as more important to their lives
- have the highest job satisfaction of any age group
- rate needs for job security as more important

- are less likely to report an intention to leave the organization
- are much less likely to leave the organization

Age stereotypes depict older people as frail and fragile, as having lost the vitality and energy necessary to make a full commitment to a career. Actually, large differences exist with respect to the health and well-being of persons in every age category. While some people remain very healthy in their eighties, and even in their nineties, others become mentally and physically old at 40. Recently, changes in lifestyles, dietary habits, and exercise patterns, along with the better medical interventions, have dramatically changed the health picture for older persons.

In summary, evidence on the performance of older workers and managers generally indicates that they perform as well as their younger counterparts on almost all criteria. Chronological age is a poor indicator of a person's mental and physical well-being and an inadequate basis for predicting vocational performance. Individual differences within age groups account for much more variation in performance than does age. Managers should carefully assess each employee's capabilities with an eye toward matching them to job requirements.

Myth #4: Older people have higher absenteeism and accident rates.

The accidents myth is totally false. Bureau of Labor Statistics data shows that occupational injuries occur at a lower rate for older workers. In many instances older workers are better risks than younger workers across a variety of jobs even when risk exposure is controlled. Some studies indicate that their accident rate is less than half that of younger workers. All managers agree that older workers tend to be more careful.

The absentee myth is essentially untrue. Older employees' overall attendance record is much better than that of younger workers. For one thing, people older than 65 are less likely than those who are younger to suffer from the *acute* illnesses that require hospitalization and absenteeism. Also, younger workers are more likely to take days off for caring for family members, for dealing with love affairs, for going to the beach, and for other "mental health" reasons. Most older workers have outlived their responsibilities for dependent children and elderly parents and are free to concentrate on their careers.

The kernel of truth in the absentee myth is that older workers are more likely to be absent for unavoidable reasons such as illness. The older we get, the more likely we are to develop *chronic* diseases and to become disabled, primarily because of heart disease, arthritis, or cancer. However, medical breakthroughs are helping people to avoid and cope with these diseases. And nearly all older persons remain healthy until the last few months of their lives (Salzberg 1983); for example:

- 95 percent of persons older than 65 live independent lives
- 95 percent of age-70 persons have no serious disabilities
- 80 percent of age-80 persons have no serious disabilities

The absentee myth is based on an image of age as inevitable decline and deterioration, which in turn is tied to a dread of aging and of dying. It causes people to deny that old age even exists for them. And the more age is denied, the more terrifying it becomes. Prejudice and discrimination toward the elderly are actually created by the American culture's obsession with and idealization of youth and by our refusal even to look at the reality of age on its own terms. Subconsciously, we think that if we can keep old people out of sight, we can keep the illusion of eternal youth and rarely have to face the fact that we all age and die.

Myth #5: Older workers are not as attractive to clients.

This myth contains the kernel of truth implied by our discussion of the American tendency to be obsessed with youth and fearful of old age. However, it overlooks the truth that beauty is in the eye of the beholder—and it's only skin deep.

Gender Differences

Since women's value is more firmly tied to looks than men's, women stand to lose the most as they age. If a man is old, ugly, and wise, he's a sage. If a woman is old, ugly, and wise, she's a hag, a witch, a crone. But in prepatriarchal societies the elder women were generally considered founts of wisdom, law, healing skills, and moral leadership, according to Betty Friedan's study. Their wrinkles would have been badges of honor, not of shame. By contrast, our society regards elder women as relatively unattractive and useless.

When men are considered in their prime, in their fifties and sixties, women are considered to be over the hill. The aging woman is often surprised and hurt by the unexpected hostility she encounters as she slips into old age. The combination of sexism and ageism turns older women into invisible citizens of the modern world. We make them invisible by rarely featuring them in films or television programs, and generally passing them by as social and professional leaders.

Media and Advertising Stereotypes

Older people are generally pictured as "ugly, toothless, sexless, incontinent, senile, confused, and helpless," and old age is so negatively stereotyped that "it has become something to dread and feel threatened by." These were the conclusions of the Gray Panthers' nationwide volunteer force called Media Watch, reported in *Advertising Age*. The sales pitches for products that promise to stop or cover up aging send the message that age is acceptable only if it passes for or acts like youth. A multibillion-dollar beauty industry exploits women's well-founded fear of looking old. Many people proclaimed a real breakthrough in the 1980s when the female stars of the TV series *Dynasty* were considered still attractive and employable at age 50. A 1993 consumer survey, reported in *Advertising Age*, found that most consumers older than 35 now believe that a woman can be beautiful at 40, or 50, and *even* past 60. This was hailed as great progress, even though it implies that women past sixty-something have no chance (*Advertising Age* 1993).

Yet the U.S. population is about one-third older persons over age 50, one-third youngsters under age 20, and one-third adults in between. Assuming youngsters are not potential customers for many of the products and services that companies sell, people 50 and older represent nearly half the potential customers that most companies should target. Companies who project an image of older persons in a positive way, with attractive, natural older role models will hit pay dirt, especially with the me-generation of baby boomers, as discussed later.

Myth #6: One That's True—You're only as old as you feel.

Remember, a myth is a symbolic saying or story whose function is to bind together the thoughts of a group and promote coordinated social action. Some myths are essentially true, and this is one of them. Scientists are discovering that aging is mainly in the mind. The best ways to slow the mental aging process are:

- maintaining a positive attitude
- remaining mentally and physically active

These activities bring us to Myth #7.

Myth #7: One That's Very True—Use it or lose it.

This myth is not only true, it's a key to staying healthy and alert as we grow older. We can retain our vitality and health best by using our minds and bodies. Physical and mental exercise, along with a healthy diet, are the specific keys. Energy levels peak in the early thirties and normally drop about 7 percent per decade, primarily because people tend to become more sedentary. But physical exercise can dramatically slow the energy drop.

Aging decline has in fact been reversed with changes in diet, exercise, lifestyle, and environment. People who reach age 65 in the 1990s are more likely to be healthy, active, and financially self-sufficient than any previous generation (Campbell, Abolafia, and Maddox 1985). We must learn to view age as continued human development, a continuation of personal growth, not of decline and decay. Staying independent and connected to people in the workplace, community, and family are crucial to vital aging and longevity. The key is to move on to new growth in the last third of life, from age 60 to 90.

PAST AND PRESENT PROFILE

In 1860 people over age 65 were less than 3 percent of the population but they had great economic and political influence relative to their proportion. They dictated the behavior of younger family members because they owned the farm or family business and they knew more than anyone about making money from it. New generations adopted the occupations and lifestyles of parents and grandparents, so older people's knowledge and experience were indispensable. They were at the center of economic and social life, from trade and commerce to finance, political organization, and religious training. By the 1930s most who lived to old age faced poverty, loneliness, and ageism, according to J.C. Hushbeck's studies (1989). What happened in between?

Separation of the Generations

Between 1860 and 1920 we moved from an agricultural to an industrial economy. Mass production led to the de-skilling of most workers. The rapid pace of work, need for stamina, and a rapid wearing-out of laborers led firms to prefer hiring younger applicants. This put older workers at a physical and technological disadvantage. As people moved to cities to get jobs, the nuclear family became the norm, housed in small quarters, and the older generation was separated from the younger.

Fewer and fewer older persons were able to be self-supporting or economically productive. Many were faced with no property, no job, and uncertain family support. Industrial pension plans were usually nonexistent or inadequate when it was time to retire. Social security and improved company pension plans have improved the retirement picture, but most retirees are still socially isolated, ghettoized, and ignored.

Current Profile

Today, people are living longer, so what constitutes "old age" is changing, and the population of older persons is growing larger by the year. Now that childbirth is safer and less frequent, women are out-living men.

How old is old?

For business purposes, we might say it's older than 40 because that's when protection from discrimination kicks in. Other government sources seem to disagree. For example, the Bureau of Labor Statistics says it's 55, but the Census Bureau says it's 65. Gerontologists say that because people live longer and remain healthier than in the past, it's now more realistic to use two age categories:

- *young-old*, currently 65 to 75, soon to be 75 to 85
- *old-old*, now older than 75, soon to be older than 85

Currently, persons who make it to age 55 without chronic illness will normally remain healthy to age 85.

How many are old?

About 13 percent of Americans are currently older than 65, a huge increase during this century, and the trend is expected to accelerate in the coming 25 years, as shown in Table 12.1.

TABLE 12.1: Proportion of Americans Over Age 65

1900	1990	2015, Projected
4%, 1 in 25	13%, 1 in 8	17%, 1 in 6
3 million	31 million	54 million

Source: U.S. Census Bureau, 1993.

Ethnic Differences

How old you live to be is affected by your ethnic heritage. Here are percentages of people older than 65 in 1990, by ethnic subgroup:

- Euro-Americans   13 percent
- Asian Americans   8 percent
- Latino Americans   8 percent
- African Americans   6 percent
- American Indians   6 percent

The Euro-American population had the highest proportion of elderly because they have higher over-65 survival rates and lower fertility rates, meaning fewer young persons.

- Who lives the longest? Euro-American women, who average age 80 at death.
- Who dies the youngest? African American men, average age 45 at death.

Women—Older and Poorer

About two-thirds of people older than 65 are women—because they live longer. The older they become, the less likely the women are to be married because their husbands die before they do. Therefore, older women are more likely to live alone, in contrast to older men, most of whom are married and living with their wives. And the women are twice as likely to live in poverty, with 16 percent classified as poor. Nationally, about 10 percent of older persons live in poverty, but in nine southern states, the rate is 20 percent or more (U.S. Census Bureau 1993).

Because women live longer and are apt to need to work, in 1998 about 255,000 women in their 70s, 80s, and even 90s were working, an 80 percent increase since 1985. But many were working because they wanted to (Working Woman 1999).

AGEISM: HOW IT WORKS AND HOW TO MOVE BEYOND IT

Ageism means that as you progress from being perceived as a middle-aged employee in the prime of life to an older employee, you are likely to be increasingly devalued, avoided, and discriminated against. Such actions are usually subtle but occasionally blatant. We need our older employees. They're the fastest-growing population group at the same time that the U.S. labor pool is shrinking. It's time for everyone in the workplace to reassess negative views of older workers. We all have a stake in how society will treat our future selves.

Impact of Ageism on Careers

The social impact of ageism can deflate your ego, but the career impact can deflate your bank account. Benson Rosen and Thomas Jerdee (1988) reported on a study sponsored by *Harvard Business Review* (HBR). Researchers found that younger managers stereotype older workers as being rigid, too old to train, declining in competence, and less creative than younger workers. When the researchers compared the ways younger managers treat 30-year-olds and 60-year-olds, they found that:

- Managers perceive older employees to be relatively inflexible and resistant to change. They therefore make much less effort to give older persons feedback about needed changes in performance.

- Managers provide very limited organization support for the career development and retraining of older employees.

- The promotion opportunities for older people are somewhat restricted, especially when the new positions demand creativity, mental alertness, or the capacity to deal with crisis situations.

How Managers Withhold Feedback and Encouragement

In this study researchers provided a case involving customer complaints about employee performance. Most of the managers said they would have an encouraging talk with a 30-year-old employee, but they would reassign a 60-year-old. Clearly the managers saw the older employee as more resistant to their influence, even though there was nothing in the case to support such a perception. Reassigning the older employee, rather than encouraging him to improve his performance, deprives the employee of the opportunity to improve his performance. Such actions make the effects of age stereotyping very difficult to overcome. By transferring older employees, managers avoid a direct test of their own assumptions about older workers' rigidity and resistance to change. Such managers cut off the opportunity to learn whether this age stereotype is valid or not.

How the "Too–Old–to–Train" Stereotype Creates Blocks

Employees over age 50 are vulnerable to problems of career obsolescence. Both managers and their older employees need to commit themselves to continuous career development in order to keep older workers' knowledge and skills up to date. One of the cases in the HBR study revealed managers' assumptions that older workers are not motivated to improve their job-related skills. These assumptions are reflected in decisions to avoid investments in the continued development of older employees. Assumptions about retirement practices can also influence these decisions. While 74 percent would allocate funds to send a 30-year-old employee to a production seminar, only 53 percent would allocate it for a 60-year-old. Managers may balk at paying for expensive training for older employees, believing they'll soon retire. But younger employees change jobs more frequently, so investment in their training may also be "wasted."

How the "Less–Creative" Stereotype Hinders

Managers are less likely to promote older employees. Managers in the study were asked to decide whether a sales rep should be promoted to a marketing director position that called for fresh solutions to challenging problems. They rated the outlook for successful performance as much less favorable for a 60-year-old candidate than for a 30-year-old, and indicated very little support for promoting the older candidate.

How the "Declining–Competence" Stereotype Discriminates

Managers are more likely to give demanding new jobs to younger workers, reflecting the stereotype that connects age with declining mental alertness and resulting nervousness. The majority of managers viewed a 30-year-old employee as more suitable for a new role calling for poise and mental alertness. The HBR study revealed a pattern in which older employees are seen as less able to cope with higher-level positions when role requirements conflict with age stereotypes. Therefore, the probability of a promotion is somewhat lower for an older employee than for an identically qualified younger person.

How to Move Beyond Ageism

Yes, the older you get, the more devaluation and discrimination you are likely to face. That's because we as Americans tend to view old age quite negatively, often equating it with loss of abilities, vitality, and attractiveness and with illness, nursing homes, and death. It's not surprising that many younger people prefer to avoid older people and the depressing thoughts their presence may trigger. But such pictures are increasingly false. To move beyond ageism, we must begin dealing with the new facts of life. We must adopt accurate, life-affirming beliefs.

The Third Age as Vital Age

We're entering an era when old age will be a full one-third of life for most people.

1. Youth is the first 30 years of life.
2. Middle age the second 30 years.
3. Old age is the third 30 years, from age 60 to 90.

Many people today are retaining great vitality throughout the Third Age, embarking on a new adventure and finding new wholeness. They have a burning need to be part of an enterprise larger than self, whether in the workplace or the community at large, to contribute to humanity, and to pass on something to the next generation.

The Need for New Beliefs

What if we reexamine our devastating stereotypes of age as do-nothing retirement, deterioration, and decline and change our beliefs? What if we begin to value older persons as fountains of wisdom, support, and vitality—as slow-burning, steady energy, now past the flash fires of youth? What if we begin to allow and expect that they will continue to grow, develop, and unfold in the last third of life as they have during the first two-thirds? Won't we have much to gain and little to lose? Wouldn't such new beliefs lay the foundation for bridging the generation gap?

BRIDGING GENERATION GAPS

Older and younger employees often experience a communication gap that is caused primarily by the differences in their experiences and values. Understanding the key themes for each age group can build a base for understanding and can reduce stereotypes, prejudice, and discrimination.

The Generation Gap

The HBR study indicates that younger managers are less likely to support older employees' training. But managers in the over-50 age category are more likely to recommend financial support to enable an older employee to attend a technical seminar. In promotion decisions, older managers are much less likely to be influenced by the candidate's age. They are equally likely to promote both a younger and older man, and they would favor the creation of a new supervisory position for both a younger and an older woman. We might conclude that an older employee has a better chance of fair treatment from an older boss. We might also conclude that the older boss has lived long enough to begin seeing that age stereotypes are not necessarily true. We all need to be aware of these kinds of generation gaps. Including older managers on any decision-making panel can provide the balance needed for fair decisions.

Generational Values and Customs

How can you understand what makes each generation tick? Learn about their key values. Each generation internalizes the cultural ethos (essence of the key values) that are typical of the larger culture at the time that generation was coming of age. They incorporate that cultural ethos as they deal with the issues of the day, and as they respond to major historical events. Table 12.2 summarizes research on the ethos of various American generations of this century, based on studies by L.J. Gann and P.J. Duignan (1986), and S.E. Jackson (1992).

TABLE 12.2: Generations and Their Cultural Ethos

Birth Years	Era	Key issues	Cultural Ethos
1930-1945	Matures	Great Depression ⟶ World War II ⟶	Surviving; security; saving Defending freedom; duty
1946-1964	Baby Boomers	Postwar ⟶ Civil rights ⟶ Me generation ⟶	Rebuilding; demanding personal freedoms; individuality; seeking personal fulfillment
1965-1975	Generation Xers	Information Age ⟶	Spanning the global village; cutting edge, fun, diversity
1975-1985	Millenniums	Planetary Shifts ⟶	Ethnic diversity, global concern, rapidly changing technology

Matures

People in the Mature generation range in age from fifty-something to seventy, a relatively small group that includes most of our current business and political leaders. They grew up in the 1930s to 1950s. Most share a strong work ethic and place a premium on job and financial security—at it's flip side employee loyalty, which they hold onto long after younger generations have given up. Some, especially ethnic minorities, are first- or second-generation immigrants who still retain many customs from their home cultures, such as dress, music, principles of family life, respect for authority figures, and patriotism. Most hold to the traditional values that Americans are know for around the world. They tend to ask, Why do young people think the world owes them a living? They believe that "when the going gets tough, the tough get going" and generally keep a stiff upper lip in the face of adversity.

Baby Boomers

Members of the Baby Boom generation are now mostly in their thirties and forties and some are turning 50. They grew up in the 1950s and 1960s and entered the workforce in the 1970s and 1980s. Their large size gives them significant social and economic clout. In their youth they tended to be either quite traditional or radical. Some are former hippies and yippies, and many are now yuppies. Some, such as the hippies, were suspicious of big business and big government. A few, such as the yippies, took to the streets to demonstrate against the Vietnam war and other political issues. Many have experimented with drugs, and their slogan in the 1960s was "Don't trust anyone over 30."

They grew up in more permissive homes, and they place great value on work that is self-actualizing. Some rejected their parents' focus on upward mobility and dedication to work. They insisted on finding and expressing their own individuality and pursuing a lifestyle that leaves ample time for the pursuit of leisure activities. Their focus on their personal development led to the designation of the "Me Generation" in the 1970s. In the 1980s, however, they encountered economic stagnation and disappointments in the workplace. Many, as yuppies, found that in order to succeed in careers they had to sacrifice the kind of home life and personal life they desired.

Baby Boomer employees are battling their own midlife crises and even at midlife are focusing on discovering the meaning of life.

Generation X'ers

Generation X members, born between 1965 and 1975, ranges in age from late twenties to early thirties in 2000. They're a smaller group than the Boomers. Some are children of hippies and other counter-culture types. Because this group is greatly divided between the haves and have-nots, clear statements about who they are have not yet emerged. One thing for sure: They're more diverse. They accept diversity and even insist on it. Most tend to be less materialistic and more idealistic than the their Yuppie predecessors. Many are from broken homes and so tend to want marriages that work and that last. Many have adopted their parents' values of personal growth and development.

Generation X workers want to avoid stress and burnout; they search for jobs that will let them have a personal life. They want stress-free fun and are attracted to anything they consider leading-edge but also like certain old things in new packages, such as the new Volkswagen Beetle.

Bruce Tulgan (1999) discovered five typical myths about Gen X'ers that help create a generation gap.

Myth #1: X'ers are disloyal. The reality is that they're wary but not disloyal. They've entered the workforce at a time following great corporate downsizings and reorganizations, so the old-fashioned employee loyalty makes no sense for them. This contrasts with older employees who tend to hold onto the ideal of loyalty until and unless betrayal experiences finally shake them loose from this attachment.

Myth #2: X'ers are arrogant. They tend to be very self-confident but not arrogant. Their parents were more likely to be divorced, both working, or more permissive than parents of previous generations. They learned to do things for themselves and to handle problems alone. They learned over and over again that if they had to, they could fend for themselves.

Myth #3: X'ers have short attention spans. They're the first generation to grow up within the information revolution. That's shaped the way they think, learn, and communicate. They prefer audio, visual, and computer over print media. They can quickly sift through, select, and assimilate information from simultaneous sources. This fast-and-loose style fits the emerging chaotic world.

Myth #4: X'ers are not willing to pay their dues. Their experience with corporate downsizing has shown that dues-paying doesn't pay off. The only source of security they believe in is themselves.

Myth #5: X'ers want instant rewards. Waiting to be rewarded poses problems for most X'ers because they've always lived in a world where everything changes faster than anyone can keep track. They do need constant feedback from employers in order to feel secure. They prefer to work in a way that produces tangible results each day.

The reality is that managers who make slight accommodations for Gen X'ers ways of doing things will find most to be hard-working, creative, and productive.

Their Achievement Style. Help them see the daily tangible results of the work. For example, break down a job into concrete, achievable parts with daily checklists so they can note what they've accomplished. Provide frequent feedback. Give specific feedback each time a task is completed, with concrete suggestions for improvement, if necessary.

Offer to be a mentor. Most welcome the chance to create long-term bonds of loyalty with teaching managers and mentors since long-term relationships with organizations are unavailable. Make sure they're learning marketable skills on the job. Give them creative challenges and opportunities to build proof of their value. This helps them build the security from within they've learned to rely on rather than on a corporation.

Their Learning Style. They like to learn on their own. Their independence and ability to assimilate information make them suited to self-study courses. Agree on the learning goals and time targets, then provide them with multiple sources of the information they need and let them go for it.

Millennium Generation

Born between 1975 and 1985 the Millennium Generation is 15- to 25-years-old in 2000. It's the most diverse in history, with 60 percent more non-Euro-Americans than in previous generations. About 30 percent are either African American, Latino American, or Asian American. More are raised in cities with a majority of non-Euro-Americans (Chideya 1999). Although some states, such as South Dakota are still 90 percent Euro-American, others such as California are no longer predominantly Euro-American.

Mellowing with Age

Younger people, ages 18 to 25, are more likely to see themselves as emotional, nervous, competitive, uncooperative, and not helpful or supportive of others. Having arguments that lead to physical blows occurs almost exclusively among the young men. People younger than 30 are much less likely to vote, to make charitable contributions regardless of income, or to participate in voluntary organizations. Spirituality plays a relatively minor role in the lives of most young people and takes on increasing significance as they age.

Older persons, regardless of generation, tend to grow mellow with age. Studies by Walter Gove of Vanderbilt University suggest that as we age, we become less self-absorbed, more cooperative and attentive to others. We function more effectively, becoming more serene and less emotional. We act in more socially accepted ways, are more community oriented, and are more likely to see others as friendly and considerate. Finally, we become more spiritual, having a stronger interest in spiritual activities and turning to spiritual beliefs that comfort us.

The Impact of Cross–Generational Work Teams

As corporate structures become more flexible and web-like, as layers of hierarchy are removed, previously segregated generations of employees find themselves working together and even rotating jobs among themselves. Another factor throwing the generations together is the entry and reentry into the workforce of middle-aged women, former retirees, and young student interns and apprentices. Four generations of workers may now find themselves working side by side. This provides rich opportunities for all of them. Younger employees have much to learn from older ones, ranging from alternative philosophies of life to practical tips gained from life experiences. Older workers can gain much from younger ones, ranging from learning about what's new to absorbing a fresh, high-energy outlook.

Strategies for Bridging Generation Gaps

Bridging the generation gap at all levels is becoming more important in the workplace because networking and relationships are more central to job performance. Here are a few bridging strategies to start your thinking. You may come up with others on your own.

Use Diverse Teams

Except at work, many young employees may have few relationships with older persons other than their parents and grandparents. One remedy for this experiential gap is to make assignments to teams and committees so that employees of different ages will work together. Studies discussed in Chapter 4 indicate that meaningful contact among diverse employees can reduce prejudice. Contact that involves working together toward meaningful goals is most likely to bridge generational differences.

Open Up Communication Lines

Be aware of communication across the generation gap. People tend to communicate within their own age groups rather than between them because they seek perspectives similar to their own and support for their opinions. Also, younger workers may shun and thus isolate older workers, creating a communication gap. Part of diversity training can be helping younger people find ways to include older workers in communication lines and vice versa.

Use Diversity Training

Training should include information that makes younger workers more aware and sensitive of older workers' needs, strengths, and potential contributions—helping them replace myths and stereotypes with facts.

Training can also include information that makes older workers more aware of their own actions that foster the generation gap and suggests alternate actions. For example, a person's image is a powerful communication tool. An image that promotes rapport usually includes dressing in style, maintaining good grooming, enjoying an active personal life, showing a warm sense of humor, *not* offering knee-jerk judgmental criticisms of fellow workers or repeating the same old comments, contributing new ideas, and giving credit to co-workers.

Diversity training should also focus on building relationship skills with older employees. Training can focus on utilizing varied generational strengths as well as individual strengths. It can also include information about the desirable traits of older employees, according to studies by Carol Ryff and others, that compare them with younger employees. For example, older workers are likely to be:

- more cheerful
- more committed to the organization and involved with their jobs

- more stable, reliable, and careful
- less likely to have accidents, be absent, or quit

Training seminars can start with a frank discussion of generational values differences and how these differences are reflected in supervisory styles and in expectations about worker loyalty, commitment, and career aspirations. Case studies that present typical specific problems in the relationships between younger and older workers can be analyzed and solutions explored. For example, problems may occur when a young woman is assigned to supervise a much older man—and in other situations where traditional status relationships are switched. Finally, training participants can develop ways to stress generational unity when working together to achieve common job goals.

THE ADEA: WHAT YOU SHOULD KNOW

Before the Age Discrimination Employment Act (ADEA) was enacted in 1976, many large companies would not hire workers older than 40 and most required retirement at age 65. The act, designed to help overcome the effects of ageism on the careers of older persons, provides guidelines in the areas of recruiting, hiring, selection, promotion, and termination. The act has had a favorable impact on older workers, with minor negative side effects for others.

Major Provisions of the Act

The ADEA as amended, is intended to:

- Protect workers over age 40 from discrimination
- Promote employment opportunities for older workers capable of meeting job requirements
- Protect nearly all employees from forced retirement at any age

It covers private employers of 20 or more persons, labor organizations, employment agencies, and all government employees.

Providing for Valid Assessments

The major exception to age requirements occurs when an age requirement is a bona fide occupation qualification (BFOQ), reasonably necessary to the normal operations of a business. Also, differential treatment of employees based on reasonable factors other than age, such as physical fitness, is permitted. The ADEA does not preclude the discharge or discipline of an older worker for good cause. For example, an employer might defend a personnel decision on the ground that the older employee could not meet performance standards or that his declining functional abilities represented a potential threat to the public safety. Careful documentation of such actions is critical if an age discrimination suit is filed. The EEOC is responsible for enforcing the ADEA.

Ending Recruiting Discrimination

An example of recruiting discrimination is the practice of focusing on college graduates. Since age tends to be highly correlated with college graduation, the policy of recruiting future managers only from the ranks of college seniors potentially discriminates against older employees with comparable credentials. A corporation would be especially vulnerable to charges of age discrimination if admission to its executive training programs were limited *exclusively* to recent college graduates.

Ending Selection Discrimination

Job application forms can no longer require applicants to state their age, nor can interviewers legally inquire about age. The issue is whether an applicant is capable of performing the job. An age limit is a BFOQ only when it can be shown that all, or almost all, persons over that age cannot meet the requirements of a specific job. A construction firm might be able to show that virtually no one over age 70 can meet the physical requirements for carrying 60-pound loads up a ladder. However, a restaurant chain or airline will have a difficult time showing that organization image, or even customer preferences for attractive young hostesses, is sufficient justification for rejecting an otherwise qualified over-40 job applicant.

Age limits are likely to be upheld as a BFOQ in jobs with stringent physical demands that also involve public safety. Accordingly, it is not uncommon to find age limits governing the selection and retirement of airline pilots, air traffic controllers, police officers, firefighters. These are jobs requiring strenuous physical exertion or work under stressful conditions, where even a slight decline in reaction time could endanger others' lives and where public safety is involved. Even in these instances, it is wise for companies to have statistical or medical data to back up decisions about physical incapacities associated with aging.

Ending Promotion Discrimination

Organizations most often get in trouble with age discrimination suits concerning promotion when they follow inconsistent promotion policies and then try to justify their decisions after an employee files a complaint. Personnel actions are more defensible when they are based on a systematic, objective, and job-related performance appraisal system.

Ending Termination Discrimination

Decisions to terminate older workers are almost always difficult because motivations for such termination can be subject to many interpretations. Perhaps the best defense against a charge of age bias is the ability to show that the decision was based on the employee's substandard performance or some similar legitimate business reason. Managers must be prepared to demonstrate that the employee's behavior was measured fairly and objectively and that the employee was given a reasonable opportunity to bring her performance up to standard. Managers should also be prepared to show that they didn't harass the employee in an attempt to "run her off."

The End of Mandatory Retirement

People who opposed the elimination of mandatory retirement pointed to the possibility that retaining older workers would delay the promotion of some younger workers. It could also block the progress of women and minorities who entered promotion pipelines only after affirmative action programs were in place for several years. These workers are often just waiting for employees in higher positions to retire so they can move up and into their jobs. Researcher Benson Rosen (1988) found that ten years after passing laws to end mandatory retirement, only about 4 percent of these younger workers had been affected, so the concerns appear unfounded.

RETIREMENT: WHETHER, WHEN, AND HOW?

It's time to overcome the myth that everyone should retire by age 65. Currently 80 percent of employees have retired by age 70, but the retirement decision is a complex one that should not be decided upon age alone. In fact, we could say the decision is a life-or-death one, and people should carefully consider the many key factors that affect retirement.

People generally view retirement as a chance to finally be free from onerous responsibility and hard work. Yet retirement means loss for many, so it may in fact lead to decline and deterioration. Typical concerns are:

- loss of the identity that comes from career roles
- loss of power—organizational power, earning power, prestige
- loss of challenge to keep developing abilities and potentials
- loss of inner fulfillment that is tied to work performance and achievement
- loss of the social ties and social status that are career-connected
- loss of involvement in the active mainstream

In our culture, prestige and self-worth are based largely on occupational status and income, especially for men. And women who haven't had careers of their own often bask in the reflected light of the husband's occupational status. For men and their wives, the sense of loss usually sets in a year or so into retirement. On the other hand, career women are less likely than men to be *defined* by their careers, but retirement can be just as traumatic for them.

In 1950, about 70 percent of men older than 65 were in the workforce. By 1985 the proportion had dropped to 33 percent, which reflected retirements triggered earlier by company mandatory retirement policies. But the 1976 ADEA forbidding mandatory retirement has resulted in an increase in the older workforce, to 67 percent in 1997. Through the years surveys have indicated that one-third of retirees would stay with the company and move on to some new type of work or different work pattern—if they could. The ADEA and private 401(k) pension plans are allowing older employees to do just that. (Bureau of Labor Statistics)

Factors that Affect the Employee's Decision

The factors that have the strongest and most consistent influence on the timing of retirement are health considerations and financial well-being. Gender and educational level also appear to affect retirement intentions. The answers to the following questions will provide insight into the likelihood of an employee choosing to retire. The three most significant questions are:

1. Can the employee afford to retire?
2. Does disability or declining health make retirement desirable?
3. Is the employee male or female?

Women tend to retire earlier than men, which may be related to the fact that women have been concentrated in lower-level jobs. Workers with less formal education tend to retire earlier, perhaps because they are clustered in more physically demanding and less intrinsically motivating jobs. Ethnicity has not been associated with patterns of early retirement. The following are some factors that have a less significant impact on retirement plans.

Over-65 men who continue to work are primarily at the bottom—or the top—of the occupational ladder. Most of those at the bottom are working from financial necessity. Those at the top work for the meaning, enjoyment, and vitality it gives them. They're more likely (than those who retire) to keep up with new developments and transmit and advance them. They also have a greater sense of their own identity and are better able to act contrary to public opinion and others' expectations.

Work = A Longer Life

You may have heard that many men die soon after retirement. Does this mean people must keep working in order to keep living? Betty Friedan's studies indicate that if retirement doesn't lead to new purposes that involve continued work or a new line of work, it often ends in early death, or is experienced as a living death. While satisfying work tends to increase longevity, unsatisfying work tends to reduce it. Depression is a typical symptom of a retirement without satisfying work and often leads to reduced immunity to disease or to suicide. In 1980, when persons 65 and older were 11 percent of the population, they committed 25 percent of reported suicides. The male-to-female suicide rate goes from three-to-one for young men and women to ten-to-one among those 65 and older. The tendency of men to define themselves by their occupational roles—and the loss of those roles—is considered a major factor in post-retirement depression and suicide (Menkler 1981).

People who experience growth, change, and aliveness after age 60—those who don't complain of boredom, stagnation, or loneliness—have several things in common:

- They're passionately committed to a career or other vital activity that uses their mature qualities of broader perspective and greater wisdom and that motivates them to keep developing a variety of abilities.
- They don't expect their most valued qualities to decline with age—such traits as trust, risk-taking, adaptability, nonconformity, and ability to live in the present moment.

- They don't need to pretend to be young but they don't think of themselves as old.
- They refuse to conform to traditional old-age stereotypes in their choice of lifestyles and friends, and they have friends of all ages.

Baby boomers are aware of the role work plays in prolonging vitality. Eighty percent say they plan to work at lease part-time during their retirement. The Social Security Administration predicts that more than 7 million people aged 65 and over will be working in 2020 (*Working Woman* 1999).

LEADERSHIP CHALLENGE: PREVENTING SKILLS OBSOLESCENCE

The most pressing problem for many of today's older workers is occupational obsolescence, which can lead to unemployment, underemployment, and lower wages.

Savvy business persons see the benefits of helping older workers move into the twenty-first century, when physical strength and endurance will not be important factors in most jobs. Factory jobs will probably account for less than 10 percent of employment after the year 2000. New jobs are being created in fields devoted to computerization, robotization, and human services, and these jobs require radically new skills.

How Skills Obsolescence Occurs

Several factors make up the job obsolescence picture:

- After age 50, age differences in years since schooling are associated with an appreciable skills disadvantage to older workers.
- Older workers tend to have less schooling than younger employees and are less likely to have degrees in business, computer, and similar high-demand fields.
- As we move from a manufacturing economy to an information and service economy, older workers' skills are too often industry-specific and not readily transferable.
- New jobs in high-tech fields call for specific kinds of education and training.
- Many companies are reluctant to invest in further training for older employees, and employees may be reluctant to invest in their own training.

Many managers hold stereotypes that older workers are harder to train and will soon retire anyway. They don't see older employees as part of a pool from which future leaders can be drawn. This may not be direct discrimination but it has the same effect. Managers assume that training for older workers has a shorter payback period. But let's look at reality.

- Turnover rates are increasingly higher for employees of all ages.
- New technologies become obsolete in ever-shorter time spans.
- More people remain relatively healthy and vital well into their 70s and 80s.
- More older workers are planning to work for many more years—if companies offer a welcoming environment that meets their needs.

These facts suggest that the exclusion of older persons from training programs may be more a habit and a result of stereotyping than strict cost-benefit thinking.

Older workers internalize these stereotypes and many are less likely to invest in extensive retraining on their own. Rosen Benson's research indicates that younger workers are willing to make greater investments on the assumption that they have more time before expected retirement to pay back the costs and to reap the financial benefits of training. Since the younger ones earn less than the older, their time-out from work in order to attend school costs them less (in terms of wages they would have received if they had continued working).

Results: Unemployment, Underemployment, Lower Wages

Skills obsolescence often leads to unemployment for older persons. During downsizing phases, older workers are more likely to lose their jobs than their younger peers (and their skills are more likely to become obsolete) because they've usually worked up to a relatively high pay scale. And once unemployed, they're likely to experience longer periods of joblessness than their younger counterparts due to obsolete job skills and age discrimination—and they're more likely to take a pay cut. Older women and minority men are likely to be hit the hardest.

How to Prevent Skills Obsolescence

Equal opportunity for older workers calls for companies to design policies that provide affordable and useful training to workers of all ages. Policies need to ensure equal access to this training, as well as to the more secure and better-paying jobs. When older workers find themselves with obsolete skills, in dead-end jobs or career ruts, their motivation and job performance are likely to decline. The potential is still there, but it's underutilized. Leaders can remedy this situation through career planning and appropriate training.

Career Planning

In these times of rapid technological change, the most important goal of career management programs may be to identify job categories where future organizational needs are likely to be low and to help employees in these jobs to plan a new career path. Organizations can prepare employees to move into high-demand career tracks compatible with their interests, skills, and aspirations.

Older employees can be encouraged to do ongoing career planning. This begins with a critical self-analysis of interests, skills, and potential. The employee should then develop short-term and long-term career goals, specific and in writing. Next comes written plans for achieving goals, including how to use strengths and overcome obstacles. Written plans help the employees and their managers to assess progress along the way. Finally, especially important for older employees, is making Plans B and C—backup plans to cover the possibility that their career progress may get seriously sidetracked.

Training to Prevent Skills Obsolescence

Technological change creates new opportunities for employees who are trained in business, technological, and scientific fields. It also leads to the displacement of middle managers and production workers, especially older workers with obsolete skills.

Preliminary evidence suggests that the training approaches most compatible with the cognitive strengths of older employees:

- Permit self-paced learning
- Focus on experiential learning rather than abstract learning, hands-on activities rather than theory alone

On the other hand, *most* people probably respond best to this type of training.

Some companies provide a tuition reimbursement plan designed to help retiring workers prepare for second careers. Senior employees begin to draw from their educational fund a few years before retirement and continue to draw from it for a few years after retirement. Employees who acquire skills in the company's "critical needs areas" may be offered post-retirement, part-time, or consulting positions.

LEADERSHIP OPPORTUNITIES: BUILDING ON OLDER PERSONS' STRENGTHS

You now know that the older population is ballooning. Baby boomers are entering their fifties, and by 2020 about one in six Americans will be older than 65. Some business leaders are preparing for the changes this implies. Some sociologists are predicting that the Boomers won't be as accepting of age stereotyping and discrimination as recent generations have been. Businesses that treat them more positively will have a definite advantage.

To build on their strengths, you can begin by understanding their needs and helping them get what they need to do a good job. You can support strategies for keeping older employees on the payroll by such actions as offering flexible career options, making fair appraisals, and making the corporate culture more welcoming. You can help them make connections with the growing over-50 marketplace.

Opportunity #1: Understand How Educational Level Affects Needs

Current changes in the nature of work can be threatening to older employees with limited skills, but they may be challenging and intriguing to other, better-educated older employees. You can help less-educated workers face their fears and make new plans. On the other hand, you can support better-educated workers in using and expanding their skills.

Recognize Fears of the Less Educated

The employment picture as seen by many older employees with limited education and skills:

- Technological change is a threat.
- Retraining is scary or unacceptable.
- Unions are not much help because they're going along with management to eliminate the old jobs and retrain for the new jobs.
- Government is not much help because its programs are also geared toward retraining.

Help these co-workers face their worst fears and become comfortable with the worst-case scenario. Lead them in understanding that age is not necessarily a barrier to handling change and learning new technological skills. Help them to make career plans for gaining new skills and knowledge and to get support for the training they need.

Support Goals of the Better Educated

Better-educated, more highly skilled older employees tend to be more flexible and to see a brighter job picture:

- They often want a few minor adjustments in their work situation.
- They may desire to work a few less hours per week.
- They often want to be freed from the prison of the 5-day, 40-hour week or the arduous commute to the workplace.
- They may wish to be liberated from the controls on time and place of work implied by traditional employment contracts.
- They may want more flexibility and discretion in their work. Many may want to work at home on a full- or part-time basis, perhaps for more than one employer.

You can help them develop arrangements for time and place of work that will allow them to continue making valuable contributions to the team and the company.

Opportunity #2: Understand Older Employees' Motivational Needs

A vicious cycle of declining motivation can affect older employees. Here are the factors:

- Managers who expect a decline in motivation among older workers might make age-based managerial decisions that in fact lead to decreased motivation for these employees.
- To the extent that an older employee perceives that his or her efforts no longer lead to promotion or other significant rewards, his or her motivation tends to gradually decline.
- Limited opportunities for development and lack of feedback about performance may further reduce the older worker's motivation.
- In today's relatively flat organizational structures, there are shorter ladders to climb and fewer promotions to give. Many ambitious employees reach career plateaus much earlier than in the past. Employees need to become aware of this fact and to be given opportunities for lateral moves to expand their career growth and development.

It's likely that lowered motivation may result, not from aging itself, but from managerial expectations and treatment of older employees. If this is so, then policy changes to eliminate discrimination against older employees represent only a first step. Additional efforts to help managers and co-workers identify age stereotypes and eliminate their effects on everyday decisions need to be made. These efforts must also deal with all the practices that tend to support and perpetuate the stereotypes.

Opportunity #3: Adopt Strategies for Meeting Needs

Some simple general strategies for understanding an older employee's concerns include listening with awareness, developing empathy for their situation in life, and helping them to manage the changes they encounter.

Listening

Listen to older workers and be a supportive sounding board. You'll learn a great deal about their strengths and problems that way, gain insights to solutions to problems, and gain from their knowledge and experience. Encourage small group meetings of older workers for the purpose of getting in touch with their interests, desires, talents, and needs and then communicating those to co-workers and management.

Developing Empathy

If you live long enough, you'll be an older person one day, if you're not already. Ask yourself, What will I do when I'm no longer "young and cute?" and then put yourself in the older person's shoes. Look for the individual personality inside the older body. Be open to many kinds of beauty. Focus on skills, experience, contribution, and performance rather than narrow ideas about physical appearance. This is a positive strategy for relating to persons of all ages.

Managing Change

Encourage older workers to stay current. Help them to respond positively to change, to develop the new skills and acquire the new information they need in the changing business environment. Many older employees need a little encouragement to help them overcome the limitations imposed by cultural myths.

In organizations where self-managing teams are replacing most of the hierarchy, help people bridge the generation gap. Help older employees to pace themselves and avoid burnout. Stamina may decrease for some, but they can still be productive workers. Learning time may take a little longer but will be mastered.

Opportunity #4: Support Corporate Culture Changes

If business leaders want to retain productive older workers, they must bring about changes in corporate culture norms. For example, we know that managers who hold age stereotypes are normally less willing to approve promotions, offer training opportunities, and work out performance problems with older workers. In fact, studies indicate that managers age 40 and over tend to be rated significantly lower than younger managers on readiness for promotion, even when education, performance, and job tenure are comparable. Such age stereotypes contribute to an organizational climate that discourages continued employment opportunities for older employees. But when companies are able to develop supportive organizational norms that encourage older workers to stay on, all middle-aged and younger workers get a clear message: *The contributions of senior employees are recognized and welcomed here* (Cox and Nkomo 1992).

Clearly, the information economy will ease the transition to longer working lives. Working with computers in service-sector occupations such as medical diagnostics or insurance services is much less demanding physically than assembly line, construction, and other manual labor. It's unrealistic for us to expect people to spend almost a third of their lives in retirement. The challenge for leaders in traditional organizations is how to tap the knowledge of their older workers while keeping promotion opportunities open for younger employees.

Adopt a Variety of Change Strategies

Here are just a few examples of the many specific actions organization leaders could take for the purpose of making the culture more welcoming to older employees:

- The achievements of older workers are recognized and publicized.
- There is a shift away from celebrating retirements and toward celebrating continued contributions.
- Managers and co-workers do *not* anticipate retirement simply because of an employee's age. After all, people may retire at 50 or 80 or any other age—and may leave for any reason at any age.
- All employees are trained to understand the ADEA and any other legal considerations governing the employment of older workers.
- All employees participate in training to overcome deep-rooted assumptions and expectations about what senior employees can and cannot do.
- Training also raises employees' awareness of the pervasive influence of age stereotypes on day-to-day interactions and decisions and helps them move beyond myths and stereotypes.
- Training provides all employees with skills to bridge communication gaps between young managers and senior employees.
- Training is designed to explore value differences and similarities between younger and older workers and to move to appreciation for the diversity of values, as well as the unity that common values provide.
- Expect and encourage creative thinking and innovative results from employees of all ages.

Value Older Employees

If the corporate culture values and supports older workers who delay their retirement, they're likely to stay longer. Your attitude has its impact, just as every employee's attitude counts, so you can influence the value that people generally place on the contributions of older workers and the belief that effective workers should be retained as long as possible. Some organizations actually encourage direct group pressure on people to retire. Other organizations encourage a more subtle expression of norms calling for early retirement. Such pressures do have a strong influence on employees' retirement decisions.

Respect Employees' Retirement Decisions

We know that companies can no longer force employees to retire, but they can and do offer them tempting rewards to retire. Failing that, they can resort to subtle pressure: lower performance evaluations, onerous job assignments, taking away responsibilities or perks, exclusion from desired projects or meetings. Finally the employee gets fed up, gives up, and retires.

Studies indicate that managers are less likely to pressure employees to retire if they view them as having some of the following traits and life situations: younger, financially troubled, likely to make a poor social adjustment to retirement, supported by the union, engaged in personal activities that are compatible with business interests, and still earning high performance ratings. Of these reasons, most experts agree that the only rational, valid reason for encouraging one employee to stay over another is higher performance ratings. This leads us to why and how an organization can hold onto its effective older employees.

Opportunity #5: Support Strategies for Retaining Older Workers

Currently more than half of Americans are out of the workforce before age 63, and 80 percent are out by the time they're 70. The goal of a retention strategy is to retain older workers as long as feasible. Such a strategy can benefit the organization and society as well as older employees.

Benefits to the organization of an effective retention strategy are that it:

- lowers pension costs
- lowers turnover rates and resulting turnover costs
- provides longer and larger paybacks for investments in training
- contributes to high employee morale
- enhances the organization's reputation in the community

Benefits to society of an effective retention strategy are that it:

- lowers social security costs
- adds to U.S. productivity and the tax base
- contributes to the social integration of the older population

Benefits to older employees of an effective retention strategy are that it:

- keeps them physically and mentally active
- maintains or enhances their self-respect
- provides them with income
- satisfies their social needs by keeping them in daily touch with other active people at work

Opportunity #6: Support Flexible Career Options

Most companies are offering senior employees the wide range of employment options they say they want. Those companies who do offer such options normally make workers retire from their current level. Then the companies hire them back at a much lower wage, often on a temporary basis.

Surveys indicate that about one-third of retirees would prefer to stay with the company and move on to a different kind of work or work pattern (Friedan 1993). They say they would postpone retirement if they were offered the right job modifications and more flexible retirement options. Permitting major job modifications could launch senior employees on something of a second career, while opening career paths for younger employees.

Many companies have only two alternatives for older employees: keep working or fully retire. More suitable options may include:

- part-time work
- job changes or restructuring
- job rotation
- job sharing
- tandem staffing

- periodic sabbaticals
- temporary assignments
- flexible scheduling
- various phaseout-to-retirement options
- contract consulting
- other creative career options

Some companies are providing training programs that focus on alternatives to complete retirement and on post-retirement employment options and second-career opportunities.

Some type of part-time work seems the natural way to make the transition from full-time work to retirement, or to deal with certain disabilities on either a temporary or long-term basis. Survey responses indicate that older workers want to retire gradually (Sandell 1987). Yet, sudden retirement, not part-time work, is typical. Why is retirement usually sudden? Primarily because so few career options are available to older employees. While many say they would prefer modified work and schedules, flexible options are seldom available. When they are, the pay is often so low that workers choose sudden retirement.

What managers personally can do to help is be flexible, choosing from the various strategies others have used or creating new ones that fit the situation.

An example of a phase-out option is to establish a company temporary employee pool. Retirees who wish to work on a part-time basis sign up. Where appropriate, the company provides refresher courses to employees who have been away from the job for some time. Retirees may be called on to fill in during vacation periods or to add their expertise to special projects. At higher levels they're hired as consultants and work on a project fee basis.

Opportunity #7: Make Fair Assessments and Performance Reviews

Leading-edge companies have clear policies for managers, teams, and co-workers: Leave myths and stereotypes behind and make realistic assessments of older persons' abilities. Be sure you are fair and objective in evaluations.

Realistically Assess Ability and Disability

Managers and co-workers are likely to misinterpret health information on older employees if they hold stereotypes regarding the declining health of older people. Identical health conditions may be perceived as more serious and disabling for older workers than for younger ones. One study indicated that when medical reports emphasize capacities or functions that an employee can successfully perform, manager's recommended continued employment. When medical reports emphasized disabilities, managers recommended part-time assignments, phaseouts, and termination—even when the health problems were not likely to interfere with ability to do the job, in some cases.

Disability laws could come into play in these instances. A systematic and comprehensive approach to health evaluations might include the following:

- Current and complete job descriptions, with emphasis on physical and psychological demands
- Medical reports that emphasize both employee capacities and limitations associated with illness or injury and that focus on job-related implications of medical problems
- Training for managers in interpreting medical reports in order to make better decisions regarding further employability
- Job redesign as one strategy for meeting the needs of senior workers with health problems

Give Fair Performance Evaluations

Good performance appraisal systems provide the accurate, objective information that managers and team co-workers need in order to make important decisions about motivating, rewarding, promoting, training, transferring, and terminating employees. Appraisals should be based only on job-related behaviors and achievements that are related to a job analysis, behavior standards, and agreed-upon measures. A management-by-objectives process is considered the most legally acceptable.

The appraisal system should generate the documentation that would be required to prove that personnel decisions comply with the law. All employees should get periodic feedback that highlights their strengths and weaknesses and explores the implications of their present performance for future career moves. This feedback should help dispel any misconceptions and misunderstandings employees may have and should help them create realistic expectations about their future with the company. Effective two-way communication between employees and their managers can usually prevent costly age discrimination suits.

The bottom line: think of the last third of life as a time of continuing growth and learning, a time when people deserve constructive performance feedback that can help them continue to improve.

Opportunity #8: Help Make Connections to the Over–50 Marketplace

The over-50 marketplace is exploding. People are living longer and older consumers tend to have more spending power than in the past, and the Baby Boom generation is turning 50. Older Americans offer a booming market in financial services, from insurance to estate planning. They are still a relatively untapped market in housing, clothing, travel, and investment services. Just as women professionals have an edge in understanding women's issues and relating to women customers, so older professionals and employees have an edge in understanding elders' issues and relating to older customers. And many older persons appreciate seeing that older employees are valued in the companies they do business with.

It's good business to retain older employees, to seek their views in designing "senior-oriented" products and services, and to position them for customer contact in the over-50 marketplace—but certainly not to limit them to these roles. The contributions people can make to the organization are not limited by age. In fact, the experiences and insights that come with age normally enhance a person's contributions. However, we may need to create a new, true myth about valuing older persons, a myth that moves younger employees to see and appreciate those contributions.

SUMMARY

The longer we live, the more likely we are to be faced with cultural devaluation, for ageism has accelerated in this century. Age myths picture older employees as an increasing problem in terms of productivity, attendance and accident rates, physical and mental ability, rigidity and dogmatism, commitment to work, and physical attractiveness. Actually, older workers are just as mentally alert and productive as others and have better attendance, accident, and turnover rates. Their physical and mental ability are retained well beyond age 70 as long as they remain in good health. In fact, people reach their mental prime at about age 60. Older workers are no more likely to be rigid and dogmatic than others, but tend to have much greater knowledge and wisdom. Healthy people retain their creativity even past the age of 100.

Generation gaps can be bridged by such strategies as using age-diverse teams and finding ways to open up communication lines between older and younger employees, and providing good diversity training.

The ADEA provides guidelines for treating older employees with fairness and giving them equal opportunities. It's designed to end age discrimination in recruiting, selection, promotion, and termination practices—and to end mandatory retirement for most jobs.

Since older workers have usually progressed to higher pay than younger ones, this can make them a layoff target during downsizing. If they do lose their jobs, they have more difficulty finding another position. If their skills are in high demand, they may have more job security than younger workers, but often their skills are becoming obsolete.

Skills obsolescence and ongoing training are major issues for those past age 50. Younger managers are often unwilling to invest in their retraining, and they themselves may not be motivated. One reason is the assumption that they'll retire before the training investment pays off. Another is the myth that older people have difficulty learning and adapting to change, even though these traits are not necessarily affected by age.

You as a business leader have many opportunities to appreciate and utilize the wealth of experience and talent older employees can offer your company. You can understand how their educational level affects their needs and how managerial expectations can affect their motivation. You can adopt specific strategies, such as empathy and change management, to meet their needs. You can support corporate cultural changes that value and respect older employees contributions. You can support strategies for retaining older workers and giving t hem flexible career options. You can give fair performance evaluations and utilize their ability to connect with the over-50 marketplace.

Skill Builder 12.1: The Case of Older Worker Wendy

You're in charge of Bache Investment's college recruiting. You cannot remember a more hectic time in your life. When you were promoted to this job, your boss told you that the job would test your energy and endurance. During the past two months, you visited 24 universities and interviewed more than 200 MBA students for entry-level investment advisor positions. The experience has been exhausting. Because of your reading schedule, you have relied heavily on your assistant *Wendy* to handle many duties that you usually attend to personally.

Since returning to the office from your recruiting trips, you have become increasingly aware of Wendy's aloofness. You sense that she is purposely avoiding you. You also noted that she quickly looks away when you question her about a late travel voucher or a missing file. A little investigating reveals that Wendy is behind in her routine responsibilities and is now over a week late with an important EEO/AA report. Wendy's failure to attend a monthly staff meeting was the last straw. You are determined to get Wendy back on track or to find someone else who is capable of managing the workload. You leave a note for Wendy, requesting that she meet you in your office at 8:45 Monday morning.

Now take the role of Wendy. You have been having doubts about your ability to manage the growing workload and about your future at Bache Investments. Returning to full-time work four years ago at age 53 represented quite a change for you. Although you had worked as an executive secretary before your marriage, your previous positions had been much less demanding than this position. At home, your husband has also noticed a recent change in your behavior. He tells you that you seem tense and short-tempered and asks if you're having problems at the office. You confide that you think your boss is subtly pressuring you to quit. You explain that he told you to complete several complex monthly EEO/AA reports without reducing your regular workload. You confess to your husband that the reports require many statistical calculations, some beyond anything you ever encountered. Completing the reports accurately seemed to take forever. You tell him how you have worked through lunch hours two and three times a week. You relate how you skipped staff meetings just to catch up on regular paperwork. You have been feeling overwhelmed and incompetent. With only six more years to go before you plan to retire, you wonder why your boss wants to force you out. Perhaps your future with the company will be resolved at the Monday morning meeting with the boss.

- If you were Wendy's manager, what would you do?
- If you were Wendy, what would you do?

Skill Builder 12.2: The Case of the Youthful Supervisor

Jose is 27 years old. From a Latino American family, his parents were strict and taught him that older people deserve great respect and are usually the ones in authority. His father was the undisputed head of the home, and his grandfather was the highly respected patriarch of a large clan. Jose has been transferred from a field assignment and promoted to team leader of a product promotions group. One of the team members, *Scott*, is in his fifties and has been with the company for nearly ten years. Scott reminds Jose of his father in some ways.

Jose must meet with Scott to make suggestions for improvements on his part of a current team project. Jose senses that Scott is somewhat defensive toward him and a little resistant to taking constructive criticism and suggestions from him.

- Jose asks you for advice. What would you say to him?

Skill Builder 12.3: The Case of Stock Broker John

Leigh is Human Resources Director for Goldman Funds, an investment firm. Her job is to hire stock brokers who have the ability to create wealth for Goldman clients and for the company. Leigh has been in this field for 20 years and spent many of those years as a stock broker herself, so she knows how demanding the job can be. Most of the stock brokers are young, unmarried, and devote 60 to 70 hours a week to their jobs. Most of them also spend several hours a week maintaining their physical fitness in order to deal with the stress of the job.

Leigh is interviewing applicants for a stock broker position that just opened up. The most unusual applicant is *John*, unusual because he's 67 years old while the other applicants are in their twenties or thirties. John had a long career in the insurance industry, with many years as a salesman, a few years as a claims adjuster, and the remaining years as an executive. John retired when he was 62, and within a year, he was extremely bored with retirement activities. He enrolled in the local university and has just completed a master's degree in finance. He earned grades that ranked him in the top 10 percent of his class.

John comes across as very personable in the interview. He tells Leigh, "I've always loved to sell, I've always loved dealing with calculated risks, and it's very important to me to get to know the clients I serve and to make a contribution through my work." Leigh is impressed, but she's concerned about how many years they can reasonably expect John to work. Leigh is also concerned about the high turnover rate that seems to come with the stock broker position. One of her goals is to lower the employee turnover rate.

- If you were Leigh, what would you do?

Skill Builder 12.4: A Case of Maggie's Way

Maggie, age 55, has been an office manager with the Pillsbury-Mason law firm chain for the past 15 years. She is extremely dependable, loyal, and committed to her job and the firm. She has received performance awards and is highly valued and respected in the firm.

Jake was hired a few months ago as an administrative assistant. He just graduated with honors and holds a brand new degree in business administration with a concentration in management. His goal is to become an office manager very quickly. He knows he has what it takes. However, he had only a few months of actual office experience before taking this job, so he's having a little difficulty adapting to his co-workers and the office environment. Jake's main frustration is that he has many good ideas, and he wants to take action on them. He knows he could run this office in a minute, but he's blocked because "Maggie's ways" control the entire office.

As the other employees say, "Maggie's Way" is sometimes confusing, but Maggie is very competent and always on top of everything. The problem is that her ways are sometimes unique, so it's difficult for new employees to understand or to find things. Her procedures generally are very simple and to the point, but sometimes they're so simple that others tend to look right over them, especially in a hectic office. On the other hand, when it comes to many procedures, Maggie insists that employees take their time, go through the proper channels, and follow her office manual. In contrast, Jake believes in getting things done efficiently, finding short cuts, avoiding time-consuming over-cautiousness, and basically getting on with it.

Jake's experience is that he has difficulty understanding many of Maggie's requests. He frequently sees the best way to handle a procedure or task, but Maggie always wants him to do it her way. When he tries to explain how a procedure could be improved upon, Maggie listens politely, but it always ends up that the procedure is done her way.

Last week, Jake was under a great deal of pressure to complete a project. He took things into his own hands, did it his way, and got it out on time. When Maggie found out, she confronted him. Tempers flared and they exchanged some heated words about each other's management style. *Stan*, one of the law partners, walked by as this exchange was going on. He's concerned. Pillsbury-Mason is known for its quiet, calm, harmonious environment.

- What are the key issues?
- If you were Stan, what would you do?
- If you were Maggie, what would you do?

REFERENCES

Advertising Age: p.S-2, "Door Ajar to Women of All Ages in Ads," October 4, 1993.

Campbell, R.T., J. Abolafia, and G. L. Maddox. "Life-Course Analysis in Social Gerontology" in *Gender and the Life Course*. New York: Aldine, 1985.

Chideya, Farai., "Shade of the Future," *Time*, February 1, 1999.

Chideya, Farai. *The Color of Our Future*, New York: Wm. Morrow & Co., 1999.

Cox, Taylor, Jr. and Stella M. Nkomo, "Candidate Age As a Factor in Promotability Ratings." *Public Personnel Management* 2: 197-210, Summer, 1992.

Friedan, Betty. *The Fountain of Age*. New York: Simon and Schuster, 1993.

Gann, L.J. and P.J. Duignan. *The Hispanics of the United States: A History*. Boulder, CO: Westview Press, 1986.

Gove, Walter R. "The Effect of Age and Gender on Deviant Behavior: A Biopsychosocial Perspective." in *Gender and the Life Course*. NY: Aldine, 1985.

Hushbeck, Judith C. *Old and Obsolete: Age Discrimination and the American Worker, 1860-1920*. New York: Garland Publishing, Inc. 1989

Jackson, Susan E. *Diversity in the Workplace*. New York: Guilford Press, 1992.

Lemonick, Michael D. and Alice Park Mankato, "The Nun Study," *TIME*: pp.54-65, May 14, 2001.

Menkler, Meredith, "Research on the Health Effects of Retirement." *Journal of Health and Social Behavior* 22: 117-130, 1981.

Mitchell, Olivia S., ed. *As the Workforce Ages*. Ithaca, New York: ILR Press, 1993.

Retirement Living, April 1976, report of survey regarding older workers.

Rosen, Benson and Thomas Jerdee. "Managing Older Workers' Careers." *Research in Personnel and Human Resources Management* 6: 37-74, 1988.

Rosen, Benson, and T. H. Jerdee. *Older Employees: New Roles for Valued Resources*. Homewood, IL: Dow Jones-Irwin, 1985.

Ryff, Carol D. "Subjective Experience of Life-Span Transitions" in *Gender and the Life Course*. New York: Aldine, 1985

Salzberg Seminar on Health, Productivity and Aging, June, 1983.

Sandell, Steven H. *The Problem Isn't Age: Work and Older Americans*. New York: Praeger, 1987.

Scripps Howard News Service, reported in *San Francisco Examiner*: D-1, May 10, 1998.

Time: pp.46-49, "Shade of the Future," Feb 1 1999.

Tulgan, Bruce. *Managing Generation X: How to Bring Out the Best in Young Talent*. New Orleans, LA: Merritt Publishing, 1997.

U.S. Census Bureau. *We . . . the American Elderly*. Department of Commerce, Washington, DC, 1993.

Working Woman: pp.54-57, "The Age of Work," October 1999.

Resources

Brain Connections, 745 Fifth Avenue, Suite 700, New York, NY 10151, a source guide to 160 organizations devoted to brain diseases and disorders.

Aging, a journal.

American Association of Retired Persons (AARP), the largest older persons' organization, which engages in research and lobbying and publishes the magazine *Modern Maturity*.

Gray Panthers, an organization.

McCabe, Jim. Consultant on Aging Workers, Technical Assistance Group, San Ramon, CA (510) 838-7277.

Older Women's League (OWL), an organization.

Waters, Elinor B. and Jane Goodman. *Empowering Older Adults*, San Francisco: Jossey-Bass, 1990. This book includes examples of corporate programs for older workers.

CHAPTER 13

Working with Persons of All Sizes and Shapes

Pretty women wonder where my secret lies.
I'm not cute or built to suit a model's fashion size.
But when I start to tell them, they think I'm telling lies.
Maya Angelou

Appearance discrimination is rampant in our society—especially for those who are "overweight." If you gain as few as 20 or 30 pounds over your "ideal" weight, you may suddenly face new career problems and even a lower income—yet about one-third of all Americans have done just that. Weight discrimination affects women more than men, probably because it is related to the beauty myth and to appearance discrimination in general. Virtually all the publicized lawsuits have been filed by women, and the support groups and organizations are created and joined primarily by women.

Between one and two million people are considered "morbidly obese" according to Marian Burros' research. They weigh at least twice as much as the top of the medically recommended "normal weight range" for persons of their height, build, and age. For adults this means people at least 100 pounds above the normal weight range.

The Terms We Use

Terms are very touchy for people who have experienced appearance bias, especially for people who are considered medically and legally "obese." Some activists prefer the term "fat" and don't like "overweight" as a label. But "fat" still offends many people, and "large" is not descriptive since it can include a tall or muscular man who may in fact have an appearance advantage. We'll use the term "obese" since we'll be discussing medical and legal implications.

Get ready to learn what it's like to be an obese person in the workplace. As you do, imagine seeing situations the way an obese person might see them. You'll also learn about other types of appearance issues. Specifically, in this chapter you'll learn:

- How typical stereotypes about obese persons compare with reality
- How fat prejudice affects obese persons
- What the Beauty Myth is and how it affects obese persons and others

- Rights that obese employees want
- Rights that most employers want to retain
- Emerging law concerning obese persons' workplace rights
- How you can help obese employees overcome barriers and contribute their strengths to the organization

Before the we explore this topic, complete Self-Awareness Activities 13.1 and 13.2.

Self-Awareness Activity 13.1: What Do You Believe about Obese Persons?

Purpose:

- to get in touch with your beliefs and stereotypes about this group of people
- to experience how judgmental beliefs affect your thinking and feeling processes
- to experience the ways in which your beliefs create your reality regarding other persons, even before you have any interaction with them

Part I. What Do You Believe about Obese Women?

Step 1. Associations

- Relax as deeply as you can: close your eyes and take a few deep breaths.
- Focus on the word "obese woman" and allow a mental picture to come up in your mind's eye. Imagine that you are this woman. Be obese woman.
- Notice your resistances to being this person, and your willingness.
- Notice the words and images that come to mind as you "see" this woman.
- Open your eyes and list 10 to 20 words in the order in which they occur to you.
- Review your list. Mark a plus beside the words that are positive, a minus beside the words that are negative, and a circle beside neutral words.

Step 2. Negative Associations

- Close your eyes and focus again on the image of the obese woman. Formulate a negative opinion or judgment, perhaps one you typically hold about such women.
- Notice your *feelings* as you see the person in this negative way. What *thoughts* come up as you focus on the image?
- Write a few sentences about your feelings and thoughts.

Step 3. Positive Associations

- Formulate a positive opinion or judgment, perhaps one you typically hold about obese women.
- Notice your *feelings* as you see the person in this positive way. What *thoughts* come up as you focus on the image?
- Write a few sentences about your feelings and thoughts.

Step 4. Insights

- Focus on the differences between your experiences when you hold negative and positive judgments or opinions. What were the differences? What meaning does this have for you, for your beliefs and feelings about people from this group, and about beliefs in general?
- Write your responses in a few sentences; include anything you like about your feelings, thoughts, and insights.

Part II. Experimenting with Opinions about Obese Men

Repeat the phases and steps in part I, this time focusing on the image of an obese man.

Next, determine your current knowledge about obese persons by completing Self-Awareness Activity 13.2. After you've completed this chapter, review your answers, determine whether your answers reflect cultural stereotypes and myths or personal biases, and make any corrections necessary.

Self-Awareness Activity 13.2: What Do You Know about Obese Americans?

Purpose: To see what you know about the issues covered in this chapter.

Instructions: Determine whether you think the following statements are basically true or false—and why. The answers are discussed in the following paragraph and throughout this chapter.

1. People become obese only because they overeat.
2. Anyone with sufficient willpower can lose excess weight.
3. People become excessively overweight because of personality problems.
4. Obese people have jolly personalities.
5. Obese employees are likely to cost employers more in health care and sick leave than employees who diet to keep their weight low.
6. Being overweight has no significant effect on career success.
7. Obese men suffer as much discrimination as obese women.
8. Obese persons are protected by law from workplace discrimination.
9. Extremely overweight people generally make poor workers.

STEREOTYPES AND REALITIES

Most of the stereotypes about obese persons are either false or distorted, partial truths. In fact, most stem from people's discomfort with obesity based on their fear of becoming obese themselves.

To get to know what it's like to be an obese person, you must understand the stereotypes they deal with every day. To bridge the divisive walls these stereotypes hold in place, you must know what they are, know other realities that balance or refute them, and move beyond myths to a more realistic view of obese persons. The goal here is to appreciate each person's unique value and to strengthen our unity as one cohesive team, organization, and culture.

Stereotype #1: People get overweight when they overeat and don't exercise.

This may be true for most people. However, obese people consume no more calories per day than other people, according to 19 out of 20 studies on this topic. To get down to normal weight range and stay there, an obese person must eat excruciatingly less than a normal-weight person, probably for life. In addition, greatly overweight people have a complex physical situation. Large size probably *causes* the inactivity of greatly overweight persons, and not the other way around. In 1993 a National Institutes of Health panel wrote that evidence increasingly indicates that overweight is not a simple disorder of willpower but a complex disorder of energy metabolism. The experts concluded that diets almost always are disasters, with dieters regaining the weight they had lost.

Stereotype #2: People are overweight because they lack willpower.

This very basic myth says that individuals should be able to control themselves, and there is something morally wrong with them if they keep giving in to fattening foods. It says that being overweight means being a weak-willed slob. It also ignores the "obesity gene" factor.

Willpower Doesn't Work in the Long Run

Choice and "willpower" are certainly an element in weight gain prevention for the average person. Since we've seen plenty of people who decided to lose weight and then did it within a few weeks, we believe that willpower is the key. What we ignore is the fact for virtually everyone who is significantly overweight gains it all back within a few months or years.

When Martin Seligman, director of clinical psychology at the University of Pennsylvania, reviewed the dieting studies, the best result he could find was one in which 13 percent of the dieters maintained their losses after three years. About 90 percent gain all or almost all their weight back within four or five years, many within a few months. It may be that the 10 percent who succeed over the long term 1) watch every bite they eat, 2) are more or less obsessed with watching their weight, and 3) were close to their natural weight anyway and would weigh only a few pounds more if they had never dieted.

The "Weight Gene" Can Mutate

Scientists at the Rockefeller Institute in New York have discovered a genetic mutation they think is responsible for at least some types of obesity (Friedman 1995). As a result of this "faulty" gene, the body's fat stores don't tell the brain how big or small they are, so the brain may not be able to properly regulate appetite, food intake, and/or food metabolism in ways that in turn regulate the body's fat stores.

Stereotype #3: Obese people just need to get on the right diet.

After years of reviewing the scientific literature on dieting and weight loss, Martin Seligman (1994) concluded that:

- Dieting may make overweight worse, not better.
- Dieting can have negative side effects, such as repeated failure and hopelessness, depression, fatigue, bulimia, and anorexia.

Stereotype #4: Being obese poses health risks; being thin does not.

Seligman's review led to less-firm conclusions about the health risks of overweight, but he makes these suggestions:

- Underweight is clearly associated with substantially greater risk of death. Staying 20 percent or more underweight, as virtually all high-fashion models do, can over time greatly reduce stamina, impair the immune system, and lead to other types of health problems.
- Mild to moderate overweight, 10 to 30 percent over so-called ideal weight, may possibly be associated with a marginal increase in mortality, particularly for those at risk for diabetes.
- Substantial obesity of 30 to 100 percent overweight possibly causes health damage and may be associated with somewhat increased mortality.
- Morbid obesity, over 100 percent overweight, may well cause premature death.

Seligman suspects, but is not yet certain, that the weight fluctuation hazard may be larger than the hazard of staying mildly overweight. Gaining weight gradually during adulthood is normal and healthy, but going on diets dramatically increases the risk of heart attacks and strokes later on. Therefore, a new eating disorder might be called "being 20 percent over your so-called ideal weight and ruining your life and health by dieting." An example is the 5'6" medium-frame woman who weighs 165 pounds instead of 135, and repeatedly gains and loses weight through dieting.

Stereotype #5: People who diet are healthier and live longer.

A study by researcher Lyn Dettmar of 466 flight attendants found that 25 percent of them weighed five pounds or more than the airline's top limit. Within this "overweight" group, half either made themselves vomit or used laxatives to lose weight. Dettmar (1990) concludes that such dieting creates more stress than the added weight would create, as well as eating disorders.

What *does* contribute to health is moderate exercise, wholesome natural foods, minimal fat and alcohol intake, eating only when hungry, and eating slowly and only until satisfied. For example, S. Blair reported on a couple of studies that revealed the importance of exercise. In a study of 13,000 people, the least-fit 20 percent had a much higher death risk than even the next-to-least-fit 20 percent. In another study using a large sample of men, the death rate of sedentary men was 30 percent higher than those who exercised moderately (Blair et al. 1988).

Weight is not always an indicator of longevity. Although people in the "normal" weight range of those insurance company weight charts *do* live longer than heavier ones, on average, how much longer is in great dispute (so is how many people are exceptions to the rule because of bone structure and muscle development). In fact, no study has compared the longevity of people who stay within their so-called ideal weight without dieting to people who maintain it with dieting. Those who constantly diet may in fact shorten their lives.

Stereotype #6: Obese people are less productive workers.

Most jobs don't require much physical activity, and there's no reason obese persons can't be just as productive as others. Activists concede that obese people are not appropriate for all jobs, such as those performed in tight quarters or those requiring certain physical abilities. Airline attendants and ballet dancers are examples. But for most jobs obese persons should not be disqualified from applying. They should have a chance to take whatever physical tests are required. If the job requires running down a track every day, let *all* the applicants show that they can run the track. In addition, employers should consider making reasonable accommodation to obese persons, as they do to persons with disabilities.

Stereotype #7: Poor persons are more likely to be obese.

The stereotype that poor persons are more likely to be fat implies that they are less informed and less in control of their lives. In fact, it's more likely obese persons make less money because they're obese than that being poor leads to a higher incidence of obesity. This is a major workplace issue that we'll discuss in detail later.

Extreme obesity can be related to physical disability. Until 1995 such persons had no legal protection from discrimination; then state courts ruled that they were protected under the Americans with Disabilities Act. Obese persons are on average just as productive as other workers, but some accommodation may need to be made on account of their size. These people have begun organizing to fight one of the few remaining types of discrimination that has gone unchallenged. They see weight discrimination as the final frontier in the civil rights struggle and hope to eventually expand the federal Civil Rights Act to cover obese people.

Whether the issue is weight, height, attractiveness, skin color, or other aspect of appearance, your goal is to learn more about experiences of various types of people. And the ultimate goal is to move beyond myths and stereotypes to working productively and profitably together.

HOW DOES FAT PREJUDICE AFFECT PEOPLE?

Perhaps the cruelest aspect of obesity prejudice is that people tend to believe the obese could become slender if they simply summoned adequate willpower and self-discipline, in other words, character. The devaluing of obese persons often has the effect of invading their privacy.

The Message: You're Inferior

Obese women say that little glances and comments they receive are often more damaging than overt discrimination, wearing away at their self-esteem and confidence, reinforcing the message most have heard since childhood: "You're inferior because you're fat." Some typical humiliations obese persons have reported include:

- Frances went to see a doctor to get treatment for what appeared to be strep throat. The doctor insisted that she weigh in, then focused more on her overweight than on her illness. He insisted that she must immediately begin to lose 75 pounds.

- Joan's companion was stopped by a policeman for speeding. He gave Joan a ticket for not wearing a seat belt, even though she explained that the belt in her friend's car wouldn't reach around her body.

- Bill was embarrassed at the grocery checkout when the women behind him commented about two items of "fattening foods" that he was buying.

- Stephanie was trying to find a job. Time after time, she would send a resume and cover letter and the phone response was enthusiastic. When she showed up for the interview, however, she often saw shocked faces and heard, "We think you're over-qualified," or "We've changed strategies."

- Karen applied for a job as a legal secretary. The attorney was impressed with her skills and told her he would hire her—if she could show a 10-pound-a-month weight loss when he weighed her in his office.

- When Jay walked into the staff meeting, two of the men jokingly grabbed their dough-nuts, implying that he might scarf them down.

- Rosita was enjoying lunch at a seafood restaurant with two co-workers. One said, "You know, Rosita, that butter you just put on your bread comes to over 100 calories." The other said, "Yes, and I noticed you ordered a salad with figs, which are loaded with calories."

One activist said, "We're the last safe prejudice. The fat person is the last person employers can safely kick around." That's changing.

When they leave their homes each day, one to two million obese Americans find themselves in a world built for small people, a world in which they're continually reminded they don't fit. Some of the problems they encounter:

- sitting: finding chairs anywhere that will accommodate them
- flying: fitting into tiny airplane seats
- going to a theater: fitting into tiny theater seats
- traveling in cars: fitting into small cars, dealing with seat belts that won't reach

The Assumption: You Are Your Body

The modern culture of dieting is based on the idea that the personality becomes the body. A related belief is, our size *does* change when we diet, so we must be able to choose it and therefore control it. For many overweight people, the misery is not so much about how they look, but that they feel to blame, that they've been bad to allow their bodies to get fat. Their fat is seen as perverse bad manners, and they can't walk to the corner store without risking insult.

Naturally-thin Sally saw naturally-obese Janice eating a cookie at lunch and commented to Aretha, "How is she going to lose weight that way?" This assumes that Janice should diet all the time, and that she *can*. It pinpoints a whole category of food that should be denied to Janice. It views Janice's unwillingness to forgo cookies as an act of rebellion. And it assumes that what Janice eats is everyone else's business.

At times obese persons feel truly reduced to being just a body and nothing more. As damaging as "conventional wisdom" about overweight has been, the more recent psychological viewpoints may be even more damaging:

- Obese people put on weight as a defense mechanism.
- They're trying to hide inside all that fat.
- They're trying to feed their hungry, empty hearts.
- They're seeking release from the loss of mother or father . . . and on and on.

One woman who was obsessed for years with keeping her weight far below its natural point said, "By fussing endlessly over my body, I ceased to live in it." She gave up dieting and entered her body again with a whole heart. She says that by letting go of dieting, she freed up mental and emotional energy and space in her life-space for more productive and joyful thoughts and activities. She will no longer pursue a thin elusive body that others say she should have. She says, "It was a terrible distraction, a sidetracking that might have lasted my whole life. By letting go, I go places."

Devaluation and Rejection

Devaluation and rejection are two of the biggest hurdles obese persons must overcome in achieving self-esteem and claiming a place in the world. To illustrate how extreme our culture is about thinness, consider a comment made in the film "The Money Pit" by reed-slim actress Shelly Long to her estranged husband Tom Hanks. "Well, I haven't been out of the house much lately; you know I put on a few pounds." The implicit message was that she felt so bad about her appearance, she had been hiding out at home, and certainly had not had any romantic encounters!

Marian Burros (1994) asked William Dietz, director of clinical nutrition at a Boston hospital, about obesity stereotypes and myths. He replied that a because of these myths, neither the government nor the health industry in this country are committed to obesity as a public health problem. He said, "We've ignored it and blamed it on gluttony and sloth." Many people believe that gluttony is a sin, and most believe it reflects laziness, lack of willpower, food addiction, and lack of self-esteem. In fact, gluttony and sloth are two of the classical "seven deadly sins." What a heavy burden to lay on anyone! But "fat activists" point out that people naturally come in different shapes and sizes and that for most obese people, obesity is a relatively uncontrollable genetic condition.

A Cultural Obsession with Thinness

What does it mean when more than 80 percent of U.S. women say they dislike their bodies? Coincidentally, 85 percent of them weigh more than the average fashion model, who in turn weighs 20 percent less than the average woman. The pressure to be very thin starts quite early for little girls. Their role model since the 1960s has been the most popular American doll of all time, Barbie. It's estimated that about one in a million women would naturally have proportions similar to Barbie's, but little girls start trying at a very young age. In fact, by age 10, about 80 percent of them have been on a diet. Later we'll discuss the tyranny of the Beauty Myth, especially for women, and obese persons' right to challenge it.

Women: The Hardest-Hit

A recent survey reported by Esther Rothblum (1993) indicates that 90 percent of employees cite acceptable weight as essential for a successful career, ranking it fourth, ahead of attractiveness and youthfulness. Intelligence, job qualifications, and education were the first three essentials. Since the stereotype of the ideal woman makes her much thinner than that of the ideal man, more women than men are affected by weight discrimination.

Rothblum also found that men must be significantly heavier than women before they experience the same discrimination. As shown in Table 13.1, employers are slightly more likely to directly urge overweight men than women employees to lose weight. But even moderately overweight women are dramatically more likely than men to experience abuse by co-workers.

TABLE 13.1: Discrimination—Men and Women Employees

Type of discrimination	Men (%)			Women (%)		
	Average	30–40% overweight	300 lbs or more overweight	Average	30–40% overweight	300 lbs or more overweight
Not being hired	–	–	42	–	31	62
Fired/pressured to resign	–	–	11	–	2	17
Urged to lose weight	15	27	69	11	33	60
Abused by co-workers	15	47	–	23	62	73
Abused by supervisors	3	13	52	2	39	45
Needed to conceal weight	–	–	17	–	10	25

Based on the research of Esther Rothblum, University of Vermont, 1993.

Alternative Beliefs

Our entire society suffers when people are forced to fit into one appearance mold. Film maker Frederico Fellini became legendary by filling his films with many colorful characters. Diverse people make films fascinating, and they also make life fascinating and rich for us, once we give up our ego judgments and relax into the diversity. When will we start accepting diversity in size and shape, all sizes and shapes, instead of believing that beauty comes in a very narrow range of acceptable packages?

You could find hundreds of positive beliefs to adopt about obese persons. Author Sally Tisdale (1993) shares her own belief:

> When I really look at the people on the street, I see a jungle of bodies, growing every which way like lush plants, growing tall and short and slender and round, hairy and hairless, dark and pale and soft and hard and glorious. They are all loved and lovable.

THE BEAUTY MYTH AND ITS IMPACT

The Beauty Myth says that good-looking people, sexually attractive people, all look a certain way. The acceptable range of body sizes and shapes—including the sizes and shapes of key body parts, such as facial features, breasts, hips, and legs—is extremely narrow and limited. And it's becoming slimmer and younger all the time, especially for women. The myth implies that the ideal woman always looks and acts about 25. When they're 15, most girls are trying to look and act 25. When they're 35, 45, and 55, many women are still trying to look and act 25. When they finally give up the impossible task, many feel invisible and ignored.

Naomi Wolf (1991), author of the book *The Beauty Myth*, argues convincingly that people in our culture didn't hate fat until women began to join forces and reject their inferior status. She says that until women got the vote "fat rounded hips and thighs and bellies were perceived as desirable and sensual." Can it be that the more powerful women become, the more pressure we unconsciously place on them to be smaller and to get rid of the curves that make their bodies different from men's?

Author Kim Chernin (1982) theorizes that we do this to women as a way of diminishing "mother power"—to wipe out the memory of the "primordial mother who rules over our childhood with her inscrutable power over life and death." Wolf adds, "A man's right to confer judgment on any woman's beauty while remaining himself unjudged . . . is the last unexamined right remaining intact from the old list of masculine privilege."

Anyone has the right to challenge the beauty myth by asking such questions as, "Who says so? Who made that rule?" in response to fashion and beauty decrees—and by asserting their human rights to consideration and respect. It's not easy, however.

Cultural Conflicts

To begin with, the weight-loss industry has billions at stake in Americans' obsession with slimness and dissatisfaction with their bodies. It has on its payrolls some of the most prominent weight-loss scientists, who publish journal articles recommending new, improved diets and warning of the health risks of being overweight. Instead of carefully evaluating their claims, and investigating the credibility of the sources, Americans tend to jump on every new diet bandwagon, shelling out billions each year for the privilege of depriving themselves of the foods they want when they want them.

Our values set up eating conflicts; for example we love fattening foods and hate fat people. Consider these random but related facts:

- Kellogg's spent $32 million per year advertising Frosted Flakes in the early 1990s, while only $34 million per year was spent for *all* U.S. obesity research.

- Advertising and commercials for calorie-rich junk foods flood the media, consumption of fast foods is increasing, and so are the overweight.

- Fast food is usually junk food—it's seductively available, convenient, cheap, and tasty.

- Americans spent $40 billion a year on diet programs and diet products in the early 1990s, double the amount spent in the early 1980s; adding diet-related foods sold in food stores, the amount was $80 billion.

In magazines, television, the movies, and shopping malls, women are constantly urged to prepare or indulge in fattening foods—by tantalizing recipes for fudge cake, smells wafting from the Mrs. Fields' cookie counter, and such. In the same media, at the same time, they're bombarded with female role models of beauty and talent who are thinner than almost all the actual women in the population.

In 1980 the average Miss America contestant weighed 6 pounds less than 1960 contestants, and the average *Playboy* centerfold became noticeably thinner. Meanwhile the average woman weighed 6 pounds more. These trends continue in the 1990s. As a people, the more obsessed we've become with diets, the more we weigh. Defining overweight as 20 percent or more above the "normal" range, we find the United States leads the industrialized nations in overweight people (Garner, Schwartz and Thompson 1980; Jeffrey, Adlis and Forster 1991).

New Self–Affirming Patterns

Recognizing that size acceptance is an issue for all women—not just large women—is a first step toward solving our nationwide eating problems, according to psychotherapists Jane Hirschmann and Carol Munter (1995). After all, it's our cultural intolerance of certain body sizes that sends us to diets in the first place. And diets often turn us into compulsive eaters or into people obsessed with food, calories, weight, and body size. Hirschmann and Munter use the following process to empower the obese women they work with to stand up for their rights:

- Stop hating your body by challenging those thoughts that put your body down. When you think, "My stomach's too big," shift to, "Who says so? Who made that rule?"

- Make friends with your body and become its loving caretaker; give your body unconditional acceptance and love.

- Become aware of concerns and needs that "bad body thoughts" might mask.

- Reclaim your appetite, dump diets, and learn to eat in response to stomach hunger instead of "mouth hunger" triggered by unconscious needs.

- Assert yourself when people insult your body or intrude into your business.

This process of challenging cultural myths includes many strategies and tactics for dealing with the complexity of overweight. The goal is to give people a solid basis for changing the way they think about their bodies, food, and eating and to establish new, self-affirming patterns.

WHAT RIGHTS DO ACTIVISTS WANT?

Obesity activists say that everyone has a right to be accepted for the person within rather than the exterior physical appearance. In the workplace people have a right to be valued for their potential and actual performance.

Rights that Affect Many

The right to be protected from weight and appearance discrimination affects an increasing number of Americans. For example, about 22 percent of adults were classified as obese by the International Obesity Task Force in 1999, up from 14 percent in 1980. And over one-third were classified as overweight. The Task Force uses body mass index (BMI) which is a ratio between height and weight, correlated with body fat. A BMI of 30 or more is considered obese, and 25 or more means overweight. Those who are the targets of extreme discrimination are referred to legally as the *morbidly obese*, and one to two million Americans, or 1.5 percent, fit this description, as shown in Figure 13.1

FIGURE 13.1: U.S. Weight Distribution 1990 (estimates)

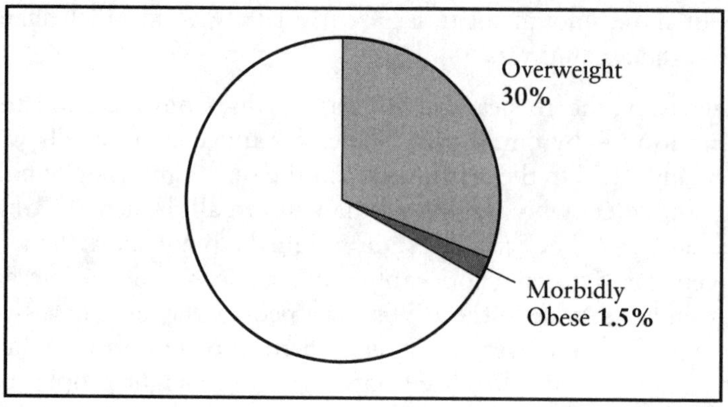

Overweight 30%

Morbidly Obese 1.5%

Source: International Obesity Task Force.

The actual proportion of overweight Americans remained at about 25 percent from 1960 to 1980. Then in the following decade, it rose to 30 percent. Obesity is increasing even faster among young people than among adults. Twenty percent overweight means about 25 pounds over for an average 5' 4" woman and 30 pounds for an average 5' 10" man. Obesity varies by ethnic group but is increasing in every group, as shown in Table 13.2.

TABLE 13.2: Americans 20 Percent or More above "Normal Weight"

	1980	1990
All Americans	25%	30%
Euro-American women	24%	33%
African American women	44%	50%
Mexican American women	44%	50%

Adapted from a report by Marian Burros, New York Times.

Some Basic Rights

Obese persons are beginning to fight discrimination. The size acceptance movement has been active for about 20 years. An underlying principle is that by accepting yourself just as you are, you develop the strength, self-esteem, and confidence to fend off the insults, attacks, and discrimination the world heaps upon obese persons. Sally Tisdale states, "Rejection can't kill you. With the right attitude, rejection can make you stronger. Don't hide out at home. Go out in the world and risk rejection."

Critics say that social preference for thinness is too ingrained in the culture to be legislated away. Activists reply that these same arguments were used for other forms of discrimination. "It's the same as saying you can't hire black salespersons because the customers won't like it, or that you can't hire women because they can't handle male customers' resistance to buying from women," says Art Stine of Michigan's Department of Civil Rights. His department investigates 10 to 20 cases of weight discrimination each year.

At least three national organizations have emerged in recent years to take up the cause of obese Americans. The activist group that's been most prominent in the media recently is the National Association to Advance Fat Acceptance (NAAFA). With 4,000 members in 75 chapters nationwide, NAAFA's goals include:

- improving the self-esteem of obese people
- ensuring their civil rights
- challenging our fat-rejecting culture through education, legislation, and the courts
- achieving equal access to employment

NAAFA leaders say they like the word *fat*. They don't like *overweight*, and they ask "Over whose weight?" They say *obesity* suggests a medical disorder. NAAFA has reclaimed the label *fat* much as some African Americans have reclaimed *nigger* and some gays the term *queer*—but these are still very controversial terms. Certainly not all obese persons agree that they want to be called fat, and most people in our culture have been conditioned to avoid calling people fat. For this reason, the most common term is the medical and legal term *obese*.

The International Size Acceptance Association (ISAA) is focusing on legal workplace rights by asking people to sign petitions to send to legislators. ISAA has attracted national news media and created some interest in this issue.

Legal Workplace Rights: Money Matters

Until recently overweight people had no legal rights for protection from employment discrimination based on weight. Those who are starting to fight back against such discrimination have been forced to resort to two related legal rights:

- protection under the ADA, which treats obesity as a disability in the workplace
- protection under the constitutional right to privacy, on the basis that personal eating habits should not affect how an employee is judged at work

Sally Smith, executive director of NAAFA, notes that one person may be 100 pounds over society's ideal, and others may be just 10. Talking to interviewer Jan Wahl, Smith said, "If employers can use it against the greatly overweight person today, what's to keep them from using it against the slightly overweight tomorrow?"

People who weigh more not only find it more difficult to get and keep jobs, they also make less money.

- One study found that businessmen sacrifice $1,000 in salary for every pound they are overweight. Obese women tend to earn less, too.
- Among women who earn more than $50,000, only 13 percent are obese, while among women in the poverty category, 30 percent are obese.

- In a study of women of all weights, Harvard sociologist Steven Gortmaker found that the overweight women, averaging 5' 3" and 200 pounds, had household incomes that averaged $6,710 below those of thinner women and that they were 10 percent more likely to live in poverty. Overweight apparently keeps people from becoming as affluent as they might otherwise become.

- Obese women are more likely than thin ones to lose socioeconomic status over the course of their adolescence and young adulthood, no matter how well they originally do on achievement tests or how affluent their families. The heavier the woman, the greater the job discrimination, according to a seven-year study of 5,000 women.

Even women of average size or only slightly heavy are often encouraged to lose weight and are more likely to be passed over for promotion than thinner women. This phenomenon is much more common for women than men.

To End Appearance Discrimination, Too

The workplace rights problem goes beyond weight discrimination to the Beauty Myth and the broader issue of appearance discrimination. Attractive people tend to earn about 5 percent more than those with average looks. And homely workers make about 7 percent less than those with average looks. That's a 12 percent pay gap between the homely and the attractive. Women considered to be unattractive are less likely to work than other women and tend to marry men with lower levels of education.

Attractive people are widely regarded as being more intelligent, friendly, honest, and confident than others, all traits that could influence employers and customers to discriminate in favor of them. Attractive children are rewarded with more praise from parents and teachers, influencing their self-esteem and confidence, both valued in the marketplace. Certain occupations cater to attractive employees more than others, but favoritism toward good looks and prejudice against homeliness is pervasive in most jobs. Even within any given occupation, good-looking people make more. When the appearance ratings of 700 MBA graduates were correlated with the salaries they were earning ten years after graduation, better-looking men made as much as $10,000 per year more (Hamermesh and Biddle 1993).

WHAT RIGHTS DO EMPLOYERS WANT TO RETAIN?

Employee appearance and size can affect the success of certain businesses. Employers want to retain the right to achieve fair, reasonable business goals. In theory, activists in the fat acceptance movement do not disagree with this principle. In practice, the two groups may disagree about what is fair and reasonable.

Some employers who run airlines, fashion stores, restaurants, beauty salons, and real estate agencies say they have a right to establish an image and hire only employees who fit that image. Civil rights advocates counter that the only criterion should be performance. One who lost 40 pounds, said, "I did my job well before, and I do it well now. Weight has nothing to do with it." Another said, "Who are employers to play God, to judge what is acceptable or beautiful? Rubens painted large women who were beautiful. It seems clear to me that hiring and promotion ought to be based on your ability to do the job."

Some employers say that customers won't do business with obese persons and that co-workers won't respect them or work well with them. Activists reject the circular reasoning and the ethics of this argument, noting it was also used to resist equal rights for minorities and women. They say it's morally unacceptable for employers themselves to discriminate against obese persons just because prejudiced customers and co-workers might discriminate against them. Such actions signal that employers accept prejudice and encourage it. Just as it is the employers' responsibility to stop sexual harassment of women and ethnic discrimination toward African Americans, it's also their responsibility to stop harassment and discrimination toward obese persons.

Some employers claim that obese employees cost more in health care and sick time. Health professionals suggest that yo-yo dieting could make both obese and thinner persons less healthy. And some obese persons are reluctant to seek medical care because doctors often don't respect them, are condescending and patronizing about their weight, and harangue them to lose weight. Others don't have health care coverage. Nevertheless, there are no respectable studies showing that obese persons cost more because of health problems.

WHAT LAWS PROTECT OBESE WORKERS?

Persons who suffer weight discrimination by employers have only recently gained some legal protection. Laws take two forms.

1. *Legislation.* The most powerful and direct are laws specifically prohibiting discrimination based on weight, height, or other aspects of physical appearance. They follow in the tradition of civil rights laws prohibiting discrimination on the basis of race, creed, color, gender, and similar characteristics.

2. *Court rulings.* Less direct are court rulings that equate obesity with disability and require employers to make reasonable accommodation for obese employees.

Most activists agree that the best protection is to add weight discrimination to the other types of discrimination prohibited by the federal and state civil rights acts.

Legislation: Civil Rights

In the late 1990s, Michigan was the only state in the country with a law that specifically protects the employment rights of overweight people. Weight and height were added to its civil rights statues. The cities of Santa Cruz, California, and Washington, D.C. are among the few local governments that have added such clauses to their civil rights laws.

Massachusetts and New York began considering legislation in 1994 that would add height and weight to civil rights statutes covering employment and housing. A similar bill failed in Texas. California's civil rights laws, while not specifically covering weight, were the basis for a million dollar court award to a 400-pound man. He had sued the automotive parts firm that had fired him after 10 years' employment. In September 1995, after a six-week trial, he was awarded back pay and reparation for emotional distress.

Right to Privacy Law

Another legal avenue is the right to privacy, based on the principle that one's personal eating or exercise habits should not affect how one is judged in the workplace. The American Civil Liberties Union has launched a national project to fight an employer trend to meddle in employees' private lives, such as their eating, drinking, and smoking habits.

Court Rulings: Disability

New Jersey law regards obesity as a disability that automatically triggers discrimination protection regardless of the cause of the obesity. In most of the states where obese employees have won their lawsuits, their cases were based on the ADA. Their attorneys claimed that obesity should be viewed as a physical disability. This is risky at best since some experts still claim that obese people could lose their excess weight if they really wanted to.

The disability argument did prevail in a federal appeals court in 1993. A woman sued the Rhode Island Department of Mental Health after she was denied a state job because at 5' 2" she weighed 320 pounds. Lawyers for the state agency said the law should not be interpreted to cover obesity because obesity "is caused by voluntary conduct and is not immutable." They argued that the plaintiff could lose weight and rid herself of any disability arising from her obesity at any time. But the judge and jury ruled that there was credible evidence that the metabolic dysfunction causing weight gain in the morbidly obese lingers even after weight loss. Their decision was upheld in a federal appeals court, which said that discrimination against the obese could constitute a violation of the ADA. The court further stated that:

> In a society that all too often confuses "slim" with "beautiful" or
> "good," morbid obesity can present formidable barriers to employment.

The court briefs and opinions don't indicate that obesity in itself is necessarily a disability. Instead, the reasoning is that when persons are discriminated against, either because their obesity limits their activities or because employers perceive obesity as a disability that limits their activities, then such persons can be protected under disability law.

EEOC Support for the Disability Approach

The Equal Employment Opportunities Commission (EEOC) filed a brief in federal appeals court in the Rhode Island case. EEOC lawyers urged the court to consider obesity just as it would view many other conditions not specifically mentioned in the ADA, based on how long the person has been affected by the condition and how difficult it would be to change. Noting that obesity isn't a "traditional" disability, the EEOC said that "although it's possible for an obese individual to lose weight, obesity is a chronic, lifelong condition." It further stated that a condition does not have to be involuntary or immutable to be covered. The EEOC did not indicate that a person must be "morbidly obese" in order to be protected from discrimination, and the ruling probably opens the door for claims from more moderately obese employees. Discrimination claims under the ADA must be filed first with the EEOC.

The idea behind the ruling is that the way persons look shouldn't affect their ability to get and keep a job. NAAFA activists say being fat doesn't necessarily mean poor health, and it's too bad that in most states their only recourse in fighting discrimination is through laws meant to protect the disabled. Several overweight persons interviewed by Jan Wahl said the predicament was offensive because most of them are not disabled and are in fact very healthy people.

LEADERSHIP CHALLENGE: MEETING WORKPLACE NEEDS

Your major challenge as a leader working with obese employees, and others that suffer from appearance discrimination, is to help them overcome the barriers they face to success in the workplace. Here's a summary of the basic needs of these employees.

- protection from discrimination and harassment by managers and employees
- respect for their privacy
- acceptance of them as they are
- appreciation of their value as human beings and of their contributions
- accommodation that will help them do their job
- fair and equal compensation

LEADERSHIP OPPORTUNITIES: BUILDING ON STRENGTHS

You have an opportunity to enlighten the corporate culture and to influence employees to move beyond the beauty myth to an appreciation of people for their inner qualities and contributions to the organization.

Opportunity #1: Look Below the Surface

You can move away from a focus on the superficial aspects of corporate employee image, such as size, shape, facial features, and other aspects of the Beauty Myth. An in-depth corporate image focuses on such inner strengths as being honest, respecting others, keeping agreements, honoring commitments, delivering the goods on time, providing top-quality service, being positive, focusing on others' strengths and contributions, seeing the humor, loving life, summoning courage, and on and on. These qualities seem old-fashioned in a way. Yet aren't they really the raw materials that leaders can skillfully draw on to create a highly motivated and committed world-class workforce?

Opportunity #2: Set Policies on Obesity Harassment and Discrimination

Employers and managers have a responsibility to stop the harassment of obese employees and to stop discriminatory actions against them. The first step is to develop policies and procedures designed to provide equal opportunity and fair treatment of obese persons. Affirmative action programs and equal opportunity policies already in place for minorities and women can be used for guidance in remedying discrimination. Company policies and procedures designed to prevent sexual harassment and to handle such cases can serve as a pattern for preventing and handling cases of obesity harassment.

Opportunity #3: Make Reasonable Accommodation

Although obese persons are not necessarily disabled, those who are greatly overweight usually need some type of accommodation. The best way to find out is to ask tactfully what can be done to help them to be as productive and successful as possible on the job. Comfortable, sturdy seating arrangements are nearly always needed and appreciated, not only at a work station or executive desk but also in meeting rooms, lounges, dining facilities, and any other place the employee frequents in the course of the job. If a company car or other transportation is provided, arrange for adequate size in seats and seat belts.

A few obese persons have difficulty getting around. The same provisions that are made for other mobility-impaired employees can be made for these employees—such as electric carts, ramps, elevators, and convenient parking.

Opportunity #4: Enlighten the Corporate Culture

You can encourage change in those company practices and habits that degrade and discriminate against obese persons through your own example, through appropriate storytelling, through making them heroines and heroes when they excel, through visibly supporting them in other ways, and through providing information and training for all employees about obesity issues. Corporate diversity training programs can include a segment on obese persons. Every employee needs to complete such a segment.

You can focus on the contributions of obese employees, and on their positive qualities. You can unfailingly respect their dignity and refuse to countenance disrespect in the form of wisecracks, jokes, put-downs, unsought advice, and similar behavior.

Opportunity #5: Consider New Marketing Opportunities

Some leaders are breaking the mold and giving talented obese persons job opportunities in such high-profile jobs as television news reporter, talk show hostess, and situation comedy star. Some say that such media personalities seem approachable, like a "next-door neighbor," and people feel comfortable with them. Business leaders need to examine this opportunity to relate to new types of customers and perhaps open up new markets.

SUMMARY

Myths and stereotypes about obese persons cause people to judge them negatively, to reject them as friends and employees, and even to invade their privacy by telling them how to lose weight. Most studies indicate that obese persons eat no more than other people, and they often have difficulty exercising because of their size. Diets don't work for most people, especially the very obese. Nearly all dieters gain back the weight. Apparently, the metabolism of some persons is different and this may be due to a mutation of the "obesity gene." Obesity poses some health risks, but so does the dieting syndrome and so does being extremely underweight.

Most jobs are sedentary, and obese employees are just as productive as others. Because of appearance bias, however, obese persons are less likely to be hired and promoted, make less money on average, and are more likely to be poor than those considered attractive by cultural standards. These standards are more stringent for women than for men, primarily because of the Beauty Myth that appearance is more important as a way of judging women. About 30 percent of Americans, or 75 million people, are considered overweight, and between one and two million are morbidly obese.

Obese employees have had no protection from job discrimination in the past, but that's changing. Nationally, the most significant development is a case won in a federal appeals court and supported by an EEOC brief that cites morbid obesity as a condition protected under the ADA. A size acceptance movement is emerging in which obese activists declare their rights to equal treatment, to equal pay, and to challenge the beauty myth. The major leadership challenge is meeting the needs of obese employees. Leadership opportunities include looking beneath surface appearances to career strengths and building upon them, setting policies that prohibit harassment and discrimination, making reasonable accommodation, enlightening the corporate culture, and considering new marketing opportunities in which persons of various sizes and shapes can be an asset.

Skill Builder 13.1: The Case of Chris, a Job Applicant

Chris is 35 years old, has two years of college, and weighs 350 pounds. In response to a newspaper ad, Chris applied and interviewed for a job at Worman's Hardware Store. He didn't get the job, but when he learned of another opening, he called the chain store's personnel coordinator, *Georgia*. Georgia told Chris the store wanted more experienced people. She also told him, "There is some concern about your weight and whether you can physically handle hauling heavy items of hardware and supplies." Chris has 10 ten years' experience in retail selling although he has never worked in a hardware store.

- If you were Chris, what would you do?
- If you were a top manager at Worman's, how would you view this situation?

Skill Builder 13.2: The Case of Laura, Public Relations Manager

Laura was 40 years old and had successfully held several managerial positions in public relations. When she applied for a job at a major East Coast medical center, she was wearing a slenderizing dark suit and had been on a strict diet for two months. She got the job but didn't report for work until a month or so later. In the meantime, Laura relaxed her diet regime. As usual after such diets, she was starved and tired and quickly went back up to her usual 230 pounds. When she arrived for her first day on the new job, *Murray*, the director of public relations blurted out, "My God, you've put on a lot of weight since we interviewed you. I'm not sure this is the image we want for the hospital."

From that day on Laura was constantly pressured to diet and watched to see if she was slimming down. Laura felt demeaned, set apart from the others, and was subjected to humiliating comments. She had an expensive professional wardrobe, but *Jan*, her boss, told her to wear only black or navy. Laura knew that meant "camouflage your size." She says, "Every time I walked into the office, I got a quick once-over to see what I was wearing and whether I had lost weight." At a staff meeting Jan asked Laura to tell everyone about the liquid diet she was starting.

For the next year Laura was successful in her job. She got national publicity for the hospital, raised large sums of money, and developed award-winning programs. Nevertheless, she was called into Jan's office one Friday afternoon and fired. Jan didn't mention her weight directly, but said, "Things that should have changed didn't change."

- What is your opinion of the way Murray and Jan handled Laura's case?
- Do you think Laura should have done anything differently?
- What do you think she should do now?

Skill Builder 13.3: Louis' Career Goals

Louis has been working for Manko's, a privately-owned printing firm for about 5 years. The firm specializes in designing and printing forms used by automobile dealers. Louis' duties include taking phone orders and arranging for the shipping of the merchandise to clients. The shipping aspect requires lifting boxes of forms. His job calls for good customer relations skills, and over the years he has helped the firm develop and retain a loyal clientele.

Louis' doctor tells him that he's about 150 pounds over his ideal weight. This has been the case for nearly all his adult life, at least since his early twenties. Louis has dieted and lost weight several times in the past years, once even losing 125 pounds. As he says, "I've tried every dieting gimmick in the book, and I always end up at about the same weight in the long run." Louis has always been somewhat self-conscious about his weight, for he was a little "pudgy" even as a child. His mother frequently cautioned him about his eating patterns, saying, "Louis, you don't need to eat seconds; you've had enough to eat." Or, "No, Louis, you don't need to eat cookies; try an apple or an orange for a snack."

Louis' weight has not been a problem at the print shop. He gets along well with the employees, as well as the customers he relates to by phone. There are four employees: a printer, two outside salespersons, and Louis, who handles everything in the office. The owner, *Bill Manko*, relies on him to keep the office running, and the salespersons rely on him to do favors for their customers, such as shipping forms ASAP, providing information about the proper type of form a customer needs, and explaining to customers how to use certain forms.

Bill tells Louis that the firm has grown enough to need another outside salesperson. He's looking for a good person. Louis realizes that the job would be a good opportunity for him to expand his career, and he decides to apply. When Louis approaches Bill about the job, Bill seems quite surprised and says, "Well, let me think about it, Louis." A few days later, Bill says to Louis, "I think you're a better asset to the company in your present job. You don't quite fit the sales rep image, and we need your know-how and knowledge of the business and the customers to handle phone orders and shipping."

- What are the key issues in this case?
- If you were Bill, what would you do?
- If you were Louis, what would you do?

Skill Builder 13.4: The Case of Helen, Travel Agent

Helen has been working for World Points Travel Agency for about a year. World Point consists of a chain of 15 travel agencies with a total of about 100 employees. When Helen interviewed for the job, the office seemed perfectly suited to her style. People seemed to like their work and enjoy a little humor. *Franko*, the manager, was very flexible about allowing her to work only 25 hours a week and to schedule her hours around her daughter's needs. He hired her on the spot.

Helen was thrilled to get the job: all she wanted was to work part time so she could spend time with her three-year-old daughter Linda, whom she has just enrolled in a good nursery school. Helen figured that a nice part-time job at a travel agency would give her a chance to get out of the house and meet people and enough money to pay Linda's school expenses.

Everyone was friendly from the beginning, and Helen was invited to join the employee's association even though part-time workers were technically not eligible for membership. The employee's association didn't negotiate contracts or require dues, but did consult with management in making policies for the agency and the employees. Little did Helen know that the actions of the group would eventually lead to her downfall.

A few weeks ago, the group suggested to management that the company's image needed to be improved. As one of them said, "We sell so many European vacation plans, we need to present a chic, updated European image." Most of the improvements involved changing the names of vacation packages and the office decor. The trouble arose when the group decided to adopt appearance standards for employees; for example: "Employees who deal directly with the public must look attractive and professional and wear outfits that reflect current European high-fashion. Employees must keep their weight within the optimal weight range for their height and bone structure."

Helen is 5'6" tall and weighs about 200 pounds. Last week, two of the women from the employee association committee that drafted the image policy met with Helen. They asked her if she would agree to bring her weight down to 160 pounds within the next six months, saying "That seems reasonable, don't you think." Helen said, "No, I don't think it's reasonable. I gained this weight three years ago when I was pregnant and then nursing my daughter. I've tried to lose it, and it's just not that easy. I'd like to lose it on my own terms and in my own time frame. To make this kind of agreement just puts too much pressure on me."

Marge, the committee chair said, "It was the employee association's idea to do this, and you are a member of our group, so you shouldn't view this as something the company is forcing on you." Helen replied, "Do you think I don't look good enough to sell European vacation plans? Don't I have a right to look the way I want to look, so long as it isn't outrageous or harmful to business?"

Marge replied, "We all know you're a highly professional worker and an attractive representative of the company. But we think the rule should apply to everyone." The others seemed to agree with Marge.

The next day Franko approached Helen and suggested changing her job duties, saying, "Helen, let's try you out at the confirmation desk. You can keep your current salary and hours and it will probably be a better fit for you." Helen objected, "Franko, I love meeting with people and I'm good at it. I don't want a strictly telephone job behind the scenes. All I'll be doing is confirming hotel and flight reservations. It would be boring, and I would go nuts."

- What are the key issues in this case?
- If you were Helen, what would you do?
- If you were Franko, what would you do?

REFERENCES

Blair, S., et al. "Physical Fitness and All-Cause Mortality"; J. Holloway, A. Beuter, and J. Duda, "Self-Efficacy and Training for Strength in Adolescent Girls"; Paffenbarger et al. "Physical Activity, All-Cause Mortality." *Journal of Applied Social Psychology* 18, 1988, 699-719.

Brown, Laura S. and Esther D. Rothblum, eds. *Overcoming Fear of Fat.* Binghamton, NY: Harrington Park Press, 1989.

Burros, Marian. "More Americans Tipping the Scales." *New York Times*, July 15, 1994.

Chernin, Kim. *The Obsession: Reflections on the Tyranny of Slenderness.* New York: Harper & Row, 1982.

Dettmar, Lyn. Chicago clinical psychologist, study conducted in 1990.

Fraser, Laura. "The Overweight Want Their Rights," *San Francisco Chronicle*, June 22, 1994, E-7.

Friedman, J. of Howard Hughes Medical Institute, Rockefeller Institute, New York, NY. See reports in *Nature* and *Discovery*, March, 1995.

Garner, D., P. Garfindek, D. Schwartz, and M. Thompson, "Cultural Expectations of Thinness in Women." *Psychological Reports* 47, 1980, 483-91.

Gortmaker, Steven, et al., "Social and Economic Consequences of Overweight in Adolescence and Young Adulthood," *New England Journal of Medicine* 329,14, September 1993, 1036-1037.

Grunwald, L. "Do I Look Fat to You?" *Discovery*, March 1995, 58-74.

Hamermesh, Daniel S. and Jeff Biddle. *Beauty and the Labour Market.* Cambridge, MA: National Bureau of Economic Research, 1993.

Hirschmann, Jane and Carol Munter. *When Women Stop Hating Their Bodies*, New York: Fawcett Columbine, 1995.

Jeffrey, R., S. Adlis, and J. Forster, "Prevalence of Dieting Among Working Men and Women." *Health Psychology* 10. 1991, 274-81.

Johnson, Carol A. *Self-Esteem Comes in All Sizes: How to Be Healthy and Happy at Your Natural Weight.* New York: Doubleday, 1995.

Kano, Susan. *Making Peace With Food* (a step-by-step guide to self-help in freeing yourself from diet and weight obsession). New York: Harper, 1989.

Lyons, Pat and Debby Burgard. *Great Shape.* Menlo Park, CA: Bull Publishing Co., 1990.

Olds, Ruthanne. *Big & Beautiful* (a book on overcoming fatphobia). Washington DC: Acropolis Books Ltd., 1992.

Polivy, Janet and Peter Herman. *Breaking the Diet Habit.* New York: Basic Books, 1983.

Rose, Laura, S. Brown and E.D. Rothblum, eds. *Life Isn't Weighed on the Bathroom Scale.* Waco, TX: WRS Group, 1994.

Rothblum, Esther D. "Weight and Acceptance on the Job," in *Life Isn't Weighed on the Bathroom Scale*, ed. Laura Rose, S. Brown and E.D. Rothblum. Waco, TX: WRS Group, 1994.

Seligman, Martin. *What You Can Change and What You Can't.* New York: Knopf, 1994.

Tisdale, Sally. "A Weight That Women Carry." *Harpers*, May 1993.

Wahl, Jan. "Taking a Female Lead." *Radiance,* fall 1994.

Wolf, Naomi. *The Beauty Myth: How Images of Beauty Are Used Against American Women.* New York: Doubleday, 1991.

Resources – Organizations and Workshops

AHELP, Association for the Health Enrichment of Large People. Annual conferences for health professionals. Joe McVoy, Ph.D., Director, AHELP, P.O. Drawer C, Radford, VA 24143.

Ample Opportunity. Organization, Portland, Oregon.

Annual Event: International No-Diet Day, May 5.

Boycott Anorexic Marketing, a Boston group founded by psychotherapist Dr. Mary Baures, who is concerned about a society that promotes eating disorders. In 1994 the group criticized the ultrathin models used by Coca-Cola and Calvin Klein and called for a boycott.

David Garner, Ph.D. Eating disorder specialist and antidiet activist.

Fed Up! Book, workshops, and support groups, by Terry Nicholetti Garrison, 233 Forest Home Drive, Ithaca, NY 14850.

Largely Positive. Workshops and support groups, manual on starting support groups, Carol Johnson, Milwaukee, Wisconsin, P.O. Box 17233, Glendale, WI 53217.

NAAFA, National Association to Advance Fat Acceptance, based in Sacramento, CA, with 4,000 members nationwide.

National Council on Size and Weight Discrimination.

Resources – Magazines and Films

Dimensions, the lifestyle magazine for men who prefer large, radiant women, and the women who want to learn about them. 7189 Capitol Station, Albany, NY 12224.

Extra! a magazine for large persons.

Fat Chance, a documentary film sponsored by the National Film Board of Canada, to be aired on public broadcasting systems.

Healthy Weight Journal (formerly *Obesity and Health*), published by Healthy Living Institute, 402 South 14 Street, Hettinger, ND.

Radiance, the magazine for large women, a sponsored project of the San Francisco Women's Center, P.O. Box 30246, Oakland, CA 94604.

CHAPTER 14

Managing Diversity: Inclusive Corporate Cultures

A diverse company is better able to sell to a diverse world.
Microsoft executive

The best approach to managing diversity is one that includes all persons and excludes none. It provides a climate that supports all types of employees. Its goal is to include all employees in the inner circle of employees who are continuously learning to create continuous improvement—in activities that contribute to the bottom-line success of the organization.

While leaders of some companies still refer to their corporate culture as a melting pot and the company as one big happy family, a new breed of leaders is moving beyond the melting pot and legal approaches to an inclusive multicultural approach. This approach builds on the best affirmative action principles and a strong corporate culture, but it goes further. Its leaders value diversity. Just as important, they consciously improve the corporate culture by making it more multicultural and inclusive. Then they develop corporate strategies, systems, and action steps that reflect that core value. These leaders are change agents who learn how to inspire others to create the changes needed to build a productive, innovative, synergistic workforce.

Before you delve into the details of this inclusive approach to managing diversity, test your knowledge by completing Self-Awareness Activity 14.1.

Self-Awareness Activity 14.1

What Do You Know about Managing Diversity?

Purpose: To see what you know about the issues covered in this chapter.
Instructions: Determine whether you think the following statements are basically true or false—and think about why. The answers will emerge in this chapter, and the summary at the end of the chapter focuses on these issues.

1. An inclusive multicultural approach to managing diversity focuses on minorities.

2. The most basic change that must take place in the organization is modifying its systems and practices to accommodate diverse employees.

3. Valuing diversity goes beyond tolerance to appreciation for all types of people.

4. The focus of employee training in the multicultural approach is on new minority employees learning about the corporate culture.

5. This inclusive approach builds upon equal opportunity principles and the current affirmative action program.

6. A key strategy for making this inclusive approach work is getting to know each individual employee.

7. The key to bringing about change is for top management to make a commitment.

Managing diversity is all about recognizing and responding effectively to the leadership challenges and opportunities you encounter in the workplace, such as the following:

- Meeting specific needs of all employees in your diverse workplace
- Creating an inclusive multicultural approach to managing diversity
- Creating an inclusive organization culture
- Including all employees in bottom-line efforts

LEADERSHIP CHALLENGE: MEETING ALL EMPLOYEES' NEEDS

Your greatest diversity challenge as a leader in today's workplace is meeting the needs of all employees—people from all the diverse groups, including Euro-American men. You must understand the many barriers facing ethnic minorities and women in most American corporations and develop strategies for dismantling them. The most important barriers are the policies and practices that systematically restrict the opportunities and rewards to nontraditional employees. To help formulate better policies and practices, you must understand not only the external barriers that diverse workers face, but also some of their typical life experiences and the resulting internal barriers.

Some of the strongest barriers to the success of diverse employees are structural blocks built by the culture and the organization. Leaders with multicultural awareness and skills can help in the struggle to break down these barriers.

Challenge #1: Changing an Incompatible Corporate Culture

To many diverse employees, the corporate culture seems unfriendly and stressful, often resulting in loneliness. At higher levels minorities, women, and employees from other diverse groups may be dramatically outnumbered by Euro-American men who treat them "differently," exclude them from social events and friendly camaraderie, and may view them as a curiosity. These newcomers sometimes report that the "insiders" watch them closely, overscrutinize their work for mistakes, withhold information, and even sabotage their work. They say they must be better than the others just to keep up. They say that when they cluster with others from their own diversity group, they may be jokingly or seriously accused of plotting against the dominant group, being divisive, or excluding others. If they remain isolated, they may be seen as arrogant or resentful. If they try to join the insiders, they may be met with stereotyping or some degree of rejection. We'll discuss this basic aspect of managing diversity in more detail later.

Challenge #2: Changing Unsuitable Organizational Systems

The most lasting and workable changes in the firm's systems and practices flow naturally from a commitment to corporate culture change. One reason AA programs have had such difficulty is that leaders rarely built them upon a commitment to corporate culture change. Once this commitment is made by a critical mass of employees, changing systems and practices becomes relatively easy. Specific suggestions are discussed later in this chapter.

Challenge #3: Ending Historical Exclusion

Nontraditional employees have traditionally been kept out of the inner circle. The American culture has traditionally sent the message that Euro-American men take the lead role in all arenas of power. Studies indicate that a key barrier is their reluctance to share power and privilege and their natural tendency to associate with people like themselves (Carr-Ruffino 1991). Savvy leaders know it's time to break this cycle by giving everyone an equal chance.

Challenge #4: Raising the Comfort Levels of Euro–American Men

An effective multicultural approach respects the concerns of all, including Euro-American men. It focuses on the leadership benefits of gaining multicultural skills in order to meet diverse employees halfway in cultural understanding and collaboration. Diversity training is essential.

Resistance to change results in backlash, as we discussed in Chapter 1 concerning affirmative action. In fact, backlash has become so prevalent that it now is the primary barrier to the diversity efforts of many major companies. When downsizing cuts job opportunities, people become especially resentful and fearful and more likely to resent any competition from diverse employees.

People tend to be most accepting and comfortable with others who are most like them. Virtually all the emotions that block goodwill toward others spring from fear, and fear in turn often springs from the unknown, from ignorance. Studying cultural differences makes people knowledgeable, diminishes their fear of the unknown, and increases their comfort level with diverse others. Learning about stereotypes and prejudice can help also, but the instructional approach must be respectful, not blaming. It must address such concerns as reverse discrimination, lowered standards and quality, erosion of income and job security, and loss of a traditional way of life.

Challenge #5: Removing Networking Barriers

For all nontraditional groups a major barrier is inability to create and manage networks. Individuals often can't get the information they need about industry trends and where the company is headed, nor handle company politics adequately. Understanding the organizational culture and the barriers it may have erected can be even more important than formal degrees, according to several surveys. In fact, courses and degrees may be less relevant to success in the executive suite than they once were because most omit these soft skills (Cox 1993; Carr-Ruffino 1991).

Challenge #6: Minimizing Conflict Among Subcultural Groups

When one underrepresented group competes with another for privileges, status, and power, infighting can occur and create a barrier for all. Managers have been known to use divide-and-conquer tactics to increase friction and infighting among diverse subgroups. The dramatic increase in hate crimes, at record levels now, indicates that backlash and infighting are problems in society at large, not just in organizations. The growing diversity in the population has increased interethnic tension. You can learn to apply the people skills you've learned here and elsewhere.

You can help to establish policies and practices that will minimize conflict. And you can lead conflict resolution efforts that bring seething problems out into the open and resolve them in ways that all can live with.

Challenge #7: Turning Around Poor Career Development Patterns

Euro-American men are often reluctant to assign nontraditional managers to those challenging, high-profile jobs that are needed to prepare people for senior management positions. They don't want people to fail, and they want the company to look good. Such assignments include leading a major start-up, troubleshooting (sometimes overseas,) serving on important task forces, taking a headquarters staff job, and taking line jobs of increasing responsibility. They involve autonomy, visibility, access to senior management, and control over significant resources. They are considered the fast track in many organizations and may be used as tests and rewards for high-potential candidates. Such career-enhancing assignments are often not available to diverse employees, who tend to be found in staff rather than line positions (Kotter 1990; U.S. Department of Labor 1991; Catalyst 1990; DiTomaso, Thompson, and Blake 1988).

You can use your influence and take the lead in showing confidence in the potential of diverse employee to handle such challenging assignments. Be willing to give those who are ready a chance, to support them every step of the way, and to give credit for their successes, achievements, and contributions.

Challenge #8: Breaking the Glass Ceiling

The U.S. Department of Labor reports that 30 percent of corporate middle management is made up of women, African Americans, and Latino Americans. These groups make up less than 5 percent of senior management, even though they're about 65 percent of the workforce. A major consulting firm surveyed nearly 1,400 senior executives, and only 29 were women and 13 were people of color, meaning 97 percent were Euro-American males (U.S. Department of Labor 1991; Korn/Ferry 1999).

Universities such as Harvard, Yale, and Princeton, which are typically considered feeder institutions for high-paying management jobs, refused to admit women as undergraduates until the 1970s. Lack of education became a widely accepted explanation for the slow movement of nontraditional employees into and through management. It's still used today despite the fact that their educational achievement has soared. It's been more than 35 years since the passage of the 1964 Civil Rights Act. It's been more than 25 years since women and minorities entered leadership-oriented programs in significant numbers. Even if it takes 15 or 20 years to develop a general manager, more minorities and women should logically be reaching the middle- and top-level jobs. Clearly, lack of qualified candidates is not the only explanation for under-representation.

On the bright side, 1999 was a breakthrough year for women and African Americans—symbolically, at least. A woman and an African American man became the first to work their way up through the ranks and become CEO of a large corporation. Carly Fiorina of Hewlett-Packard (Fortune 100) and Lloyd Ward of Maytag (Fortune 1000).

LEADERSHIP OPPORTUNITY #1: CREATE AN INCLUSIVE MULTICULTURAL APPROACH

The inclusive approach is a diversity-within-unity approach, as indicated in Figure 14.1. Unity is provided through a strong corporate culture that focuses on the best niche for the organization to fill and on the purpose of the organization, as well as on valuing diversity. And diversity is provided for through a strong emphasis on appreciating each individual—respecting the uniqueness of every employee, including values, lifestyles, and cultural heritage. Above all, the multicultural approach is an inclusive approach. No one is excluded simply because he or she was not born a member of the ingroup—or has changed physically in ways that don't affect basic job performance.

Leaders encourage the organization to adapt in ways that support all types of employees, and they help all employees become oriented to the organization, a two-way street. Corporate leaders make certain the organization's values and norms accommodate a wide range of workers. They make sure that everyone has a chance to build multicultural skills and to update and refine them continually.

This inclusive approach aims to support and empower all employees in learning, stretching, and moving up because leaders pay attention to this issue at the individual, interpersonal, and organizational levels. Leaders develop strategies to bring all employees into the "Inner Circle" and remove barriers to inclusion, as shown in Table 14.1. The multicultural approach is also about making sure that the systems and practices of the organization support employee empowerment, through natural evolvement so that stop-and-go types of AA programs are unnecessary. It's a comprehensive managerial process for developing an environment that works for all employees. Empowering the total workforce is achieved through such strategies as pushing decision making down to lower levels, organizing self-managing work teams, providing adequate education, and supporting career development.

TABLE 14.1: Managing Inclusion at All Levels

Inclusive Strategies	Barriers to Inclusion
Personal Level	
Become aware of prejudice and other barriers to valuing diversity	Stereotypes, prejudices
Learn about other cultures and groups	Past experiences and influences
Serve as an example, walk the talk	Stereotyped expectations and perceptions
Participate in managing diversity	Feelings that tend to separate, divide
Interpersonal Level	
Facilitate communication and interactions in ways that value diversity	Cultural differences
Encourage participation	Group differences
Share your perspective	Myths
Facilitate unique contributions	Relationship patterns based on exclusion
Resolve conflicts in ways that value diversity	
Accept responsibility for developing common ground	
Organizational Level	
All employees have access to networks and focus groups	Individuals who get away with discriminating and excluding
All employees take a proactive role in managing diversity and creating a more diverse workplace culture	A culture that values or allows exclusion
	Work structures, policies, and practices that discriminate and exclude
All employees are included in the Inner Circle that contributes to the bottom-line success of the company	
All employees give feedback to teams and management	
All employees are encouraged to contribute to change	

This type of diversity management is not about Euro-American males managing women and minorities, nor is it about focusing on women and minorities to the exclusion of Euro-American men. It's about all managers empowering whoever is in their workforce. This inclusive approach focuses on understanding individuals and valuing the cultural background they came from. It's about respecting that heritage without assuming that a particular individual adheres to all aspects of the heritage. It's about asking questions in a sensitive, respectful manner based on your expanded knowledge and awareness of cultural differences. This approach views diverse employees as persons who can enrich the work team or organization, who can interact with others to create innovative sparks, entrepreneurial genius, and total-quality performance. It is symbolized in figure 14.1.

FIGURE 14.1: Diverse Groups within a Strong Corporate Culture: Diversity within Unity

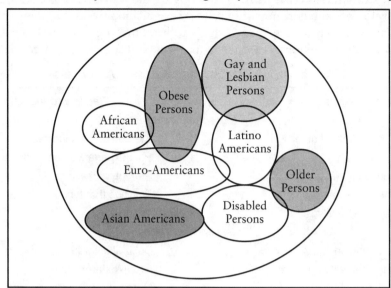

Key Aspects of a Multicultural Approach

The most important activities for building a multicultural approach are:

- Modify the corporate culture toward a multi-culture that incorporates the values and customs of all the subculture—essential foundation for all other changes
- Include all employees in bottom-line efforts
- Build on equal opportunity and affirmative action principles
- Adapt corporate systems and practices that respect members of all subcultures
- Address concerns and resistances some people may have to this inclusive approach
- Build consensus for changing to an inclusive culture

LEADERSHIP OPPORTUNITY #2:
CREATE AN INCLUSIVE CULTURE

Valuing diversity is first of all a bottom-line issue because it's the first step in getting all employees on a path to contributing to bottom-line success. That's because valuing diversity is at the heart of such issues as conflict resolution, negotiation, employee relationships, employee empowerment, leadership effectiveness, continuous learning, continuous improvement, productivity, total quality management, synergistic teams, and trust building. Given the potential payoffs, companies can't afford to be satisfied with outdated corporate cultures that exclude many potential contributors.

Changing the corporate culture is most effective, of course, when top management makes a commitment to shifting the culture in ways that accommodate, motivate, and empower all employees. The ultimate goal is for everyone to grow and develop, to be effective and productive, to interact to create a synergy that sparks innovation and commitment. But any person anywhere in the organization can have an influence toward change. Wherever you are on your career path, you can accept a leadership role in this kind of change. The most powerful change starts in the basic cultural elements:

- *values* that build respect for all kinds of persons and that build trust—a high value for diversity
- *heroines and heroes*, role models of success from all the diverse groups

- *stories*, myths, and legends about diverse heroes and heroines and new ways of succeeding in an inclusive organization
- *rituals*, ways of doing things and ways of interacting with each other, that expand to include the ways typical of all groups
- *ceremonies* that are meaningful to people of all groups, that incorporate the customs of all groups, that recognize people from all groups
- *symbols* and slogans that touch people from all groups and that communicate an inclusive worldview

Culture change is the basis for all other organizational change. Lasting change must come from inside the organization—and from the foundation of core beliefs and values. Role modeling and persuasion are the best methods of leading change, while coercion doesn't really work at all. When key leaders in all areas and at all levels become committed to change, this critical mass will bring along most other employees in its wake.

Freedom to Be Authentic

Every person and every human culture needs to express who they are. The strong desire of many former communist countries and ethnic groups to claim a separate culture reflects this universal need. When groups unite to achieve certain common purposes, they can greatly increase their power. But when they can't find ways to accommodate cultural differences and blend them into a group strength, they lose their joint power. At the corporate level such groups may simply lose the opportunity to achieve greater goals, but at the societal level, they may deteriorate into anarchy and bloodshed, as happened in the Los Angeles riots and in Bosnia.

Whether in a national culture or a corporate culture, people are more productive and enthusiastic when they have the freedom to express their own values and determine their own lifestyle. The most effective organizations learn how to combine and balance the drive for individual freedom and achievement with the drive for belongingness and group affiliation. And they focus on building and maintaining trust, the essential ingredient.

Beyond the Melting Pot: Free Choice and Cultural Enrichment

The most positively powerful aspects of American acculturation patterns have been described by Nathan Glazer (1970) and Stephen Burman (1995) as our willingness to informally recognize that diverse members have a desire and a right to self-development, acculturation, or integration at their own chosen rate. Diverse groups have a right to an integrated or independent economic base, to social, religious and political institutions, and to political recognition as part of a united country. This has been the American genius for embracing diversity within a common unity.

Creating an inclusive corporate culture means dealing with these cultural realities. The evidence on acculturation patterns among Asians and Latinos in the United States indicates that substantial identity with the root national cultures remains even after three or more generations of citizenship. The least effective policy an organization can pursue is to insist that members of any group give up cherished beliefs and practices. People always resist such pressure—usually by going underground and then engaging in passive aggressive behavior. Of course covert behavior is much more difficult to deal with than open, direct behavior (Deshpande et al 1986; Allport 1954).

Since cultural accommodation is a two-way street, the process is subtle and complex and trying to force it on any of the parties may create as many problems as it solves. The best approach is to allow people the freedom to assimilate into the mainstream culture and the corporate culture to the extent they desire and to retain their cultural heritage as they see fit. This approach must rest on appreciating differences and respecting each person's cultural heritage and their decisions about what to retain. Cultural change takes time, and a relaxed, accepting attitude allows the shifts to occur with minimal friction.

When ethnic groups retain those distinctive and colorful ways that they treasure, the organization is enriched. Each individual decides those aspects of their ethnic cuisine, art, the philosophical and spiritual beliefs, myths and stories that they want to hold dear and to express. When people are allowed and encouraged to preserve these treasures, they become more interesting and valuable to the whole organization and to the nation. They "prevent drab standardization in a culture dominated by advertising, brand names, malls, and sedative television" (Cox 1993, 84).

Leadership Traits

Unlike people who stereotype, leaders who value differences tend to:

- base beliefs about characteristics of culture groups on a systematic study of reliable sources of data
- acknowledge that people within an ethnic group vary and that they have many voices and many individual styles and patterns
- resist the tendency to evaluate differences
- avoid negative connotations

A multicultural approach enhances acceptance, tolerance, and understanding of differences.

Education for All

The inclusive multicultural approach is a relatively new concept for many employees. Training is normally needed at all levels of the organization for positive change to occur. Training usually begins at the top, since top management must thoroughly understand the concept and apply it consistently in their own thinking and acting. Training sessions tend to focus on the ways that people are both alike and different in values, attitudes, behavior styles, ways of thinking, and cultural background. Common goals of the educational programs are for participants to:

- expand their awareness and acceptance of cultural and individual commonalities and differences
- understand the nature and dynamics of cultural and individual differences
- explore their own feelings and attitudes about people they view as "different"
- identify ways that differences might be tapped as workplace assets
- build better work relations with people from all societal groups

This approach leads people to appreciate the value, richness, and creativity that can flow from a diverse workforce. It focuses on helping everyone to better understand some key commonalities and differences among employees from various groups and how differences can be valuable to the organization. It exhibits real concern and commitment to providing a corporate culture where people from all groups can thrive. When employees thrive, the company tends to thrive, as Microsoft has shown.

LEADERSHIP OPPORTUNITY #3: INCLUDE ALL EMPLOYEES IN BOTTOM-LINE EFFORTS

Continuous improvement is highly valued in most organizations these days. Although Americans tend to prefer dramatic breakthroughs, decisive victories, and clear "wins," leaders have learned that small incremental improvements are much easier to come by. They can also lead to comparable or greater success over time. One of the most powerful benefits of a continuous improvement approach and process is that it inevitably leads to continuous learning for the employees who are included in it. In fact many leaders are convinced that the successful organization these days must be a learning organization. Since organizations are people first and foremost, this means that successful organizations must be staffed by employees who are continuously learning.

Showcase: Microsoft
A Valuing Diversity Culture

Microsoft focuses on valuing diversity and creating a corporate culture that reflects that value. This view has been productive and profitable for the firm, which grew from a start-up to the largest software firm in the world in a few short years. Microsoft has a diversity program that is proactive. Program leaders want to know when people feel unwelcome at work, when they're worried about things outside of work, or anything else that could stand in the way of top performance. A diversity staff implements diversity training programs, updates benefits policies, and investigates cases of discrimination and harassment.

The company's Diversity Advisory Council includes representatives from employee groups of gay persons, women, persons with disabilities, Jewish Americans, African Americans, Latino Americans, American Indians, and Asian Indian Americans, and it expands as new groups form. The council helps formulate policy, identify problems, and create the best possible working environment for all employees. Microsoft's diversity manager says the council helps to boost productivity and to stem turnover, adding millions to company profits.

Microsoft's management also understands that it takes more than a nondiscrimination clause and diversity groups to achieve a supportive environment for all groups. Some people are intolerant, and the company needs specific training programs to help people become more aware of the nature of prejudice, the facts about various groups, and of alternative ways of believing and interacting.

Microsoft wants to tap into the different needs and backgrounds of employees to use their talents, to use the various perspectives they bring, based on who they are. For example, a Microsoft marketing goal is to put a computer on every desk in every home. To do that, the company needs to know who these consumers are and what they're like. The philosophy:

> *We must make our products accessible to all types of consumers,*
> *and therefore we must market them differently to each group. A*
> *diverse company is better able to sell to a diverse world.*

Make an Inclusive Learning Loop

The cycle of continuous learning that leads to continuous improvement and that also results from efforts to continuously improve is sometimes called the learning loop because one process feeds into the other, as shown in figure 14.3. Imagine ongoing learning loops leading to ever-higher levels of learning and improvement as an ongoing spiral.

FIGURE 14.3: Learning Loops

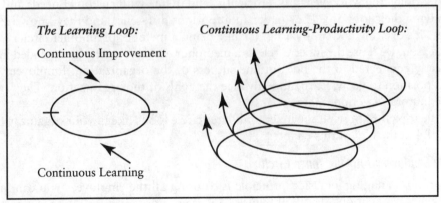

The Learning Loop:
Continuous Improvement
Continuous Learning

Continuous Learning-Productivity Loop:

One aspect of continuous learning might be called the ARC of improvement, standing for a process of analyzing, resolving, and changing as follows.

Analyze current process, practices, and results by asking: What happened that was effective or ineffective? Why did it happen? What needs to happen?

Resolve problems and find better ways of doing things by asking: How can we bring about what needs to happen? How can we prevent problems from recurring? How can we the handle the situation differently in the future?

Change. Get agreement on what will change. Give support for the change.

The story in the showcase of continuous improvement that follows helps to illustrate the concept.

Showcase: Continuous Improvement

A Miami construction firm won a contract to "gut and rebuild the interior" of a 1930s hotel, to bring it up to modern standards but keep its Art Deco charm. The design and construction teams decided to complete one floor at a time, starting with the first floor of rooms, moving floor by floor to the tenth floor at the top, and finally to the lobby. When they finished the first floor, all were very proud of the results. The rooms looked great, and the work had been completed efficiently, effectively, and on time. It was so good they could have repeated exactly the same process for the other floors. Instead, they used the learning loop and engaged in a process of continuous improvement. They analyzed what could be done better, faster, more effectively, and more efficiently as well as how they could better coordinate tasks, combine them, reschedule them, and make similar improvements. When they finished the second floor, it was even better in quality and appearance than the first floor and had been completed more efficiently. Continuing to learn from their experiences on each floor, the teams finally surveyed the completed tenth floor, which they had done in record time. Everyone agreed that this was the best floor yet. The team leader had an idea: "Let's go back down to the first floor now and compare the results." The workers were amazed. The tenth floor was so superior to the first that they were actually a little embarrassed about the first floor.

Make an Inclusive Inner Circle

All learning loops are not equally beneficial or productive. We all know people who become extremely efficient at filling out forms, filing papers, operating computer programs, and other activities—that are largely a waste of time. At best, these employees aren't contributing much to the bottom-line success of the organization, nor to their personal career success.

Employees who work on projects and tasks that *do* contribute directly to the quality of the organization's products and services are fortunate. The more improvement they create and the more they learn about doing the work elegantly, efficiently, and in line with customer needs and preferences, the more satisfying their jobs are. They make an important difference and they know it. That's more than fulfilling—it's exciting and motivating. It's like being a member of an inner circle.

For this reason, we'll use the Inner Circle as a metaphor employees who are included in those learning loops directly connected to the bottom line success of the organization. Employees in the Inner Circle are in a position to grow, learn, and advance the goals of the organization. They're "where the action is," the important action, that is.

To get a clear picture of what the inner and outer circle looks like in your organization, complete Skill Builder 14.4 at the end of this chapter.

Bring All Employees into the Inner Circle

An important managing inclusion principle is to bring all the employees you can into the Inner Circle and its key learning loops. Think of Figure 14.3 as your organization. Who is a part of the inner circle and who is left out? If bottom-line success is your most important priority, it makes sense to get all the employees working toward it. Learning how to do this is a key managing diversity skill. Here are some suggestions:

- Specify the skills and capabilities that are required.
- Get to know all the employees, their weaknesses and strengths.
- Develop strategies to overcome the obstacles that stand in the way, to bridge the gaps between necessary skills and capabilities and those the employee now has.
- Provide them with required knowledge and skills

Give All Employees Quality Treatment

An important managing inclusion principle is to bring all the employees you can into the Inner Circle and its key learning loops. Think of the figure 12.5 as your organization. Who is a part of the inner circle and who is left out? If bottom-line success is your most important priority, it makes sense to get all the employees working toward it. Learning how to do this is a key managing diversity skill. Here are some suggestions:

- Believe in each employee and communicate that belief
- Explicitly communicate high standards and high expectations
- Promote a respect for diversity
- Show each person that he or she is important to you and the organization
- Provide support to *all* employees.
- Value people through your procedures and practices
- Teach people the basis of success in the organization, including the unwritten rules; be an effective mentor.
- Lead people to engage in learning loops and bring them into bottom-line learning loops

LEADERSHIP OPPORTUNITY #4: BUILD ON EQUAL OPPORTUNITY PRINCIPLES

While a multicultural approach goes beyond affirmative action programs, it does not ignore equal opportunity principles or abandon AA programs. It does build on lessons business leaders have learned about how to make AA work most effectively for all groups.

Revitalize the Affirmative Action System

The first step toward a multicultural approach is to review the company's AA policies and procedures. Top leaders can start revitalizing the AA system by communicating that it must be respected by everyone. Violation of AA policy should be treated as seriously as violation of other important corporate policies. Senior management needs to regularly monitor the organization to be sure diversity goals are being met. Employment data should be organized by gender and ethnic group status. It should show minority groups and women as a percentage of

- total employees in each job category
- total management pool
- each level of management

The organization's grievance process for handling individual cases of discrimination should be reviewed to make sure it's fair, effective, and credible. Management needs to systematically review grievance files to detect patterns of mistreatment or discrimination.

Every aspect of an employee's career path is affected by company policies and practices regarding equal opportunity and affirmative action. In Chapter 3 we discussed some of the leadership challenges for eliminating discrimination from these practices. The following checklist can guide your efforts toward revitalizing your company's practices.

Recruiting. Focus on two key principles: (1) Go where diverse employees are to recruit applicants for all types and levels of jobs. (2) Make sure that word-of-mouth recruitment reaches all types of potential applicants. In order to find diverse applicants, do the following:

- Go to universities that have large numbers of minority students. Contact all types of minority student organizations, give them job postings, go to their job fairs, speak at their meetings.

- Get lists of various types of minority organizations—community, social, professional, business, etc. Make regular and systematic contact with the formal and informal leaders of these organizations.

- Ask qualified persons from minority groups to apply for open positions. As long as a 1992 ruling of the federal Sixth Circuit Court holds up, this is legal if it helps the firm to recruit minorities as a part of an effort to fairly balance their workforce. It's still illegal to take the next step and offer a job at that point (*HRM Ideas* 1992).

- Encourage your own minority employees to spread the word among their friends, family, and other contacts. Reward them for helping to recruit minority employees.

- Identify and solve applicants' transportation problems, where appropriate.

Screening. Be sure that all job criteria—such as experience, degrees, and certificates—are really good predictors of job success and don't unreasonably exclude certain groups whose members could succeed. Be sure all tests and exams are valid. Be sure that such barriers as arrest records, poor credit records, or subjective evaluations by prejudiced individuals do not unfairly discriminate against certain minorities.

Compensating. Set goals to achieve equitable salaries and perquisites across all cultural groups. Eliminate practices that lead to lower salaries and perquisites for some groups.

Integrating. Set goals to acquire a reasonably balanced staff in all corporate areas and at all levels, to eliminate "pink ghettoes," "gay ghettos," "minority jobs," etc.

Evaluating. Find ways to eliminate performance evaluation that is colored by bias, stereotyping, or prejudice. For example, have a diverse panel of employees or managers perform important performance evaluations, especially those that affect promotions.

Training and development. Monitor and track all employees' career paths and progress toward achieving their career goals. A diverse panel should make decisions about who will be offered training and development opportunities, especially those opportunities designed to prepare people for promotion.

Promoting. A panel of diverse employees is more likely to make unbiased promotion decisions than is a homogeneous panel or an individual decision maker. Publicize the criteria for promotion, demystify the process. When everyone understands what it takes, those working toward promotion can better focus their attention and energy.

Dismissing. Laying off and firing are the most difficult aspects of dealing with employees. The difficult goal is to find procedures that don't unfairly discriminate against minorities who were unable to get better jobs until recently and therefore have little seniority, older workers who have been loyal to the company and have seniority, or any other group.

Learn from Past Lessons

Among the contributions AA has made to the workplace are the lessons it has taught us about what does and doesn't work in managing diversity. Even though it's important to consider common issues, patterns, and themes of each subcultural group, it's also important to deal with each person as an individual. Everything leaders do should encourage the minority person to take an achieving, team-oriented outlook, never a victim mentality.

Set high but realistic AA goals. Progress in revitalizing AA is slow and incremental. Neither managers nor employees should expect a quick fix. Most AA programs have to be refined and refined, and some may be judged unsuccessful and terminated.

Identify job requirements as opposed to preferences, conveniences, or traditions. Creating a diverse workforce is about enhancing the organization's capability to tap the potential of a diverse group of employees. Set the right goals for the AA program, and keep asking whether all systems and practices are helping to achieve those goals.

Reexamine job standards but keep them high. Ensure that hiring and performance standards are as clear and job-related as possible. They must be common across groups to be perceived as fair.

Test assumptions and support claims. Management should test the assumptions underlying personnel policies and be able to support the claims they make about the effects of systems and programs.

Encourage an achiever self-concept, not a victim self-concept. Every U.S. group, except for Euro-American men, has been disadvantaged in the workplace by stereotypes, prejudice, and discrimination. In that sense they have been and still are victims of the system, but the victim argument produces negative side effects. Victims must have persecutors, which implies that Euro-American men are collectively guilty of oppression. Resentment grows as victim and oppressor accuse each other of injustice in the pursuit of self-interest. Relying on the status of victim to obtain rights or favors is demeaning and self-destructive to the victims because it focuses on what they don't have instead of building on what they can and do have.

A more positive approach is for minorities to focus on setting personal career goals and then on developing the strengths, talents, initiative, and contacts needed to achieve those goals. The only way to become social and economic equals is to act like and demand treatment as equals. This means building skills, showing initiative, and persevering despite real and sometimes unfair obstacles. But just as Euro-American men need some support from the system, so do minorities. While there may be a few who can muster what it takes to overcome huge barriers and climb past the middle-management level, companies should not demand or expect such superhuman efforts. Organizations must also do their share in removing unnecessary barriers and providing reasonable support.

Use leadership, not coercion. True leadership inspires positive change but doesn't force or coerce it. Coerced change usually leads to low morale, cynicism, and covert resistance. One leadership approach is to establish core groups for the purpose of bringing about change, for example to explore group differences and to promote effective communication and team building. Then management can encourage the formation of similar core groups through voluntary employee participation.

Stress uniqueness, not just common group characteristics. Be aware of the common group characteristics you're likely to encounter in different groups, but avoid a new type of stereotyping. Be open to the variance, or diversity, of individuals, and never automatically assume that a person is representative of his or her group. Be aware of the wide range of differences among individuals from a particular group.

Treat group characteristics as important, but not "special." Respect group differences in beliefs, skills, and so forth, but don't put them on a pedestal as more important than other differences among employees. An emphasis on group differences rather individual differences can divide the workforce, invite blame and resentment, and risk the development of a we/them mentality. Group differences should be handled as factors in meeting business objectives, not as ends in themselves.

Tailor treatment to individuals, not to groups. Develop individuals, not groups, but at the same time address the particular characteristics or disadvantages found disproportionately in some ethnic or gender groups. Programs to assist and develop employees should not be conditioned on group status unless there is a compelling reason to do so. Target programs to the specific strengths and weaknesses, advantages and disadvantages of individuals. Special career tracks for African Americans or women can be demeaning to them and arouse resentment among others. Flexible jobs or benefits packages may be especially important to women but must be generally available to all employees. Compensatory treatment should be provided on the basis of individual, not group, characteristics. Basing rights on ethnicity or gender should be used only as a last resort.

LEADERSHIP OPPORTUNITY #5: MODIFY CORPORATE SYSTEMS AND PRACTICES

Top management controls the resources and has the decision-making authority to make the multicultural approach work. Top managers influence people whose prejudice is embedded in a set of beliefs and values that often includes respect for authority. They can favorably influence organization do's and don'ts that subtly guide egalitarian interpersonal behavior. All levels must support the multicultural approach, if it is to succeed. To manage the diversity, all leaders must be committed to creating unity among diverse employees. Management must include unity issues when they conduct a diversity audit to see what's needed. Then they have the basis for developing and implementing a plan that coordinates all major systems and practices (Thomas 1991; Cox 1993; Morrison 1992).

Address Unity Issues

Diverse organizations often have unity problems, and therefore building a strong corporate culture is essential to overcoming these problems. Typical issues are finding common ground, maintaining group cohesiveness, and communicating through cultural barriers. Any diversity audit should address these issues.

Find common ground. Too much diversity in work teams, management groups, or any type of problem-solving group can be especially dysfunctional. When communication barriers, style conflicts, and points of view lack even a core of commonality, decision making may become impossible. Leaders can provide that core of commonality by fostering a corporate culture that's strong enough for all groups to feel connected to common values, heroes, myths, rituals, ceremonies, and other cultural anchors (Shephard 1964).

Maintain group cohesiveness. While group cohesiveness has many advantages, higher productivity is not necessarily one of them. Research has *not* shown that cohesiveness alone improves the work performance of groups. Highly cohesive groups are just as likely to have lower productivity as they are to be more productive. The best way to improve cohesiveness *and* productivity is to find common ground and work toward common goals. Leaders can encourage this through the ways they establish and lead work teams (Arnold and Feldman 1986).

Avoid communication breakdown. When a group becomes diverse, misunderstandings may increase, conflict and anxiety may rise, and members may feel less comfortable with being in the group. These effects may combine to make decision making more difficult and time-consuming. In these respects culturally diverse work groups are more difficult to manage effectively than homogeneous work groups. The challenge is to manage in such a way that you maximize the potential benefits of diversity while minimizing the potential difficulties.

Building a strong culture that focuses on corporate niche and also values diversity is a complex, ongoing effort. It means paying special attention to the values, norms, grapevine, heroes, rituals, and ceremonies that make up the culture. It means becoming a role model who vividly shows by actions and words what the company stands for. Two strategies that can be especially powerful in building a strong diversity culture are using self-managing teams and assigning managers as culture catalysts.

Use self-managing teams. The multicultural approach leads to a new type of organization that better suits the needs of today's workers. People are more effective when they feel in control of their destinies. The strongest motivating force for today's workers is peer-group pressure, the primary control mechanism for teams. Strong cultures, which are necessary for bonding self-managing groups into a productive whole organization, are most easily built in smaller units. The electronic equipment that links teams is far cheaper than layers of middle management.

Make managers culture catalysts. The role of managers will focus more and more on creating sparks in the corporate culture. They make culture change happen without forcing it. They build, enunciate, and promote a strong culture that bonds people together, giving people a core of common beliefs and values, a sense of common purpose.

Conduct a Diversity Audit

One of the first steps in developing a multicultural approach is to conduct a diversity audit to get feedback from employees about how they're affected by the systems and the culture. Interview questions can be based on the following types of general questions:

- Why do employees select and remain with the organization?
- What has determined their success?
- How do they assess the quality of work assignments and supervision they've received?
- What barriers hamper further upward mobility?
- How do they view the firm's overall success in managing diversity?
- Do the company's systems and practices work naturally for everyone? If not, why don't they? What must the organization do to make them work naturally for everyone?
- Will the cultural assumptions of this organization allow us to take the necessary corrective action? If not, what cultural changes must we encourage?

Leaders must examine each system in detail and identify patterns that hinder multiculturalism. They must:

- determine what is generating problem patterns
- determine what to do to eliminate the undesirable patterns and convert the system to a facilitating factor
- develop a plan for implementing the system changes

The multicultural approach calls for changing the systems and then encouraging the culture to naturally change as a result. For example, we know that since companies changed their hiring and promotion systems to allow women into management positions, corporate values and norms have changed so that people no longer are disturbed or upset when women are hired or promoted into those jobs—at least at the lower management levels.

As new people join the organization, informal customs and practices that have been comfortable for Euro-American men may need modifying in order to meet the needs of new employees. Formal practices may also need change: flexible work scheduling, working at home, family leave, child-care provisions. The recurring questions should be: How can we meet the needs and preferences of diverse employees? How can we enhance their strengths and elicit the unique contributions they might make.

Do some research on what has worked for other organizations. For example, a field experiment assessed the impact of flextime use on absentee rates and worker performance. Both short-term and long-term absences declined significantly. Three out of four worker efficiency measures increased significantly under flextime (Kim and Campagna 1981).

Develop a Diversity Plan

A diversity audit can provide the company with a profile of the organization's diversity. It can inform leaders about diverse employees' values and needs through information from surveys, focus groups, interviews, task forces, and similar sources. Leaders can then describe the future state they need to create in these areas:

- matching people and jobs
- managing reward and performance
- informing and involving people
- supporting lifestyles and life needs

The diversity audit provides information for analyzing the present state—where the company is now in each of these areas. The next step is to define the gap between this present state and desired future state. What needs to be done to bridge the gap? Leaders can then plan and manage transitions from the present state to the desired future state.

Suppose you were asked to recommend a plan for a multicultural approach to diversity for your organization. What would you include? Of course, you'd want to tailor the plan to fit your particular organization's needs, after conducting an audit. But there are certain actions that are typical of the most excellent companies for diversity. You'd want to seriously consider the following actions.

Set diversity goals. Set annual diversity goals for hiring and promotion in both staff and line jobs, for each division. To overcome the barriers inherent in being an isolated token minority, the goals should aim for a critical mass of each type of diverse worker in each area. To this end, management should consider clustering members of the same ethnic or gender group in particular work teams, departments, offices, or facilities—as a transitional procedure—in areas central to the mission of the organization, where jobs carry high status and wages. This can enhance the performance and retention of diverse employees.

The best way to ensure that diverse workers' needs and preferences are met is to promote enough members of each category up through all levels of the organization. When diverse managers gain power over significant arenas of decision making, substantive changes that meet the needs of other diverse workers will occur more naturally.

For example, the managers who understand best what Asian American employees value and need are the Asian American managers, and women managers have the greatest insight into needs of women employees.

Aim for a diverse board. Encourage the board of directors to include women and minorities in proportion to the workforce and customer base. Board decisions need to reflect a wide range of views.

Use diversity specialists. Make someone responsible for diversity issues. It may be an officer, a staff manager, or an entire department. In addition, establish a task force or committee that addresses diversity issues. Consider using a diversity consultant for specific needs.

Provide diversity training. Provide diversity training for every person, especially managers, every year. Incorporate appropriate diversity training into new employee orientation.

Develop for promotability. Determine what must be done to retain and promote diverse employees. The organization must first discover and then create the conditions under which women and ethnic groups can thrive at all levels of the organization. Hire entry-level people who have enough skills and experience that they have a good chance to advance. Provide a basic level of support—that is, encouragement, training, resources—to all new employees. Encourage mentoring, career tracking, and other career development strategies. Rotate supervisors in order to expose new employees to different management styles and to expose supervisors to a range of employee skills and concerns. Systematically monitor all terminations, transfers, and promotions as part of an effort to retain and promote women and ethnic employees. Provide appropriate skills training to meet the needs of minority and women employees.

Provide internships and scholarships. Set up internship programs for minority and women students, to give them some training and exposure to the company, and to enhance recruiting efforts. Consider providing scholarship programs for members of targeted groups, both as an indirect recruiting device and as part of community outreach.

Reward diversity gains. When hiring and promoting Euro-American men, include criteria that predict their contribution to the organization's AA and multicultural goals. Before hiring, look for evidence that predicts their ability to function effectively in an organization that is achieving those goals. Examples of predictive experience include experience working in multicultural settings, being supervised by a woman or ethnic manager, collaborating on multicultural work teams, having resided in a racially integrated neighborhood, providing help with child care for employees, successfully balancing job and family responsibilities. Predictive educational experience might include attending equal status, interracial schools, studying with diverse teachers, belong to school groups with diverse members, attending courses or workshops on multicultural or non-Western cultural topics, and speaking another language.

Hold every manager responsible for the progress and success of their diverse employees. Performance in this area should be part of performance evaluation and rewards. Promotion criteria can be expanded to include success in helping diverse employees thrive in the organization. Examples of specific actions include finding, hiring, promoting, encouraging, and sponsoring diverse employees.

Encourage support groups. Help minorities and women to establish support groups for purposes of networking, mentoring, supporting, and influencing company decisions. Provide some company funds to these groups for bringing in speakers, holding events, and similar activities.

Set diversity contracting goals. Create minority and women's vendor-supplier programs and use minority contractors, minority-owned banks, law firms, and other minority-owned business services for specified percentages of the annual purchasing budget.

Use community outreach. Connect with minority and women's organizations in the community. Establish a continuing dialogue for making job referrals, posting job openings, making charitable contributions, and similar activities.

Implement a Diversity Plan: Success Factors

Key success factors of the multicultural approach center around treating people as respected individuals and giving feedback in a culturally sensitive manner. It's important to get to know people as individuals, as well as part of a particular cultural group, to give feedback sensitively based on that knowledge, and to set the tone for creativity to occur (Thomas 1991; Gottfredson 1992; Morrison 1992).

Get to Know the Individual

Take time to get to know each employee, as well as his or her subcultural group. The more you learn about each person, the better you will be able to collaborate with that person as an individual and as part of a work team. What you don't know may keep you from doing your own job effectively. Here are some suggestions that may help.

- *Avoid appearance stereotypes.* Don't assume race or ethnicity from appearance alone. Many Latinos have Asian features, and many Blacks have Latino, Jamaican, or other origins and strongly distinguish themselves from African Americans. Bi-ethnic persons' cultural backgrounds are not easy to determine from appearance only.

- *Avoid ethnic stereotypes.* Don't assume that all foreign or minority workers are impoverished or deprived. Get to know the background of each one.

- *Put emotions in perspective.* Don't take emotional outbursts personally. Ask, are emotional outbursts a normal way of responding to the situation in that person's culture? Remember, also, that newcomers often experience a phase of frustration and anger during the adaptation phase.

- *Discover other people's values.* Watch how they behave. When someone behaves consistently in similar circumstances, it suggests a value at work.

- *Clarify which values apply in each situation.* Identify precisely which value or values are at play in a given situation. It is one thing to know that a person values family ties more than you do. It is more difficult to recognize that the family ties value is at stake when that person is absent from work for what would seem like a trivial family matter to you. Your tendency may be to judge by your standards for consistent attendance at work rather than by his standards of family loyalty.

- *Apply employee values to work enhancement.* Look for the positive side of the other persons values—not only how that value is positive in the other's culture, but also how that same value could be applied in ways that are consistent with organization values and objectives. Apply the value to the job at hand. How can you bring the person's value into play so that it help achieve job objectives? For example, when you need teamwork to accomplish something previously done by individuals, the person from a tightly woven culture is likely to rise to the occasion.

- *Apply relevant training.* Determine each new employee's knowledge of the system, and train each one accordingly. Has this employee faced the complexities of the U.S. corporate system before? You may need to train some employees in very basic ways.

- *Determine each employee's primary thinking pattern.* Determine their primary thinking pattern. If you see that abstract and hypothetical thinking is not familiar to them, try using examples, stories, and hands-on experience.

- *Determine each employee's primary learning pattern.* Be patient while employees are in the process of gaining necessary knowledge and experience. You may have to answer more questions, even very basic ones, than you would with Euro-American male employees.

- *Reinforce successful new behavior.* Choose reinforcers, recognition, and rewards that the recipients value as such. Give them in a way that is in line with that person's values.

- *Understand cultural style differences.* For example, learn to accept compliments gracefully and without suspicion; take them in stride. Some cultures use compliments and flattery as a normal, polite way of interacting.

Give Feedback Sensitively

People from tightly woven cultures often have some difficulty giving and getting feedback in the direct style used in most organizations and by most U.S. managers and workers. Many Asians and Middle Easterners have been taught never to confront others directly. And other European groups, such as the British, tend to be more subtle when communicating about performance. In the United States, feedback is a standard part of performance assessment and an integral part of management and creative collaboration. Your style can either respect or violate the values of harmony and consensus as practiced in some other cultures. Here are some suggestions for giving feedback sensitively.

- *Choose the right time and place.* What is culturally appropriate for giving feedback to this employee? Shall it be in a formal or informal session? Directly or using a third party? In private or in a group? Oral or written or both?

- *Clarify your commitment to the person receiving or giving feedback.* Stress the results you are working toward and the importance of the process of asking for, giving, and getting feedback.

- *Specifically describe behavior.* Tell the other person what you have seen or understand them to have said or done. Keep in mind possible cultural differences that may affect behavior.

- *Give positive acknowledgment.* Tell what stands out for you or excites you about what the other person did or said.

- *Give supporting information.* Share information, data, or facts that you have that pertain to what the other person has done.

- *Give an I-message.* Openly and frankly share your opinions and preferences as your own. Avoid talking in terms of absolute rights and wrongs.

- *Open up possibilities.* Share ideas and suggestions you have for the other's work or performance.

- *Share your experience.* Tell about your experience with activities or work similar to the recipient's.

- *Offer clear expectations.* Be clear about what you mutually agreed upon in the past or are now asking the other person to do.

- *Use creative questioning.* Raise questions that clarify the content or direction of the recipient's performance. Questioning can bring out cultural differences.

- *Give support.* Offer support, resources, and information to enable the other person to fulfill their agreements and meet your expectations.

- *Summarize.* Recognize what each of you has contributed during and after this feedback session.

- *Ask for feedback.* Get feedback on how the other has received your feedback. Listen for clues about cultural or individual differences that may affect the situation.

Giving feedback about job performance is crucial to employees' success and can help to build trust or destroy it. Therefore, becoming aware of cultural differences concerning evaluation, appraisal, and criticism is crucial to your success as a leader.

Set the Stage for Creativity

A key advantage of a diverse workforce is the increased potential for creativity and innovation. To tap this potential, leaders must set the stage for creativity to occur. Research indicates that the following factors foster creativity in diverse groups (Miller 1992).

- Create a nonjudgmental environment that encourages people to risk exploration without having to produce a "winner" every time.

- Avoid judgmental words such as good, bad, better, best, mistake—words that kill creativity.

- Cultivate an appreciation of bizarre questions and ideas without negatively labeling them as weird or crazy.

- Produce a noncompetitive atmosphere that focuses on performance and end results, rather than on the how-tos of creative discovery.

- Foster a cooperative spirit that encourages people to learn from each other and to delight in each others' success.

- Provide reasonable, organic structure and discipline to bring out creativity.

- Have fun! Encourage people to get carried away by the sheer fun of creating something.

- Support employees in ways that allow them to release their anxieties about whether their creation is good enough.

Overcome Resistance

Growing a multicultural organization is challenging because the barriers are many, the guidelines are still being tested, and the barriers to a particular talented employee achieving his or her full potential are complex. But when we look at the changing face of organizations today and compare that with what we saw in the 1950s, we know that many barriers have already been overcome. If we want our organizations to change and are willing to devote the energy to it, we can make remarkable progress. Success is more likely if leaders are aware of typical resistances of top managers and employees, as well as typical managerial problems in implementing a multicultural approach.

Resistance from the Top

Typical reasons top managements give for not managing diversity are rooted in lack of information about diversity, short-range planning, and a lack of commitment:

- It costs too much.
- We can't find enough qualified minorities.
- We should hire the best person.
- We don't believe in reverse discrimination.
- Enough progress has been made.

- It's time to just be gender-neutral and color-blind.
- We have too many priorities that are more crucial than diversity.
- It's too much work to make the needed changes.
- Our organization is just too large to make the needed changes.
- A focus on diversity is divisive; we focus on being one big happy family.

This "divisive" rationalization is so common and erects such a rigid barrier to multiculturalism that it's worth pursuing. Here are some variations on that theme.

Divisive Rationale 1: We shouldn't focus on differences. Some people think that if we look at how cultures differ, we won't see how they're alike and therefore we won't find a common ground of unity. But learning about other cultures and valuing cultural differences need not be a barrier to unity. We can always connect with others for many reasons, including these.

- Anthropologists assure us that humans are more alike than they are different.
- Psychologists point out that we all have needs for survival, security, belonging, recognition, and self-actualization; we differ only in the ways we go about fulfilling these needs.

Therefore, we can value diversity and still find common ground almost everywhere, if that's our intent.

Divisive Rationale 2: We don't want to stereotype people. For an opinion to be a stereotype, it must be *rigid*, not taking into account individual differences within a group. Learning about cultural patterns and typical beliefs and values should provide *flexible general guidelines* to help us understand what makes people act they way they do—to know the right questions to ask people when problems arise. We must always keep in mind that general guidelines do not apply equally to every person from a culture, just as no one of us conforms to exactly the same beliefs and behaviors within our own culture.

Divisive Rationale 3: We don't want to be racist or sexist. Actually, not admitting differences is probably more ethnocentric than is exploring and respecting differences. After all, if we're all alike, who are we like, which culture? What culture represents the norm to which we all should conform? The unconscious assumption is that it's our own, of course. It's a way of saying, "People are basically alike—like me."

Divisive Rationale 4: Focusing on similarities is easier. Life seems easier, in the short run, if we assume that everyone is alike. Dealing with diverse people means dealing with complexity and uncertainty, and it may seem easier to settle for "we're all basically alike." But if misunderstandings are based on cultural differences, then ignoring differences keeps us from getting at the root of the problem, which in turn can build and fester.

Summarizing these tendencies to avoid the diversity issue, President Clinton's race advisory board chair, John Hope Franklin, said that stereotypes actually remain because Americans cling to the idea that it's best to try to ignore race. That, in turn, forces people to bury—and therefore harbor within—beliefs they form from stereotypes they heard at school, in the media, and from family members. Franklin, an African American leader, said: "The idea that we should aspire to a 'colorblind' society is an impediment to reducing racial stereotyping. Given that research has demonstrated that the best way to reduce racial stereotyping is to be conscious about racial differences, it is important to present a thoughtful alternative to the 'colorblind society' concept" (Clinton 1998).

The bottom line: Companies that avoid addressing diversity adequately are short-sighted and in the long run will probably regret having fallen behind in the race to build and keep a staff of highly qualified people. Many just don't understand the advantages of managing diversity effectively.

Typical Implementation Problems

Some typical management problems in implementing a diversity plan include:

- top-down, directive management style, which doesn't provide for a two-way acculturation and adaptation, nor dialogue about what diverse employees need and want

- overconcern with getting tasks done and underconcern with the people doing them
- narrow view of diversity that focuses only on minorities and women rather than all employees, or only on increasing the numbers of minorities and women rather than taking a comprehensive multicultural approach
- short-term, results orientation: "We met our diversity goals for the year"
- lack of strategic perspective; a focus on daily operational concerns
- lack of leadership to develop the vision of an empowered diverse workforce, to articulate a strategy to gain competitive advantage, and to build and maintain systems and practices that support the vision and strategy

Employee Resistance

Typical reasons that employees resist managing-diversity efforts include:

- lack of motivation—people not understanding the business rationale for moving ahead with managing diversity, how it will affect the productivity and viability of their departments and the organization
- belief in the melting pot, that people should adapt and be one big happy family
- ignorance about culture, and its potential as an effective tool for empowering employees
- prejudice and stereotyping
- affirmative action backlash, and suspicion that any new diversity approach is an effort to sneak AA in through the back door
- risk aversion, unwillingness to risk the experimentation and changes that managing diversity requires
- lack of power, knowledge, or skills in managing diversity on the part of those managers and employees who want to become change agents
- responsibility overload—managers believing they don't have the time or energy for another initiative, not seeing how managing diversity can help them achieve their goals, rather than being a distraction

Knowing the resistances can help you plan for overcoming them. This knowledge can also help you analyze why the diversity efforts are not working as well as expected. The barriers list can become a checklist for figuring out why.

LEADERSHIP OPPORTUNITY #6: BUILD CONSENSUS FOR CHANGE

Creating change is always a leadership challenge. First, build on current needs and desires for change within the organization. Second, work through your own issues around change and help others work through theirs. Third, recognize and avoid typical change traps. Finally, identify and develop conscious change agents who can in turn help you build a critical mass of people committed to making the needed changes.

Build on the Organizational Need and Desire to Change

Most organizations have many values and practices from the past, as well as current pressures and future concerns, that facilitate a multicultural approach. Among these are:

- a strong corporate culture that values diversity
- a well-planned and well-administered AA program

- Awareness of limitations of AA efforts, including backlash and stigma problems—managers are looking for a better way to create equal opportunity
- a prior substantial investment in managing diversity—management has a stake in making the investment pay off
- a good track record for diversity—the company already perceives itself as diverse
- the organization's pride in being a fair and equitable employer
- legal, moral, and social responsibility concerns
- intense competition that forces managers to examine all possibilities for enhancing productivity and effectiveness
- an increasingly diverse workforce with fewer available qualified recruits.
- employees' unwillingness to be assimilated and their comfort and pride with their diversity

These are the motivators that you can build on, the desires and needs for change that can help your multicultural approach become a winner.

Work Through Change Issues

Building consensus requires networking with employees who are good candidates for becoming conscious change agents. Working through your own change issues can prepare you to help others open up to positive change. What if we could address the bottom-line concerns of all the major corporate players, or stakeholders, about changing the corporation? What if you could help them clear away all their reservations to supporting the changes? Answering the provocative questions that are posed in Skill Builder 14.2 may get your creative juices flowing. Even more important, you may come up with just the right questions for your organization to address.

Avoid Typical Change Traps

Change agents need specific skills. When you venture into new territory, from the known to the unknown, the going can be rough. Most of us need some guidance from people who've been there before. Here are some typical traps you'll want to avoid (Terry 1990).

- Believing there is one best way. Focus on the end result; the paths leading there may be many.
- Adopting a label, such as "diversity manager" or "change agent" but avoiding the real struggle. We must do the work.
- Not realizing that many people are unable to comprehend and/or accept these ideas. We must deal with people according to where they are in their own development and take it one step at a time.
- Focusing only on the *reasons* change is needed or only on change actions themselves. Both theory and action are needed.
- Holding Euro-American men responsible for solving the problem of prejudice. *All* stakeholders must be deeply involved in any solution.
- Becoming self-righteous, impressed by your own virtue. Remember to look at where you've been and where you're going.
- Believing we have a choice about whether to change or not.

This last trap deserves further comment. Our choice is not whether change will take place but whether we'll make it happen, watch it happen, or ask "What happened?" Savvy leaders take a proactive stance toward change, looking for opportunities and dealing with challenges. You as a leader can help people to understand that change is the constant in life. The world keeps changing whether we approve or not. An increasingly diverse workforce is a fact of life. Therefore, when we speak of creating organizational change and building consensus for change, we're talking about anticipating and recognizing changes that are already in motion and responding positively. We're speaking of making things happen in ways that build trust and cooperation rather than resisting the changing diversity of the workplace and proceeding as though it doesn't exist. A personal and organizational commitment to respect all types of employees and to support them in their career development is a proactive response to this change—one that's good for all employees and for the organization.

Develop Conscious Change Agents

If we seriously want to eliminate prejudicial injustice in America, instead of pretending to ignore color and other differences, we must be color conscious in a radically new way, according to African American consultant Robert Terry (1990). Euro-Americans must understand their ingroups' role in creating the crisis and in resolving it, taking such actions as the following:

- Become a conscious agent of change—recognize that new directions are possible.
- Seek ethical clarity—know what you want your organization, and America, to stand for and why.
- Identify the various forms and expressions of prejudice—know who we are and have been, and why.
- Develop long-range change strategies to eliminate and move beyond prejudice—to experience what a truly equitable organization might be.
- Discern the appropriate day-to-day tactics—assess your power for change.
- Experiment, test, and refine a personal lifestyle that expresses your newly affirmed values—experience who you might be.

Making a personal commitment to bring about change is the first step to becoming a conscious change agent. The next step is to become conscious of what needs changing. To be conscious is to be always actively aware of ourselves in relation to other people and things around us. Skill Builder 14.3 focuses on becoming conscious of how changes in beliefs lead to changes in actions.

Core beliefs about a situation can either lock us into limited options or solutions or they can open the door to different ways of seeing the past and present, and a different guide for future action. For example, if we see African Americans as the problem, then both our attitudes and behaviors will flow from that belief about the situation. If we believe that the Euro-American culture and privileged Euro-Americans are the problem, then it becomes possible to explore new behavior and reevaluate earlier attitudes. We may see that people from both cultures need to take responsibility for bringing about change. The most important question for each person is, "What can I do to bring about needed change?"

Once you've decided what you can do, the next step is making a personal commitment to help bring about positive change, as set out in Skill Builder 14.3. As a leader you have significant opportunities to take personal stands and to follow through with personal actions, no matter how small, toward creating positive change. You may need to go against the norms of the corporate culture, which is always challenging. But if your stands and your actions are consistently supportive of, for example, Latino American or gay employees as basically equal and valuable human beings, then your actions build a bridge over centuries of mistrust to the other side, to mutual respect and trust.

SUMMARY

Meeting the needs of all types of employees is the ultimate challenge for diversity leaders. The needs include working in a corporate culture that's comfortable for them, in an organization whose systems and practices support their career development. They need to align with a company that has ended practices that have historically excluded minorities from higher levels. Managing diversity means also meeting Euro-American males' needs for becoming comfortable with diverse persons holding leadership and peer roles. Diverse employees need to develop networks of contacts and accept career development opportunities, allowing them to break through the glass ceiling.

A successful multicultural approach must be all-inclusive and must deal with employees as individuals, taking into account their cultural and experiential background against the backdrop of a diverse society. It's crucial to move the corporate culture toward a valuing-diversity culture that goes beyond tolerance to appreciation—for all types of employees. It gives people the freedom to be themselves and to make some choices about which aspects of their culture and background they want to retain. It's based on building multicultural skills and providing diversity education for all employees.

Including all employees in the bottom-line efforts of the organization not only boosts organizational success, it also meets the needs of diverse employees. Continuous improvement feeds into continuous learning, and also results from it, creating an ongoing learning loop. Those learning loops that are directly connected to improvement of key products and services are the ones that generate excitement and satisfaction for employees. The Inner Circle is a metaphor for employees involved in such learning loops.

Building on equal opportunity principles is another key aspect of the multicultural approach. Leaders first revitalize the AA system currently in place, using past lessons we've learned about what works and what doesn't. A good diversity audit becomes the basis for developing and implementing a diversity plan. A key strategy for making the multicultural approach work is getting to know employees as individuals, taking into consideration their cultural and experiential background within the context of a diverse society. Leaders can overcome the resistance of other leaders and employees to the multicultural approach by understanding typical reasons given in the past and adopting the strategies others have used successfully to move beyond such resistance.

Building consensus for change is essential to successfully implementing the multicultural approach. While the commitment of top management is the first step, lasting change requires the consensus of a critical mass of employees. As a leader you can start the change process by building on those factors already at work within the organization that motivate people toward change. You can work through your own change issues and help others to do the same. You can anticipate some typical change traps in order to avoid them. Eventually you must develop others as conscious change agents who will in turn influence yet others toward positive change. This builds a critical mass of employees with a commitment to creating a valuing-diversity culture with a multicultural orientation.

Skill Builder 14.1: A Question of Change

Purpose: To stimulate thinking about ways to make your workplace more supportive of all employees.

Instructions: Record your responses and any additional insights, including further questions that could lead to creative solutions for your particular organization, perhaps for all organizations. If you don't work for a large organization now, think of past organizations you've worked for or have been a part of, such as a university or school.

Step 1. Consider the viewpoints of all stakeholders

Who are the stakeholders that have widely varying viewpoints in your organization? Examples might be sales employees, women in the accounting department, African American employees, Euro-American managers. A) List the stakeholders, each on a separate page. B) Under each stakeholder, write a one-line statement that you think represents that group's general viewpoint. C) Under each one-liner, list the major corporate changes you think people in that group might want.

Step 2. Develop a concept of culture

Imagine that everyone in the organization agreed that the underlying problem of prejudice and inequity is rooted in the current corporate culture. What effect would this have?

Step 3. Identify barriers to mutual respect and trust

If you and other key people conducted a long, hard, critical examination of "why we haven't been able or willing to value and appreciate our diversity," what barriers do you think you would find?

Step 4. Take responsibility for personal growth
Imagine that most of the employees worked deeply with their beliefs and feelings about prejudice and diversity? Would this eliminate most of the barriers noted in step 3? What barriers would remain?

Step 5. Influence culture change

- Would this process be enough to begin some positive change in corporate values, norms, structures, and power? What specific changes might occur? What else would be needed?

- Is there any evidence of overt or subtle paternalism, threats, or punishment in the organization? Be specific.

- Would this process be enough to begin shifting this pattern? How might this evolve? What else would be needed?

- Could this process lead to collaboration based on mutual trust, as peers committed to solving a common problem within a common framework? How might this evolve? What else would be needed?

Skill Builder 14.2: Beliefs about What Needs Changing

Purpose: To become aware of the role and power of individuals changing their beliefs.
Step 1. How can we become conscious of what needs changing? We might start by examining some core beliefs, attitudes, thoughts, feelings, decisions and day-to-day action choices. Examine this core belief:
Belief #1: *America is the great melting pot. If African Americans can't succeed in business, it's not because Euro-American managers and co-workers don't welcome them. It's because they don't have what it takes to succeed.*
Based on this belief, what needs to be done in the workplace? In society in general? What ideas come to mind? Record them.
Step 2. Now think about this alternate core belief:
Belief #2: *American culture, systems, institutions, and beliefs are what block African Americans from succeeding in business. The stereotypes, prejudice, institutionalized discrimination, and personal discrimination of Euro-Americans are the problem.*
Based on this alternate belief, what needs to be done in the workplace? In society in general? What ideas come to mind? Record them.
Step 3. Jot down your insights regarding the difference a belief makes.

Skill Builder 14.3: Making a Commitment for Change

Purpose: To make a written commitment to help change the workplace toward valuing diversity and eliminating discrimination.
Step 1. List at least three personal stands you're committed to taking:
Step 2. List at least three personal actions you're committed to taking.

Skill Builder 14.4: Who's in the Inner Circle?

Purpose: To get a clear picture of insiders and outsiders in your organization.
Step 1. Think of the organization where you work. Think about which employees are involved in continuous improvement and continuous learning—in learning loops that directly affect the success of the organization, its bottom-line results. In other words, think about which employees are included in the Inner Circles?

Step 2. Place symbols, such as triangles or circles, inside the Inner Circle that represent employees you know. You might use a different symbol, incorporating colored ink or pencil, for each employee—or a different symbol for each work team, unit, or department that's in the Inner Circle.

Step 3. Which employees are not included in the Inner Circle? They may be in learning loops, but not those that make a real difference. Draw symbols for those employees in the area outside the Inner Circle below.

Step 4. What does this picture say to you about your organization?

- About its effectiveness in managing diversity?
- About its effectiveness in utilizing all its human resources?
- About its effectively in developing all its employees potential for contribution?

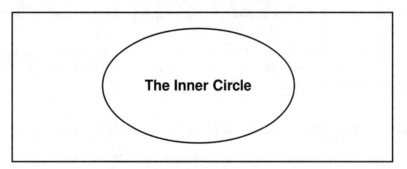

Skill Builder 14.5: The Case of a Skills Gap at Lights Plus

Phyllis went to a Lights Plus store to buy some track lights she had seen advertised at a special reduced price. *Henry*, an African American salesperson, waited on her. Phyllis explained that the track lights were the only lighting in her home office and she needed lots of light throughout the room. Henry told her the sale track lights were very good lights, very popular. He went to the stock room to get the lights and tracks, couldn't find the tracks, and returned to tell Phyllis that they didn't have them in stock. Instead of giving up, Phyllis insisted on knowing if they could be obtained for her, so Henry asked the manager *Mark* about getting the tracks. Mark felt sure there were some tracks in the stock room and quickly found them. A sale was made. When Phyllis called in an electrician to install the lights, he pointed out that they gave small spots of very intense light and were not too effective for general lighting. In addition they were much more expensive than the general-lighting type. Phyllis decided to return them and wait for the general-lighting type to go on sale.

A month or so later Lights Plus advertised at half price the type of track lights Phyllis needed. She called the store near her to be sure they were still on sale and were in stock. When she walked into the store, Henry greeted her. He showed her the sale track lights, which were packaged in boxes, picked up a couple of boxes, and took them to the cash register. When he entered the transaction, Henry saw that the price displayed on the register was the regular price, not the sale price. Henry said, "Well, these lights are $59.99 a package." Phyllis was exasperated. She said, "Then I don't want them. I don't know why the woman who answered the phone here about an hour ago told me they were still on sale. If she had told me they were now regular price, I wouldn't have made the trip." Henry said nothing and Phyllis left the store, shaking her head.

Driving home, Phyllis recalled her last trip to Lights Plus. Henry had been uninformed about where to find merchandise in the stock room. "Maybe he's uninformed about prices too," she thought. She turned the corner, went back to the store, and asked to speak to the manager. When she explained the price problem, Mark replied, "Oh, yes, that's just one of those computer glitches. Somehow the sale information didn't get into the current computer file. No problem, you can have the track lights at the sale price." When Mark went to pick up the packets, he said, "Now some of these sets are black and some are white, even though the pictures on all the boxes show white lights." Phyllis thought, "Why didn't Henry tell me that? Without that information, I had a fifty-fifty chance of bringing home lights of the wrong color." (Note: The top management of Lights Plus has expressed the company's top-priority objective this way: "Customer satisfaction is the target.")

- In what ways did Henry fail to meet the company's target?
- Describe the gap between Henry's skills and capabilities and the required skills and capabilities. What do you think Henry should do?
- Was Mark effective in managing inclusion? Giving quality treatment? Applying the ARC of improvement? What do you think Mark should do?
- What cultural differences might explain the problems that occurred in this case?

Skill Builder 14.6: The Case of a "Diverse" Corporate Culture

Sharon is a 22 year old college student looking for a part-time job to help pay her school expenses. She interviews for a part-time receptionist job in a medical clinic. When *George*, the office manager, meets Sharon, he feels that she will "melt right into the company culture." The support staff is diverse, consisting of 11 Asian Americans, 6 African Americans, 4 Euro-Americans, and 8 Latino Americans. George believes that given her enthusiasm, Sharon will get along well with her co-workers, and given her educational background, he's sure she can perform the job duties. He offers her the job and she accepts.

Her first day on the job Sharon is introduced to all the staff members. She immediately feels as if she's part of the family. Her co-workers are very friendly, and each of them makes her feel welcome and comfortable. Sharon is assigned to report to *Tiffany*, an African American supervisor. From the first day Sharon notices that the staff in fact does not act like a family when it's time for coffee breaks and lunch. Actually the staff is pretty segregated. The African Americans sip and munch together, while the Asian Americans form their own group, speaking Cantonese. Meantime, the Latino Americans get together and speak Spanish. Tiffany leads Sharon straight to the African American group and they welcome her.

As Sharon and Tiffany get to know each other, Sharon reveals that her father is African American and her mother is Asian American. They divorced when Sharon was only three and Sharon has not seen much of her father since the divorce. Sharon doesn't have many African American friends. "Most of them seem to take the attitude that I'm not black enough," she says. "I think they're referring to the way I express myself rather than my skin color. I know I look more African American than Asian American. But I do speak Cantonese and of course my thinking is much like my mom's."

One day Sharon asks Tiffany, "Why do people go off into their own little ethnic groups all the time? They never seem to intermingle except on the job, only enough to get the work done." Tiffany replies, "Just human nature, I guess. We don't try to get people to intermingle. We just leave well enough alone. People get along pretty well now. If we try to get more interaction, they might start fighting, who knows?"

Now, a few weeks later, Sharon feels ignored by her African American co-workers and a little uncomfortable with them. She knows it's because she seems withdrawn and reserved to them, like she's holding back. But it's just the Asian way. Sharon tries a few times to join the Asian American group, even speaking Cantonese with them. At first they're surprised and interested in knowing more about her. But now they too tend to ignore her. Somehow she doesn't quite fit in with them either.

Sharon is feeling lonely. Every day she sits at the front desk, taking incoming calls, recording messages, and greeting patients. Sometimes Tiffany helps her out. But even when they're working side by side, they don't have many personal conversations any more. When her afternoon shift is over, Sharon goes home with few interesting stories to tell her mother—a few about patients, but none about co-workers. Sharon is thinking about looking for another job. Tiffany notices that Sharon is not as enthusiastic as she was when she first took the job. Even George has noticed a difference in Sharon's attitude.

- What are the key issues in this case?
- If you were Sharon, what would you do?
- If you were Tiffany, what would you do?
- If you were George, what would you do?

A CONCLUDING ACKNOWLEDGMENT OF YOUR ACHIEVEMENT

Congratulations! If you've worked your way through this book, you now have a solid foundation for becoming a diversity leader and a conscious change agent. You've begun building a most valuable set of multicultural skills. In Chapter 1 you learned that you would proceed through five skill-building steps, and now you've completed those steps.

Steps You've Completed in Building Your Multicultural Skills

Step 1. You've become aware of culture and its pervasive influence.

Step 2. You've learned more about your own culture.

Step 3. You recognize your own biases, the ways in which you stereotype, assume, judge, and discriminate.

Step 4. You've learned about other cultures you encounter in the workplace so you can recognize when cultural differences may be at the root of problems and so you can appreciate the contributions people from diverse cultures can make to the work situation.

Step 5. You've started building your interaction skills and you've practiced some new behaviors, using self-awareness activities and skill builder case studies.

Being a diversity leader can be difficult and complex. You often must intuit your way into the murky unknown as change in the workplace accelerates. But the effort is so worthwhile, and success is so rewarding—and you now have some tools for doing it.

Managing diversity is the challenge of the new millennium—for our communities and our planet as well as for our workplaces. Do we want join a world of prejudice, bigotry, hatred, rage, riots, terrorism, and war? Or do we want to join in our common humanity and work through our differences so we can achieve great things together in peace and harmony? If we want harmony, then common sense tells us that workplace and community discrimination against whole groups of people must come to an end.

Managing diversity is also the opportunity for the new millennium. It offers opportunities to grow personally and collectively, to learn new ways of collaborating, to create a synergy that sparks innovation and accelerates human knowledge and achievement. Let's welcome these changes for the opportunities they open up and for the challenges that motivate us to keep sharpening our diversity skills.

REFERENCES

Allport, G. W. *The Nature of Prejudice.* Boston: Addison-Wesley Publishing Company, Inc., 1954.

Arnold, H. and D. Feldman. *Organizational Behavior.* New York: McGraw-Hill, 1986.

Blanchard, F.A., and F.J. Crosby, Eds. *Affirmative Action in Perspective.* New York: Springer-Verlag, 1989.

Blank, Renee and Sandra Slipp, *Voices of Diversity.* New York: Amacom, 1994.

Burman, Stephen. *The Black Progress Question.* Thousand Oaks, CA: Sage, 1995.

Carr-Ruffino, N., et al. "Legal Aspects of Women's Advancement" in *Woman Power*. Thousand Oaks, CA: Sage, 1991.

Carr-Ruffino, Norma. "U.S. Women: Breaking Through the Glass Ceiling." *Women in Management Review* 6, no. 5, 1991.

Catalyst. *Women in Corporate Management*. New York: Catalyst, 1990.

"Clinton Urged to Drop 'Colorblind' Concept," *Associated Press*, June 24, 1998.

Cox, Taylor. *Cultural Diversity in Organizations*. San Francisco: Berrett-Koehler, 1993.

Deshpande, Hoyer, and J. Donthu. "The Study of Ethnic Affiliation." *Journal of Consumer Research* 13, 1986, 214-220.

DiTomaso, N., D.E. Thompson, and D.H. Blake. "Corporate Perspectives on the Advancement of Minority Managers" in *Ensuring Minority Success in Corporate Management*. New York: Plenum, 1988.

Fernandez, J.P. *Managing a Diverse workforce*. New York: Simon & Schuster, 1991.

Glazer, Nathan and D.P. Moynihan, Eds., *Beyond the Melting Pot*, 2nd ed.. Cambridge, MA: MIT Press, 1970.

Gentile, Mary. *Managerial Excellence Through Diversity*. Chicago: Irwin, 1996.

Gottfredson. "Dilemmas in Developing Diversity Programs" in *Diversity in the Workplace*. New York: Guilford, 1992.

Graham, Lawrence. *The Best Companies for Minorities*. New York: Penguin, 1993.

Helgeson, Sally. *The Web of Inclusion*. New York: Doubleday, 1995.

Henderson, George. *Cultural Diversity in the Workplace*. Westport CT: Praeger, 1994.

HRM Ideas & Trends in Personnel, No. 272. Commerce Clearing House, April 1992, 53.

Jackson, Susan, Ed. *Diversity in the Workplace*. New York: Gilford, 1992.

Kim, J.S., and A.F. Campagna. "Effects of Flextime on Employee Attendance and Performance." *Academy of Management Journal* 24, 1981, 729-741.

Korn/Ferry International, "Diversity in the Executive Suites: Good News and Bad News," www.kornferry.com/diversit.htm, 1999.

Kotter, J.P. "What Leaders Really Do," *Harvard Business Review*, May-June 1990, 103-111.

Miller, Brian. "Adult Sexual Resocialization" in *Sociology of Homosexuality*. New York: Garland, 1992.

Morrison, Ann, R.P. White, and E. Van Velsor. *Breaking the Glass Ceiling*. Reading, MA: Addison-Wesley, 1987.

Morrison, Ann. *The New Leaders*. San Francisco: Jossey-Bass, 1992.

Shephard, C. R. *Small Groups*. San Francisco: Chandler Publishing, 1964.

Terry, Robert W. *For Whites Only*. Grand Rapids, MI: William B. Eerdmans Publishing Company, 1970, 1990.

Thiederman, Sondra. Bridging Cultural Barriers for Corporate Success. New York: Lexington Books, 1991.

Thomas, Roosevelt. "From Affirmative Action to Affirming Diversity." *Harvard Business Review* 68, 2, 1990, 107-117.

Thomas, Roosevelt. *Beyond Race & Gender*. New York: AMACOM, 1991.

U.S. Department of Labor. *A Report on the Glass Ceiling Initiative*. 1991.

Other Resources

The following materials address the political correctness issue:
Gates, H.L., Jr. *Loose Canons*. New York: Oxford University Press, 1992.

Graff, Gerald. *Beyond the Culture Wars: How Teaching the Conflicts Can Revitalize American Education*. W.W. Norton, 1992.

The diversity training materials that follow are available from:

Managing Diversity, JALMC, P. O. Box 819, Jamestown, NY 14702

Banks, G. *The Human Diversity Workshop.*

Dickerson-Jones, Terri. *50 Activities for Diversity Training.*

Dickerson-Jones, Terri. *50 Activities for Managing Cultural Diversity.*

Directory of Diversity Recruitment

Fyock, C. *Cultural Diversity: Challenges and Opportunities.*

Gardenswartz, L. and A. Rowe. *Managing Diversity: A Complete Desk Reference and Planning Guide* and *The Diversity Tool Kit.*

Managing Diversity, a monthly newsletter.

Myers, S. and J. Lambert. *Diversity Icebreakers: A Trainer's Guide.*

Turkewych, C. and H. Guerreiro-Klinowski. *Intercultural Interviewing.*